Great American Railroad Stations

Janet Greenstein Potter

PRESERVATION
PRESS

JOHN WILEY & SONS, INC.

New York • Chichester • Brisbane • Toronto • Singapore

This publication is designed to provide accurate and
authoritative information in regard to the subject
matter covered. It is sold with the understanding that
the publisher is not engaged in rendering legal, accounting,
or other professional services. If legal advice or other
expert assistance is required, the services of a competent
professional person should be sought.

Library of Congress Cataloging-in-Publication Data:

Potter, Janet Greenstein.
    Great American railroad stations / Janet Greenstein Potter.
        p.   cm.
    Includes bibliographical references and index.
    ISBN 0-471-14389-6 (pbk. : alk. paper)
    1. Railroad stations—United States.   I. Title.
Preservation in the United States.   II. Title.
TF302.U54P68   1996
385′ .314′ 0973—dc20   95-51432

Printed in the United States of America

10 9 8 7 6 5 4 3 2

Contents

* * *

MIDWEST
291

SOUTHWEST
413

WEST
457

Foreword

By Senator Daniel Patrick Moynihan

★ ★ ★

In 1963, New York City's Pennsylvania Station was torn down and dumped in the Jersey Meadows—without apology, without protest. Herbert Muschamp, the architecture critic of the *New York Times,* has written, with good reason, that this "was one of the greatest traumas New York City ever suffered." Some good came of it: The Landmarks Preservation Commission was set up, and the preservation movement took on a forward-looking cast—less nostalgia and more finding new uses for old treasures. Yet, Mr. Muschamp continued, "though the loss of the old Penn Station shocked the City to its senses, the idea persists that the shock may have come too late to save it." The City, that is. More than a building is at stake here.

In Washington D.C., Union Station almost met the same fate, but we saved it. In 1981, I could see from my office in the Senate a tree growing in the roof—the building had literally "gone to seed." We managed to pass legislation; and, through the good offices of then Secretary of Transportation Elizabeth H. Dole, the station became a roaring intermodal success, a nexus of intercity rail lines. subway service, taxis, buses, private cars, bicyclists, pedestrians, and (a Washington exclusive) tourmobiles. And all this with some of the best shopping and dining in the city.

We had learned something in Washington, and we applied it to the next transportation bill. Congress passed and President Bush signed the Intermodal Surface Transportation Efficiency Act of 1991 (mercifully known by its acronym, ISTEA). Robert A. Roe of New Jersey was the bill's manager in the House; "Intermodal" is his word. I was the Senate manager; "Efficiency" is mine. The long title was our way of saying that the long era of building the Interstate Highway System—the idea began at the 1939 World's Fair in Flushing Meadows—was over. The time had come for integrating transport systems and paying attention to costs. The late W. Graham Claytor, Jr., president of Amtrak, spotted it right away. Moments after ISTEA became law, he wrote to ask if I would like to see a model of his concept for a new Pennsylvania Station.

For years, Amtrak had been struggling with what to do with the original Pennsylvania Station's replacement "facility," a hole in the ground with Madison Square Garden on top.

It had never worked even before it started to stink. Yet on any weekday, half a million people—the population of Wyoming—grope their way through it. The facility also handles the commuter lines and the subway lines, and ridership on all modes is increasing, leading to the prediction of pedestrian gridlock within a decade. Then the U.S. Postal Service went high-tech, and Mr. Claytor saw an opportunity.

The original Pennsylvania Station, modeled on the Baths of Caracalla, opened in 1910. It is a Beaux Arts masterpiece by McKim, Mead, and White. Eight years later, substantially the same building, designed by the same firm, of the same materials and the same dimensions, and substantially the same purpose, in this case moving the mail by rail, opened across Eighth Avenue. Known as the James A. Farley Post Office, it is a National Historic Landmark, so designated in 1965 as a direct result of the preservation law born of the destruction of its sibling, Pennsylvania Station. And because it had acquired a new high-tech facility several blocks away, the Postal Service was vacating. Mr. Claytor developed a brilliant plan to refurbish the building and to move Amtrak into its central court, newly glazed and once again a magnificent gateway to New York City. Once again a decent railroad station.

With the passage of ISTEA, there were funds available; after all, this was the quintessential intermodal project. President Clinton came on board, making room for $100 million in his budget. Mayor Giuliani and Governor Pataki put up another $100 million, and on September 1, 1995, the Pennsylvania Station Redevelopment Corporation was formed to raise the remaining $115 million through private means. There is money to be made in creating a great train station.

On the Northeast Corridor, first Philadelphia, then Washington, and now Boston came up against the same problems and solved them with brilliantly refurbished structures, such as Daniel Burnham's gateway to the city of Washington. Only New York remained diminished. Now enter a time machine, turn back the clock, re-create Pennsylvania Station in the great Farley Post Office atop the same tracks, athwart the same transportation systems—intercity and suburban rail, subway, bus, taxi, sidewalks of old. All anew!

David Reisman once remarked that America is the land of the second chance. By God, here is one.

Preface

★ ★ ★

When I was a little girl living in Wilmington, Del., my father traveled once a week to his company's office in New York City. Every Wednesday about 5 p.m., he phoned my mother to tell us whether to meet him at the "Pennsy" or the "B&O" station. In those days, right after World War II, there were two railroads carrying passengers between Washington and New York with varying routes and schedules. Both of their Wilmington depots were designed by renowned Philadelphia architect Frank Furness.

Greeting my father at the station glows as one of the brightest memories of my childhood—especially if his choice that day was the Baltimore & Ohio station on Delaware Avenue. The tracks were elevated as they came through town; and for that reason Furness split the building vertically between street and track level, and then linked both parts with a great, sloping roof. My mother and I climbed the wide covered stairway outside the station to reach the platform. Slowed by my short-legged two-step, we struggled to reach the top before the train thundered into the station. At track level, I watched eagerly as trainmen lifted the trap doors and exposed the steps descending from each coach; from my child's vantage point, I strained to spot my father among the other double-breasted suits and fedoras getting off the train. Being lifted into the air, I felt not only the safe haven of my father's arms, but also the drama of a railroad station—a precious moment surely influenced by the role setting plays in life's journey of memories.

Years later, I discovered this same depot had once borne witness to the arrival of my stylishly dressed, but frazzled, maternal grandmother and her six children. The B&O station was the final stop on their 1908 emigration from Russia. The connecting link between family and depot stretched back longer than I realized. Yet my children will never know the B&O station, a building that embodied so much collective memory. In 1960, Furness's baroque, skylit gem was obliterated—sacrificed to become the parking lot of a supermarket.

The other Wilmington depot, Pennsylvania Station, is still standing, renovated in 1984 by Amtrak. At least I can visit 50 percent of my childhood images in a tangible way. But for most communities in the United States, not even one depot remains where a person can go home again.

To my mind, railroad stations are the most fanciful class of buildings in America. Preparing for this guide, I examined hundreds of books and photograph collections, as I sought early pictures of tiny depots and huge terminals. I often gasped, turning the page in

Early view of the Baltimore & Ohio station in Wilmington, Del. Its location was the southwest corner of Delaware Avenue and North Dupont Street.

wonderment at the intricacies of imagination that designers applied to the practical needs of a railroad station. My eyes scanned the captions looking for that ugly word "demolished," which unfortunately appeared below painfully breathtaking designs. Even when the word was absent, I could not be sure the building was still standing. Hundreds are lost each year, victims of wrecking balls or that most cowardly form of aggression—arson.

We do not go into art museums, take the paintings off the wall, throw them to the ground, and stomp on them, or invite a hack artist to paint over the canvas. Yet society so often allows masterpieces of architecture—compact and charming or grand and inspiring—to be destroyed or altered as though real estate ownership supersedes any other value system. What is worse, once we raze them, our fine old buildings can no longer be replaced with others of equal or superior majesty. The best railroad stations were conceived in the dreams of architects and civil engineers, and then brought to life by talented craftspeople. In the last 50 years, we have lost the ability to duplicate such architecture, whether because of cost, forgotten skills, or a bent toward soulless functionalism. This guidebook is a tribute not only to those who built these stations, but also to the railroaders who worked within the depot and on the platform—advising travelers, loading freight and baggage, and directing the safe passage of trains. Besides celebrating the depots that people have rescued against difficult odds, my selections also highlight many stations that still need salvation. At every depot we visit, whether a train stops there or not, we honor our own memories and those of the generations before us, whose comings and goings nearly always included a train.

Acknowledgments

This work, covering the entire country, commanded the assistance of far more than a thousand contacts. My first thanks go to the often unsung librarians, from villages to major cities and universities, from all-volunteer to professional historical societies, whose sleuthing through books and files brought forth many of the interesting details and photographs that enhance this book. To them, as well as the many other people who helped with information on specific stations, I extend my cross-country voice of appreciation.

Every project has its early cheerleaders, whose encouragement boosts the concept into reality. A key supporter was Timothy P. Gardner, then vice-president of passenger marketing at Amtrak. Tim was instrumental in the rebirth of Union Station in Washington, D.C. His subsequent endorsement of my plan to bring the topic of depot preservation to a national audience was a significant contribution to *Great American Railroad Stations*. Another important consultant was John P. Hankey, former chief curator of the B&O Railroad Museum. His suggestions about reading material and our conversations on 19th-century station life headed me in the right direction.

My biggest individual "thank you" goes to Herbert H. Harwood, whose acquaintance I made while working on this book and whose contribution became that of a steadfast, trusted friend. Herb initially agreed to help with Delaware and Maryland, but his knowledge of all the mid-Atlantic states and railroad history in general soon made him my consultant on many places and topics. He served as both an anchor and a touchstone in my striving for accuracy and clarity. During the long process of research, evaluation, and writing, Herb's scholarship, common sense, talent as a photographer, and sense of humor combined into the best single advisor I could hope to find.

I would also like to recognize the representatives of state historic preservation offices, who provided evaluations and depot surveys. Many answered follow-up questions or gave advice on sources for photographs. A partial listing of those involved appears below.

Alabama: Melanie Betz. Alaska: Joan M. Antonson. Arizona: Reba N. Wells. Arkansas: Mark Christ. California: Marilyn Lortie. Colorado: Dale Heckendorn, Barbara Norgren, and Holly Wilson. Connecticut: John Herzan. Delaware: Stephen Del Sordo and Alice H. Guerrant. Florida: William Thurston. Georgia: Kenneth H. Thomas. Hawaii: Don Hibbard. Idaho: Belinda Henry Davis. Illinois: Ann V. Swallow. Indiana: Paul Diebold. Iowa: Ralph Christian, Amanda Lehman, and Lynda Wessel. Kansas: Martha Hagendorn-Krass. Kentucky: Marty Perry. Louisiana: Patricia Duncan and Jonathan Fricker. Maine: Kirk Mohney. Maryland: Ronald

Andrews. Massachusetts: Douglas Kelleher. Michigan: Kathryn B. Eckert. Minnesota: Susan Roth. Mississippi: Todd Sanders. Missouri: Mark A. Miles. Montana: Pat Bik and Chere Jiusto. Nebraska: Carol Ahlgren. Nevada: Ron James and Michelle McFadden. New Hampshire: Parker Potter. New Jersey: Dan Saunders. New Mexico: Mary Ann Anders. New York: John Bonafide, Kathleen La Frank, Mark Peckham, and Clare Ross. North Carolina: Michael Southern. North Dakota: Lauren McCroskey. Ohio: John E. Rau. Oklahoma: Susan Allen. Oregon: Elizabeth Walton Potter. Pennsylvania: Dan Deibler, Douglas Reynolds, and William Sisson. Rhode Island: Ann Angelone. South Carolina: J. Tracy Power. South Dakota: Michael A. Bedeau. Tennessee: Claudette Stager. Texas: James W. Steely. Utah: Roger Roper. Vermont: Elsa Gilbertson. Virginia: Joseph S. White. West Virginia: Rodney Collins. Washington: David M. Hansen. Wisconsin: Joe DeRose. Wyoming: Sheila Bricher-Wade.

I also solicited recommendations from historians and depot supporters in every state and region. Many responded with a devotion that far exceeded my requests. They generously provided detailed lists, portions of unpublished manuscripts, or photographic images. All were available for questions and for checking sections of the completed manuscript. To these industrious "captains" goes my special thanks:

Charles Albi, J. Leonard Bachelder, John Ballweber, Henry E. Bender, Mark J. Camp, Frank W. Campbell, Charles B. Castner, Mark J. Cedak, David B. Clarke, Rebecca Conard, Thomas W. Dixon, Larry E. Easton, Vernon J. Glover, Gene M. Gressley, John E. Gruber, Lee Gustafson, David Harris, William F. Howes, Robert C. Jones, David R. Kovl, Robert F. Lord, Rick W. Mills, Herman Page, Francis H. Parker, William A. Pollard, James N. Price, James J. Reisdorff, Philip C. Serpico, Dwight A. Smith, Charles H. Stats, Donald R. Traser, Timothy C. Truscott, Robert A. Trennert, Ralph Ward, Thornton H. Waite, George C. Werner, and Kyle K. Wyatt.

Other knowledgeable scholars and preservationists provided general guidance, supplied their own previous research, or read portions of the manuscript. They include:

Richard D. Adkins, Jerry Angier, Fred Arone, Carlos P. Avery, Christopher T. Baer, Sam Breck, Frank A. Brooks, Keith L. Bryant, Gordon Chappell, Bruce Clouette, R. Richard Conard, Carl W. Condit, Dan Cupper, George Drury, William D. Edson, Kenton Forest, James Frederickson, Franklin Garrett, H. Roger Grant, Frances C. Gretes, Constance Grieff, Paul Hammond, Don L. Hofsommer, Harvie Jones, Walter Kidney, James E. Kranefeld, Frederick Love, John Luebs, Albro Martin, Constance L. Menninger, Diane Miller, F. Stewart Mitchell, William S. Osborn, Richard Palmer, G. William Schafer, Mac Sebree, Thomas Shook, Mark Smith, Don Snoddy, Dennis Stuart, Thomas T. Taber, Preston Thayer, George E. Thomas, J. Craig Thorpe, Gregg M. Turner, Nancy Webster, Warren W. Wing, William L. Withuhn, and Ron Ziel.

For wading through (or letting me wade through) their wide-ranging collections of photographs, I am most grateful to the following keepers of the archives:

Charles Bates (Allen County Historical Society); Anne Calhoun (B&O Railroad Museum); Mary Anne Burns Duffy (West Chester University); Ellen Halteman and Kevin Bunker (California State Railroad Museum); Terry Keenan (Syracuse University); Joyce W. Koeneman (Association of American Railroads); Jacqueline J. Pryor (Railway & Locomotive Historical Society Collection); Marilyn Ibach (Library of Congress); William W. Kratville (Union Pacific Historical Museum); William F. Lang (Free Library of Philadelphia); Scott A. Rappe, AIA (Graham, Anderson, Probst & White); Linda Ries (Pennsylvania State Archives); John R. Signor (Southern Pacific Lines); Christie K. Stanley (Kansas State Historical Society); Richard

W. Symmes (Walker Transportation Collection); John M. Williams and Barbara Hull (Hagley Museum and Library); Paul Woehrmann (Milwaukee Public Library); and William E. Worthington (Smithsonian Institution). The following private collectors also deserve my thanks: Howard Goodwin, Herbert H. Harwood, Roberta Niesz, William T. Turner, the late John P. Vander Maas, Frank Weer, and John Willever.

Specialists from the world of passenger transportation shared their knowledge of transportation and of their companies' historic resources. I am grateful for assistance from the following:

Amtrak: Clifford Black, Deborah Hare, Ruth Ludeman, Sue S. Martin, Patricia P. Kelly, W. Douglas Varn, and especially Bruce Heard—for his infectious enthusiasm, networking assistance, and his fund of historical information. California Department of Transportation: John W. Snyder. New Jersey Transit: David Koenig. New York Metropolitan Transportation Authority: David Florio and Jeanne Giordano.

Two long-established railroad historical societies were particularly helpful both through their many publications and through the personal assistance of their members. My appreciation extends to many chapters of the National Railway Historical Society, with individual thanks to Larry Eastwood, Frank Tatnall and especially Lynn Burshtin, whose graciousness and skill facilitated my in-depth visits to the society's library in Philadelphia. I also am very grateful to the Railroad Station Historical Society, especially William and Janet Rapp.

People who assisted me in specialized areas, and whom I thank, include: Robert M. Vogel, formerly of the Smithsonian Institution, for his consultations on engineering questions; Alice Kent Schooler, for fostering my love of architectural history and for solving a number of stylistic puzzles presented by various depots; Edward H. Weber, for generously printing a bounty of his wonderful photographs; and Theodore Xaras and Frank Weer, for their encyclopedic knowledge of railroad stations in the Philadelphia area and railroading in general.

The following individuals were most cooperative in accommodating my sometimes voluminous requests for information:

Orden Lantz (National Register of Historic Places); Gray Fitzsimons (Historic American Engineering Record and Historic American Buildings Survey); Sally Sims Stokes (National Trust for Historic Preservation Library); and Barbara Pahl (National Trust Mountain/Plains Regional Office).

I am grateful to Garry Greenstein, for sharing his in-depth knowledge of antique automobiles to help me date old photographs, and Norman Dodge, for his priceless, early-on championing of my literary aspirations.

For their zeal and care in the production of this book, I thank Suzanne Dane, Walter Schwarz, and past and present staff members of The Preservation Press: Peter Lindeman, Amanda Miller, Milagros Torres, Janet Walker, and Mary Alice Yates.

On the home front, I reserve the most profound gratitude for my rainbow of a daughter. From our inspiring trip to Washington Union Station when she was but a little girl through the years of research and writing that followed, she demonstrated a remarkably mature editorial sense and an affectionate understanding of my preoccupation with railroad stations.

An Oregon Railway & Navigation Company train and crew at the station in Dayton, Wash., c. 1890–95.

100 Years of Glory

★ ★ ★

ailroad stations were once as common as today's zip codes, at least one for every community. From roughly 1830 to 1930, train transportation was the catalyst of America's booming geographic and economic expansion. Railroads dominated the landscape and controlled a massive new cross-country flow of life and commodities. When people spoke of "the road," they usually meant the railroad; and by "car," they meant a rail car. Wagon roads—bumpy, rutted channels of mud or swirling dust in warm weather—were totally impassable in the blizzards of winter. Until well into the 20th century, only the streets of major cities bore the firmness of bricks, cobblestones, or asphalt. In myriad small towns, the main thoroughfare, whether paved or unpaved, carried the proud name "Railroad Avenue;" because at its helm lay the most crucial building in town—symbol of prosperity and faith in the future—the railroad station.

Hundreds of railroad companies operated passenger and freight service along the quarter-million miles of track that linked America's communities, from farm villages to small mining towns to highly industrialized cities. Although rivers were important to transportation, especially in a north-south direction, only the railroad overcame topography by conquering mountains, valleys, and bodies of water. Time and space expanded with a leap unparalleled before in history. From their trunk lines, railroads branched off to feed thousands of communities across the growing country, communities whose economic development was so tied to the railroad that town and station name were frequently the same: College Station, Tex.; Hopewell Junction, N.Y.; Genesee Depot, Wis.; Lake Station, Ind., among many others.

Because the United States today has only one intercity passenger carrier (Amtrak) plus a couple of dozen commuter lines and major freight haulers, relatively few people born in the last 50 years know more than a hobby's-worth of information about life in the railroad era. In the late 20th century, automobiles, trucks, airplanes, and electronic transmissions reign supreme. During the preceding era, railroading filled the combined transportation and communication shoes of all these specialized enterprises. Train tracks and

1

rail yards—not highways and parking lots—webbed the nation. People frequented the railroad station as commonly as modern folks drive onto a freeway ramp, board a plane, accept delivery of a package, or push buttons on their telephones.

For decades, travelers passed through America's railroad stations for purposes as routine as going to work or shopping and as momentous as departing for college, a homestead out West, or the front lines of war. In dramatic fantasy, depots have served as emotion-charged settings for novels and motion pictures. In dramatic reality, they were battle targets, forums for political oratory, and haunts of escaping criminals. Railroad stations reflected the diverse and shifting society around them. They made a distinct comment about the prosperity, hard times, or values of a community. From whimsical to majestic, from rural to urban, their styles varied as much as the ever-changing tastes of traveling Americans.

Main waiting room in Pennsylvania Station, New York City, during World War II. Huge images of railroad workers and the armed forces hang above the crowds.

"Old Ironsides," Matthias Baldwin's first full-size locomotive, pulling a Philadelphia, Germantown & Norristown train past the depot (now gone) at 9th and Green streets in Philadelphia. Each carriage bore a different paint scheme; for example, gold in combination with blue, green, or sage.

Evolved during the last grand age of travel, the era of steamship and steam train, the railway station was an essential ingredient of every traveler's itinerary. Yet in the 1830s, when the first United States railroads chugged forth along the Eastern seaboard, there was no thought given to such a particular building type. Until then, people and freight had been transported exclusively by river current, animal, or wind power. Sailing ships, pack mules, stage coaches, freight wagons, or the latest innovation—canal barges— moved the nation. Even the primitive "railways," established by British miners in the 1600s for carting coal, depended on four-footed creatures and gravity for motive power. Not until 1804, when Englishman Richard Trevithick combined a steam engine with a tramway (boxlike wagons running on rails) did self-generated, mechanically-powered locomotion become a reality. In America, some of the early lines like the Baltimore & Ohio Railroad and the Athens branch of the Georgia Railroad started out horse drawn. But soon fledgling steam locomotives amazed people by pulling open carriages, connected with chains, over iron-topped wooden rails. They traveled at terrifying speeds of 10 or 20 miles per hour.

Scrambling to raise capital for tracks and equipment, railroads had little interest in constructing passenger depots; they loaded and unloaded travelers at buildings that pre-dated the iron horse—stagecoach inns, general stores, or taverns. Furthermore, a "sta-tion" might have no station building or "depot" at all. In many rural places, just a gravel path and a signpost were a stopping place for the train (a practice that carried well beyond the incipient days of railroading). In some cities like Philadelphia, the timetable described the station as a street corner, similar to a bus stop today. Railroads often built the freight depot first, while the passengers waited on an open platform or in a crude shed. It was important to shield farm products and building materials; windblown and drenched people were a less urgent problem.

On the east coast, between the 1830s and 1870s, a number of the buildings constructed specifically as passenger train stops—were it not for their trackside location—would have been scarcely distinguishable from regular houses. Often, except for the

The c. 1850s Philadelphia, Germantown & Norristown station at Nicetown (in Philadelphia) looked very much like a residence. This photo was taken c. 1890, about 12 years before the building was replaced by the second of three consecutive depots. (None remains today.)

ticket office, most of the space was living quarters for the agent's family. If travelers were fortunate, the ticket seller let them wait in the parlor, rather than restricting them to the cold front porch. Dating from the 1870s, two of these residential-style depots (built on a line that became part of the Pennsylvania Railroad) remain at Morstein (enlarged in 1889) and Kirkland, both near West Chester, Pa.

Another early solution to the mixed needs of railroading was the "train barn"—with shape similar to a livestock and grain shelter. Designed as much to protect the locomotive and short string of cars as the passengers, it encased the ticket office, waiting rooms, and as many as seven tracks. The one still standing in New Albany, Ind., is a rare example. Used as a warehouse today, it still has two tracks running into the building.

Stoughton, Mass. Resembling a wooden barn, this structure combined (under one roof) an enginehouse with a freight and passenger station. Photographed c. 1880, it stood at the end of Railroad Avenue. The station was demolished after an 1888 stone depot was built at the foot of Wyman Street. (see Massachusetts, page 95.)

In the mid-19th century, when trains traveled only in daylight, the doors at either end of the train barn were closed at night, with the shiny, fancy locomotive bedded securely inside. Commonly built of wood, train barns were often ignited by sparks from the engines they supposedly guarded—and were, in fact, anything but a safe resting place.

As locomotives became more powerful and could pull longer chains of cars, the trains outgrew their stables. Small homelike stations also became outmoded (although many continued in service) as they grew overcrowded with passengers and freight. Depot designs, especially for small towns, evolved with now familiar "railroad station" characteristics. The typical depot acquired a Janus-like quality, with one face turned inward toward the community it served, and another face turned outward toward the railroad tracks and world horizons—a building where the back door was just as important as the

Northern Railroad of New Jersey station at Tenafly, N.J., c. 1910.

Identical track and street sides are not uncommon to depots.

In the parlance of railroading, the track side is "the front."

front. Indeed, which was which? There usually were multiple doors, to enable simultaneous ingress and egress of crowds at train time. In the freight section, large warehouse doors directly opposite each other permitted goods to be passed street to track side and vice versa. The building also had a clear outdoor component—a busy platform where people and goods waited to be loaded onto trains. At minimum, partial shelter was required. The porch roof of the early dwelling-type stations evolved into deep platform overhangs. They extended out from the building and were supported by brackets or freestanding posts. These platforms and canopies were the most defining feature of most railroad stations. The platform was a bridge between the humanly scaled building and the giant-sized, earth-shaking transport that skirted its boundaries. Growing ever longer as the railroad era progressed to accommodate increasingly longer trains, the platform accounted for the extremely horizontal character of many stations. Lastly, a nearly ubiquitous, polygonal bay window enabled the station agent to monitor activities on the platform and down the track.

Activity inside and around a station depended on how active that particular stop was along the line. At a lightly serviced, unheated flag stop—where the train did not halt unless it was signaled by a passenger holding out a flag or lantern—travelers might spend many cold, boring hours, or even overnight, waiting for the train, with no idea why it was late or when it would arrive. At a busy station, with a fully authorized railroad agent in charge, the depot surpassed the general store as the community's gathering spot. It was the place where political views, gossip, and problem-solving ideas were exchanged around the fireplace or pot-bellied stove. Today, people turn on the television or go to a shopping mall for recreation. In the railroad era, people went down to the depot. In a world without parcel post or private delivery services, ordering from one of the catalog companies like Sears, Roebuck or Montgomery Ward meant a trip to the railroad station to see if a new dress or an urgently needed tool had arrived. Time spent scrutinizing the passengers getting off the train, whether the arrival was a dry goods salesman, a new school teacher, or a suspicious unknown person, provided the curious with a mouthful of news to spread. The departing parties were no less interesting: a student off to boarding school, a young woman escaping scandal, a criminal being escorted to jail. Newspaper reporters regarded the depot as a good source for leads, a place where observation and interviews generated the most current stories in town.

Some communities were serviced only by local or "accommodation" trains. These towns were way stations, less important intermediary points, where express and long-distance trains did not stop. Gawking townspeople went down to the depot just to witness the bell-clanging "Limited" tear through the station and to speculate on what famous people might be aboard. In some places, school recessed or court adjourned to partake of the event. Spectators held onto their hats while the powerful train sucked the air right out of the station. Then the semaphore blade shifted or the signal light changed color. The rushing, self-contained world of the train—that day's excitement—was gone. It was a time of fast mail trains and pokey milk runs, of funeral caravans and circus trains—a time when baseball teams and even Santa Claus came by rail.

THE AGENT AND THE TELEGRAPH

The station agent, on rare occasions female, was typically the sole or ranking on-site employee of the powerful railroad — and shown as much respect as the mayor, pastor, or physician. A seasoned agent combined the roles of ambassador, confidante, travel agent, safety engineer, and commerce booster. Among his specific duties were selling tickets, supervising freight and express shipments, announcing train departures and arrivals, stoking the heat stove, washing windows, sweeping the floor, repairing tools, bookkeeping, evicting hoboes, and picking up mail sacks tossed from speeding trains. Skilled with words and numbers, the agent also had to be well-versed in geography to route passengers through the many connections that constituted most long-distance trips. Frequently the small-town agent was also the postmaster. He sometimes ran a concession stand, where he sold flowers or travelers aids to earn extra money. Richard Sears, who later teamed with Mr. Roebuck, started his retail career while an agent at North Redwood, Minn., when he capitalized on a shipment of wristwatches abandoned at the station.

Most railroads favored family men for station agent positions; they were considered more likely to remain sober and stable. Paying a modest rent and available 24 hours a day for emergencies, the agent and his family often lived in part of the building, with lace curtains at the window and children playing around the baggage carts, freight scales, and farmers' milk cans that cluttered the platform. The small-town depot retained a homey quality despite the periodic ground trembling noise and constant coal-dusty smell of steam railroading. In off-peak hours, some depots

Chicago, Burlington & Quincy agent John G. Hohl sitting at his desk in the Wahoo, Neb., depot. The year is 1906.

From c. 1890 to 1917, William Codner was an agent for the Hocking Valley Railway (later Chesapeake & Ohio system) at Canal Winchester, Ohio. About 1908, Mr. Codner's son snapped this picture of him mowing the station lawn.

did double duty as town meeting halls (Greer, S.C.), or housed Sunday church services (Union Station in Jackson, Mich.).

In the midst of an already hectic, detail-filled job, the agent performed yet another task—one that affected the safe operation of trains along what were principally single track lines, ripe for collisions. That pivotal role was "operator," a function made possible by Samuel B. Morse's contrivance, the electromagnetic telegraph, first tested in 1844 along the B&O Railroad's right-of-way between Washington, D.C., and Baltimore. In the earliest days of railroading, only the locomotive engineer's strict adherence to the printed schedule and accompanying rules had kept adequate spacing between trains to prevent both rear-end and head-on accidents. If a train was delayed, on-board crews had no way to communicate with each other. Workers often had to pull off the main track and hold their train on a siding for an indeterminate amount of time, while guessing whether to continue waiting or risk proceeding toward a collision. In 1851, after a chance realization by an Erie Railroad superintendent, the telegraph advanced from its initial routine communications function. It became the critical link in a somewhat complicated system for controlling train movements. As word of delays was relayed by telegraph between dispatchers and agents along the line, dispatchers could order new meeting and passing locations that would override the timetable.

With no radio communications available in those days, the crew aboard a train could only get these detailed instructions in person—upon arrival at a depot or tower. The operator notified the crew whether instructions were waiting by shifting indicators on the lighted semaphore known as "the order board" (at a depot, it was positioned outside the agent's bay window or on the roof). He changed the signal either by running outside to work pulleys below the semaphore or by manipulating big levers within his office. The engineer and conductor knew from the signal whether to come inside to sign for new orders or wait in the tall locomotive cab for the agent to hand up thin sheets of instructions called "flimsies." Sometimes the train barely slowed for the orders, held out on a bamboo hoop or (later) a long Y-shaped fork for a crew member to grab as the train skimmed by.

Boswell, Ind., 1949. The agent is "hooping up" orders to an eastbound New York, Chicago & St. Louis ("Nickel Plate") train traveling from Peoria, Ill., to Lima, Ohio.

The "Morse man" also conveyed general news and personal messages to the local populace. In the days before long-distance telephone service or radio, and when out-of-town newspapers could take 24 hours to arrive, the station agent was the local news anchor; each train conductor was a field reporter. Election tallies, baseball scores, grain and livestock quotations, accident reports, announcements of births and deaths came tapping out in a mysterious code that the esteemed station agent was specially trained to send and decipher. Gossip spread quickly among "depot loungers," who knew that the most interesting place to loiter was down at the station. The agent produced and directed the show. Most train tickets today are sold through vending machines, at convenience stores, or over the phone. The small-town station agent is a nearly extinct occupation.

GROWTH AND EXPANSION

In the second half of the 19th century, "agent-operator" and other railroad careers were up and coming vocations—similar to the outpouring of jobs created by the computer industry a hundred years later. Telegraph wires paralleling the tracks marched symbiotically across the nation, as railroads advanced the rapid westward expansion of industry, commerce, and population. Struggling to raise the massive capital needed for laying track and buying equipment, some railroads obtained United States government land grants, which provided them with both land for a right-of-way and surplus to sell to settlers. Companies plopped depots and telegraphers in sparsely inhabited areas where population and business were merely predictions. Immigrants, traveling on cheap one-way tickets west, arrived

Workers erecting the telegraph line through Weber Canyon, east of Ogden, Utah. This stretch of Union Pacific track was part of the nation's first transcontinental railroad.

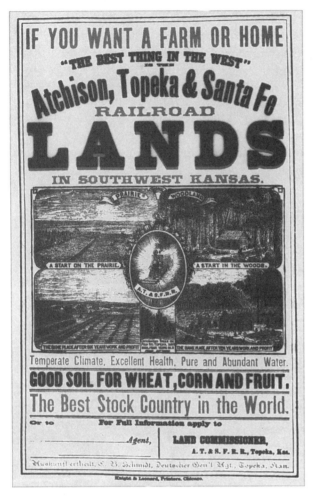

The Atchison, Topeka & Santa Fe enticed settlers to southwest Kansas with posters promising "Temperate Climate. Excellent Health. Pure and Abundant Water."

at towns deliberately planted by the railroad where none had been before. In a newly platted railroad town, lots were sold from the first building constructed, which was either the land office or the depot, standing at one end of the main street. In farm towns that had been established before the railroad era, residents pressed politicians and railroads to bring a train stop to their communities. They knew that having a station meant ease and speed in shipping goods and receiving supplies; and that in a competitive world, towns without train service could wither and die. Having a station was particularly important at a county seat, the place where people went to pay taxes or transact other official business, and most desirably, spend money with local merchants. A county seat without a train stop could be outmaneuvered by a competing location and lose its valuable courthouse-town designation.

In the East, stations typically were injected into established communities, although sometimes land speculators built the stations in undeveloped suburban areas in order to attract buyers. By the post–Civil War years, eastern stations were customarily fine, architect-designed buildings, constructed of jigsawed and ornamented wood or durable masonry. In the West, railroad companies were rushing to lay track across vast, inhospitable territory. They were short on funds and could never be certain which new towns would boom. Early depots were small frame shacks—often no more than box cars with their trucks removed, set down next to the track. They were dimensioned to fit easily on railroad flat cars and were only one-story high to squeeze under bridges and through tunnels. Easily hoisted onto the train by company-owned cranes, they could be transported to a new site after a more permanent or substantial building was constructed. Simple wooden depots had another pragmatic advantage—they were cheap to replace if destroyed by fire or storm.

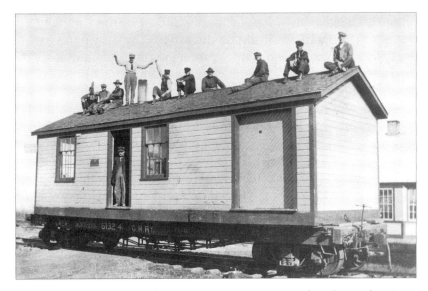

La Bolt, S.D., c. 1913. After constructing a new wooden depot, the Great Northern transported the old portable version down the rails to another location. (The second depot is now gone, destroyed some time after passenger service ended in 1957.)

STANDARDIZATION

In the 19th century, burgeoning railroad business made it necessary to establish a quick, inexpensive way to put up urgently needed depots. To a new industrial age, when interchangeable parts and machine-sawn wood defined taste and style, standardized depot design was just the ticket. As far back as 1867, railroads began standardizing and testing everything from locomotive parts to the juice yields of particular oranges used in dining cars. Most railroads had stock depot blueprints—several different styles in perhaps three different sizes each—that could be tailored to a particular location's traffic, importance,

The smallest version of C&O Standard Design No. 3, first drawn in 1892. The agent's office (behind the bay window) was flanked by a single waiting room and a freight room.

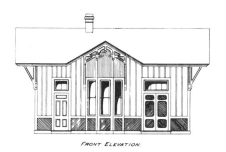

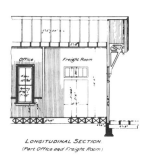

and land contours. These plans were easily constructed by the company's own "bridges and buildings gangs," sometimes using modular parts. By modifying a standard design, railroads could eliminate monotonous duplication for travelers and satisfy the concerns of towns wanting a gussied-up depot. Dormers, ridge cresting, roof brackets, and finials provided distinctive differences for little money.

On the other hand, by repeating design elements and colors that would distinguish their depots from those of other companies, railroads practiced one of the first examples of corporate identity campaigns, the logotyping of architecture. For example, a standard depot of the Atchison, Topeka & Santa Fe was readily recognized by the beveled agent's bay window with gabled dormer. Paint schemes had an equally strong impact. They varied from the chocolate and vanilla flavors of the Reading Company to the dark red and yellow gold of wooden, first generation Illinois Central stations. Some companies used multiple shades of green or yellow, and others painted their depots in polychromes of three to five colors. Tenants in adjacent, railroad-owned buildings often discovered that their leases required painting their store, hotel, or grain elevator in colors to match the depot. Blocks of identically shaded buildings made abundantly clear which railroad held sway in a given town. Howard Johnson restaurants with their orange roofs and McDonald's with their golden arches owe an advertising and design debt to railroad stations.

With nearly daily mergers and buy-outs among railroads, visual consistency for all depots on a particular line was the exception as much as the norm. Sometimes the structures on one particular branch line resembled each other, but not any other depots on the larger railroad. This family likeness can be an architectural clue to the station's beginnings on a predecessor or subsidiary railroad. When one railroad took over another, they often slapped a corporate paint scheme on the newly acquired depots to announce the buildings' current ownership. Going a step further, the Chicago, Burlington & Quincy, a railroad made up of numerous predecessors, actually had a standard brick veneer and stucco remodeling design, such as the one it used in 1929 at Corning, Iowa.

Identical buildings were most common in the Midwest and West. The lines in pioneer territories were built by fewer railroads than in the East and in a competitive hurry. A great many station stops were planned simultaneously over vast territory. Another reason for the template building process was technological development; the first western stations date from a later time than in the East—from the 1870s to 1890s as compared to the 1840s to 1870s. Later in the 19th century, machine-driven, prefabricated production affected design. Although the East tended to have more one-of-a-kind buildings, early depots built from the same or similar blueprints were not uncommon; but finding two or more of the buildings still standing is rather rare. Hopewell and Pennington, both in New Jersey, were built by the Delaware & Bound Brook (later the Reading Company) as a matched set, except for the difference in construction material—brick versus stone. Ridgway, Pa., and Springville, N.Y., on the old Buffalo, Rochester & Pittsburgh, are twin sisters more than 100 miles apart. Designs were sometimes copied or casually traded among railroads, via plans printed in publications like *Railway Age* or by draftsmen changing employers and taking ideas with them. Freelance architects who worked for

Bearing a distinct resemblance to each other, these two depots were constructed on unrelated lines. Although choices such as type of masonry and window design differ, the outlines of the buildings are very similar.

1920s view of the brick and stone station at Bucyrus, Ohio, built by the Ohio Central (later New York Central).

Early view of the stone depot at Fort Payne, Ala., built by the Alabama Great Southern (later Southern Railway).

multiple railroads occasionally imprinted a similar vision on different clients, thus giving riders a well-founded case of déjà vu. The same building might pop up on unrelated lines. For example, a depot at Elmsford, N.Y. (now a restaurant), built by the New York & Northern, bears a striking resemblance to another 1880s station at Great Meadows, N.J., built by the Lehigh & Hudson River and now listed in the National Register of Historic Places. The depots at Bucyrus, Ohio, on the Ohio Central and at Fort Payne, Ala., on the Alabama Great Southern (both also listed in the National Register) are look-alikes a decade apart in different regions of the country.

STYLES, TIME, AND HOSPITALITY

Although numerous railroad stations were designed by famous private practice architects such as Frank Furness, Henry Hobson Richardson, and Daniel H. Burnham, no single architect dominated the design evolution of railroad stations. In fact, most depots were the in-house products of civil engineers or architects on the railroad staff. A few well-known architects became associated with particular railroads, for example Frank Milburn for the Southern Railway or E. Francis Baldwin for the Baltimore & Ohio. Frank Furness, the most prolific station architect, worked his brilliance on three mighty railroads, the Pennsylvania, the Reading, and the B&O. Unfortunately, the biggest and best of many architect-designed stations have been demolished. Of the approximately 180 depots that came from the drawing board of Frank Furness, not more than 18 are left. Only one is of any substantive size—the former Pennsylvania Railroad station at

Philadelphia architect Frank Furness c. 1891.

Designed by Frank Furness for the Philadelphia & Reading, the Mt. Airy station (completed in 1883) still serves as a commuter stop in northwest Philadelphia. This c. 1885 photo shows the deep porch roof, now cut back. The covered stairway and dormered pavilion in the background (both gone) led up to Devon Street.

Wilmington, Del., which ranked among his least elaborate confections (and may be more the work of his partner, Allen Evans). H. H. Richardson's name is often associated with railroad depots because of the popularity of Richardsonian Romanesque as a station style; but the actual number of bona fide Richardson depots was really quite small, and just a handful remain. Far more were designed by his successors, Shepley, Rutan, and Coolidge, after Richardson died in 1886, when only in his late forties. Many of these architectural giants vied with each other for commissions; Frank Furness, for example, lost two momentous Pennsylvania Railroad competitions, one to Burnham in Pittsburgh and the other to Charles McKim in New York City.

The majority of style and technology concepts originated in Europe and took decades to reach the United States. While large and elegant railway stations were being constructed in European cities as early as the 1830s, comparable American structures were not begun until the late 1860s. Sophisticated designs were soon applied to midsize stations as well, particularly those found at county seats, where the populace doggedly petitioned the railroad for depots appropriate in size and style to the self-assessed importance of their community. The chamber of commerce frequently took the lead in these successful campaigns, by insisting on more prestigious masonry to replace less substantial or ornately "old-fashioned" frame depots. This public relations lobbying resulted in the demolition of some very fanciful stations that many people would treasure today. In a further ironic development, when economic prosperity receded in the middle to late 20th century, and many of these communities lost their train service entirely, the depots were converted to chamber of commerce offices.

Although some railroad executives believed that luxurious stations increased ridership, just as many balked at spending money on costly items not directly revenue-productive. Architects and local citizens usually had to prod corporate directors into paying for anything not strictly functional. One of these items was a feature imported from Europe, the bell or clock tower, which often elevated the railroad station above the church spire or courthouse steeple, perhaps symbolically as well as physically. Uniform and precise time—the factor that so rigidly shapes our lives today—was a contrivance of railroading. Adhering to schedules in the early days was at best hit or miss, with scores of contiguous areas operating on their own individual time, gauged by the sun's movement across the sky. In 1869, there were more than 80 different time regions in the United States. Efficient and safe railroad operations necessitated dividing the country into Standard Railway Time Zones (Eastern, Central, Mountain, and Pacific). This plan was designed by the industry and effected in 1883, when 600 railroads converted to railway time. So all-pervasive was railroading's influence, that Americans swiftly adjusted to the arrangement—even though these zones were not formally adopted by the United States government until 1918. Punctuality soon became an American obsession, with railroads as the nation's timekeeper. Every Thursday at noon, Western Union flashed the correct time across the telegraph wires. People synchronized their wind-up pocket watches or their newfangled "wrist" watches according to the freshly adjusted station clock. Bigger and more ornate clock faces appeared on the increasingly taller depot towers of America's

The clock tower on Union Station in Worcester, Mass., was designed by architects Ware and Van Brunt. Built c. 1875, the depot went out of service in 1911, after the Boston & Albany constructed a new Union Station just across Washington Square (*see* page 100). This photo was taken c. 1906.

cities and towns; while the tower itself, symbol of accomplishment and aspiration, served compositionally as a vertical counterpoint to the long, low station.

American depots were similar to European railway stations in another way—inclusion of hotels and "refreshment saloons" in the layout of selected locations. These amenities were essential before the 1880s, when dining and sleeping cars—"hotels on wheels"—came into frequent usage (particularly in America, where the distance between cities was great). Prior to that time, travelers who wanted a comfortable night's sleep had to disembark at one of the hotels positioned at intervals along the line. For food, unless they brought their own, passengers were dependent on young "train butchers" or "butches" who hawked snacks, reading material, and sundries from the station platforms or aboard the trains. Another alternative was a hurried meal of abominable, over-priced food at one of the intermittent "eating houses" that were scheduled stops along the way. The early eating house stations (especially in the east) were mostly obsolete by the 1890s, and few of these buildings exist today. Starrucca House in Susquehanna, Pa., and the Merwinsville Hotel in New Milford, Conn., are finely preserved examples.

This practice of incorporating a hotel or restaurant into the station was reborn and expanded in the West under the consummate entrepreneurship of Fred Harvey, whose establishments were known on railroad timetables by the more elegant phrase "dining stations." His company debuted modestly in 1876 in Topeka, Kans., and grew to a chain of establishments stretching from Chicago to California. The elegant Harvey House accommodations, with buildings and interiors often designed by the innovative architect and highly theatrical interior decorator, Mary Colter, were supplemented by super-efficient Harvey food service, both aboard trains and at the stations. Transcontinental travel became infinitely more pleasurable; and the tourist business of the Atchison, Topeka & Santa Fe —Fred Harvey's principal promoters— became notably more profitable.

The dining room at Starrucca House, photographed c. 1875-1880. It was part of the eating-house station and hotel at Susquehanna, Pa., along the main line of the Erie Railroad.

Although many Harvey hotels have been razed, several still stand in various stages of deterioration or preservation, such as those in Waynoka, Okla.; Williams and Winslow, Ariz.; and Barstow, Calif. La Fonda, one mile east of the original Santa Fe, N.M., passenger station, has been in continuous operation since the 1920s. The Harvey House restaurants, with wholesome "Harvey Girl" waitresses and food so fine that locals went down to the depot for Sunday dinner, closed one by one over the years, many during the economic downturn of the 1930s. (There were also well-known meal stops operated by other entrepreneurs such as the J. J. Grier Company that are often casually, but erroneously referred to today as "Harvey Houses.") Strong nostalgic interest in them remains. Despite Oklahoma's being a state without passenger service, riders on scenic excursion trains can still alight for a meal at the Harvey House restaurant in the old Hugo depot, which was restored in 1983.

Harvey Houses and adjacent stations were frequently built in the various Spanish Colonial styles that were particularly popular in the Southwest. Nationwide, every archi-

This Italianate-style Baltimore & Ohio passenger station was located at New Jersey Avenue and C Street, N.W., in Washington, D.C. It was razed after the 1907 Union Station was built.

tectural fashion from Dutch Colonial to Elizabethan Revival, from Prairie School to Art Deco, manifested itself in a railroad station somewhere. In a country struggling for its architectural identity and influenced by whatever designs poured from showcases like the Philadelphia Centennial Exposition of 1876 or the Chicago World's Columbian Exposition of 1893, each new endeavor was heralded as the consummate railroad style. The passage of time has crowned Italianate the winner, with its asymmetry, arched windows, square bell towers, and bold brackets—the outline most readily used today to symbolize "railroad station" in nostalgic Christmas card drawings and model railroad dioramas. In actuality, Italianate was only one of many styles applied to depots and not necessarily the most prevalent.

The City Beautiful Movement, partly an outgrowth of the 1893 Chicago fair, heavily influenced railroad station design in metropolitan areas of the late 19th and early 20th centuries. It was a nationwide planning concept that sought to rectify the clutter and ugliness of gritty American cities, with its supporters advocating tree-lined parkways bordered by light-colored, monumental public buildings. Often set back from the street by broad plazas, City Beautiful stations were designed on a scale that dwarfed the passengers who swept their long skirts and velvet-collared top coats through the portals. Beaux Arts and Classical Revival styles flourished in this atmosphere, with the most successful results achieved in buildings like D. H. Burnham and Company's Union Station in Washington, D.C. When less gifted architects tried their hand at imperial splendor, they sometimes produced porticoed railroad stations that looked more like places to make a bank deposit than take a train.

Union Station, Washington, D.C., c. 1920s. The "City Beautiful" setting included a Beaux Arts post office (left of the station), designed by Daniel H. Burnham's firm and completed in 1914.

STATION LAYOUT AND DESIGN

Because railroad stations combined architecture with the churning energy of massive trains, they were more alive than mere buildings. Whether a tiny, three-sided shelter or a terminal the size of city block, a railroad station was configured so that a long, enormous powerhouse could go directly past it, under it, over it, or sometimes right through it. This interplay between structure and train demanded a number of special design considerations. The principal one was the location and position of the tracks. Except at the end of a line, most railroad stations were "side-loading" with the track running parallel to the building and only a few inches or feet from the platform's edge. Differences occurred because of topography or the desire to avoid having railway and street traffic meet on the same horizontal plane—known as a "grade crossing." Once railroads were entrenched

Grade level crossing at the Georgia Railroad station in Conyers, Ga., 1953.

in an area, the desire to "separate grades"—putting street and rail traffic (or sometimes two rail lines) on different levels—was one of the most common reasons for building new stations. In some locations, tracks were depressed below grade level, and passengers descended interior or exterior stairs from the depot to reach track level. If the tracks were elevated above street level, there were essentially three options: have passengers climb from a street-level depot to reach the tracks; elevate the depot as well as the tracks; or build a multilevel depot with an upstairs waiting room. The latter two arrangements made it less likely that travelers would miss their trains.

Two variations existed for side-loading stations. "Island" depots had a platform and tracks on both sides of the building, which made loading and unloading passengers more efficient, but created the necessity for a way to get people over or under the tracks to reach the street. A tunnel under the tracks or an overhead walkway was the answer. Passengers also had to use subterranean passageways or elevated footbridges when a station was "two-sided," which meant it had two depot buildings—one on the inbound side and one on the outbound side. These were found most frequently at commuter stops like Southport and Fairfield, Conn. (extant). More often, only one of the two sides had a complete building with a ticket seller. That was the inbound side, where commuting workers and shoppers waited for trains into the city; the outbound side was just a sheltered platform. A rare, extant example of safe passageway, is found at the Allen Lane station in Philadelphia, which has maintained its covered stairs and pedestrian overpass for more than 110 years.

Allen Lane station in Philadelphia, October 1969. A Penn Central commuter train, heading outbound, passes under the pedestrian bridge. Built on a single 38-foot steel span, this covered walkway was added to the station in 1912. An 1885 brick depot (increased from one to two stories by the Pennsylvania Railroad in 1891) is located up a set of stairs to the right—on the outbound, rather than the more typical inbound side.

Kingsland station, Lyndhurst, N.J., in 1918. The Delaware, Lackawanna & Western built this c. 1904 depot on a bridge spanning a railroad cut. Today Kingsland is the first stop out of Hoboken, N.J., on New Jersey Transit's Port Jervis line.

In contrast to the more conventional side-loading stations, sometimes the train actually went across the roof of the building. Examples are the Pennsylvania Railroad stations in Wilmington, Del., and Newark, N.J., where viaducts were constructed to bring the tracks in directly above the stations. Other stations were built with raised portions straddling the tracks, like the PRR stations in Baltimore, Md., Harrisburg and Lancaster, Pa., and the Kansas City Union Station in Missouri (all extant). Often the reason for this configuration was the unavailability of land on either side of the tracks. Small stations at Kingsland (Lyndhurst), N.J., and Ossining, N.Y., sit in their entirety on bridges; the trains pass beneath them.

The word "terminal" indicated a major junction point or the end of the line; although to many people it connoted a large, metropolitan depot, typically designed with broader, grander strokes than a country or suburban depot. "Terminal" also implied that some servicing of locomotive and railroad cars was undertaken nearby. In a side-loading terminal on a busy line, with the tracks running parallel to the building, people had to walk across multiple tracks to reach their designated train for departure, or to reach the depot upon arrival. For this reason, an alternative design was often more desirable, one that included a "head house," so called because it was at the head of all the tracks, and sat perpendicular rather than parallel to them. The end of each track abutted the waiting rooms or an intermediary concourse, and passengers could walk along a platform beside each track to arrive at their rail cars. Sometimes station design combined a head house and dead-end tracks with very active through tracks—for example, at the 1907 Union Station in Washington, D.C., which is still in service.

Whether a terminal was side-loading or "stub-end," arriving trains needed not only servicing, but also turning to head the opposite direction. Methods to turn trains included: a looping track (which requires extensive ground space); a "wye" (where tracks are arranged like the letter Y with a connecting segment between the two arms); and "switching" (in which locomotives rearrange the components of a train). The particular disadvantage to a stub-end situation was that after a train deposited its passengers, it had to either back out of the station or be pulled out by a switch engine. The decision to construct either a side-loading or head house station was often a given, not a real choice, and was rooted in the amount of available acreage, pre-existing street arrangements, and track orientation. A certain amount of flexibility had to occur between the city planners and the railroad. Substantial changes in street layouts resulted when new stations were built in major metropolises, like Washington, Cincinnati, and New York; but these alterations were not without limitations and occurred at tremendous expense.

The type and size of depot often depended more on growth predictions than the town's current population. Bad estimates sometimes produced disproportionately large stations, like those at Wadley, Ala., and Clifton, Ariz. On the other hand, a substantial depot at a junction might have appeared out of scale with the community but, in fact, the crowds of passengers changing trains justified the size. This was the case with Union Station in Durand, Mich., built in 1905 and still standing. Vacation spots and college towns

Trains of both the Grand Trunk and Ann Arbor railroads posed for this 1905 photo at Union Station in Durand, Mich. This highly active junction point necessitated building a large depot in a small town.

often had extra large depots to accommodate the seasonal surge of travelers. For most successful communities, railroad stations during their heyday became overused in 10 to 20 years—just like new highways today, which fill to capacity with automobiles shortly after they are completed.

Separate freight and passenger depots existed only when business warranted having two buildings and more employees to staff them. Small-town America was saturated with "combination depots," where freight and passenger service stayed under one roof and under the supervision of one agent, whose office was efficiently located in the middle of a sometimes exceedingly long building. The freight section was often much larger than the passenger waiting room and opened both onto the track and the street, where wagons and teams of horses (and later motor trucks) pulled up to load and unload. Its wide doorways, outside platform, and interior workspace were ideally at a level even with the floor of a railroad box car, for less back-breaking work. Thus, the platform at a combination station was bilevel—lower at one end to accommodate passengers and higher at the other for loading freight. The interior of the freight space was unfinished, or at best had wainscoting rising about seven feet high, to guard the walls from being banged by cargo. For a similar reason, if a depot was built of wood or brick, often the exterior was faced with stone up to windowsill height, to prevent damage from baggage carts or crates.

The passenger side sometimes had a single waiting room. More often, the depot had two waiting rooms—segregated by gender—in a time when society felt it necessary to protect women from the vulgar male population. A dignified gentlemen traveling with a lady might accompany her to the women's waiting room, but no respectable woman

Fresh flowers and potted ferns soften the ladies' waiting room at Seattle Union Station, May 20, 1911.

entered the men's smoking, spitting, and swearing arena. According to an early 19th-century newspaper, the men's waiting room was "packed with a mixture of all colors and nationalities, and a combined odor of pipes, garlic, Limburger [cheese], beer . . . strong enough to upset a locomotive." To further shield the gentler sex, the men's "toilet room" frequently could be entered only from outside the building. This arrangement was inconvenient for male passengers, but it kept railroad workers, teamsters, omnibus drivers, and local riffraff from entering the waiting room areas. Today's euphemism "rest room" stems from the ladies' "retiring room," which was an inner sanctum beyond the waiting room area, where rocking chairs and ottomans made longer waits between trains more comfortable. Even when the more modern concept of a "general" waiting room evolved (found more often after the turn of the 20th century), a separate retiring room was still provided for women and, in many cases, a men's smoking room as well. The general waiting rooms in small towns were simply furnished, with pewlike wooden benches lining the wainscoted walls (or back to back versions in the room's center), a clock, stove or radiator, and a rack of travel brochures and railroad timetables. Gas wall sconces or chandeliers and early electric lights provided illumination. The station agent's office had a ticket window that opened into a central vestibule or into each waiting room. Some agent's offices were leanly furnished and tidy; others were crammed and cluttered with a desk, cash drawer, telegraph equipment, possibly an upright typewriter, and piles of paperwork.

Great Northern agent Harry Ellis, c. 1910, in his fully appointed office at the Solway, Minn., station. (This depot still exists, but was relocated about 1970 to County Route 16, 3.5 miles southeast of town.) In evidence are telegraph equipment, a telephone, a typewriter, and a hoop the agent took outside for passing orders to train crews.

In 1904, the Baltimore & Ohio completed a new facility (now gone) at Locust Point Pier, Baltimore. It was designed to handle the arrival of steamships loaded with thousands of immigrants. Nearly one-half of the pier's upper portion was the railroad depot. After inspection and processing by government officials, these Polish immigrants were waiting for their train.

In the segregated South, there was an additional waiting room for "colored" travelers, which was commonly accessible only from an outside entrance and usually not further subdivided by sex, often with one toilet room for everybody. If the station master's office did not have a separate ticket window opening into the colored waiting room, then purchases had to be made from outside.

During railroad's golden era, immigrants ("emigrants" in earlier parlance) arrived from Europe or Asia and, except for those who remained in their port of entry, fanned quickly across the country. They were confined to their own railroad cars and waiting rooms, partly to keep the newcomers separated from the already washed and assimilated "Americans," and partly to supervise their language and travel needs. After being processed at facilities like Castle Garden or Ellis Island, a railroad station was usually the first American building the immigrants entered. As they traversed the states and territories, their language and native costumes added to the fascinating sights and sounds locals encountered down at the depot. At larger stations, special lunch rooms were provided (to keep greenhorns from being swindled) along with laundry facilities, and offices for land grant agents. With a peculiar inversion of terminology found only in America, native Indians were forced to ride in the "emigrants" section of trains and share their station facilities.

Virtually everything and everyone came and went exclusively by rail: correspondence, small packages, people, animals, seeds, produce, coal, lumber, and the latest fashions. Depending on the amount of traffic, a depot had auxiliary rooms or a separate building for other services like baggage handling (including coffins traveling at one-half passenger fare) or mail sorting. Shipment of parcels, trunks, money, and individual items was conducted at busier stations by the express agent, who worked for companies such as American Express, Adams Express, or Wells Fargo, housed in the depot or in a separate express building. At smaller stations, the ticket clerk was often a dual agent, employed by both the railroad and the express company. "Express" was loaded onto passenger (not freight) trains, either in the baggage car or in special cars owned by the express companies.

Streetside entrance for ex-press shipments, Seaboard Air Line station in West Palm Beach, Fla.

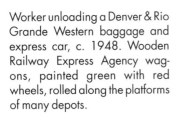

Worker unloading a Denver & Rio Grande Western baggage and express car, c. 1948. Wooden Railway Express Agency wagons, painted green with red wheels, rolled along the platforms of many depots.

This wooden water tank serviced locomotives of the Delaware, Lackawanna & Western. The tank and three-stall roundhouse (both now gone) stood at Ithaca, N.Y.

Outside the depot, other buildings supporting the railroad were found on the grounds or a ways down the track, such as coaling stations and water tanks (to supply the ingredients for making steam) and shanties for crossing guards or watchmen. Signal towers stood where the number of tracks and traffic warranted complex safety controls. Except for very short lines, railroads were (and still are) divided into operating units called "divisions." If the depot was at one of many "division points," typically 100 miles

The Reading Company station at Quakertown, Pa., still stands today, but this crossing guard shanty is long gone. Among the items on the tower were warning bells, a chimney for the coal-fired heat stove, and a stop sign (which the watchman held up in front of street traffic).

apart along the line, the building was substantial in size and usually housed railroad offices on the second floor. At division points, crew and equipment changes occurred. Cars were repaired and switched, and trains dispatched. Each division was further divided into sections about five to 15 miles long, which was the length of line that a "section gang" could maintain and repair. Crew members and division workers rested and lived in bunk or "section houses." (In some parts of the country "section house" meant a tool storage facility.) The section foreman often lived with his family in a home right by the depot, and sometimes took in his "gang" as boarders. Y.M.C.A.s, subsidized by the railroad, were built next to many division point stations and provided inexpensive worker housing. One of these still stands at Hinton, W.Va.

Roundhouse (now gone) at Albany, Ga., c. 1930. Poised for rotation on the turntable, an Atlantic Coast Line locomotive and coal tender.

Dominating the divisions' rail yards were rectangular enginehouses or roundhouses (so called even if they incorporated only a segment of a circle) used for storing and maintaining locomotives; ash pits for coal's residue; and storage houses for oil and sand (the latter used for creating friction on the tracks). Once so essential to the scene at division point stations, few of these original facilities remain today. The increasing preference for diesel locomotives in the 1930s and 1940s completely dethroned "King Steam" by 1960. Although some buildings were converted into service facilities for diesel equipment (which requires relatively low maintenance), railroads centralized their repair sites and typically razed steam-era shops. Scattered remnants of these complexes linger today mostly as industrial artifacts. One rare exception is the three-quarter roundhouse still in use for locomotive repair in Anaconda, Mont., on the aptly named Rarus Railway. A few other roundhouses have been preserved or resurrected by steam tourist railroads or museums. The city of Aurora, Ill., took on an unusual project when it adapted a roundhouse and locomotive shop into a transportation and visitors center.

Various commercial facilities dependent on the railroad rimmed many depots, even those of modest size. Among the most common were grain elevators, ice and coal suppliers, lumberyards, and hotels for "drummers" (traveling salesmen). If departing travelers did not walk to the depot, they parked horse and wagon at the nearby livery stable, which also served as the carriage-for-hire facility to accommodate arriving passengers.

At first, stations did not have identifying signs on their exteriors. Unless the brakeman stuck his head in the coach and called out the station name—and he frequently forgot—travelers had to guess if this was their point of debarkation. Experts at stopping the train with hand brakes on the roof of each car, but sloppy with enunciation, brakemen garbled the announcements they did remember. Eventually, signboards were posted at the gable ends of the depot. Across the front of the building, signs took a form commonly visible in old photographs, with the name of the station stop in the center, destination and mileage for opposite directions (usually terminal points) at each end of the sign. The blue and white signs of Western Union, which eventually wiped out all competing telegraph companies, were nailed to depots across the nation. In later years, these emblems were joined by the ubiquitous "Bell" symbol for public telephone—extremely important in an era when only a tiny fraction of homes or businesses had phone service. Advertising posters spread unchecked. Travelers could be tempted by signs on depot walls to chew "The Real Thing: Wrigley's Spearmint" all the way from Jersey City to Port Jervis.

A gallery of advertising posters wrapped around this long-gone Erie Railroad station at Circleville, N.Y.

LANDSCAPING

Because the depot was a place of pride and the gateway to their community, local citizens, and sometimes the railroads themselves, created gardenlike settings to welcome the traveler. Knowing that beautification programs attracted riders, railroads set up horticultural competitions and awarded prizes to the best station gardens. Quite often, the name of the stop was spelled out with marigolds and daisies or with stones painted white. Landscapers transformed muddy, equipment-strewn station grounds into tidy lawns and rock gardens. Ornamental fountains bubbled next to weeping beech trees and bright azaleas that lined the depots' carriage and pedestrian approaches. Shrubbery hid visually displeasing ele-

Trenton Junction, N.J.

Beside the tracks, the Reading Company planted a formal garden worthy of a castle, July 1914.

In 1929, the railroad replaced this whimsical wooden depot (built in 1882) with a new one clad in brick. The Trenton Junction stop was then renamed West Trenton (served today by trains of the Southeastern Pennsylvania Transportation Authority).

ments from passengers eyes along the immediate right-of-way, and carefully positioned hedges prevented snow from drifting onto the track.

In warm climates like California and Florida, inside waiting rooms tended to be small, while breezeways and courtyards with benches, palm, and banyan trees established open-air gathering spots for passengers. Most companies had sense enough to emphasize regional species, although the Union Pacific attempted to grow deciduous trees in Wyoming. Civic authorities in many communities placed a modest town park right next to the depot, which provided a pleasant waiting area for overflow crowds. Although most of these have been swallowed by urban expansion, Depot Park still exists in Santa Rosa, Calif., where it was laid out on railroad property in 1904 and is maintained by the city today.

Station landscaping was a corporate-level concern for the railroads. In the 1880s, the Boston & Albany hired landscape architect Frederick Law Olmsted, designer of New York's Central Park, to plan the grounds for a series of new stations designed by his Brookline, Mass., neighbor, Henry Hobson Richardson. At stops along the "Newton Circuit," a commuter line linking wealthy Boston suburbs, Olmsted planted wild roses, bridal wreath, Japanese ivy, and a canopy of shade trees. His examples inspired railroad gardening programs all over the country, some of which included greenhouses to provide fresh flowers for dining cars. During the 1920s, at the Outer Station in Reading, Pa. (1874; destroyed by fire in 1978), the Reading Company's staff gardener transplanted 14,000 flowers each June from the railroad's hothouse. They were laid out in fleur-de-lis patterns and arranged to form the corporate logo. At a station in Niles, Mich., horticulturists spelled out the town's name in flowers each spring, while goldfish swam in the depot pond. Agents at many smaller stations earned extra money selling bouquets from the gardens they tended. Depot beautification persists today in a number of communities that still have train service, although it has become almost always the purview of volunteer gardeners rather than the town or railroads. In 1990, a garden club in Deland, Fla., sold personalized bricks, thereby raising enough money to pave sidewalks around the town's renovated depot, plant irrigated shrubbery, and erect a gazebo. Unfortunately, the gardens at most depots that still have passenger service were destroyed during the 1950s when they were blacktopped for parking lots.

Gardens were particularly prevalent at commuter stations that ringed large cities like Boston, New York, Philadelphia, and Chicago. In the era of railroad rather than automobile suburbs, commuters generally lived within walking distance of the station; little space was devoted to vehicular parking. When a new suburb was planned, the developer often constructed a depot as the very first building. The city people who came to inspect the sample houses and select a plot of ground came by rail; a fine depot indicated that a fine community would be built to match. The community's most influential citizens —among them railroad executives and stockholders—departed for work each morning from these stations. They demanded depots that would reflect a progressive and cultivated community. Viewing them as extensions of their elegant suburban homes and wanting to impress guests arriving by train, wealthy suburbanites sometimes contributed personal funds to build depots of sufficient distinction. Today, even without their former lawns, these small, but architecturally sophisticated stations are among the earliest and best preserved passenger stations, especially in concentrated numbers, and the ones most likely to be functioning as originally built. At one time, most of them also had separate freight houses, but few of these diminutive suburban freight depots exist today. A precious example is the wooden, Frank Furness freight station at Noble outside Philadelphia. The Reading Company replaced the corresponding passenger station with a masonry building in 1901, as part of an ongoing "upgrade" that destroyed many of Furness's more stimulating wooden depots.

RAILWAY PALACES AND THE LONG-SPAN TRAIN SHED

The majority of railroads were concerned with their primary money maker—hauling freight—but passenger service was the place to earn public relations stripes. Within the big city centers, railroads battled to outdo each other by constructing the most up-to-date and extravagant station facilities. The volume of traffic seemed to be multiplying with no end in sight, which justified ever bigger yards and terminals. Engaged in an all-encompassing rivalry, more aggressive than the competition between today's automobile makers, a railway "palace" was a good place to display power, wealth, and efficiency—to dazzle both stockholders and the public. In railroad's gilded age, before World War I, opulence earned respect rather than being regarded as undemocratic. The railroads lavished money on a game of architectural one-upsmanship by competing to build the most spectacular monuments to their arrogant success.

The outstanding feature of early railway palaces was an engineering masterpiece called the train "shed." Its lean-to kind of name bore no resemblance to the structure's reality. In some cases soaring more than 100 feet above the trains, covering as many as 32 tracks, and extending over 1,000 feet in length, the "long-span train shed" was an outgrowth of the early, much smaller train "barn." The barn had enclosed the ticket office, waiting rooms, and several tracks; the shed was distinguished by its separation from the waiting room and ticket office structure. It covered only the tracks and platforms. Each designer's challenge was to shelter these under a single roof span, although many sheds used a combination of two or more spans.

Interior of the train shed at Reading Terminal, Philadelphia, c. 1900. Today the arched, single span, which once sheltered 13 tracks, stretches over part of a 1990s convention center.

By combining the wonders of engineering with dazzling architecture, railway palaces became industrial shrines of monumental scale. The shed was attached to a multistoried head house, the equivalent of a mini-city that incorporated not only ticket offices and grand waiting rooms, but also bathing and changing facilities, barber shops, reading rooms, pipe organs, oyster bars, elegant restaurants, private dining rooms, and dozens of retail stores. Extensive train travel involved frequent and sometimes long layovers. For well-heeled vacationers, this was a leisurely era, when the transportation experience was as significant to travel pleasure as the destination. People moved comfortably within the

Artisans who had recently worked on the Chicago World's Columbian Exposition of 1893 brought their talents to the main waiting room of Union Station, Nashville, Tenn. Decorative elements included stained glass, marble, mosaic tile, ornamental plaster, wrought iron, and brass. Beyond the archways bordering the balcony were offices of the Louisville & Nashville.

rhythms and ambience of a railway palace (in total contrast to the impatience of travelers waiting out a "delay" in today's plastic airport seats). Although station amenities were largely directed toward intercity passengers, some metropolitan stations had to simultaneously handle the needs of everyday commuters, who were indeed in a hurry. In the best designs, passage through the building went smoothly, planned by architects who had no previous examples for handling crowds other than cathedrals and theaters. In the worst arrangements, mazelike spaces slowed and frustrated surges of commuters.

Efficient designs for the movement of people began with the civil engineer's conceptions about the movement of trains, specifically the layout of tracks in the switching yards where trains were made up, or in the station's "throat" where the tracks converged before fanning out to approach the shed. When poorly engineered, these elements translated into congestion in the head house, which might be erroneously blamed on the architect. From the windows of the railroad's corporate offices, frequently housed in the upper stories of the head house, executives could bear immediate witness to how well their thousands of dollars in design fees had been spent. Outside the station, a hubbub of streetcars, baggage delivery trucks, and horse-drawn cabs and carriages pulled past the porticoes or through the porte-cocheres. Another constant in and around the station was the United States mail, which was loaded onto specially designed rail cars sometimes trav-

The throat of Boston South Station. In 1930, the tracks terminated under 14 individual platform canopies, which replaced the origional triple-span train shed. Plumes of steam indicate the location of trains.

eling as all-mail trains or at the front end of fast passenger trains. Often, the mail was sorted en route. By the 20th century, post offices were deliberately located alongside the passenger stations of big cities like New York and Philadelphia, where elevators, roof-mounted chutes, and underground passages secured the swift movement of mailbags between the buildings.

The head house and the train shed typically bore little stylistic resemblance to each other. The former was conceived in the architect's dreams; the latter was the province of the civil engineer. Utilized in midsize stations as well as giant railway palaces, the first sheds were made of wood. If they survived the threat of fire, they deteriorated rapidly from exposure to sulfurous steam given off by idling locomotives. Change was initiated in 1851, when a revolutionary exhibition hall, the Crystal Palace, was built in London. The vast floor space roofed by traceries of iron and glass stunned 19th-century visitors, who lived in a world of thick masonry walls, modestly sized windows, and somber decor. The

Crystal Palace concept—exclude the elements, but let in the light—was soon applied to translucent, platform-sheltering vaults of railroad pride. Engineers seized upon the use of cast iron as a structural material and competed to exceed each new record for the widest single-span train shed in the world.

St. Pancras Station in London, begun in 1863, set the example for the great long-span shed at Grand Central Depot in New York City, which was completed in 1871 on the site of today's Grand Central Terminal. The showpiece of Cornelius Vanderbilt's New York Central empire, the train shed and head house formed America's first imposing station designed in the European tradition. The train shed, the largest interior space on the North American continent at the time, ranked as the nation's second most popular building attraction (after the Capitol in Washington). The entire complex was obsolete within three decades, and after major remodeling in the 1890s was replaced in 1913 by the current landmark on Park Avenue.

Essentially a roofed outdoor space, at most walled on three sides and open to the elements at one end, a train shed was an impressive structure, but excessively costly to build,

The first Grand Central Depot in New York City. Designed by architect John B. Snook, the head house contained totally separate waiting and baggage rooms for each of the three railroads it served. To transfer, passengers had to go outside and reenter by another door.

requiring the use of traveling scaffolding. It was also a nightmare to maintain. The highly corrosive fumes emitted by coal-burning engines weakened the structural iron framework, while soot blackened the glass. Both the railroads and the public lost their early enthusiasm for these engineering gems. The theory that great height and louvered ventilators would dispel the noxious fumes proved too dependent on the caprice of wind and temperature. The train shed was cold or stifling during extreme weather conditions, and always dark and smoky. Bad acoustics caused other problems; passengers' ears were assaulted by railroad workers shouting to make themselves heard above the noisy locomotive engines, gongs, and whistles. Stepping lively to avoid battalions of luggage, mail, and express carts wheeled along the platforms, passengers were blasted by steam from the train and splatted by dirty drips from chronically leaking skylights. The acrid, cinder-filled air drifted from the shed into the palatial waiting rooms of the head house.

The initial blow to the long-span train shed was dealt by a civil engineer named Lincoln Bush, whose patented namesake, the Bush shed, was first installed in 1906 at the Delaware, Lackawanna & Western's Railroad and ferry terminal in Hoboken, N.J. A modular concept (infinitely expansible in length and width), the Bush shed was a series of narrow, low vaults, only 16 feet above the rails. Each of the multiple spans covered two adjacent tracks and a half-platform on each side; they were joined together to provide nearly total shelter from the elements. Constructed of steel, protected by a covering of reinforced concrete and copper, the Bush shed withstood the deleterious effects of steam emissions. For safer breathing, the fumes escaped through slots opening a few inches above the locomotive smokestacks. Skylights paralleled the slots and illuminated the platforms; in contrast to the glass canopies of long-span sheds, they could be easily reached for cleaning. What is more, construction costs were halved.

By 1914, Bush sheds had been installed in 12 stations, some of them at new facilities like Pennsylvania Station in Baltimore, and others as replacements for the great long-span sheds, like at the Central Railroad of New Jersey terminal in Jersey City. (Both

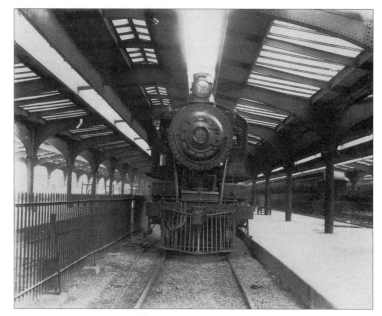

Delaware, Lackawanna & Western locomotive No. 969 inside the 1906 Bush shed at Hoboken, N.J. Steam escaped through slots in the skylit roof; one vent was positioned above each track.

examples are extant, although the one in Jersey City is no longer in railroad use.) As an actively practiced engineering concept, the Bush shed lasted only about a dozen years. Its popularity was soon overtaken by the freestanding "butterfly" or "umbrella" platform sheds supported by center poles (modern versions are used even today at newly built railroad stations or retrofits). The stand-alone sheds were even more economical and easily expandable, but offered minimal protection from wind and rain—and less aesthetic satisfaction than their grand ancestors.

The second blow to long-span train sheds came from the electrification of rail lines which occurred in a number of metropolitan areas. Until the late 19th century, steam trains traveled city streets at grade level or sometimes on elevated viaducts, but rarely underground. The smoke from a steam train going through a long tunnel choked the passengers; even worse, it temporarily blinded the locomotive engineer. In heavily traveled areas, with drivers who could see neither signals nor tracks ahead, trains collided with fatal results, like the 1902 rear-end smashup in the Park Avenue tunnel leading to the old Grand Central.

The tracks at surface level posed another dilemma. They cut dangerous, disruptive swathes through business and residential neighborhoods. Railroads not only consumed and divided valuable downtown real estate, they also caused horrific accidents as trains crisscrossed streets filled with horse-drawn wagons, automobiles, and pedestrians. Whistles, massive noise, cinders, and soot offended both residents and visitors. From earliest rail history, cities struggled with this problem, sometimes by directing railroads to uncouple the locomotive and pull the train into or out of town under real horse power. Various ordinances were passed that permitted steam engines to traverse the community only at night; or, as late as the 1930s, required a flag-carrying guard to ride horseback ahead of the train, while he escorted the monster through town.

The technological capability to electrify rail lines, albeit prohibitively expensive in most areas, meant that tracks could be tun-

November 1916, Danville, Pa. A boy on a bicycle watches Delaware, Lackawanna & Western "camelback" locomotive No. 928 ease across the street.

Original configuration of the train shed at Mount Royal Station in Baltimore. (In the late 1930s, the railroad extended this shed northward, toward the camera.) An overhead third rail provided electricity for eastbound trains coming up through the Howard Street Tunnel.

neled under city streets to provide sootless, smoke-free stations and train-free city thoroughfares. Equally important to railroad executives, electrification converted their aboveground track space into buildable, income-producing real estate. The first electrification occurred in the Howard Street tunnel under downtown Baltimore in 1895. The tunnel fed into the Baltimore & Ohio's splendid new Mt. Royal Station, completed the following year and still standing today. Although Mt. Royal was constructed with a midsize train shed, subsequent electrified stations—in particular New York City's Pennsylvania Station (1910) and Grand Central Terminal (1913)—would have no need for sheds, because all trains arrived underground. Existing sheds continued to be used for decades after the advent of electrification. In Philadelphia, the Reading Company electrified commuter service in the early 1930s, but continued to run long-distance steam or diesel trains into the shed of its 1893 terminal. The five-span shed at St. Louis Union Station, completed the same year as Reading Terminal, was never electrified at all. (Both of these sheds still stand, but the stations are no longer used for train service.)

The last long-span American train shed was completed by the Pennsylvania Railroad at Pittsburgh in 1903 (the shed was razed in 1947). Architects then borrowed the train shed form for other spaces in the great city stations. They transferred the elements of vaulted interiors, exposed trusses, and vast expanses of glass to the grand halls and concourses. The concourse, a transitional territory between tracks and head house, provided for the circulation of crowds. At Union Station in Washington, D.C., the concourse was literally big enough to accommodate an army.

UNION STATIONS

A busy metropolitan station might easily process 500 to 700 trains per day. Some cities, and even small towns, had as many as seven railroads serving passengers, each with its own station. The network of tracks threading through the city streets caused massive congestion and consumed blocks of land needed for other purposes. Separate stations were expensive to operate. A "union" station was formed when two or more railroads agreed to unify their needs and share costs by bringing their trains into or alongside the same depot. Getting old rivals to enter a cooperative venture was sometimes quite difficult. In Seattle, Charles Mellon of the Northern Pacific and James J. Hill of the Great Northern squabbled for a decade over location, architect, and design for a joint station. Modestly sized communities such as North Canaan, Conn., and Iowa Falls, Iowa, also built union stations. There were various kinds of landlord-tenant relationships. The most typical arrangement for larger stations involved a "union terminal company," jointly owned by whichever railroads used the station. This company oversaw construction and operation of the facility. The individual railroads paid use fees based on the amount of business conducted.

Viewed from Broadway, the Romanesque-arched entrance to Union Station in Nashville, Tenn.

Once a union station was built, the railroads routinely demolished the old stations it replaced. In Washington, D.C., the opening of Union Station meant the destruction of B&O's New Jersey Avenue station and the Baltimore & Potomac station (Pennsylvania Railroad subsidiary) on the Washington Mall—fine buildings that modern day preservationists would fight to keep standing. Railroads had numerous other reasons for tearing down and putting up stations, among them was the elimination of grade crossings (by moving, raising, or depressing the tracks) to avoid the traffic-stopping face-offs between automobile and train, where so many accidents occurred. Depots were often in the way of these adjustments and fell to the wrecking ball. Major fluctuations in passenger or freight traffic, increases in community wealth, and changes in architectural taste caused the razing of many other early stations; although small passenger or combination stations were sometimes saved by conversion to freight-only use, for example in Fort Payne, Ala., and Cherokee, Iowa. Accidental fires were an extremely common reason for depot loss, brought on by heat stoves, gas lanterns, and sparking locomotives. Not infrequently, stations were demolished by derailments or runaway trains. For all these reasons, many of the railroad stations that exist today, including those discussed in the regional section of this guidebook, are second- or even fifth-generation buildings.

These early losses occurred within the context of a culture that was still predominately railroad oriented, as part of the ebb and flow of station construction, destruction, and rebuilding. By the 1920s, this situation began to change as powerful forces—all severely negative for railroading—combined to revolutionize the way America moved people,

In 1889, when the Northern Railroad of New Jersey built a new passenger depot at Englewood, N.J., this older depot (photographed c. 1910) was converted to a freight station. The more substantial new station still stands, but its tower has been drastically altered.

Columbus & Hocking Valley station in Canal Winchester, Ohio. Because the preceding depot burned, the agent and two other safety-conscious men are testing the water pressure at the new station.

In 1942, a fruit-carrying freight train derailed at the Grand Trunk Western station in Lansing, Mich. Instead of finishing off the demolition with a wrecking ball, the railroad rebuilt the station to its original appearance.

things, and information. The door-to-door convenience of automobile travel seized middle-class families, and they parked millions of affordable, mass-produced automobiles in newly built garages. Buses and trucks, winners of rate and fare wars with railroads, rolled along on recently paved highways funded by state and federal governments, while the privately owned railroad infrastructure deteriorated. Sea traffic through the Panama

By the end of the first quarter of the 20th century, the internal combustion engine had begun altering transportation modes and land use patterns across the country. Automobiles dominate this street scene in Detroit, Mich.

Canal swallowed an increasing share of railroad business. Nascent commercial airlines revved up previews of the streaking speeds that would become routine a few decades hence. Long-distance telephone service and radio transmissions made instantaneous connections commonplace. The simple marriage of railroad to telegraph multiplied into an intercontinental extended family of transportation and communication systems, which compressed space and time more dramatically than the once startling transition from animal power to steam-driven locomotion. With all these changes, after less than a century of domination (in many parts of the country a mere half-century), the seemingly invincible railroad industry began a slow and tedious decline, taking down with it thousands of the nation's most charming, dynamic, and beloved buildings—the great American railroad stations.

Beyond the Great Depression

✻ ✻ ✻

The Great Depression of the 1930s accelerated the deferred maintenance and demolition by neglect that were gradually destroying the bulk of America's railroad stations. Just a handful of outstanding new ones pierced the shabbiness, like the Art Deco delights in Fort Worth, Tex. (1931), Cincinnati (1933), and Newark, N.J. (1935). In a brief resurgence of activity during World War II, the crowd-handling prowess of railroad stations was put to the ultimate test. Masses of soldiers, off to war or home on leave, jostled throngs of civilians who had been forced back to the

Art Deco in massing and style, the Texas & Pacific station, Fort Worth, Tex.

1944. Above the ground floor were both railroad and commercial offices.

Detail surmounting the main entrance.

rails by gasoline and tire shortages. When the war ended, misguided optimism about the future of passenger service engendered construction of new stations like the lackluster New Orleans Union Terminal (1954) and the small, but more visually stimulating Chesapeake & Ohio station in Prince, W.Va. (1946). The last half of the 20th century brought forth essentially unimaginative passenger shelters and corrugated metal freight houses. Railroad station design and fabrication of any brilliant or innovative nature would never happen again.

For the expanding post-war population of the 1950s, the ideal place to live was a brand new tract house in the suburbs. Easily obtained GI mortgages were used to buy ranch- and split-level-style houses in subdivisions that could only be reached by automobile. These purchases translated into fewer people buying tickets at the railroad station. The building type fell victim to a no-frills world that saw most rail travel as outmoded, unfashionable, and inconvenient. A number of "name trains" like the *Twentieth Century Limited* were refurbished after the war (and even some new trains established) to make another decade or two of luxury runs across the country; but wartime air power, which exploded into a peacetime, commercial aviation industry, skeletonized what was left of long-distance rail travel. Municipalities spent millions of dollars for new public airports that increased regional business and bolstered civic images. Meanwhile, train depots, the province of financially strapped private railroads, decayed into urban ruins.

A road-building frenzy, initiated by a congressional bill in 1944 was reinforced with the Interstate Highway Act of 1956, which designated funds for constructing a nationwide, signal-free road system that could transport troops and materials swiftly by truck in case of war. Joined to state-supported turnpikes and freeways, this network ensured that America's landscape would soon be blanketed by a lava flow of macadam and concrete. The narrow corridors of steel rails that once were within walking distance of most homeowners' front doors—and within 25 miles of almost every farm—were summarily dismantled and sold for scrap.

Pennsylvania Railroad station, Ardmore, Pa., c. 1920s. Built in 1873 along the railroad's prestigious main line just outside Philadelphia, the depot was demolished in 1957. Its one-story replacement is a masonry box devoid of character.

The railroads, losing riders and passenger service revenue at a relentless pace, petitioned regulatory agencies to be let off the passenger-carrying hook. Critics accused the railroads of deliberately maintaining poor and infre-

Atchison, Topeka & Santa Fe
station in Arkansas City, Kans.

1888 version.

1951 replacement
depot embodies the
era's severe, strictly
functional design.

quent passenger service to scare riders away and better their own case for total abandonment of people-hauling. For certain, railroads used low or no maintenance as the guid-
ing principles for dealing with depots. In the extravagant, financially draining big-city stations, the railroads sought to offset expenses by introducing billboards, pay toilets, and
tawdry concession stands. Small-town depots were stripped of their ornate elements,
their second stories were knocked off, or they were totally smashed to the ground. One
form of demolition involved cabling the building to two locomotives and having them pull
in either direction—a tug-of-war in which the parents murder the child. Or municipalities helped out by burning the depots for fire-fighting exercises. If they were replaced at
all, it was by dreary, nondescript boxes. Along Philadelphia's Main Line, about the time
the United States rocket-launched the first satellites, such venerable, active depots as
Ardmore, Bryn Mawr, and Paoli were pulled down. These delicious slices of gingerbread
were supplanted by tasteless, tan brick stations that lacked even the simple charm of a
wooden depot on the western prairie. During the 1950s and 1960s, there was little public outcry over the loss of these old-fashioned buildings. "Victorian" was a synonym for
"monstrosity." In 1956, Carroll L. V. Meeks cheerfully published his classic architectural
study, *The Railroad Station.* Eight years later, upon the 1964 second printing, he lamented
that his treatise, begun as a history, had become an obituary.

PENNSYLVANIA STATION

Carroll Meeks died in 1966. A loss that must have broken his heart—and the hearts of many Americans—was the 1963 shocking, vulgar destruction of Pennsylvania Station in New York City. As the gateway to America's premier metropolis, Penn Station's disappearance from the cityscape still jars the souls of those who knew this beauty. Imagine arriving in New York harbor to find the Statue of Liberty gone, and worse, replaced by a giant plastic Kewpie doll. The station's clandestinely planned demolition was so unconscionable, so large scale, but so casual, that the death of Penn Station gave birth to much of the local and national landmark legislation that followed.

Pennsylvania Station, New York City.

Photo taken from the roof of Macy's department store, February 1910 (prior to the station's full-service opening that November). In the foreground, site preparation for the Hotel Pennsylvania, 7th Avenue and 33rd Street.

The concourse, still under construction, September 1910.

Built during the first decade of the 20th century, Pennsylvania Station was the brainchild of Alexander Cassatt, the forward thinking president of the Pennsylvania Railroad. He was determined to get his trains onto the island of Manhattan, by going over or under the lower Hudson River, which had defied anything but ferry access for more than 30 years. Rail travel on the PRR from the south and west ended on the New Jersey shore, where passengers, including Cassatt himself, had to cross the cold and choppy Hudson on a boat. By the early 1900s, improved tunneling techniques and electrified trains enabled Cassatt to conquer not only the Hudson but the East River as well. The mighty Pennsy now had a purely rail route from New Jersey to Long Island and on to New England via the Hell Gate Bridge.

The workers, called "sandhogs," who tunneled both under the rivers and Manhattan Island itself, had as their destination 32nd Street between 7th and 8th Avenues. At that location, architect Charles F. McKim (McKim, Mead, and White) was supervising construction of a railway palace wrapped in beige travertine, pink Milford granite, and scintillating glass-on-steel framing that was conceived to last for generations. McKim turned to the Continent for design inspiration. His artistry and genius incorporated visions of Sir John Sloane's Bank of England and Bernini's colonnade at the piazza of St. Peter's for the station's facade. On the interior, a colossal main waiting room, modeled after the tepidarium at the Roman baths of Caracalla, nearly overwhelmed travelers with its six-story-high Corinthian columns but nary a bench to rest on. By day, this awesome space was bathed in downward rays of natural light from clerestory windows beneath the vaulted

In the main waiting room, irreplaceable majesty.

The waiting room, its floor strewn with rubble, midway through demolition in 1964.

and coffered ceiling. In the evening, candelabra-topped iron lampposts, anchored in marble, lit the way to McKim's graceful steel and glass canopied concourse, where the industrialized world of American rail transport intersected ancient Rome.

Exhausted by illnesses and personal tragedies, neither Alexander Cassatt nor Charles McKim lived to see the festive opening day in 1910, when 100,000 dazzled sightseers arrived to watch from the concourse, suspended above the tracks, as the first trains arrived and departed. The building itself, so substantial and sublime, would not live beyond the ignominious seventh decade of the 20th century.

By the 1950s, Penn Station was layered with thick soot, masking the beautiful pink and beige tones of its masonry. Then the usual sort of disrespectful things happened that plagued America's grandest railroad architecture, most notably the intrusion of an enormous, glaring ticket counter enclosure, cabled to the waiting room's towering ceiling and blocking the entrance to the concourse. Up the grand marble staircase, an arcade of elegant shops was scarred by the installation of modern storefronts. And in a final, ironic show of contempt, elevated displays of new automobiles invaded the station.

Meanwhile, the Pennsylvania Railroad was making secret plans to rid itself of this now gray elephant. Desperate for financial transfusions to their ailing business, Pennsy executives sold the station's air rights—a death warrant with the stroke of a corporate pen. The railroad would continue to own only the tracks beneath the surface. In exchange, the Pennsy got a quarter interest in the relocated Madison Square Garden sports complex that was built atop a new, low-ceilinged, fluorescently lit, below ground station—the bargain basement mockery of a once glorious structure. Pennsy's "strictly business" minds saw architecture only as real estate value; and although there had been public relations rhetoric about "giving" to the community when the structure was built, there was no corresponding sense of guilt about "taking" it away.

Once spread triumphantly over eight city blocks, Pennsylvania Station was demolished starting in October 1963, a heinous task that dragged on for two years. Generally speaking, historic preservation was scarcely a phrase in the vocabulary of Manhattan residents, even those who considered themselves culturally aware. The recently formed New York City Landmarks Preservation Commission was not yet vested with power. Just a handful of prominent architects tried to stop the obliteration of this national treasure, but they found themselves whistling in a darkened railway tunnel with no light at the end. Only after the sculptural maidens carved by Adolph Weinman lay dumped among debris in the New Jersey Meadowlands, only after the six stone eagles that once perched above the portico had found various new homes (grounded in front of the new sports complex or guarding shopping malls), and only after travelers took their first train to or from the fit-for-trolls successor station, did people really notice that they had failed to protect a building they unknowingly cherished. That shortsightedness, coupled with the absence of adequate legislation, effectively pulverized an architectural masterpiece. In the long view, the strength of the New York City Landmarks Preservation laws—a national model for fighting urban desecration—was fueled by Penn Station's demise; but what a grievous price to pay.

Save the Depot!

✯ ✯ ✯

By the mid-1960s, the smattering of American preservationists who had opposed the destruction of New York City's Pennsylvania Station had grown into a modest army, embattled against the ravages, not of war, but a decade of government "urban renewal" programs—the perversion of the City Beautiful concept a half-century earlier. Most of America's midsize to large metropolitan railroad stations were destroyed between the 1950s and 1970s. Maintenance costs, the escalating value of downtown real estate, and the opportunity to sell air rights above railroad-owned property continued to decimate the ranks. Glass-roofed sheds and concourses were especially strong candidates for demolition.

Outraged when federal funds were used to wipe out entire neighborhoods, preservationists campaigned for passage of the National Historic Preservation Act, which became law in October 1966, exactly three years after the first wrecking ball struck Penn Station. Amended numerous times since then,

In April 1974, this "April Fools'" cartoon appeared in *Preservation News,* published by the National Trust for Historic Preservation.

49

the legislation was designed to reverse the epidemic destruction of treasured landmarks. It established an Advisory Council on Historic Preservation (at first part of the National Park Service; after 1976, an independent federal agency) to advise the President and Congress on preservation matters. The council's initial task was to draw up guidelines for protective review of any projects involving historic properties and the use of federal funds, and for resolution of conflicts that might arise. This review process would be applied to properties listed in the National Register of Historic Places—the expansion of an earlier inventory of districts, sites, structures, and objects significant in American history, architecture, archeology, and culture. The secretary of the interior, through the National Park Service, was assigned to oversee the National Register and authorized to grant matching funds for states to survey their historic sites. Subsequently, the National Register became a tool for identifying recipients of financial aid used to acquire, preserve, and develop historic properties, including depots, during the 1970s.

The Tax Reform Act of 1976 and the Economic Recovery Act of 1981 offered investors generous tax incentives for participating in projects that did not demolish historic buildings, but rather restored them. Numerous railroad stations in various sizes were renovated under guidelines set forth by the secretary of the interior. These projects established benchmarks for creatively and appropriately designed adaptive uses. Among those were Union Station in St. Louis, Mo., accommodating a hotel, restaurants, and stores; a small

At Union Depot in Galveston, Tex., a museum called the Center for Transportation and Commerce re-creates the 1930s ambience of its preserved waiting room. Visitors use audio tapes to eavesdrop on imaginary conversations typical of the era. This collection of 36 life-size figures is the work of Ivan and Elliott Schwartz of New York City.

depot in Higginsville, Mo., adapted to an antiques shop and later a museum; an 1880s Richardsonian Romanesque station in Battle Creek, Mich., remade into a restaurant; a Great Northern depot in Aberdeen, S.D., transformed into professional offices; and the apartment house conversion of Pennsylvania Station in Pittsburgh. Unfortunately, the Tax Reform Act of 1986, which was more like a deforming action, substantially weakened the benefits available to outside investors in such projects. The loss of these tax credits had a drastically negative effect on historic preservation and no doubt resulted in many depots being poorly remodeled, remaining abandoned, or reduced to dust.

Amtrak's Broadway Limited departing Chicago, November 14, 1971. Behind the locomotive of this "rainbow train" is a motley collection of cars acquired from at least four different railroads.

AMTRAK

While federal preservation laws were being written in Washington, and local ordinances were being thrashed out in scattered places across the country, nearly 150 years of historic rail operations were coming to an end. Passenger service was about to experience a total overhaul that would affect thousands of railroad stations. Virtually all private rail carriers had ceased to invest capital in passenger equipment or services, let alone depots. In 1968, a last-ditch merger occurred between fierce old rivals, the Pennsylvania Railroad and the New York Central. But by 1970, Penn Central had filed for bankruptcy; and passenger operations, even in the more heavily traveled northeast corridor, were in a dramatically obvious crisis. Foreseeing that passenger service in the United States would surely and shortly dwindle to zero, Congress created the National Railroad Passenger Corporation commonly known as Amtrak, which began operations in May 1971 (over a network much reduced even from the immediately preceding years).

For decades, airline and highway industries had been government subsidized, albeit indirectly, through construction and maintenance of airports and the federal highway system, while rail companies had to dig solely into their own threadbare pockets. After passage of the Rail Passenger Service Act, Amtrak was eligible for direct federal funds to underpin its new for-profit corporation (virtually all of Amtrak's stock today is held by the United States Department of Transportation). Congress valued at least some level of passenger service and recognized (with some lapses in comprehension) that no country in modern times expects this form of transportation to stand completely on its own.

Within eight years, all of America's remaining trunk lines had gone out of the passenger business or had conveyed their passenger service to Amtrak. Such well-known names as Union Pacific and Atchison, Topeka & Santa Fe—railroads that had brought new settlers to the West and later carried tourists to see the natural wonders of America—became freight-only railroads. Today, except for most of the northeast corridor and a stretch in the Midwest, Amtrak operates principally over the trackages of these freight railroads (and in some cases commuter railroads). Amtrak stops at more than 500 locations, but owns only 13 percent of the depots, some of which are just plastic shelters. The balance are owned by various entities, from freight lines to municipalities to private parties; and frequently, the owner of the depot building, the land beneath it, and the platform are not the same. (Preservationists typically must unravel and satisfy this tangled knot of title holders, when they attempt to acquire a depot.)

The formation of Amtrak ultimately benefited the preservation of railroad depots beyond the obvious reason—providing a train ride to the station—but not without passing through some very rough times. At first, virtually all of the depots were owned by railroads that still ran freight over the tracks, like the Chicago & North Western or Burlington Northern. As passenger service was reorganized, Amtrak phased out unprofitable station stops, and the freight-only lines categorized many depots as "surplus," i.e. candidates for demolition. (The railroad euphemism is "removal.") Structures in countless places were lost, although many communities scrambled to find alternate uses. In certain cases, the smaller buildings stayed in railroad service, but they were used for equipment storage or office space by freight-only lines, rather than having any passenger function. The big-city depots, even if Amtrak still serviced the area, mostly suffered neglect. Amtrak frequently occupied only a small portion of the building, or built an inelegant shelter next door, or moved the station stop to the suburbs. Fortunately, for one heavily traveled region, a congressional appropriation in 1974 authorized the Northeast Corridor Improvement Project. Over the next ten years, Amtrak upgraded trackage and cooperated in ventures with public and private parties to restore historic stations in eight cities: Boston, New Haven, New London, Newark, Philadelphia, Wilmington, Baltimore, and Washington, D.C. By contrast, the list of large stations felled by dynamite or the wrecking ball during the 1970s would fill several pages (the smaller ones, a volume). Most communities no longer had train service, and the white knight of adaptive use rode into only a few big cities like St. Louis and Cincinnati.

The former Pennsylvania Railroad station, Wilmington, Del., in 1984. As part of the Northeast Corridor Improvement Project, Amtrak rebuilt the station's sidewalk canopy to closely match the original.

At historically significant stations where passenger service continued, Amtrak generally lacked the funds to cover depot improvements on its own. The railroad was sometimes able to participate in joint projects with other railroads (freight only) that still owned the buildings or with local governments and citizens groups. In Orlando, Fla., more than 1,200 volunteers and 60 businesses donated labor and materials to beautify the Sligh Boulevard Station; Amtrak covered approximately 15 percent of the total cost. On a large scale, the massive restoration of Union Station in Washington, D.C., was a cooperative venture of Amtrak, federal and city governments, and a commercial developer.

In the early Nineties, the fortunate citizens of several communities witnessed an unexpected near-miracle. Passenger service was restored to places where it had been discontinued, seemingly never to return. Because Greeley, Colo., and Evanston, Wyo., had preserved their depots, the buildings were available for rededication as scheduled stops on Amtrak's Pioneer Route. In Los Angeles, commuters now wait for new light rail trains near the 1904 Watts Pacific Electric depot, now listed in the National Register of Historic Places. Restored and adapted to office use in 1989, it had not experi-

Located at 103rd Street and Grandee Avenue, the former Pacific Electric depot at Watts (Los Angeles) in 1906.

enced the whoosh of a train for 40 years. These examples demonstrate the importance of preserving not only the building but also the right-of-way (once abandoned, ownership usually reverts to adjacent landowners). Recreational "rail trails" are one productive alternative. A 1983 federal "railbanking" law allows unused railroad corridors to be set aside for future train use, while serving as biking, walking, and horseback riding trails for the interim. Upwards of 7,000 miles in about 600 projects have been railbanked in this fashion. Rail corridors vary nationally from 30 to 200 feet wide, in some cases providing enough space for a "rail plus trail," should train service be reestablished.

INTERMODAL SURFACE TRANSPORTATION EFFICIENCY ACT

In the 1980s, when grants-in-aid became generally unavailable, tax incentives for historic rehabilitation in some cases took up the slack, until undermined by the 1986 Tax Reform Act. While preservationists continued to fight for reinstatement of beneficial tax credits, another form of financial rescue for depots was provided by the Intermodal Surface Transportation Efficiency Act. Passed by Congress in late 1991 (and promptly dubbed "iced tea"), ISTEA made available $155 billion in federal funds for transportation projects over six years. Approximately $3 billion were earmarked as "enhancement funds" which could be used for restoring facilities on historic transportation corridors—including active and inactive railroad stations. In 1993, the National Trust for Historic Preservation, in cooperation with several transportation and conservation organizations, held a series of workshops on ISTEA to discuss funding acquisition and project implementation. Since that time, many communities continue to be successful in obtaining ISTEA funds for buying and restoring their depots. In a typical arrangement, the federal government's contribution is 80 percent, with the balance coming from various local sources. Ventures range from small local museums and "rail-trail" headquarters to full-blown, active passenger stations, often with a mixed-use component. Numerous examples appear in the regional section of this guidebook.

Yet while positive legislative and reorganizational procedures have been instituted in high places—and some depots have been saved—abandonment, neglect, and demolition continue their unabated assault on many of America's railroad stations. The statistics tell the story. By 1916, America had reached its peak in track mileage—about 264,000 miles of main and branch lines, rail yards, and sidings. That same year, John A. Droege, general superintendent of the New York, New Haven & Hartford, published a book called *Passenger Terminals and Trains.* He placed the number of passenger or combined passenger and freight stations at 85,000. (Droege covered strictly freight depots in another volume.) At a workshop sponsored by the National Endowment for the Arts in 1974, the National Park Service estimated that 20,000 railroad stations remained, although the study was not specific about the type of stations considered. Informal research accumulated by the author of *Great American Railroad Stations* suggests that by the early 1990s, not more than 12,000 depots existed—an average of about 250 per state or 15 percent of the 1916 figure.

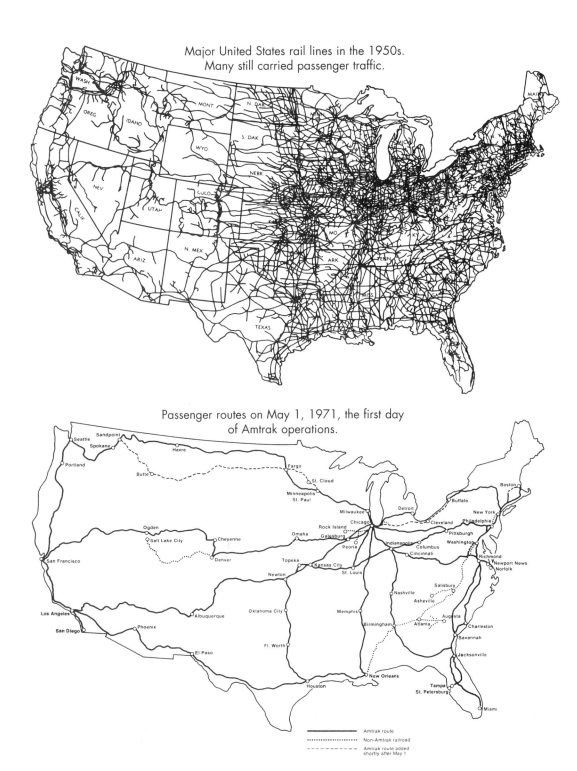

Major United States rail lines in the 1950s.
Many still carried passenger traffic.

Passenger routes on May 1, 1971, the first day
of Amtrak operations.

——————— Amtrak route

·················· Non-Amtrak railroad

– – – – – – – Amtrak route added
shortly after May 1

A comparison of these two maps shows the acute decline in passenger service that occurred within just two decades.

As the number of historic depots continues to decline, a different statistic is on the upswing—railroad stations restored and adaptively used for purposes other than rail travel, or with train service as just one component of a multiuse facility. Of the railroad stations that remain, many are in better condition now than they were for decades; but a substantial portion linger in abused or endangered circumstances. More small to medium-size stations than large ones are at risk, simply because quantitatively they once saturated the country. Of the huge metropolitan terminals, virtually all have been either demolished or restored, with the exception of two in serious jeopardy: Central Terminal in Buffalo, N.Y., and the Michigan Central station in Detroit. These two are in the hands of private developers and have seen numerous proposals put forth for years without resolution. Eventually, railroad stations will fall into one of only two categories: rehabilitated or nonexistent (including those altered beyond recognition). Preservationists are working hard to beat the bulldozer and put more depots into the first category. This undertaking, given a substantial boost by ISTEA, requires creative transportation, urban, and economic planning combined with tenacity and diplomacy.

TRACKS TO THE FUTURE

Railroad depots represent a unique building type, part of a collective memory. Even for people born in the years after railroading's preeminence, in a time when the family car (frequently a "station wagon") had clearly replaced the locomotive as the romantic symbol of the open road, trains and railroad stations populate the landscape of our culture. Appearing often in feature films—*Silver Streak, Murder on the Orient Express, Union Depot*—and the idioms of speech—"whistle stop," "asleep at the switch," "jerkwater (or tank) town"—steam railroading myth and terminology manage to infiltrate our computerized, fiber optic lives. Impressionable preschoolers enter the world of railroads through a public television program based on a 1940s British story about Thomas the Tank

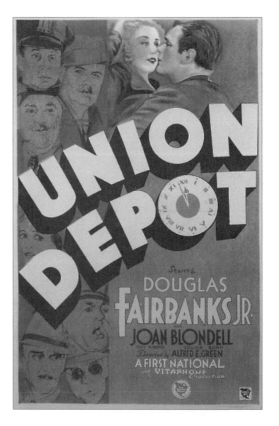

Dozens of subplots crisscross in the 1932 movie *Union Depot.* Throughout its history, the motion picture industry has used sets and, more often, actual locations for hundreds of railroad station scenes.

Engine. Called *Shining Time Station*, the program's loyal audience may never see a real train nor live within 300 miles of a passenger-carrying track. Whether people ride trains or not, the depot symbolizes journey, anticipation, adventure, and mystery—not a place to stand still, but a building that represents movement, speed, and change—primary components of America's traditional outlook on life. Because of this embedded, unspoken tug at our dreams, the depot often becomes a rallying point for historic preservation.

Crossing socioeconomic boundaries, a "Save the Depot!" campaign is commonly the first preservation project a community attempts, with a wide variety of individuals contributing strategy, money, influence, materials, and labor to do the job. The station sometimes serves as the cornerstone for a large-scale historic and commercial revitalization that follows. In other communities, the depot is the only historic building left in town, the sole structural connection to their boomtown past and therefore an intense focus of pride, despite its typically plain face. In a country where just a few generations back, one in every six nonagrarian jobs was with the railroad, millions of people have fathers, grandfathers, aunts, and uncles who worked for the industry. The humblest depot maintains a sense of place, the last link to a once powerful heritage. The yearning to preserve their stations is so fierce that some communities have heroically rebuilt depots completely gutted by fire. In Grass Lake, Mich., citizens used original specifications to reconstruct their former depot, rather than let the remaining walls be bulldozed after fire fighters put

Michigan Central station, Grass Lake, Mich.

June 22, 1980, the day after a fire devastated the depot.

Rebuilding completed, 1991. Measured drawings, which had been made in the 1970s, enabled workers to re-create the contour of the roof. The cost of the depot's reconstruction was paid for in part by private contributions totaling $100,000. Each donor's name was incised in a new brick walkway.

out the blaze. Churches are the only other nonresidential building type with so much symbolic value that if destroyed, they inspire exacting reproduction. And most depots are not even needed for their original purpose.

Railroad stations have been the subject of frequent preservation battles across the country, which often center around a problem peculiar to this building type. Many old stations in small communities, though not in railroad use, are still sited along active freight lines. Upon hearing rumors of imminent demolition, or watching the station decay from neglect, residents come knocking on corporate doors with a request that the railroad sell, donate, or lease them the station. In particular, the big "Class I" railroads tend to refuse. They express a generalized fear (not valid in every case) that a building transferred to community use incurs increased risks of safety and liability, because visitors or children will wander onto the tracks. Sometimes installation of a fence, sealing off doorways, or pulling the building back a few hundred yards resolves the conflict; although these steps seriously interfere with the contextual relationship of the depot to the very rails that brought life to its door.

MOVE IT OR LOSE IT

Historically, at times of track realignments or facility upgrades, railroads often moved the old depot for use in a new location (still along the rails). A variation on this pattern continues today when preservationists find that relocation (typically away from the rails) is the only route to the building's survival. Railroads tended to move their depots by train; now the transport is usually by truck. Easy portability means that certain stations have been relocated as many as six times, usually a combination of railroad and preservation moves over the years. Sometimes the trip is long distance (one depot in Nebraska was moved 90 miles to a museum); sometimes just a few hundred feet. In the best (but rarest) circumstances, the move involves renewed life as a regular train stop, as with a 1990s project for the old "Big Four" depot in Lafayette, Ind., (*see* page 312).

The most common new location is a municipal park, a move that saves the building but destroys any integrity of setting or industrial association. Sometimes a stretch of evocative, go-nowhere track is laid down to recreate a proper juxtaposition, with a locomotive or caboose parked outside the door to maintain a sense of scale. (Ideally this piece of equipment is from a compatible period and railroad.) In a less static fashion, tourist railroads can provide a very appropriate new use for old stations. Typically summer-only operations, run either as nonprofit avocational pursuits or by freight lines looking for extra revenue, these round-trip scenic cruises provide an excellent opportunity to board a train from a historic depot, although amidst an atmosphere probably more serene and sanitized than what existed in the railroad era. One example is an 1891 depot in New Hope, Pa. After spending time off-site as a hunting lodge, it was moved back to the tracks, placed somewhat closer to the extant freight house, and restored as part of a steam-train operation.

The passenger depot at New Hope, Pa., c. 1930s, still bearing its Philadelphia & Reading weather vane. Originally located on Bridge Street and Railroad Avenue, it was moved in the early 1950s to a wooded area for use as a clubhouse. The following decade, the depot was moved to Bridge and Stockton streets, near the extant freight house, to service a tourist railroad.

The pressure to relocate a depot can occasionally be lifted by citizens offering to pay the insurance premiums or by finding an occupant with limited visitor traffic, like a small office or commercial venture. But citizens should be aware that railroads tend to be more cooperative when local authorities are involved in any proposals put forward. They are comforted by the idea that civic powers will remain accountable even if citizens groups dissolve. In some cases, a railroad is readily willing to sell or donate the depot, but will only rent the land—with the proviso that the ground lease can be terminated on short notice. This situation falls somewhere between a mixed blessing and an outright predicament for the group that wants to find a use for the depot. Few people want to invest in restoring or occupying a building where the ground can virtually be pulled out from under them.

STATE AND LOCAL SOLUTIONS

A number of states, such as California, New Mexico, and Michigan, have established programs that make multimodal use of their depots—as the junction for train, bus, taxi, and senior citizen van services. These facilities have frequently stimulated commercial renewal that has spread to surrounding properties. In Kalamazoo, Mich., a state grant facilitated the full restoration of a handsome 1887 depot to be a center for Amtrak, the city transit system, and various commercial concerns. Other paths to preservation involve transit authorities—for example, those in New Jersey and southeastern Pennsylvania—that have developed successful policies for renting space in their historic depots. Tenants are offered low rent in exchange for agreeing to rehabilitate and maintain the buildings. Commuters are allowed access to the platforms and sometimes to conventional or dual-purpose waiting rooms. If train service has been discontinued, but the building is still owned by a railroad or transit authority, a lease in exchange for maintenance can keep the structure in good condition, banked for a future time when rail service may resume.

Local governments play a crucial role in the preservation of any historic structure. Listing a building in the National Register of Historic Places denotes a building's significance on the state or national level and is often an important step in obtaining grants or tax benefits. But contrary to a commonly held misperception, National Register listing will not prevent the demolition of a building. United States law requires a review process for National Register properties only if proposed changes or demolition involve federal funding, licensing, ownership, or management. Even this review does not guarantee that the building will be properly preserved or restored. Furthermore, only a portion of significant structures are listed in the National Register. Concerned citizens must understand that the power to issue or not issue a demolition permit rests at the local level. Zoning laws, preservation ordinances, and bold planning departments can make the difference between a restored railroad station and a pile of memories carted to the dump. Last minute heroics rarely save a building. The time to act is well before a preservation crisis, by surveying historic railroad stations and passing legislation on the local frontier, where more communities need to be drawing their lines in the sand.

Depot preservation continues to be affected by the bankruptcies, consolidation, or automation of today's freight railroads. Economic streamlining brings two direct dangers: (1) abandonment of infrequently used branch lines and their associated buildings and (2) disposal of surplus buildings along active routes. Citizens need to prepare for these possibilities by maintaining contact with the railroads and with congressional legislators, and also by understanding how state property tax laws impact depot preservation. Local groups should delineate viable (and ideally self-sufficient) economic plans, study the possible liability issues, and seek advice from their state historic preservation officer on how to proceed.

Once the station is in hand, whatever the planned use, rehabilitators face a challenge to maintain or reestablish some element of railroading context. Even if the depot stays on its original site, the tracks may be gone, and rarely do any pieces of associated architecture stand nearby. Over the years, depot platforms and canopies were cut back to accommodate bigger locomotives, taller freight cars, and mechanized track maintenance equipment. Cupolas, dormers, and clock towers were seen as upkeep problems by financially struggling railroads and as antiquated gewgaws by streamline-minded, post–World War II generations. Agents were no longer needed and neither were their bay windows. Once dispatchers (increasingly computer-assisted) started controlling train traffic from centralized locations, depot "order boards" and other hand-operated signals became obsolete. The replacement of any of these features by today's owners or occupants, especially the platform and the roof that shades it, re-creates for the visitor a sense that this was a place for waiting, for boarding, for going somewhere on a train. In most depots, the roof is the chief visual element, not the walls. The original architects put much thought into the design and choice of materials of this building component. Reproducing the same look is critical to the restoration process, despite the expense. The village of Greenport recognized this fact when it obtained a matching grant from the state of New York to restore its 1892 Long Island Rail Road station. Completed in time for the building's centennial, work included extending the handsome trefoil-bracketed overhang, which had previously been cut back by one-third.

Other platforms and overhangs will not fare so well in the future, as federal legislation and new transportation policies change the look of many active depots in the 1990s. In historical configurations, after the train pulled into the station, passengers descended steps that hung from each car's vestibule. (The conductor held out a helping hand.) Today, mini- or full-size, high-level platforms, flush with the floor of the rail car, are being installed at virtually all active passenger stations, a transformation dictated both by federal laws about handicapped access and by the carriers' desire to quickly load and unload riders "subway style." Unless well-considered plans are tailored for each location, this change adversely affects the building's visual and historical relationship to the platform. In New Canaan, Conn., a group of residents are considering raising an 1868 wooden depot to put the building back on proper terms with today's elevated commuter platform. Another negative impact on a depot's appearance can occur (as it did at New Canaan) when the railroad determines that an overhanging canopy must be shortened or removed to accommodate the new platform-to-train relationship.

Many depot interiors have suffered over time as well, whether the building remains in railroad use or has been adapted to other purposes. Traffic is drastically reduced at most of the stations that continue to serve passengers, and often interior space has been adjusted to save energy or accommodate additional uses. In other cases, freight-only railroads are the exclusive users of former passenger stations. Although technically still in railroad use, these depots house activity very different from former times, even from old freight station operations. Because "less-than-carload" shipments go by truck, these

Station at New Canaan, Conn., built by the New Canaan Railroad (later New York, New Haven & Hartford). This early 20th-century view shows the original relationship of tracks to platform level and depot.

depots now house maintenance equipment or computerized railroad offices, not goods in transit. Freight railroads often reposition or add interior walls, or they block up doors and windows. Similar problems can occur with adaptive use, because of the relative ease with which a depot's open spaces can be reconfigured. A depot may say "railroad station" on the outside, but pure "delicatessen," or "dentist's office" on the inside. Preservationists who acquire depots with remodeled interiors can contribute to architectural correctness by reintroducing original features such as partitions, ceiling height, and woodwork. Painting with authentic colors and installing period light fixtures and benches help bring back the flavor of the railroad world.

Another challenge in adaptive use arises from the fact that many depots lacked a connecting hallway. The only way from one room to another, or from downstairs to upstairs, was by going outside and reentering through another exterior door or taking the outside stairs. The best cure for this problem is to find a mixture of uses where separate access serves as an advantage.

CLOSING THE LOOP

Commercial occupants of depots have found that even small displays of "railroadiana" such as timetables, telegraph equipment, lanterns, a freight scale, and ticket cubbyholes remind people that a train once stopped at this location. At a current commuter stop along the old Pennsylvania Railroad in Chestnut Hill (part of Philadelphia), two ticket stubs found during conversion of the waiting room to a bank are framed and posted on the wall. The first reads: *From Chestnut Hill to Brooklyn via Short Line. One Corpse. $2.39.* The other reads:

Early view of the Pennsylvania Railroad station at Chestnut Hill in Philadelphia. A commuter station now called Chestnut Hill West, the depot houses a ticket office and a bank branch. Its spire and central dormer are missing, but covered stairs still lead to a canopied, historic trolley stop.

White Hall station, Bryn Mawr, Pa. This photo was taken in 1870, just before the Pennsylvania Railroad realigned the old Philadelphia & Columbia tracks and built a new Bryn Mawr passenger station. The new station (a handsome Wilson Brothers design; razed c. 1963) was positioned a half-mile northeast of White Hall. The White Hall depot, now owned by a hospital, is still on its original site at County Line Road and Old Railroad Avenue (the paved-over P&C right-of-way).

Mr. James Hopkins. 2 Horses. 2 Carriages. 1 Attendant. from Chestnut Hill to Atlantic City via Delaware River Bridge. $26.69. Apparently Mr. Hopkins's fare covered not only himself, but also shipment of his private vehicles—in much the same fashion as travelers today place themselves and their cars aboard Amtrak's Florida-bound *Auto Train.* These artifacts remind us of the building's history and provide a tangible, primary-source contact with the past.

Although not categorized or labeled as such back then, mixed and adaptive use of railroad stations occurred even in the 19th century. The 1885 railroad station in Millis, Mass., was built with multiuse intentions; municipal offices and a library filled the second floor. Today the building serves exclusively as the town hall. Probably the oldest adaptive use on record is the station at White Hall, now part of Bryn Mawr, Pa. Built in the late 1850s, it was the stop for the White Hall hotel a few hundred yards away, where Philadelphians came to escape the heat and disease of the summer city. About 1870, the Pennsylvania Railroad, which had bought the state-owned Philadelphia & Columbia, realigned the track and eliminated the White Hall stop. The old depot was converted to an isolation ward for the Bryn Mawr Hospital (which uses it today for a volunteer-run thrift shop). After 125

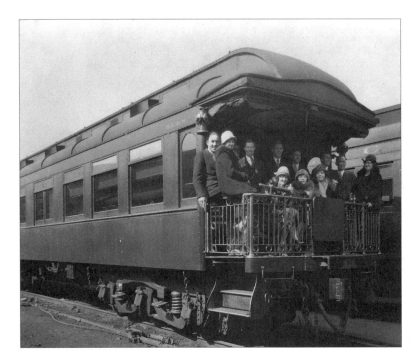

Saving a depot connects people to an earlier time, when most long-distance travel involved the excitement of taking a train. In this c. 1930 photo, a group of stylish passengers is about to depart from the Lackawanna Ferry and Railroad Terminal, Hoboken, N.J.

years of adaptive use, the building still looks like a railroad station, although the depot's entrance was opposite the side currently used. An 1870 brick station in Tonawanda, N.Y., began its saga of reuse in 1922. The New York Central relocated its tracks to the other side of town, and the old depot was converted to a meeting place for the American Legion and the Boy Scouts. In 1935, the city library took over the building. Thirty years later the old depot went through another adaptation to become a museum.

By the 1990s, adaptive use was more than the age-old practical inclination to "make do;" it had become a trend—and the only way to stop the loss of a building type declining rapidly in numbers. The most common uses found today, either in single or mixed use, are restaurant, office, museum, library, store, art gallery, bank, visitors center, dwelling, and community meeting space. In many ways, the depot has gone full circle, from the old days as informal clubhouse and social center to new life as space where local theater groups give plays and brides and grooms hold wedding receptions. The National Council on the Aging has a program called Discovery Through the Humanities, a series of discussion groups for older citizens. With a bittersweet twist, many of these oral history sessions gather at depots converted to senior centers. Railroading is one of the most passionately discussed topics; although ironically, the only means of transportation to the station is by car. In the most satisfying situations, adaptive use is combined with a train stop, where locomotives still lumber to a halt outside the door. A conductor calls "All Aboard!" beckoning passengers to a ride down the long steel rails to yet another depot—where strangers, loved ones, work, adventure, sadness, and joy are waiting to meet us at the station.

Guide to the Guide

✵ ✵ ✵

ew extant railroad stations have not been altered or relocated, whether during their active years, decades of abandonment, or conversion to adaptive use. The buildings highlighted in this book—principally passenger stations (or combination freight and passenger)—are rarely fully intact; and their functions often differ widely from their original uses. Individually and as a collection, they were chosen for the story they tell about the era when railroading was central to America's growth and everyday existence, as well as the story of their new roles within today's automobile-oriented society. The author hopes that with a little guidance from this book, both armchair tourists and actual sightseers can imagine the stations (dating from about 1830 to 1950) as they once appeared, including the elements that gave the buildings life—travelers and trains; workers who sold tickets and tapped out telegrams; and crates and baggage carts that bumped along the platforms. Many of these depots were ravaged over the years by modernization, vandalism, or fire. But preservation-minded communities and entrepreneurs resisted the easy solution (polishing the building off with a bulldozer) and seized the opportunity to integrate the old with the new, thus safeguarding a measure of historic texture for the neighborhood. It is no exaggeration to say that without these people, scarcely any depots would remain. Other stations listed in this book may merit such sympathetic treatment, yet still await rescue. They are trapped in the web of financial constraints, apathy, and lack of imagination that have doomed tens of thousands of stations before them. For some of these highly endangered depots, inclusion in this book may turn out to be their last hurrah.

The volume is divided by region and then alphabetically by state and town. (A number of extant depots have been moved to other municipalities or even other states. They are listed according to their current location.) The invention of the automobile made individualized travel plans a reality. One could leave home and go directly to the destination—in one conveyance and at any hour. This fluidity, especially once superhighways were developed, nearly destroyed United States passenger train service. Except in metropolitan areas, train service today is nonexistent or infrequent. With some irony, the only possible or practical way to visit most entries in this book is by car. An address or intersection is provided within the information that heads each depot's profile. Visitors may enjoy searching the area for additional stations. Street maps (especially for places that still have tracks) and old railroad maps are useful in the gumshoe process—just follow the rails or abandoned right-of-ways and keep an eye out for that "railroad station" look.

Below the address is the name, if available, of the person or firm responsible for the station's design. This slot is restricted to architects or civil engineers whose work on the building could be documented with some certainty. Frequently, the signature found on a depot blueprint is simply the stamp of approval from the railroad's chief civil engineer, whom researchers sometimes mistakenly identify as the architect. Credit has been given, the author hopes accurately, to the proper talent. The date noted is the year the depot was completed or went into service.

Each entry identifies the name of the railroad at the time the depot was built, as well as the more commonly known (usually bigger) railroad that owned or dominated the station in later years. Physical descriptions were taken, where possible, from early newspaper articles, to give today's reader a vision of the depots as they were in their heyday. Details are provided not only to demonstrate the extensive attention once paid to the aesthetics of transportation buildings, but also to provide clues for the visitor's understanding of what remains. To put the buildings in context, notations are made of related structures found on (or near) the station site and of certain other depots known to be in (or lost from) the community. If "NR" or "NR District" appears in the entry, the building is listed in the National Register of Historic Places. "NHL" or "NHL District" is a far more exclusive designation, indicating National Historic Landmark status—an honor bestowed on only about 20 depots in the country.

Gathered primarily in 1992 and 1993, information on ownership and use will ideally serve three purposes: (1) to aid readers planning a station tour, (2) to generate ideas for "save the depot" groups, and (3) to give historians an overview of the late 20th-century status of these buildings. Within the brackets at the end of each entry are two notations. The first is the title holder to the depot structure itself (but not necessarily the land, platforms, or tracks). The second notation is the current function—sometimes appearing incongruous next to the owner's name (especially if the building is leased from a freight railroad)—ranging from continued use as a passenger train stop to totally nonrailroad enterprises. *Train stop/npa* means that although boarding and disembarking occur at this site, there is "no passenger access" to the depot. (In some cases, the building may in fact be open to the public, for example, as a restaurant, but does not provide waiting space for travelers.) *Depot museum* means the management has tried to recreate the appearance of an active station (as contrasted to a museum exhibiting collections of art, railroadiana, local history artifacts, and so forth). *Railroad use* reflects any one of a number of freight railroad uses, such as signal repair headquarters, bunk house, or communications center; but the phrase does not mean a freight depot (in the now obsolete sense of a shipping point).

Readers are advised that a depot's seemingly secure status can be rapidly altered. In December 1994, Amtrak announced plans for substantial changes in service that include both elimination of routes and reductions in frequency. Certain stations in this book that are currently listed as train stops will be deactivated and thus in need of adaptive use. The story of depot preservation remains forever under revision.

Signal for Caution: A depot along an active right-of-way presents the best possible context for experiencing a great railroad station. Please use care on your adventures and respect rules about safety. Have a wonderful trip, but make sure to Stop, Look, and Listen for the Locomotive!

New England

The combined railroad station and municipal building at Millis, Mass., sporting a stone chimney and tower.

Connecticut

Connecticut depots provide a good contrast between architect-designed masonry stations in midsize cities and small wooden depots in picturesque New England villages. Especially noteworthy is a virtually intact collection of country depots between New Milford and North Canaan, which can be reached by car from U.S. Route 7.

CORNWALL

CORNWALL BRIDGE STATION

Poppleswamp Brook and Kent roads, off
　U.S. Route 7
1886

Subject of a painting by Eric Sloane, the Cornwall Bridge station sits on the Housatonic Railroad (now a freight line) where the tracks parallel the river. The station stop was named for the 1841 covered bridge that stood a few hundred yards upstream, until it floated by— destroyed in a 1936 ice jam. Three relatively harmonious dormers on the depot's track side are modern additions; missing decorative pendants and incised bargeboards are echoed in the original lacy roof brackets. To accommodate passengers on the once busy line (part of the New York, New Haven & Hartford), the

Cornwall Bridge station when its decorative wood-working was intact.

station platform formerly extended about three times the building's length. Further north along the tracks, the stations at West Cornwall and Falls Village stand in equally authentic settings. NR. [Privately owned. Antiques shop.]

DANBURY

DANBURY UNION STATION

White Street and Patriot Drive
1903

In the early 20th century, in excess of 50 passenger trains a day stopped at Danbury to serve more than 50 local hat-making firms and the only high school in the region. Built by the New York, New Haven & Hartford, which had acquired control of three major lines that served Danbury, the buff and brown brick station comprised a group of polyganol pavilions. An extensive, bracketed platform canopy (removed by the 1950s) followed the curve of the tracks. Today, on the inside, the original benches, matchstick wainscoting, ticket window, and brick fireplace remain. In late 1992, the city of Danbury gave the state of Connecticut some land to be used for a new commuter stop a quarter-mile away. In exchange, the city obtained title to the old station. Upon receipt of ISTEA funds, the city began restoring the building to its 1903 appearance (including the canopy) for a new role as the Danbury Railway Museum. The depot once

Platform canopies in place at Danbury Union Station c. 1905.

played another part—as a location in the 1951 Hitchcock film *Strangers on a Train*. NR. [City of Danbury. Museum.]

HARTFORD

UNION STATION
One Union Place
George Keller
Shepley, Rutan, and Coolidge
1889

In 1987, Hartford Union Station had its second, or perhaps third, resurrection. Richardsonian Romanesque in design, the building was con- ceived by local architect George Keller, but actually executed by the firm of Shepley, Rutan, and Coolidge (successor to Henry Hobson Richardson). Built in 1889, it replaced an earlier station at Spruce and Asylum streets, an elongated train barn with imposing Italianate towers. Two railroads used the new depot: New York, New Haven & Hartford and New York & New England. It was constructed by Orlando Norcross, who was known as "Richardson's Master Builder," because he was responsible for so many of the renowned architects's buildings. In 1914, this second station, constructed of Portland, Conn., brownstone, was gutted by a fire that destroyed the gabled

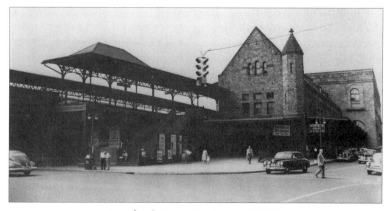

Hartford Union Station c. 1950.

roof on the buildng's main portion. Refurbished with a flat steel roof in the center and a new interior (including decorative plasterwork, iron and brass railings, and a glass and marble vestibule), the station rose from the ashes only to be threatened in the 1960s by diminished ridership and a deteriorating neighborhood. Fortunately, a cooperative venture between the public and private sector, which took two decades and $20 million to achieve success, gave the station new life in the 1980s as a transportation and commercial center. Intercity trains still stop at Union Station, having been reconfigured by architects to meet contemporary needs. One of the two original platform sheds has been relocated to street level; its iron trusses and fancy spirals now shelter bus riders. The station is adjacent to Bushnell Park, which is ornamented by the Soldiers' and Sailors' Memorial Arch—another George Keller creation. NR. [Greater Hartford Transit District. Transportation center, restaurant, and mixed commercial.]

KENT

KENT RAILROAD STATION
East side of U.S. Route 7 in town center
c. 1872

"Milk trains" picked up dairy farmers' full cans at frequent stops along America's rural rail lines and brought them back empty at the end of the day. In the era before bus transportation, Kent students took the milk train on a lovely ride paralleling the Housatonic River to and from high school in New Milford. Trains of the New York, New Haven & Hartford (successor to the original Housatonic Railroad) also hauled away produce and brought in passengers bound for children's camps and summer inns, including the station hotel that stood on the site now occupied by the library. Regular passenger service on this line ended in 1971. With simple lines and board and batten siding, the

Passengers and milk cans on the platform at Kent.

exterior of the Kent station is essentially unchanged. The building still stands just a few feet from the one remaining track. [Privately owned. Art gallery.]

NEW HAVEN

UNION STATION
Union Avenue
Cass Gilbert
1920

The New York, New Haven & Hartford (the "New Haven") covered the entire state of Connecticut and the eastern portion of Massachusetts. Because so many other railroads were absorbed into its system, the New Haven was known as "The Consolidated." Its thick blanket of branch lines effectively blocked most competition. Home offices were near (and later in) New Haven Union Station built by Cass Gilbert, which replaced one that burned in 1918. Gilbert, who began his career with the New York City firm of McKim, Mead, and White, established his own office at the age of 21 in St. Paul, Minn. Among his lifetime commissions were the 60-story Woolworth Building —the tallest building in the world in 1912— and the United States Supreme Court Building completed in 1935. His design for Union

Station's cast-stone and brick exterior emphasized simplicity and symmetry. Inside, a wealth of limestone and travertine were in fact mostly fool-the-eye plaster castings. The south end once housed a ladies' retiring room, men's smoking room, and dressing rooms; a deluxe dining room was on the second floor.

After the building closed in 1973, passengers had access only to a pedestrian tunnel from street to tracks. During the 1980s Northeast Corridor Improvement Project, architects devised a new pattern for taking passengers to track level and restored Union Station's three-story-high center section, including original spherical light fixtures suspended from a gold and white coffered ceiling. Two interior balconies that had been enclosed during World War II for a U.S.O. lounge and later used for offices were returned to Gilbert's open configuration. NR. [State of Connecticut. Transportation center.]

NEW LONDON

UNION STATION
27 Water Street at the foot of State Street
Henry Hobson Richardson
1887

New London Union Station represents one of the last commissions of noted architect Henry Hobson Richardson, who died in 1886 at age 47. When Richardson began practicing architecture in the mid-1860s, his designs reflected the Victorian Gothic and Second Empire styles that dominated the time. His distinctive variation on another style, Romanesque Revival, began to develop in the 1870s and became known as "Richardsonian Romanesque." Characterized by monumental massing, rusticated stonework, broad rounded arches, and sweeping rooflines, the Richardsonian look broke with the verticality of preceding styles. His ideas were well

On the plaza side of New London Union Station, horse-drawn carraiges circle a monument (still standing today) that honors Civil War soldiers.

suited to the strength and horizontality most depots required, and these concepts influenced railroad station design in numbers far exceeding the architect's actual commissions. Upon his death, Richardson's practice passed to his three assistants, Shepley, Rutan, and Coolidge, whose firm completed Richardson's unfinished projects and produced many station designs of its own. The popularity of Richardsonian Romanesque faded with the coming of the City Beautiful Movement in the 1890s, principally because it could not accommodate the demands of skeletal construction without abandoning its most distinguishing features.

First used in early 1888, Union Station was built to serve the New York, New Haven & Hartford and the New London Northern (later Central Vermont) railroads. A simple rectangle with a hipped roof, the only ornamentation was the patterned brickwork and carving on the red sandstone blocks. A trackside canopy once projected from the building, but was replaced by a freestanding metal one. In the 1960s, Union Station became the focus of a decade long preservation battle, when urban renewal advocates threatened demolition. They considered the building an eyesore blocking their view of the Thames River. After a group of citizens undertook a feasibility study, efforts to save the station coalesced into a successful mid-1970s rehabilitation. Additional floors were inserted into the two-and-a-half-story structure. Amtrak took a lease on the basement level and part of the original waiting room. The balance of the building was adapted to restaurant and office use. Richardson's decorative brickwork was chemically cleaned and repointed. Interior oak trim was restored, while original wainscoting was salvaged to cover the surfaces of a new mezzanine wall and the Amtrak ticket booth. NR. [State of Connecticut. Transportation center and commercial.]

NEW MILFORD

MERWINSVILLE HOTEL
Brown's Forge Road off U.S. Route 7
   in Gaylordsville
1843

In 1837, an enterprising man named Sylvanus Merwin discovered that a railroad would be built through his village. He purchased land

Track side c. 1940s.

Agent Ed Hurd (son-in-law of Sylvanus Merwin) and his entourage c. 1890s.

on the east side of the Housatonic River and erected a hotel in anticipation of business the trains would bring. When railroad representatives arrived to negotiate with Merwin for purchase of the right-of-way, he demanded that his hotel be used as a meal stop named after him. Once the Housatonic Railroad agreed, Merwin built an addition on the south side of the hotel to house a waiting room and ticket office—with himself as the station agent. The Houatonic became part of the New York, New Haven & Hartford (the "New Haven") in 1892.

Merwin's son-in-law, Ed Hurd, was the next agent. About 1905, the railroad decided to reassign the position to a younger man; Hurd told the New Haven to get itself a new station. After using a ticket office built onto the freight house just south of the hotel, the NYNH&H replaced that configuration with a conventional station in 1915. The stop's name was soon changed to Gaylordsville. (The Gaylordsville depot is now relocated a half-mile south along the track and made into a residence.) The Merwinsville Hotel was reused first as a dwelling and later as a warehouse. A quickly contained fire in the late 1960s sparked local citizens' interest in buying and saving the building, which is now listed in the National Register of Historic Places. This painstaking project, still ongoing, includes rebuilding the foundation and restoring the third-floor ballroom, as well as the railroad ticket office. The line was once double-tracked, and the train came within inches of the hotel. (One track remains today and is used for freight.) The back porch, from which passengers boarded the train after a 20-minute meal stop, remains intact in this tiny New England village. Another National Register depot, one stop south in New Milford's town center, is well cared for by volunteers; although its defining platform canopies, decorative trim, and interior partitions have not been restored. NR. [Merwinsville Hotel Restoration, Inc. Museum.]

NORTH CANAAN

CANAAN UNION DEPOT
Combined U.S. Routes 7 and 44, village of Canaan
1872

Designed by a railroad civil engineer, Union Depot in Canaan was at an important junction of the Connecticut Western and the Housatonic railroads (both later absorbed by the New Haven system). Of frame construction with board and batten siding, the depot comprised two 90-foot-long wings joined at right angles by a three-story tower. Typical of junction stations, each railroad's wing faced its respective line, but shared the corner. Telegraphers (responsible for transmitting train orders) operated out of the handsome octagonal tower, where windows on each face provided a long, high view down the tracks.

Passenger service ended in 1971. The depot stood nearly vacant for more than a decade, as it passed through a number of private hands. In 1980, the state of Connecticut "railbanked" 35 miles of Housatonic track, a legally proven method for preserving the right-of-way for future use. A new freight line was chartered in

Canaan Union Depot c. 1915.

1983, which today hauls logging products and plastic. When it occasionally operates a tourist excursion, the railroad sells tickets from the old window cage. Inside the agents bay at the foot of the tower, big signal levers are still present; the exterior apparatus is gone. Although out of context in its current position, a rare shanty was moved to the grounds for preservation. It sheltered a guard in the days before automatic crossing gates. A steel water tower stands at its original trackside location. NR. [Privately owned. Freight line office, restaurant, and commercial.]

OLD SAYBROOK

OLD SAYBROOK RAILROAD STATION

455 Boston Post Road

1873

Old Saybrook was known in the late 19th century as Saybrook Junction, because the station stood "on the diamond" (a descriptive railroad term for the spot where lines cross) of the Shore Line Railroad (New Haven system) and the Connecticut Valley Railroad. The boomerang-shaped, wooden passenger station is now incorporated into the Saybrook Junction Market Place, along with the freight depot (relocated from another track alignment). Part of the depot was converted to a restaurant by enclosing the platform area; the ceiling of the canopy is visible on the inside. A 1913 wooden signal tower remains diagonally across from the station house. It replaced an earlier tower on the south side of the tracks that was destroyed when a passenger train derailed. The signal operator was killed in that accident. He is buried in a cemetery next to the new tower, which ceased operations in 1983. The north-south tracks are now owned by a steam tourist railroad operating out of nearby Essex, but the tracks no longer extend south of the junction to waterside Saybrook Point. [Amtrak. Train stop and restaurant.]

WALLINGFORD

WALLINGFORD RAILROAD STATION
37 Hall Avenue off Colony Street
1871

With both its mansard roof and platform canopy supported by large iron *C* brackets, the Second Empire–style Wallingford passenger station bears a strong resemblance to the smaller station still standing at Windsor and the more elaborate but demolished station at Stamford. The Wallingford depot was built by the Hartford & New Haven in the year before it merged with the New York & New Haven. Just beyond its 100th birthday, in 1972, the station became a rehabilitation project for students at the Yale School of Architecture. Seized by a modernizing mentality — and to meet the request of their client (the town) — these design pupils set about to divide space and make the second story functional. In the process, they removed the depot's original finishes, ceiling medallions, and stenciled wall frieze, and lowered the first floor ceiling at the north end. Today the building serves as the town's continuing education center. Extensive exterior repairs in the early Nineties — more sensitive to a preservation ethic — included reslating the rosette patterns between the dormers and roofing the platform canopy with appropriate standing-seam metal. The basement still shows signs of an arched, masonry tunnel that ran under the tracks to reach the freight depot (razed in the 1920s). NR. [Town of Wallingford. Train stop/npa and education center.]

WATERBURY

UNION STATION
389 Meadow Street
McKim, Mead, and White
1909

In the early 1900s, an executive of the New York, New Haven & Hartford made a trip to Italy, where he fell in love with the Gothic city hall of Siena. He came back insisting that the firm of McKim, Mead, and White add a campanile to its design for Waterbury Union Station, a restrained Renaissance Revival building. Thus, a 245-foot-high, clock-faced bell tower stretches like a skinny, gargoyle-encrusted giant from the two-story center section. Replacing a smaller Italianate depot built in 1887, the brick and granite station was built as part of a project to double-track the line and eliminate grade crossings.

In the 1950s, Union Station was acquired by a newspaper publisher and adapted for new use — a surprising and fortunate move in an era when demolition was the norm. The railroad retained the right to maintain a rent-free passenger area in some portion of the building. Today Metro North, a commuter line operating partly on former NYNH&H trackage, uses an

Waterbury Union Station c. 1940.

enclosed space under the old platform canopy as a waiting room. The former Railway Express wing is rented to a freight line; a modern printing plant is attached to the north end. The *Waterbury Republican–American* occupies the south wing's former restaurant and baggage room and the main portion of the building. Small-paned windows in round arches rise the full height of the former waiting room, although their drama has been compromised by insertion of a second floor. Journalists working on this level get a good view of the vaulted tile ceiling. In 1916, citizens raised money to have a bell installed in the tower. Its clock-synchronized chiming still floats out to the hills around Waterbury; at noisy street level, 318 steps below, people can barely hear the ringing. Tower climbs are available by pre-arrangement. NR. [Privately owned. Train stop and offices.]

Maine

In sparsely populated Maine, railroads hauled more lumber and potatoes than people; nonetheless, the lines were important in bringing both tourists and French Canadian settlers to the state. Most depots were built of wood with restrained details. Portland, Bangor, and Lewiston had substantial masonry stations, but these splendid landmarks were all destroyed after passenger trains ceased running in Maine. The 30-year dry spell of no passenger service that commenced in the 1960s may end soon; a new Boston to Portland extension of Amtrak is contemplated for the late 1990s.

BOOTHBAY

FREEPORT RAILROAD STATION
State Route 27, 8 miles from U.S. Route 1
c. 1912

The nonprofit Railway Village in Boothbay is the kind of museum some people call a "building zoo." The Freeport station was relocated to this re-created New England village in 1964, after the Maine Central Railroad sold it to the museum's founder. At the old ticket window, visitors buy passage to a 15-minute steam train ride through a covered bridge and past a dozen or so restored railroad structures, including signal towers, crossing shanties, a flagstop depot from St. George, Maine, and the Thorndike station from the Belfast & Moosehead Lake Railroad. The wooden Freeport depot is equipped with a rooftop signal mast. [Railway Village. Tourist train stop.]

Freeport station on its original site.

BROOKS

BROOKS RAILROAD STATION
Off State Route 7 at the tracks
1896

The original potbellied stove still warms the old Belfast & Moosehead Lake Railroad station in Brooks. After the Maine Central stopped using this line in the 1920s, the B&ML took over freight and regular passenger service and kept them going for more than three decades. In 1987, the B&ML restarted—this time operating tourist excursions that travel along the Penobscot Bay and through Maine woods and farmland. The Brooks station is the refreshment stop. Volunteers slide hot dogs through the old ticket window to visitors snacking in a waiting room rimmed by wooden benches. Sun illuminates the upper window sash filled with stained glass; on dull days, early light fixtures brighten the depot. A side track still loops around behind the building. Tracks like these were used for unloading freight cars. The freight house, which was northwest of the passenger station, is gone. The depot at Unity, 12 miles west, is the only other B&ML station left on its original site. [Belfast & Moosehead Lake Railroad. Museum and tourist train stop.]

BUCKSPORT

BUCKSPORT RAILROAD STATION
Main Street at the foot of Mechanic Street
1874

Built at a time when railroads were tying small towns into the coastal main line from Boston to Canada, the station at Bucksport sits with its back to the waterfront. Doors and windows have Italianate pediments and fine dentil molding with a small bracket at either side. Bolder brackets support the deep, overhanging eaves. Since the 1960s, volunteers have replaced the building's foundation, floor, and roof. Some interior wainscoting remains. A potbellied

stove from another location was donated by the Maine Central (a successor to the narrow gauge Bucksport & Bangor), when the station was being rehabilitated. Today the tracks (used for freight) end about 300 yards short of the depot. NR. [Bucksport Historical Society, Inc. Local history museum.]

GARDINER

GARDINER RAILROAD STATION
51 Maine Avenue
George Burnham
1911

Once a stop for Maine Central trains with names like *Pine Tree Limited* and *The Scoot* (a commuter train for shoemakers), the brick and granite Gardiner station replaced a c. 1852 wooden depot. Built just south of the present structure, the old depot was at the entrance to a covered bridge across the Kennebec River. The architect for the new station, George Burnham, also designed the Cumberland County Courthouse in Portland, where he practiced. After the last passenger run in 1960, the railroad depot became an auto parts store—its mahogany ceiling hidden by acoustical tiles. In the late 1980s, the building's raised basement was converted to a kitchen and dining hall for senior citizens while the main floor became office space. The tracks are gone. NR. [Privately owned. Commercial.]

Early trackside view of the Gardiner station.

GREENVILLE

GREENVILLE JUNCTION STATION
State Route 15, west of Greenville
c. 1890

At Greenville Junction, a viaduct carried the Canadian Pacific Railroad over a spur of the Bangor & Aroostook line (the "BAR"). BAR trains took passengers to a nearby wharf, where they transferred to steamboats bound for resorts on Moosehead Lake. Although the BAR waterfront station is gone, the CP depot at the junction remains. A witch's hat roof tops the rounded, former ladies' waiting room, where benches once circled the wall. Most of the depot housed freight operations. An identical plan was used for the stop at Lancaster (St. John), New Brunswick. Today, just one train of Canada's nationalized passenger service, known as VIA Rail, stops at Greenville Junction (in the middle of the night). The depot's future is uncertain. [Canadian Pacific, Ltd. Train stop/npa and vacant.]

OAKFIELD

OAKFIELD RAILROAD STATION
Station Street
c. 1911

The first Oakfield station was moved to Smyrna Mills about 1910, to make way for a new depot on the Bangor & Aroostook (the "BAR"). In 1941, the second station was itself relocated— a few hundred yards south to facilitate a grade crossing improvement. Situated at the southern end of a large classification yard (where trains were made up), the depot was at the junction of two BAR lines. After passenger service ended in 1961, freight personnel continued to use the building. Twenty-five years later, the local historical society acquired the depot from BAR. The group's work included reconstruction of the platform shelter and new blades for the semaphore. The depot's interior had retained most of its original pressed tin ceilings and walls. Fortunately the group was able to locate a source for the same pattern and restore the

Greenville Junction station on the banks of Moosehead Lake.

one room that had been stripped. Exterior walls retain the original clapboarding and diagonal sheathing. Freight trains continue to use the tracks. [Oakfield Historical Society. Railroad and local history museum.]

PARIS

SOUTH PARIS STATION
Main Street and Western Avenue
1889

Because of abundant forests, most small-town stations in Maine were wooden. In the village of South Paris, the station was built of brick to replace an old depot dating from the mid-19th century. Situated along the Grand Trunk Railway, "Canada's winter road to the sea," the station saw its last regular passenger service in 1962 (operated by the Canadian National Railway). Today, freight trains of the St. Lawrence & Atlantic run past the empty, one-story building, which is is capped by a jerkinhead, or hipped gable, roof with ornamental wooden brackets. The depot was purchased by a commercial concern in the early 1990s, but the new owners have not announced their intentions. [Privately owned. Vacant.]

PHILLIPS

PHILLIPS RAILROAD STATION
Depot Street off Main and Pleasant streets
1905

When railroads were first laid out, "the gauge," or distance between the rails, varied from line to line, from about two feet to six feet wide. Passengers and freight had to be unloaded and reloaded into different cars nearly every time they transferred to another line, which could be several times in a long trip. Scarcely anyone seemed to be contemplating an integrated system. Some folks even advocated the deliberate use of an obscure width; members of the New York State legislature were pleased that the Erie Railroad's broad gauge of six feet would keep competitors off their tracks. The Grand Trunk Railway, which originated in Canada, believed using an odd gauge would prevent the United States from invading by rail. In the 1860s, Congress passed a law declaring that all rails over public domain from the Missouri River to the Pacific Ocean would be 4 feet, 8½ inches apart, a distance that eventually became "standard gauge" throughout the country.

1920s view of the Phillips station.

One of the reasons for building a narrower gauge was topography—for example, a narrow mountain right-of-way—but cost reduction was also important. With a frugal Yankee mentality, numerous companies in Maine built railroads only two feet wide. Five of these miniature lines were consolidated in 1908 as the Sandy River & Rangeley Lakes Railroad, whose headquarters were at Phillips. Replacing an earlier train barn, or "covered station" as this configuration was called in New England, the 1905 Phillips depot was built on a curve and decorated with a pointy cupola. Across the tracks, SR&RL built a car barn and blacksmith shop that still exist. The 10-stall roundhouse and machine shop were destroyed by fire (after having been converted to factory use). When an American Legion post took over the remaining buildings, it rearranged openings and put up plywood paneling in the depot. The local historical society hopes to acquire the passenger depot and restore the interior for a museum. The freight station has been relocated seven times; it now rests nearby at the Sandy River & Rangeley Lakes Railroad Park, where it has been completely restored, along with a tiny depot that was moved from Sanders Mill. [Privately owned. Meeting space.]

RANGELEY

MARBLES STATION
Hotel Road off Main Street
c. 1906

The Rangeley Lake House was owned by John G. Marble, whose spring supplied the mineral water that made this resort famous. Hunting and fishing opportunities were another tourist draw. In 1906, Marble persuaded the Phillips & Rangeley Railroad to extend its narrow gauge line from the wooden Rangeley depot to the hotel's north wharf. (In later years, the Rangeley depot became a bakery and then was destroyed by fire.) An architect (reportedly from Lewiston) drew plans for a new train stop named Marbles, which overlooked Rangeley Lake. For decades, day-trippers stepping off the train could rent row boats or canoes outside the depot's door. A two-story corner tower gave the stone depot a gatehouse look, as though it guarded the large hotel rising high behind it. Today, the tracks are gone as is the hotel, which ceased operations in the late 1950s and was demolished. [Privately owned. Residence.]

A fleet of rowboats awaited vacationers arriving at the Marbles station.

Rockland station, on Penobscot Bay, was the terminus of the Maine Central line from Brunswick.

ROCKLAND

ROCKLAND RAILROAD STATION
4 Union Street
Coolidge and Shattuck
1918

One of the partners in H. H. Richardson's successor firm, Shepley, Rutan, and Coolidge, formed a new partnership in 1916 called Coolidge and Shattuck. Among its first commissions was the brick and granite Rockland station. Built by the Maine Central Railroad, it replaced an earlier depot along the old Knox & Lincoln line. In the

1950s, the building was converted to municipal offices with a dropped ceiling hiding its vaulted interior space. Two ornate iron lamps still flank the columned entrance. Green and gray slate shingles cover the roof. NR. [City of Rockland. Municipal offices.]

WELLS

WELLS BEACH STATION
Depot Street, off State Route 109
c. 1900

Trains leaving Wells hauled out granite, farm produce, fish, and clams. They brought in mail, kerosene, coal, and tourists. Replacing a smaller 1872 depot, the completely shingle-sided Wells Beach station was built in a gambrel-roofed Colonial Revival style sometime between 1890 and 1905. A century later, if Amtrak returns to Maine, its trains will fly by here and stop at a new transportation center in Wells. Back when Boston & Maine passenger trains plied this route, the next stop north was The Elms, built in 1888 specifically to accommodate the farm of George Lord, president of the railroad. Originally resembling the 1872 Wells Beach station, The Elms now houses an antiquarian book store along busy Route 1. [Privately owned. Residence.]

Early 20th-century view of the Wells Beach station. To meet the train, most people still went to the depot on foot or by horse-drawn vehicle. A lone automobile is visible on the left.

YARMOUTH

YARMOUTH RAILROAD STATION
Main Street (State Route 115)
1906

By 1967, the Village Improvement Society had maintained the village green in front of the Yarmouth Grand Trunk station for half a century. When the Canadian National Railway (successor to the Grand Trunk) threatened to demolish the building, the society became the new owners of a depot with a granite base, shingle sides, and a need for loving care. Built to succeed an 1849 wooden building, the station had a women's waiting room with a large fireplace, studded by sparkling samples of Maine minerals. The society 's fund-raising events, including house tours, provided the money for restoration. In 1979, the depot was leased to a florist, who helps keep the well-tended station in full bloom. When a freight train comes through Yarmouth, automobile traffic still backs up on Main Street. Eighty railroad miles to the northwest at Gorham, N.H., stands a very similar, rounded-end Grand Trunk depot, which has found new life as a museum. NR. [Yarmouth Village Improvement Society. Retail.]

A rounded end was common to this Grand Trunk design, as seen at the Yarmouth station.

Massachusetts

Massachusetts was the adopted home of architect Henry Hobson Richardson. His variation on an earlier Romanesque Revival style (dubbed "Richardsonian Romanesque"), whether from his own drawing board or the hands of his imitators, makes a concentrated appearance in the state's remaining railroad stations. Wood or stone were the chosen materials for most depots in Massachusetts. Slate roofs with copper cresting offered durability and refinement, especially in the more cosmopolitan Boston area.

ATHOL

ATHOL RAILROAD STATION
South Street off Main
1873

Originally a two-story building, the Athol station lost its upper floor in an 1893 fire. It was rebuilt with a slate, hipped roof and a clock tower. The initials FRR for Fitchburg Railroad were applied to the tower and worked into the stained glass window transoms on the track side. Passengers of the Springfield, Athol & Northeastern (later the Boston & Albany) also used this union station. Since the early 1980s, a private owner has been working on restoration, including removal of the suspended ceiling to expose the original 17-foot-high vault. Many of the interior partitions were removed when the building was previously converted to a tavern; the current owner has reintroduced the separate, cedar-trimmed men's and women's waiting rooms. He hopes to restore at least one example of the stained glass transoms, most of which were smashed by vandals. The tower's timepiece, by famous Boston clockmaker E. Howard, is safely in storage. The exterior brick walls are painted maroon with cream trim, colors of the Boston & Maine, which succeeded the Fitchburg line. The brick freight station next door is in commercial use. A half-mile east along this active freight track, a vacant, three-stall roundhouse retains its turntable pivot. [Privately owned. Vacant—for lease.]

ATTLEBORO

ATTLEBORO INBOUND AND OUTBOUND STATIONS
1 and 3 Mill Street
1906 and 1908

On the New York, New Haven & Hartford, between New York and Boston, a full depot on both sides of the tracks was a common arrangement. Attleboro has the only intact pair in the Boston area. On the east side of the tracks heading for Boston, the story-and-a-half, brick "inbound" station was built in 1906. A terracotta tile roof extended out into deep eaves on the east and west, and then stretched north and south of the building, to form the platform shelter. During a 1986 rehabilitation, a portion of the waiting room was partitioned off for transit authority offices, but the original ceiling height, arched windows, and wooden trim remain. NR. [Massachusetts Bay Transportation Authority. Train stop and offices.]

The 1908 station on the west side has a full-story granite lower level, once used to receive incoming freight (largely textiles and jewelry), which was then raised by elevator to track level. Most passengers headed for

Providence, R.I., used exterior stairs from Mill Street to reach the main waiting room and platform. The upper story-and-a-half are red brick with rough-cut granite sills. Palladian windows harmonize with those of its depot-mate across the tracks. A 1984 fire destroyed the southern half of the interior (former express, baggage, and telegraph rooms) and the roof, but the oak-trimmed waiting room was not seriously damaged. Commuters do not have access to the building. NR. [Privately owned. Commercial.]

BELMONT

BELMONT RAILROAD STATION
Common Street and Concord Avenue
1908

About 1907, a Belmont farmer and his dray horses hauled 365 tons of field stone to this site, for construction of a new railroad station. It was the fourth in a sequence of depots set approximately on this location. The Boston & Maine had begun work on a stone viaduct in 1906 to raise the tracks above street level. Constructed as part of the same project, this rustic, Tudor Cottage–style depot was built with a series of rhythmically stepped arches and columns. They encased a ramp and stairways to the upper level (now partially enclosed). By the mid-1950s, the Boston & Maine cited decreased ridership as a reason to raze the depot. The Lions Club persuaded the railroad to avoid demolition costs and sell the building instead. Across the street sits the very first Fitchburg Railroad (B&M predecessor) depot. It was built in 1853, during an era when Belmont exported ice, clay, and strawberries; tourists and commuters were a later import. This one-room, octagonal structure, now owned by the local historical society, was relocated twice before coming to rest opposite one of its successors. [Privately owned. Train stop/npa and meeting hall.]

Early postcard view of the Belmont station.

BEVERLY

BEVERLY DEPOT
10 Park Street
Bradford Lee Gilbert
1897

Beverly's third station was designed by Bradford Lee Gilbert, whose most significant railroad commission was the Illinois Central station in Chicago (built in 1893 to service the rush of tourists to the World's Columbian Exposition, and razed in the 1970s). The Beverly depot was quite a colorful place when it opened, with a main section of yellow brick trimmed in brownstone, red brick for the baggage wing, and a red tile roof. A fireplace was installed in the southern end of the general waiting room, which featured a Knoxville marble water fountain as its centerpiece. The Beverly Improvement Society lent its assistance to the Boston & Maine by planting trees and shrubs in the adjacent Depot Square. Thirty-three workers once staffed the busy depot; but by 1965, not even a ticket seller was employed. After a fire damaged the former baggage room in 1971, the new private owner converted the building to a restaurant. Included in the railroad memorabilia that decorate the eatery are benches and lanterns salvaged from Boston's South Station. A special zoning provision requires that the owners provide parking spaces and a heated waiting area for commuters. NR. [Privately owned. Train stop and restaurant.]

BOSTON

SOUTH STATION
Atlantic Avenue and Summer Street
Shepley, Rutan, and Coolidge
1898

Boston's South Station once handled nearly twice as many passengers per year as New York City's Grand Central Terminal. Its construction, undertaken by the Boston Terminal

Pre-1901 view of Boston South Station. The electrically-lit pylon (now gone) honored Admiral George Dewey, Spanish-American War hero.

Company to replace four smaller stations, necessitated a complete reworking of the surrounding streets. A triple-span shed (replaced in 1930 by butterfly canopies) covered 28 stub-end tracks. They terminated at a winged head house that fronted atypically on the point of an intersection. South Station (so named to be distinguished from Boston's North Station) served the Boston & Albany and the New York, New Haven & Hartford and its subsidiaries.

By the 1960s, pigeons were roosting in the station's neglected interior; and the Boston Redevelopment Authority was poised to raze the head house. A delay in getting demolition funds created a window of time that enabled parts of the building to be spared. Ownership was eventually assigned to the local transit authority, which participated in a joint venture to rehabilitate the battered structure. The Atlantic Avenue flank, which had been amputated in anticipation of total demolition, was partly rebuilt by using Stony Creek granite from the original quarry in Connecticut. Although both wings of the station are now half the length they were when trains first arrived on New Year's Day 1899, the Classical Revival facade is essentially intact. A 14-foot-diameter clock sits above the roofline, surmounted by a stone eagle. Inside, a dramatically designed, modern-day food court occupies the old concourse area. A new wall of glass, 235 feet wide, provides diners with a panoramic view onto the tracks. The Amtrak ticket office is now in a portion of the original waiting room; the ornate coffered ceiling is still visible. NR. [Massachusetts Bay Transportation Authority. Multimodal center, restaurants, and offices.]

BOURNE

BUZZARDS BAY STATION
70 Main Street
c. 1912

When the New York, New Haven & Hartford built its new brick and stucco depot, Buzzards Bay was already a busy Cape Cod junction point and rail yard. A matching red-tile-roof signal tower (extant) was thoroughly modern; its switches operated electrically. Freight

Buzzards Bay signal tower and depot in 1959.

Early view of the Chatham station.

depots were built adjacent to the nearby Cape Cod Canal that was just about to be completed. The entrance to the passenger station was flanked by classic columns. Diamond-shaped panes filled not only every window but even the transoms above the baggage-loading doors. By 1964, passenger service was suspended. The depot sat along a bend in the tracks, with platform canopies that angled slightly, conforming to the curvature. When a street across from the station was realigned in the 1970s, the northwest canopy was shortened to only one section. The chamber of commerce took over the entire building, sprucing it up with volunteer labor backed by donations of cash and materials. The old ticket booth became a window used for distributing tourist information. In the 1980s, Amtrak reinstated summer service to the depot, which is now also a stop for the Cape Cod Scenic Railroad. Just behind the station stands a famous 1935 railroad bridge, sporting twin, turreted towers. Other noteworthy Bourne depots are found at Cataumet, Grey Gables, and Monument Beach. [Commonwealth of Massachusetts. Train stop/npa, offices, and hospitality center.]

CHATHAM

CHATHAM RAILROAD STATION
Depot Road
1887

For nearly 25 years, while Chatham campaigned to get an existing Cape Cod rail line to service the town, passengers were forced to use the plodding stagecoach to complete the trip from Harwich—what would later be a seven-mile, 18-minute train ride. Locals finally formed their own railroad company, with the town of Chatham as the largest stockholder, and hired the Old Colony Line to lay tracks and operate the trains. By 1937, the New York, New Haven & Hartford, which had absorbed the Old Colony, halted both passenger and freight service to Chatham. The Chatham Railroad naturally went bankrupt. The engine house with turntable, car house, tool and hand-car shed, and the water tower with windmill were destroyed or converted to storage; the rails were sold for scrap. The passenger depot stood mostly idle until 1956, when a former Chatham resident purchased the building and donated it to the town. His stipulation was that it be operated as a museum. The Queen Anne building is dominated by a bold, polygonal tower with the agent's bay at its base. Its Stick Style details are carefully highlighted in dark red against a light yellow background. A 12-foot-high waiting room occupies most of the interior floor space. The ticket office features the original agent's desk and equipment. NR. [Town of Chatham. Railroad museum.]

CHESTER

CHESTER RAILROAD STATION
Main Street off U.S. Route 20
c. 1850

Boston & Albany (successor to the Western Railroad) replaced most of its wooden stations with stone, but Chester escaped the upgrading epidemic. Much later, nearly 150 years after its construction, this old "eating house" station was scheduled for demolition by Conrail. A local group rescued the depot and moved it across the tracks and 100 feet south, but did not turn it around. The street side now faces the tracks. Typical of very early depots, the station did not have a bay window. As part of the

Chester station c. 1910. A morning train is headed west toward Pittsfield, Mass., and Albany, N.Y.

restoration process, the Chester Foundation will remove a loading door that was added in the 1950s, when this passenger station was converted to freight use. Volunteers are uncertain of the depot's construction date, although telegrams and posters found within the building date from the 1850s. Two associated structures remain standing west of the depot—a six-stall brick roundhouse and a coaling tower. [Chester Foundation. Vacant—future railroad and local history museum.]

EASTON

OLD COLONY RAILROAD STATION
80 Mechanic Street, village of North Easton
Henry Hobson Richardson
1884

In the 19th century, the Ames family of North Easton operated the world's largest shovel factory. Frederick Ames was a director of the Old Colony Railroad. He personally commissioned his friend, H. H. Richardson, to design a new railroad station, which Ames then conveyed as a gift to the railroad. (The Ames family gave North Easton other extant Richardson buildings including the library.) Another Frederick—the famous Mr. Olmsted—landscaped the station grounds. The building is covered by a broad, hipped roof of slate, which originally swept dramatically into a long platform canopy, now missing. On the street side, a round-arched porte-cochere of brownstone-trimmed granite faces Langwater, an Ames estate. Carved wild animals ornament the east side of the depot, including snarling wolves and dragons (the latter are on the underside of the carriageway roof). Lion heads decorate the armrests of trackside benches. In 1958, the New York, New Haven & Hartford (Old Colony's successor) ceased passenger service and closed the depot. Ten years later, the Ames

Engraving of the North Easton station from the *History of the Old Colony Railroad*, published in 1893.

family bought its deteriorating gift back from the railroad and donated it to the town's historical society. Members unboarded the windows and doors and began an ongoing restoration project to provide exhibit and meeting space in the old station. A short stretch of track remains. NR. NHL District. [Easton Historical Society. Museum and community center.]

FRAMINGHAM

FRAMINGHAM RAILROAD STATION
Waverly Street at Concord Street
Henry Hobson Richardson
1885

When H. H. Richardson designed this gray and red granite passenger depot, the village was called South Framingham. He got the commission through Boston & Albany directors, James Rumrill and Charles Sargent; the former was a Harvard College chum, the latter lived across the street from Richardson's home in Brookline. Of the nine stations Richardson designed for

the line, this was probably the biggest and most active. A trademark of his stations was the steeply pitched, hipped roof that extended into a platform canopy. As with most of the larger designs, Richardson added dormers to light the waiting room. It would otherwise have been quite dark because the deep overhang blocks a significant amount of sunlight from the first floor windows. Framingham's dormers are surrounded by carved lion heads; below, the bow-front agent's window is set with bull's-eye glass panes. Dominated by a fireplace, the large waiting room has a double-height ceiling of exposed truss construction and walls sheathed in narrow vertical boards. The original floor plan included a dining room with a buffet, a serving room with upstairs kitchen, and a smoking room. When the station was built, there were lines going in about six directions from Framingham, as well as connections to two trolley lines. A century later, the depot was sadly deteriorated (part of the roof collapsed in 1978), until saved by adaptive use. NR. [Privately owned. Train stop/npa and restaurant.]

Drawing of the Holyoke station from the *Railroad Gazette,* April 1, 1887.

HOLYOKE

HOLYOKE RAILROAD STATION
Lyman Street at Bowers Street
Henry Hobson Richardson
1885

H. H.. Richardson's friendship with James Rumrill, who was a director of the Connecticut River Railroad as well as the Boston & Albany, led to the architect's commission for a large station at Holyoke. Similar to the one at Framingham, the depot was built with a two-story interior lit by broad dormers. A ladies' retiring room, a telegraph room, and a special room for "emigrants" flanked the general waiting area. By 1967, the Boston & Maine, successor to the Connecticut River, had ended passenger service to Holyoke. Sturdily constructed of brownstone-trimmed granite, the depot has been converted to an auto parts store, whose alterations, including installation of a second floor, appear to be reversible. The design is similar to a union station in Chatham, N.Y., which was the work of Richardson's successors. Still owned by a freight railroad, Chatham (NR) has been nearly vacant for decades. [Privately owned. Commercial]

LEE

LEE RAILROAD STATION
Railroad and Elm streets
1893

The Lee station looks like a New England saltbox house, simply because the entire platform canopy is missing. When that was in place, it not only sheltered passengers but also completed the now lopsided roofline. Built by the New York, New Haven & Hartford in Stick Style, the standard design depot retains its original double set of fretwork banisters, the rectangular agent's bay, and the combination of horizontal and diagonal wooden siding. Inside, beneath an 18-foot ceiling, are walls of yellow pine with black walnut trim. The original ticket window and old safe remain; the latter is decorated with Hudson River scenes. [Privately owned. Restaurant.]

LEOMINSTER

LEOMINSTER RAILROAD STATION
24 Columbia Street
1878

In 1873, citizens of Leominster petitioned the Boston, Clinton, Fitchburg & New Bedford Railroad for a new station. According to a contemporary article, they figured that annual freight and passenger tariffs of $98,000 a year entitled them to more than "the miserable apology for a depot . . . a disgrace to both the town and the railroad corporation." Their demands were met. In 1878, the newspaper reported construction of a granite-trimmed, brick depot with a 70-foot-high tower—"not showy, but neat, comely, and substantial." The building was heated by two furnaces, instead of stoves, and was lighted by gas. The interior was trimmed with ash and walnut. Pine doors led to fully furnished dressing rooms off each waiting room. Fixed settees that hugged the walls had leather-board seats of local manufacture. Suddenly sentimental, the community worried about the fate of the "battered and familiar" 30-year-old wooden depot and were pleased

when a private citizen removed it to a site by Monoosnock Brook. (An early example of adaptive use—for manufacturing combs—it was not razed until about 1930.) The New York, New Haven & Hartford took over this line and continued regular passenger service to Leominster through 1931. The depot then served for many years as an express agency. [Privately owned. Commercial.]

LEXINGTON

LEXINGTON DEPOT
10 Depot Square (Massachusetts Avenue)
c. 1850, 1918

New Englanders call this early type of depot a "covered station"—known also as a train barn. At Lexington, an arched passageway for trains accounted for half the depot, which until the 1970s still had its slate roof. Most likely built by the Lexington & West Cambridge about 1850, it was damaged by fire in 1917. When town officials convinced the successor railroad, Boston & Maine, to renovate rather than demolish, the clapboard-sided Italianate station acquired a

Leominster station, sited on a curve.

1940s trackside view of the "covered station" at Lexington.

new Colonial Revival cupola and colonnade, designed by William Roger Greeley. As many as 44 trains a day traveling from Lexington to Boston stopped here; by the late 1950's, the number was down to one each way. The building was then converted to a bank (although train service continued until 1977) with a totally altered interior. Despite some window changes, the exterior maintains the look of a train barn. Originally, one track went under the roof and one ran outside the arched shed. Today, bicyclists pedal through the shed as they ride along the former right-of-way, now a recreational trail. [Privately owned. Bank.]

MILLIS

LANSING MILLIS MEMORIAL BUILDING
64 Exchange Street
1886

Lansing Millis, born in 1823, was a prominent New England railroad man and chairman of the Town Board of Selectmen. He also owned Oak Grove Farm in East Medway (the original name of the community), which shipped milk to Boston. Soon after he died in 1885, his heirs called a town meeting, and made a special request. They asked permission to erect a

building to Lansing Millis's memory that would house the New York & New England Railroad station on the first floor and a public library and town offices on the second. They invited the general public and Mr. Millis's former business associates to contribute special stones for inclusion in the walls. Dotting the depot's cylindrical tower are memorial stones carved with the initials of Millis's business interests and an unusual field stone, contributed by a farmer, that was used in its original location as a tethering ring. On the north side of the station are found a lion-head stone and another from a grist mill dated 1690. Passenger service on the New York, New Haven & Hartford (second successor to the NY&NE) ended in 1967. Today, tracks still run next to the depot, but no trains. [Town of Millis. Municipal offices.]

NEWTON

NEWTON CENTRE STATION
South side of Union Street
Shepley, Rutan, and Coolidge
1891

Shortly after 1900, the tracks at Newton Centre were depressed to eliminate a nearby grade crossing. A cut was made in front of the depot

The Lansing Millis Memorial Building included a library on the second floor. (For exterior view, *see* page 67.)

and the platform shelter was extended downward to meet the new track level. The changes were visually compatible with the extant granite building, which had been built a decade earlier to replace a wooden depot across the tracks. Shed dormers were added to accompany the original, hooded versions and bring light into the now deeper canopy. Newton Centre was one of the largest of the "Newton Circuit" suburban stops planned by the Boston & Albany, all of which were designed by H. H. Richardson or his successors. Just a handful are extant. Chestnut Hill, which was among the finest, was demolished about 1959 to make a bigger parking lot for commuters. At Newton Centre, in 1987, the depot was sympathetically reconfigured, aided by rehabilitation tax credits. Unfortunately, a freestanding baggage building of matching stone was subsequently dismantled and incompatibly incorporated into a commercial building. [Massachusetts Bay Transportation Authority. Train stop, coffee shop, and retail.]

WOODLAND STATION
1897 Washington Street
Henry Hobson Richardson
1886

Woodland is a bona fide Richardson depot, although he died before construction began. Peculiar to this design was the porch, set into the building, rather than extending out beyond it. Dormers were not needed, because there was no platform shelter to block the light. Woodland had a single waiting room, ticket office, and baggage room. Outside, passengers sat on stone seats under the sloping roof. Similar designs in granite and brownstone were built at Eliot (1888; razed for a commuter parking lot) and Wellesley Farms (1894; NR, but damaged by fire). The Boston & Albany placed Woodland in an unsettled suburb expressly to attract new residents. Today, the track and depot are surrounded by a golf course, and commuters wait at a nearby, modern shelter. [Privately owned. Storage.]

NORTHAMPTON

UNION STATION
125 Pleasant Street (off Strong Avenue)
1897

More than 2,000 people came to inspect Northampton Union Station when it opened on a Sunday in 1897. They were duly impressed by the Longmeadow brownstone and buff brick exterior, Italian marble floors, and incandescent lighting. The station's construction was paid for by the Boston & Maine, with the New York, New Haven & Hartford sharing maintenance costs. The station was part of a $1 million grade separation project that involved much wrangling over where to place the building. Tracks ran on both sides of this island station. A platform canopy, which protected passengers waiting on both the east and west sides of the depot, extended several hundred feet to the bridges over Main Street.

By the 1960s, the station had been altered for private offices; Amtrak passengers waited in a small shelter erected to the south. Conversion to a restaurant in the mid-1980s was accompanied by the city's creation of a covered walkway along an abandoned railroad bed, which made the building accessible both to a municipal parking lot and to Main Street. The city also rehabilitated an entrance to the depot through the long-closed "subway" (an underground pedestrian tunnel), popular in earlier times for "promenading." Inside the red-tile-roof depot, restaurateurs restored the old waiting room, with its hooded fireplace and cathedral ceiling, to become the main dining room. The ticket office was turned into a private booth; the baggage room holds banquet space. NR district. [Privately owned. Restaurant.]

PALMER

UNION STATION
West end of Depot Street
Henry Hobson Richardson
1884

In 1882, H. H. Richardson designed a trapezoidal depot to fill a wedge-shaped site between tracks used by the Boston & Albany and the Central Vermont railroads. The Flynt Company was awarded the construction contract because of the quality of granite available from its Monson, Mass., quarry and previous successful work on St. Paul's Universalist Church in Palmer. The station was designed with typical Richardsonian curved spaces and rounded arches. A two-story waiting room was flanked by a dining room, kitchen, and two agents' offices to the west; a baggage room, ticket office, and men's smoking room bordered the opposite side. A semicircular, glassed-in Western Union office protruded from the north wall of the waiting room. Interior finishes were pressed brick to a height of six feet with molded red oak sheathing above. Conductors' rooms were on the second floor. Outside, the hipped roof was extended on

Waiting room with rounded ticket office, Palmer Union Station, 1959

all four sides to form dormered porches, which have since been altered, along with the trackside canopies. The station served as a transfer point for long-distance travelers and for immigrants employed in area textile mills. During World War I, Union Station was a stopping point for troops on their way to join ships docked in New London Harbor. The one-acre Union Station Park, designed by Frederick Law Olmsted, had a stone grotto with a pool and fountain, which were filled in about 1950. Two decades later, all passenger service had ceased; the building became a pool hall and luncheonette. The current owner hopes to obtain funds for the depot's restoration. Freight and passenger trains use the tracks. NR. [Privately owned. Vacant.]

STOCKBRIDGE

STOCKBRIDGE RAILROAD STATION
Half-mile south of town center on U.S. Route 7
McKim, Mead, and White
1893

In the late 1880s, the Laurel Hill Civic Association got tired of badgering the Housatonic Railroad (soon part of the New York, New Haven & Hartford) for a new depot and began raising funds itself. The group contributed half the cost of a fine stone station. Designed in English Gothic Revival style by New York City's McKim, Mead, and White, the Stockbridge station served passengers until it was leased from the railroad and converted to a discotheque in the mid-1960s. A few years later, the club's manager was driving by at 4:30 a.m., when he spotted flames breaking through the roof. The fire gutted the interior, and the "New Haven" announced plans to level the building. The railroad finally yielded to public pressure and a purchase offer from the same man who discovered the fire. He and his wife worked to re-create a railroad flavor in the gift shop they then opened in the former depot. Since that time the building has housed various commercial ventures. [Privately owned. Restaurant.]

STOUGHTON

STOUGHTON RAILROAD STATION
53 Wyman Street
Charles Brigham
1888

Stoughton's three preceding stations succumbed to the gamut of depot destruction possibilities; they were consecutively burned down, blown down, and torn down. The architect for the current building, known for his later work on the Massachusetts State House, was originally a partner in the Boston firm of Sturgis and Brigham. The Stoughton station, built of locally quarried granite, was used by commuters on the Boston & Providence, which eventually became part of the New York, New Haven & Hartford. Brigham designed the depot with a 62-foot-high, stone clock tower

slit by narrow, lancet windows and topped with a slate roof. A 12-sided ladies' waiting room fanned out of the depot's west side. Exposed timbers arched upwards to a carved oculus in the ceiling's center. Fireplaces adorned both the men's and ladies' waiting rooms. In 1924, an express train traveling from Taunton to Boston derailed and crashed through the depot. The engine overturned in the ladies' waiting room; amazingly, there were no fatalities. Two young boys who wanted to see a "real crash" had caused the disaster by placing four large spikes on the tracks. In the 1960s, a plan for Stoughton's urban renewal—conceived by supposedly more mature minds—included total demolition of the depot. Fortunately, a local committee, to honor the nation's Bicentennial, coordinated a rescue effort that brought together a number of groups and financial resources. Restoration began in the mid-1970s. Work included refurbishing the mechanism of the E. Howard clock and fabricating four new dials. The depot is maintained by the town of Stoughton. NR. [Massachusetts Bay Transportation Authority. Train stop.]

Stoughton station in December 1946.

Tourists clamber onto the roof of a transfer vehicle at the Swampscott station, 1910.

SWAMPSCOTT

SWAMPSCOTT RAILROAD STATION
Railroad Avenue and Burrill Street
c. 1873

The Swampscott station suffers from being on the wrong side of the tracks. Today's suburban Swampscott was originally a summer resort. The depot was therefore placed adjacent to the outbound, rather than inbound, track to accommodate trains filled with tourists arriving from New York and Boston. Loaded with luggage and trunks, they needed shelter while waiting for horse-cart transfers to nearby luxury hotels. Other reasons for the depot's location on the southeast side of the Eastern Railroad track (later Boston & Maine) were convenience for loading freight and relative lack of land on the northwest side (just room for a small shelter, which is now gone). In modern times, commuters wait in the morning on the inbound side, across the tracks from the depot. The building is leased to a community service group who did some repairs, but has no funds for restoration. Missing from the exterior are the dormers, clock, and decorations that once graced the double roof line. [Massachusetts Bay Transportation Authority. Vacant.]

WALPOLE

WALPOLE CENTER RAILROAD STATION
West Street off Elm Street (State Route 27)
1883

The Walpole union station was designed to fit within the X-shaped junction of two railroads: the New York & New England and the Old Colony (both later New York, New Haven & Hartford). The depot's two wings formed a 112-degree angle, anchored by a two-story tower with spired roof. Covered by both vertical and horizontal boards, the depot was spruced up by volunteers in the 1970s and is essentially unaltered. Passengers still wait on the old oak benches and buy their tickets at the original window. A round radiator, common to many depots, sends out warmth from the center of the room. The window sash were once painted in imitation cherry graining, now covered over.

A large wooden signal tower, just west of the depot, was demolished in 1946. In the neighboring village of South Walpole, the station has been converted to a post office. [Massachusetts Bay Transportation Authority. Train Stop.]

WARREN

WARREN RAILROAD STATION
Railroad Square off Main Street
Shepley, Rutan, and Coolidge
1892

When the present owner of Warren's Boston & Albany station converted it to a real estate office, he was careful to leave partitions in place, including those of the American Express section, and to not disturb the mahogany trim. The original grates to the ticket windows were put in storage. In the future, this rockface granite, trimmed-in-brownstone depot could easily be restored by simply removing the dropped ceiling and reopening closed-off windows. Built by H. H. Richardson's successors, it has eyelid dormers, characteristic of his style. The station visually anchors the town common and stands opposite the Richardsonian Romanesque public library. The depot was constructed in the 1890s as part of a project to eliminate two grade crossings. At that time, the brick freight depot was relocated to the west; it still stands on Maple Street. Both freight and passenger trains use the tracks. Another extant building (now a residence) that has been moved to Bacon Street is believed to have been the first of Warren's three successive railroad stations. [Privately owned. Office.]

WAYLAND

WAYLAND DEPOT
1 Cochituate Road
1881

The roof overhang on the Wayland depot is so deep that its Stick Style supporting brackets reach halfway down the wall. Built by the Massachusetts Central Railroad (a Boston & Maine predecessor), it had become a taxi stand by the 1960s. Decorative architraves above the doors and windows lightly embellish this classic example of a board and batten country station. Purchased by the town in the early 1970s, the depot was restored just in time for its cen-

Early 1900s view of the Warren station.

Wayland depot in 1882.

tennial. It is leased to a nonprofit group, Wayland Depot, Inc. To the east, the 1881 freight house still stands. The tracks and a round water tower are gone. NR District. [Town of Wayland. Gift shop.]

WEST BROOKFIELD

WESTERN RAILROAD DEPOT
Ware Street near Milk Street
c. 1845–47

West Brookfield's wooden, Gothic Revival depot (possibly the second of three consecutive stations) was a scheduled eating stop for its first three or four decades. It was built by the Western Railroad, which opened in 1839. The station's 75-foot-long refreshment room was entered through a full-width portico of three ogee arches, each topped with a fleur-de-lis motif. These ornamentations still exist, as well as Gothic panels and tracery found on doors and windows. The depot was relocated to the present site after the Boston & Albany (successor to the Western) constructed a new stone passenger station at Front and Central streets in 1884. At first converted to a grain warehouse, the wooden depot is used today by an oil company for storage, while maintaining a remarkable percentage of its early exterior features. It may be one of the oldest depots left in

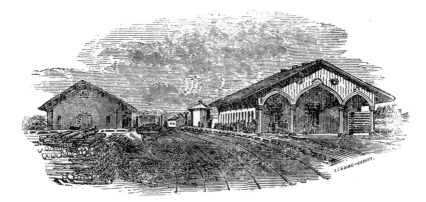

Western Railroad depot at West Brookfield, from an 1847 publication.

the United States. The Richardsonian Roman-esque stone successor station, which sits about 500 yards away on the track's north side, was remodeled by the town for use as a senior center. [Privately owned. Warehouse.]

WESTFIELD

BOSTON & ALBANY STATION
Depot Square, State Route 10 and U.S.
  Route 202
1879

When the Boston & Albany opened its new station at Westfield, the local newspaper was particularly impressed that the building had indoor plumbing, not surprisingly lacking in the preceding station. The two-story depot with decorative brickwork and handsome carved double brackets was trimmed inside with pine and black walnut. A covered platform connected the station to the New Haven & Northampton depot (razed in the 1940s), which sat at right angles to the B&A. After passenger service ended in 1955, the depot was converted to a series of unsympathetic commercial uses. In the early Nineties, a new owner and a group of town officials worked out financing with three area banks to do a first-class renovation of the depot. Their work included repairs to the slate roof and pressure washing to remove white paint from the brick walls. [Privately owned. Offices.]

WILLIAMSTOWN

WILLIAMSTOWN RAILROAD STATION
370 Cole Avenue at North Hoosac Road
1898

At one time, Williamstown was the site of a large Boston & Maine rail yard with a nine-stall round-house and machine shops. Built to replace an 1859 wooden depot that burned, the core of this cut-stone station has an unusual half-hexagon shape topped by a triangular dormer with a fanlight insert. The slate roof extends northwest to shelter the former passenger platform and south-east to meet a covered walkway that connects with the separate baggage building. Deep eaves are supported both by wooden brackets and stone arches. Despite many years of use by a commercial enterprise, the interior, including the ticket window, is essentially undisturbed. About a quarter-mile northwest, the somewhat altered freight house sits near two remarkably intact coal storage complexes. When they were operational, a bucket system was used to raise home-heating coal from hopper cars to the tops of the silos. The coal was then discharged down chutes to delivery trucks. [Privately owned. Offices.]

WORCESTER

UNION STATION
Washington Square
Samuel Huckel, Jr. (Watson and Huckel)
1911

The second Union Station in Worcester replaced one built about 1875 that had a wondrously high, medieval clock tower. The head house of the old station, designed by Ware and Van Brunt, remained across the street from the present one until demolished in 1959 for Interstate 290. Part of a broad scheme to eliminate grade crossings by constructing underpasses and viaducts, the new station was built and owned by the Boston & Albany, with space rented to the New York, New Haven & Hartford and to the Boston & Maine. The names of all three railroads were carved above the main entrance. Designed by a Philadelphia architect in a predominantly French Renaissance style, the station featured twin white marble towers that extended 175 feet above street level. Topped by minarets and adorned with balconies and lion heads, these exquisite towers were unfortunately removed within a few decades because the foundations proved insecure. Passengers entered the main waiting room through pedimented doorways flanked by Ionic columns. Walls of marble and soft-tinted Caen Stone

Worcester Union Station on its completion in 1911. In the left foregroud is the tower of the preceding Union Station (*see* page 16).

(a cementitious product, scored to look like stone from Normandy, France) soothed travelers under an elliptical-arched ceiling lined with stained glass panels.

In the mid-1950s, the 128-by-80-foot room was sealed off; by 1972, all passenger service at this location had ended. Today, much of the roof has collapsed onto the terrazzo floors, thick with rubble and the ill effects of small fires set by vandals. Contemplating using the station for a multimodal transportation center, the Worcester Regional Transit Authority undertook a major feasibility study in the early Nineties. The building proved to be structurally healthy, and acquisition by the city is under consideration. ISTEA funds have been committed to this project, which may include restortation of the twin towers. [Privately owned. Vacant.]

New Hampshire

New Hampshire's few city-size stations, such as Manchester, Nashua, and Concord, were gone by the 1960s. Most of the extant depots in this heavily forested state are wooden, built by predecessors of the Boston & Maine, which dominated New Hampshire by the late 1800s. Over the years, increases in tourist traffic had the biggest impact on determining the size and number of passenger stations.

ALTON

ALTON BAY RAILROAD STATION
12 miles north of Rochester, on State Route 11
1907

Waters of Lake Winnipesaukee lap under the veranda of the Alton Bay station, once a transfer point for passengers going from train to steamboat. After rail operations ceased in the mid-1930s and the tracks were removed, the Boston & Maine sold the depot to the town. The shingle-sided station, looking very much like a summer cottage, is maintained through a combination of grants, municipal appropriations, private donations, and volunteer labor. Improvement projects have included painting the depot in original colors of buff and green, restoring the operational semaphore, and introducing a boardwalk and park setting into the surrounding area called Depot Square. The interior floor plan has been modified somewhat to accommodate modern needs, but the woodwork and diamond-shaped window panes are essentially intact. A restored, 1,200-passenger vessel, the *Mt. Washington*—namesake of the original paddle-wheeler that burned—still docks next to the station. NR. [Town of Alton. Community and tourist information center.]

ANDOVER

POTTER PLACE DEPOT
Depot and Cilleyville roads, off State Route 11
1874

Named after former land owner, Richard Potter, a ventriloquist and magician of 19th-century renown, Potter Place is a tiny locale of nebulous

Potter Place depot c. 1932.

boundaries. Its frame depot, built by the Northern Railroad, was the boarding place for trips to Boston or Concord. Students bound for nearby New London Academy (now Colby–Sawyer College) arrived by train at Potter Place and were taxied to school by carriage or sleigh. A room for handling milk shipments stretched across the northwest end of the station. Express and baggage were also serviced from the passenger depot; freight, from a separate building (still standing). The Northern's successor, Boston & Maine, sold Potter Place Depot in 1961. The last of several interim owners donated the depot to the local historical society in 1983. Typical Stick Style, the one-story building has exterior walls divided into rectangular panels of vertical and horizontal boards. Bandsawn ornamentation drips from sheltering eaves that are more than five feet deep. Inside, the ticket office contains intact telegraph equipment, as well as levers to the roof-mounted signal mast. Still a few feet from the tracks, the depot remains in a relatively undisturbed setting that once included a water tower and a bunk house. NR. [Andover Historical Society. Local history museum.]

BETHLEHEM

MAPLEWOOD DEPOT
Maplewood Road, approximately .25 mile off
  U.S. Route 302
c. 1881

The Maplewood depot was built of wood in the heart of the White Mountains, a tourist region whose 19th-century grand hotels were reached by train. Passengers arrived on the Profile & Franconia Notch (later the Boston & Maine), a three-foot-gauge railroad. The line (changed to standard gauge in 1897) was abandoned in 1924; the Maplewood Hotel burned in the 1960s. Today, the Maplewood depot sits isolated and derelict. Once piercing the dense growth of oak and maple trees with a church-like spire, the depot is bereft of its cupola and its platform canopies. The building needs immediate rescue. [Privately owned. Vacant.]

Nestled in the woods, Maplewood depot c. 1903.

Early view of the Crawford station with its covered wooden platform (now gone).

CARROLL

CRAWFORD RAILROAD STATION

U.S. Route 302 in Bretton Woods, northwest of
 Saco Pond
1891

At 1,900 feet above sea level, the Crawford station stood as the highest depot on the Maine Central's Mountain Division. The station serviced the 1859 Crawford House Hotel, which burned in 1977. Located just beyond the gateway to Crawford Notch—a natural gorge widened for railroad traffic in 1875—the depot's Queen Anne charm included an octagonal tower and a canted fireplace bay. The station was sheathed in wooden siding and patterned shingles. Inside were birch floors, colored glass window panes, and a terra-cotta hearth. Today, the depot is well maintained, although the semaphore that extended from the tower is gone, along with the freestanding covered platform and an ancillary building (probably for baggage). At nearby Bretton Woods, the Fabyan station (now a restaurant), has detailing similar to the siding and wooden brackets of the Crawford depot. NR. [Appalachian Mountain Club. Tourist and hiking information center.]

CONWAY

NORTH CONWAY DEPOT

Merged U.S. Route 302 and State Route 16,
 center of North Conway
Nathaniel J. Bradlee
1874

Small circular windows once ornamented the twin rectangular towers of the North Conway depot. A Victorian interpretation of Russian provincial architecture, it was designed by the same Boston architect responsible for Union Station in Portland, Maine (1888; razed 1961). Built by a predecessor of the Boston & Maine (the Portsmouth, Great Falls & Conway), the depot flourished for three-quarters of a century, during a time when hauling summer tourists, winter skiers, and lumber were prof-

North Conway depot with original tower details c. 1886.

itable railroad enterprises. A big round clock in the central dormer kept time, which would someday tick dangerously close to the building's 11th hour. After the station closed in the early 1960s, the depot's supporters struggled through a decade of uncertainty. Finally a court decision enabled a group of investors to form a tourist railroad, which now uses the depot as its operating headquarters and point of departure. A museum, gift shop, and snack bar occupy the original baggage and waiting rooms. After tearing out a 1914 heating system, the railroad installed appropriate potbellied stoves (although propane heaters do most of the work). The exterior is painted yellow with white trim; the terne-metal portions of the roof are red. A four-stall roundhouse, believed built at the same time as the station, is colored to match. Its turntable operates with a compressed air motor, powered by air brakes of the locomotives. A freight house and section house stand to the northeast. Depot Park, originally owned by the railroad and now deeded to the town, creates a grassy buffer between the highway and the station. NR. [Conway Scenic Railroad. Tourist train stop.]

DURHAM

Durham Railroad Station
3 Depot Road
1896

About 1910, East Lynn, Mass., got a new depot; the old one was dismantled—yellow brick by yellow brick—and moved by the Boston & Maine to Durham. Replacing a wooden depot, it was reassembled on its stone base and enlarged. The station served as a busy University of New Hampshire stop, until passenger service ceased in the 1960s. The college purchased the depot from the railroad and converted it to a nonprofit restaurant. Students working toward culinary arts degrees use the depot as their real-world laboratory, where burgers and ice cream are dished out beneath the high wooden ceiling. Outside, a signal mast is still anchored to the trackside dormer that pierces the slate roof. There are rumblings of new passenger service to Boston; perhaps the Durham depot sign—now displayed in the dairy bar—will again be posted outside. [University of New Hampshire. Restaurant.]

Postcard view of the Laconia station.

LACONIA

LACONIA RAILROAD STATION
11 Veterans Square (Church Street)
Bradford Lee Gilbert
1892

The Laconia station's high style and relatively large scale are attributed to the influence of Charles A. Busiel. A Laconia native, he was managing director of the Concord & Montreal (soon part of the Boston & Maine) and was elected governor of New Hampshire in 1895. Bradford Lee Gilbert of New York City designed the depot in a Romanesque Revival style with round-headed openings and a prominent porte-cochere. The light gray granite body and red sandstone trim were set with red mortar; the roof was gray slate with copper flashing. A central three-story rotunda served as the general waiting room, with a ceiling of carved wood, a marble floor, and stained glass windows. In the 1960s and 1970s, the rotunda and southwest wing (which had been the agent's office and ladies' waiting room) were used as a police station and courtroom. During this period, part of the platform area was enclosed to become chamber of commerce offices. The now restored rotunda area and a portion of the northeast wing (former men's smoking room and baggage area) are vacant. NR. [Privately owned. Chamber of commerce, restaurant, and retail.]

NEW BOSTON

NEW BOSTON RAILROAD STATION
Depot Street off State Route 13
Bradford Lee Gilbert
1893, 1895

In 1893, a group of local men built a five-mile rail line from Parkers Station to the village of New Boston. These entrepreneurs immediately leased the line to the Concord & Montreal (soon to become the Boston & Maine). Early one morning, just two years later, the fieldstone and stucco New Boston depot caught fire; nothing remained but the walls and part of the roof. Quickly rebuilt, including its shingled wooden turret, the station continued in operation until the mid-1930s, when the tracks were removed. For $200, a local group bought the depot, which was used consecutively for community meetings, overflow classroom space, and church services. Today it is the police station; the tur-

At the New Boston station, an exposed stone chimney pierces a pseudo-half-timbered gable.

ret and trim are painted constabulary blue. Although the interior now has extra partitions and a false ceiling, the huge stone fireplace remains in view. The water tank and roundhouse are gone. [New Boston Playground Association. Police station.]

NORTH HAMPTON

NORTH HAMPTON RAILROAD STATION
206 Atlantic Avenue
1870

In the late 1980s, a local architectural firm won a statewide award for its adaptation of the little North Hampton depot. Converting the building to its own offices, the firm designed new dormers, clerestory windows, and an artificial lighting system compatible with the flavor and structural identity of a railroad station. The lower portion of the double-level roof still extends eight feet from the building, although the covered waiting platform is long gone. A signal mast with original colored lenses and reproduction blades remains anchored outside the agent's bay. The adjacent tracks are used by the Boston & Maine (now a freight line), which succeeded the Eastern Railroad in 1885. Passenger service ended in 1965. When the

Early view of the North Hampton station complete with its wooden platform and free-standing canopy.

B&M sold the building, a restriction was placed in the deed, requiring the depot's owners to provide shelter, if passenger service ever returns. [Privately owned. Offices—for sale.]

SANDOWN

SANDOWN RAILROAD STATION
Depot Road and Main Street
c. 1874

When land was surveyed for the Nashua & Rochester Railroad, a shrewd farmer granted permission for the right-of-way on condition that "I or one of my heirs will always be station agent." If the station were ever shut down, his heirs would receive $300. In the mid-1930s, the Boston & Maine closed the Sandown depot— and paid farmer Hubbard's descendants their money. For more than 40 years thereafter, the wooden country station suffered various abuses caused by salt and highway equipment storage, vandalism, and aborted renovation projects. In the late Seventies, citizens formed a historical society for the express purpose of restoring the depot. The group's labors included locating a similar depot being torn down and salvaging enough materials to refurbish Sandown; although the station today remains devoid of its bandsawn bargeboards and brick chimney. The B&M donated an abandoned stretch of track, which members hauled away and reinstalled at the depot. Several pieces of historical track maintenance equipment are parked at the depot: two flanger cars, a three-wheeled velocipede, and a gasoline powered "put-put." The right-of-way is now a recreational "rail trail." NR. [Sandown Historical Society. Local history and railroad museum.]

WOLFEBORO

WOLFEBORO RAILROAD STATION
Railroad Avenue off Main Street
1872

Wolfeboro, at the northeast corner of Lake Winnepesaukee, was a stop on the Eastern Railroad (later the Boston & Maine). In the

Two men (one probably the agent) and a little girl on the track side of the Sandown station.

Eastern Railroad locomotive No. 87 at the Wolfeboro station c. 1880.

1970s, a local rail enthusiasts club undertook restoration of the once gingerbread-laden depot, which had lost all its distinguishing features. The group rebuilt the platform canopy and a 20-foot tall steeple. A high school industrial arts class took on the project of reproducing the 10 missing dormers. The paint manufacturer who supplied the exterior stain was so taken with the depot that he featured it on a company calendar. It was a proud day when a painstakingly fabricated locomotive-shaped weather vane, just like the one visible in old photos, was hoisted atop the steeple. Then in 1987, the Wolfeboro depot was struck by light-

ning. Damage from the ensuing fire was repaired by the town government, which also remodeled the waiting room for office space. The express room is unchanged; the separate freight house (now privately owned) is used for storage. An additional depot built in 1900 at the old steamboat landing—Wolfeboro Lake station—is visible from the "in town" depot. Today it houses an ice cream parlor. The community's name was originally spelled "Wolfeborough," but was apparently shortened to better fit the railroad timetable. [Town of Wolfeboro. Chamber of commerce and nursery school.]

Rhode Island

Providence's 1899 Romanesque Revival Union Station—part of a five-building complex—was a candidate for restoration under the Northeast Corridor Improvement Project, when it was gutted by fire in the 1980s. After Amtrak relocated just south of the capitol, a private corporation began the heroic project of working its office needs into Union Station's shell. Rhode Island's next largest extant station, Pawtucket–Central Falls, is seriously endangered. The modest number of village and small-town depots that remain standing once earned their revenue from the textile industry, agriculture, and tourism.

PAWTUCKET

PAWTUCKET–CENTRAL FALLS RAILROAD STATION

307 Broad Street
H. W. Mellor
1915

Vandalized and neglected for decades, the passenger station in Pawtucket has lost many of its architectural features: copper roof, stained glass skylights, iron and glass porte-cochere, marble wainscoting, and terra-cotta shields painted with locomotives and other railroad

Pawtucket-Central Falls station.

1916 postcard view.

Covered stairs once gave passengers access to the platforms. Today the endangered building is unused, although trains still pass under it.

motifs. The building was designed by a New York, New Haven & Hartford staff member and constructed by the well-known Norcross Brothers firm, whose workers applied red tapestry brick and cast-stone trim to a structural steel frame. A union station (also serving the Providence & Worcester), it replaced depots in both Pawtucket and its sister city, Central Falls, after a special legislative commission forced the smaller sibling to cooperate in the venture. As many as 140 trains a days once stopped at Pawtucket; but by 1959, the station was closed. Straddling active tracks, the depot today faces an added threat. Amtrak trains are being electrified between New Haven, Conn., and Boston (requiring overhead wiring), and freight trains are shifting toward the use of double-decker cars. Both of these modernization procedures create height problems, because trains pass *under* the Pawtucket depot. To resolve this situation, the tracks would have to be lowered and a new use found for the building, whose once elegant spaces still hold the promise of rebirth. [Privately owned. Vacant.]

SOUTH KINGSTOWN

KINGSTON RAILROAD STATION
Railroad Avenue in the village of West Kingston
1875

Erected by the New York, Providence & Boston, the Kingston station was also the western terminus of the Narragansett Pier Railroad. By the early 1970s, Kingston's freight house and baggage-express building had been demolished; the frame passenger station was deteriorating from a quarter-century of neglect. Local citizens managed to pull together enough funds and volunteer labor to patch leaks, replace rotted wood, and paint the exterior. Over the years they held periodic cleanups at the station, while lobbying the state to invest in nonhighway transportation alternatives. They also directed the temporary relocation of an early 20th-century switching tower that had been visually separated from the depot (since 1936) by construction of the Route 138 overpass.

Kingston station during its first year of operation, before arrival of the Narragansett Pier Railroad.

In 1988, an accidental fire caused severe damage to the finely detailed main waiting room and ticket office. Friends of the Kingston Railroad Station obtained a grant from the National Trust for Historic Preservation to assess funding and restoration options. In the early Nineties, the state was awarded ISTEA funding to establish a multimodal center at the Kingston station, with a substantial portion of the funds going to restore the depot. The building will have to be moved back from the tracks somewhat, partly to accommodate a new high-level platform. The historic signal tower will be replaced north of the depot, similar to its original location. Kingston's first station (c. 1837) stood about one-half mile north of this location on the opposite side of the tracks. NR. [Amtrak —pending transfer of ownership to state of Rhode Island. Train stop.]

PEACE DALE RAILROAD STATION
Railroad Street in the village of Peace Dale
c. 1876

Only eight miles long, the Narragansett Pier Railroad began operating in the 1870s to bring raw cotton and wool to the local textile mills, as well as large quantities of coal needed to generate steam for the machinery. The railroad also encouraged development of fashionable resorts at the Narragansett Pier beaches. The unusual design of the Peace Dale station came from ideas supplied by a member of the Hazard family—owners of the railroad, the Peace Dale Mill, and beachfront property. A small frame structure, it had a curious monitor-on-hip roof with delicate metal tracery and a center chimney (which are gone). Its broad eaves sheltered the platform on four sides. Headquarters for the superintendent and dispatcher, Peace Dale also had an engine house and turntable. Whitewashed stones, set off by scarlet begonias every spring, spelled out the station name. After passenger traffic diminished in the 1920s, the NPRR operated "rail

Peace Dale station in 1915. The monitor-on-hip roof, covered in wooden shingles, once had fancy ridge cresting and a chimney.

buses" (gasoline-powered track vehicles— some versions were also highway-capable), until service ended altogether in the 1950s. In 1981, the tracks and three steel trestles at Peace Dale were dismantled. NR District. [Privately owned. Apartments.]

WESTERLY

WESTERLY RAILROAD STATION
14 Railroad Avenue
1912

Westerly's Spanish Colonial Revival station was built to replace the original wooden depot dating from around 1837. Construction of the new brick and stucco building coincided with the elimination of a grade crossing. The tracks were relocated to the north, and an automobile underpass was built at Canal Street. Initials of the New York, New Haven & Hartford were worked into the ornate terra-cotta decorations of the station's central dormer, designed to contain a clock. A double-tiered, tile roof was supported on the bottom level by a round-arched, open arcade. Just west of the depot, a separate, hipped roof structure created an open-air waiting room. To the east, a similar but enclosed shelter provided access to a pedes-

Passengers once waited under a curved canopy (now gone) at the Westerly station.

trian tunnel under the tracks. In essentially unaltered condition (even the benches remain), the station suffers today from deferred maintenance and vandalism. The state department of transportation is in the process of acquiring the building, which will be rehabilitated. NR District. [Amtrak—pending transfer of ownership to state of Rhode Island. Train stop.]

WOONSOCKET

WOONSOCKET RAILROAD STATION
Depot Square
1882

After the Blackstone Canal collected its last toll in the 1840s, the new Providence & Worcester Railroad converted much of the old towpath to a track bed. The current Queen Anne–style depot replaced the original wooden one that burned. The design is attributed to the railroad's chief engineer, John Waldo Ellis, whose office went up in the smoke. Both street and trackside entrances were centered below a large cross gable, embellished with decorative brickwork, terra-cotta, and stained-glass oculus windows. A square clock tower with a tall, pyramidal hipped roof was topped by a loco-

motive-pattern weather vane. The east end of the depot shared a wall with a historic commercial building (razed in the 1960s).

The New York, New Haven & Hartford, which had leased the P&W, canceled passenger service in the early 1950s. About 20 years later, P&W reincorporated as an independent freight line, using the Woonsocket station (restored after a 1970s fire) for its accounting and computer department, until moving out in 1990. After the subsequent private owner lost it to foreclosure, the building was acquired by the state department of transportation with the aid of ISTEA funds. The state bus system and a division of the National Park Service will use the office space. Archaeological artifacts, collected from various highway projects, will be reposed in the basement. The main hall, with its architectural features restored, will return to waiting room status. Plans for the exterior include applying a simulated slate roof and reproducing the missing iron cresting. The weather vane—stolen once, recovered, and then sold by the developer—will be duplicated and installed with an alarm system. Freight trains still use the tracks, which may someday bear the weight of a new commuter service as well. NR District. [State of Rhode Island. Vacant—future multimodal center.]

Vermont

As in most other New England states, railroads supported the growth of farm business and textile manufacturing. Vermont railroads also hauled lumber from the northern part of the state and marble from the south. Fine woods and marble added character and elegance to the interiors of Vermont depots.

BENNINGTON

BENNINGTON RAILROAD STATION
Depot and River streets
William C. Bull
1898

A depot where even the conductors' toilet room was wainscoted in marble, the new Bennington station was described by a contemporary newspaper as "the handsomest and most artistic in the State." Designed by a prominent local architect in Richardsonian Romanesque style, the depot was constructed of rock-faced blue marble crowned with a slate roof. Built by the Bennington & Rutland (later Rutland Railroad), it replaced an 1850s wooden structure. Although much of the interior fabric has been removed or damaged, the former ladies' waiting room best maintains the level of elegance this depot exhibited, despite its branch line status. (The main line from New York to Montreal passed through a smaller village, North Bennington.) Women entered through an opening that is still flanked by wooden columns with stylized Corinthian capitals. Walls have cherry-stained paneling and a molded cornice. The paneled breast of the polished marble fireplace rises to meet a 12-foot-high ceiling. After passenger service ended in 1933, the depot was leased for a series of commercial uses, including an automobile dealership. An unsympathetic restaurant conversion occurred about 1970, but fortunately, the current owner's style emphasizes the remaining historic character. As with many depot-restaurant adaptations, the porte-cochere and part of the platform area are enclosed for dining space. Freight trains still ply the tracks. NR. [Privately owned. Restaurant.]

This view of the Bennington station shows the original appearance of the platform canopy, rounded-end waiting room, and porte-cochere.

North Bennington station with the original hooded, double window.

NORTH BENNINGTON RAILROAD STATION
Main Street at the railroad tracks
1880

Replacing an earlier wooden depot, the Bennington & Rutland station in North Bennington was an important junction with the Troy & Boston (later Boston & Maine). By mid-20th century, this handsome brick building on a foundation of cut marble blocks was abandoned, derelict, and in the path of a highway project—which fortunately fell through. Two local citizens offered to buy and restore the building if the village would accept title and maintain the structure. Restoration work, which uncovered vividly toned wainscoting of cherry and chestnut, included rebuilding the clock-faced cupola that had burned in the early 1900s. A comparison with early photographs shows that only the hooded double window was not reproduced according to the original design. Brick chimneys with decorative niches anchor both ends of the mansard roof, which is

shingled in alternating shades of light and dark gray. Village administrators and the architect who invested both money and talent in the rescue project share space in the former station. The state of Vermont owns the land under the depot and the tracks on which the Vermont Railway runs freight trains. Northeast of the passenger depot stands a separately owned, rounded-end brick freight house. NR. [Village of North Bennington. Offices.]

BRATTLEBORO

UNION STATION
Main and Vernon streets
1916

In the mid-1960s, after the Central Vermont and Boston & Maine railroads terminated passenger service, Brattleboro's selectmen were ready to demolish Union Station. A group of citizens convinced the city to lease the building to them for one dollar a year and the promise of massive volunteer labor. The restored landmark opened in 1972 to provide space for art exhibits, lectures, and occasional concerts. Built of locally quarried stone with a slate roof, Union Station replaced an ornate brick depot dating from 1880. An even earlier station, a modest frame structure, still stands across the tracks. Inside Union Station's waiting room, the focal point is a set of wide marble stairs rising through a large archway. They originally led to a footbridge across the tracks. When the bridge was removed long ago, the exterior doorway was blocked off. The museum recently opened the wall by installing a period-appropriate window that gives a view onto the Connecticut River and the mountains beyond. The former men's and ladies' waiting rooms house rotating art and historical exhibits; the station's lower level accommodates a small Amtrak waiting room. NR. [Town of Brattleboro. Train stop, museum, and art center.]

BRIGHTON

ISLAND POND STATION
Main Street (State Routes 114 and 105), village of Island Pond
1904

In the mid-1800s, the village of Island Pond emerged as something of a foreign outpost on Vermont soil. At the halfway point between Montreal, Quebec, and Portland, Maine, Island Pond's welfare was economically and politically tied to the prosperity of Canada's Grand Trunk Railway. The two-and-a-half-story brick passenger depot and customs office is all that remains of a once great complex of switching yards and servicing and crew facilities. Set on a high, rusticated stone base, the exterior of the depot is virtually intact, including the platform canopy and parapeted three-story tower. Canadian National Railways passenger service (Grand Trunk's parent) ceased using the depot

Island Pond depot in July 1949. The shadow of a wooden footbridge stretches across the station's many tracks.

Burlington Union Station c. 1916.

in the early 1960s; it was used for freight crews of the St. Lawrence & Atlantic Railroad until 1989. The town of Brighton is restoring the station to house a bank, tourist information center, and the Island Pond Historical Society. Trains run nearby, but the tracks in front of the depot are gone. NR District. [Town of Brighton. Mixed use.]

BURLINGTON

UNION STATION
One Main Street
Fellheimer and Long
1916

Burlington's Union Station was known for many years as "the Green Mountain Power Company," which occupied much of the three-level depot from 1940 until the mid-1980s. Designed by New York City architects Fellheimer and Long (whose depot commissions later included major terminals in Buffalo, New York, and Cincinnati), the station had a glass-enclosed pedestrian overpass, four through tracks, and canopied platforms. One of

its joint tenants, the Central Vermont, discontinued passenger operations in 1938; the Rutland Railroad followed suit in 1953. The building's brick exterior, ornate grillwork, and medallions of Mercury are essentially intact; but the interior, replete with Vermont white marble walls and coffered ceiling, was destroyed long ago. Union Station now anchors a waterfront redevelopment area. [Privately owned. Artists' gallery and studios; little theater; small businesses; and homeless "day station."]

CHESTER

CHESTER RAILROAD STATION
State Route 103, village of Chester Depot
1872

When the Rutland Railroad went out of business in 1961, the state bought the right-of-way and leased the Rutland–Bellows Falls portion to a new company, the Green Mountain Railroad. This operational freight line hauls talc, historically an important local product. In summer, it also transports tourists on excursions along the banks of the Connecticut and Williams rivers to a railroad station in the village of Chester Depot. Restored with a new floor and sill, the painted-brick station has a flared and bracketed canopy extending from all four walls. Stylistically, the depot resembles two Central Vermont Railway stations in the National Register—Bethel (now a tavern) and Randolph (now a gift shop)—which also have arched windows, corbeled cornices, and triptych windows in the gable ends, but were shorn of their platform canopies decades ago. The similarities are not surprising; CV controlled the Rutland from about 1871 until 1896. [Green Mountain Railroad. Tourist train stop.]

GREENSBORO

GREENSBORO BEND DEPOT
Main Street, village of Greensboro Bend
1872

The village of Greensboro Bend derived its name from its location—midpoint on a loop in the east-west mainline of the St. Johnsbury & Lake Champlain Railroad, between St. Johnsbury and Swanton. Livestock, maple syrup, hides, and Christmas trees were among the commodities exported from Greensboro Bend. Tourists were imported in the summer, particularly those bound for Caspian Lake. A wooden water tower and a long stretch of coal sheds once stood near the depot. As a 1976 Bicentennial project, volunteers painted the depot's Stick Style exterior, but all proposals to use this long-vacant building have fallen through. A covered breezeway still connects the passenger depot to an 1896 freight house. The Morrisville depot (20 miles west) had similar ornamentation to Greensboro Bend, but much of Morrisville (now a restaurant) has been covered over with modern shingles. NR. [State of Vermont. Vacant.]

HARTFORD

WHITE RIVER JUNCTION STATION
Railroad Row in White River Junction
1937

Although not many travelers originated or ended their trips at White River Junction, anyone going by train from New York or Boston to Montreal

White River Junction station in 1973 was topped by a replacement of the original locomotive weather vane.

invariably passed through the station. So much switching of equipment occurred at this point that trains seldom arrived and departed with the same locomotive. The current Colonial Revival station succeeded a number of predecessors, starting from the mid-19th century, each destroyed by fire. Wedged between the tracks of the Boston & Maine and Central Vermont railroads, the depot had a gable pediment above the northeast entrance (B&M) and a fan window on the southwest side (CV). The large northwest wing held the baggage service; the smaller southeast wing contained the waiting room. Above the depot's copper roof, a domed cupola was topped with a locomotive weather vane (stolen in the mid-1950s). The station's restaurant was beloved for its New England specialties; travelers deliberately arranged itineraries with time for a meal stop. Today, one daily visit by Amtrak is the only passenger train activity at the station. NR District. [Jointly owned by Guilford Transportation and Central Vermont Railway. Train stop—for sale.]

NEW HAVEN

NEW HAVEN JUNCTION DEPOT
Junction of U.S. Route 7 and State Route 17
1868

Built by the Rutland Railroad, the story-and-a-half New Haven Junction depot served also as a crossing point for the short line Bristol Railroad from 1892 to 1930. The corbeled, round-headed arches above the door and window openings add distinction to this simple, well-restored depot of variegated red brick. Typical of early stations, it lacks an agent's bay. The tracks come startlingly close to the building. A rooftop-mounted signal with colored lenses is intact. When the state acquired the Rutland in the 1970s, it conveyed ownership of this "surplus" structure to the historic preservation office, which leases it to a con-

struction and landscaping concern. NR. [Vermont Division for Historic Preservation. Commercial.]

NORTHFIELD

NORTHFIELD DEPOT
West end of Depot Square
1852

Northfield was the first headquarters for the Vermont Central Railway (later Central Vermont), until the management relocated to St. Albans in the 1860s. The brick depot, which replaced one that burned at age four, is one of the few remaining structures from an early complex of roundhouses, repair shops, offices, and company housing. Since the surprisingly early date of 1866, a bank has leased space in the building, at first sharing it with the railroad and now as the sole occupant. The station was in deteriorating condition by 1899. Its two large wings were removed, and Stick Style ornamentation applied. A small agent's office remains inside with original wainscoting and signal levers (the outside mast is gone). The bank manager works from the old station agent's desk. NR. [Central Vermont Railway. Bank.]

ROYALTON

SOUTH ROYALTON RAILROAD STATION
Railroad Street, facing South Royalton's
    village green
c. 1886

In 1886, after a serious fire destroyed all of South Royalton's stores, several houses, and the freight depot, the Central Vermont Railway participated in reconstruction plans for the community. The railroad moved the tracks back from the village green, rendering it twice the previous size, and remodeled the old pas-

Depot Square in Northfield.

senger depot into a freight house. A new story-and-a-half passenger station was built in Queen Anne style, with walls of brick, wooden shingles, and clapboarding, and a roof covered in slate. Supported by brackets, a pent roof with belcast eaves (curved to resemble the edge of a bell) wrapped around all four sides the station. On the south and north walls, light was admitted through two horseshoe-arched windows of stained and leaded glass. In the mid-1960s, the railroad vacated the building, which was converted at first to a mixture of community and commercial purposes. The interior retains its depot decor, with artifacts like old railroad lanterns and an oil can set against wainscoted walls. A baggage cart is positioned outside. NR District. [Central Vermont Railway. Bank.]

ST. ALBANS

CENTRAL VERMONT RAILWAY HEADQUARTERS
Lake & Federal streets
1860s–1920s

The Central Vermont Railway headquarters complex was begun about 1863, following the consolidation of several shorter lines into a

through system from Boston to Montreal. Approximately one-dozen historical structures survive, including a three-story, mansard roof office building, a freight station, various maintenance and repair shops, and one of two roundhouses. The 1963 demolition of the four-track train shed and depot (which abutted the office building) sadly compromised the near-perfect historical integrity of this site. Amtrak uses a former switch house (c. 1900) for its waiting room. NR. [Central Vermont Railway. Train stop and freight railroad headquarters.]

ST. JOHNSBURY

ST. JOHNSBURY RAILROAD STATION
Opposite Railroad Street Park
R. E. Glancey
1883

Designed by a local architect-builder, the St. Johnsbury station was at the junction of lines connecting southern New England with Quebec, and western Vermont with Maine. As a union station, it originally served three railroads: the Connecticut & Passumpsic Rivers, the St. Johnsbury & Lake Champlain, and a prede-

St. Johnsbury station.

Early streetside view.

Attached and freestanding platform canopies were intact in 1949.

cessor of the Maine Central. The St. Johnsbury site functions today as a junction for modern freight lines, while the passenger depot is used for a pizza shop, stores, and offices. The two-and-a-half-story brick building is roofed with slate shingles. Ornamental lightning rods poke upward from the ridge line and dormers, but most of the metal roof cresting is gone. A long, covered platform once stretched east from the depot and was connected to a one-story express building (razed). The depot's streetside entranceway is a well designed reproduction of the original. A fire in the 1980s damaged the station's upper stories, but they were subsequently repaired. St. Johnsbury's roundhouse is gone, and the freight station has been swallowed by a supermarket.

St. Johnsbury was the home of Thaddeus Fairbanks, 19th-century inventor of the famous platform scales that were manufactured in the town. In the early 1900s, St. Johnsbury repeatedly won a "depot beautification" prize for gardening work in a park area just south of the passenger station. Part of its display was a large set of platform scales filled with plants. NR. [Privately owned. Commercial.]

SHELBURNE

SHELBURNE RAILROAD STATION

U.S. Route 7, on the grounds of Shelburne Museum
Robert H. Robertson
c. 1890

One-time physician Dr. W. Seward Webb was the son-in-law of railroad magnate, William Henry Vanderbilt. He also served as president of the St. Lawrence & Adirondack Railway (later Rutland Railroad) and the Wagner Palace Car Company. Exploring the United States in his private train, Webb fell in love with the green rolling beauty of Vermont. He commissioned his architect friend Robert H. Robertson to design the major buildings on his new 4,000-acre estate, as well as the nearby Shelburne station. Builder of one of New York's first skyscrapers, Robertson had already designed depots for the Hudson Valley Railroad. The Shelburne station was one of his standard plans. Although this stop was used by the general public, it was sited so as to be most convenient to Webb's family and guests. In 1953, Webb's descendants transferred ownership of the Shingle Style depot to their previously established Shelburne Museum. After relocating and meticulously restoring the depot, museum employees constructed a detached wooden shed, similar to the type that was known to house Dr. Webb's private railroad car. [Shelburne Museum. Depot museum.]

Shelburne station in 1897 on its original site.

Windsor station with the Ami B. Young Courthouse in the background.

WINDSOR

WINDSOR RAILROAD STATION
Depot Avenue off Main Street
c. 1905

Replacing a two-story wooden station across the tracks, Windsor's hipped roof, brick depot was built by the Central Vermont Railway and jointly used by Boston & Maine's Connecticut Valley line. All doors and windows have rounded arches. Elaborately carved brackets support the six-foot-deep platform canopy. Above both the gabled street entrance and the trackside dormer, wooden cutouts cast pleasing shadows on the walls. Inside, below a coved, southern white pine ceiling and dentilled cornice, iron bars protect the former station agent's ticket window. Although no travelers had disembarked at Windsor since 1966, passing trains continued to give the building a familiar shake. In 1995, the community persuaded Amtrak to make Windsor a stop on its new *Vermonter* service. NR District. [Central Vermont Railway. Train stop/npa and restaurant.].

Mid-Atlantic

Western Maryland Railway station (foreground) and office building at Union Bridge, Md., 1956. Hanging on the signal mast are hoops and forks which the agent used for handing up train orders to on-board crews.

Delaware

Delaware's principal municipality, Wilmington, lies virtually centered between New York and Washington on the highly traveled Northeast Corridor. Train service was historically dominated by the Pennsylvania Railroad, headquartered in nearby Philadelphia. Other than a fairly large station in Wilmington and a mid-size one in Newark (home of the University of Delaware), the remaining stations are—and were—in rural settings.

CLAYTON

CLAYTON RAILROAD STATION
Bassett Street
c. 1855

The Italianate-style Clayton depot is the best Delaware example of a very early standardized design. A smaller version stands at Felton (NR District), but the roof has been altered. United States Secretary of State John M. Clayton initiated the original charter of the line, known as the Delaware Railroad (financially controlled by the Philadelphia, Wilmington & Baltimore and later the Pennsylvania Railroad). The Clayton station was built of brick and, unlike Felton, lacked an agent's bay. Its double doors and small-paned windows were all topped with molded arches and fanlights. Pierced by two ridge chimneys with decorative tops, the roof had wide eaves supported by brackets. Inside, the floor was brick. By 1868, the depot was surrounded by a freight house, an express office, an eating saloon, a hotel, and several stores. After 1885, Clayton became a division headquarters and one of the Delmarva Peninsula's

Early postcard view of the Clayton station shows two chimneys on the depot and a platform canopy (to the right), all now gone.

largest railroad centers, although the general area remained agricultural. Passenger service ended in the 1950s. NR. [Privately owned. Antiques store—for sale.]

DOVER

DOVER RAILROAD STATION
West end of Loockerman Street
c. 1856, 1911

The Philadelphia, Wilmington & Baltimore first reached the state capital at Dover in 1856. Traffic generated by abundant peach crops and by the Civil War contributed to the line's prosperity. In 1911, the Pennsylvania Railroad (PW&B successor) expanded and remodeled the Dover station into a more elaborate Georgian Revival style. Enlarged again in the 1950s, it was altered two decades later for justice of the peace offices. The state is considering a commuter service between Wilmington and Dover, with the old depot as a new multimodal center. NR District. [State of Delaware. Magisterial courtrooms and offices.]

MONTCHANIN

MONTCHANIN RAILROAD STATION AND POST OFFICE
Montchanin Road (State Route 100) at Rockland Road
1889

Wilmington and the surrounding estate area (known locally as "chateau country") has been the domain of the French-born du Pont family since the early 1800s. Montchanin was one of four stations on the Wilmington & Northern Railroad (later the Reading system) that were named after places in France or for family members. Colonel Henry A. du Pont was the president and general manager of the Wilmington & Northern, a line useful for moving black powder and anthracite between the Du Pont Company's mills in Wilmington and coal mines in Pennsylvania. Montchanin, originally called Du Pont Station, was also the local post office. A two-story frame structure with a terne-metal roof and a porte-cochere, the Montchanin depot sits today along a freight line, in a setting little changed over the years.

Dover station after its 1911 expansion.

Just a few minutes north is the former Winterthur station and post office (now a visiting scholars residence on the grounds of the du Pont family's famous estate-turned-museum), from which the W&N hauled passengers and Winterthur Farms' milk to Wilmington. NR District. [Privately owned. Post office, sandwich shop, and apartment.]

NEWARK

PENNSYLVANIA RAILROAD STATION

State Route 896, 1.5 miles north of I-95 (swing back under the railroad overpass)

S. C. Fuller

1877

Through the 1950s, greenhouses and gardens surrounding its Newark station supplied cut flowers for dining cars on the Pennsylvania Railroad. As replacement for a frame structure, the depot was designed by the chief engineer of the Philadelphia, Wilmington & Baltimore—a Pennsy predecessor. Newark was located at the junction of two PRR lines, one stretching down the Delmarva Peninsula and another shooting out to Harrisburg, Pa. A small freight house and stockyard complex stood opposite the passenger depot. A story-and-a-half high, the depot's exterior was dominated by large gable dormers and Gothic arched windows. It was originally roofed in black slate that coordinated with the patterned red brickwork mortared in black. The first floor contained men's and ladies' waiting rooms, a ticket and telegraph office, a baggage room, and the agent's kitchen. His family's sitting room and three bedrooms were upstairs.

In the 1980s, the city of Newark purchased the depot from Amtrak and performed a major renovation. Work included restoration of the interior partitions and exterior porches. Elements still missing are most of the bargeboards, decorative iron scrollwork, and exterior double doors. Newark's Baltimore & Ohio station, designed by Frank Furness, was demolished right after World War II. NR. [City of Newark. Train stop, offices, and historical society museum.]

Postcard view of the PRR station in Newark. The building on the left was for storage of baggage, mail bags, and probably express shipments. The station wagon belonged to a transfer company, a service which transported luggage and steamer trunks between passengers' homes and the station.

B&O station at South Market and Water streets, Wilmington, July 1946.

WILMINGTON

BALTIMORE & OHIO RAILROAD STATION
South Market and Water streets
Frank Furness
1888

Few people realize that just one block from Wilmington's old Pennsylvania Railroad station (now Amtrak) stands the hulk of a Baltimore & Ohio branch line depot designed by Frank Furness. The tracks were originally laid by the Wilmington & Western, whose trains made it no further west than 18 miles—just over the state border into Landenberg, Pa. B&O's two-story, brick and wood-sided passenger depot had one of Furness's typical multifaceted rooflines, punctuated by chimneys and dormers. A very large freight house stood nearby, but eventually freight service was transferred to the passenger depot.

By the early 1990s, after decades of vacancy and vagrants, compounded by a fire, the boarded-up station looked to be beyond hope. But a feasibility study conducted by the city determined that the building was essentially sound and that interior details like the two fireplaces were intact. As part of a revitalization program along the Christiana River waterfront,

the city acquired the depot from CSX Transportation. Title to the structure may be conveyed to the Delaware Rail Administration for a transportation-related use, but a major complication to on-site restoration remains. CSX retains ownership to the plot of land under the depot, which it could sell to yet another party. [City of Wilmington. Vacant.]

PENNSYLVANIA RAILROAD STATION AND OFFICE BUILDING
French Street and Martin Luther King, Jr., Blvd.
Furness, Evans and Company
1908

By the early 1900s, Wilmington's waterfront area (confluence of Delaware and Christiana rivers) was clanking with heavy industry, notably shipbuilding and world-famous fabrication of opulent railroad cars. The Philadelphia, Baltimore & Washington (Pennsylvania Railroad subsidiary) serviced these businesses and also accommodated two passengers routes—part of the New York to Washington, D.C., run and a branch line down the Delmarva Peninsula. About 1900, the Pennsy decided to elevate the main line tracks through Wilmington, which was accomplished by constructing a four-mile-long, brick-arched

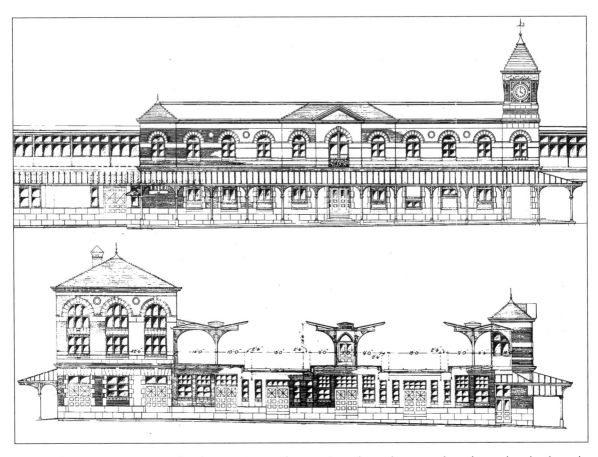

Wilmington PRR station. Taken from a 1905 trade magazine, these elevations show the viaduct that brought trains to the station's upper level. (For photo, *see* page 53.)

viaduct. Workers completed a four-and-a-half story PRR office building in 1905 (extant). Next, they demolished a substantial and highly ornate depot—only about 25-years-old—to make way for a new brick station, trimmed with stone and capped by a tile roof. Its dominant feature was a three-story-high tower with four clock faces and terra-cotta festoons. The tracks, running literally across the top and center of the depot, split the second floor into separately roofed facilities.

Through the years, a layer of shabbiness and grime spread over the Wilmington station, which volunteers in the 1970s tried to counteract by slapping on mad brush strokes of bright-colored paint. Fortunately, the Wilmington station became part of the Northeast Corridor Improvement Project; it was reconfigured and restored by professionals in 1984. A new main waiting room and ticket office were established on the street level, with a ceiling of exposed, riveted trusses and metal decking. Most trains now depart from a center island reached by escalator. An old stairway with brass rails and acorn finials leads up to the side platforms and pre-rehabilitation main floor. Here the original waiting room—with coffered ceiling, original cylindrical radiators, benches, and chandeliers—awaits a new use and occupant. NR. [Amtrak. Train stop.]

District of Columbia

In the early 1900s, the United States Senate Park Commission approved a plan for renewing the open spaces and sparkle that were part of Pierre L'Enfant's 1792 design for the nation's capital. Of crucial concern was removal of the noisy, sooty stations and confusion of tracks that cluttered the vistas of the Washington Mall. A single new station would serve all seven railroads coming into the city. Devising the scheme was a prestigious group: architect Charles F. McKim (soon to design New York City's Pennsylvania Station); sculptor Augustus Saint-Gaudens; landscaping genius Frederick Law Olmsted; and Daniel H. Burnham, whose firm created the plan's magnificent linchpin, Union Station.

WASHINGTON

UNION STATION

Intersection of Massachusetts and Louisiana
    avenues and First Street, N.E.
William Peirce Anderson (D. H. Burnham and
    Company)
1907

Since its rededication in 1988, Union Station ranks as one of the country's premier rescue and preservation stories, notably because it combines a well-conceived new use of spaces with the building's original function. The exhilaration of entering Union Station's beautifully restored, nine-story-high waiting room is magnified by the knowledge that beyond the concourse filled with "festival marketplace" shops and eateries, one can still buy a ticket and board a train.

Union Station was built on the edge of a shantytown called Swampoodle; workers filled the marshy soil with four million cubic yards of dirt. Construction of the barrel-vaulted Main Hall required use of 100-foot-high traveling scaffolding—the same technique that was employed 80 years later to replaster, paint, and gild the coffered ceiling. This area was the ticketing and central waiting area, where passengers sat on high-backed, individually heated mahogany benches. (Today, the space is free of

seats and used as a giant vestibule and dining area that frequently accommodates special events.) Through the rear doors of the Main Hall, travelers entered the concourse—an unheated, covered arena, two-and-one-half times the length of a football field. From the concourse, conductors ushered passengers through ornate, iron gateways leading to 20 train platforms (a total of 33 upper- and lower-level tracks). In the late 20th century, the now enclosed concourse and a newly created mezzanine level envelop a modern ticket counter, stores, and restaurants. In the redevelopment process, the basement below the concourse was excavated five feet deeper for use as a movie theater complex and food court. Union Station's visitors can also dine, in more luxurious fashion, in the old Presidential Reception Suite (built in response to fears of railroad station assassinations), the East Hall (site of the earlier Savarin Restaurant), or the former baggage room (northwest corner of the station). Amtrak's waiting area is in a new concourse beyond the original one. Upper floors of the station's wings still contain offices.

The elegance of today's Union Station belies the saga of assaults the building endured. In 1953, just a few days before President Dwight D. Eisenhower's inauguration, the brakes failed on a 400-passenger train from Boston. The *Federal Express* hurled into the station and crashed through the con-

Early interior views of Washington Union Station. (For exterior view, *see* page 19.)

Main Hall with its mahogany benches c. 1914.

Savarin Restaurant c. 1907. Today this is a retail space known as the East Hall.

course floor, right where the Amtrak ticket counter stands today. Astoundingly, no one was killed and within 36 hours, workers had covered over the gaping hole and restored operations. In the late 1960s, a deliberate crater was carved into Union Station's waiting room floor. As part of a government folly called the National Visitors Center, a multi-image slide show was entombed in an immense pit that cruelly disfigured the Main

Hall. Train passengers waited in a shack behind the real terminal. In 1980, further damage befell Union Station, when in the midst of open-roof repairs, a tremendous storm inundated the exposed interior.

Ronald Reagan's first inaugural gala was the last event held at the National Visitors Center; the doors closed permanently in 1981. While rodents, pigeons, and toadstools invaded the building, Congress hatched a new plan for Union Station that involved Amtrak, a commercial developer, and various government

agencies. The Beaux Arts, granite-clad masterpiece was given a new life—and a new, old floor (white marble with red squares found to duplicate the original). Cleaned and polished, the Roman soldiers of sculptor Louis St.-Gaudens (Augustus's brother) stand vigil over the Main Hall, whose majesty never fails to impress either a first-time or frequent visitor. NR. [United States Department of Transportation (leased to Union Station Redevelopment Corporation). Train stop and commercial.]

Maryland

Maryland is known as "the cradle of American railroading," because of a pioneering run by the Baltimore & Ohio in 1830. Despite the notorious loss more than 140 years later of the Queen City Station and Hotel in Cumberland (razed by the B&O), Maryland has managed to save a remarkable variety of early depots, especially in the Baltimore area. These structures give a physical presence to the transportation saga. A respectable number of stations remain standing that were designed by Ephraim Francis Baldwin, who worked chiefly for a powerful triumvirate of institutions: the Roman Catholic Church, the state of Maryland, and the B&O Railroad.

BALTIMORE

CAMDEN STATION
Howard and Camden streets
John R. Niernsee and J. Crawford Neilson
1856, 1865 (wings added)

In 1992, America's classic spectator sport brought new life to an old depot. The Maryland Stadium Authority chose a run-down railroad yard west of the Inner Harbor as the site for Baltimore's new baseball stadium. Its construction included restoration of both Camden Station and the 1,000-foot-long, eight-story-high Baltimore & Ohio warehouse. In the mid-19th century, the B&O showcased its burgeon-

ing transportation empire in the elaborate Camden passenger station and company headquarters (designed by the Baltimore architectural firm where E. Francis Baldwin was serving his apprenticeship). A mixture in brick of Georgian, Greek Revival, and the newly popular Italianate, Camden Station was the hub of the B&O, which—until 1873—was the only rail line serving Washington from the north. Its 185-foot-high central tower (shortened into a cupola in the 1870s) made it the tallest building in Baltimore. At the start of the Civil War, the station's telegraph brought first news of the firing on Fort Sumpter. One week later, Union soldiers barricaded themselves inside Camden Station, after a deadly brawl between the 6th

Camden Station c. 1870 with its original central tower.

Massachusetts Regiment and a mob of southern sympathizers.

A century later, shorn of all three towers, Camden Station had fallen into decay and disuse; although commuter trains continued to discharge passengers at the platform. The 1990s restoration included reconstructing the towers, recreating the west wing and the third story of the east wing, and using tinted concrete to replace missing brownstone elements. The waiting room, which had been enlarged and redecorated to welcome the Democratic National Convention of 1912, retains oak paneling and marble wainscoting from that era. The brick and stone B&O warehouse is now the Baltimore Orioles' executive offices and social space. The actual train stop is relocated one block south. Used temporarily as exhibit space, the old depot needs a permanent occupant. NR. [Maryland Stadium Authority. Vacant—for lease.]

MOUNT CLARE STATION
Pratt and Poppleton streets
c. 1851

For many years erroneously dated as 1830, and thus billed as America's oldest depot, the brick, polygonal-shaped Mount Clare Station served originally as a small ticketing site and office building. Although not Mount Clare's first depot, its location marks the formal inauguration of revenue-generating rail service in the United States. Precisely at 9 a.m. on May 22, 1830, a "train" of four individually horse-drawn cars traveled along the rails from Mount Clare to Ellicott's Mills, 13 miles west. The Baltimore & Ohio soon replaced, where possible, the

Mount Clare in 1953. This view shows the roundhouse, ticket office, and annex just before the complex became the B&O Railroad Museum.

muscle power of real horses with the steam power of "iron horses." Because these smoking engines were not permitted in downtown Baltimore, trains were broken up or reassembled at Mount Clare; and the individual cars pulled by horse between there and the Pratt and Light Street Station. In 1953, the B&O opened a museum on the Mount Clare site, which comprises the depot, an 1884 passenger car roundhouse (now used to display locomotives and railroad cars), and a handsome office annex (1884, enlarged about 1892). Designed by E. Francis Baldwin, the spectacular brick roundhouse is 235 feet in diameter and soars

123 feet to the top of the cupola. A functioning wood-floored turntable is used today for rotating the displays, which date back to the 1830s. NR. NHL. [B&O Railroad Museum. Museum.]

MOUNT ROYAL STATION
Cathedral Street and West Mount Royal
    Avenue
Baldwin and Pennington
1896

In the 1960s, the Maryland Institute raised more than a million dollars to purchase the Mount Royal Station and convert it to an annex

Mount Royal Station.

The clock tower soars above the neighborhood c. 1900.

B&O publicity photo of the waiting room, 1950s.

for the institute's College of Art. The chosen architectural firm subsequently won an award from the American Institute of Architects for its skillful adaptation. Although the height of the former men's and ladies' waiting rooms was sacrificed to create two floors, central passage between them was kept 37 feet high. The stamped metal ceiling, mosaic marble floor, and most of the decorative ironwork were preserved. The baggage room and platform areas were enclosed for studio space, with extensive use of glass and skylights maintaining a feeling of spaciousness. The limestone-trimmed granite exterior, which layers Renaissance Revival onto a Romanesque design, remains intact, including the 150-foot-high tower with an eight-day, E. Howard clock. Parallel to the head house, a nearly 800-foot-long, iron train shed covers two remaining tracks, still used by a freight railroad. The building sits below street level, between two tunnels that carry train traffic into the shed. E. Francis Baldwin and his partner (after 1883), Josias Pennington, were the original designers of this Baltimore & Ohio station. NR. NHL. [Maryland Institute, College of Art. Library, gallery, and studios.]

PENNSYLVANIA STATION
North Charles Street near Lanvale Street
Kenneth M. Murchison
1911

Kenneth Murchison designed a number of American railroad stations, including Union Terminal in Jacksonville, Fla., and stations in Johnstown and Scranton, Pa. (all extant). In 1909, he won a competition instituted by the Pennsylvania Railroad for a new union station in Baltimore to be used by three of its subsidiaries plus (by trackage rights) the Western Maryland. The station succeeded two earlier union stations, one from 1873 and an 1886 replacement. The latter was deemed "primitive and inconvenient" by the Commission to Improve Railroad Facilities in Baltimore; it was

Pennsylvania Station in Baltimore, 1985. Restored, stained glass skylights brighten the waiting room.

also unsafe because passengers had to cross the tracks to reach the trains or the depot. Murchison solved this problem by elevating the station above the tracks and providing stairways down to each platform.

Built of pink Milford granite, Pennsylvania Station contains two great public spaces. A balcony wraps around the two-story, 100-foot-long main hall surfaced in Sicilian and Pentelic marble. The waiting room has a triple-domed ceiling with stained glass skylights. Blacked-out during World War II, they were restored during the 1980s Northeast Corridor Improvement Project. Two of the original mahogany benches with attached candelabra fill one end of the room opposite the ticketing alcove (the old marble ticket counter with iron grilles was modernized in 1925 and 1957). A concourse, at right angles to the waiting room, stretches over the tracks and combines additional waiting space with the more typical circulation function. Features include large windows and fully intact, glazed terra-cotta border tiles and water fountain from Cincinnati's Rookwood Pottery. The track area contains one of the nation's few remaining Bush train sheds. (Murchison and civil engineer Lincoln Bush also collaborated on the extant railroad and ferry terminal in Hoboken, N.J.). Only one of the station's two identical 1910 signal towers remains standing, and that survivor is in the path of an impending light rail line. NR. [Amtrak. Train stop.]

PRESIDENT STREET STATION
President and Fleet streets
1850

Until recently, the fate of the President Street Station (a crumbling brick ruin with a partially collapsed roof) seemed hopeless, but the future may be brighter. Built by the Philadelphia, Wilmington & Baltimore (later the Pennsylvania Railroad), it served as a passenger station until 1873, when a union depot was built on Charles Street (site of today's Amtrak station). Subsequently used as a freight station and then a warehouse, the building has been vacant

since the 1970s. A series of arson fires destroyed the 1913 wooden train shed (replacement for the original barrel-vaulted shed) and damaged the head house.

Similar to a long-gone sister terminal in Philadelphia, President Street was probably the work of civil engineer George A. Parker, who spanned both the train shed and head house with "tied trussed" arches. Historically, President Street Station is associated with the Civil War riots of April 1861, which occurred when Union soldiers en route from Philadelphia to Washington attempted to transfer (by horse-drawn railroad cars) from this depot to the one on Camden Street. An angry mob attacked the troops, with numerous casualties on both sides. Today a wasteland of vacant lots, the area around President Street Station was once packed with residential and industrial buildings. The city acquired the depot in 1979 for part of a freeway extension (that was never built). By the late Eighties, the Inner Harbor revitalization a few blocks away had spread toward President Street; in 1991, a combination of private and public money was used to stabilize the remaining head house. The city is contemplating installation of a museum in the facility. NR. [City of Baltimore. Vacant.]

Engraving of President Street Station from an 1858 railroad guide.

BROOKLANDVILLE

BROOKLANDVILLE RAILROAD STATION
Falls and Hillside roads
c. 1905

In the early 1830s, the Baltimore & Susquehanna (later the Pennsylvania Railroad) began horse-drawn operations. (Its trains would not be pulled by steam engines for nearly two decades.) Brooklandville passengers waited at an 1832 inn, Brooklandville House (NR), along the Falls Turnpike Road. The inn was constructed opposite the site where—decades later—a station house would be built. Replacing a simple open shed, the new 20th-century depot included dwelling space for the agent at the west end of the first floor and on all of the second. A brick base, up to windowsill level, was surmounted by decorative half-timbering. The station served country estates north of Baltimore like Gramercy Mansion (1902; extant), built by Pennsylvania Railroad president, Alexander Cassatt for his daughter. Only one other depot remains on the old PRR Green Spring branch—the nearby Stevenson station. Passenger service ended in 1933; the tracks are gone. [Privately owned. Residence.]

BRUNSWICK

BRUNSWICK RAILROAD STATION
End of South Maple Avenue
Baldwin and Pennington
1891

Situated on the Potomac River, Brunswick was originally a canal town called Berlin. The Baltimore & Ohio renamed the community and made it a division point. Brunswick's story-and-a-half wooden depot had trackside dormers filled with Palladian windows and colored panes. Located originally on 7th Avenue (to serve a new suburb that developed only minimal activity), the station was later picked up and moved to the center of town, when the main depot proved inadequate. In the early 1990s, MARC (the state-owned commuter line that leases the depot from the city) restored the interior and painted the exterior in the original colors of reddish brown with dark brown trim. The "white" waiting room serves passengers; the former "colored" waiting room is a MARC office. A wooden, railroad Y.M.C.A. in Queen Anne style was part of this historic district, but the building burned in 1980. Southeast of the depot, on the other side of the tracks, stands a deteriorating, 12-stall, brick roundhouse. The community is trying to acquire the roundhouse from CSX Transportation, but the company claims that the building's location between two tracks makes liability an insolvable issue. NR District. [City of Brunswick. Train stop]

CHESAPEAKE BEACH

CHESAPEAKE BEACH STATION
Mears Avenue
c. 1898

Just before the turn of the 20th century, Colorado railroad builders Otto Mears and David Moffat decided to build a small eastern railroad from the District of Columbia to what they planned as a gambling resort on the Chesapeake Bay. The casino never materialized (no gambling allowed in Calvert County), and the race track Mears built was for naught. Just south of the depot, a more innocent amusement park provided a destination for passengers; but the Chesapeake Beach Railway never operated in the black. In 1935, train service ceased, and the tracks were removed. The depot served consecutively as a bus station, a repair shop for slot machines, and storage space for the restaurant next door. The amusement park was dismantled in the mid-

1970s. The following decade, the depot was restored as a railway museum. Its porch, which had been closed off with cinder blocks, was reopened; and workers found enough upright posts to pattern replacements. Precise paint color restoration was achieved through microscopic analysis. The style of architecture, with its low hipped tower, is reminiscent of designs found on Colorado railroad stations. Bay waters lap a few hundred yards from the building—the only depot left of the fizzled Chesapeake Beach Railway. NR. [Privately owned. Railroad museum.]

CUMBERLAND

WESTERN MARYLAND STATION

Canal Street

C. M. Anderson

1913

After the 1971 notorious destruction of the Baltimore & Ohio's Queen City Railroad Station and Hotel, the depot built by the Western Maryland Railway gained greater prominence—it became the sole physical tie to Cumberland's railroad past. The three-story, brick, division point depot was built on a bank of Will's Creek, near the terminus of the Chesapeake & Ohio Canal. Baltimore architect C. M. Anderson encircled the roofline with a massive modillioned cornice. He interspersed 12 formal dormers with four tall chimneys. After passenger service to Cumberland ended in the late 1950s, the building continued to function as railroad operating offices. By the time the city acquired the depot—with oak woodwork in the spacious waiting room painted green—it had been abandoned for nearly a decade. Grant money and matching funds were used for restoration, including the wooden canopy, which today shelters passengers waiting for excursion trains. Ownership of the depot was transferred to a nonprofit group in 1984. An identical division point station at Hagerstown (NR) was built the same year as Cumberland and functions now as police headquarters. NR. [Western Maryland Station Center, Inc. Tourist train stop; county tourist information center; art gallery; transportation and industrial museum; and canal museum.]

Cumberland WM station in 1946, when the island platform canopy was still in place.

Steaming past the Patapsco Hotel, a B&O train is about to stop at the Ellicott City station.

ELLICOTT CITY

ELLICOTT CITY RAILROAD STATION
Maryland Avenue and Main Street
c. 1831

Thirteen miles west of Baltimore on the Patapsco River, Ellicott's Mills (later Ellicott City) was the first terminus of the nation's first regularly scheduled passenger service—the Baltimore & Ohio. Used originally as a combination freight house, engine house, and operations office, the depot did not handle passengers until 1856. (The extant Patapsco Hotel across the street was the initial passenger stop.) In 1830, the exciting 26-mile round trip cost 75 cents and took three hours. The depot's thick stone walls are still topped today by a gable roof, cupola, and brick chimneys. A bracketed roof extension on the track side shelters the platform. Of additional note nearby: an 1885 freight depot; a portion of the 1830 Oliver Viaduct north of the station; and one partially excavated turntable. NR. [Historic Ellicott City. Museum.]

FREDERICK

FREDERICK RAILROAD STATION
South Market and East All Saints streets
1854

In January 1853, the Baltimore & Ohio finally made it to the Ohio River. The railroad's 25-year-long objective to cross the Appalachian Mountains had been met, and it started building more substantial stations back home. Frederick is the sole survivor of several Italianate buildings constructed by the B&O in the early 1850s. It supplanted an 1831 depot, one block east, which remained standing until 1911. The new, two-story brick station was later expanded—apparently by the annexation of a neighboring Federal-style townhouse. The depot is anchored at the corner by a three-story tower with a low pyramidal roof. B&O discontinued train service in 1949. Today, the building is fully restored on the exterior; the interior was renovated to house low income services. In the early Nineties, the city built a new homeless shelter, attached directly to the former depot. NR. [City of Frederick. Community Center.]

FROSTBURG

FROSTBURG DEPOT
19 Depot Street, off East Main Street
E. Francis Baldwin
1891

In the late 19th century, Frostburg supported an unusual combination of coal mining and mountain tourism. Today, a tourist railroad winds 16 miles through the hills and valleys of western Maryland, with a stop at the Frostburg station. Built by the Cumberland & Pennsylvania Railroad, the depot (which saw its last regular passenger service in 1942) was abandoned by the Western Maryland Railway in 1973. By the time the current owner took title at a bankruptcy sale in 1982, the former combination freight and

passenger depot had been roughed up by a stint as a motorcycle repair shop. Converted to a restaurant, the freight room is now a dining area, where a glass wall provides customers a view of trackside activities. A cocktail bar is installed in the former waiting room, and sundaes are dished out from the old agent's office turned into an ice cream parlor. The site includes a working locomotive turntable, an 1800s warehouse now sheltering a collection of antique carriages, and a railroad workers' hotel used today for gift shops. NR District. [Privately owned. Restaurant and tourist train stop.]

GAITHERSBURG

GAITHERSBURG RAILROAD STATION
Southeast of Summit and East Diamond
    avenues
E. Francis Baldwin
1884

The Baltimore & Ohio established a station at Gaithersburg in 1872, although it probably had only a freight building. After the passenger depot was built 12 years later, the center of business activity shifted from Frederick Avenue to

WM steam locomotive No. 1103 at the Frostburg depot, 1950.

WM diesel locomotive No. 7548 at the Gaithersburg station (built by the B&O). The brick freight house is visible in the center of this 1981 photo.

the area near the station. Buildings surrounding the depot were typical of most 19th-century station sites: feed and fertilizer stores, a flour mill and grain warehouse, livery stables and blacksmith, a bank, and a barber. E. Francis Baldwin designed the Gaithersburg station in Queen Anne style, with ornamental brick and a slate roof. The steeply pitched gabled roof of the agent's bay perched prominently above the depot. The interior was divided into men's and ladies' waiting rooms and warmed by potbellied stoves. Wooden benches on cast iron frames—still in use today—had tin inserts lettered with "B&O RR." The city restored both the interior and exterior of the building in the late 1980s, including outside trim colors of beige and reddish brown. The nearby brick freight house is used as meeting and exhibit space. Many other depots of Baldwin's design shared stylistic similarities to Gaithersburg, including the active station at Laurel (restored in 1993 after a fire) and Sykesville (now a restaurant). NR. [City of Gaithersburg. Train stop, museum, and trackmen's storage.]

LUTHERVILLE

LUTHERVILLE RAILROAD STATION
Front Street
c. 1876

Lutherville was a planned community—one of the country's earliest railroad suburbs, established in 1852. The two-story stone station with a gambrel roof—typical of American barns but unusual for a depot—replaced a more rudimentary passenger station. Built by the Northern Central Railway (later the Pennsylvania Railroad), it may have served as a combined depot and hotel. A second-story porch once stretched along the trackside facade; large shade trees still border the tracks. The rails now accommodate a rapid transit line. One stop south of Lutherville was the Sherwood station (later called Riderwood). Built in 1905 and recently determined to be a Frank Furness design, Riderwood—like Lutherville—is now a dwelling. [Privately owned. Residence.]

OAKLAND

OAKLAND RAILROAD STATION
Liberty Street
E. Francis Baldwin
c. 1885

Garrett County was named for John W. Garrett, president of the Baltimore & Ohio. Replacing the village name of "Slab Town" with Oakland about 1850, the B&O laid out streets and 64 lots. Oakland became the county seat in 1872. Soon after, it evolved into a successful mountain resort when the grand Oakland Hotel opened in 1876 (razed 1911) just across the Little Youghiogheny River from the station. A new masonry depot replaced the old wooden one, which was relocated to Altamont. Although the date stone just under the peaked roof reads 1884, the Oakland station was probably not completed until 1885. One of E. Francis Baldwin's more elaborate Queen Anne–style depots, its most notable feature was a circular tower topped with a haystack-

Still served by passenger trains when this 1960 photo was taken, the Oakland station had a small fleet of baggage wagons parked on the platform.

shaped, slate roof. The main construction material—several different kinds of molded brick—was embellished by decorative half-timbering, fish-scale shingles, stone trim, and stained glass. Except for a short-lived revival by Amtrak, passenger service ended in 1971. The town is trying to acquire the building for a museum and information center. NR. [CSX Transportation. Storage.]

PERRYVILLE

PERRYVILLE RAILROAD STATION
650 Broad Street
1905

On the track side of the Perryville station, the platform canopy is incorporated into the depot's surprisingly formal design. The canopy divides the second-story fanlights from the tripartite windows below. This Palladian theme was established most prominently in the projecting central pavilion (the lower window is now converted to a doorway). Originally, the depot's slate roof was dotted with ornamental "snow cleats" (current cleats are replacements and slate shingles are gone), both to reinforce the Colonial Revival style and to prevent a one-piece snow slide from collapsing the platform canopy. During World War II, Perryville was especially crowded with sailors en route to the United States Naval Training Center at Bainbridge. Built by the Philadelphia, Baltimore & Washington (Pennsylvania Railroad system), the Perryville station is virtually identical to a depot at Northumberland, Pa. (now a restaurant). Perryville was rehabilitated in the early 1990s for use on a new commuter line from Baltimore. [Amtrak owned. MARC stop.]

POINT OF ROCKS

POINT OF ROCKS RAILROAD STATION

South side of State Route 28 (east of U.S. Route 15)
E. Francis Baldwin
c. 1873–75

In the 1830s, both the Baltimore & Ohio Railroad and its competitor, the Chesapeake & Ohio Canal, were constructing routes west from Point of Rocks—and fighting over access. The legal system resolved the dispute in favor of the canal. The race between the artificial waterway and the up-start train tracks would proceed in tandem, along a narrow strip of land between the Potomac River and the Catoctin Mountains. The triangular Point of Rocks depot was later built on a wedge-shaped piece of ground between the Metropolitan branch of the B&O to Washington, D.C., and the original main line to Baltimore. It was designed during E. Francis Baldwin's tenure as head of the B&O architectural department. The Gothic Revival building actually consists of two parts; the rear section is a few years older. Brick walls striped with bands of granite are accented by sandstone and granite arches. A variety of dormer styles pierce both the hipped roof and the four-story tower at the depot's apex. In 1931, the station was struck by lightning that seriously damaged the roof and second floor. The B&O, in an unusual Depression-era show of respect for architecture, restored the building's original appearance. NR. [CSX Transportation. Train stop/npa and headquarters for track maintenance crews.]

ROCKVILLE

ROCKVILLE RAILROAD STATION

98 Baltimore Road at Church Street
E. Francis Baldwin
1873

In the late 19th century, the railroad enabled Rockville to expand both as a resort town and as a Washington suburb. About 90 years later, the Rockville station earned consumer recognition as the prototype for a scale-model version manufactured by the Atlas Company. But when a new rapid-transit system came to Rockville in the early 1980s, the old Baltimore & Ohio station was in its way. Rather than being demolished, the brick

Point of Rocks depot. In the foreground, tracks to Washington, D.C.

NORTHEAST (TRACK) ELEVATION

SOUTHEAST STATION ELEVATION

MATERIALS:
FOUNDATIONS: STONE WITH WATER TABLE
EXTERIOR WALLS: BRICK WITH STONE BELT COURSES
EAVES: WOOD
ROOF: SLATE
PORCH: WOOD

Rockville passenger and freight depots. This drawing was made in 1977, before the buildings were relocated.

passenger depot and separate freight house were relocated about 35 feet west and turned to face downtown. With stone-trimmed Gothic-style windows, jerkinhead dormers, and a steeply pitched roof of variegated slate, the depot has become the unofficial historic preservation symbol for the city. NR. [Privately owned. Offices.]

UNION BRIDGE

WESTERN MARYLAND STATION AND OFFICE BUILDING
North end of Main Street
1902

At the turn of the 20th century, the Western Maryland Railway had its headquarters in a two-story brick building at Union Bridge, which was first reached by rail in 1862. A story-and-a-half depot, in matching Classical Revival style, was linked to the offices by a platform canopy. Scrolled brackets and limestone braces supported the trackside shelter. Many of the windows in both buildings, including those of the depot's large gabled dormer, were accented by limestone keystones. About 1915, the railroad moved its car and engine shops to Hagerstown; and Union Bridge operated mostly as a terminal point for commuter trains. Today, the office building is owned and used by a railway historical society for its museum. The depot is owned and used by a freight railroad, with a small space leased to an excursion line. NR. [Western Maryland Railway Historical Society and Maryland Midland Railroad. Mixed use and tourist train stop.] *See photo* page 123.

New Jersey

After the Civil War, many suburbs and oceanside resorts in New Jersey were created by joint ventures between real estate owners and railroads, who wanted to expand beyond their mostly freight operations. The majority of passenger stations they built concentrated on commuter amenities, rather than facilities for long-distance travelers. In the early 20th century, both increasing patronage and grade separation projects made replacement depots necessary. When state-owned New Jersey Transit was formed in 1979, its rail division inherited about 150 aging stations. A recipient of federal funds, New Jersey Transit had to follow specific guidelines for handling historic properties. As a consequence, more than 50 stations have been placed in the National Register; a significant number continue to undergo restoration. By leasing out excess space, New Jersey Transit obtains additional revenue and encourages new uses for historic structures. Most importantly, a tenant who rents an entire depot is often required to provide commuter waiting space; the building thus retains a measure of its original use.

BERNARDSVILLE

BERNARDSVILLE RAILROAD STATION
U.S. Route 202
c. 1902

In 1905, the advertising department of the Delaware, Lackawanna & Western encouraged customers to try the pleasing summer weather found in New Jersey's suburbs: "the air dry and bracing . . . at night laden with the delicious odor of pine and hemlock." Today commuters can step within the Bernardsville depot's Greek Revival interior for breakfast or to cash a check before boarding a train. In the mid-1980s, New Jersey Transit committed the common preservation crime of sandblasting the depot's Richardsonian Romanesque exterior of pink stone. Acknowledging the error, the agency wisely hired a full-time preservation specialist to henceforth oversee its many historic depots. NR. [New Jersey Transit. Train stop, delicatessen, and bank.]

BLOOMFIELD

BLOOMFIELD RAILROAD STATION
West of Lackawanna Plaza, between
    Washington Street and Glenwood Avenue
William H. Botsford
1912

The Delaware, Lackawanna & Western used reinforced concrete not only for the railroad viaduct, but also for the inbound and outbound buildings at Bloomfield. Except for the green glazed pantiles on the roof, Bloomfield's extremely modern look was a stark departure from conventional depots. Its design was conceived by William H. Botsford and implemented by Frank J. Nies, head of the DL&W's architecture and engineering staff. In 1994, the long platform shelter and small waiting room on the inbound side suffered a fire; its future is uncertain. In the more substantial outbound building, the track-level waiting room is closed; but the first first floor is used commercially. NR.

Early view of the Bloomfield station shows concrete retaining walls and ramps.

[Inbound, owned by New Jersey Transit; outbound, privately owned. Train stop/npa and pizza parlor.]

BOUND BROOK

BOUND BROOK RAILROAD STATION
East Main Street at Hamilton Street
1913

Because of its proximity to the Delaware & Raritan Canal, Bound Brook became an early 19th-century industrial center. In 1913, the Central Railroad of New Jersey replaced its frame depot with a new Classical Revival station of limestone-trimmed red brick. (The demolished building was very similar to the depot standing today at Red Bank.) Inside, red quarry tile wainscoting surmounted a gray and tan terrazzo floor with a black border. In the mid-1980s, a local man who owned a cafe across the street watched commuters waiting in the icy cold outside the vacant depot. After a complete rehabilitation, aided by state and federal grants, the building became his new restaurant, and now warms commuters at 6 a.m. Inspired by this showcase restoration, Bound Brook established a local historic district surrounding the depot. NR. [New Jersey Transit. Train stop and restaurant.]

EAST ORANGE

EAST ORANGE RAILROAD STATION
65 City Hall Plaza
Frank J. Nies
1922

The East Orange station was constructed as part of a massive grade separation project, the same year as the next stop west, Brick Church (1922; extant). The tracks and platforms at East Orange were built above a columned viaduct, 800 feet long and 75 feet wide. The second floor of the brick and concrete depot abutted track level. Additional station facilities and automobile parking were provided beneath the deck. William H. Truesdale, President of the Delaware,

July 1925 streetside view of the East Orange depot.

Lackawanna & Western, liked each station to have a distinct stylistic character. East Orange, unusual for its Jacobean Revival elements, fulfilled his wishes. Today the depot is being considered for a restaurant, which may also provide a waiting space for passengers. NR. [New Jersey Transit. Train stop/npa—for rent.]

ELIZABETH

CENTRAL RAILROAD OF NEW JERSEY STATION
West Grand Street between Broad and
   Union streets
Bruce Price
1893

Some of Bruce Price's original drawings are serving as a guide for contemplated restoration of the Elizabeth station. He designed the Central Railroad of New Jersey station a few years before his elegant Windsor Station in Montreal, Canada. At Elizabeth both the CNJ and the Pennsylvania Railroad undertook a monumental track elevation and station improvement project between 1891 and 1894. Their tracks crossed just east of this station. (Although the 1894 PRR station was destroyed after a 1970 fire, the Pennsy's tracks are part of Amtrak's "Northeast Corridor.") With a turreted, 75-foot-tall clock tower, the CNJ depot was a landmark to passengers on both lines. In 1967, the CNJ's main line commuter service was rerouted; the Elizabeth stop declined in importance and was soon eliminated. The buff brick, Romanesque Revival building, roofed in slate, has suffered over the years from alteration, neglect, vandalism, and several fires, and is now boarded up. Mixed-use development under consideration for this area would include restoring the depot. NR. [New Jersey Transit. Vacant.]

FAR HILLS

FAR HILLS RAILROAD STATION
U.S. Route 202
1914

For its early 20th-century suburban stations, the Delaware, Lackawanna & Western tended toward a standard design—a low rectangular, hipped roof structure with a loggia at one or both ends, best described as Renaissance Revival with Arts & Crafts influences. Variations occurred in scale, material, and trim. Far Hills, in

Elizabeth CNJ station, August 1950.

an area of elite estates, was unusual for its execution in concrete. The 1916 brick station at Morris Plains is nearly identical. Like the station at Bound Brook, the Far Hills depot-turned-restaurant opens at 6 a.m. to accommodate commuters. NR. [New Jersey Transit. Train stop and restaurant.]

GLEN RIDGE

DELAWARE, LACKAWANNA & WESTERN STATION
Ridge Avenue off Bloomfield Avenue
Jesse H. Lockwood
1887

Architect Jesse H. Lockwood took advantage of the 18-foot-deep, sandstone cut through which the Delaware, Lackawanna & Western passed. His two-level design flowed down a steep

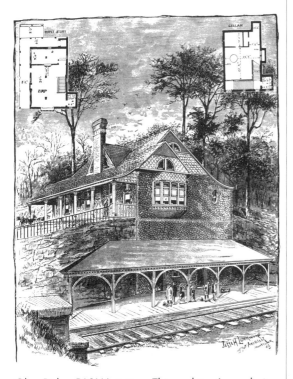

Glen Ridge DL&W station. This architect's rendering shows the original platform canopy.

embankment to the covered platform below. (The current canopy dates from a 1913 double-tracking and depot expansion project.) A wagon road was even with the upper story of the building, which also served as the post office. The station's Queen Anne style blended well with the surrounding houses (some of which are used today for commercial purposes). Its walls were blue-black fieldstone; the roof was slate. Nearby on Benson Street, the former Erie Railroad station—long appreciated for its exquisite Palladian dormers—lost its original roof in a late 1980s fire. NR. [New Jersey Transit. Train stop/npa—for rent.]

HADDON HEIGHTS

HADDON HEIGHTS RAILROAD STATION
Atlantic and Station avenues
c. 1890

In the late 19th century, Haddon Heights was a new suburban community, planned to draw middle class families from nearby Camden and from big-city Philadelphia. A local businessman persuaded the Atlantic City Railroad (later Pennsylvania–Reading Seashore Lines) to construct a station in the center of his holdings, along a broad avenue leading to residential streets. As built, the Queen Anne design was identical to depots at West Collingswood and Audubon (both extant); Haddon Heights's open-air waiting area was removed many years ago. A three-sided shelter protected pass-engers waiting on the other side of the tracks. Across the street stood a brick freight station (now a beauty parlor), saved in the 1980s when the local historical commission resisted demolition plans put forth by Conrail. In the early 1990s, an Eagle Scout took on the ambitious project of painting the wooden siding and repairing the polychrome slate roof of the former passenger station. NR District. [Consolidated Rail Corporation (Conrail). Repair shop for railroad switches.]

Lackawanna Ferry Terminal and Railroad Station, Hoboken.

Waiting room, March 1917. Just out of view is the Tiffany glass ceiling.

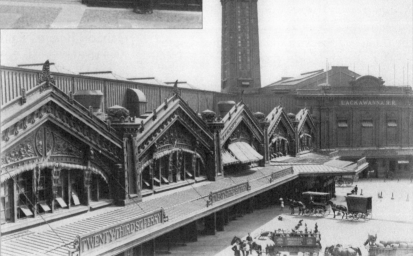

Horse-drawn commercial vehicles wait to board the ferry. The entrance to the railroad station is on the right.

HOBOKEN

LACKAWANNA FERRY AND RAILROAD TERMINAL
Foot of Hudson Place
Kenneth W. Murchison
1907 (entire complex opened)

When ferryboats from Ellis Island crossed the Hudson River to Hoboken, immigrants landed at an ornate, copper-clad festival of a building—

part ferry terminal, part railroad station. Some of the immigrants boarded trains to the coalfields of Pennsylvania and beyond; others settled in New Jersey and joined the enormous work force of ferry commuters into Manhattan. The Lackawanna Terminal, built by the Delaware, Lackawanna & Western, was consecutively the fifth on the site, and one of seven combination ferry and railroad facilities that operated simultaneously on the west shore of the river.

The entire ferry concourse and part of the train concourse and waiting room were built over water, on a concrete platform supported by 13,000 wooden pilings. Copper sheathing applied to the terminal's steel and concrete frame was not only visually striking, but also notably lightweight in contrast to masonry veneer. Murchison hoped the copper would conceal cracks caused either by settlement or the shock of ferryboats banging into the building. The station's 22-story clock tower (dismantled long ago and replaced by a radio antenna) was a Hudson River landmark, illuminated by electricity. The two-level, 500-foot-long ferry concourse was placed at a 120-degree angle to the attached railroad station, reconciling the direct frontage on the Hudson with the path of pre-existing rails. Double-decker ferries discharged passengers at the upper level and wagon teams to the floor below. The innovative Bush shed (covering 14 tracks over nearly five acres) and a railroad Y.M.C.A. (added later) were built on solid ground. Ornamental details of the head house were late French Baroque, designed by Kenneth Murchison, who studied at the Ecole des Beaux-Arts in Paris.

In 1981, New Jersey Transit, whose trains and buses now use this terminal, began an ongoing restoration of the entire complex. Uncovering the spectacular Tiffany glass ceiling of the 50-foot-high waiting room was simple and inexpensive compared to future tasks of stabilizing the terminal's underwater foundation (which is being attacked by marine organisms thriving in the improved water quality of the Hudson) and the copper cladding (which is being lifted by wind and vandalism). The huge upper ferry concourse is ornamented with classical detailing and the remnants of six Tiffany skylights. Years ago, from a balcony on the southern end, patrons at one of the terminal's two restaurants had a fine view of the river. Vacant and currently closed to the public, the enormous space is ripe for adaptive use. A

very large, adjacent trolley terminal was demolished in 1949; trolley tracks are still embedded in the cobblestone streets outside. In 1989, a new eight-minutes-to-Manhattan ferry service was established. It departs from a wharf in front of the 1904 Pullman Building and Immigrant Station (adjacent to the train concourse) that serves today as the ticket office and waiting area for ferry passengers. Used by 60,000 commuters a day, the Hoboken Terminal area is an inspiring example of in-progress, waterfront revitalization. NR. [New Jersey Transit. Multimodal transportation center and commercial.]

JERSEY CITY

CENTRAL RAILROAD OF NEW JERSEY FERRY AND RAILROAD TERMINAL
Liberty State Park
Peabody and Stearns
1889, 1914

The Central Railroad of New Jersey Terminal stands on ground once completely covered by water. Called Communipaw Cove, it was filled during the 1860s when the first terminal was constructed. (Ferry service from Communipaw to Manhattan began two centuries earlier in 1661.) In 1889, a new terminal was completed, designed to accommodate the vast number of passengers transferring between ferry slips at the Hudson River's edge and the railroad. This kind of maritime terminal, with intermodal handling of ferry and train traffic, was most prevalent in the New York–New Jersey Harbor, the San Francisco Bay, and the Philadelphia-Camden waterfront. The configuration tackled complex circulation problems, including the loading of vehicular traffic (at first horse-drawn) onto the ferries. The Jersey City complex was the work of two entities: the railroad staff, who engineered the train shed, ferry house, and wood-piling foundations; and the

Single-decker ferry slips, seen here, were constructed in 1889 at the CNJ Ferry and Railroad Terminal, Jersey City. In 1914, a new two-level ferry facility was completed. It provided passengers with direct access to double-decker boats and created passageways to the new Bush train shed.

prominent Boston architectural firm, Peabody and Stearns, that designed the head house. Styled like a French Renaissance chateau, the terminal included separate waiting rooms for immigrants arriving from Ellis Island, many of whom (between 1892 and 1954) came through this building.

Besides the CNJ, the facility served passenger trains of the Baltimore & Ohio and the Reading Company. By the 1930s, the terminal's business began declining — hurt by the Depression, the reduced immigrant flow, and new ways to get over and under the Hudson River. In 1967, passenger traffic was rerouted through Newark, and the Jersey City Terminal closed down. Its once immense complex of service and repair facilities, thawing sheds, float bridges, ferry sheds, and docks is now gone. The three-story head house and the severely deteriorated Bush shed (which in 1914 replaced the original long-span train shed) are essentially what remains. With all gritty traces of railroading erased, including the tracks, the

terminal is surrounded today by a park. The Romanesque Revival main waiting room has been restored with its dramatic ceiling of exposed steel trusses embellished by metal star bursts and rosettes (applied to the connectors). Metal brackets, with patterned perforations, support a gallery that rims the room. Cream-colored, glazed brick walls envelop a completely unfurnished space (no benches needed anymore) — a flexible arena used for everything from historical exhibits to dog shows. New stained glass ceiling panels replicate in feeling the skylight of the former ladies' waiting room, now combined with the old ticket office into a small auditorium. A wide stairway to the second floor meets an abrupt ending — the blocked up former entrance to the huge ferry terminal, which was built in 1914 and demolished in 1980. The state has reconstructed two wharves to accommodate a tourist ferry service linking this site with various historic points in New York Harbor, such as Ellis Island and the Statue of Liberty. NR. [State of New Jersey. Exhibit and special event space.]

LAMBERTVILLE

LAMBERTVILLE RAILROAD STATION
11 Bridge Street
Thomas U. Walter
c. 1873

Begun in 1851, the Belvidere–Delaware Railroad paralleled the Delaware & Raritan Canal (extant). The Pennsylvania Railroad, which swallowed the B–D in 1872, hired a noted Philadelphia architect to build a replacement for the c. 1820 residence that had served as a depot. Thomas U. Walter — famous for the dome of the United States Capitol — designed a two-and-a-half story stone station with four jerkinhead wall dormers, jerkinhead gables, Italianate arched windows, and Stick Style brackets. At the roof ridge was a wooden cupola topped by an obelisk. The upper floors were

Early view of the Lambertville station, bordering the Delaware & Raritan Canal.

division offices. In the early 1980s, after two decades of abandonment and failed plans, the depot was restored and converted to a restaurant. The owner rebuilt the platform and canopy, which now provide both a place to dine and to board a tourist train. Two railroad box cars serve as the kitchen. NR District. [Privately owned. Restaurant and tourist train stop.]

LITTLE SILVER

LITTLE SILVER RAILROAD STATION
Sycamore and Branch avenues
1890

Although the depot at Little Silver has suffered from sandblasting and rearranged partitions, it serves more commuters and trains than ever before. Built on the New York & Long Branch, a line jointly operated by the Central Railroad of New Jersey and the Pennsylvania Railroad, the simple Richardsonian Romanesque depot still has its steeply pitched slate roof with sharply

flared eaves, supported by heavy timber brackets on stone corbels. The recently expanded waiting room rises to roof height, distinguished by a pair of queen post trusses. Diamond-shaped panes fill the upper window sash. As part of an unofficial campaign for restoration funds, the devoted newsstand tenant once kept a "contributions fishbowl" next to the coffee urn. NR. [Borough of Little Silver. Train stop.]

A bicycle leans against the wall at the Little Silver station.

MADISON

MADISON RAILROAD STATION
Kings Road
1916

Serving two universities, the Madison station was appropriately conceived in Collegiate Gothic style by a succession of Delaware, Lackawanna & Western architects. (The initial designer, William H. Botsford, died on the Titanic; Frank J. Nies's staff revised the plan.) An earlier depot and numerous houses were demolished for the track elevation project that included a new, two-level, slate-roofed station with a rock-faced stone veneer. Today, the *L*-shaped depot still extends one leg toward its stone porte-cochere. In the waiting room, medieval-style chandeliers hang from a ceiling of exposed arch trusses. A platform canopy extends from the building and stretches down the tracks to the former express building. The complex includes a matching outbound shelter across the tracks and a matching freight house to the northwest (now a Y.M.C.A.). NR. [New Jersey Transit. Train stop and vacant commercial space.]

MANASQUAN

MANASQUAN RAILROAD STATION
East Main Street
1877

The wooden station at the seacoast village of Manasquan (originally just plain "Squan") was built by ships' carpenters. Building materials are reported to have been salvaged from the 1876 Philadelphia Centennial Exposition. Originally constructed at Sea Plain (now Spring Lake), the New York & Long Branch depot was transported on flat cars to its present location in 1880. The existing platform canopy likely dates from that time. An identical depot stood at a stop called Avon by the Sea–Neptune City, but was razed c. 1966.

Steadily deteriorating, Manasquan was rescued by a Save Our Station campaign initiated in 1984 and was subsequently leased to the town. Donations from contractors and individuals enabled exterior restoration (minus the gingerbread and one of two chimneys) to be completed for the borough's 1987 centennial. The baggage room is now the commuter waiting room and taxi office. Other spaces have been assigned to a variety of community uses. [New Jersey Transit. Train stop, museum, chamber of commerce, and offices.]

MAPLEWOOD

MAPLEWOOD RAILROAD STATION
Dunnell Road
c. 1902

The addition of a third track at the turn of the century required a new station for Maplewood. The staff of the Delaware, Lackawanna & Western designed an eclectic depot that captured architectural elements from the surrounding neighborhoods: Romanesque rock-faced brick, a Queen Anne hexagonal tower, and Tudor Revival half-timbering. The floor plan included a men's smoking room and a Union News facility. In 1914–15, the third track was relocated next to the embankment. A tunnel was built to connect the main station with a new island platform and the stair pavilion on the outbound side. [New Jersey Transit. Train stop.]

MORRISTOWN

DELAWARE, LACKAWANNA & WESTERN STATION
Morris Avenue at Elm Street
1913

As a county seat and an important stop for Delaware, Lackawanna & Western trains from Buffalo, N.Y., Morristown merited a grander

The estatelike approach to the Morristown DL&W station.

station than nearby communities. Located at a junction with the little Morristown & Erie Railroad (which had its own depot), the "Lackawanna" station was built as part of a track elevation project. Passengers approached the new inbound and outbound depots via curving, vehicular driveways, framed between brick gateposts with decorative globe lights (four of these pillars remain today). A heavily landscaped plaza appealed especially to commuters walking to the station.

Designed by the railroad's architectural team (under Frank J. Nies) in a Renaissance Revival style, the buildings were clad in buff brick, laid in Flemish bond with dark headers. Green glazed tiles covered the steel truss and concrete slab roof. Round-arched door and window openings were interspersed with several large oculus windows. A copper and glass canopy, supported by chains and ornamented scroll brackets, sheltered the streetside entrance. The high-ceilinged waiting room, with its large, polygonal ticket office, contained oak woodwork and terrazzo floors bordered in marble. Shaded lamps, mounted onto wooden benches, and matching wall sconces (now missing) provided artificial light. On the station's east end was a baggage room. Today, the roundhouse and freight house are gone;

but across the tracks, the outbound station and a dilapidated express building (scheduled for rehabilitation) remain. NR. [New Jersey Transit. Train stop.]

NEWARK

DELAWARE, LACKAWANNA & WESTERN STATION
Lackawanna Avenue near the intersection of
   University Avenue and Broad Street
Frank J. Nies
1903

The Delaware, Lackawanna & Western's Newark station was constructed as part of a track elevation and depression project that eliminated 27 grade crossings. Each had been protected by crossing gates and a watchman. The brick and limestone, Renaissance Revival depot was anchored on the southeast corner by an 80-foot-tall campanile, faced with three clocks set in cartouches. Pilasters and round arches framed the oversized windows, supplemented by two monumental, hipped roof dormers on the street side. An entrance at the foot of the tower led up to a mezzanine level, housing the ticket agent and coffee shop. Classical detailing included columns decorated by plas-

Early view of the Newark DL&W station. Canopies sheltered the sidewalk and the elevated train platforms.

ter cartouches, monogrammed with DL&W. The third floor, at track level, comprised the waiting room, railroad offices, and express room. Platform canopies sheltered both sides of the tracks. A two-level outbound station, reached by an underground passageway, stylistically matched the inbound building. Very much intact and still in use today as a commuter stop, known as "Newark Broad Street," the station once also served long-distance trains headed toward Buffalo, N.Y., and points west. The separate freight station is gone. NR. [New Jersey Transit. Train stop.]

PENNSYLVANIA STATION
Raymond Plaza West at Market Street
McKim, Mead, and White
1935

In 1929, the city of Newark and the Pennsylvania Railroad agreed on a major multimodal center to facilitate connections between elec-

trified commuter and long-distance rail lines, a subway, a rapid transit line, and taxi and bus service. Engineers drew plans for three boulevards to create improved access to the site, and a tunnel leading to a new post office building. A key element in the project was a viaduct carrying multiple levels of train tracks (both conventional and rapid transit) right across the roof of the station's concourse. Trains made roof-level stops under a huge, skylit, steel canopy, where aluminum-clad waiting rooms sheltered passengers, many of whom used Newark as a transfer point. Faced in buff brick and terracotta, the viaduct extended northeast and southwest of the depot, with openings beneath for pedestrians and vehicles. Fluted columns flanking each arched passageway were topped by stylized granite eagles. The northeast end of the viaduct fed into two new lift bridges across the Passaic River.

The station building, clad in Indiana gray limestone and rubbed pink granite, replaced an

1889 multiturreted depot on Market Street. Designed in the 1930s by McKim, Mead and White (after all the founders had died), the classically organized, Art Deco extravaganza was restored five decades later as part of the Northeast Corridor Improvement Project. Arching above the station's main entrance marquee is a heroically scaled window embellished by carved stonework rosettes. The marquee's underside is decorated with swirls of light bulbs and stars, surrounding a burnished aluminum sunburst. Inside the station, a 75-foot-long marble and travertine main waiting room has Art Deco details on virtually everything: the mail box and the water fountain; the border of the terrazzo floor; and the high wooden benches,

where, on the end panels, acanthus leaves mingle with the PRR logo. Natural light from floor-to-ceiling windows is supplemented by four, 800-pound hanging globes (two are replicas), decorated with zodiac symbols circling white-bronze equators. Thirteen large plaster medallions rim the room, each celebrating an aspect of transportation history from the canoe to the airplane. New ticketing facilities and the central information kiosk are essentially the only nonoriginal elements. In the mid-1990s, New Jersey Transit (the station's operator) began a five-year improvement project that includes a new concourse and some fine tuning of the previous historic restoration. NR. [Privately owned. Multimodal transportation center and commercial.]

Newark Pennsylvania Station.

One of twin Art Deco entrances, 1984.

Beneath an entrance marquee, a lighted sunburst.

ORADELL

Oradell Railroad Station
Maple and Oradell avenues
1890

After the new Oradell station was built, the preceding board and batten depot (standing across the tracks) was relocated 100 yards north for use as a freight house (since demolished). The New Jersey & New York (a subsidiary of the Erie Railroad) covered the sides of the Queen Anne–style depot with scalloped wooden shingles; the attached Wells Fargo express building, with clapboards. On the ridge of the gable-on-hip roof sat a short rectangular tower, capped by an octagonal spire and fronted by a gable dormer. Today, chimneys, finials, roof cresting, and panes of colored glass are missing, as is the gabled porte-cochere. The trackside stairs once stretched full-width between two of the turned wooden columns supporting the broad, wraparound porch. The interior, with men's and ladies' waiting rooms

and a 16-foot-high ceiling, was altered somewhat in 1913 to add indoor plumbing. NR. [Borough of Oradell. Train stop and florist.]

PARK RIDGE

Park Ridge Railroad Station
Hawthorne and Park avenues
1872

In the 1870s, when the Hackensack & New York Extension Railroad (soon to be the New Jersey & New York) announced a route that would bypass Park Ridge, residents offered to finance construction of a depot. Their inducement was well-received, and train service came to town. Opening day receipts were $3.50. In 1981, contractors announced that the crumbling Carpenter Gothic depot, empty for 20 years, was a candidate for bulldozing. A local man called on neighbors to bring their shovels and hammers to a string of depot renovation rallies, which included elevating the entire building to

After entering the streetside porte-cochere, departing passengers could either walk through the Oradell depot or around the covered porch to reach the tracks.

A separate freight depot stood northeast of the Park Ridge passenger station.

install a new foundation. Donated funds, materials, and labor reproduced the depot's distinctive flared-eaves cupola, which sits astride a new slate roof, drained by copper gutters and down spouts. The interior was originally divided into three spaces, but has since been stripped of its partitions. A matching board and batten freight house stood northeast of the passenger depot. NR. [Ownership in dispute. Train stop/npa and community meeting space.]

PENNINGTON

PENNINGTON RAILROAD STATION
Franklin Avenue and Green Street
1882

The Delaware & Bound Brook (later part of the Reading system) inaugurated service to Pennington in 1876. To celebrate, the railroad gave 700 people free round trips to the Centennial Exposition in Philadelphia. A sandstone station house was completed six years later. Two-and-a-half-stories high with a mansard roof, the building had a strongly domestic appearance; only the deep platform canopy, extending around all four sides, gave it a distinctly "railroad station" dimension. The roof was circumscribed by lacy iron railings. A wide staircase led down to the loading platform. Painted in browns and ochres, the depot was surrounded by landscaped grounds with flower beds. A large fountain in the center of the lawn operated on summer afternoons. For years,

Pennington station, 1953.

farmers brought their milk cans just in time for the 6:45 a.m. train. Cattle unloaded at the depot were driven right through the streets of town. In the early 1900s, 50 trains a day stopped at Pennington; in the mid-1960s, all service was discontinued. After a decade or so of vacancy, the station was converted to dwelling units. Residential development now surrounds the building; the remaining track carries freight trains. The former Hopewell station, 4.7 railroad miles northeast of Pennington, is a twin design, but made of brick. NR. [Privately owned. Apartments.]

PERTH AMBOY

PERTH AMBOY RAILROAD STATION
Elm Street between Smith and Market streets
1927

Today's Perth Amboy station was built by the New York & Long Branch Railroad as the direct result of a grade separation project. The preceding station (1875) was similar to the Red Bank depot (see below). The new station comprised red brick inbound and outbound structures, each built against an embankment. They were linked at the second story by a riveted steel pedestrian bridge that still stretches high above the four tracks. Italian Renaissance Revival features include loggia arches (now mostly closed in) with terra-cotta surrounds and rosettes. Spanish tile roofing covers the extensive platform canopies. In the early 1990s, the community of Perth Amboy began a major study to prepare the station buildings for some form of adaptive use compatible with commuter services. NR. [New Jersey Transit. Train stop.]

RED BANK

NEW YORK & LONG BRANCH STATION
Between Monmouth and Oakland streets,
  off Bridge Avenue
c. 1877

In the 1870s, two lines crossed at Red Bank — the New Jersey Southern and the New York & Long Branch. After 1879, both lines were con-

One commuter is wearing a top hat in this early view of the Red Bank NY&LB station.

trolled by the Central Railroad of New Jersey (builder of the NY&LB). The old NJS depot, two blocks north, was converted to a freight office (demolished in 1947). Passengers from both lines then used the NY&LB station, which was similar to at least six other depots built by the CNJ. The two-story wooden structure contained an octagonal ticket office and men's and ladies' waiting rooms. Upstairs living quarters for the agent were later converted to railroad offices. Various woods were used in the depot: hemlock structural framing, white pine clapboards, maple floors, and chestnut doors. Patterned slate shingles covered the roof; a 25-foot-wide canopy sheltered 168 feet of platform.

Because many of Wall Street's financial leaders commuted from Red Bank, liveried chauffeurs often met the evening trains. Probably the most famous arrivals at Red Bank were Britain's King George VI and Queen Elizabeth, during a 1939 visit to the United States. Six years later, the station was shorn of its exterior ornamental woodwork. For three decades, the depot remained denuded, until the borough of Red Bank hired an architect to study old photographs and re-create the Carpenter Gothic gingerbread. The Dutch Boy Paint Company contributed materials to restore the cream, brown, and rust color scheme. New Jersey Transit plans a full-scale restoration of the platform canopy and the depot's interior for the late 1990s. NR. [New Jersey Transit. Train stop.]

RUTHERFORD

RUTHERFORD RAILROAD STATION
Station Square
Charles W. Buchholz
1898

With its hyphenlike loggias and circular belvedere, the Rutherford station presents a warm-climate face not typical of northern New Jersey. The "spa image" of this area, once

Rutherford station, 1908, plastered with advertising.

known as "Boiling Spring," may have inspired the design, credited to the chief engineer of the Erie Railroad's New York Division. Built of limestone-trimmed orange brick, the Renaissance Revival depot originally had a Spanish tile roof (now slate). Door and window transoms have oval tracery with yellow and green glass. The classically detailed interior has a wooden, coffered ceiling and an imposing fireplace. Providing compositional balance to the end opposite the belvedere, the former express section is home to a cab service. Two other depots preceded this one, sited with a view of the Manhattan skyline. NR. [New Jersey Transit. Train stop and taxi headquarters.]

SOMERVILLE

SOMERVILLE RAILROAD STATION
Veterans Memorial Drive West
Frank V. Bodine
1890

In 1926, the tracks were move slightly away from the Somerville depot and elevated onto a fill. Wooden platforming adjacent to the building was replaced with concrete and an additional, automobile-accessible porte-cochere added. Canopied shelters were erected on both sides of new island platforms. Although the

Side view of the Somerville station c. 1938.

depot was altered at that time—particularly the streetside, double-arched entranceway—most of the structure's Jersey sandstone and wood-shingle exterior remained intact. Designed by a New Jersey architect, with contrasting towers and various roof levels covered in slate, the station was at the junction of two Central Railroad of New Jersey lines. The second floor housed railroad offices; downstairs, the waiting room had a 25-foot-high ceiling. [Privately owned. Train stop/npa and commercial.]

TENAFLY

TENAFLY RAILROAD STATION
North of Clinton Avenue and the railroad track
Daniel Topping Atwood
1874

The cost of the new Tenafly station (replacing a wooden one that was relocated and converted to freight-only use) was equally shared by three parties: the Northern Railroad of New Jersey (part of the Erie Railroad), the townspeople, and a local man who also donated the land. The depot's architect, Daniel Atwood,

practiced in nearby New York City and had a suburban office in Tenafly. His one-story High Victorian design was executed in three shades of rock-faced, native sandstone—pink, tan, and gray. The station was not only symmetrical; its track and street sides were virtually identical. A large, ornate cupola with diminutive pitched dormers nestled between the polygonal roofs of back-to-back center bays. The trackside bay held the agent's office; the streetside bay, the ladies' waiting room. Full-scale pitched dormers let light into the depot's high-ceilinged rooms. Exterior door and window treatments included Gothic arches and miniature Romanesque details. The building was actually completed in 1873, but bickering over construction payments delayed opening until the following year. At first, the attached platform canopy was supported by square posts; but they obstructed movement and were soon replaced by complex brackets. Another early change was the track dimension. In 1878, the six-foot-gauge Northern line was relaid to standard gauge. Starting about 1910, the streetside of the station was a trolley reversal point, from which streetcars headed down to ferries on the Hudson River.

The borough purchased the depot in the early 1960s; passenger service ended in 1966. Since then, tenants have ranged from clothing stores and an art gallery to the current occupant, a beauty parlor. A new slate roof was installed in the early Eighties. In 1994, with the help of a matching state grant, the borough began further restoration of the exterior, to include reconstruction of the missing platform canopy (removed in the early 1960s) and the fancy roof cresting. Freight trains use the one remaining track. NR. [Borough of Tenafly. Commercial.] *For photos, see page 5.*

WALDWICK

WALDWICK RAILROAD STATION

Hewson Avenue and Prospect Street
c. 1887

Despite having its wooden siding stuccoed over, the Waldwick station retains its original Stick Style ornamentation, including roof cresting, finials, and the post and beam detailing of projecting gables. Corbeled chimneys and windows bordered with square panes are derived from Queen Anne style. Original interior features include diamond-shaped stone-tile flooring,

Waldwick station with its original wooden siding, 1908.

wooden benches, and a ticket window with an iron grille. For many years, the depot's exterior was painted in two shades of green, to match the Erie passenger cars. The architect may have been "A. Mordecai," who signed the blueprints for a number of Erie Railroad stations; among them was Port Jervis, N.Y., (1892; extant). Until a few decades ago, a large coach yard and a four-stall engine house stood just north of the station. A 19th-century signal tower (NR), clad in wooden siding and shingles, remains on the west side of the tracks. Waldwick was once an important shipping center for the local berry crop. After rapid suburbanization in the 1950s, commuter service increased proportionately. NR. [New Jersey Transit. Train stop and vacant commercial space.]

WENONAH

WENONAH RAILROAD STATION

East Mantua and North East avenues
1893

A planned community, Wenonah was started by the Mantua Land & Improvement Company. Its president — Civil War general William Sewell — was also on the board of the West Jersey & Seashore (a Pennsylvania Railroad subsidiary). In the early 1890s, after outgrowing an 1869 wooden depot, the WJ&S moved the building across the street to stand beside the post office, where it remains today as a private dwelling. The railroad constructed a new English Cottage–style depot with a brick first story and half-timbering applied to the stuccoed upper portion. The second floor contained three bedrooms for the agent's family; the lower floor comprised the kitchen, living room, waiting room, and ticket office. A separate baggage building stood across Mantua Avenue, on the east side of the tracks.

In the 1970s, the railroad attempted to sell the property for use as a sandwich shop. Wenonah's mayor discovered that by virtue of an

1890s agreement, a portion of the station's land had reverted to the borough when passenger service ended in 1971. Following litigation, the municipality purchased the structure, complete with resident pigeons and leaking roof. Restoration (mostly donated labor and materials) was completed in time for the 1976 Bicentennial. The facility is available free of charge to all community groups. Freight trains use the one remaining track. [Borough of Wenonah. Meeting space, courtroom, and offices.]

WHITE HOUSE STATION

WHITE HOUSE RAILROAD STATION
Main Street
Bradford Lee Gilbert
1890

Stylistically, the depot at White House Station is derived from H. H. Richardson's widely pub-

lished design for Auburndale, Mass., (1881; razed 1960s). Built by the Central Railroad of New Jersey at a junction with the little Rockaway Valley Railroad, the one-story, combination passenger and freight depot featured a semioctagonal open portico with Romanesque detailing. A slate roof sheltered the walls of uncoursed stone rubble. In the early 1980s, more than 200 residents rescued their vacant and deteriorating station with seven months of arduous labor. The township's first-ever library was installed in the old depot, which retains a massive stone fireplace in the former ladies' waiting room, wrought iron grilles on the ticket windows, and stained glass transoms. As with most New Jersey Transit leases, the tenant is required to provide crack-of-dawn waiting space for commuters. In this case, passengers wait amdist picture books in the children's section. NR. [New Jersey Transit. Train stop and library.]

The depot at White House Station with its slate roofing (since replaced) and water tank, 1950s.

New York

New York State serves a four-course meal of railroad stations: from tiny country flag stops to midsize city stations; from sophisticated suburban depots to the world famous Grand Central Terminal. Of particular note are the many Westchester County stations, still sheltering commuters, who board trains from new, somewhat disfiguring, high-level platforms.

ALBANY

UNION STATION
Peter D. Kiernan Plaza on Broadway
Shepley, Rutan, and Coolidge
1900

In 1956, New York Central announced plans to close 406 passenger stations as "excess and obsolete" property. Albany Union Station—also used by the Delaware & Hudson—was on the list. Albany's mayor, ironically a great-grandson of the Central's founder, managed to keep the station open for another decade. Within months of the 1968 closing, copper flashing was stripped by vandals. Rain and snow soon waterlogged the ornamental plaster. Mahogany trim mildewed, structural steel corroded, and small trees sprouted on the roof. The state, which had taken custody of the building, sold off every transportable interior fixture during a 1971 auction. Finally, public sentiment forced the state to spend $1 million on a new roof and stabilization. In 1984, the nearly three-decade wait for a new use had a happy ending, when Norstar Bancorp purchased Union Station and began renovating it for company headquarters. Restoration architects faced the challenge of doubling the floor space while maintaining the grandeur. An ingenious solution for the 56-foot-high central waiting room was to raise the floor 12 feet (providing data-processing

Early streetside view showing trolley tracks at Albany Union Station.

space below) and move the two-story cast-iron galleries 15 feet inward to add offices. An extra story was gained in the north and south wings by extending the newly established floor level through the tall baggage and restaurant areas. A parking garage was built on the site of the boarding platforms. In 1986, thousands of people came to the grand opening of the former station, whose Beaux Arts, pink granite facade was cleaned and polished for the occasion. NR. [Privately owned. Offices.]

ARDSLEY-ON-HUDSON

ARDSLEY-ON-HUDSON RAILROAD STATION
Ardsley Avenue and Hudson Road,
    village of Irvington
McKim, Mead, and White
1895

The New York Central's Ardsley-on-Hudson station was constructed to match the adjacent "Casino," a golf and country club that opened the following year. Members such as John D. Rockefeller, J. Pierpoint Morgan, and Cornelius Vanderbilt had the choice of coming by train or by yacht up the Hudson River. Using a combination of granite, brick, wood, and stucco, the architects mixed Shingle Style—especially in the tower—with elements of Tudor and Romanesque Revival. The arched pedestrian footbridge, built in 1911, now connects the station to a 1930s apartment complex, which replaced the demolished country club. [Privately owned. Train stop, post office, and residence.]

BINGHAMTON

DELAWARE, LACKAWANNA & WESTERN STATION
Chenango and Lewis streets
Samuel W. Huckel, Jr.
1901

In railroading's heyday, station stops made during the wee hours did not necessarily inconvenience passengers. Before departure or after arrival, sleeping cars stood immobile on a siding with their human cargo snoozing inside. At the Delaware, Lackawanna & Western station in Binghamton, a brick structure directly east of the passenger depot housed a boiler, used to

Binghamton DL&W passenger station c. 1917. Across the tracks is the parapeted gable of the freight depot.

convey steam heat to these parked sleepers. Built at the same time as the depot and still standing, the steam plant was also designed by Philadelphian Samuel Huckel and featured segmental-arched doorways and windows, brick corbeling, and an octagonal chimney. The depot itself, of Italian Renaissance style, was clad in brick and stone, with a tile roof and a five-story-high campanile. By the early 1970s, the passenger station, once bustling with railroad offices and a restaurant, was scarcely used. Most of its platform canopy was removed or cut back. In the 1980s, a local architectural firm purchased the depot and began restoration. Work on the roof and tower was supplemented on the inside by refinishing the old Union News facility and the ticket windows.

Located in central New York, near the Pennsylvania border, Binghamton was once a key railroad center and junction point for freight and passengers alike. Other notable railroad buildings in the historic district include the former Erie Railroad freight house and the Delaware & Hudson's combination station. (The DL&W freight house was razed in 1990 to make way for a baseball stadium.) Today, besides its office and retail use, the DL&W passenger depot is headquarters for the Susquehanna Valley Chapter of the National Railway Historical Society, whose vintage rail cars are being restored in the former passenger-car yard area. Immediately south stands one of Marconi's 1913 "wireless telegraph" towers used in a pilot program for transmitting messages between a fixed point and a moving train. NR District. [Privately owned. Commercial.]

VESTAL RAILROAD STATION
328 Vestal Parkway East, 10 miles west of
    Binghamton
1881

When the first mail sack arrived at the Vestal depot, it contained eight letters. Less than a century later, postal bags were considerably

Vestal station on its original site, 1958.

weightier but trucks and planes were moving the mail, and many stations were obsolete. In the mid-1970s, the town of Vestal purchased the former Delaware, Lackawanna & Western passenger and freight station for relocation to its library grounds. The municipality restored the Gothic Revival board and batten building, with its broadly extended eaves, curlicue supports, and multiple pendants, for presentation to the local historical society. Once a typical design for DL&W country depots, Vestal is virtually identical to another rare survivor at Painted Post (1882; now adjacent to a rail trail). [Vestal Historical Society. Railroad and local history museum.]

BRIARCLIFF MANOR

BRIARCLIFF MANOR RAILROAD STATION
Off State Route 9A in Law Park
c. 1915

In the 19th century, this area was known as Whitsons. One of its residents was a once-poor immigrant from England, Walter Law, who had become a partner in the famous home furnishings business, W&J Sloan. He changed the name of the village to Briarcliff Manor and paid for a new railroad station. It was designed to match the theme of his nearby home, Briarcliff Lodge (today part of Kings College). Once a stop on New York Central's Putnam Division, Briarcliff Manor was built in a pseudo-medieval style of stucco and half-timbering. Inside, Mission-style tables and chairs rested on oriental rugs. The depot was purchased by the village in 1959. The right-of-way is now a biking and jogging trail. [Jointly owned: Village of Briarcliff Manor and the Library Board. Library.]

BRONXVILLE

BRONXVILLE RAILROAD STATION
Pondfield Road
1916

For the Bronxville station, the design staff of the New York Central apparently was inspired by the Gramatan Hotel (1905; razed in 1972), which stood across the street from the depot. The third station in an area once called Underhill's Crossing, it was built as part of a grade separation project on the Harlem Division. Of fairly elaborate Mission style, the depot had a polygonal waiting room, parapeted walls, and flat buttresses topped with little tile roofs. The caduceus-and-helmet motif above the window symbolized the swiftness of Mercury. Today, the speed conscious commuter railroad has replaced the original loading area with a high-level platform. Behind the station, the elegant houses of the turn-of-the-century development, Lawrence Park, line the brick and cobblestone streets. [Village of Bronxville. Train stop and newsstand.]

BUFFALO

CENTRAL TERMINAL
495 Paderewski Drive
Fellheimer and Wagner
1930

Completed six months before Wall Street's Black Friday, Buffalo Central Terminal would

see many black days of its own by the 1980s. Midpoint on the New York Central's main line between New York and Chicago, Buffalo was considered the railroad gateway to the Midwest, as well as Niagra Falls and Toronto. The city was served by more than eight railroads, which could never agree on the construction of a union station. The biggest, New York Central, promised for decades to build a new downtown station and correct serious grade crossing problems. Instead, the railroad cleared a few hundred homesites in an eastside residential area—a decentralized, airport-like location, more than two miles from the heart of the city—and there constructed a vertical shaft of Art Deco inventiveness.

Designed by Alfred Fellheimer and Steward Wagner, the terminal proper was a rectangular structure roofed by two intersecting barrel vaults. Extending from this central mass was a 450-foot-long train concourse and a 362-foot-long baggage and mail wing. A 271-foot-high, stepped-back, office tower soared from the station's northwest corner. The main floor of the terminal was placed 21 feet above track level, thereby solving a side station's biggest problem—passengers having to cross the tracks. A series of ramps (which Fellheimer preferred to the Beaux Arts–style grand stairway or the newer escalator—considered too slow) kept pedestrian, baggage, and mail circulation smooth; although the distances were somewhat hard on shoe leather. The Art Deco grand concourse was ornamented with four-color terrazzo flooring, marble ticket counters, and finials in fleur-de-lis and papyrus-leaf patterns. Its vaulted ceiling was covered with a special sound-deadening, but tedious to apply clay tile, perfected by the Guastavino family. The Spanish-flavored general waiting room was embellished with bas-relief medallions of state landmarks. Decorative metalwork separated the huge dining hall into three areas.

Except for World War II crowds (who picked souvenir fur off the stuffed buffalo in

Buffalo Central Terminal soon after it went into service.

the concourse), Central Station's traffic never reached anticipated levels. The station was on the New York Central's 1956 list of depots for sale, but there were no takers. In 1979, the same year passenger service ended, a private party bought the depot, but then lost it, still undeveloped, at a tax auction seven years later. By then, the concourse had been gouged to permit passage of piggyback freight cars on the tracks below. The next owner proceeded to sell off the station's interior artifacts, while rain and snow penetrated broken windows. Various legal battles involving the city, the current owner, and two prospective buyers have so far achieved no resolution. Buffalo had several other historic stations; they are all gone. NR. [Privately owned. Vacant.]

CHAPPAQUA

CHAPPAQUA RAILROAD STATION
Depot Plaza off South Greeley Avenue, hamlet of Chappaqua
1902

Almost every building in Chappaqua is named after Horace Greeley, the 19th-century journalist and political crusader, who established an experimental farm and family retreat in the area. His daughter donated more than two acres of farmland for the new depot and small

park, with the covenant that Depot Plaza remain open space in perpetuity. Built of fieldstone, the depot had a tile roof extending over the platform and the airy porte-cochere. Chappaqua was a stop on the upper Harlem Division of the New York Central, whose president lived in the village at the time the depot was built. Its design (but not materials) is similar to other extant depots from the drawing board of the New York Central staff: Mount Kisco, Bedford Hills, and Katonah. NR District. [Town of New Castle. Train stop.]

FORT EDWARD

FORT EDWARD RAILROAD STATION
East and Wing streets
1900

Similar to other Delaware & Hudson depots at Altamont (NR) and Westport (now a little theater), the Fort Edward station is built of brick to windowsill level with wooden siding above. It replaced a finely detailed, 1880 wooden station that was torn down. The polygonal southern end (former waiting room) is pierced at the eaves by one of many large wall dormers (now boarded up), which once lit the double-height interior. A pyramid-capped cupola still straddles the slate-covered roof, but the depot's window openings have been drasti-

Upcoming restoration will return the Delaware & Hudson station in Fort Edward to this early appearance.

cally altered. Inside, wainscoting has been covered with wallboard and a false ceiling installed.

In late 1994, the Fort Edward Development Corporation was awarded $450,000 in ISTEA and state funds to restore the depot's original appearance. Passengers who had been left out in the elements will now have access to a waiting room with historical displays. Travel connections will be available to the Glens Falls Transit System. The development agency has submitted an agreement to purchase the depot from its freight railroad owner. [CP Rail System. Train stop/npa and vacant.]

GENEVA

GENEVA RAILROAD STATION
Sherrill Street
1893

Geneva was a major junction and division point for the Lehigh Valley Railroad. Its large, Romanesque Revival station had walls of red brick resting on a high base of gray stone. Daylight entered upstairs offices through a variety of windows, dormers, and at least one skylight. Passengers waited inside under a vaulted ceiling and outside under a freestand-

Geneva station with an array of early 20th-century transportation modes: trolley, auto, horse-drawn cab, and steam train.

ing platform canopy. A restaurant occupied the west end of the depot. After train service ended in 1961, the building was largely abandoned for many years. Vandalism and ice took a heavy toll. In the mid-1980s, after Conrail had already let the contract for demolition, a local resident bought the depot and with the help of his wife and several craftspeople, jacked up and stabilized floors, restored crumbling exterior brick arches, and put on a new roof. Plans are to use the depot for a small business incubator. [Privately owned. Vacant.]

GREENE

GREENE RAILROAD STATION
4 Washington Street
1914

About 1990, a real estate firm in the village of Greene adapted a 1914 brick, Prairie Style depot to be its new office. The owners maintained the sense of a railroad station by restoring the original light fixtures, copper gutters, freight scale, ticket window, and station master's desk. They duplicated original signage and had wooden storm windows made to cover the ribbon style sash. When the Delaware, Lackawanna & Western built this depot, its frame station on Cherry Street, with deeply overhanging roof and fanciful brackets, was converted to a freight house. The owners of the brick depot have purchased the wooden station as well, although concerns over cost and structural soundness may inhibit preservation. Freight trains still ply the tracks. [Privately owned. Office.]

GREENPORT

GREENPORT RAILROAD STATION
Third and Wiggins streets
1892

The Long Island Rail Road was chartered in 1834 to provide a boat-rail connection between New York City and Boston. A direct, overland route through Connecticut was thought unfeasible for construction—too hilly with too many rivers to cross. In the 1850s, after another railroad proved this topography could in fact be conquered, the LIRR sought replacement business by promoting village settlements along its right-of-way, eastward through Long Island. By the 1920s, the LIRR (then part of the Pennsylvania Railroad system) was the biggest commuter conveyor in the United States.

A busy waterfront community with steamboat connections, Greenport was the eastern terminus of the main line. In 1892, brick passenger and freight depots were built to replace earlier wooden ones. A century later, the passenger station, including benches embossed with the letters LIRR, was partially restored by the village (see "Save the Depot!" page 60), which leases the property from the railroad. The community plans to convert the building (as yet missing its fancy iron roof cresting) to a maritime museum. A volunteer group operates a railroad and local history museum in the freight house. Although the roundhouse is gone, a 19th-century turntable (reconfigured in the early 20th century) still has its original air-powered traction motor, which may be returned to operation for a proposed steam excursion train. NR. [Long Island Rail Road. Train stop/npa and museum site.]

HARTSDALE

HARTSDALE RAILROAD STATION
East Hartsdale Avenue
Warren and Wetmore
1915

The station at Hartsdale was designed by one of the two firms that had just completed Grand Central Terminal, Warren and Wetmore. Here in suburban Westchester County, the architects achieved a rustic, half-timbered appearance by using a modern material for the infill, reinforced concrete. Inside, a fireplace accented the

Industrial design and the look of old England contrast in this trackside view of the Hartsdale station.

cozy, cottagelike interior. Another station on the New York Central's Harlem Division, Scarsdale (1904; extant), was quite similar in shape and pseudo-medieval style. Scarsdale was from the drawing board of Grand Central's initial design team, Reed and Stem. [Privately owned. Train stop.]

HUDSON

HUDSON RAILROAD STATION
69 South Front Street
1874

The Hudson station has had two rehabilitations: one by the New York Central's "bridges and buildings" crew in 1941 and one in the Amtrak era. During the 1941 modernization, the platform canopy was shorn from the walls, as was the "too Victorian" iron roof cresting. The depot was painted in the company's standard color scheme, light green (applied to the brick body) with dark green trim. Interior changes included elimination of the men's smoking room and the "decidedly old-fash-

ioned" waiting room settees. The 1992 project aimed for the 1874 look—very similar to the extant station at Peekskill, 73 miles south. Work was coordinated by the city, which is committed to recapturing the community's 19th-century style and flavor—when Hudson's woolen mills, brick manufacturing, and apple

Except for the platform canopy, the track side of the Hudson station, c. 1890, was a mirror image of the street side.

growing and whaling industries were at their peak. Besides expanding the depot's waiting room and refinishing the woodwork, restoration architects re-created the metal canopies and one of two chimneys, applied a red and gray slate roof with original rosette patterns, reproduced the fancy cresting, and reclaimed the red stained brick. A mixture of state and federal funds with support from Amtrak footed the bill. About two blocks south of the passenger station, on the same side of the tracks, stands a large masonry freight depot with a monitor roof. [Amtrak. Train stop.]

HYDE PARK

HYDE PARK RAILROAD STATION
River Road
Warren and Wetmore
1914

Commanding an expansive view of the Hudson River at Crum Elbow Creek, the Hyde Park station was in the hometown of future President Franklin Roosevelt. (The first depot burned about 1912.) During Roosevelt's years of national prominence, high profile visitors departing from this small depot included Winston Churchill and King George VI of England. In 1957, the New York Central closed the building. Scheduled for demolition in the mid-1970s, the depot was rescued when the Hudson Valley Railroad Society offered to restore and maintain it on a $1 per year lease from the town. The group repaired the hipped, red tile roof, which sits atop walls of red brick laid in Flemish bond, and re-created the ticket office (out of pine for economy's sake). A baggage room flanks the waiting room, which has exposed brickwork, wooden rafters, and a clay tile floor—all typical of the Mission style. A nearby pavilion, owned by the Lions Club, was originally the freight station, now minus its walls. Both passenger and freight trains fly past

the inactive station, which once had a siding (just to the south) for parking private rail cars belonging to the Roosevelt and Vanderbilt families. Paralleling the Hudson River and going past the station, a historic walking trail connects the Roosevelt and Vanderbilt mansions. The depot has appeared in three movies: *North by Northwest, Eleanor and Franklin,* and *Tootsie.* Hyde Park shares stylistic similarities with Poughkeepsie, an imposing four-story depot, still in passenger service at the next stop south. NR. [Town of Hyde Park. Museum and community meeting space.]

ITHACA

LEHIGH VALLEY RAILROAD STATION
West Buffalo Street and Taughannock
    Boulevard
A. B. Wood
1898

In 1966, five years after the last Lehigh Valley passenger train left Ithaca, patrons walked through the depot's pedimented porte-cochere and found a new restaurant that preserved much of the past. Designed originally by a local architect, the yellow and tan brick station has Colonial Revival detailing with a Romanesque feeling in the use of arches, rock-faced stone, and general mass. The platform area has been glassed in and leads to a string of railroad cars parked outside, used as supplementary dining rooms. Inside, a cocktail bar runs along the old ticket counter, backed by Corinthian columns. The former baggage room (now a service area) is reportedly part of an earlier depot. A large wooden freight house, located just northeast of the passenger station, was demolished for construction of Route 96 in the mid-1970s. Another Ithaca passenger station stands one block to the south—the Delaware, Lackawanna & Western (1919; now a bus depot). NR. [Privately owned. Restaurant.]

MAMARONECK

MAMARONECK RAILROAD STATION
Station Plaza off Mamaroneck Avenue
1888

In pre-Hollywood days, Mamaroneck was the year-round home of the motion picture industry and the summer home of many wealthy Manhattanites. The first Mamaroneck station was a wooden Gothic Revival depot, located on the site of today's parking lot. To eliminate the grade crossing on Mamaroneck Avenue, the New York, New Haven & Hartford elevated the tracks and built a new depot at track level. A High Victorian polychrome effect was achieved through the use of a stone base, brick walls, and unglazed terra-cotta friezes. Stone bands above the windows, now dingy, were once bright white. In 1926, two tracks were added for trains of the New York, Westchester & Boston, and the depot was moved down to street level. Stairways and a pedestrian tunnel (now closed) were built for passenger access. To adjust to its new location, the depot's arched porte-cochere was eliminated, and the roof line was extended to form the present wide eaves. With its strong architectural integrity—including an elegant fireplace and central tower—the depot merits restoration, currently under consideration. [Metropolitan Transportation Authority. Train stop.]

MARTISCO

MARTISCO RAILROAD STATION
East of State Route 174, between the towns of
  Marcellus and Camillus
1870

Just west of Syracuse, the Auburn & Syracuse (later the New York Central) built a red brick two-story depot at a stop it called "Marcellus." Renamed Martisco in 1905, the station (successor to a wooden depot) was once the busy workplace of an agent, telegraph operator, baggageman, and yardworker. The agent's

Marcellus (later Martisco) station, 1875.

family had bedrooms upstairs. Its other living quarters were in a one-story, matching annex on the west end, razed in 1949. Passenger service ended in 1958, and the depot's fanlight-topped, brick-arched windows were boarded over. Six years later, the NYC put Martisco on the demolition list. Fortunately, a group dedicated to railroad history purchased the depot and renewed everything from the roof to the electrical system. The brick, painted long ago by the railroad, is still light green. [Central New York Chapter, National Railway Historical Society. Railroad museum.]

MIDDLETOWN

ERIE RAILROAD STATION
James Street off North Street
George E. Archer
1897

Designed by a railroad staff architect, the Erie depot in Middletown was a robust Romanesque Revival building of yellow brick with a red tile roof. Its broad, arched entranceways were formed by multiple ribbons of brick. Inside, a massive, exposed fireplace chimney stretched to the top of the vaulted ceiling. Today, the depot is being incorporated into a new library,

Erie Railroad station in Middletown. On the street side were tracks used by interurbans and trolleys.

to be built on the site of the tracks, which were torn out in 1983. The preserved waiting area will become the periodical reading room; the baggage and express section, which was originally connected to the depot by a covered passageway, will become a workspace. One of the depot's exterior walls — wisely left exposed rather than covered over — will now be an interior wall of the library. [Middletown Enlarged City School District. Public library.]

NEW YORK, ONTARIO & WESTERN STATION
Low Avenue off Wickham Avenue
Bradford Lee Gilbert
1893

When the New York, Ontario & Western Railway ("O&W") outgrew its 1873 Wickham Avenue station, the wooden depot was hauled down the street and converted to a hotel, since demolished. (Another early station, the 1872 Main Street depot, still stands on its original site.) At Wickham Avenue, a substantial new depot was built from two products hauled on the line, Hudson River brick and Scranton sandstone. The station was enlarged in 1905 by adding the north tower. Because the O&W never had on-board food service, all trains stopped at Middletown. Hungry passengers en route from Manhattan to resorts in the Catskill Mountains mobbed the depot's famous Seeholzer's Restaurant. In 1919, after repairing damage from a serious restaurant fire, O&W added two stories to the depot's central portion and moved its general offices from New York City to Middletown. The 544-mile O&W was abandoned in 1957. Today, just a few miles of track, used by freight trains, extend past the depot. [Privately owned. Offices and dance studio.]

Middletown O&W station decorated for the Fire Parade, October 1899.

MUNNSVILLE

MUNNS DEPOT
Off I-48 between Syracuse and Little Falls,
    at the foot of Station Road
1870

In the 1880s, when the New York & Oswego Midland Rail Road became the New York, Ontario & Western, the Munnsville station name was shortened to Munns. The cupola and bay window were added in the 1890s, along with an expanded freight section, to handle larger shipments of hops. After the depot was abandoned in 1957, a farmer cut into the south wall—to make an opening for his tractor. In 1989, the current owner began a single-handed, labor-of-love restoration, which included not only substantial structural repairs, but also installing an old "O&W" train order signal, replacing one removed in 1935. Although no longer roofed in slate, the depot is painted with its 1890s scheme of olive for the board and batten siding, mint green trim, and red window sash. The interior, warmed by two potbellied stoves, has a fully equipped telegraph desk. Although the tracks are gone, the depot still commands a fine view of the Stockbridge Valley. [Privately owned. Depot museum.]

NEW ROCHELLE

QUAKER RIDGE STATION
Stratton Road off Weaver Street
Fellheimer and Long, Allen H. Stem,
    Associated Architects
1912

Just south of the New Rochelle–Scarsdale border, the Quaker Ridge station and tracks were built upon an artificial embankment. The New York, Westchester & Boston placed this "island" depot between its inbound and outbound track. Access to the masonry building and platform

Quaker Ridge station, 1912. The arched opening was an entrance to the pedestrian tunnel, which in turn gave access to the elevated depot.

was solely through ornate, street-level arches that led to an under-track, pedestrian passageway. From the center of this tunnel, passengers climbed a set of stairs to reach the interior of the station. Now part of a residence, the once open archways are secured with doors, which enable the artist-owner to still use the old tunnel for reaching his home and studio. The former train platform serves as a gallery to display his sculptures. Passenger service ended in 1938, and the tracks were scrapped two years later. Because of foliage, Mohegan Avenue is the best vantage point for viewing the depot. [Privately owned. Residence.]

NEW YORK CITY: THE BRONX

EAST 180TH STREET STATION
481 Morris Park Avenue
Fellheimer and Long, Allen H. Stem,
    Associated Architects
1912

The north central Bronx was sparsely populated when the progressive New York, Westchester & Boston Railway opened its all-electric, heavy

Street side of East 180th Street station, 1950.

duty suburban line in 1912. Built without any grade crossings and using all high-level platforms, the NYW&B was a paragon of efficiency. Instead of collecting tickets on the train, the railroad used a European method—color-coded tickets deposited in a "chopper" box (an early paper shredder) at the destination station. Mediterranean styling was used for all the original stations. NYW&B's three-story company headquarters and station facing Morris Park Avenue resembled an Italian villa with towers, an arcaded loggia, and a red tile roof. A long viaduct of exceptionally heavy steel was integrated into the station's construction. Coach yards and a repair shop were nearby. Although conventional train service ceased nearly 60 years ago, the station is now the gateway to an adjacent subway stop. NR. [City of New York. Transit authority offices.]

NEW YORK CITY: MANHATTAN

GRAND CENTRAL TERMINAL
East 42nd Street and Park Avenue
Reed and Stem
Warren and Wetmore
1913

By the late 1800s, the New York Central had already outgrown its 1871, Second Empire–style "Grand Central Depot" and great train shed.

The railroad tried lowering certain stretches of track through the city and massively remodeling the station, but those actions did not alleviate the core problems: inadequacy of the rail yard, traffic disruptions and dangers inherent to a surface level station, and smoke and cinders offensive to people living along the tracks. The answer to these difficulties was found in the new field of electric traction, which had been used on street railways for a dozen years, but scarcely applied to heavy, main line railroads. William J. Wilgus, chief civil engineer for the New York Central, conceived the brilliant innovations that were applied to the new facility—an all-electric, underground, double-level station (commuter trains on the lower level) with a terminal building above. This plan had added value—it would free up 30 blocks of Manhattan real estate for lucrative development and restore the crosstown streets from 45th to 55th Street. In 1903, the New York Central awarded the design contract for the terminal building to Reed and Stem of St. Paul, Minn. Charles A. Reed (Wilgus's brother-in-law) developed an elevated "circumferential plaza" that wrapped Park Avenue around the outside of the building, rather than having the terminal straddle the street as others proposed. Inside, innovative ramping moved pedestrians between two below-ground concourses (lined with stores) and street level. Whitney Warren, whose firm collaborated with

Grand Central Terminal, 1930s. Looming behind it, the tower of the New York Central Building.

(some say "muscled out") Reed and Stem, designed the Beaux Arts facade of Stony Creek granite and Bedford limestone.

Since opening day in 1913, when 150,000 people came to tour the new building, Grand Central Terminal has survived a legal challenge to its landmark status, the controversial construction of the 59-story Pan Am Building just north of the main concourse, and the trivialization of its magnificent interior. In 1989, the Metropolitan Transportation Authority embarked on a limited rehabilitation program, including restoration of the original waiting room, wainscoted in Botticino marble and illuminated by ornate, bronze chandeliers suspended from a 50-foot ceiling. The station's principal space, the main concourse, is paved with Tennessee marble and brightened by great arched windows. Above the central information booth with its famous, four-faced golden clock, the great vaulted ceiling is painted with 2,500 stars of the Mediterranean winter sky. Originally the zodiac figures were outlined in gold on cerulean blue, with the stars lit from behind. This surface was covered over in 1945 with panels painted to approximate the underlying artistry. A begrimed muddy green today, the ceiling awaits return to its heavenly colors. Full restoration of the concourse and historic exterior storefronts was unlikely, until a landmark day in 1993, when a restructured, 110-year lease was signed between the M.T.A. and the terminal's owner, Penn Central Corporation (surviving real estate vestige of the defunct railroad). Penn Central relinquished any remaining right to construct an office tower above the terminal (an old idea it was again considering) and gave full control over improvements to the M.T.A. The transit authority expects to complete restoration, funded partly by ISTEA, in the mid-1990s. NR. NHL. [Privately owned. Train stop and commercial space.]

NEW YORK CITY: QUEENS

JAMAICA STATION
Sultphin Boulevard and Archer Avenue
    in Jamaica
Kenneth M. Murchison
1913

Daily, thousands of passengers changed trains at Jamaica, the busy hub of the Long Island Rail Road commuter line (part of the Pennsylvania Railroad after 1900 and now a subsidiary of the Metropolitan Transit Authority). In 1908, a plan was devised to rearrange and elevate tracks both in the yards and through the community. This immense project not only eliminated numerous grade crossings, but also prepared Jamaica for an upcoming change. Soon most lines west (and many east) would be electrified, with direct access to Manhattan via tunnels under the East River. Built as part of this transition, the new four-story terminal (designed to support eight upper stories) had a steel skeleton sheathed in brick and terra-cotta with a pattern of triple windows repeated on each floor. Plans filed prior to construction describe a main waiting room decorated with Rookwood faience tile, but this area was altered in the 1950s. The upper floors remain headquarters for the Long Island Rail Road, making this one of the few midsize stations in the country with its spaces still used as built. [Long Island Rail Road. Train stop and railroad offices.]

NORTH TARRYTOWN

PHILIPSE MANOR RAILROAD STATION
Riverside Drive in the village of North
    Tarrytown
c. 1910

About 1900, plans were made for a new residential area on a bluff above the Hudson River to be called Philipse Manor. A promotional brochure promised 25 trains a day, but the service did not materialize. In order to get his lots sold, the frustrated developer finally built a depot and donated it to the New York Central. The station's rusticated stone, in shades of orange-brown, light gray, and pink, formed a solid base for the visual interplay of pseudo-half-timbering, multiple roof heights, and diamond-paned windows. The lower level of the station was used for freight; the ticket office and octagonal waiting room were on the second story, at street level. Red tile pavers formed the hearth of a rock-faced granite fireplace, set amidst simulated paneling and a beamed ceiling. Despite being boarded up today, the building remains a fine example of Tudor Revival depot architecture. Nearby, on the river side, a one-ton cast-iron eagle still spreads its 12-foot wings, just a few flaps from the depot. Once part of a 16-bird flock, it originally perched on Manhattan's old Grand Central (the 1900 remodeled station; razed 1910). NR. [Metropolitan Transportation Authority. Train stop/npa and vacant.]

PLATTSBURGH

PLATTSBURGH RAILROAD STATION
Bridge Street
Albert W. Fuller (Fuller and Wheeler)
1886

Built by the Delaware & Hudson, the Plattsburgh station was a union depot, serving the Chateaugay Railroad as well (the two lines crossed at South Junction). When the depot opened, a local newspaper called it "a good example of the modern composite style of architecture" (what today we might call a Victorian hodge-podge). The upper floor contained a 36-foot-square "Railroad Association Reading Room . . . supplied with papers and periodicals for the benefit of the employees of the company." Albany architect Albert Fuller trimmed the brick building with Longmeadow brownstone and chose black slate for the roof.

Trucks and wagons had access to the lower-level track side of the Plattsburgh station.

In 1980, when private investors bought the Plattsburgh station from the Delaware & Hudson, it was virtually abandoned, except for one small Amtrak waiting room at track level. Restored according to the Secretary of the Interior's Standards, the project qualified for rehabilitation tax credits. It consists of a four-story section topped by a square turret in each corner, and a three-story section with a poly-

sided turret bearing the D&H emblem. The depot slopes down an embankment, with the full basement opening onto a canopied boarding platform. Inside on the main level, the original, oak-trimmed waiting room has been converted to commercial office space. A small CP Rail System yard (stretching from the north and east sides of the depot) contains a brick, former machine shop. Plattsburgh's roundhouse was destroyed by fire in 1992. [Privately owned. Train stop, restaurant, and offices.]

PORT HENRY

PORT HENRY RAILROAD STATION
South Main Street
Fuller and Wheeler
1888

A contemporary newspaper article described the new Port Henry depot, sited near the banks of Lake Champlain, as being built in the "modern Gothic Style." Designed by Albany architects, the depot was constructed entirely of stone with a slate roof. A polygonal tower separated the entrances to the ladies' waiting room (north door) and the men's (south door). Broad,

Port Henry station, July 1925.

arched windows let in the light. The newspaper predicted that once the flower beds were planted around this Delaware & Hudson station, travelers might think they were instead riding on the mighty Pennsylvania Railroad—"where every depot building is a miniature villa or baronial castle embowered as a small garden of Eden." In the 1980s, a senior citizens group arranged to rent the building from the railroad—at no cost—in exchange for providing upkeep, utilities, and a waiting room. [CP Rail System—to be conveyed to the town of Moriah. Train stop, senior center, and nutrition center.]

PORT JERVIS

ERIE RAILROAD STATION

Jersey Avenue at Fowler Street
1892

Port Jervis's second Erie Railroad station burned the day after Christmas 1890, less than a year after its construction. The 1892 successor depot, also brick, incorporated a second floor for division offices, whose separate building had been destroyed in the fire. A prominent square tower with a pyramidal, slate-covered roof projected from the track side of the depot. The 10-foot roof overhang was supported by heavy timber trusses. The depot's design is attributed to "A. Mordecai," whose name is associated with a number of other Erie stations, including Waldwick, N.J.

Abandoned in 1974, the station suffered from a subsequent decade of failed private enterprise plans. Finally, the Minisink Valley Historical Society and the Depot Preservation Society used an entire arsenal of fund-raising techniques from bake sales to a 10,000-space "depot birthday book" (a $5 contribution bought a listing). They came within $2,000 of the purchase price; a local bank donated the balance. Further donations, grants, and bank loans amounting to $1 million helped restore the interior to its 1912 appearance—including

Erie Railroad station at Port Jervis, May 1908.

the waiting room's coffered ceiling—and provided landscaping and new mechanical systems. In 1993, two local businesspeople purchased the station. They now lease the adjacent express building to Conrail for a trainmaster's office. The depot's baggage room, ticket office, restaurant, and upstairs offices are being converted to commercial use. The owners would like to have commuter rail (and also local bus) passengers use the waiting room. A track realignment would be required, because train passengers currently board from a platform behind a nearby fast food restaurant. Were this laudable shift to occur, the Depot Preservation Society Museum, currently housed in the waiting room, could remain appropriately and informatively in place. NR. [Privately owned. Museum and commercial.]

ROCHESTER

INDUSTRY DEPOT

282 Rush–Scottsville Road (State Route 251),
   south of Rochester
1909

Built by the Erie Railroad, the depot at Industry (the stop was named for a nearby state school) is a well-restored example of a modest wooden

Industry. The separate freight station on the left (now gone) may have been the relocated and reconfigured predecessor of the passenger station . The wires above the tracks supplied power to local electric trains which the Erie operated from 1909 to the early 1930s, in addition to its through steam service.

passenger station. The first depot on this site was built about 1853 when the station was called Scottsville. Last used for passenger service in 1941, the current building (which once had a slate roof) was completely abandoned in 1957. A railway preservation group acquired it a dozen years later. In great disrepair, the depot had be jacked up, so that its rotten sills could be replaced. Among the station's original features are the wainscoting and intact agent's office; the semaphore and wood-burning stove were salvaged from other Erie stations. Numerous pieces of railroad equipment and artifacts are on display. [Rochester Chapter, National Railway Historical Society. Depot museum.]

LEHIGH VALLEY RAILROAD STATION
99 Court Street
F. D. Hyde
1905

The Lehigh Valley Railroad station was built on a bridge over the Genesee River and the Johnson–Seymour Millrace. The Erie Canal, which also used the bridge, passed to the east of the depot. Several other railroads had elaborate depots in the immediate vicinity; the Lehigh

Valley is the only one that remains. Designed by a New York City architect, the essentially two-story building is clad in mustard yellow brick with thin mortar joints tinted red. The roof was originally red tile. A sandstone watertable runs around the building with a battered wall of split red paving brick below. The trim is painted in original colors of dark green, light green, and red. A terra-cotta panel with the initials L.V.R.R. and the date 1905 ornaments a French Renaissance–style corner tower. Passenger service ended in the 1950s. After a stint as a bus depot and an era of crumbling vacancy, the station became a night club and is today a catering facility. A platform, now enclosed, joins the passenger station to the freight house, which has been converted to the kitchen. The station once had a stub-end train shed and a rail yard. NR District. [Privately owned. Commercial.]

ST. JAMES

ST. JAMES RAILROAD STATION
Lake and Railroad avenues
1873

Originally surrounded by farmland, the St. James station is a rare survivor of the numerous

Carpenter Gothic window details on the St. James station were fully intact when this c. 1940s picture was taken.

board and batten depots erected during the 1860s and 1870s by the Long Island Rail Road. Each gable peak was once topped by an ornate finial that matched a similar motif above the windows. Carpenter Gothic brackets supported the roof and the door and window cornices. Today on the inside, tongue and groove walls still surround a potbellied stove. Outside, an automatic ticket dispenser stands on the site of the demolished freight station. Local residents, concerned about the deteriorating condition and lack of maintenance, would like the passenger depot donated to Suffolk County. NR District. [Long Island Rail Road. Train stop.]

SALAMANCA

BUFFALO, ROCHESTER & PITTSBURGH STATION
170 Main Street, downtown
1912

Salamanca's Buffalo, Rochester & Pittsburgh (later the Baltimore & Ohio) stub-end passenger station is built of brick in a Romanesque Revival style. Double horseshoe, sandstone archways on both track and street sides lead to a vaulted waiting room trimmed with red oak. A 1912 brick freight house sits at right angles to the passenger depot. Much of the community of Salamanca is on the Seneca Indian Reservation. The town's name was changed from "Hemlock" to honor the Spanish Marquis of Salamanca, who was involved in financing the Erie Railroad prior to the Civil War. (The former Erie passenger station still stands across the street from the BR&P.) In 1980, the Salamanca Rail Museum Association acquired and restored the one-story depot for exhibits on local railroads and for displays of equipment. In a deliberate hunt for original depot furnishings, the group located the old Salamanca agent's desk. This downtown depot was at the end of a one-and-a-half-mile spur. The former East Salamanca passenger depot (a large and ornate structure) remains on the main line and is used by a freight railroad for office space and equipment storage. [Salamanca Industrial Development Agency. Railroad museum.]

SARANAC LAKE

UNION DEPOT
Depot Street
1903

When fresh air was the only known cure for tuberculosis, passengers arriving at Saranac Lake for treatment were often confronted with coffins being loaded for departure. Built by the Delaware & Hudson, the station combined a stone base, shingle siding, and a massive, pseudo-half-timbered, gable dormer. The New York Central, which jointly used the station, purchased this portion of the D&H line in 1946 and tore off the cupola, some small dormers, and the railing above the porte-cochere. The platform canopy had been removed about seven years earlier. Passenger service was dis-

Saranac Lake depot, 1919.

continued in 1965; freight, in 1972. (The tracks remain and are targeted for a tourist line.) The state leases the depot to a preservation group that recycles building materials. Both Saranac Lake and the next stop on the line—Lake Placid—are part of the 118-mile-long "Adirondack Railroad District" being proposed for National Register status. Stretching from Utica to Lake Placid, the area presents a prime example of wilderness railroading, in this case built to exploit logging and open the region to tourism. The Lake Placid depot (now a historical society museum) is a more subdued version of Saranac Lake. Despite a similar loss of cupola and platform canopy, Lake Placid retains its slate roof and freight house. [New York Department of Transportation. Warehouse.]

SOUTHAMPTON

SHINNECOCK HILLS DEPOT

Hill Station Road, Shinnecock Hills
1887

The Long Island Rail Road's president built Shinnecock Hills as a combination depot and real estate sales office. Its open tower provided a panoramic view of 3,200 acres of barren land, some of which would become summer home sites for people escaping the heat of Pittsburgh and New York City. LIRR trains continued stopping at the shingle-sided depot until the 1930s; its summer-only post office function lingered through the 1960s. Boarded up and about to be burned for a fire-fighting exercise, the depot was rescued to become a private residence. The tower, now glassed in, is a circular bedroom adjacent to an active LIRR track. [Privately owned. Residence.]

Shinnecock Hills depot, 1923.

SOUTHAMPTON RAILROAD STATION
Railroad Plaza, east of North Main Street
Bradford Lee Gilbert
1902

Turn-of-the-century Southampton was an area of ocean beaches and lush farmland that attracted New York City high society. Visitors to the resort hotels and owners of 30-room summer "cottages" arrived by train (often pulling private rail cars) to an embarrassingly primitive, 1870s wooden depot. The leaders of the community petitioned the Long Island Rail Road for a more substantial structure. They were rewarded with a Bradford Lee Gilbert creation—clad in an unusual combination of oyster shells accented by brick. The long platform canopy, upheld by pillars and scrolled brackets, had a small express building at each end until after World War II. Inside the depot today, a pedimented Palladian window, paneled wainscoting, curved-end benches, and a working fireplace provide a fine space for waiting. The wooden freight building still stands opposite the passenger depot. NR District. [Long Island Rail Road. Train stop.]

SPRINGVILLE

SPRINGVILLE RAILROAD STATION
227 West Main Street (at Depot Street)
1911

When the modern day owners of the Springville depot found the original blueprints and some used brick, they were able to rebuild the station's chimney, which had been damaged by two lightning strikes. The interior of the depot had fared better; most of the built-in benches for the men's and ladies' waiting rooms, the station agent's oak furniture, the ticket window, original plumbing fixtures, and wainscoting were intact. Built by the Buffalo, Rochester & Pittsburgh (later Baltimore &

Ohio), the depot replaced an 1883 wooden one that stood across the tracks. Its brick walls with cast stone trim, the polyganol central pavilion, and numerous dormers were all topped by tile roofs with flaring eaves. A stone panel carved with the station name and the date 1910 (the year construction began) was placed above the entranceway. Designed by the railroad's engineering department, the depot was built in response to increased traffic from a new commuter service. By 1955, passenger service had ended. In 1993, its owners received a state award for historic preservation. Still on an active freight line, the Springville depot is identical to one in Ridgway, Pa. (now a fast food restaurant). NR. [Privately owned. Gift store.]

SYRACUSE

NEW YORK CENTRAL STATION
Erie Boulevard
1936

The Art Deco–style New York Central station in Syracuse was built as part of a 1936 track elevation project. Its opening meant the closing of a wonderful 1898 Richardsonian Romanesque station at the corner of South Franklin and West Washington streets (razed 1939). Six 1,500-foot-long covered platforms extended to either side of the new brick-and-limestone-clad structure. Ornamented on the street side with bas reliefs of famous trains—the *DeWitt Clinton* and the *Twentieth Century Limited*—this Depression-era station served rail passengers for only a quarter-century. In 1962, after the New York Central built a new station in East Syracuse, the old one got a dose of plywood paneling and a dropped ceiling—poison as yet untreated by the antidote of restoration. Syracuse's other passenger station, the Delaware, Lackawanna & Western (c. 1942), is now offices. [Privately owned. Bus depot and commercial.]

TUXEDO PARK

TUXEDO PARK RAILROAD STATION
Orange Turnpike (State Route 17)
Bruce Price
c. 1886

In 1885, Peter Lorillard, heir to a snuff and tobacco empire, founded a king-size hunting and fishing club and game preserve on a 13,000-acre property his family had owned since the early 1800s. It was served by an Erie Railroad station in Tuxedo Park Village (now the hamlet of Tuxedo Park). The depot's architect was Bruce Price, whose daughter, etiquette expert Emily Post, moved into the upper crust community of houses constructed by the Tuxedo Park Association. Besides the depot, Price also designed Lorillard's house and gate house, the post office, and a number of workers' dwellings. In 1915, a freight train derailed into the station, which necessitated rebuilding the two-story tower. Many exterior details are intact today, including the triangular vents and the weather vane, although the original wooden siding and patterned shingles have been stuc-

coed. Stained glass transoms surmount the swinging doors that once divided the men's and ladies' waiting rooms. A matching freight station stood directly across the tracks. [Town of Tuxedo. Train stop/npa and police station.]

UTICA

UNION STATION
Main Street between Railroad and First streets
Stem and Fellheimer
1914

Once an important fording point on the Mohawk River, Utica has a long transportation history that covers Indian trails, early turnpikes, canals, and Union Station's current use as a multimodal center (train, bus, and taxi). The depot was designed in Beaux Arts style for the New York Central, and within a year, used also by the Delaware, Lackawanna & Western and the New York, Ontario & Western. Various railroad and commercial offices occupied the upper floors. Allen Stem (of Grand Central fame) and his new partner, Alfred Fellheimer (previous partner Charles

Tuxedo Park station when its balcony and roof ornamentation were intact.

Utica Union Station c. 1914.

Reed had died in 1911), chose cut stone and gray brick with limestone details for the station's three-story exterior. Above the streetside colonnade, they placed an ornate clock surrounded by eagles. The barrel-vaulted main hall, with a coffered ceiling in the seating area, contained both square and round columns of marble (most were veneered). Union Station's noted restaurant had an expansive marble counter, which is still in use, although the room is now partitioned. On the building's track side, only one full-size section remains of the original umbrella canopies. NR. [Oneida County. Transportation center, restaurant, and commercial.]

YONKERS

YONKERS RAILROAD STATION
Larkin Plaza, foot of Dock Street and Wells Avenue
Warren and Wetmore
1911

Located in lower Westchester County, the Yonkers station is the third on the same site. The spot was originally chosen for its proximity to steamboat wharves and commercial docks at the confluence of the Hudson and Nepperhan rivers. The center section of the current Beaux Arts building has a monumentally scaled, arched window. Smaller windows of similar shape light the depot's two wings, which are ornamented by diamond-patterned brickwork and elaborate, paired brackets. Inside, a Guastavino-tiled entrance rotunda leads to the former New York Central waiting room, decorated with brickwork and terra-cotta shields. [Privately owned. Train stop.]

Yonkers station, distinguished by fine brickwork and bold ornamentation.

Yorktown Heights station, 1953.

YORKTOWN HEIGHTS

YORKTOWN HEIGHTS RAILROAD STATION
Commerce Street
c. 1877–86

The Yorktown Heights station was placed within a triangular piece of ground that included a grassy plot used for grazing cattle awaiting shipment by rail. A standard design of the New York & Northern (later New York Central's Putnam Division), Yorktown Heights had sister stations at Millwood (extant) and Baldwin Place (razed). Board and batten construction, clapboarding, and a variety of applied horizontal and vertical boards achieved a primitive half-timbered effect. In the 1930s, a brick chimney on the north facade replaced one that had been positioned at the center of the roof. Floor-to-ceiling oak paneling, built-in benches, and a double Dutch door between the waiting and baggage rooms outfitted the interior. After passenger service ended in 1958, the building alternated between debilitating commercial uses and vacancy, until the town began restoration in 1976. Fortunately a local official had the foresight to store the original light fixtures and station sign, which were reinstalled at the depot. NR. [Town of Yorktown Heights. Vacant.]

Pennsylvania

Pennsylvania covers virtually the entire gamut of railroad station history. Examples include 18th-century inns, once used as train stops; early depots that looked just like houses; 19th-century suburban stations, still in active service; and big-city railway palaces. Home state of the giant Pennsylvania Railroad (one of the country's most powerful corporations) and the Reading Company (hauler of anthracite coal to fuel the Industrial Revolution), Pennsylvania had wealth and population density — the typical ingredients of great passenger stations. Of special note are the approximately 100 historic stations in and around Philadelphia, now owned by a regional train, trolley, subway, and bus operation (a surprisingly intact, early multimodal network). Most are still active or awaiting a possible return to service. Many have space to spare. Through a "lease-and-maintain" program begun in 1982, the Southeastern Pennsylvania Transportation Authority (SEPTA) offers liberal long-term rentals in exchange for the tenants' repair and maintenance of the depots.

ALIQUIPPA

ALIQUIPPA RAILROAD STATION
111 Station Street
1911

The Pittsburgh & Lake Erie (New York Central System) grew wealthy hauling coal and steel. For Aliquippa (the stop was then called Woodlawn), it built a new brick depot trimmed with stone and rose-colored terracotta. The Tudor Revival exterior encased an Arts and Crafts–style interior, divided by wooden partitions with leaded glass sidelights and transoms. Located northwest of Pittsburgh, the depot was restored in the 1970s by a company descended from Jones and Laughlin Steel (an early and very important customer of the P&LE). Workers rebuilt the roof with clay tiles from the demolished freight house, whose remains were found lying in a nearby field. Freight trains use the tracks. NR. [Privately owned. Offices.]

ALLENTOWN

ALLENTOWN TERMINAL RAILROAD DEPOT
Race and Hamilton streets
1890

The Allentown Terminal Railroad was only three miles long. Jointly owned by the Central Railroad of New Jersey and the Philadelphia & Reading (later the Reading Company), it brought these railroad services into the heart of the city. The red brick station, although one-story high, was imposing. A steeply pitched roof had ornate cresting and was pierced by a tall, four-sided clock tower. Passengers waited under a freestanding umbrella canopy. After the station closed in 1972, vandals and arsonists took over. In 1981, the depot, with its rounded-end waiting room, was converted to a restaurant. It now anchors a new commercial area — fitted into an old industrial district of silk mills, boilerworks, and worker housing. Across the street, a large hotel that opened within a year of the railroad station is still standing. A half-block west was the Lehigh Valley Railroad station, demolished in the name of urban renewal after LV passenger service ended in 1962. [Privately owned. Restaurant.]

BETHLEHEM

CENTRAL RAILROAD OF NEW JERSEY STATION
Lehigh and Main streets
c. 1874

In the 1870s, the Lehigh & Susquehanna (leased to the Central Railroad of New Jersey) built a story-and-a-half, essentially Second Empire–style depot next to the Lehigh Canal. (Today the water supports an occasional canoeist while many joggers tread the old towpath.) The depot's mansard-roof attic space, which likely contained agent's living quarters, was expanded by a very large Queen Anne–style dormer. Looking out the windows in 1912, the agent's family would have seen Teddy Roosevelt giving a speech from the back of a special train. In 1962, with guidance from Historic Bethlehem, Inc., the Jaycees decided to restore the brick depot, which had closed three years earlier. The property continued to be railroad owned, even when converted to a dining establishment in the Seventies. About

1982, a subsequent restaurateur saved the freight house from demolition when he purchased it and the passenger station from Conrail. The Jaycees still meet on the upper floor. The tracks remain. Across the Lehigh River, Bethlehem Union Station (once used by the Reading and the Lehigh Valley railroads) may be rehabilitated with ISTEA funds. NR District. [Privately owned. Restaurant.]

CHADDS FORD

COSSART STATION
State Route 100, 2.2 miles south of U.S. Route 1
1929

Cossart was named for Marie Cossart, who was an ancestor of Henry A. du Pont—head of the Wilmington & Northern (later the Reading Company). Replacing a frame station that burned, the current stone building was constructed by the gentleman farmer whose huge estate still exists across the road. The depot could easily be mistaken for a Pennsylvania farmhouse, except for the arched breezeway (once used for storing milk cans) that goes through the center of the building to the track.

CNJ station at Bethlehem, September 1951.

Cossart station c. 1940s.

Pocopson station. No element belies the building's current use as a veterinary clinic, as seen in this trackside view, 1993. Patients enter through a handsome porte-cochere on the eastern side of the depot.

The original floor plan included a waiting room with a fireplace and the agent's kitchen on the first floor; the balance of his family's living quarters were on the second floor. Today, short line freight trains pass a few feet from the depot, still in its rural setting. [Privately owned. Apartments.]

POCOPSON STATION
State Route 926 and Pocopson Road
1893

Three stops north of Cossart, at Pocopson, waiting still occurs in the old waiting room, but the meowing and barking customers are not buying any tickets. They are about to enter the former railroad agent's office for a veterinary examination. Exterior walls of the meticulously preserved depot combine pale green serpentine stone and fish-scale wooden shingles. Interior wainscoting and trim, including bull's-eye corners on the door and window frames, are intact, as well as the shelf used to hold a traveler's possessions while purchasing a ticket. The upper floor once provided living quarters for the agent, who watched the track from the depot's two-story rounded tower. On the grounds, a serpentine water well and an early outhouse com-

plete this very authentic site along the track. [Privately owned. Clinic and residence.]

CHESTER

PENNSYLVANIA RAILROAD STATION
6th Street between Avenue of the States and Welsh Street
William Holmes Cookman
1903

The river industries adjacent to Chester, just on the edge of Philadelphia, provided a large share of the ships, planes, and supplies needed during both World Wars. Chester's Pennsylvania Railroad station was used not only by workers, but also government inspectors and dignitaries, and troops embarking from nearby steamer docks. It was built during a massive project to both eliminate grade crossings and increase the number of tracks on the New York–Washington main line. The design was an early work of William Cookman, prolific PRR staff architect. Walls of Kittatinny brick laid in Flemish bond were trimmed with bluestone. Both the depot roof and the platform canopies were copper. Inside,

Early view of the PRR station in Chester. Except for the extensive overhang to provide shelter for passengers, the depot resembled a mansion.

woodwork and benches were cherry-stained mahogany; floors and wainscoting were marble. Today, the Classical Revival building retains its architectural integrity, but is in deplorable condition. A minority business organization is trying to obtain the building for restoration as a commercial and transportation center. Chester's Baltimore & Ohio station, designed by Frank Furness, was demolished about 1960 to facilitate construction of Interstate 95. [Amtrak owned. SEPTA train and bus stop.]

CORAOPOLIS

CORAOPOLIS RAILROAD STATION
Neville Avenue at Mill Street
Shepley, Rutan, and Coolidge
1895

The Pittsburgh & Lake Erie's main business was hauling coal for steel companies, but it also did a good job of moving people through the Allegheny Valley. Designed by H. H. Richardson's successors, the Coraopolis depot has a massive trackside tower with a triple

arch motif that thrusts into the platform overhang. The canopy extends to the adjacent brick freight house. Roman buff brick and red sandstone walls are sheltered by a slate roof. Each window's half-moon transom was once filled with stained glass. In 1916, a porte-cochere was added on the Mill Street side. The railroad altered the interior several times, including converting the ladies' waiting room and the men's smoking room into rest rooms. After P&LE passenger trains stopped running in the 1970s, the depot was used as an auto parts store. The current owners are slowly restoring the building—including a typical Richards-onian feature, its very large eyebrow dormer—in the hope of finding a compatible adaptive use. [Privately owned. Warehouse.]

ELKINS PARK

ELKINS PARK STATION
Spring and Park avenues
Cope and Stewardson
1899

William Elkins was a financial giant of the late 19th century. He owned utility companies nationwide, most of the trolley lines in Philadelphia, and extensive real estate. Outside the Philadelphia city limits, he and builder William T. B. Roberts developed the land around Elkins's country home, in an area previously known as Ogontz Park. Because the closest stations—Ogontz (1874; extant on Old York Road) and Ashbourne (now gone)—were not perfectly convenient, Elkins made an offer to the Philadelphia & Reading: He would build a handsome new station if the railroad would relocate its train stop to the center of his project. To design it, Elkins chose a local firm (especially famous nationwide for collegiate architecture), Cope and Stewardson. The station's gray schist and limestone trim were the principal materials of the great houses in surrounding suburbs. The roof was originally red tile (slate today). An octagonal stone tower dominated the track side. A porte-cochere extended from the broad roof overhang to the driveway; another was attached to the small waiting room on the outbound side of the tracks.

Today, the main semicircular waiting room—with its paneled wainscoting, great fireplace, and open trussed ceiling—is a private office. Commuters seek shelter in the former ladies' waiting room. The station, originally called just "Elkins," is part of the local transit authority's "lease and maintain" program. Businesses are given an incentive to renovate decrepit stations by trading rent for improvement costs. The next stop south, Melrose Park (gutted by fire; razed 1991) was a smaller version of Elkins Park. The next station north, Jenkintown (1931; extant as a train stop and restaurant), was designed by Horace Trumbauer, architect for the magnificent Lynnewood Hall—home to William Elkins's business partner, Peter Widener. NR. [Southeastern Pennsylvania Transportation Authority. Train stop and office.]

ERIE

UNION STATION
14th and Peach streets
Fellheimer and Wagner
1927

From the start, Erie's second Union Station (used by two of the city's four railroads) had trouble getting on its feet and staying there. Plans were made in 1915 to eliminate numerous grade crossings and replace an 1866 depot, but momentum was interrupted by World War I. The station opened 12 years later to a band concert and a big Saturday night dance. Among its amenities were a waiting room with terrazzo floors and marble wainscoting, a restaurant,

and a barber shop. The express section held a huge refrigerator and brine vault to accommodate the tons of fish shipped daily from Lake Erie. Two years later, the Depression hit. The rough-textured brick building, in various shades of beige and brown with terra-cotta trim, flourished only during World War II. Beginning in the 1950s, the New York Central (the major user) and the Pennsylvania Railroad either eliminated or severely curtailed passenger service. Amtrak later suspended operations altogether, until reinstating the *Lake Shore Limited* in 1975. Offices gradually emptied in the 1960s and 1970s, as freight sales and servicing shifted to other cities. By the Nineties, the station's owner (Conrail) was looking for demolition contractors. Fortunately, commercial development brought new life to the building. [Privately owned. Train stop, restaurant, and commercial.]

EXTON

MORSTEIN STATION
408 King Road, west of Ship Road
c. 1870s

In 1899, when prominent maritime lawyer, John F. Lewis, built a summer home called Morstein, the name of the nearby railroad station was changed to match. Both buildings are now on the property of an environmental consulting firm that restored the station in 1988. The core of the building is the two-story brick section, which is a prime example of the early "dwelling-type" depot—it looked just like a house. An 1899 wooden addition to the west provided a ticket office and a waiting room. Built by the West Chester & Philadelphia (later the Pennsylvania Railroad), Morstein housed the ticket agent's family and the post office as well. The tracks, which paralleled King Road south of the depot, are gone. NR. [Privately owned. Office.]

GETTYSBURG

WESTERN MARYLAND STATION
35 Carlisle Street
1858

In early July 1863, the day after the Battle of Gettysburg, trains arrived at the depot on Carlisle Street to evacuate the wounded. Four months later, Abraham Lincoln disembarked to deliver "a few appropriate remarks" at the now-famous dedication of a military cemetery. Built by the Hanover Junction, Hanover & Gettysburg (later the Western Maryland), the Italianate station had painted brick walls and a bell-tower cupola. Typical of many early stations, its two-story head house sat perpendicular to the tracks, with a one-story section and shed that stretched along the rails. The last passenger train departed in 1942; freight trains still use the tracks. Another station, built by the Gettysburg & Harrisburg (later the Reading Company) in 1884, stands on North Washington Street and is used by a tourist railroad. [CSX Transportation. Tourist information center.]

At the Gettysburg WM station, 1962, the arrival of an excursion train sponsored by the the Baltimore Chapter of the National Railway Historical Society.

GLEN MILLS

GLEN MILLS RAILROAD STATION
Glen Mills Road, east of Cheyney Road
c. 1881

Citing, lack of funds for bridge repair, the region's transit authority shut down service on its line through Glen Mills in 1986. Subsequently, the Thornbury Historical Society used a combination of citizens' donations and state funds to restore the depot, built by the Philadelphia, Wilmington & Baltimore (later the Pennsylvania Railroad). Fancy red and black brickwork accent the depot's one-and-a-half stories. A distinctly Gothic feel is conveyed by the pointed arches of the windows and the flared, steeply pitched dormers. The upper floor and part of the first floor (once the agent's living quarters) are rented as an apartment; former waiting and ticketing areas provide meeting and museum space. Should train service return, travelers will again stand on the covered porch of this station, still very much in its original country setting. The historical society also restored a dilapidated, three-sided shelter (1891) at the next station west, a flag stop called Locksley. NR District. Southeastern Pennsylvania Transpor-tation Authority. Mixed use.]

GREENSBURG

GREENSBURG RAILROAD STATION
Harrison Avenue and Ehalt Street
William Holmes Cookman
1911

Greensburg was an early stop on the Pennsylvania Railroad; its first depot was built in the 1850s. The grade west from Greensburg was very steep. Before pulling out of the station, trains sometimes backed up to get a running start. To overcome this problem, the track was elevated during 1909–10. William Cookman of the PRR staff designed a new

Tower atop the Greensburg station, 1970, with PRR emblems in the ovals that once held clocks.

Jacobean Revival–style depot, built of brick with stone trim and a slate roof. The wide, elaborate porte-cochere bore a 1910 date stone (the building opened the following year) within a scrolled cartouche. The station's tall, square tower—capped by a copper-domed roof and finials—once had four clock faces (for awhile replaced by PRR emblems). Decorated with stone scrollwork and finials, five gable dormers brought light into the story-and-a-half passenger section. An arched, brick gable and hooded dormers accented the baggage building. Two wide, concourselike tunnels provided passageway under the main line tracks.

After 1971, the station was essentially abandoned for 22 years. Then in 1993, following a decade of failed attempts by private developers, the nonprofit Westmoreland Trust and local leaders were able to acquire the station and make restoration plans. ISTEA funds played a key role. Once the ravages of neglect, weather, vandalism, and a 1980s fire are reversed, the building will be reopened for Amtrak passengers (who currently have access only to the tunnels). Contemplated additional uses include a restaurant, visitors center, retail shops, and historical society headquarters. NR [Westmoreland Trust. Train stop/npa and vacant.]

HARRISBURG

PENNSYLVANIA RAILROAD STATION
Aberdeen and Market streets (automobile access from 4th and Chestnut streets)
1887

In 1893, throngs of locals visited the Pennsylvania Railroad's Harrisburg station to witness the Liberty Bell passing through to the Chicago World's Columbian Exposition. By 1970, the station—just blocks from the capitol building—was a run-down bus and train depot that people hesitated to enter. After a six-year search for funding, the Harrisburg Redevelopment Authority implemented a 1980s plan to reconfigure the site and restore the building. To make space for a much needed pedestrian plaza, the authority repositioned the bus shelters, each of which was then covered with a platform canopy salvaged from an unused train track. Two landmark train sheds, one contemporary with the head house and the other c. 1896, were saved. Their structural system is based on a truss patented by Albert Fink in 1854. Amtrak had begun dismantling the sheds, until halted by the state historic preservation officer in 1976. The long-covered skylights have been reglazed, and the roofs are now painted "Tuscan red," the historic color of Pennsylvania Railroad rolling stock. The brick walls of the three-story, gambrel-roofed head house (remodeled after a serious 1904 fire) sit on a rock-faced sandstone base. Ornate fireplaces (with PRR emblems in the cast iron fire backs) anchor both ends of the main lobby, which is paneled in oak. The upper stories are leased to a developer, who took advantage of rehabilitation tax credits in the conversion to commercial office space. Many awards have been bestowed on this project, which contributed greatly to the revitalization of downtown Harrisburg. NR. NHL. [Amtrak. Transportation center and offices.]

HUNTINGDON

UNION DEPOT
4th and Allegheny streets
1872

The Juniata River follows an unusual east-west course through the mountains of central Pennsylvania. Its valley was a natural path for an early turnpike, a canal, and later the railroads. Huntingdon Union Depot, built by the Pennsylvania Railroad, also served the Huntingdon & Broad Top Mountain. Long and shallow (140 by 25 feet), the brick building has twin Italianate windows in each of its 13 bays. Vacant for about 30 years, the passenger station began coming back to life in 1993, when the current owners started rehabilitation. They purchased it from Amtrak (which stops at a boxy shelter next door) for yet-to-be-determined commercial purposes. The extant eastbound

shelter, on the other side of the tracks, is available from Conrail to anyone willing to move it. A hundred yards west of Union Depot stands Hunt Tower, a two-story, brick and frame PRR signal tower from the 1890s. Rendered surplus by a 1985 changeover to computerized traffic controls, Hunt Tower was about to be razed by Conrail when local leaders rescued it. Now part of a downtown revitalization project, the tower was acquired and restored by Huntingdon's Main Street Program for mixed use as a dispatcher's office for paratransit services accommodating the disabled and the elderly, a visitors center, and a transportation museum. NR District. [Privately owned. Vacant.]

JIM THORPE

CENTRAL RAILROAD OF NEW JERSEY STATION
Susquehanna Street and Broadway
1888

Jim Thorpe was originally known as Mauch Chunk (the name was changed in the 1950s to honor an Olympic athlete). From 1891 until after World War I, the Central Railroad of New Jersey popularized a concept made possible by rail

CNJ station at Jim Thorpe, September 1951.

A c. 1940s bus makes a stop at the Johnstown PRR station in 1970.

travel—the "day trip." One destination was this little town in the Poconos, advertised as the "Switzerland of Pennsylvania." The depot's three-story cylindrical tower housed the ladies' waiting room on its first floor; a two-story vaulted space in the main section was for men. Built of sculpted red brick, accented by a series of Romanesque arches, the station had a red tile roof. In the 1970s, the depot was refurbished as part of a public works project; in the process, some partitions were shifted or removed. Jim Thorpe's Lehigh Valley Railroad station was burned in the 1960s for a fire-fighting exercise and replaced by a supermarket. NR. [Carbon County. Tourist information center, bank, freight railroad office, and tourist train stop.]

JOHNSTOWN

PENNSYLVANIA RAILROAD STATION
47 Walnut Street
Kenneth M. Murchison
1916

Two blocks west of the Johnstown Flood Museum stands a former Pennsylvania Railroad station. Its architect, Kenneth Murchison (responsible for the Baltimore PRR station five years earlier), incorporated multistory sandstone columns and a 45-foot-high Guastavino-tiled vault into this comparitively small, Roman Revival design. PENNSYLVANIA is spelled out

in bronze above both the east portico (original entrance for trolley riders) and south portal (vehicular courtyard). Interior finishes of the red brick station include marble, terra-cotta, and terrazzo. The impressive canopies for the elevated train platforms are gone.

In the 1980s, a supply company purchased the building. (It continues to use the baggage and express areas for storage.) The following decade, to free the main waiting room for some future adaptive use, Amtrak relocated its ticket office to one of two underground concourses linking the depot to the tracks. This concourse also houses a permanent exhibit on regional history, installed by the Johnstown Area Heritage Association, a professional organization spearheading the depot's ongoing restoration. The former PRR freight house, now used commercially, is one mile east of the passenger station. NR. [Privately owned. Train stop, warehouse, and partly vacant.]

LEBANON

CORNWALL & LEBANON STATION
161 North 8th Street
George Watson Hewitt
1885, 1912

The Cornwall & Lebanon was an ore-carrying short line railroad, 22 miles long. Its unexpectedly grand passenger station at Lebanon

Early view of the Lebanon C&L station and its train shed.

was paid for by iron-ore millionaire Robert Coleman. Philadelphia architect George Hewitt combined brownstone, brick, and terracotta into a Victorian feast of Chateauesque, Flemish, and Romanesque elements. In 1912, the south wing was added for express offices and the interior was remodeled. Oak wainscoting, the paneled ceiling, and two operational fireplaces date from that time. Passenger service on the line (acquired by the Pennsylvania Railroad) ended in the 1930s. The station served as a bus depot during World War II. Demolition nearly occurred in the 1970s, after a dress factory occupant closed down. (The station's iron train shed was already long gone.) A local

man purchased the depot for his insurance business. By restoring the building to standards set by the secretary of the interior, he was able to obtain rehabilitation tax credits. NR. [Privately owned. Commercial.]

PHILADELPHIA & READING STATION

250 North 8th Street
Joseph M. Wilson (Wilson Brothers and
    Company)
1901

Catty-corner from the Cornwall & Lebanon station, the Philadelphia & Reading built a new depot designed by Joseph M. Wilson, whose

The crossing gate is down at the Lebanon P&R station.

architectural and engineering firm worked on Philadelphia's Reading Terminal. An unbroken sweep of slate roofing unified the depot's two sections. The smaller east end once housed the baggage room and offices of the telegrapher and yardmaster. Equal-sized men's and ladies' waiting rooms filled the west end. On the exterior, each section had belcast, hipped gable dormers. Rising about 75 feet above the story-and-a-half station was an octagonal tower. The eight sides each held a Gothic window, trimmed by horizontal striping of brick and cut stone. Passenger service ended in 1963. Converted to a bank in the late Seventies, the station retains not only its architectural features, but also the landscaped grounds and the rumble of freight trains passing by. An open-air waiting space that once stood between the depot's two sections is now the drive-through teller area, paved with cobblestones found during modern driveway excavations. The Farmers Trust Company (now Farmers Trust Bank) put on a new slate roof and chemically cleaned the masonry to bring out its golden glow. NR. [Privately owned. Bank.]

MORTON

MORTON RAILROAD STATION
Yale Avenue, just west of State Route 420 and
    Morton Avenue
Wilson Brothers and Company (attributed to
    William Lightfoot Price)
1880

Although its second-story windows are boarded up, Morton is a well-preserved, Victorian Gothic depot. Located on a Philadelphia commuter line, it was built by the Philadelphia, Wilmington, & Baltimore (soon part of the Pennsylvania Railroad). The depot's two stories of dark red brick were originally pointed with black mortar. Large gable dormers, which pierce the steeply pitched roof, are decorated with bargeboards patterned after medieval roof trusses. Across the tracks, the outbound shelter (c. 1909) has fancy millwork and jigsawed griffins typical of other

PRR depots in the area. Completing this suburban station complex is a rather substantial, board and batten freight house. [Southeastern Pennsylvania Transportation Authority. Train stop.]

NORTH EAST

NORTH EAST RAILROAD STATION
Wall and Robinson streets
1899

Still sited adjacent to active tracks, the North East station is an example of a once fairly common design on the Lake Shore & Michigan Southern (New York Central System). Like many masonry depots on the line, it replaced a 30-year-old wooden station. At North East, when the new station was built, the 1869 frame building was moved 400 feet west and turned 180 degrees to become the freight and express station. Threatened with demolition less than 70 years later, the passenger depot was rescued by a preservation-minded group, who managed to save the 1869 depot as well. By excavating a basement under the brick and stone passenger station, the members created usable office and library space for their new museum without altering the depot's external appearance. The depot retains its trademark Palladian dormer, although the original slate roofing is gone. Similar depots exist in Ohio at Conneaut, Delta, and Stryker and at Sturgis, Mich. [Lake Shore Chapter, National Railway Historical Society. Museum.]

PHILADELPHIA

GRAVERS STATION
East Gravers Lane and Anderson Street
Frank Furness
c. 1883

Frank Furness designed about 125 projects for the Philadelphia & Reading (later the Reading Company) between 1879 and 1887. Gravers, also known as Gravers Lane, is one of the few

Early photo of the station on Gravers Lane in Philadelphia, when this line had yet to be double tracked. (For photo of Mt. Airy station, *see* page 14.)

that remain. Its quirky array of materials, textures, patterns, and levels accumulate into a painfully tantalizing vision of the architect's lost creations. The track side is dominated by a three-story, semiellipsoidal tower that carries both gable and shed dormers. In the 1960s, a storm destroyed the station's extremely deep platform canopy, which had extended from the waiting room down a wide flight of stairs. Years later, after winning a trail-blazing struggle with the local transit authority, the Chestnut Hill Historical Society restored the brick and timber station, including the missing overhang. The group plans to refurbish the small waiting room for an adaptive use. Gravers is lovingly maintained by its tenant, the son of the last ticket agent; his family still occupies the building's original two-story apartment. Two stops south is another Furness depot, Mt. Airy (NR), whose long porch roof was shortened many years ago when the tracks were raised several feet and the stairs eliminated. This northwestern section of Philadelphia was also served by Pennsylvania Railroad commuter trains. These former Reading and PRR branch lines (both

now operated by SEPTA) still terminate at Chestnut Hill, which has several historic depots within walking distance of Gravers. NR. [Southeastern Pennsylvania Transportation Authority. Train stop/npa and residence.]

NORTH PHILADELPHIA STATION
2900 North Broad Street at Glenwood Avenue
Theophilus P. Chandler
1901

Germantown Junction, the original name of the North Philadelphia station, was at the intersection of a Pennsylvania Railroad local line to Chestnut Hill and its main line tracks to New York City. It was designed by Philadelphia socialite and architect Theophilus Chandler, who trained in Paris and designed more than 15 stations for both the Reading and Pennsylvania railroads. He chose the French Chateauesque style—common for the homes of millionaires, but used infrequently for railroad architecture. An intra-regional connecting facility (in contrast to a center city terminal), the large brick two-story station replaced an outmoded depot from the 1870s.

Major changes to the station between 1912 and 1915 included excavating a lower level, relocating the ticket office and waiting room to the second floor, and installing a restaurant on the upper floor. When the PRR's 30th Street Station was completed in the 1930s, failure to build a looping track at that site meant North Philadelphia continued for decades as the railroad's principal Philadelphia stop for trains traveling between New York and the Midwest. By the time Amtrak acquired the station in 1976, the building had been fire damaged and had big holes in the roof. Filthy, deteriorated, and graffiti-covered, the depot closed completely in 1990, although trains continued to stop. Amtrak built a modern station on the north side of the tracks. The railroad constructed new platforms, restored the old canopies, and regraded the parking lot (thus putting the main floor of the historic depot back to its original level). A supermarket will be built on part of the site; Amtrak still seeks a retail tenant for the 1901 building. An adjacent former streetcar depot, reached by a covered walkway, is scheduled to become a police mini-station. Three blocks south on North Broad Street stands a 1929 neo-Grec Reading Company station, harshly converted to hotel and now abandoned. The Reading and PRR

stations were connected until the 1960s by a passenger tunnel (part of the Broad Street Subway). [Amtrak. Train stop/npa — for lease.]

OVERBROOK STATION
City Avenue and 63rd Street
1858

In the 1820s, threatened by New York competition from the Erie Canal, the Pennsylvania legislature commissioned a transportation network that was known as the State Road (or Main Line) of Public Works. The chain, which extended from Philadelphia to Pittsburgh, consisted of canals, railroads, inclined planes (assisted by stationary steam engines), and tunnels. The initial railroad portion, named for its termini, was called the Philadelphia & Columbia. In 1857, the state sold the line to the Pennsylvania Railroad.

Still in operation today, Overbrook is one of the oldest passenger stations in continuous use along the PRR "Main Line" (a phrase that became synonymous with the upper crust Philadelphia suburbs the railroad served). The core of the wooden depot (which for much of its life also housed the local post office) looks very much as it did, mid-19th century. The two-story section was the agent's residence, perpendicu-

Early view of the PRR North Philadelphia station.

Overbrook station before the c.1880s addition of platform canopies.

lar to the tracks. Parallel to the rails was a one-story section with an open porch, providing passengers with homelike protection from the elements. Overbrook's long platform canopy was likely added when the line was expanded to four tracks in the 1880s. Reached by an 1884 pedestrian tunnel, the outbound shelter has flared eaves supported by ornate brackets. The adjacent, brick signal tower dates from c. 1915, when the line was electrified. In 1993, after many years as a boarded-up embarrassment, the Overbrook station received funds from several sources, including ISTEA, to begin a three-year, $3 million restoration and site improvement project. Ideally, adaptive uses will be combined with the original function—a waiting room and ticket office. A small stream runs under the tracks—hence the name "Overbrook." NR District. [Amtrak owned. SEPTA train stop/npa]

QUEEN LANE STATION
Wissahickon Avenue and Queen Lane
W. Bleddyn Powell
1885

In 1882, the Pennsylvania Railroad formed a subsidiary, the Philadelphia, Germantown & Chestnut Hill, to push a second commuter line into relatively undeveloped sections of north and northwestern Philadelphia. (The Philadelphia & Reading had already arrived.) Ten passenger depots, all designed by W. Bleddyn Powell, were built expressly for PRR's Chestnut Hill branch. Today, seven remain. Their original appearance ranged from similar to identical Victorian brick stations. Queen Lane began life as a one-story twin to Westmoreland (razed in the 1950s). In 1890, a second story was added to accommodate the agent's family. A century later, the station is remarkably intact. Covered wooden stairs still lead down to the canopied platform (originally wooden, then brick, and now macadam). The main depot was built on the outbound side of the tracks, which are still spanned by an iron

footbridge. Protecting passengers with its roof and wooden sides, the overpass leads to a gingerbread-embellished inbound shelter. A group of area residents, in coordination with the station's owners, promotes the ongoing restoration. [Southeastern Pennsylvania Transportation Authority. Train stop.]

READING TERMINAL
Market and 12th streets
Francis Harry Kimball
Wilson Brothers and Company
1893

Situated on a corner, the Reading Terminal's eight-story, Italian Renaissance head house had right-angle facades of pink brick, ornamented with richly detailed cream-colored terra-cotta. A pink granite basement and first story anchored the building, which was crowned by a copper cornice and roof balustrade (replaced now with a plain brick parapet). The station eventually consolidated passenger services from three separate depots of the Philadelphia & Reading (soon the Reading Company), whose main offices occupied the upper floors. The half-basement level contained retail enterprises; the first story housed ticketing and baggage services. A viaduct carried the Reading's tracks into Philadelphia. From the second-floor waiting room, passengers walked a 50-foot-wide, skylit concourse to reach the cavernous stub-end train shed—a single clear span of 256 feet, which was a record-breaking achievement at the time and remains a landmark today. A New Yorker, Francis H. Kimball, collaborated in his design for the station with the Wilson Brothers and Company, an architectural and engineering firm in Philadelphia, which contributed its talents to many significant railroad buildings—in particular the superb Broad Street Station (1881 portion) a few blocks away (razed in 1952).

Passenger service ended in 1984. A decade later, when the Reading Terminal became part of Philadelphia's new convention

Reading Terminal.

Head house with its original cornice
and balustrade.

Train shed, early 1900s. The lower level contained a very large, bustling market (still in operation today). Trains entered on the upper level.
(For interior view of shed, *see* photo on page 32.)

center, the train shed was transformed into a vast ceremonial hall, with an upper level inserted at one end. Its roof trusses remain exposed; the skylights, 95 feet above floor level, were partially restored (the ceiling was originally 60 percent glass). The head house, which the city did not acquire from the Reading Company until 1993, is expected to become retail stores and offices—and once again the entrance to the shed area.

In the 1890s, when the Philadelphia & Reading decided on the new terminal's location, it faced a dilemma. Two extremely large and very busy retail market houses stood at the intersection of 12th and Market streets. Because acquisition and demolition required satisfying the merchants and their loyal customers, the P&R agreed to build a street-level market within the iron train shed. The new market was located directly beneath the tracks, which were 25 feet above street grade; the rumble of trains overhead mingled with the shouts of purveyors, whose delicacies ranged from oysters to Amish pies. In the early 1990s, during the train shed's incorporation into the convention center, Philadelphians feared disturbance—or worse, gentrification—of the market. After massive lobbying efforts, special leasing policies were developed to keep the market's character intact. NR. NHL. [City of Philadelphia. Convention Center.]

SUBURBAN STATION
16th Street and John F. Kennedy Boulevard
Graham, Anderson, Probst and White
1930

By the 1920s, the Pennsylvania Railroad realized the critical need for redesigning its path through Philadelphia. About half of the average 500 trains per day were "through" trains. Tracks into the central station on Broad Street (built in 1881, enlarged in 1893) came to a dead end, which meant trains had to reverse direction out of the station and follow a circuitous route back to the main line before continuing their journeys. In addition, the three-quarter-mile-long "Chinese Wall"—an elevated track bed once hailed as

16th Street entrance to Suburban Station, 1930s.

progress—was a nightmarish bottleneck. Besides causing congestion on the rails, the one-block-wide wall consumed 18 acres of valuable real estate. To make matters worse, its low street underpasses obstructed traffic and frustrated development of additional land further north.

To remedy these problems, the PRR undertook a project (begun in the 1920s, but not completed until the 1960s) known as the Philadelphia Improvements. Among its features were a new station west of the Schuylkill River at 30th Street; a Herculean track, bridge, tunnel, and electrification project; and the demolition of Broad Street Station and its extensive approach. Because the location at 30th Street—fine for through trains—would be unsatisfactory for commuters into center city, one of the first stages of the project was a new "Broad Street Suburban Station," as it was originally called. Located one block west of the main Broad Street Station (which was not razed until 1952), the Suburban Station complex was a different concept: a 20-story-high, conventional office building with 12 acres of below-ground concourse and track area. At Suburban Station, the railroad took on a new role—developer of commercial real estate. Designed by a famous Chicago firm, the office tower's Art Deco styling was carried, in a limited fashion, to the concourse below, where acres of retail shops served both office workers and commuters. NR. [Multiple owners. Train stop, office tower, and retail.]

30TH STREET STATION
30th and Market streets
Alfred Shaw (Graham, Anderson, Probst
    and White)
1933

Philadelphia was the home city of the mighty Pennsylvania, America's biggest railroad. At the company's new regional headquarters along the Schuylkill River, Alfred Shaw sought to proclaim this greatness through a neoclassical design interpreted in Alabama limestone.

30th Street Station.

Architect's rendering of 30th Street facade. The Schuylkill River is in the foreground.

Seventy-one-foot-high Corinthian columns formed impressive porticoes on both the east and west facades. Linchpin of the Philadelphia Improvements project, Pennsylvania Station, or "30th Street" as it came to be called, was multilevel. On the north side, a skylit upper level served commuter trains—with passengers sheltered by massive, curved umbrella sheds. At street level, a palatial, combination concourse and waiting room extended transversely above the underground, long-distance tracks. Visitors to the new station (fully opened in 1933) found a familiar, allegorical plaque on the wall—*Spirit of Transportation*, transplanted from Broad Street Station. Sculpted in 1895 by Karl Bitter, who had named it *Progress of Transportation*, the figures included a boy carrying a primitive concept of an airplane; four decades later an updated title was essential. Placed in an auxiliary waiting room (today a benchless passageway), this piece of public art was joined in 1952 by a 37-foot-high memorial sculpture, just inside the east entrance. Beneath Walker Hancock's bronze angel carrying a fallen soldier, artisans embossed—letter by letter—the names of 1,307 PRR employees killed in World War II.

In 1988, Amtrak undertook a major restoration of 30th Street—one of the busiest stations

World War II memorial framed by huge columns.

in the country. Among the projects were cleaning of the main concourse's gilded columns of marble and Roman travertine; repair of the red, cream, and gold coffered ceiling (98 feet above the Tennessee marble floor); restoration of 324 bronze and glass light fixtures (including ten 18-foot-long cylindrical chandeliers); reopening the former ticket lobby; and replacement of original storefront designs. In 1991, a few months after the project was completed, a nearly disastrous fire broke out that caused extensive smoke and water damage—requiring many of the craftspeople to return for an unexpected encore. NR. [Amtrak. Train stop, railroad offices, and commercial space.]

PHOENIXVILLE

PHILADELPHIA & READING STATION
4 Bridge Street (State Route 29)
c. 1858–1865

In the early 1800s, the village of Phoenixville acquired its name from the famous Phoenix Iron Works (later the Phoenix Steel Corporation). Mid-century, the Philadelphia & Reading (later the Reading Company) built a depot with tracks on two sides. Out front was the main line; the Pickering Valley branch line passed behind the depot and through the yards of the steel mill. The Reading hauled massive amounts of anthracite coal to the Phoenix blast furnaces, which stood below the hilltop passenger station. Built of pinkish stone, the depot had Italianate

Phoenixville P&R station. This end view shows the original height of the twin Italianate towers.

towers (originally twice the present height and capped with graceful spires) and two large rose windows. Elaborately curved iron brackets supported the platform canopy that sheltered all four sides of the depot. The canopy was dotted by iron "snow cleats" to keep one-piece snow slides from falling onto waiting passengers. The depot's large baggage room was reportedly the scene of a ball celebrating the end of the Civil War. Train service ceased in 1981. Another Phoenixville passenger station, built for the Pennsylvania Railroad (c. 1883), burned in 1985. [Privately owned. Catering facility.]

PITTSBURGH

PENNSYLVANIA STATION
Grant Street and Liberty Avenue
D. H. Burnham and Company
1903

Pennsylvania Station (once known as Union Station) was built on a constricted site that had been the location of three previous depots, including a combination station-hotel that railroad workers set afire during 1877 labor riots. The western terminus within its namesake state, Pennsylvania Station served several lines that were part of the PRR system. At the center of Daniel Burnham's three-part, front-to-back design was a high-rise railroad office building, which nearly obscured its rear appendage, a huge, long-span shed (demolished in 1947). Extending out from the main facade and shaped like a circle within a square, an outdoor rotunda (referred to even on original plans as "the cabstand") created a wholly unexpected entranceway to the station. Constructed of brown terracotta on a steel truss framework, the rotunda was ornamented with late 18th-century French detail: cartouches, guilloche bands, and urns. Beneath the fabulous domed ceiling, elaborately decorated pendentives bore the names of the four major cities served by the PRR: Philadelphia, Pittsburgh, New York, and Chicago.

Pittsburgh PRR station.

A curving driveway swept up to the cabstand. In the foreground of this c.1905 photo are storage tracks for railroad cars and the "Panhandle" tracks to St. Louis.

View from inside the ornate cabstand with its domed ceiling.

For many years, it was a common nighttime practice to outline—in light bulbs—the entire head house, the rotunda's great arches, and a two-story-high PRR emblem. In the 1970s, it was a frequent daytime practice to speculate about the fate of the soot-stained, vacant station. (Amtrak was already in a new facility behind the building.) Scaffolding was erected to catch broken pieces of terra-cotta cornice before they fell on passers-by. Fortunately, in the mid-1980s, when substantial rehabilitation tax credits were still available, Pennsylvania Station was converted to a 242-unit apartment complex, with its rotunda and waiting room rescued in the process. Another ornate station on Liberty Avenue did not survive—the Wabash Terminal (1904, designed by Theodore C. Link), which stood on the triangle at Ferry Street; it was razed in 1955. NR. [Privately owned. Apartment building.]

PITTSBURGH & LAKE ERIE STATION
Smithfield Street Bridge and West Carson Street
William George Burns
1901

The approximately 50-acre Pittsburgh & Lake Erie complex is situated at the foot of Mt. Washington, directly across the Monongahela River from Pittsburgh's central business district. When the distinguished Pittsburgh History & Landmarks Foundation signed a lease for the property in 1976, two structures appended to the passenger station were already gone: a remarkable bridge-spanning trolley shelter (razed in 1967) and the immense long-span train shed (razed in 1935). Five remaining buildings, from the years 1897 to 1917, including the centerpiece passenger station, were gradually adapted to a variety of commercial uses. The terminal building, clad in brown-

Pittsburgh P&LE station.

The cornice includes a bas-relief of P&LE locomotive No.135 set between two date stones (1879, the year the railroad opened to traffic, and 1900, the year before the station was actually completed).

Perfect symmetry in the newly opened waiting room c.1901.

stone, golden brown brick, and terra-cotta, was designed originally by a local architect who had just relocated from Toronto. Today on the inside, 72,000 square feet of new office space surround the breathtaking former waiting room and vestibule. Gilt, mosaic, and mostly faux marble layer nearly every inch of the two-story-high space, which is extended further by a great tunnel vault, filled with recessed panels of stained glass. This area, plus the loading dock, baggage room, and ticket office were converted to a restaurant in 1978.

By the mid-1980s, the entire complex of former railroad buildings had become known as Station Square. With retail shops, offices, and restaurants installed in the former Shovel Transfer Warehouse, the area went from being a run-down, out-of-the-way neighborhood to attracting more than three million people a year. Serving as a gateway to the station is the adjacent Smithfield Street Bridge, Gustav Lindenthal's 1883 lenticular truss span (NR); Frank Furness's 1888 Baltimore & Ohio depot once stood at the other end. Bordering Station

Square on the west is the Duquesne Heights Incline and to the east, the Monongahela Incline (both NR). These cable railways, which still provide rapid transit straight up Mt. Washington, have noteworthy lower- and upper-level stations. NR. [Privately owned. Mixed use.]

POTTSTOWN

READING COMPANY STATION
High Street between Hanover and York streets
1929

Pottstown, a sophisticated example of a mid-size station, opened in November 1929, just after the Black Friday stock market crash and in the twilight of railroading's golden era. Today, bank tellers cash checks from behind four old ticket windows in the classically formal waiting room. An ornate clock decorates the west wall. At the room's opposite end, the words Union News Company are still painted above a window that now opens into an office. On the streetside exterior, a large copper canopy is suspended by chains from the mouths of terra-cotta lions. The trackside facade is virtually identical, with the same style pedimented doorway, except that READING COMPANY is incised in a terra-cotta panel above three, two-story-high windows. A local bank rescued the seriously deteriorated building in 1988, after nearly 12 years of vacancy.

Probably designed by the railroad's chief engineer, Clark Dillenbeck, the depot was begun in 1928, as indicated by the date stone between the main building and the baggage and office wing. The gray stone walls are protected by a green glazed terra-cotta roof. Framing of the extensive steel platform canopy remains—entirely uncovered, like an umbrella without the cloth. Across the tracks, the former freight station is now adapted for offices. The historic Shuler House Hotel once stood directly in front of the passenger depot; in 1972, borough officials used federal urban renewal funds to demolish it. The weed-filled lot is still empty. The Pennsylvania Railroad station, located four blocks away, was razed c. 1960. NR. [Privately owned. Bank and commercial offices.]

QUAKERTOWN

QUAKERTOWN RAILROAD STATION
East Broad and Front streets
c. 1902

In the 1930s, farmers were still driving pigs and cattle through the streets of Quakertown to reach the railroad station on the old North Pennsylvania line, by then part of the Reading Company. In 1981, passenger service ended when the current transit authority eliminated all non-electrified service out of Philadelphia. Eight years later, a serious arson fire burned through the depot's roof. After repulsing demolition plans for two years, a local preservation group had fire fighters pump five feet of water from the basement. Members began stabilizing the building; but full-scale restoration has stalled, partly for lack of a tenant or a user (which sometimes translates into difficulty obtaining grant money). Reactivation of passenger service via a newly contemplated light rail system may turn the tide. Just to the north, the matching stone freight station is currently leased to a commercial concern; a huge, hand-

Reading Company station at Pottstown, August 1929. The new depot and track work were nearly complete.

operated "pillar" crane for unloading flat cars still stands nearby. [Southeastern Pennsylvania Transportation Authority. Vacant.] *For photo see* page 27.

ROCKHILL FURNACE

ORBISONIA STATION
Off U.S. Route 522, north of the Pennsylvania Turnpike
1906

The East Broad Top Railroad is a narrow gauge line (three feet wide) established in the early 1870s and used principally for hauling iron ore and later coal. Today, tourists are hauled via original steam equipment along five miles of the nearly intact 33-mile-long main line. A National Historic Landmark, the railroad gives visitors a sense of railroading as it was 60 years ago. The passenger station and general office building at Orbisonia is a simple two-story clapboard structure. Among the many other extant buildings on the line are a brick roundhouse; a stone shop building filled with belt-driven machinery; a wooden sand house; a human-powered turntable; a company store; and three more passenger stations. Preservationists spent the early 1990s fighting

Orbisonia station c.1907, before construction of the platform canopy (added by 1911).

a string of proposed 12-story, high-tension towers that would have adversely affected the scenic views along the East Broad Top right-of-way. The tower project was canceled, but the ongoing need for a suitable management entity to protect this irreplaceable resource has not abated. Among the alternatives being studied by regional, state, and federal agencies is a linear park—ideally one that retains the tracks and the train. NR. NHL. [Privately owned. Tourist train stop.]

SAYRE

SAYRE RAILROAD STATION
1 Lehigh Avenue
1882

In 1871, trains of the Pennsylvania & New York Canal and Railroad Company (a subsidiary of the Lehigh Valley) were busy transporting passengers and massive amounts of anthracite coal. Railroad baron Asa Packer decided to build a roundhouse for the Northern Division at South Central Junction, soon renamed Sayre for the LV's original chief civil engineer. The first depot, a wooden structure, burned down when a kerosene lantern exploded in 1875. The railroad constructed a temporary station and an ornate, three-story office building (razed c. 1950). Both the office and the new permanent brick depot were landscaped with trees and flower gardens, bordered by wooden fencing. The station's High Victorian Gothic style, with Queen Anne motifs, was relatively sophisticated for this up-country setting near the New York border. The community received many visitors who came to Sayre for treatment at the well-known medical facility begun in the ex-home of Robert Packer (Asa's son). Passenger service ended in 1961. Fifteen years later, the remaining freight service of the LV was absorbed by Conrail, which subsequently sold the depot. On the second floor, a railroad museum retains many LV artifacts. The first

Baggage wagons, milk cans, and small boys were among the fixtures found outside the Sayre station.

floor has been used variously as a restaurant and a store. [Privately owned. Railroad museum and commercial.]

SCRANTON

DELAWARE, LACKAWANNA, AND WESTERN STATION
Lackawanna and Jefferson avenues
Kenneth M. Murchison
1908

The Delaware, Lackawanna & Western not only hauled anthracite coal, it owned or leased coal fields north and west of Scranton. Early 20th-century profits enabled the railroad to build a French Renaissance-style depot clad in Indiana limestone, fronted on both sides by massive columns. Atop the five-story building (a sixth story was added in 1923), a large clock was flanked by sculpted eagles. A 20-foot-deep canopy wrapped around three sides of the building. On the track side, Lincoln Bush, chief engineer of the "Lackawanna," installed two, recently invented, smokeless sheds. (The one remaining, albeit truncated, shed has been enclosed as part of the current restaurant.) The main waiting room, two-and-a-half stories high,

was decorated not only with several kinds of imported marble, but also with more than 30 faience panels representing scenes along the Lackawanna line. Daytime lighting came from the barrel vaulted ceiling of leaded glass; at night, lights concealed behind the cornice provided illumination. (In 1983, when the long-empty building was converted to a hotel, the damaged ceiling was left mostly open with a view to the steel trusses above; the current owner is restoring all the glass.) Railroad offices occupied the upper floors. Northwest of the passen-

Scranton DL&W station shortly after opening.

ger station is the 67-acre DL&W yard complex, now the Steamtown National Historic Site, which includes 13 structures dating from 1865 to 1939. Scranton was also serviced by the Central Railroad of New Jersey, whose passenger terminal burned in 1910. The CNJ's turreted, vacant freight station (NR) still stands at the western end of Lackawanna Avenue. NR. [Privately owned. Hotel and restaurant.]

STRASBURG

EAST STRASBURG STATION
Route 741, one mile east of Strasburg
c. 1882

In 1960, after more than a century of operation, the Strasburg Rail Road needed a depot for its new tourist operation. In the old tradition of recycling railroad stations, it bought an about-to-be-abandoned depot. Hauled in nine sections from East Petersburg, the Stick Style depot (plus octagonal outhouse) was reassembled and restored—including the corbeled brick chimney—at the East Strasburg terminus. (Metal roof cresting was long gone and not replaced.) Attributed to noted architect Frank

J Tower, relocated to Strasburg and restored. The locomotive is Strasburg Rail Road No. 89.

Furness, it was built originally by the Reading & Columbia (later the Reading Company). Just west of the depot stands another important piece of railroad architecture—a Pennsylvania Railroad signal tower that once controlled a crossing at Lemoyne. Abandoned by Conrail in 1983, the c. 1885 structure was disassembled and moved 50 miles by the Lancaster Chapter of the National Railway Historical Society. Members painted "J" Tower its original light and dark umber with red accents and installed an antique set of "interlocking" equipment. (Interlocking is an assemblage of devices that controls signals and switches in a pre-established or "locked" sequence to ensure the safe movement of trains.) Directly across Route 741 from the tower and depot is the state-operated Railroad Museum of Pennsylvania. [Strasburg Rail Road. Tourist train stop.]

SUSQUEHANNA

SUSQUEHANNA DEPOT (STARRUCCA HOUSE)
Depot Street
1865

The brick railroad station-hotel, known as Starrucca House, stretched along the Erie Railroad's main line. It was 40 feet deep and 327 feet long. Beneath two large cross gables on the track side, travelers entered a 120-foot-long dining room—a two-and-a-half-story, navelike hall with ribbed vaulting, pointed Gothic windows, and carved wooden balconies. The dining hall filled the central third of the building; hotel rooms occupied the remaining second and third floor space. Its design has been attributed to a formally trained architect, E. J. M. Derrick. Sleeping and dining cars ended the need for station-hotels; by 1903, the restaurant and bedrooms had become a railroad Y.M.C.A. and division offices. A second floor was inserted into the banquet hall. At some point, two Romanesque Revival roof towers, which provided ventilation to the dining hall, were removed. The adjacent car mainte-

Susquehanna. Early view of Starrucca House with its two Italianate towers (now gone) and a rail car used as an annex. (For interior view, *see* page 17.)

nance shops were mostly destroyed by fire in the Seventies and later demolished. Today, the station-hotel has reverted to feeding people, but they come by car—the tracks are used by freight trains only. In the late 1980s, the current owner removed the added floors and restored the dining hall's high ceiling. He also intends to return the hotel rooms to their original use. The new, elevated crossing shanty in the parking lot is patterned after an 1860s Wisconsin prototype. One mile east in Lanesboro, the famous Starrucca Viaduct (1848) still carries trains 1,040 feet across the Starrucca Creek Valley. NR. [Privately owned. Restaurant.]

TAMAQUA

TAMAQUA RAILROAD STATION
West Broad Street (U.S. Route 209) between
    Berwick and Railroad streets
1874, 1880, 1885

A lovely park with flowers planted by the Reading Company once bordered the Tamaqua station. Replacing a nearby smaller depot that burned, the new Italianate brick building with a terne metal roof was built in three sections. The first addition (1880) created a T-shaped plan with a restaurant and kitchen. The second addition, five years later, was the

freight house. A scheduled meal stop on the route between Philadelphia and Williamsport, the depot was originally heated by fireplaces and stoves that sprouted eight chimneys (removed in the 1920s). A magnificent 1857 roundhouse that once stood to the north was replaced in the 1890s by a new enginehouse— in turn replaced in the 1960s by a shopping center. The last passenger train pulled out in 1963; the railroad vacated the building in 1980. A dozen years later, a preservation-minded group bought the depot from a developer to thwart demolition. The group is gradually restoring it, including repairs to the men's waiting room, damaged in a suspicious fire. A steam tourist train stops here periodically. NR. [Save Our Station, Inc. Vacant.]

Tamaqua station, August 1952.

VALLEY FORGE

VALLEY FORGE RAILROAD STATION

Valley Forge National Historic Park (west end, off State Route 23)

c. 1911

Contrary to the erroneous assumption of many 20th-century visitors to Valley Forge, George Washington did not arrive in the winter of 1777 by train. Located directly behind the general's headquarters, the Valley Forge depot was built about 1911 by the Reading Company in exchange for a narrow strip of land, which it needed for increasing its main line tracks to four. The railroad agreed to erect a structure costing not less than $10,000, with covered platforms, a steamboat landing (for the Schuylkill River), and a passenger tunnel under the tracks. Today, the well-preserved station with walls of coursed, rubble stone still has its slate roof. Among the classical exterior details are console-type brackets supporting the porch roof and several kinds of cornice molding. On the inside, the barrel-vaulted waiting room has tiered paneling covering the walls to ceiling height, a fireplace with a white marble surround and hearth, and four handsome wooden benches. Raised panel wainscoting formalizes the baggage and rest rooms, as well as the ticket office, which retains its frosted window, marble shelf, and original cupboards.

After the nation's 200th birthday celebration in 1976, the depot was taken out of railroad service and used for a time as headquarters for the park police. Eventually it became a meeting space. The next stop east, the c. 1904 Port Kennedy station, had been closed in 1966, but then reopened for the Bicentennial with a new name—Valley Forge. Deactivated again in the early 1980s, wooden Port Kennedy (still wearing its confusing Valley Forge sign) stands unoccupied today at the east end of the park. NR District. NHL District. [National Park Service. School programs facility.]

WHITE DEER

WHITE DEER STATION

Depot Road, off U.S. Route 15

1912

The stone and brick White Deer station replaced a brick depot that burned in 1911. It was sited on an "island" between two sets of tracks: the standard gauge Reading Company (the "Reading") to the east; the narrow gauge

Park side of the Valley Forge station.

White Deer station, June 1914.

White Deer & Logantown to the west. Freight was loaded from both sides of the building. An Elizabethan-style dormer over the Reading-side agent's bay was supplemented by Tudor Revival dormers over each railroad's freight door. When an all-volunteer restoration project began in the early 1970s, the depot was deteriorated but intact, including the oak woodwork. Tracks (inactive) remain only on the Reading side of the depot. [Central Pennsylvania Chapter, National Railway Historical Society. Meeting space and museum.]

WILKES-BARRE

CENTRAL RAILROAD OF NEW JERSEY STATION
33 Wilkes-Barre Boulevard
c. 1869

Passenger service to the Central Railroad of New Jersey station in Wilkes-Barre ended in 1963; by the mid-Seventies, the derelict building was condemned. A local businessperson rescued the depot by doing a restaurant conversion, in which 10-foot-wide ceiling holes were repaired and missing parts of the interior were reproduced. The two-and-a-half-story brick station, topped by a high, octagonal cupola, became the bar and offices of the restaurant. Dining takes place in the enclosed platform and in train cars connected to the depot. It was built by the Lehigh & Susquehanna Railroad (part of the Lehigh Coal & Navigation Company). Today, automobiles roll on the four-lane highway that replaced the railroad right-of-way. NR. [Privately owned. Restaurant.]

Wilkes-Barre CNJ station, 1930s.

Numerous posters, including one for the musical *HAIR*, are affixed to the Wynnewood station in this February 1971 view.

WYNNEWOOD

WYNNEWOOD RAILROAD STATION

East Wynnewood and Penn roads
c. 1870

In the 19th century, a score of depots were built to serve the wealthy patrons of the Pennsylvania Railroad's Paoli Local commuter line west of Philadelphia. Paralleling Route 30, two-thirds of the stations remain standing today, in widely varying states of preservation or disrepair. (Unfortunately, three of the most significant — Ardmore, the Bryn Mawr passenger station, and Paoli — were razed.) Wynnewood is the most intact of a handful constructed in an early standard design that lacked an agent's bay. Similar depots were built at stops then known as Villa Nova [*sic*], Haverford College (westbound), Radnor, and Elm (renamed Narberth; now gone). At Wynnewood, the cross gables of the inbound stone depot are each pierced by a diamond-shaped opening. A long canopy shelters the train platform, which is laid in herringbone-patterned brick. To reach the wooden

outbound station, travelers descend to a brick, barrel-vaulted pedestrian tunnel under the tracks. Both the outbound and inbound platform canopies have gable elements filled with wooden cutouts. Ornate iron fencing above the tunnel stairs is identical to that used elsewhere along the line.

Nine quick stops west of Wynnewood is the oft-photographed Strafford station, with its bold criss-cross of applied decoration. Strafford presents a somewhat peculiar streetside face, because it was relocated at least twice during the 1800s. The last move placed the once ground-level depot adjacent to elevated tracks, which necessitated the addition of a lower story. The next stop west of Strafford is Devon, an English Cottage–style depot of stone and patterned shingles. Complete with Queen Anne window panes, carved brick chimneys, and an outbound station, the Devon depot is essentially intact, but in urgent need of restoration. In contrast, Wynnewood is tended today by the local civic association, which provides landscaping expertise and coordinates maintenance. [Amtrak owned. SEPTA train stop.]

West Virginia

West Virginia was dominated by three railroads: the Baltimore & Ohio in the north and the Chesapeake & Ohio and the Norfolk & Western in both the middle and southern portions. A number of the best extant stations are in the Appalachian Mountains, which run diagonally through the eastern half of the state. Parts of the state were ruggedly inaccessible until the railroad arrived and provided a new way to move people, coal, and lumber.

ALDERSON

ALDERSON RAILROAD STATION
1 C&O Plaza (at Railroad Avenue)
1896

More than 100 stations were built by the Chesapeake & Ohio using this once-common passenger station design. Alderson is the best surviving example of the half-dozen that remain. Adopted in 1892 and used until about 1910, the pattern was executed in inexpensive board and batten construction. A bit of fanciness was supplied by the decorative barge-boards on both the dormered agent's bay and the end gables. Built by division carpenters,

the Alderson station was expanded in 1917 to create more space for express shipments. Waiting rooms, which had originally segregated men from women, were reassigned by race. In 1957, the freight house standing to the east was demolished, and freight operations moved in with passenger services. In the early Seventies, the depot became a municipal warehouse. When Amtrak resumed service to Alderson the following decade, the beaded board waiting room was reopened to passengers. With the help of ISTEA funds awarded in 1994, the town will convert the balance of the station into a visitors center, community heritage display, and conference room. About 75 miles northeast of Alderson, the Marlinton

Young men and old gathered at the Alderson station, 1910. A newsboy, once a fixture at many depots, stands in the foreground.

Track side of the Charleston C&O station c.1910. In the background, the bridge over the Kanawha River.

depot (former C&O Greenbrier Branch), is a similar standard design. Marlinton has been painted pre-1923 C&O colors of yellow with white trim and converted to a visitors center. NR District. [Town of Alderson. Train stop and warehouse.]

CHARLESTON

CHESAPEAKE & OHIO STATION
305 MacCorkle Avenue (south end of South Side Bridge)
1906

Sitting across the Kanawha River from the state capital district, Charleston's Chesapeake & Ohio station once had first- and second-floor waiting rooms. The main entrance was on the upper story, which passengers reached directly from South Side Bridge. The first story was at track level, where a long platform canopy sheltered travelers. About the time MacCorkle Avenue was constructed in 1933, C&O began substantial alterations to the stone and yellow brick building, trimmed in terra-cotta. Many years of

unsympathetic treatment ensued, which were reversed by a 1987 adaptation to commercial space. The rehabilitation architect incorporated the station's arched windows, interior balcony, and high ceilings into his design and retained the red tile roof. Using found parts, he was able to resurrect—on a smaller scale—the grand staircase that the C&O removed in 1962. Amtrak, which leases space in the former express area, may relocate altogether, if a possible change in train routing occurs. Charleston's Union Station is gone. [Privately owned. Train stop, restaurant, and offices.]

GRAFTON

GRAFTON STATION AND HOTEL
40 and 100 East Main Street
M. A. Long
1911

Grafton House, a combination station and hotel, was erected in 1857, the year after the town was incorporated. Located on the Baltimore & Ohio main line, Grafton played a

Grafton station and hotel.

Willard Hotel under construction, 1911. The mansard roof had not yet been built.

Streetside view of the station, mid-1930s. The hotel is on the left.

key role during the Civil War. Later, as bituminous coal mines developed south of Grafton, this junction became an assembly point for coal trains going east. In 1911, the brick dual-purpose station-hotel (which stood at track level) was replaced with side-by-side structures. M. A. Long of Baltimore, who was on the B&O staff at the time, designed a brick and cut stone depot in the Beaux Arts style, with ornate facades for both Main Street and the tracks. Fabulous Christmastime displays of model trains were a yearly feature in the classically detailed waiting room. Passengers reached the tracks, one level below, via an exterior, covered stairway.

Built of identical materials, the depot's six-story neighbor, the Willard Hotel (named for the B&O's president) had a mansard roof, with finely detailed windows (now devoid of decoration). The top floor contained a ballroom. Last used to house railroad workers, the hotel is cur-

rently empty. In 1994, the city began negotiating to buy the depot and hotel from CSX Transportation, whose workers still have offices in the station. NR District. [CSX Transportation. Complex mostly vacant.]

HINTON

CHESAPEAKE & OHIO STATION
Front Street
1890

An 1880 editorial in a local paper published harsh words about Hinton's first depot: "The so-called reception room is without doubt the blackest, greasiest, dirtiest, filthiest, most disgusting place in the whole town. . . ." Nine years later, the Chesapeake & Ohio replaced the small frame building with a two-story brick station roofed in slate. On a hill behind it, the C&O

housed workers in a railroad Y.M.C.A. The "Y" burned in late 1911 and was replaced by a brick version (used today as a senior center). The depot itself was partially destroyed by fire in 1913. An undamaged lunch room stayed open for business; temporary division point offices were installed at the Y.M.C.A. Rebuilt and then expanded over the years, the passenger depot was part of a major rail yard wedged between the mountains and the New River (now within the New River Gorge National Park). Today, only a few tracks remain. A quarter-mile west of the empty passenger station stands a dilapidated freight house (built on a different grade, now trackless). NR District. [CSX Transportation, Inc. Train stop/npa, vacant.]

HUNTINGTON

CHESAPEAKE & OHIO STATION
6th Avenue between 9th and 10th streets
1913

In the early 20th century, the Chesapeake & Ohio's rapidly increasing passenger business merited construction of nine updated stations, built of brick and scattered through Kentucky, Virginia, and West Virginia. The chosen style was Colonial Revival, seen as a suitable match for the historic battlefields, natural wonders, and ancient mineral springs that patriotic Americans wanted to visit. Huntington was the most important C&O town, and eventually became West Virginia's largest city. Huntington's first station was constructed in 1873, when the railroad laid out the streets. It was built of stone in Second Empire style and stood just west of the current building. Sheltered by a hipped, red tile roof, the new station was entered on the street side through a three-story-high pedimented portico. A series of arched windows on the first floor were echoed in magnification by a very tall round-arched window, stretching from the second floor to the top of the trackside gabled dormer. In 1983, Amtrak moved to a new, smaller building across the yard, and the old station's platform canopy was removed. A statue of Collis P. Huntington—a key player in construction of the first transcontinental rail connection and later president of the C&O—once adorned the streetside lawn. Sculpted by J. Gutzon Borglum of Mt. Rushmore fame, it now stands outside a former competitor's building, the Baltimore & Ohio depot (NR) on 2nd Avenue, which has been converted to a restaurant. [CSX Transportation, Inc. Railroad offices.].

Huntington C&O station c. 1925. The passenger train is westbound, pulled by locomotive No. 454.

Martinsburg c. 1910. CV&M was controlled by the Cumberland Valley of Pennsylvania when this photo was taken.

MARTINSBURG

CUMBERLAND VALLEY & MARTINSBURG STATION
535 West King Street, west of U.S. Route 11
c. 1890

After the Cumberland Valley & Martinsburg (later the Pennsylvania Railroad) built a new brick and wood-shingle station, the old one became freight only. A cross between Richardsonian Romanesque and Queen Anne styles, the passenger depot had broad arches, a jerkinhead roof, and corbeled chimneys (now plain). Today, freight trains still travel past the building, which is being considered for a restaurant. Both Amtrak and MARC (a commuter line) stop at another location, the former Baltimore & Ohio station on East Martin Street. That structure began life in 1849 as the Berkeley Hotel. It was acquired by the B&O, after Confederate troops destroyed the actual depot, and later was substantially expanded. The 11-acre B&O complex includes a brick and cast-iron roundhouse built in 1866; its 1872 companion was destroyed in 1990 by arson. NR District. [Winchester & Western Railroad. Vacant.]

PHILIPPI

PHILIPPI RAILROAD STATION
U.S. Route 250 (Main Street)
1911

In November 1985, just five months after the Barbour County Historical Society completed four years of fund raising and restoration (using early 1900s specifications), a flood

As with many stations, Philippi was situated adjacent to a grade crossing.

washed over the Philippi depot. Work began anew on the Mission-style building of buff brick, trimmed with light-colored stone. At the roof line, curvilinear parapets bracket the gable dormers, each faced with a round window. The roof was originally red tile, which the historical society hopes to restore. Interior trim is oak. The west elevation of this county seat depot faces the famous Philippi two-lane covered bridge (1852; NR), spanning the Tygart Valley River. The Baltimore & Ohio eliminated passenger service to Philippi in 1956. Freight trains still use the tracks. The line originated in 1884 as the narrow gauge Grafton & Greenbrier. NR. [City of Philippi. Local history museum.]

PRINCE

PRINCE RAILROAD STATION
State Route Route 41, 10 miles north of Beckley
1946

Robert R. Young, the feisty Texan who controlled the Chesapeake & Ohio, wanted everything about his railroad to be very up-to-date. The Prince station combined Art Moderne features like streamlined, rounded corners with the window walls of International Style. Built of brick with a flat concrete roof, it replaced a c. 1915 depot. The waiting room featured a huge photo mural of a local coal mine, and a rounded ticket counter built of blond wood and travertine. Chessie the Cat was the C&O's advertising symbol from the 1930s into the 1970s; passengers were invited to "sleep like a kitten and wake up fresh as a daisy" on modern air-conditioned trains. Chessie's tiled image was set into the waiting room floor. Above the rounded-end, concrete platform canopy, the station name appeared in stainless steel letters. Prince was the prototype for a depot replacement campaign, but the program was aborted by the post–World War II downturn in business. [CSX Transportation, Inc. Train stop.]

SHEPHERDSTOWN

SHEPHERDSTOWN RAILROAD STATION
Between German and High streets, west
of the tracks
1908

In 1982, Norfolk Southern Corporation acquired Norfolk & Western (builder of the Shepherdstown station) and the Southern Railway. The new company policy was to demolish all unused railroad buildings within 40 feet from either side of the right-of-way's center line. Shepherdstown, where passenger service had ended in the Fifties, was on the demolition list. Then in the early 1990s, a local historical commission arranged to buy a piece of land adjacent to the right-of-way. The group plans to relocate the Shepherdstown depot, with its large, decoratively half-timbered gable, 40 feet to the north and 28 feet further from the track. It will be placed on a new full basement, partially above ground; the lower level will become a health clinic. With an added hallway, the main floor will be converted to a community center. If a contemplated commuter service between Washington, D.C., and Hagerstown, Md., comes through, the depot could again see passengers, for whom the long-gone platform canopy would need to be restored. Among extant stations of similar design are Williamson in West Virginia and Farmville (NR District), Luray, Salem, and Suffolk in Virginia. NR District. [Corporation of Shepherdstown. Vacant—future health clinic and community center.]

THURMOND

THURMOND RAILROAD STATION
State Route 25, just over the Thurmond Bridge
1904

In the early 1990s, the National Park Service acquired the former Chesapeake & Ohio passenger station in Thurmond from CSX

Positioned next to the bridge over the New River, the Thurmond station c. 1920.

Transportation. Plans are to develop the entire historic district as a typical railroad and mining town of the early 20th century. Situated at a gateway to the New River Gorge, the depot is undergoing total restoration by the NPS. Plans include using it for a museum and interpretative center, with the waiting room available to Amtrak passengers.

Something like a Venice canal, the only "street" in Thurmond was the railroad, whose yards were wedged on a flood plain between Beury Mountain and the river. The town itself was built onto the mountainside. Because of the huge amount of coal-handling, Thurmond was once the C&O's most lucrative station. The current building replaced a c. 1892 design that burned down. The second floor of the new board and batten depot, reached only by an exterior stairway, had offices not only for the usual railroad workers like the yardmaster, track supervisor, and telegraph operator, but

also for coal buyers. The first floor contained waiting rooms, a ticket office, baggage and express rooms, a lunch stand, and a news counter. A separate freight station (razed in the 1950s) was perpendicular to the passenger depot and cantilevered over the river for lack of ground space. An early 20th-century engine-house operated three shifts a day with about 75 men. (Stabilized by the National Park Service, who planned to restore it, the enginehouse was destroyed by fire in 1993.) Adjacent to the depot, a c. 1910 railroad bridge was augmented about 1920 with an automobile cartway cantilevered onto the upstream side. The bridge is still the only access to Thurmond.

The town's heyday as a railroad center diminished in the 1950s, with the change from steam to diesel; today, CSX operates its freight service out of a trailer. White-water rafting is now Thurmond's major "industry." The Thurmond station was used prominently in the

1987 motion picture *Matewan*. NR District. [National Park Service. Train stop/npa and future museum.]

WHEELING

WHEELING RAILROAD STATION
16th and Market streets
M. A. Long
1908

On a momentous New Year's Day, 1853, the first train rolled into Wheeling. After 25 years of financial and engineering struggles, the Baltimore & Ohio had at last crossed the mountains and reached the Ohio River. Both the population of Wheeling and the business of the B&O increased dramatically during the Civil War and into the 20th Century. In 1908, an imposing new station was built, designed in Beaux Arts style by M. A. Long, who also did the B&O station and hotel in Grafton. Each of the ornate central pavilion's three entrances was topped by a cartouche bearing B&O initials. Both the main section and the limestone and brick wings had mansard roofs covered with tile. Forty dormers admitted light to this attic space. After passenger service ceased in 1961, the building was used commercially, until made part of a community college 15 years later. The interior was radically altered, including insertion of a second floor into the original waiting space. In the late 80s, the abutting viaduct and track system, which once brought trains to the second-story platform, was removed. The depot has become an ironic monument to the B&O—a handsome facade with the railroad's full name carved above tall, arched windows—but no other evidence of the town's railroad heritage in sight. NR. [State College System of West Virginia. School.]

WHITE SULPHUR SPRINGS

WHITE SULPHUR SPRINGS RAILROAD STATION
West Main Street
1930

Before the Civil War era, White Sulphur Springs began attracting people who sought the benefits of its mineral waters. The Chesapeake & Ohio arrived in 1869; it bought the resort in 1910. Two years later, the C&O built a new hotel called the Greenbrier (replacing one known as "Old White"), with its entrance set directly across the street from the station. Two wooden stations preceded the red brick depot that stands today. For many years, the C&O used a nostalgia-based promotional theme, claiming it was "George Washington's Railroad" (he was president of a canal company that the C&O absorbed). Colonial Revival style was a perfect architectural vehicle for this vision, as evidenced by subtle classical details on the 700-foot-long platform canopy that still exists. Lengthy trains carrying guests from eastern cities dropped off their sleeping cars in the small rail yard that once stood nearby. The Pullmans were then connected to steam and electricity for the still slumbering passengers. That yard is now a parking lot, devoid of tracks except for one (a looping track that swings behind the depot and back to the main line). In 1990, after a decade as the resort's real estate office, the depot was restored to its 1930 appearance and reopened for passenger business. Its design is said to derive from an early 19th-century cottage that stood on the hotel grounds. The depot's simplicity distinguishes it from more typical, porticoed Colonial Revival stations. A wooden freight station, located to the east and on a separate grade, still stands. [CSX Transportation. Train stop and special events facility.]

South

Straight ahead, the train shed and head house of Main Street Station, Richmond, Va. On the left, Chesapeake & Ohio tracks; on the right, the Seaboard Air Line. In the left background of this 1950s photo, Interstate 95 is ominously under construction.

Alabama

Nineteenth-century Alabama consisted mostly of small towns spread over great distances; large depots were rare. Of the three big-city stations that once stood simultaneously, two remain—in Montgomery and Mobile. The Birmingham station, an elaborate composition of pavilions, towers, and domes, was demolished in 1969.

CULLMAN

CULLMAN RAILROAD STATION
309 1st Avenue, N.E.
1913

In the 1870s, a political refugee named John Cullman decided to establish a German colony on 349,000 acres of land he optioned from the Louisville & Nashville Railroad. A gridiron plan was laid out for a new town, with the railroad right-of-way as the central axis. When Cullman died in 1895, his will directed that $15,000 be used for lowering the railroad tracks to eliminate noise and smoke through the town. His wishes were not followed until 1911, when L&N began laying a second track along its realigned route. A half-mile from the old depot the railroad built a new station, designed by its chief engineer's office. Its stucco-clad, Spanish Colonial Revival style was unusual both for L&N and for the area. Originally a racially segregated passenger station, the building spent its last railroad years as a freight agency. A 15-year-long negotiation to save the depot was not concluded until 1991, when the city bought the land, and CSX Transportation donated the building. During all those years, citizens demonstrated their commitment to preservation through numerous fund-raising events. The entire process was boosted toward con-

clusion in 1993 with the receipt of ISTEA dollars. The depot's new use has not been decided. NR. [City of Cullman. Vacant.]

EUFAULA

EUFAULA DEPOT
South Randolph Avenue
George Whipple
1872

Designed by a local architect for the Vicksburg & Brunswick (later Central of Georgia), Eufaula's combination freight and passenger station was eclipsed in 1891 by a new depot in another location (since razed). Thereafter, the 1872 building served principally as a freight station. Its overhanging roof is supported on four sides by wooden brackets, in turn upheld by brick pilasters that tie into the roof trusses. In the shelter of the southside canopy, early 20th-century advertising remains clearly painted onto the bricks. The depot's numerous tall windows are round-arched on the exterior, but squared on the interior, with original blinds. The first roof was wood-shingle, but the current one is metal. Used as a retailer's warehouse for decades, the depot was acquired in the 1980s by a church. Its crumbling brick walls need repair. Freight trains still use the tracks. NR District. [Privately owned. Storage and recreational facility.]

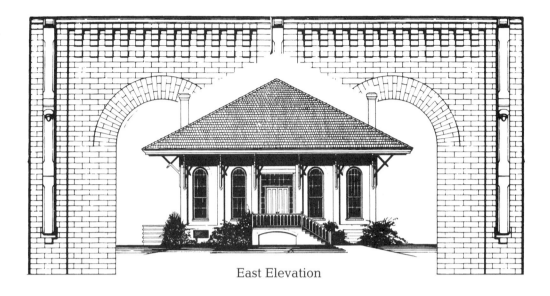

East Elevation

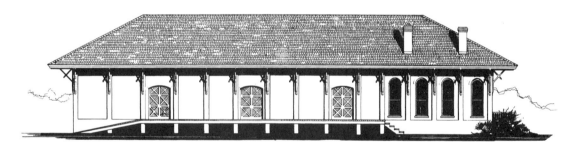

Eufaula depot. Artist's conception of the east (top) and south elevations if restored.

EVERGREEN

EVERGREEN DEPOT
Front and Cooper streets
1907

As a county seat, Evergreen warranted a large version of this standard design Louisville & Nashville station. Many similar depots built about 1900 were demolished during the 1960s. Fortunately for Evergreen, the Murder Creek Historical Society acquired and restored the depot, which it then donated to the city. The one-story wooden station has three sections, each with a hipped roof, a gable dormer, and wide eaves supported by deep brackets. The former freight room serves as a community meeting space. Other areas house the chamber of commerce and a shop dedicated to selling local crafts. Although passenger service was initially discontinued in 1971, Amtrak returned in 1989. Two other stations of the same standard design stand in Mississippi at Ocean Springs (chamber of commerce and art gallery) and Pascagoula (train stop and cultural facility). NR. [City of Evergreen. Train stop and mixed use.]

FORT PAYNE

FORT PAYNE RAILROAD STATION
Northeast 5th Street (State Route 35)
Charles C. Taylor
1891

In the late 1800s, the economy and population of Fort Payne boomed with the discoveries of iron ore, limestone, and coal. When the Alabama Great Southern constructed an elegant new passenger station, the old combination depot became freight-only. Although the design has been attributed to the railroad's chief engineer, it was essentially the work of Cincinnati architect Charles C. Taylor. A nearly identical depot (made of brick and stone) still stands in Bucyrus, Ohio, built by the Ohio Central. Fort Payne's native gray sandstone was trimmed with pink granite and capped by black slate and terne metal roofing. A corner tower with a "candle snuffer" spire housed the ladies' waiting room in the lower portion, accented by a fireplace.

Interior ceilings were more than 14 feet high, with exposed beams of hand-hewn pine. In the early 1970s the Southern Railway (successor to AGS) discontinued passenger service. The railroad donated the depot to a local volunteer group that had formed solely to preserve the building. The depot was rededicated in 1986. NR. [Landmarks of DeKalb Museum, Inc. Depot museum.] (For photo, *see* page 13)

HUNTSVILLE

HUNTSVILLE DEPOT
320 Church Street
1860

In 1862, Union troops captured the station at Huntsville, a division point on the critical Memphis & Charleston Railroad. The passenger depot was used as a temporary prison, set in the Huntsville yard amidst the enginehouse, machine shop, and two car shops. In 1912, the

Wood-sided passenger cars at the Huntsville depot c. 1880s.

depot's interior was remodeled by the Southern Railway, which had acquired the line in 1898. Passenger service ended in 1967. Just a few years later, the depot was in the path of an interstate highway. National Register listing forced a remapping of the highway and helped save the nearly roofless depot. During the process of restoration and conversion to a museum, Civil War graffiti were uncovered and carefully preserved. A local architectural firm used a then-innovative process of computer enhancement to study an 1880s photograph that identified missing elements on the two-and-a-half-story brick depot. Across the tracks stands an 1856 freight station (until recently in record-breaking continuous operation), which the city intends to acquire for adaptive use. NR. [City of Huntsville. Museum of railroading, commerce, and industry.]

LAFAYETTE

LAFAYETTE DEPOT
1st Avenue West, off 1st Street West
1908

After Lafayette's wooden depot burned, the Central of Georgia built a brick station with a belcast, tile roof. In the early 1980s, Norfolk Southern Corporation (a modern freight railroad) donated the depot to the county, but retained title to the land. Wooden wainscoting and other fine millwork accent the former passenger section and the agent's office. In the freight end, brick walls and sliding doors bear the names of old businesses. Back when the depot was in active operation, railroad workers unloaded goods from the freight cars into these assigned spots. When wagon drivers arrived they could easily locate the right shipment. Today the railroad tracks are used only for local transport of pulpwood, and the depot's freight platform is gone. [County of Chambers. Local history museum.]

MOBILE

UNION DEPOT
Beauregard and Water streets
Philip Thornton Marye
1907

In the late 19th century the Southern Railway obtained a majority stock position in the Mobile & Ohio; Union Depot was a joint project of the two railroads. It was designed in a Spanish Colonial Revival style by P. Thornton Marye, head of a large Georgia architectural firm, known for the Atlanta Terminal Station (1905; razed 1971) and numerous public buildings throughout the South. Delicate sculptural details punctuated the surface of the beige brick Mobile Union Depot, which was crowned by a large, octagonal dome surmounted by a lantern. Roofed in red mission tile, the L-shaped structure featured baroque sculptural elements including cartouches and plant, animal, and human forms. Along the entrance arcade, six gargoyles served as rainspouts. In 1940, the depot became commonly known as the GM&O (Gulf, Mobile & Ohio) station, after one of the several railroad mergers that affected its history. Passenger service ended in 1958. The interior (already radically altered in the 1940s) was partitioned for railroad offices, which remained until the Eighties. Although the

Mobile Union Depot c. 1940.

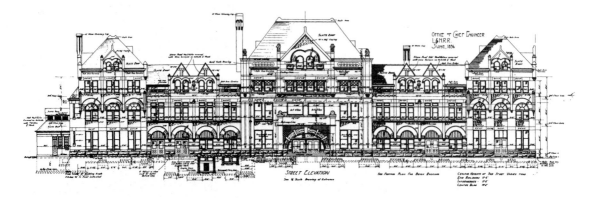

Architect's street elevation for Montgomery Union Station.

depot's National Register status played a role in defeating a raised highway along the waterfront, that road now passes at grade level before the empty station, isolating it from the rest of the city. Freight trains use the numerous remaining tracks. Suggestions abound for an adaptive use, but the depot's future is very uncertain. NR. [Privately owned. Vacant.]

MONTGOMERY

UNION STATION
300 Water Street (at Lee Street)
Benjamin Bosworth Smith
1898

Prior to the construction of Union Station, Montgomery was served by a small, two-story frame structure. A local architect designed the new depot complex principally for the Louisville & Nashville, although several other lines also stopped at this "through" station. Its three-and-a-half stories of brick and stone blended the massing of Victorian Gothic with details from Romanesque Revival. Enhanced with stained glass and terra-cotta elements, the wide Roman arch of the streetside porte-cochere was duplicated on the track side. This Roman arch motif was repeated dozens of times throughout the exterior. The first-floor layout included a general waiting room (two stories high with a balcony), ladies' and "colored" waiting rooms, and a restaurant. A two-story baggage building anchored the east end; a freestanding mail and express office was constructed to the west in 1913. Across Water Street was a huge, complementary design freight station (now gone).

Parallel to the station house stands one of the country's few surviving, midsize train sheds. Originally covered in slate, its gable roof is supported by 25 Pratt trusses of timber, wrought iron, and cast iron. The central monitor was built with a glass roof to admit light, while lowered sides allowed the escape of locomotive smoke. After Amtrak suspended service to Montgomery in 1979, the L&N requested that the city tear off the shed's roof and decking (described as a safety hazard). The swiftly ensuing deterioration was reversed in the early 1980s, when the shed was rehabilitated by the Landmarks Foundation (with help from the National Trust Endangered Properties Fund). With its four tracks removed, the shed was converted to a 600-foot-long shelter used for parking during the week and for special events on week-ends. Work on the complex included stripping green paint off the depot's copper canopy; using toothbrushes and toothpicks to get white concrete-based paint off the "buttered-joint" masonry (so called for its very narrow ribbons of mortar); and reinstalling the shed's multicolored glass panes. Adapted to commercial space, the depot went through several hands, foreclosure, and vacancy, until new owners took over in 1993. They plan to build a hotel the adjacent parking lot. About 200 yards east of the historic depot, Amtrak (which reinstated service in 1989) uses part of a renovated grain silo for its station. NR. NHL. [Depot privately owned. Restaurant and offices. Shed owned by City of Montgomery]

PIEDMONT

PIEDMONT DEPOT
North Center Avenue
1868

When the Selma, Rome & Dalton built its combination freight and passenger station at Piedmont, the town was called Cross Plains. Passenger service ended in the late 1950s, although the depot was used for freight purposes by the Southern Railway until 1981. The Piedmont Historical Society restored and manages the board and batten building, which is repainted gray, a color described in an early

Piedmont depot as a museum, 1994.

newspaper article. Fireplaces (now bricked in) were the original heating source in the square, high-ceilinged passenger section. Most of the door and window openings are topped by a slight Italianate arch. A long freight house, with a lower roof, extends perpendicular to the passenger section—a common configuration for stations in the mid-19th century. The tracks are gone. An endangered depot at Oxford is quite similar to Piedmont. NR. [City of Piedmont. Local history museum.]

STEVENSON

STEVENSON RAILROAD DEPOT AND HOTEL
Main Street
c. 1872

Stevenson owes its existence to the railroads; it was founded by and named for the first president of the Nashville & Chattanooga. In the 1850s, shortly after the town was surveyed and lots were sold, the Memphis & Charleston was also completed, making Stevenson a junction —soon to be a strategic military position during the Civil War. About 1872, the two railroads shared in the cost of a new, brick passenger depot. Company records indicate that some alterations were made about 1887, which may have included the odd tower room mounted across the roof of the main structure. Its pedimented parapets are stylistically incompatible with the simple Italianate depot below. Heated by fireplaces, the interior comprised several areas: baggage and express; ticket and dispatcher's office; and "white" and "colored" waiting rooms. Built about the same time, the brick Stevenson Hotel was connected to the depot by a 30-foot-long covered walkway. The dining room, referred to at the time as "great" in size (27 feet by 57 feet), was located behind the lobby. Eight large guest rooms filled the second floor. After passenger service ended in 1976, a local group prevented demolition of the passenger depot by restoring the building and opening a museum. The 65,000 visitors per year (remarkable for a town whose population is only 2,300) experience a bit of railroad reality—the building shakes as freight trains go by. NR. [Depot, owned by the city of Stevenson. Museum.] [Hotel, privately owned. Restaurant.]

TUSCALOOSA

LOUISVILLE & NASHVILLE STATION
301 Greensboro Avenue
1912

When the Louisville & Nashville extended its tracks to Tuscaloosa, it built a small neoclassical station of limestone-trimmed yellow brick. Used as a bus depot from about 1940 to 1965, the building retains its three entrance awnings and cornices (all made of copper), mirror-image Palladian doorways, and parapeted roof. Red tiles still cover the steeply pitched roof of the east end. Seventeen blocks to the south is the current Amtrak stop (minus its tile roof and freestanding butterfly shed)—a 1911 Alabama Great Southern (Southern Railway system) station built in a Queen Anne style to replace a

depot from 1873. NR District. [Privately owned. Restaurant and night club.]

WADLEY

WADLEY DEPOT
Tallapoosa Street
1908

In the early 1900s, entrepreneur Fuller E. Calloway was seeking a new location for a textile mill. He needed river and railroad access. While traveling on a stretch of the Atlanta, Birmingham & Atlantic (later the Atlantic Coast Line), he spotted his first choice—a location that would soon become Wadley. He bought much property, built a house, and platted the town, which he named after a construction foreman on the railroad. But before any mill construction began, a dispute with local bankers caused Calloway to move on to Georgia. The little town of Wadley was left with a disproportionately large depot, intended for textile-generated traffic that never materialized. Built in a Spanish Colonial Revival style, the stuccoed depot received an orange tile roof and leaded glass windows. Interior spaces

Tuscaloosa L&N station when its platform canopy was intact.

included a freight section, "white" and "colored" waiting rooms, a telegraph office, and an express room. After passenger service ended the station became freight-only, and then just a warehouse. In the 1980s, CSX Transportation, whose trains still use the tracks, donated the building to the community. The city is now trying to acquire the land under and around the depot and has applied for ISTEA funds to rehabilitate the building. The administration intends to create a combination city hall, police department, and senior citizens facility. A virtually identical vacant depot stands 12 miles to the east at Roanoke. [City of Wadley. Vacant.]

Arkansas

Many of the intact depots in Arkansas are built of brick, made from readily available local clay. Principally second generation stations, most of the extant structures in the state date from the early 20th century, when a wave of depot modernization and fireproofing occurred. In the 1970s, Arkansas was one of the first states to compile a field survey of remaining stations—a project several states have now undertaken.

BRINKLEY

UNION STATION
East Cypress Street and New Orleans Avenue
1912

Brinkley was originally called Lick Skillet. The name was changed in 1872 to honor the president of the Memphis & Little Rock Railroad. Union Station was built by a successor line, the Chicago, Rock Island & Pacific; the Cotton Belt and the Missouri Pacific railroads were tenants. Its Mediterrean Revival style incorporated elements standard to "Rock Island" stations: a red ceramic tile roof, stepped brick parapets at the gable ends, and segmental-arched windows with concrete keystones. A week after the station was fully open, a crowd of 500 gathered to see ex-President Theodore Roosevelt's special train make a brief stop as it passed through on the way to Memphis, Tenn.

A number of nearby hotels catered to railroad clientele. After a tornado and a fire successively destroyed two wooden Brinkley Houses, a city alderman constructed the 1915 brick and concrete Rusher Hotel (NR). It included a "sample room" for display use by traveling salesmen. Ten years later, local citizens persuaded the railroad to develop a park (extant) connecting the station to the hotel. In the 1980s, the hotel—which had spent a few decades as a pool hall and liquor store with apartments above—was restored by a local couple (as the Great Southern Hotel). They later acquired both Union Station and the Cotton Belt freight depot, to prevent their demolition. NR District. [Privately owned. Vacant.]

EUREKA SPRINGS

EUREKA SPRINGS DEPOT
299 North Main Street (State Route 23 North)
1913

Long known by Indians and settlers alike, the medicinal waters of Eureka Springs became more accessible after railroad tracks reached

Eureka Springs depot with its large outdoor waiting area.

the area in 1883. The depot standing today was built of locally quarried stone by the Missouri & North Arkansas to replace a frame structure. Its roof has two parapeted gables and a square, hipped-roof cupola. Passenger service ended in 1946. Subsequent nonrailroad uses included stints as a bottling plant and a furniture factory. In 1981, the depot was refurbished for use in the television miniseries *The Blue and the Gray*. About the same time, a newly formed scenic railroad began using the depot as its base of operations. [Privately owned. Tourist train stop and offices.]

FAYETTEVILLE

FAYETTEVILLE DEPOT
550 West Dickson Street
c. 1897, 1925

In the early 1880s, the town of Fayetteville was so anxious to obtain passenger service that it raised $8,000 in promotional funds and $2,500 toward a depot. The first station burned and was replaced by the core of today's building — a former combination freight and passenger depot. After World War I, the St. Louis–San Francisco Railroad (the "Frisco") adopted a Spanish Colonial Revival style for promoting travel to California. When the Fayetteville station seemed too small to accommodate a seasonal influx of university students, the railroad expanded and remodeled it with stuccoed brick walls, a red tile roof, and finial-topped curvilinear parapets. The old conical-spired tower was replaced by a tile-roofed dormer. Inside, a massive, oak Fred Harvey newsstand was installed in the "white" waiting room, located down a narrow hallway from the "colored" waiting room. The enlargement was ill-timed; the late 1920s brought fewer passengers not more. Following World War II, paved roads in northwestern Arkansas and plane travel put further pressure on the Frisco. The last passenger train left Fayetteville in 1965. (The depot stayed in railroad use until 1982.) Current revitalization surrounding the building — including a branch bank that operates out of a Pullman car and a caboose — may bring a new use to the old station. A local businessman has obtained a 40-year lease from the owner and is seeking an appropriate subtenant. The Fayetteville station is similar to one in Poplar Bluff, Mo., (now a railroad museum) built in 1928 to replace one destroyed by a tornado. NR. [Burlington Northern Railroad Company. Vacant — for sublease.]

HOT SPRINGS

MISSOURI PACIFIC DEPOT
Broadway and Market Street
c. 1917

The one depot remaining in Hot Springs was built about the time the Missouri Pacific absorbed the St. Louis, Iron Mountain & Southern. Along with gambling, Hot Springs's therapeutic waters had already made the area a popular mountain resort—accessible by train after 1875. With a one-story, triangular plan to fit a V-shaped plot of ground, the 1917 brick passenger depot was rimmed with full-height, round-arched windows and similarly scaled open archways. Hot Springs was the terminus of a branch line from Benton, and the tracks stub-ended on the south side of the station. During a 1970s restaurant conversion, additions were made to the depot, including placement of a fixed railroad car at the east end of the building. The depot's clay tile roof still sports a tall Italianate tower, although the brick chimney is gone. In 1995, with the help of ISTEA funds, the city purchased the former MP rail yard and the station, which will be restored to its original appearance. Hot Springs was also served by the Chicago, Rock Island & Pacific, whose handsome depot was demolished about 1960 for the civic center. NR. [City of Hot Springs. Future transportation center and headquarters for recreational trail.]

LITTLE ROCK

CHOCTAW OKLAHOMA & GULF STATION
1010 East 3rd Street
c. 1899

Having discovered that historic preservation pays, The Spaghetti Warehouse restaurant chain deliberately seeks out and adapts old buildings for new dining facilities. Their 1990 conversion of the old Choctaw, Oklahoma & Gulf station (later Chicago, Rock Island & Pacific) brought back life to a space that had been closed for three decades. The brick passenger depot features an ornate, below-cornice frieze with terra-cotta embellishments of fruits, vegetables, flowers, and wheat. Its original floor plan included a 40-foot-high main waiting room, a dining hall, baggage room, and railroad offices. Adaptive use was made possible largely by rehabilitation tax credits available at the time the project was conceived. NR. [Privately owned. Restaurant.]

Post card view of the MP depot in Hot Springs.

Choctaw, Oklahoma & Gulf station in Little Rock, 1960. THE CHOCTAW ROUTE, molded in terra-cotta, is set within a shallow dormer.

UNION STATION

Markham and Victory streets
E. M. Tucker
1921

Union Station is a misnomer because the intent to unite three railroads as joint occupants failed; this Little Rock station served the Missouri Pacific Railroad only. The third station on the same site, it replaced a depot designed by Theodore C. Link (architect for St. Louis Union Station). In 1920, Link's gable-roofed creation suffered a ruinous fire, leaving nothing but the clock tower and loggia. These features were incorporated into the current Renaissance Revival structure of limestone-trimmed gray brick. The designer is presumed to have been a member of the railroad staff. Four stories high, the depot's 100,000 square feet were adapted in the 1970s to commercial use and then completely revamped in the Nineties. Amtrak's waiting space is now on the lowest level. The original waiting room, featuring a terrazzo floor and marble-tiled columns, is a children's museum. NR. [Privately owned. Train stop, museum, restaurants, and commercial.]

Little Rock Union Station, 1924.

LONOKE

LONOKE DEPOT
U.S. Route 70 and Center Street
1912

Lonoke became a train stop after Union forces destroyed the line through Brownsville in the Civil War. In 1910, the Retail Merchants and Businessmen Association wrote to the Chicago, Rock Island & Pacific to ask that it replace an 1899 frame depot with a more adequate building. Two years later, on the opposite side of the single track, the "Rock Island" built a red brick depot with parapeted gables and a steeply pitched, red tile roof. Among the items shipped from this combination freight and passenger depot were rice, cotton, soybeans, flour, and lumber. Acquired by the city in 1984 and restored by the Lonoke County Historical Society, the station retains most of its original features, including paving bricks, terrazzo floors, and wavy glass window panes. The complete signal mast remains on the roof. It was reached by a ladder that went to a tiny rooftop porch, probably a perch for changing light bulbs or making repairs. Lonoke is typical of early 20th-century Rock Island depots, particularly ones extant at North Little Rock (1913; NR) and Fordyce (c. 1925). Although inactive, the track remains. NR. [City of Lonoke. Court room and civic center.]

MAMMOTH SPRING

MAMMOTH SPRING DEPOT
On the access road to Mammoth Spring
   State Park
1886

This community was named for the huge underground spring that is the sole source for Spring River. By 1908, the tourist industry of Mammoth Spring—made possible by the 1883 arrival of the railroad—supported three large hotels and

an opera house. Its brick, Queen Anne depot was built by the Kansas City, Fort Scott & Memphis (later the St. Louis & San Francisco). With columns bearing elaborate fish and frog motifs, a breezeway linked the passenger section to the freight end. A variety of dormer styles brought light to the story-and-a-half depot. Passenger service ended in 1968. Located within a state park, the former depot is still sited along an active freight line in the Ozark Mountains. The railroad may soon donate the building to the state. NR. [Burlington Northern Railroad. Transportation museum.]

MENA

MENA DEPOT
524 Sherwood Avenue
1920

The town of Mena was named for Filomina De Goeijen, wife of an investor in the Kansas City, Pittsburgh & Gulf (later Kansas City Southern). A close friend of the De Goeijens and founder of the line, Arthur Stilwell, was an expert at advance salesmanship. In 1896, as a result of his publicized, boastful promise to lay 40 miles of track in 40 days, thousands of people were already waiting when the first train arrived in the newly created town and division point of Mena. The original, rather elaborate frame depot was torn down when the 1920 Mediterranean Revival station took its place. By this time, Mena was a county seat, although no longer a division point. The new station, designed by an architect on the railroad staff, was built of dark red brick, mortared in black, above a cut stone base. A covered outdoor waiting area had wide entrances and monolithic concrete settees lining the walls. The interior consisted of a main waiting room with Mission-style oak settees, an express agency (at the extreme west end), and a large baggage room with a "colored" waiting area in one corner. In 1987, the railroad sold the depot to the city of Mena, whose citizens had already begun renovation using only donated funds, labor, and materials. The tracks are still used by freight trains. NR. [City of Mena. Museum and chamber of commerce.]

TEXARKANA

UNION STATION
101 West Front Street
E. M. Tucker
1930

Texarkana's station was designed by the same person who worked on Union Station in Little Rock. But unlike the situation in the state capital, this depot truly served more than one railroad. Missouri Pacific, Texas & Pacific, St. Louis Southwestern (the Cotton Belt Route), and Kansas City Southern united to form the Union Station Trust. The first passenger facility in Texarkana had been at the Marquand Hotel, which burned in 1886. A union station was built in 1890 on the same site as today's build-

ing. Proposals for a new station and accompanying post office building were tabled by World War I, but reinstituted soon after the railroads returned to private operation in 1920 (the federal government ran the railroads during the war). Music, orations, a parade, a banquet, and dancing accompanied the 1930 opening. Schools declared a holiday.

The buff brick, Italian Renaissance style station was designed with triple Roman arches filled by windows stretching to the top of the third story. A stone frieze was inscribed UNION STATION, with a clock centered above the classically detailed cornice. Materials used inside included enameled brick, decorative terra-cotta, marble, terrazzo, and cast bronze. The second story comprised the main waiting room, baggage and ticketing facilities. Features deemed unusual were showers in the white men's toilet room and a baby bath in the women's retiring room. A midway extended over the six passenger tracks, accessed by three flights of stairs. Baggage, express, and local mail were handled from the station's lower level. Although the depot's architect provided room for a dining facility,

1987 artist's conception of Texarkana Union Station in the 1930s.

The Warren station was being used for freight railroad purposes when this photo was taken in 1975. Passenger service had ended nearly three decades earlier.

none materialized for 60 years. In 1990, a restaurant finally opened in the intended space. Its owners use the depot's main lobby for special events, while Amtrak occupies the lower level. The station straddles the state line separating Texas and Arkansas, a location mandated by Congress in 1876. NR. [Privately owned. Train stop and restaurant.]

WARREN

WARREN RAILROAD STATION
325 West Cedar Street (at Elm Street)
1909

The 16-mile-long Warren & Ouachita Valley Railway linked Warren with the Chicago, Rock Island & Pacific station in Banks. The railroad was built principally for servicing two large lumber mills. Appropriately, the Warren station was made of wood. Two years after opening, it was almost totally destroyed by fire. The reconstructed version—covered with wooden siding and shingles—had a two-story section for the waiting room and offices, with a one-story freight house extending perpendicularly from the rear. The numerous doors and windows were variously embellished by fanlights, rectangular sidelights, and wide transoms. When the "Rock Island" purchased the short line W&OV in 1948, passenger service was terminated. This portion of the line has been operated since the late Seventies by a lumber company subsidiary. Inside the depot, the wooden ceiling and walls are covered over with modern materials. NR. [Warren & Saline River Railroad. Railroad offices.]

Florida

Railroads came relatively late to Florida; few were constructed before the Civil War. The state's most vigorous era of railroad expansion occurred in the 1880s, with the development of Henry M. Flagler's Florida East Coast Railway and Henry B. Plant's system that eventually became part of the Atlantic Coast Line. Between 1880 and 1920, many small railroads were consolidated into larger companies, which were essentially content with the facilities at hand, typically one-story frame structures. Although tourism was important (especially to Flagler, who owned a string of resort hotels), the chief economic focus was on freight, not passengers. Bulky items like bales of cotton or crates of oranges were stored briefly in nearby warehouses; few of these structures survive.

DEERFIELD BEACH

SEABOARD AIR LINE STATION
1300 West Hillsboro Boulevard
Gustav A. Maass (Harvey and Clarke)
1927

The Seaboard Air Line station was similar to other warm-weather depots designed in the Mediterranean Revival style, which featured cool stucco walls and covered outdoor waiting areas. Especially popular in Florida during the 1920s and 1930s, the style suggested grandeur, refinement, and foreign culture—qualities appealing to tourists and retirees. Before 1898, Deerfield Beach was known as Hillsboro, and then until 1939, as simply Deerfield. The first railroad to arrive was the Florida East Coast in 1896, which provided a shipping route for crops like pineapples, peppers, and beans. In 1926, a competitor to the FEC arrived on the scene—the Seaboard Air Line. SAL hired a prominent local architect to design several stations besides Deerfield, including Boynton Beach and Delray Beach (both extant). Deerfield's combination freight and passenger station had separate entrances and waiting areas for "white" and "colored" travelers. The depot's design was dominated by an arched loggia and two square pyramid-roofed towers, covered in red tiles. Surrounded today by a parking lot and commercial buildings, the depot once enjoyed a rural setting amidst pines, palmettos, and produce sheds. Restored in the early 1990s, the depot serves both Amtrak and a new commuter line. NR. [Florida Department of Transportation. Train stop.]

JACKSONVILLE

UNION TERMINAL
West end of Water Street (at Park Street)
Kenneth M. Murchison
1919

Jacksonville's Union Terminal was the largest and busiest in Florida and acted as the rail gateway to the state. Originally, a baggage facility linked the new terminal to the old 1898 Union Station (burned in 1979). New Yorker Kenneth Murchison won the architects' competition with his Beaux Arts design executed in limestone-clad, reinforced concrete. The streetside entrance was a portico of 14 colossal limestone columns. Passengers walked through a barrel-vaulted waiting room to catch trains of the four principal railroads that the station

Jacksonville Union Terminal, 1921.

served: Atlantic Coast Line, Southern Railway, Florida East Coast, and Seaboard Air Line (united for construction and maintenance purposes as the Jacksonville Terminal Company). Today, Amtrak stops outside of town. The 1919 terminal was converted to a convention center in 1986, with an addition built on the former track and platform area. The 75-foot-high waiting room retains its marble floors and a few of the benches. Ticket windows are used for convention registration, and interpretative exhibits depict the history of the station. NR. [City of Jacksonville. Convention center.]

KISSIMMEE

KISSIMMEE RAILROAD STATION
416 Pleasant Street
c. 1910

Kissimmee may be Disney World territory today; but when this depot was built, the area was known best for vast cattle ranches and citrus groves. Constructed by the Atlantic Coast Line (one of three railroads that served Kissimmee), the wooden combination freight and passenger station had a typical Florida open-air waiting room. A signal mast protruded from the depot's trackside dormer; a cupola ventilated the roof

ridge. The station became idle in the early 1970s, until Amtrak reinaugurated service in 1976. Ten years later, the chamber of commerce announced its commitment to restoring the embarrassingly derelict building and began the process of inviting donations of cash and services. All donors—ranging from Amtrak to the many school children who gave one dollar—were issued a "stock certificate" with an artist's vision of the restored depot and a proclamation about preserving a landmark. At a special reverse auction, area businesses bid against each other to supply the materials requested by the chamber. In 1988, the fruits of the all-volunteer effort were completed, and the depot was rededicated. Mickey Mouse was among the "dignitaries" who participated in the ribbon-cutting ceremony. [CSX Transportation, Inc. Train stop.]

MILTON

MILTON DEPOT
206 Henry Street
1909

The Milton depot was built according to a Louisville & Nashville standard plan called "Special Combination Station." Sheathed in horizontal wooden siding and roofed in red tile, it had three waiting rooms (segregated by race and gender), a baggage room, and a freight section. In 1917, a long canopy (now gone) was added above the platform, and two of the waiting rooms were combined to make space for indoor plumbing. Because of heavy traffic during World War II (especially from nearby Whiting Field), the agent's office was enlarged by taking square footage from the white waiting room.

In 1974 (three years after passenger service ended), a historical society formed to save the depot and rehabilitate it for the nation's Bicentennial. In 1991, the West Florida Chapter of the National Railway Historical Society (the depot's current occupant) matched a state grant that was used for major restoration work and creation of a museum. Volunteers painted the exterior with an L&N scheme of blue-gray, olive, and white that was used from the late 1930s until the mid-1950s. The beaded boards and other fine millwork of the interior are now appropriate earth colors. Long brackets support the roof which still bears its ornamental ridge caps. (The roof tiles have been temporarily replaced with red composition shingles.) The train order signal, restored to functional status, lights up at night. Inside, a desk with working telegraph equipment further re-creates a realistic atmosphere, as do the freight and Amtrak trains that travel on the main line tracks outside the door. NR. [Santa Rosa County Historical Society. Depot museum and special events facility.]

NAPLES

NAPLES DEPOT
1051 Fifth Avenue, South
L. Philips Clarke
1926

Naples's origin as a Seaboard Air Line station (building sold to Atlantic Coast Line in 1942) is evidenced by its physical similarity to Deerfield Beach. Contrast lies in the preservation story— Naples has been without train service since 1971. In the late 1970s, a massive "Save the Depot" campaign raised enough money to purchase this expensive piece of Florida real estate and convert it to a civic and cultural center. Landscaped with many original trees, the once-abandoned, Mediterranean Revival–style building is now financially self-sustaining. Money for maintenance is acquired through moderate room rental fees, membership dues, an endowment fund, and a gift shop called "End of the Line" (with no way to turn around, trains had to back up the entire 30 miles to Fort Myers). Except for two short segments of display track, the rails are gone. NR. [Southwest Heritage, Inc. Museum; banquet and meeting facility.]

OCALA

UNION STATION
North Magnolia Avenue
c. 1917

Referred to as Union Station when it was built, the Ocala combination freight and passenger depot was at the junction of two railroads: the Atlantic Coast Line (track still used by a short line) and the Seaboard Air Line (track now used by CSX Transportation and Amtrak). The corner of the wooden depot has a broad, polygonal tower, which enabled operators to see up and down both main lines. Wooden platform canopies still stretch along each side of the depot, which fits squarely into the intersection of the tracks, known as a "diamond" in railroad jargon. In the early 20th century, Ocala shipped phosphate, livestock, and truck farm vegetables. Warehouses, banks, and other commercial buildings surrounded the station, some of which remain. The city of Ocala would like to acquire the depot for a possible multimodal center. [CSX Transportation, Inc. Train stop—for sale.]

OPA-LOCKA

OPA-LOCKA RAILROAD STATION

325 Ali Baba Avenue
Bernhardt Emil Muller
Harvey and Clarke
1927

In 1993, a week before a clean-up operation was to begin, a serious and suspicious blaze struck the Opa-Locka station, already heavily damaged by a 1982 fire, termites, and trees growing inside. Seven decades earlier, the Moorish fantasy was conceived by New York City architect Bernhardt Muller, and modified by the Florida firm of Harvey and Clarke. Muller was a friend of Glenn H. Curtiss, a pioneer aviator who developed the city and encouraged the Seaboard Air Line to extend its railroad to include Opa-Locka—the first stop between Miami and West Palm Beach. Muller designed 86 buildings for the Opa-Locka

Twin Moorish entranceways at the Opa-Locka station.

Company and considered the depot one of his best. A combination passenger and freight station of reinforced concrete and stucco, it was distinguished by elaborate polychrome tile work, a crenellated parapet, and a pair of small domes. When the first train arrived in Opa-Locka, the community held an Arabian Nights pageant. Subsequently, a popular local pastime was to put on Arabian garb, go down to the depot, and wave to trains passing through. After passenger service ended, the depot served as office space until the first fire, which was followed by a decade of abandonment. In 1995, the Dade Heritage Trust sold the depot; the new owner took over the reins of restoration. Tri-Rail Commuter Rail Authority is building a new station just west of the old depot, which it will assist in restoring. NR. [City of Opa-Locka. Vacant.]

ORLANDO

ATLANTIC COAST LINE STATION

1400 Sligh Boulevard
M. A. Griffith
1927

According to a 1927 newspaper article that appeared when the Atlantic Coast Line station formally opened, the railroad sent architect M. A. Griffith (presumably a staff member) on a predesign trip to the Southwest. His study of various types of Spanish Colonial architecture resulted in the Orlando station's trackside colonnade and massive entranceway flanked by bell towers. The depot was originally racially segregated. Today, the "white" waiting room (used by Amtrak passengers) still has copper chandeliers and a floor of large, terra-cotta tiles. Bent oak slats wrap around the corners of the room to form perimeter benches. In the room's center, back-to-back seating once sandwiched islands of light fixtures that now are gone. The "colored" waiting room is used today for storage. In the 1990s, the Orlando station benefited from a city sponsored beautification program called "Adopt-a-Spot." Organized partly by the

WEST ELEVATION
TRACK SIDE

Atlantic Coast Line (later Seaboard Coast Line) station on Sligh Boulevard in Orlando.

Jaycees, and with both financial and employee help from Amtrak, 1,200 volunteers worked on projects like scraping and painting the depot, refinishing the benches, and installing cabinets and curtains in the rest rooms. [CSX Transportation. Train stop.]

CHURCH STREET STATION
76 West Church Street
c. 1890

In the late 1800s, the South Florida Railroad opened the Orlando area to large-scale development. The population jumped from approximately 200 people in 1880 to 3,000 in 1890. Church Street Station was built by Henry B. Plant, whose system of railroads became part of the Atlantic Coast Line about 1900. The brick and wooden complex consisted of an office and baggage building, a passenger depot, and a freight house. A three-story conical tower, an onion-shaped cupola, and eyebrow dormers were among the architectural features. In the 1970s, with its exterior spruced up, the station was incorporated into a larger entertainment complex. The former main waiting room still has a Gothic Victorian fireplace, exposed beams, and large windows. A light rail system planned for Orlando may include the old Church Street Station as one of its stops. NR. [Privately owned. Retail.]

PENSACOLA

LOUISVILLE & NASHVILLE STATION
239 North Alcaniz Street
1913

The new Louisville & Nashville station was constructed during Pensacola's pre–World War I building boom in anticipation of increased business from the soon-to-open Panama Canal. Replacing a wooden depot on Tarragona Street, the new masonry building consisted of a two-story passenger station and a one-story express wing. Its buff brick first story was accented by mortar tinted to match the terra-cotta trim; the second story was stuccoed. The waiting room was finished in terrazzo, white marble, and oak.

Early view of Church Street Station in Orlando.

Pensacola L&N station c. 1920.

Passenger service to Pensacola was discontinued in 1971 (Amtrak resumed service in 1993, but at another location), and the depot eventually became part of a hotel complex. A tower of rooms was built behind the station. The waiting room and second floor offices were adapted to serve as the hotel's lobby, restaurant, ballroom, and meeting room. An elevated highway ramp now passes in front of the building. NR. [Privately owned. Hotel component.]

TAMPA

UNION STATION
601 North Nebraska Boulevard
J. F. Leitner
1912

In 1911, the Atlantic Coast Line and the Seaboard Air Line formed the Tampa Union Station Company. A year later, the *Tampa Tribune* hailed the station's gala opening as one of the city's premier social events. The Beaux Arts building was designed by J. F. Leitner (possibly on the railroad staff), whose choice of reddish brown brick, terra-cotta, and light-colored stone created a striking contrast in textures and coloration. Inside, the main waiting room was augmented by smoking and retiring rooms, with an abundance of cast bronze, electric light fixtures. Their verd antique finish was duplicated on the interior hardware. Knobs and escutcheons were monogrammed.

By the 1980s, the building—once the hub of West Florida tourist traffic—was in such disre-

Travelers wait for local transportation in front of Tampa Union Station, 1922.

pair that Amtrak relocated to a prefabricated structure placed behind it. Condemned by the city as unfit for use, Union Station was rotting inside from a combination of standing water in the basement and a roof partially collapsed into the lobby. In 1991, an all-volunteer, nonprofit group succeeded in purchasing the depot and a baggage handling building from CSX Transportation. With funding from five sources, including ISTEA, it began rehabilitation two years later. Plans call for Amtrak's reuse of the depot, which will also have rentable commercial space. A future high-speed line from Orlando, now under study, may turn Union Station into a multimodal facility. NR. [Tampa Union Station Preservation and Redevelopment, Inc. Train stop/npa.]

WEST PALM BEACH

SEABOARD AIR LINE STATION
Datura Street and Tamarind Avenue
L. Philips Clarke (Harvey and Clarke)
1925

The firm of Harvey and Clarke designed 35 Seaboard Air Line depots in Florida. The Spanish Baroque passenger station at West Palm Beach received special attention, partly because important stockholders maintained homes nearby. Roofed in red clay tiles, the building had walls clad in structural terra-cotta tile and stucco. Ornamentation came from cast stone and plaster details, such as elaborate acanthus scrolls and medallions.

West Palm Beach Seaboard Air Line station.

Fireplace, north waiting room.

Main streetside entrance, 1972.

Adjacent to the main entrance, a three-story bell tower featured a cast balustrade in front of each arched opening. The platform canopy had a pecky cypress soffit, copper gutters, and a red tile roof. Rising from the quarry tile floor of the waiting room was a palatial fireplace. By the early 1990s, after decades of continuous use as a passenger station, the depot was suffering from a leaking roof and sloppy alterations. The city of West Palm Beach used state grant money to repair the building—the first-ever restoration project for the municipality. The former baggage and express room was converted to a waiting area for passengers traveling on Amtrak and the new commuter line to Miami. The balance of the building will be put to a commercial use, with the tenant participating in the interior restoration. NR. [City of West Palm Beach. Train stop and commercial.]

Georgia

In the 19th century, few of Georgia's antebellum depots survived Sherman's Civil War "March to the Sea." In the next century, neither Terminal Station in Atlanta nor Union Depot in Savannah survived post–World War II "progress." Today an 1869 Georgia Railroad freight depot, reportedly the oldest building in Atlanta's downtown area, is used as a prominent civic meeting space; but it lacks the original upper floor and cupola, which were destroyed in a 1935 fire.

ALBANY

UNION DEPOT
100 Roosevelt Avenue (east end)
1913

A wide brick street with unused trolley tracks extends between Albany's Union Depot (Prairie Style) and the c. World War I express building (Mission style). This street was realigned and paved in 1913 as the approach to the new passenger depot. Albany's first station, constructed in 1857, still stands just north of the express building. Its roof, supported by massive timber trusses, extends into wide, sheltering eaves. After the new station was built, the old one was used from 1913 to 1959 by a wholesale grocer—an early adaptive use. The 1913 Union Depot, which once had a highly popular restaurant in the south pavilion, lost its tile roof, porte-cochere, and dormers in a 1940 tornado. After World War II, five railroads continued to serve Albany; but by 1971, passenger service had ended. Eight years later, a preservation-minded, nonprofit organization purchased the buildings. This complex of brick buildings survived the flood of 1994, although the interior collections were seriously damaged. NR District. [Thronateeska Heritage Foundation. Museum and planetarium.]

ATLANTA

BROOKWOOD STATION
1688 Peachtree Street, N.W. (at Deering Road)
Neel Reid (Hentz, Reid, and Adler)
1918

Originally known as Peachtree Station, the depot at Brookwood was a suburban stop—a convenience for Pullman travelers departing from the immediately surrounding and lovely residential neighborhood. The Southern Railway expected the small depot to relieve a measure of congestion at the downtown Terminal Station (1905; razed in 1972). Today, Brookwood Station is the only passenger depot left in Atlanta. Ironically, the accommodation is inadequate for the current 130,000 Amtrak passengers per year, and the city is considering building a new multimodal terminal on the approximate site of Union Station (1930; razed in 1971). Executed in brick and limestone, Brookwood Station exhibits the fine classical detailing for which Atlanta architect Neel Reid was known. A statue (by Daniel Chester French) of Samuel Spencer, first president of the Southern Railway, was relocated to a small garden at Brookwood after Terminal Station was demolished. The depot is now bordered by an interstate highway in a commercial neighborhood. [Norfolk Southern Corporation. Train stop.]

BARNESVILLE

BARNESVILLE DEPOT
Plaza Way and Main Street
1913

Originally the intersection of two Indian trails, Barnesville became a busy shipping point on one of Georgia's first railroads, the so-called Monroe line, later absorbed by the Central of Georgia. In 1913, after being pressured by the citizenry, CofG built a new brick depot. Designed by the railroad's chief engineer, it replaced a smaller stone structure. Seven years later, when news came that Barnesville was selected as the seat of a newly formed county, citizens congregated at the depot to welcome emissaries who had lobbied on their behalf at the state capital. Passenger service ended in

1971, and two years later the depot's owners (by then the Southern Railway) planned to demolish it. Ever the campaigners, Barnesville residents organized a "Save the Depot" crusade. In the late Seventies, they leased the ground from the Southern's successor, Norfolk Southern, which donated the building. The local historical society's restoration included installation of a new tile roof. NR. [Barnesville–Lamar County Historical Society, Inc. Meeting space.]

COLUMBUS

UNION STATION
1200 Sixth Avenue
Bruce and Morgan
1901

Union Station, also called Sixth Avenue Station, was built by the Central of Georgia. Tenants included several smaller lines that later became part of the Southern Railway and the Seaboard Air Line. The two-story, red brick and granite landmark was designed in a Romanesque Revival style by an Atlanta firm. Eight decades later, it was saved from demolition through the combined efforts of the Historic Columbus Foundation, the Southern Railway, the local government, and thousands of individuals. New owners, Total System Services (a national credit card firm), renewed much of the building's remaining features, including three original fireplaces and one of two ornate fountains. Missing items were duplicated where feasible, such as the pressed tin ceiling of the 34-foot-high waiting room and the E. Howard clock. The owner conscientiously distinguishes real from replica; details of the restoration project are described in a booklet about the station, which the corporation gives to new employees and business guests. NR District. [Privately owned. Corporate headquarters.]

In this early view, horse-drawn vehicles await arrivals at Columbus Union Station.

CONYERS

Conyers Depot

Railroad and Center streets
c. 1891

Conyers was named after a physician who granted the Georgia Railroad a right-of-way through his plantation during the 1840s. The first two depots burned—one in 1855 and the other (by General Sherman) in 1864. The county seat since 1870 and a cotton mill town, Conyers developed in a wedge shape between the courthouse and the railroad. Combining freight and passenger operations, the depot also serviced the three-mile-long Milstead Railroad. The Conyers depot design is attributed to New York architect Bradford Lee Gilbert, who had several commissions in Georgia during the 1890s. Made of wood, it had a two-story center section flanked by one-story wings. After passenger service ended in 1972, the railroad slated the depot for demolition. It was saved when local residents arranged to have the city lease it from the railroad; the Rockdale Historical Society became the sublessee. Among the authentic interior items that have been retained are benches, shoeshine chairs, and freight scales. Outside, a 1920s locomotive known locally as the Milstead Dinky is on display. NR District. [CSX Transportation. Museum and little theater.] (For photo, *see* page 19.)

CRAWFORD

Crawford Depot

U.S. Route 78, in town center
c. 1848

For about five years after the Athens Branch of the Georgia Railroad was completed, horses pulled the trains. The animals were switched every 10 miles, and Crawford was one of the relay stations. On early railroads (especially horse-drawn), rails sometimes rested not on wooden ties, but on granite blocks—readily available in this area. In 1847, the Athens Branch converted to steam. The blocks were not practical under the weight of locomotives and were replaced by wooden ties. According to oral history, the Lithonia granite blocks were reused to build a new Crawford depot. Holes in the two-foot-thick walls indicate where bolts would have joined stones to rails. Today, the depot is essentially intact; although the fireplace is closed up, the freight platform is roofed over, and plywood paneling covers some of the

Crawford depot, August 1976.

Eagles guard the entrance to Macon Terminal Station
c. 1940s.

interior walls. The freight area is used as an auditorium. NR. [Chamber of commerce and community meeting space.]

MACON

TERMINAL STATION
East end of Cherry Street (at 5th Street)
Alfred Fellheimer
1916

In 1913, the Macon chamber of commerce began campaigning for a union station. At that time, the city had 15 railroads (trunk and branch lines) entering the city and four passenger stations. To build the new station, three of the major railroads formed the Macon Terminal Company: Central of Georgia; Southern Railway; and Georgia, Southern & Florida. New tracks and approaches were laid out, but there were construction delays caused by a World War I shortage of steel. New York City architect Alfred Fellheimer created a Beaux Arts design, executed in Indiana limestone with a dark red, cement tile roof. Two blocks long, the depot had an impressive main archway, flanked by Ionic columns. The interior, outfitted with pink Tennessee marble, Tiffany fixtures, and ornamental plaster, had extensive passenger facilities that were racially segregated. All passengers reached the tracks via a pedestrian tunnel called a "subway," also lined with Tennessee marble and wide enough to accommodate seating. The train platforms were sheltered with up-to-date butterfly sheds. After passenger service ended in 1971, the four-story station was nearly demolished for an office and retail complex; the four limestone eagles atop the entrance columns were given away to a private school. In 1977, hoping to find a redevelopment solution, the city bought Terminal Station from the Southern Railway. Five years later, it was acquired by the Georgia Power Company for its headquarters. The four eagles came home to roost. Other historically significant railroad structures in the immediate area include overpasses, trestles, and the Central of Georgia repair complex (1910; endangered). NR District. [Privately owned. Utility company offices, convention bureau, and visitors center.]

RINGGOLD

RINGGOLD RAILROAD STATION
U.S. Route 41
c. 1850

When the railroad came through in the mid-19th century, the town of Cross Roads was renamed Ringgold to honor a Mexican War hero. It soon became the seat of a newly formed county. Built by the state-owned Western & Atlantic Railroad (later Louisville & Nashville), the Ringgold station was the busiest stop between Chattanooga and Atlanta. Wheat was an important export before the advent of mid-western farms. In 1863, following the Civil War Battle of Ringgold, the depot survived Yankee orders to burn the town. Heavily damaged nonetheless—possibly by an explosion—the

depot's native sandstone walls were repaired later with limestone blocks. At some point, the once low-pitched hipped roof was changed to flat.

In the 1980s, after many years of the depot's vacancy, the nonprofit Ringgold Depot Preservation Corporation began the still ongoing process of restoring the building. Its work has included a new roof and extension of the eaves, which the railroad had cut back. The largest part of the depot, the freight section, retains its cast-iron scales, supported by Doric fluted columns and a full entablature. Plans are to make this a rental space, outfitted with a stage and a dance floor, to obtain income for further preservation. Along the same tracks the brick depots at Dalton (1852; NR; now a restaurant) and Calhoun (c. 1853; NR) also survived the war. NR. [City of Ringgold. Community meeting space.]

SAVANNAH

CENTRAL OF GEORGIA STATION
303 Martin Luther King, Jr., Boulevard
1860–76

Railroads brought seemingly endless bales of cotton from the hinterlands to Savannah, which thus became an important 19th-century port city. The Central of Georgia outgrew its Savannah facilities by 1850. Superintendent William M. Wadley, planned a new, integrated complex with not only passenger and freight depots, but also facilities for the construction and repair of locomotives and rolling stock. The Federal-style, red-brick head house was begun before the Civil War, but not completed until 1876. Its stub-end train shed (1861) was designed by German immigrant, Augustus Schwaab, a civil engineer on the railroad staff, who later became a prominent Savannah builder. The shed's trusses were composed of timber, wrought iron, and cast iron—more

Central of Georgia station in Savannah, 1975 drawings.

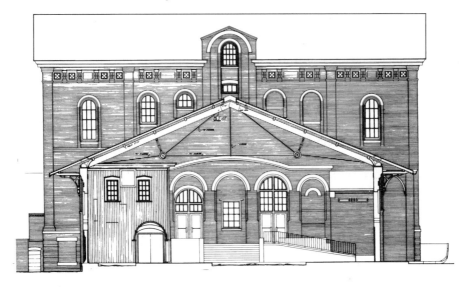

A view through the shed, toward the east wall of the head house. The closed-in wooden section on the left was the commissary. The ramp on the right led to the mail room. Today this ramp provides wheelchair access to the museum.

This elevation shows the south side of the head house and train shed. The iron gates provided direct passenger access to the shed. On the north side of the shed was the yard used for storing raw cotton.

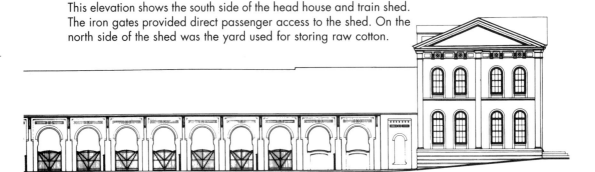

characteristic of European practices than American construction.

In the early 1970s, Amtrak took over passenger service and decided to move its stop to an outlying area. The entire historic station complex reverted back to the city. The head house was converted to a visitors center and offices, with a restaurant in the train shed. In the Nineties, the shed was readapted to become the Savannah History Museum. Other former railroad buildings in the 40-acre site include engineering offices (1856; now used by the Savannah College of Art and Design), freight houses, paint shops, and a roundhouse (open to the public). Perhaps the most extraordinary structure is an ornate, circular water tower with an antebellum privy. NR. NHL. [City of Savannah. Mixed use.]

WINDER

WINDER DEPOT
Broad and Porter streets
1912

Winder was originally a crossroads hamlet called Jug Tavern. In 1893, a year after the first Seaboard Air Line train arrived, citizens petitioned for a name change, to honor John H. Winder, the railroad's general manager. Classified as "Type 7 Standard Plan," the current building was constructed of salmon-colored brick with limestone trim, Palladian windows, and a polychrome tile roof. Deep eaves extended on all four sides. A combination freight and passenger station, it once had a loading platform and a freight dock on the south side. The interior retains the former ticket office and three fireplaces. Freight trains still use the tracks, which are now separated from the depot by a low brick wall. NR. [City of Winder. Chamber of commerce.]

Kentucky

Most of the extant Kentucky depots were built by the Chesapeake & Ohio or the Louisville & Nashville, two of the four railroads that dominated the state. Relatively few remain from the Illinois Central or the Southern Railway. The majority of intact stations are located at county seats.

ASHLAND

CHESAPEAKE & OHIO PASSENGER AND FREIGHT STATIONS
Carter Avenue between 10th and 11th streets
Graham, Anderson, Probst and White
1925

Standing two blocks east of its 1925 successor, Ashland's first Chesapeake & Ohio passenger depot (c. 1900) was a simple but elegant stone building. By the 1920s, steel had brought rapid industrial and population expansion to Ashland. Traveling on a right-of-way known as Railroad Alley, a large number of freight trains crossed the city's streets and continuously interfered with the movement of automobiles and trucks. In 1923, the city and the C&O reached an agreement for a new passenger terminal and a reassignment of routing for freight trains. The 1925 station site consumed more than seven acres. Built in Renaissance Revival style, the new three-story brick depot had racially segregated waiting rooms and a restaurant on the first floor. The newsstand, beloved by children, sold glass locomotives filled with jelly beans. Division offices occupied the upper floors. Passenger operations ceased in 1975 when Amtrak relocated to a new station five miles east of Ashland. Two years later, conversion of the old depot into a financial institution began. The general waiting room with its 25-foot-high vaulted ceiling became the main banking area. Although the tracks were removed, two platform canopies were restructured as covered parking areas. An old passenger car now serves as the bank's board room.

A few blocks north of the passenger depot, the former C&O brick freight station stands along the riverfront at 15th Street. About 1990, the city acquired the building from CSX Transportation (C&O's successor). ISTEA funds awarded in 1993 will enable the city to reconfigure the vacant freight depot into a transportation center. The municipal bus system will be headquartered here and possibly intercity buses, as well. Amtrak intends to relocate its passenger stop to this location, thus creating one of the few times in railroad history that a freight station has been converted to passenger service (the reverse being quite common). [Passenger station, privately owned. Bank.] [Freight station, city owned. Vacant—future transportation center.]

BOWLING GREEN

BOWLING GREEN RAILROAD STATION
Kentucky Street and 4th Avenue
1925

Several blocks north of its preceding station, the Louisville & Nashville built a large, Classical Revival depot of native Bowling Green stone. An asphalt driveway looped between Station Park and the entranceway. Formally treated with a set of two-story-high Ionic columns, the streetside facade displayed a series of tall arched windows and a pedimented, tile roof. When the first train rolled in, about 600 people were waiting to celebrate. Numerous speeches were followed with dancing to music by the Crystal Theatre Orchestra. Visitors inspected the general waiting room (with tiled floor and wainscoting), the dining room, and the ladies' retiring room (replete with settees and an iron crib). A covered platform extended from the depot's track side; a butterfly shed sheltered people waiting on the other side of the tracks. Passenger service ended in 1979. More than a decade later, after passing through several hands, the frequently vandalized building was purchased by a non-

profit organization, whose goal was initially to prevent demolition and ultimately to find a permanent user. [Operation Pride. Vacant.]

COVINGTON

COVINGTON RAILROAD STATION
Pike and Russell streets
1922

Between 1900 and 1910, the increasing number of trains crossing Covington's streets caused inefficient railroad operations and hazardous conditions. Construction of a new depot (the old one was at 8th and Russell) began prior to final plans for grade separation. As a consequence, the Louisville & Nashville designed the depot to accommodate both the old grade-level tracks and the future raised rails. The entire depot and grade separation project, not completed until 1929, was supervised by the Chesapeake & Ohio, which shared the station. The red brick Georgian Revival building had segregated waiting rooms at street level, with stairs and elevators rising to the elevated tracks. The high-ceilinged central portion was flanked by two-story wings. When the current owner obtained the building in the late 1980s, it had been abandoned for two decades. The roof had collapsed,

Covington station c. 1938.

Landscaping enhanced Henderson Union Station.

pigeons were homesteading, and the ticket booth was gone. One back-to-back bench remained. The depot was restored using rehabilitation tax credits. Work included repairing the metal entrance canopy and moving red clay roof tiles from the back of the building to the front and sides, to preserve the visible areas. [Privately owned. Commercial.]

HENDERSON

UNION STATION
East 4th and Clark streets
1901

The bulldozer was already on the premises in 1980, when the local historical society rescued Union Station, also commonly known as the L&N (Louisville & Nashville) Depot. The historical society was able to buy the building for $1 from the railroad, but not the land it sat upon. That acquisition followed in a few years when a local couple bought the ground and donated it to the historical society.

Union Station was originally built and owned by the L&N, but also used by the Louisville, Henderson & St. Louis (later absorbed by L&N), and the Illinois Central. A single-story, cut stone and red brick structure, the depot had an elaborate entrance. Passengers walked first through an iron portecochere to a rounded stone archway, resting on red marble columns with foliated capitals. Rising from this entrance was a tall campanile, capped by a hipped roof and ornate finial. The depot's roof was slate; the wide eaves were supported by curvilinear wooden brackets. Richly embellished with marble and classical moldings, the interior had three waiting rooms: general (which essentially meant white men), white women (with semicircular bay window, fireplace, and rocking chairs), and unisex "colored." Outside, a long freestanding canopy sheltered the platform, running between the tracks and the landscaped, parklike grounds.

After passenger service ended in 1971, the depot was used by the L&N for crew training and offices, until the building was literally condemned by the city. Neglect compounded by vandalism had taken its toll on tile floors, marble wainscoting, and stained glass windows (some of which were reportedly removed for storage in Louisville, but have never reappeared). The historical society—using unpaid labor from the general community, a vocational school, and the district court's community service program—has now made enough headway in the depot's restoration to move its office into the building. It intends to eventually add a research center, museum, and special events facility. NR. [Henderson County Genealogical and Historical Society. Office and largely vacant.]

HOPKINSVILLE

LOUISVILLE & NASHVILLE STATION
425 East 9th Street
1892

After an earlier depot burned, the Louisville & Nashville built a new Hopkinsville station, with a slate roof and delicate ridge cresting. Contemporary newspapers described the style as Swiss Gothic. The body of the depot was sheathed in horizontal and vertical ornamental boarding. Friezes comprising paneled squares decorated both the circular agent's office and

the octagonal, ogee-curved tower. Gabled hoods ventilated the attic space. Adding a Queen Anne flavor, small, stained glass panes bordered the upper window sash and the glass door panels. In 1909, an addition was built at the south end for the American Express Company; and the entire depot was stuccoed to create what was considered a more imposing appearance.

Among the famous people who arrived at the Hopkinsville station were Buffalo Bill Cody, Carrie Nation, John Philip Sousa and his band, Booker T. Washington, William Jennings Bryan, Captain Eddie Rickenbacker, and Ethel Barrymore. Located north of Fort Campbell, Hopkinsville was at its busiest during World War II, when troop strength ran as high as 100,000 soldiers. After passenger service ended in 1971, the depot remained in freight railroad use, until acquired by the city in the early Eighties. The interior was restored essentially to its 1909 appearance, retaining the three ticket windows that opened into the general, ladies', and "colored" waiting rooms. Outside, the 1909 wooden platform canopy, which interfered with the passage of modern freight cars, was removed. A brick freight depot (1905) still stands across the tracks, well maintained by its private owners. NR. [City of Hopkinsville. Civic offices.]

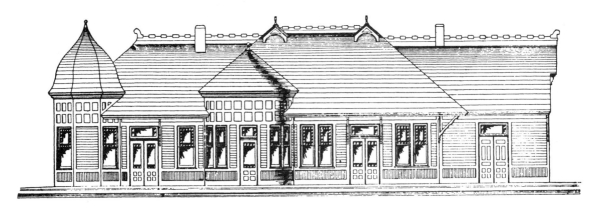

Trackside elevation of the Hopkinsville L&N station.

LOUISVILLE

Union Station

Broadway between 10th and 11th streets
F. W. Mowbray
1891, 1905

Owned exclusively by the Louisville & Nashville, Union Station was used by three other railroads: the Pennsylvania; the Louisville, Henderson & St. Louis; and the Chicago, Indianapolis & Louisville (the "Monon Route"). A stub-end terminal, it was part of a complex that included L&N's general office building. (L&N's later office building, constructed in 1907 and 1930, is still standing.) The architect, F. W. Mowbray, emigrated at age 24 from England to Philadelphia, where he worked on designs for the 1876 Centennial Exposition. Following a move to New York, he associated with various railroads and later went into private practice. He was chief architect for L&N at the time of Union Station's completion.

Union Station had massive brick walls clad in limestone with a tower at each corner. One tower was five stories high with four clock faces and miniature dormers. Both the north and south facades contained art-glass rose windows, 20 feet in diameter. The barrel-vaulted waiting room reached the full height of the building, three stories plus mansard roof. A month after the grand opening, Sarah Bernhardt agreed to try her famous voice in the cavernous space, where her dramatic rendition bounced (displeasingly) off Tennessee marble wainscoting and the wrought-iron balcony railing. In 1905, a sweeping fire broke out in the northwest tower. The featured sound in that event was the stained glass skylight crashing to the mosaic tile floor. Most of the interior was rebuilt in an amazing five months — including the timber structural system — using original plans and specifications. The depot's train shed, believed to be the work of noted engineer Albert Fink, had clerestory windows and stained glass in the gabled end. Nearly all of the shed was demolished in 1973; passenger service ended three

Louisville Union Station c. 1940.

years later. In 1978, the L&N sold the station to the city. NR. [Transit Authority of River City. Offices.]

MAYSVILLE

Chesapeake & Ohio Station

End of Rosemary Clooney Boulevard
1918

The Maysville Chesapeake & Ohio station exhibits a number of refined features typical of the Colonial Revival style: red brick laid in Flemish bond, brick quoins at each corner, a pedimented entrance porch, Tuscan and Ionic columns, a cornice with egg-and-dart molding, tripartite windows, keystoned lintels, and a corbeled chimney stack. A matching, former express and baggage structure stands to the west. The depot retains a portion of its wide platform canopy, supported by double columns. The platform itself once extended far down the track to accommodate long, main line trains. A twin depot at Pikeville (1924; now city hall) stood on a C&O branch line, thus requiring

Maysville exhibits the Colonial Revival style typical of the C&O.

only a short platform. Maysville was also served by the Louisville & Nashville. [CSX Transportation. Train stop.]

OWENSBORO

UNION STATION
1035 Frederica Street
John Bacon Hutchings and Henry Franklin
    Hawes
1906

About 1900, three railroads served Owensboro: Louisville & Nashville; Louisville, Henderson & St. Louis; and Illinois Central. City and state leaders began to pressure the trio to build a union station. Three depots were inconvenient for travelers making transfers and for the various express companies, as well as the Owensboro post office that had to meet all trains bearing mail cars. L&N handled construction of a new one-story, jointly used building, which had 16-inch-thick brick walls above a limestone base. Separated from the street by a small park, the depot beckoned passengers down a granite walkway and through a broad, gabled entrance. The floor plan resembled that of the Hopkinsville station, which had a baggage room, ticket office, and general, "colored," and ladies' waiting rooms. A steeply pitched roof flowed into polygonal north and south bays, lit by arched windows. Apparently the exterior was designed by independent architects and the interior by L&N staff members.

In the early 1930s, L&N built a long, perpendicular two-story addition to handle increasing freight traffic. By 1958, all passenger service was discontinued. Over the next two decades, when not vacant, the depot served intermittently as a railroad office, pizza parlor, and discotheque. With sensitivity to original materials and partitions, a real estate firm renovated the interior space in 1982. On the outside, craftspeople repointed the masonry and installed a new clay tile roof. NR. [Privately owned. Offices—for sale.]

PARIS

PARIS DEPOT
Winchester Street at 10th Street
1882

The Paris depot was a modified version of a Louisville & Nashville standard plan. Also used by the Frankfort & Cincinnati, the one-story passenger station had a waiting room, ticket office, and baggage room. A terne metal roof with wooden cresting surmounted walls clad in both horizontal shiplap and vertical boards. A covered platform, three times the length of the depot, extended down the track. The street side bordered a small park. In the late 1970s, CSX Transportation leased the depot to the city, which used it for a senior center. The following decade, a restaurant subleased the space. The brick freight house, once a shipping site for hemp, bluegrass seed, and valuable racehorses, stands to the north. A mile away to the southeast, the former L&N roundhouse is used today by a short line. NR. [CSX Transportation. Restaurant.]

Louisiana

Louisiana railroad construction did not begin in earnest until the 1880s. The rice and lumber booms—so important to Louisiana's economy—were made possible by a well-developed network of tracks. About 50 depots are believed to survive in Louisiana; most are post–World War I.

ARCADIA

ARCADIA RAILROAD DEPOT
800 block of North Railroad Avenue
1910

In the early 1980s, after watching the vacant Arcadia depot grow more derelict by the day, an Arcadia resident convinced the city to buy it from the Illinois Central Railroad. Built by the Vicksburg, Shreveport & Pacific, the board and batten station had a freight room with exposed roof trusses, a ticket office, and racially segregated waiting rooms with beaded board walls. A wide canopy still extends around all four sides of the building. The loading dock was recently rebuilt (its railing is a modern concession to visitors' safety.) NR. [Town of Arcadia. Museum.]

BATON ROUGE

YAZOO & MISSISSIPPI VALLEY DEPOT
100 South River Road
1925

The Baton Rouge Yazoo & Mississippi Valley depot (Illinois Central system) saw its last passenger trains in the late 1960s, upon departure of tenant railroad Missouri Pacific. Set between the Old State Capitol and the Mississippi River, the brick depot is fronted by 10 classical columns and capped by a frieze incised with the original railroad's name. Converted by the city to the Louisiana Arts and Science Center Riverside in 1976, the building's new use triggered Baton Rouge's waterfront revitalization. Preserved in the process were the depot's terrazzo floors and wainscoting, as well as doors, windows, and woodwork. To increase space, new wings were built and the train platform enclosed. The west wall of the depot is now an interior wall of a two-story art gallery, built over the old passenger tracks. The former express office is an auditorium, and the two waiting rooms contain hands-on exhibits for children. Displays include a model train layout and a full-size steam locomotive with four cars. The freight tracks are still active. NR.[City of Baton Rouge. Museum.]

DEQUINCY

KANSAS CITY SOUTHERN DEPOT
Lake Charles Avenue
1923

In the 1920s, the Kansas City Southern remodeled or replaced several facilities in western Louisiana. Its choice for stylistic upgrade was Spanish Colonial Revival, used most purely at the new depot in DeQuincy. The KCS line forked at the station, with the main line heading toward Texas and a spur line going to Lake Charles. Tracks passed the

DeQuincy KCS depot, 1930s.

depot on both the north and south sides (as they still do today). The building was brick at its base (to windowsill height) with stuccoed wooden lath above. Laid out in a cruciform plan, the depot had a two-story center section with curvilinear parapets. During World War II, a dispatcher eyed the tracks from the round-arched windows of the upper floor, reached only by an exterior stairway. Flanking the ticket office, one-story wings held a "colored" waiting room and baggage area on the west end with a high-ceilinged "white" waiting room on the east. Interior finishes included tile floors, brick wainscoting, and plaster walls. Several wood-burning stoves provided the original heat source. An open-air waiting room with built-in concrete benches was the social center of the community. In 1974, KCS conveyed the depot to the city. Preservation and management have been handled since then by the DeQuincy Railroad Museum, which installed a new red tile roof in the early Nineties. NR. [City of DeQuincy. Museum, special events facility, and chamber of commerce.]

HAMMOND

HAMMOND RAILROAD DEPOT
Northwest Railroad Avenue
J. A. Taggart
1912

In the late 1800s, a cooperative effort between a land company and the Illinois Central Railroad brought many midwestern families to Hammond. The town soon prospered when it began growing a hardy variety of strawberries that could survive long-distance shipment by rail. As wealth increased, wooden commercial structures were replaced with brick. Hammond's new combination freight and passenger depot was designed by J. A. Taggart of the railroad staff. A herringbone-pattern brick platform led to segregated waiting and lunch rooms with cypress ceilings, maple floors, and pine fixtures. An iron finial crowned the Queen Anne–style, polygonal turret which surmounted the tile roof.

In 1989, the chamber of commerce purchased the depot; the north end will eventu-

Hammond depot, June 1969.

ally become its home. When a local party donated the land beneath the depot in 1995, the building's future was secured. Amtrak occupies the original waiting room, and the local "clerk of court" uses the former restaurant section. Four blocks south stands the predecessor depot. Relocated and converted to freight-only in 1912, that building (now a flea market) retains its huge old scales. NR District. [Privately owned. Train stop and offices.]

NATCHITOCHES

NATCHITOCHES RAILROAD DEPOT
6th Street (near Church Street)
1926

Reminiscent of a 16th-century northern Italian villa, Natchitoches's Texas & Pacific depot consists of a two-story main block flanked by extended one-story wings. A small arcaded loggia joins twin square towers. Ornamenting

Street side of Natchitoches depot, nearing end of construction.

the building are Persian columns, an elaborate parapet, and multicolor glazed terra-cotta in various designs. The roof was originally red tile. Passenger service ended in the 1960s. The city, which serves as the parish seat, would like to convert the depot to a black cultural museum. A predecessor T&P depot, two blocks east, has become city hall. NR. [City of Natchitoches. Vacant.]

ZACHARY

ZACHARY RAILROAD DEPOT
4434 West Central Avenue
1885, 1918, 1926

The railroad created the town of Zachary and remained the focal point of its development until the 1940s. The town was named for a man who owned a farm through which the Louisville, New Orleans & Texas passed. About 1883, in a barter with the railroad, Darel Zachary gave it a strip of land, 50 feet wide by 650 feet long, in exchange for the eponymous honor. The original depot was a modest board and batten structure. In two remodelings, the railroad (acquired by the Yazoo & Mississippi Valley) doubled the building's length, added a bay window, and covered the exterior with clapboards and beaded boards. After passenger service ended in 1950, the depot remained in freight and other railroad use for three decades. In 1983, a former Zachary postmaster —who remembered the mail being carted in a wheelbarrow from the station to the post office —bought the depot and its land from the Illinois Central Gulf Railroad. Earning rehabilitation tax credits, he restored the station, now painted yellow (a color used at some earlier point). A tenant was obtained not only for the depot, but also for the 1945 caboose (now a beauty parlor) that the owner placed on the property. The signal mast remains along the track, which is still plied by freight trains. NR. [Privately owned. Office.]

Mississippi

Consolidating several southern railroad lines in the 1870s, the Illinois Central dominated Mississippi, especially in a north-south direction. Most Mississippi stations were standard designs built of wood, located in very small towns. Not many remain.

ABERDEEN

ABERDEEN DEPOT
West Commerce and Matubba streets
c. 1869

After the Civil War, the community of Aberdeen contracted with the Mobile & Ohio to run a branch line into its town. The two-story depot, which probably dates from that time, is flanked by one-story wings. A rear appendage from the late 19th century was once accompanied by a platform. Sheathed mostly in clapboards, the essentially Italianate station, with segmental-arched windows, has Stick Style elements in the gables. The building is in poor condition, marred by installation of corrugated-metal sliding doors and the removal of interior partitions dating from when it was used to store farm equipment. For years people referred to this as a barn, unaware that it was originally a station. The tracks are gone. In 1982, because of the high cost of demolition, the Mississippi antiquities law, and pressure from the local historical society, the depot escaped destruction by the city. It remains at risk. NR. [City of Aberdeen. Storage.]

BAY ST. LOUIS

BAY ST. LOUIS RAILROAD STATION
303 South Railroad Avenue
1929

Bounded on three sides by water, Bay St. Louis became a popular tourist destination, aided by the railroad's arrival in 1872. The current two-story Mission-style station, built by the Louisville & Nashville, replaced a wooden one that burned. Division offices were on the second floor. After L&N passenger service ceased in 1964, the depot functioned as freight offices. In 1993, when Amtrak extended the *Sunset Limited* route through Mississippi, the station

was resurrected as a passenger stop. The city purchased the land from CSX Transportation, which then donated the depot in exchange for a new building. After receiving funding (primarily ISTEA) for rehabilitation and for improving the station grounds, the city enlisted the help of volunteers to restore the original garden plan and establish a walking trail into the historic downtown area. The depot will not only serve passengers, but also provide space for commercial and educational needs. NR District. [City of Bay St. Louis. Train stop and future mixed use.]

HOLLY SPRINGS

MISSISSIPPI CENTRAL DEPOT
540 East Van Dorn Avenue
1858, 1886

A Civil War survivor, the Holly Springs Mississippi Central depot was enlarged on the east side in 1886. The steep roof, with many hipped dormers and both tent-roof and pyra-

Mississippi Central depot in Holly Springs, from the *Biographical and Historical Memoirs of Mississippi*, published in 1891.

midal-roof towers, contributed a Chateauesque flavor to the elegant brick station-hotel. Interior spaces included waiting rooms (segregated by race and gender) and 20 guest rooms. A French chef from New Orleans prepared wild game for the 125-seat dining room–ballroom, where locals came to dance on Saturday night. Until 1926, the depot also served the St. Louis & San Francisco (which departed to a new station). After the railroad stopped running the hotel, it leased the building to a succession of independent operators. Then in the late 1940s, a new owner installed a cage-making factory on the first floor and his family upstairs (his descendants still reside in the depot). The northwest and southwest wings were joined via an added roof and wall to form a courtyard. Standing to the north and still in railroad use is a brick freight depot, once part of a larger complex that included a roundhouse and machine shops. NR District. [Privately owned. Residence.]

JACKSON

ILLINOIS CENTRAL STATION
300 West Capitol Street
c. 1927

Jackson was once served by seven railroads, three of which were transcontinental trunk lines. One of these, the Illinois Central, completed a tremendous track elevation project in the mid-1920s. As a consequence, it built a new, two-story brick station in Renaissance Revival style with classical ornamentation executed in concrete. Amtrak still uses the original waiting room. Trains arrive at the upper level, past a one-story wing to the west. Across the street stands the elegant Edwards Hotel (1923). Twelve stories high and very popular in railroading's heyday, the hotel has been vacant for decades and is now owned by the city redevelopment authority. NR District. [Illinois Central Railroad. Train stop and freight railroad offices.]

Jackson IC station c. 1936.

NEW ORLEANS GREAT NORTHERN DEPOT
618 East Pearl Street
1927

Known for the first 13 years of its life as the NOGN (New Orleans Great Northern) depot, this facility was actually built as a union passenger station. It also served the Gulf, Mobile & Northern, and the two railroads built a joint freight depot as well. After a few railroad acquisitions and a 1940 merger occurred, the station found itself with a new name, the Gulf, Mobile & Ohio (later Illinois Central Gulf). In 1939, the rather prosaic, red brick depot was remodeled to coordinate with the famous *Rebel* train, which had been inaugurated in 1935. The *Rebel* was the first streamlined, diesel-powered passenger train in the south. On the station's exterior, workers removed decorative metal brackets from under the deep eaves and converted two square brick pillars facing Pearl Street to round columns. On the inside, the depot received glass block transoms and chrome door hardware for the "white" waiting room and a new curved wall for the ticket office (currently a rest room). A victim of the nationwide, post–World War II decline in rail traffic, the depot stopped serving passengers in 1954 —only 15 years after the remodeling. The state of Mississippi bought the building in 1981 and adapted it as state historic preservation offices. To re-create a 1939 look, the Mississippi Department of Archives and History painted the interior three shades of blue on the first floor, with a red pinstripe on the chair rail, and used a peach and maroon combination on the second floor. The exterior columns are painted in bands of red, silver, and gray—a 1939 scheme, chosen originally to complement the colors of the *Rebel.* NR listing pending. [State of Mississippi. Offices.]

LAKE

LAKE DEPOT
Brooks Street between Church
    and Wilkins streets
c. 1890

Belonging to the Southern Railroad of Mississippi, the first Lake depot (plus the turntable, roundhouse, water tank, and machine shop) were destroyed during the Civil War. A century later, the current building (probably constructed by the Alabama & Vicksburg) was closed and likewise on its way to destruction. It was initially saved by a local woman, who pur-

chased the depot from the Illinois Central in 1971. The railroad gave her 90 days to remove the three-room station, which was subsequently "stored" for 13 years on a property near the tracks. In 1980, it was donated to the citizens of Lake, who moved the depot to the present location, 150 feet south of the original site. With cookbook sales and auctions, the Rose Garden Club has raised and spent about $30,000 restoring the Queen Anne–style, wooden station. Multiple layers and different textures of wood, small-paned windows, ornate milled brackets, and fancy cutwork are among the building's finer details. An identical depot stood at Hickory (razed c. 1970). NR. [Town of Lake. Community meeting rooms and museum.]

NATCHEZ

YAZOO & MISSISSIPPI VALLEY DEPOT
200 Broadway
c. 1910

Poised on a bluff above the Mississippi River, the former Yazoo & Mississippi Valley depot has a narrow, covered promenade across the

Lake depot on its original site.

A train coming through the unpaved streets of Natchez to the Y&MV depot.

full streetside elevation. This open-air space gives a Mediterranean flavor to an essentially English Cottage–style building. The depot's gray brick walls, with a half-timbered effect, are topped by a red, ceramic tile roof. The former station became a restaurant in the 1970s. The following decade, another Natchez depot, known as Canal Street Station (Mississippi Central), was converted to commercial use, with the help of rehabilitation tax credits. [City of Natchez. Restaurant.]

VICKSBURG

VICKSBURG RAILROAD STATION
500 Grove Street (at Levee Street)
D. H. Burnham and Company
1907

The original, large wooden depot at Vicksburg overlooked the Yazoo River Diversion Canal, which branched off from the Mississippi River. When the canal overflowed slightly, the tracks

At the Vicksburg station, February 1917, a midwinter vacation party for IC employees.

went under water. (This situation continued until 1924, when a sea wall was built.) The first depot was replaced by a Georgian Revival station, one-half block north, constructed by the Yazoo & Mississippi Valley (Illinois Central system). D. H. Burnham and Company of Chicago designed a very formal, red brick station, with a steeply pitched gambrel roof, gable dormers, and a prominent wooden campanile. On the street side, a central freestanding portico with a balustrade was supported by two-story-high Tuscan columns. Similar columns upheld the circular, one-story south portico that was reached via French doors from the "white" waiting room. Identical chimney mantelpieces decorated the fireplaces in each of the segregated waiting rooms. Railroad offices occupied the second floor.

Also known as the Levee Street Station, the depot said good-by to its last passenger train about 1950. After the Illinois Central Gulf (a 1972 merger) sold the station in the late Seventies, it was converted to a restaurant and commercial space. In a more recent adaptation, it became a dialysis treatment center with apartments above. Most of the architectural features remain. Long, sheltered platforms once extended down both the inbound and outbound side of the tracks, which are still used by freight trains. NR. [Privately owned. Mixed use.]

North Carolina

Early depots in North Carolina's small towns were typically made of wood; most all had to be rebuilt after the Civil War. In the late 19th and early 20th centuries, when the tobacco, cotton-growing, textile, and furniture industries flourished, masonry stations began replacing frame ones, especially in the increasingly urban areas. In the western mountain resorts, the railroads built stations to accommodate and impress the tourist trade. Today virtually all of North Carolina's midsize, metropolitan stations have been demolished or heavily altered. In contrast, the state department of transportation, with the help of ISTEA funds, has decided to refurbish the passenger stations that remain in active use.

APEX

UNION DEPOT
220 North Salem Street (at Center Street)
c. 1915

Known as Log Pond before the tracks arrived, Apex was renamed apparently for being the highest elevation on the railroad. After a c. 1913 fire destroyed the original wooden depot, the Seaboard Air Line designed a new brick passenger station to be shared with the Durham & Southern Railway. Trimmed in brown sand-stone and roofed with metal shingles, the depot had segmental arches above its windows and doors. The trackside agent's bay broke through the belcast hipped roof to form a dormer, lit by diamond-paned, Queen Anne–style casements. The "white" and "colored" waiting rooms and the ladies' lounge featured fireplaces with paneled overmantels of neoclassical design. About 1970, a decade after passenger service ended, the town acquired Union Depot and converted it to a library (CSX Transportation holds title to the land). Because construction of a regional library is planned for the 1990s, a new use will have to be found for the old depot. Freight trains still travel the tracks. NR. [Town of Apex. Library—soon to be vacated.]

ASHEVILLE

BILTMORE RAILROAD STATION
One Biltmore Plaza
Richard Morris Hunt
1896

Biltmore Station was one of four structures designed by Richard Morris Hunt for George Vanderbilt's medieval-style village near the famous Biltmore Estate. (George was the grandson of railroad magnate Cornelius Vanderbilt.) Located both in a mountain resort area and at the junction of two Southern Railway lines, the one-story passenger depot was clad in decorative half-timbering and pebbledash stucco above a brick water table. The low hipped roof extended into wide eaves and a central porte-cochere. Inside, the ticket office separated two waiting rooms. The west end was the baggage area. Diamond-shaped window panes and a prominent fireplace reinforced the Tudor Revival flavor. Biltmore's freight station stood across the tracks. In 1968, the town's other passenger stop, called Asheville Station (on Depot Street) closed; the Biltmore stop was renamed "Asheville." Although, regular passenger service ended in 1975, freight trains still travel the tracks. A roundhouse, in active use, stands about one mile to the west on Meadow Road. NR District. [Privately owned. Restaurant.]

BURLINGTON

BURLINGTON DEPOT
200 South Main Street
1905, 1921

Picking up and relocating depots was a common occurrence, usually involving frame buildings. The brick station in Burlington (successor to a wooden depot that burned) has been moved twice. The first move occurred in the early 1920s, when the Southern Railway (which leased trackage and real estate from the North Carolina Railroad) eliminated a grade crossing. After moving the depot to a site just west of Main Street, it enlarged the station to include a ladies' retiring room, baggage room, and express office. SR passenger service to Burlington ended in 1968, but was reinstated in 1971 by Amtrak.

In the late Seventies, the NCRR donated the depot to the city, but insisted on its removal from the right-of-way. At its new location about one block from the tracks, the depot became the focal point of a revitalized downtown area. The Elizabethan Revival turret above the former agent's bay window now faces the street. Used for offices, classes, meetings, exhibits, and special events, the depot was restored from its foundation to the tip of its weather vane. Two early brick buildings of the North Carolina Railroad—a foundry (1858) and an enginehouse (1870)—still stand across the tracks from the depot's original site on North Main Street. The state department of transportation is considering recycling the old enginehouse into a station for Amtrak trains, which currently stop at a plastic shelter—plopped on the brick depot's second location. NR. [City of Burlington. Mixed use.]

FAYETTEVILLE

ATLANTIC COAST LINE STATION
472 Hay Street (at Hillsborough Street)
1911

The rail yard near Fayetteville's Atlantic Coast Line station once included a freight depot, a turntable, and tool and bunkhouses. The Dutch Colonial Revival passenger station was built of red brick laid in Flemish bond with a gambrel roof. Original blueprints show a streetside entrance sheltered by a glass and metal canopy. Above the door, the transom was filled with a double union jack motif, repeated (along with cannonballs) on a balustrade above the two-story agent's bay. In the early 1990s, the city completed a total rehabilitation of the exterior, including a new slate roof. The next stage, interior renovation, may bring forth an adaptive use for space not occupied by Amtrak. Three blocks southeast on Maxwell Street stands a c. 1890 Romanesque Revival station (NR) of the Cape Fear & Yadkin Valley Railway. Available for rescue (for sale by the city), the CF&YV depot is currently a warehouse, following its previous use as a horse barn. NR. [City of Fayetteville. Train stop and partly vacant.]

GREENSBORO

SOUTHERN RAILWAY STATION
East Washington Street (at Church Street)
Fellheimer and Wagner
1927

Ten thousand people (nearly one-fourth of the city's population) walked through Greensboro's new station on opening day in April 1927. Constructed by the Southern Railway, this union depot was also used by the Atlantic & Yadkin. The preceding station on South Elm Street, constructed in 1899 (and still standing), was converted after a 1927 fire into division offices. Besides a larger building, site improvements at the new station included long butterfly-canopied platforms (now gone) and the elimination of two grade crossings. The porticoed "white people's" entrance to the red-brick head house had 26-foot-high limestone Ionic columns. With a lighted map of the Southern Railway system at one end, the station's concourse was flanked by racially segregated waiting and dining rooms. Other amenities included a drug store, newsstand, and barber shop. Baggage and mail were handled from an annex; express, from a separate building. New York architects Fellheimer and Wagner also designed the similarly styled, but smaller scale, Union Station at Winston-Salem (1926), which is now an automobile repair shop.

In 1979, after the Southern Railway built a new station (with space for Amtrak in one end) a few miles west of Greensboro, it donated the old depot to the city. The municipality then leased the building to Friends of the Depot, which stabilized the structure and kept it occupied while seeking a permanent adaptive use. These efforts bore fruition. In 1993, the city began planning a new multimodal center reusing the station. [City of Greensboro. Special events facility, model railroad museum, and future transportation center.]

Greensboro SR station nearing completion c. 1927.

Hamlet station. In the background is the railroad-owned SAL Hotel (now gone).

HAMLET

HAMLET RAILROAD STATION
Two Main Street, south of U.S. Route 74
1900

The Hamlet station was an important junction for the Seaboard Air Line — a major connecting point between northeastern states and the deep south. Its two-story, frame structure formed an L shape, fitting into one quadrant of the right-angle intersection. The "legs" of the station were of unequal length. A large, round pavilion at the corner contained the waiting room; the second floor housed division offices. The pavilion's "witch's hat" roof had a brim supported by triangular braces. An even wider overhang skirted the semicircular first floor and then stretched down the tracks. In 1944, a year when many World War II troops passed through the station, the depot was enlarged with a brick, two-story wing. Today most of the passengers are guests headed for nearby resorts. Selma Union Station was another North Carolina junction depot (Atlantic Coast Line and Southern Railway) which — like Hamlet — faced a track intersection. Abandoned in the 1960s, Selma was renovated upon Amtrak's return in the Eighties. NR. [CSX Transportation. Train stop and railroad museum.]

HENDERSONVILLE

HENDERSONVILLE DEPOT
7th Avenue and Maple Street
c. 1903, c. 1915

When the Spartanburg & Asheville (later the Southern Railway) arrived from South Carolina in 1879, Hendersonville was transformed from a turnpike town to a railroad town. Middle-class tourism followed, as still-standing boarding houses and the c. 1915 Station Hotel testify. The community's early 20th-century wooden depot with a hipped roof and deeply splayed eaves was enlarged about 1915. Just a half-century later (1968), passenger service to this county seat in the Blue Ridge Mountains ended. The depot's dormers and platform canopies were subsequently removed. In 1988, total demolition was prevented when the city and a group of citizens negotiated an arrangement with Norfolk Southern (Southern Railway's successor). The railroad agreed to lease the land and donate the building. Restoration is an ongoing project, using contributed materials, volunteer labor, and occasionally the community service of convicted traffic-law violators. The station is painted a version of standard Southern Railway colors: dark green, harvest gold, and cream. The freight area has a large model railroad display; additional uses for the building have not been decided on. More than two dozen brick commercial buildings, dating from the late 19th century, fan out from the depot, which has a block of original brick street paving beside it. NR District. [City of Hendersonville. Partially vacant.]

HIGH POINT

HIGH POINT RAILROAD STATION
100 West High Avenue (at Main Street)
1907

High Point was the highest point surveyed on the old North Carolina Railroad. In 1895, NCRR granted a 99-year operating lease to the Southern Railway, which built a replacement station in High Point right where the tracks crossed the old Western and Fayetteville Plank Road (now Main Street). Of stone and brick, with an orange-red tile roof, the depot had very deep eaves, exaggerating its actual size. The building was originally level with the tracks, which were depressed through town in the late 1930s. A baggage elevator and overhead walkway were added at that time.

Most of the depot was used for a restaurant in the 1970s and early 1980s, followed by years of vacancy, vagrants, and vandalism. (Amtrak's two trains stopped between 1 and 3 a.m.) In late 1990, the Amtrak caretaker decided it was time to turn the building's fate around. By personally forging a coalition between the High Point Preservation Society and state and city officials (the city obtained a long-term lease from NCRR), he spearheaded a successful bid for ISTEA funds. They will be used to restore the depot's early appearance, including original paint colors, and to re-extend the truncated, track level platform canopy. The freight house (later used as an express building) that stood across the tracks was demolished in the 1970s. Another High Point freight station, built by the High Point, Randelman, Asheboro & Southern, is used today by a freight forwarding operation on Depot Place. [North Carolina Railroad. Train stop and community meeting space.]

RALEIGH

SEABOARD AIR LINE STATION
707 Semart Drive
1942

Up until 1942, Seaboard Air Line passenger trains stopped at Raleigh Union Station (standing today, but heavily altered), which was also used by the Southern Railway and the old Norfolk Southern (a predecessor of the modern corporation by the same name). The position of

High Point station when the tracks were still at depot level.

Union Station, sited at the end of a 1,400-foot Seaboard spur, forced both north and south-bound trains to make a time-consuming backing-up movement. Moreover, World War II–era trains were so long that while in the station, they projected past a crossover and blocked one (or both) main line tracks. Seaboard therefore decided to build itself a separate passenger station, adjacent to the main line. Original specifications for the one-story, brick building had to be altered because of stringent government limitations on the use of wartime materials. Two examples are the columns for the platform canopies (instead of being structural steel, they were wood sheathed in scrap metal) and the flashing (galvanized iron substituted for copper). Twin Colonial Revival-style entrance porticoes led to separate "white" and "colored" waiting rooms. Buff-colored walls, a molded plaster frieze, and terrazzo floors were lit by highly touted "modern" fluorescent fixtures. A ticket office, newsstand, baggage and mail rooms, segregated toilet rooms, and an outdoor waiting alcove completed the floor plan. A dining room was added later to take care of the troops.

In 1986, Amtrak rerouted its trains and moved its stop from the old Seaboard station to another 1940s Colonial Revival building, the Southern Railway depot on Cabarrus Street (which had been without passenger service since 1964). A garden supply company then produced an award-winning adaptive use plan for the Seaboard station, even incorporating the umbrella-type platform canopies into the design. [Privately owned. Commercial.]

RURAL HALL

RURAL HALL DEPOT
Depot Street, near 2nd Street
1888

Rural Hall was a disembarkation point for the resort hotels of the Sauratown Mountains. Originally constructed for the Cape Fear & Yadkin Valley Railway, the depot was used also

Freight end of the Rural Hall depot.

by the Richmond & Danville, whose tracks ran along the west side of the station. (By the end of the 19th century, both lines had become part of the Southern Railway.) The one-story depot was sheathed in German siding of southern yellow pine. The agent's office was centered between the freight section at the southeast end and the "white" and "colored" waiting rooms to the northwest. After passenger service ended in the mid-1950s, the Southern Railway used the station solely for freight operations. It opened a new brick depot in 1980 and planned to demolish the wooden one. Instead, local citizens relocated the depot 200 feet south to a similar site — with trains still passing on opposite sides of the building. NR. [Privately owned. Offices and railroad museum.]

SALISBURY

SALISBURY RAILROAD STATION
Depot and Liberty streets
Frank Pierce Milburn
1908

Kentucky-born Frank Milburn designed about 19 stations for the Southern Railway and allied systems from 1902 to 1917. Two blocks long,

Salisbury station.

Early view, based on architect's drawings.

Track side, nearing the end of construction. This view shows a portion of the high center shed that stretched from the lower shed to an island shed (out of view).

his Salisbury station was an eclectic design combining curvilinear parapeted gables, a variety of Palladian windows, and a red tile roof. A two-course water table divided the depot's dark-red brick base from the tan brick body. A massive square tower, which reportedly once held the building's water supply, had gargoyles accenting each corner. An observation deck rimmed the perimeter of the tower; in its center was the yardmaster's office. The ticket office was in the tower's base. The station's story-and-a-half main block held a large waiting room (to which the ticket office was later moved). It was racially segregated by a wrought iron railing, and the holes from the posts are still visible in the polychromed tile

floor. The smaller north wing held railroad and telegrapher's offices, and baggage and mail rooms. A shed roof, running the length of the station's eastern elevation, sheltered the train platform.

Owned jointly by the Southern Railway and the North Carolina Railroad, the depot replaced a dilapidated, pre–Civil War station that stood a short distance away. By the 1970s, the newer depot was itself deteriorated (to the point of abandonment) and Milburn's matching express building had been demolished. Two decades and many pigeons later, the Historic Salisbury Foundation began restoring the passenger station. Amtrak left its nearby glassed-in shelter and now occupies renovated space in the north wing, which also houses the owner's offices, a visitors bureau, and a stock broker. The waiting room is available for special events. In the mid-1990s, ISTEA funding was obtained to allow for restoration of the restaurant area and for a platform canopy for Amtrak. Across the street, a former railroad hotel is now a flourishing retirement home. Less than a quarter-mile north, the separate freight station is used by a commercial concern. NR. [Historic Salisbury Foundation. Train stop and mixed use.]

SPENCER

BARBER JUNCTION DEPOT
411 South Salisbury Avenue (U.S. Highway 29)
1898

The Barber Junction depot was originally located at the intersection of two Southern Railway lines. Eliminated as a passenger stop in 1968, it was relocated in 1980 to a nearby historic complex known as the Spencer Shops —once a major Southern Railway division point, yard, and shop site. Three miles from the Salisbury depot (*see* above), this 57-acre transportation museum includes a 37-bay roundhouse (undergoing restoration and scheduled to be opened to the public in 1996) and eight other substantial buildings. The former Barber Junction depot is now painted on the exterior in the Southern's standard scheme (1925–45) for wooden stations—green with yellow trim. Essentially restored, but not yet open on a regular basis, the depot's baggage room, once-segregated waiting rooms, and agent's office are used for special events. Plans include turning the station into the ticket office for the entire complex, once the roundhouse work is completed. NR District. [State of North Carolina. Part of the North Carolina Transportation Museum.]

THOMASVILLE

THOMASVILLE RAILROAD STATION
West Main Street
c. 1871

When the North Carolina Railroad arrived at Thomasville in 1855, the first passenger service operated from a hotel. Near the end of the Civil War, Confederate cavalry drove off Union raiders, thus saving the railroad and the town from destruction. An upsurge in prosperity after the war (buggy, hat, and barrel factories as well as tobacco production) encouraged the railroad and the town to build a new passenger depot. About 1871, the same year the North Carolina Railroad was leased to the Richmond & Danville, a station was constructed on the south side of the tracks, near what is now Fisher Ferry Street. By 1904, textiles pushed the economy to further prosperity, and local businesspeople demanded a new depot from the Southern Railway (Richmond & Danville's successor). When an Elizabethan Revival brick station opened in 1912, the old wooden one was moved straight across the tracks and turned 90 degrees to become the office portion of a freight depot that was probably already there.

In 1975, both the brick passenger station and the warehouse end of the freight depot were razed. The Southern Railway then donated the original one-room, wooden station to the community. The Thomasville Historical Society raised money for the depot's restoration, and with the aid of the town, turned the building another 90 degrees. The agent's bay now faces north as it once did, although it is pointed toward the street rather than the tracks. The depot is clad in both vertical boards and German siding, with a lacy, sawnwork frieze band at the eaves. Inside, narrow beaded boards sheath the station's single room, which has a replacement floor of old pine. NR. [City of Thomasville. Special events facility.]

South Carolina

By the early 20th century, South Carolina was dominated by three railroads: the Southern Railway, the Atlantic Coast Line, and the Seaboard Air Line. Amalgams of many smaller lines, the first two tended to have depots of varying appearance. Latecomer to the scene, the Seaboard, had a more consistent corporate style.

BELTON

SOUTHERN RAILWAY STATION
West side of the Public Square
c. 1910

Belton was a junction point for two lines of the Southern Railway. In 1911, 68 trains or trolleys a day were available to passengers arriving at the new brick station. Designed by the railroad's chief engineer, the one-story freight and passenger depot had an Elizabethan flavor. Its most prominent feature was a polygonal tower with diamond-shaped window panes. Massive diagonal brackets supported the flared eaves of the hipped roof. Most of the freight-loading platform was removed in the 1950s. After passenger service ended the following decade, the depot was used as a railroad office. In the late Seventies, to prevent its demolition, the city acquired a lease for the building, which is used today for the public library, community center, and two museums. An extant Southern Railway depot at Westminster (NR) is smaller than the one at Belton, but essentially the same design. Belton once had another station, the Piedmont & Northern (originally an interurban railroad, later acquired by the Seaboard Coast Line), which stood on the west side of town. NR. [Norfolk Southern Corporation. Mixed use.]

BRANCHVILLE

BRANCHVILLE RAILROAD STATION
Freedom Road (formerly North Main Street)
1877

Branchville was an "eating station," where, during a brief layover, travelers were summoned to dinner by a bell rung on the platform. Built by the South Carolina Canal & Railroad Company, the passenger station was at a junction of the Charleston to Hamburg main line and a branch line to Columbia. Set within the east leg of the wye, the depot had tracks running on two sides of the building. In 1910, the Southern Railway (successor to the SCC&RR) added another waiting room. After passenger service ended 52 years later, the Southern leased the depot to the town. The station's stewards, the Branchville Railroad Shrine and Museum, rebuilt the 1910 covered walkways, which the railroad had torn off. The replacements are narrower than the original ones—to allow for passage of wider freight trains. Connected to the waiting rooms and ticket office by a breezeway, the dining room and kitchen have been restored to the 1870–80 period. Authentic communication equipment was reinstalled in the telegraph office. NR. [Norfolk Southern Corporation. Railroad museum and restaurant.]

COLUMBIA

SOUTH CAROLINA CANAL & RAILROAD COMPANY DEPOT

800 Gervais Street
c. 1846–53, 1867

The West Gervais Street Historic District creates a gateway to the city. Reached most dramatically by traveling across the Congaree River, Gervais Street is lined with commercial buildings from the 19th and early 20th centuries. Ahead and up the hill sits the state capitol. Within this area, in the mid-19th century, the South Carolina Canal & Railroad Company built a brick Italianate depot. The plan was typical of the era and locale—a two-story office portion facing the street with a long, one-story warehouse, perpendicular and to the rear. The depot was rebuilt in 1867, after being partially burned during the Civil War. Used only as a freight station in its later railroad operations, it may have originally served passengers as well. At 902 Gervais Street stands a former Seaboard Cost Line station (c. 1903), converted to restaurants. The similarly styled, c. 1892 Columbia, Newberry & Laurens depot (later SCL) at 630 Gervais was demolished in the 1980s. NR District. [Privately owned. Commercial.]

UNION STATION

401 Main Street
Frank Pierce Milburn
1902

Union Station was built for the joint use of the Atlantic Coast Line and the Southern Railway. A mile from downtown and approached from a red brick driveway, the four-acre site was surrounded by railroad tracks and green fields. Frank Milburn, who later designed the State House dome, produced his usual eclectic creation—this time with a Jacobean-inspired exterior of stepped gables and towering chimneys. Inside the two-and-a-half-story depot, a high coffered ceiling, acanthus-topped pilasters, terrazzo floors, and large windows provided elegance and airiness to the waiting room. Mail was processed in a large separate building (burned in 1977) which matched the style and material (flecked brick trimmed in stone) of the main depot. Both ACL and SR passenger service had ended by 1968. The current adaptive use, for which the original interior paint colors were reproduced, was facilitated economically by rehabilitation tax credits. NR. [Privately owned. Restaurant and night club.]

Columbia Union Station c. 1905.

NINETY SIX

NINETY SIX RAILROAD STATION
State Route 34, center of town
c. 1900–1910

c. 1980 pencil sketch of the Ninety Six station, adapted to community use.

Settled along an Indian trading route, the town of Ninety Six supposedly was named for the distance it stood (in miles) from a Cherokee village in the Blue Ridge Mountains. Whatever the truth may be, the hyphen was lost along the way. Originally a Southern Railway combination freight and passenger station, Ninety Six is leased today by the town for use as a senior center, community center, and economic development office. The 1978 adaptation was accomplished without compromising the depot's architectural integrity. Elements found in the ticket office, waiting room, and freight section include six-foot-high wooden wainscoting, exposed ceiling beams, and oak floors. Multiple sets of sliding doors and hardware in the freight room are intact and functional. Outside, the steeply pitched hipped roof is pierced by an Elizabethan-style dormer with "union jack" window muntins. Segmental arches top the door and window openings. The track was abandoned in 1993. [Norfolk Southern Corporation. Mixed use.]

Tennessee

During the Civil War, Union forces seized Tennessee's railroads for their importance as supply lines, and railroad depots for their significance as communication centers. Because of this high strategic value, some stations were in fact destroyed by retreating Confederates. The Southern Railway and the Louisville & Nashville dominated the state, and a number of their more prominent early 20th-century stations remain standing.

CHATTANOOGA

TERMINAL STATION
1400 Market Street
Don Barber
1909

Ironically, in 1973, the same year that the now successfully restored Terminal Station was entered into the National Register of Historic Places, another Chattanooga landmark, Union Depot, was taken off the list due to demolition. Terminal Station was saved by a group of 24 private investors determined to revitalize downtown Chattanooga, who offered the Southern Railway a financial stake in the redevelopment process. Centerpiece of the 30-acre project, Terminal Station was originally the work of New York architect Don Barber. In 1900, while a student at the Paris Ecole des

Chattanooga Terminal Station, shortly after opening.

Beaux-Arts, Barber won a prize for "best designed railroad station for a large city." He later submitted this drawing to the Southern Railway, which chose it for the new Chattanooga Terminal Station. The railroad asked him to alter the interior by modeling it after a bank in Manhattan. Completed in June 1908, the station did not open until December 1909, because of a court battle concerning railroad overpasses.

The station's red brick entrance arch, considered one of the largest in the world, leads to the main waiting room. After 1961, the grand hall's 85-foot-high dome was blocked from view, because the railroad put in a false ceiling to save on heating costs. When the space was converted to a restaurant in the early 1970s, this intrusion was removed. In 1989, a second group of investors took over the complex. They undid the restaurant and duplicated the original paint scheme and marble floor of the waiting room. It now serves as gateway to the entire hospitality and vacation center. The baggage area is used for dining. The old train platforms, sheltered by butterfly sheds, lead to modern hotel buildings, supplemented by 48 Pullman cars converted to guest accommodations. Former freight warehouses have been recycled into a convention center and retail shops. NR. [Privately owned. Mixed use.]

COLUMBIA

UNION STATION
Depot Street
1902

Columbia Union Station, used principally by the Louisville & Nashville, was the community's third successive depot installation. (The previous one was converted to freight-only and then razed in 1960.) Two-and-half-stories of brick walls faced with Bowling Green limestone formed the station's central section, which featured a pair of round entrance arches. Designed in a vernacular Romanesque Revival style, this combination freight and passenger station had a central waiting room with paneled oak wainscoting, pilasters with molded capitals, and a paneled ceiling with plaster rosettes. The "colored" waiting room had ornamental window surrounds, cove molding, a mosaic tile floor, and a marble baseboard. A broad, paneled stairway led to the second floor, which was used for offices, storerooms, and at one point, an apartment for the agent's family. A one-story wing to the west contained the ladies' waiting room; the east wing handled baggage and express. Each section of the building had a slate-covered, hipped roof. Formal gardens flanked two sides of the station, whose trackside platform was removed long ago. A county seat depot, Union Station had numerous important visitors, including William Howard Taft, General John Pershing, Buffalo Bill, evangelist Billy Sunday, and William Jennings Bryan. Passenger service ended in 1954 (express shipments a decade later), after which time the station remained in occasional railroad use. In 1986, a private party purchased and stabilized the deteriorating but intact depot. NR. [Privately owned. Vacant—for rent.]

ERWIN

ERWIN DEPOT

Nolichucky Avenue and Union Street
1925

For 35 years, beginning with the railroad's arrival in 1890, the Erwin depot was a converted boxcar. In 1924, the Atlantic Coast Line and the Louisville & Nashville railroads jointly leased the properties of the Carolina, Clinchfield & Ohio; they named the operating organization the Clinchfield Railroad. The following year, the engineering department designed and built a red brick, division point depot. It had a two-story central portion (waiting room and ticket office) roofed with Spanish terra-cotta tiles. The north wing housed baggage and express; the south wing

contained a second waiting area and the trainmen's room. The streetside, arched entranceway was shaded by a marquee detailed with opal and blue stained glass.

The depot was used by the railroad's signal department after passenger service ended in 1954. More than three decades later, a local citizen acquired the depot from CSX Transportation and donated it to the community along with money for conversion to a library. ISTEA funds awarded in 1994 will be used to restore the exterior. Inside, mahogany window frames and beaded ceiling beams remain, as well as the brass ticket counter and baggage scales. A general office building, constructed at the same time as the depot, still stands to the south. NR. [Colonel J. F. Toney Memorial Library Board. Vacant—future library.]

ETOWAH

ETOWAH DEPOT

U.S. Route 411
1906

Early in the 20th century, the Louisville & Nashville completed a line from Cincinnati to Atlanta via Knoxville. The railroad acquired 1,454 acres for a new town and division point at Etowah. The complex included a turntable and roundhouse, engine and car repair shops, a 66-

An unidentified, large group of men poses at the Etowah depot, 1907.

room Y.M.C.A., and a community center. Offices for the division superintendent and the master mechanic were on the second floor of the 15-room wooden passenger depot. Covered by a slate roof pierced by six gable dormers, the station was entered on the street side through a double-lane porte-cochere. During both the First and Second World Wars, its lunch room was converted to a troop canteen, serving free coffee and sandwiches almost around the clock. Abandoned in 1974, the depot was purchased four years later by the city. Restoration was completed in 1980. NR. [City of Etowah. Railroad museum.]

KNOXVILLE

LOUISVILLE & NASHVILLE STATION

700 Western Avenue, N.W. (at South
    Broadway)
1905

When the new Louisville & Nashville station opened in Knoxville, elaborate brick paving and retaining walls with wrought-iron balus-

trades created the automobile entranceway. Accessed via a plaza-level ramp from Western Avenue, the stub-end passenger station was sited along the east bank of the Second Creek Valley. It was designed by L&N's engineering department in Louisville, headed by Richard Montfort (who is credited with Nashville Union Station), and was built of red brick accented with limestone. The main corner pavilion of the L-shaped station had a steeply pitched, clay tile roof topped by an iron finial. Large, curvilinear dormers faced each street. The central waiting room was outfitted with oak benches and marble wainscoting. In the west wing, the "colored" waiting room was adjacent to the ladies' waiting room, which included couches, writing desks, and a fireplace. With direct street entrances for the general public, the east wing contained a coffee shop and an elegant dining room enhanced by a coffered ceiling and decorative plaster moldings. The station's upper floors housed L&N offices. Facilities for baggage and express, located below street level, opened onto platforms protected by butterfly sheds. Because the Southern Railway controlled the best access route into Knoxville,

Knoxville L&N station. This correspondence was mailed on July 4, 1907, during an era when postcards did not yet have divided backs (to create separate spaces for the address and message). Messages were only permitted on the picture side.

the L&N was forced into an awkward track arrangement—all through trains turned on a wye at West Knoxville and then backed one mile into the station.

Passenger service ended in 1968. After the L&N vacated the building seven years later, large-scale deterioration and vandalism occurred. Restored for the 1982 World's Fair, at which time the extensive stained glass windows were reproduced, the depot is currently used for commercial purposes, as is the adjacent freight station (NR). The freight house was completed in 1923, built within the shell of a burned-out 1904 depot. It too was restored for the World's Fair. All tracks and platforms are gone. The passenger station was a setting for the 1962 movie *All the Way Home*. NR. [Privately owned. Commercial.]

SOUTHERN RAILWAY STATION
306 Depot Avenue
Frank Pierce Milburn
1903

Designed by Frank Milburn, the Southern Railway station in Knoxville anchors a district of 81 historic commercial or light industrial buildings (some still in original use). The buff brick passenger station, with stepped gables and Palladian motifs, lost its magnificent clock tower in a 1945 modernization program. Passenger service ended in 1970. Five years later the railroad sold the station, which subsequently went through 13 years of ownership transfers, aborted plans, and damaging fires. In 1988, the depot was auctioned to a partnership that succeeded in doing a historically sensitive office conversion. The grand entrance hall retains its ornate scrolled cornice and coffered ceiling, although the twin staircases were turned 90 degrees to accommodate current needs. Outside, one butterfly shed with jigsawed wooden supports remains along the tracks. An adjacent brick freight depot, also designed by Milburn, is part of the same office complex. NR District. [Privately owned. Offices.]

Knoxville SR station with its clock tower (now gone).

NASHVILLE

UNION STATION
10th Avenue South at Broadway
Richard Montfort
1900

In 1893, the Louisville & Nashville and its affiliate, the Nashville, Chattanooga & St. Louis, formed a "terminal company" to build a union station. For five years, the city and the terminal company fought over a newly depressed right-of-way, which became known as "railroad gulch." Financial panics, strikes, epidemics, and floods exacerbated the delay. Richard Montfort, head of L&N's civil engineering department, is credited with the building's design, although he left no proof beyond his official title on the blueprints. The station was apparently modeled after H. H. Richardson's Allegheny Courthouse in Pittsburgh. Constructed of Bowling Green limestone, the building had a 219-foot tower containing an innovative (but never accurate) gigantic digital clock, the pet project of Major Eugene Castner Lewis, president of the terminal company. A 17-foot-high statue of Mercury balanced on tiptoe above the tower's crowning finial (he fell to the tracks in 1952). The station's

Nashville Union Station.

One of two fireplaces in the ornate waiting room.

Early 1900s. Freight station (left) echoes the style of the imposing passenger terminal.

grounds included two cement pools filled with alligators from Florida; in winter, they slept in the boiler room.

The main waiting area had a stained glass skylight stretching the entire length of the three-story-high, barrel-vaulted ceiling. Marble and stone fireplaces anchored each end of the room. Frescoes and bas-reliefs illustrated the topics of farm products, natural resources, time, progress, and transportation. Covering the tracks, a gable-roofed, long-span train shed (similar to that of Union Station in Louisville, Ky.) was supported by steel and timber trusses. Along the roof ridge, a central monitor let in light; a curtain wall of stained glass covered the gable end. Because through trains entered the station's basement level, a smoke tower was added to the rear of the depot. The station became vacant in the mid-1970s and was transferred to the General Services Administration—a controversial move and an utter failure. Not properly sealed against avian intrusion, the building suffered more than $1 million

damage from pigeon droppings. It was converted to a hotel in 1986. The deteriorating train shed is being considered for reuse in a proposed mass transit project. NR. NHL. [Privately owned. Hotel.]

SPRING CITY

SPRING CITY DEPOT
Front Street
c. 1908

The Spring City depot was a short distance from the Rhea Springs resort (now gone) and its therapeutic waters. Located along the Southern Railway's Cincinnati to Chattanooga line, the concrete and red brick station superseded a wooden one that stood a block south. The trackside cross gable was ornamented with an unusual two-tone brick checkerboard pattern, filling out the space between twin arched windows and the keystoned arch above. The roof was red tile.

Forty freight trains a day still pass by the station, which went out of passenger service in the 1950s (freight service continued a while longer). Although the chamber of commerce occupies an old caboose parked next door, the depot itself is vacant and deteriorating. Determined to save the building—reportedly the only depot left in the county—a local committee has been lobbying the railroad. The group would like to have the depot donated to the town, but the insurance premium (often a major hurdle in depot acquisition) remains an issue. Future use may be as a museum and community meeting space. [Norfolk Southern Corporation. Vacant.]

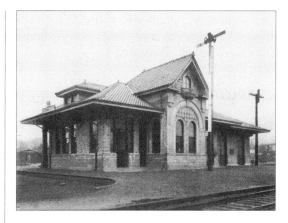

Spring City depot, 1913.

Virginia

Virginia had two grand railway stations (both in Richmond), and they are still standing. Most depots were frame or brick, one story high. The state's three longest railroads—the Southern, the Chesapeake & Ohio, and the Norfolk & Western—tended to build cookie-cutter depots from standard plans. At Petersburg, one of the state's earliest depots, constructed by the South Side Railroad (later N&W), survived the Civil War, but was flattened during a 1993 tornado.

ALEXANDRIA

UNION STATION
110 Callahan Drive
1905

In the early 20th century, a solution was needed for two related areas of congestion: the freight yards within Washington, D.C., and the bottleneck at Alexandria (adjacent to the nation's capital), where several major north-south lines converged. As part of an improvement project that included the huge Potomac Yard and a new track alignment, Alexandria received a union passenger station in Federal Revival style. The red brick depot was separated from the baggage building by an open breezeway. Seven pedimented dormers brought light through the slate roof. The station was built by the Washington Southern Railway Company (later part of the Richmond, Fredericksburg & Potomac) and served Chesapeake & Ohio and Southern Railway trains, as well. The building had extensive, attached platform canopies, a portion of which were reconstructed in 1982, although without the original heavy timber trusses and terne metal roofing. Inside today, extant features include a checkerboard, ceramic tile floor and delicate fanlight transoms. Alexandria is Virginia's busiest passenger station, although the many other rail-related buildings and switching yards are gone. [RFP Corporation. Train stop.]

CHARLOTTESVILLE

CHESAPEAKE & OHIO STATION
600 East Water Street
1905

Charlottesville is proud of being Thomas Jefferson territory, as reflected in the choice of a Colonial Revival design for the Chesapeake & Ohio station. For many years, the C&O made two stops in town. Besides having its own depot, the C&O shared a union station (today's Amtrak stop) with the Southern Railway. Early in the 20th century, after much complaining by city council about C&O's inadequate wooden depot, the railroad's engineering department designed a new building of red brick trimmed with granite and Kentucky freestone. The streetside portico had tall Ionic columns, shielding a Federal-style doorway flanked by arched windows. Racially segregated waiting rooms and the ticket office filled the first floor; offices for the dispatcher, yardmaster, and trainmaster were upstairs. Two one-story wings housed the baggage area and the employees' reading and resting room. Throughout the years, interior modifications and enlargement of the east wing added more office space. The flat-roofed platform shed (originally 500 feet long) is now enclosed and may become retail space. C&O sold the depot in the 1980s. [Privately owned. Offices.]

CHRISTIANSBURG

CHRISTIANSBURG DEPOT
Cambria and Depot streets
1868

After the original Christiansburg depot was destroyed in an 1864 Union raid, the Virginia & Tennessee built a post–Civil War replacement.

In 1906, when a new depot (used today by Norfolk Southern) was built just to the east, the old board and batten station was converted to freight-only. From then on, it was commonly called the Cambria Freight Station. (Cambria is now within Christiansburg's town limits.) The track bed was raised slightly in 1906, causing awkward changes to the depot's floor levels, doorways, and five fireplaces. At the same time, the station received an addition, which was destroyed two years later by a runaway train. Today, the principal facade of the depot faces open space in the Cambria Historic District. At the heart of the U-shaped building, a two-story Italianate tower with a Palladian window rises between projecting, one-story wings. A long freight section extends from the rear of the building, parallel to the tracks, in a fashion typical of many mid-19th-century depots.

In 1983, after two decades in various private hands, the seriously deteriorated depot was about to be demolished by the town. The current owner rescued the station, which he uses for a publishing and retail business. He lives in the freight section. A similar, but less intact depot stands further southwest on the line, at Rural Retreat. NR. [Privately owned. Mixed use.]

MANASSAS

MANASSAS RAILROAD STATION
9500 West Street
1915

Manassas became a junction town in the mid-19th century, when the Orange & Alexandria intersected with the Manassas Gap Railroad. The current brick depot, built by the Southern Railway (and also used by the Chesapeake & Ohio), traces its lineage to what was described in 1861 as no more than a "rudely constructed building." Destroyed during the Civil War, it was succeeded by new versions in 1871 and

1904. Today's brick station reportedly incorporates the walls of its predecessor, which burned in 1914. The high, hipped roof flows into wide eaves, supported by long brackets and posts. Accented by tiny dormers, a central octagonal turret is flanked by full-size dormers that echo its style and pitch. Between 1925 and 1933, many Manassas residents traveled by train to their offices in Washington, D.C. In the Nineties, commuter service was reestablished via the new Virginia Railway Express, augmenting the depot's function as an Amtrak stop. The city, which acquired the building after Norfolk Southern departed, is seeking funding to restore the interior as a waiting room and visitors center. NR District. [City of Manassas. Train stop/npa.]

MINERAL

MINERAL RAILROAD STATION
First Street
c. 1890

Originally called Tolersville Station, Mineral was renamed after 1890 for resources discovered in the area, such as gold, copper, and sul-

fur. Sheathed in clapboards above a board and batten base, this Chesapeake & Ohio depot apparently was built with a transom above every door and window (now filled in). Jigsawed brackets supported the deep eaves. The interior consisted of a waiting room, freight section, and two small offices, with a lengthwise expansion made c. 1900. Passenger service ended in the 1950s. The building serves today as headquarters for signal and track maintenance personnel. Another intact C&O depot—built in a standard design common from 1892 to 1908—stands at the county seat, Louisa. [CSX Transportation. Railroad use.]

MONTPELIER STATION

MONTPELIER STATION DEPOT
State Route 20, 4 miles west of Orange
1910

The famous 18th-century residence, Montpelier, was built by the father of President James Madison, who inherited the home. The dwelling and 1,400 acres were purchased in 1900 by William duPont, who sold a right-of-way through his estate to the Southern Railway—provided

Mineral station c. 1940.

that the railroad would make Montpelier Station a scheduled stop. Employees from the estate built the wooden depot according to drawings supplied by the Southern's engineering department. Topped with a belcast roof, the station was clad in German siding and heated by stoves. Hipped dormers with diamond-shaped panes supplied daylight to a four-room apartment on the second floor.

Every Monday morning, duPont boarded a train here for a weekly commute to his office in Wilmington, Del. His daughter, Marion duPont Scott (raised at Montpelier and heir to the estate, including the depot), shipped thoroughbred horses from a siding that also accommodated the private rail cars of her guests and the unloading of coal. (The sidetrack, now disconnected from the main line, and a wooden coal dock remain.) After regular passenger service ended in 1929 (it was a flag stop as late as the 1960s), the post office portion of the depot expanded into the former "colored" waiting room. In 1981, the British Broadcasting Corporation filmed the Montpelier Station depot (disguised as Greenwood, which was actually on the Chesapeake & Ohio) in a documentary series about Lady Nancy Astor.

Two years later, Mrs. Scott died and Montpelier became a museum property. The old "white" waiting room, unused today, retains its original furniture. Passenger and freight trains continue to use the one remaining main line track. NR. [National Trust for Historic Preservation. Post office.]

THE PLAINS

THE PLAINS DEPOT
Stuart Street
1914

Outside The Plains depot, freight trains still pound the track on a route laid out in 1852 by the Manassas Gap Railroad (later the Southern Railway). In 1979, the railroad sold the brick station to a salvage company for $10. As dismantling began, a group of local citizens, including the mayor, began 11th-hour negotiations with the wreckers to sell them the building. Half the roof had been lifted off before an agreement was reached. The group then spent four years raising the funds for restoration,

Passengers are ready for boarding at The Plains station c. 1916. Against a pole on the left are two calves.

Depot "loungers" sit under a tree at the Pulaski station.

which included replicating the roof tiles. The Georgia pine interior and the diamond-shaped window muntins survived the near demolition. Fully self-supporting today, the depot houses several offices and a "library" of bottled wines belonging to a local viticulture association. One former waiting room houses a scale-model train layout depicting a portion of the Southern Railway's main line. Skylights were added to the trackside portion of the roof, to facilitate installation of an apartment in the attic space. An old freight house, which originally was the passenger station, is still standing next door. The Southern Railway applied a similar Elizabethan flavor to other depots such as Chatham; the Hull Street passenger station in Richmond; Hickory and Reidsville, N.C.; and Gainesville, Ga., (all extant). [Save the R.R. Station, Inc. Mixed use.]

PULASKI

PULASKI RAILROAD STATION

Washington Avenue and Dora Highway
c. 1888

Originally just a water stop on the Virginia & Tennessee (later the Norfolk & Western), Pulaski was first known as Martin's Tank. In the late 1880s, the railroad purchased land from the Martin family to build a new station, located nearer the newly platted town center. It was also just west of the grand Maple Shade Inn (1884; razed in 1963 for a shopping center). Diagonally opposite the depot, the railroad laid out a large park, which is maintained today by the town. The long, one-story station of coursed rubble stone contained men's and ladies' waiting rooms, sheathed in beaded, tongue-and-groove boards and warmed by fireplaces. Numerous changes occurred over the years; for example, in 1903 the station size was doubled to add baggage and express areas. About 1914, the gender-segregated waiting rooms were converted to "white" and "colored."

In the late 1980s, witnessing the building's near "demolition by neglect," the town acquired the property from the Norfolk Southern Corporation. Painstaking restoration included rebuilding the dormers and slate roof, which had been removed about 25 years earlier. When cost predictions exceeded expectations, a private fund-raising committee substantially augmented the town's treasury. In the first phase of rehabilitation, volunteers contributed more than 900 hours of labor—some expended on painting the depot's interior the original Norfolk & Western colors. Adaptively used for a museum, the chamber of commerce, and community meeting space, the former station sits along the New River Trail State Park, a "rail trail" that, at the depot, skirts active freight tracks. NR District. [Town of Pulaski. Mixed use.]

RAPIDAN

RAPIDAN RAILROAD STATION
County Route 615
1887

Originally known as Rapid Anne, this passenger station and post office was built by the Richmond & Danville (later the Southern Railway) to replace one dating from 1866. The clapboard-and-shingle-covered depot stood on a main line until the rails were moved about 1903. (A c. 1911 Rapidan station on the relocated line was demolished in 1975.) Its plan was common to at least six other stations in the state. A deep, two story-section was perpendicular to the track, with one-story wings paralleling the rails. Under the slate-covered roof, a large porch allowed passengers to wait in the shade. Queen Anne small panes bordered the upper window

sash in red, blue, green, and amber glass. A wooden freight station (which may have been built by the Orange & Alexandria Railroad in the 1850s) and a section foreman's house still stand. [Privately owned. Residence.]

RICHMOND

BROAD STREET STATION
2500 West Broad Street
John Russell Pope
1919

Problems with grade crossings, track layout, and track capacity necessitated construction of the new "Union Station of Richmond" (the building's original name, which is still visible on the entrance). Built for two railroads—the Richmond, Fredericksburg & Potomac and the Atlantic Coast Line—the station was commonly called "Broad Street" to distinguish it from Richmond's other major rail facility on Main Street. The Richmond Terminal Railway Company operated the station, which was designed by renowned New York architect John Russell Pope. His work on Washington,

1920s aerial view of Broad Street Station in Richmond.

Elevated tracks (for through trains) skirted both sides of Main Street Station in Richmond. The station was configured with a combination of through and stub-end tracks. (For view of track approach, *see* page 223.)

D.C., structures like the Jefferson Memorial and the National Gallery of Art are reflected in the neoclassical appearance of Broad Street. Clad in limestone, the three-story-high, Doric-columned entranceway was surmounted by a full entablature and a parapet. Behind it, a 105-foot-high dome sheltered the marble and limestone waiting room. Suspended from the ceiling, a huge glass and bronze globe outlined the earth's continents along with zodiacal signs. As in many towns and cities, the station dining room was popular with the nontraveling public, as well as ticket holders. Flanking the rotunda were symmetrical wings housing extensive railroad offices. Trains arrived below the concourse level at platforms covered by butterfly sheds, supported by cast-iron Ionic columns. In the mid-1970s, Amtrak dedicated a new station west of the city, and Broad Street became the Science Museum of Virginia. The up-front, convenient parking area was part of Pope's original concept for the station. NR. [Commonwealth of Virginia. Museum.]

MAIN STREET STATION
1520 East Main Street (at East Franklin Street)
Wilson, Harris, and Richards
1901

Built on the site of the old St. Charles Hotel, Main Street was a union station for the Chesapeake & Ohio and the Seaboard Air Line (the latter moved to Broad Street Station in 1959). Designed by a Philadelphia architectural and engineering firm (successor to the Wilson Brothers), the French Renaissance–style station had a first story of rough-hewn stone. The upper stories were veneered in a tile that resembled old Roman brick. Embellished with stone and terra-cotta, two rows of dormers pierced the steeply pitched tile roof. Each clock face of the six-story-high corner tower was surrounded by scrolls, cherubic faces, and fluted columns. The ground floor contained service facilities such as mail and baggage. Because the tracks entered the city on viaducts, the main waiting room was at the second level; high wrought-iron fencing separated it from the gable-end train shed. Surmounted by a double monitor and sheltering six sets of stub-end tracks, the shed roof had 13-foot-deep eaves. These overhangs protected passengers using through tracks located just outside the walls. The upper floors of the head house contained railroad offices and a Y.M.C.A. for train crews.

In the mid-1970s, Amtrak vacated Main Street Station, which had suffered badly in the James River floods of 1969 and 1972. After the train shed's wooden roof caught fire several times, it was removed leaving only the skeleton. In 1983, just two weeks before a shopping mall conversion was scheduled to begin, a fire destroyed the upper two floors of the head house (which were part of the attic space) and damaged the clock tower. The adaptive use went forward. The depot's steeply pitched roof and dormers were replicated, including newly manufactured clay tiles from the original mold; the shed's roof was renewed in metal. Two years after the complex reopened, its poorly marketed commercial enterprise failed. In 1988, the state bought the building. The train shed is being used temporarily for state offices; the head house is partially occupied by a restaurant. In the early Nineties, a task force began studying the feasibility of having Amtrak and a high-speed rail line come into downtown Richmond, with a stop at Main Street Station. The only currently available, major north-south transportation directly into the city is via Interstate 95. Ironically, it passes within 75 feet of the station —and disrupts the original view of the head house. NR. NHL. [Commonwealth of Virginia. Restaurant and offices.]

STAUNTON

STAUNTON RAILROAD STATION
1 Middlebrook Avenue (at South Augusta Street)
T. J. Collins
1902

The Staunton Chesapeake & Ohio complex sits at the base of a steep hill, opposite a continuous row of late 19th-century brick warehouses. Designed by a Staunton firm, the beige brick passenger depot had a triple arcade, stone trim, and spoke-patterned windows. (Stylized bull's-eye windows, above the arcade, were stuccoed over at some point.) By the mid-1980s, the depot's one-and-a-half stories had suffered decades of vandalism and fires. After long negotiations with the railroad, a husband-and-wife team bought the station. Within it, they

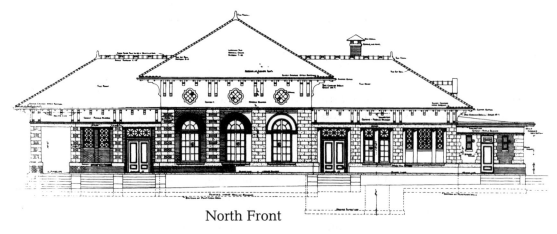

North Front

Architect's c.1902 drawing for the Staunton station.

Several appropriate "station wagons" are among the automobiles parked at the Williamsburg station, 1945.

installed the salvaged interior of an old drug store and soda fountain. They enclosed the train platform for their cafe's main seating area and then leased out the separate freight depot to another restaurateur and Amtrak. Other extant structures on the site include a late 19th-century, Queen Anne–style signal tower (C&O standard plan); a c.1925 steel water tank; and a c.1905 cast-iron footbridge over the tracks. The depot's owners have also purchased the adjacent Greek Revival–style American Hotel (built in 1854; converted to a warehouse in 1890), which they plan to turn back into an inn. NR District. [Privately owned. Train stop, restaurants, and antiques shop.]

WILLIAMSBURG

WILLIAMSBURG RAILROAD STATION
North Boundary Street
c. 1935

In 1926, when John D. Rockefeller began restoring Colonial Williamsburg, a 1907 Chesapeake & Ohio station was located behind the Governor's Palace. It was a red brick, Colonial Revival–style building, successor to a two-story, wooden depot from 1881. The Colonial Williamsburg Foundation wanted to restore the palace's gardens. Within a decade, the railroad's engineering department had realigned the right-of-way and designed a new and bigger one-story station. Also in Colonial Revival style, it was placed one-third-mile to the west, adjacent to the historic area. Materials from the dismantled first brick depot were incorporated into the second one. With a very steep roof, the station's central portion was anchored at both ends by chimneys. Wings provided an additional waiting area plus baggage and express services. Styled like early lanterns, electrified fixtures lit the interior, which had walls of buff-colored glazed brick, walnut trim, and quarry tile flooring. The wide train platform, sheltered by curving umbrella canopies, was reached directly from each waiting room. Westbound passengers waited under a wooden shelter (now gone). Today, the station serves Amtrak, intercity buses, and a car rental agency. The design is almost identical to that of Paintsville, Ky. [Colonial Williamsburg Foundation. Transportation center.]

Winchester B&O station on a January day in 1964.

WINCHESTER

BALTIMORE & OHIO RAILROAD STATION
East Piccadilly and Kent streets
E. Francis Baldwin
1893

Passenger service to Winchester ended a half-century ago. Leased now to a short line railroad, the former Baltimore & Ohio station needs repair. Although the cupola, eyebrow dormers, and wood-shingled polygonal tower are intact, the slate roof and mortar of this brownstone building are deteriorating. Local citizens and city planners would like to revitalize the depot, which is across the street from a complex of vacant 19th-century woolen mills, also in need of restoration. About three blocks north along the track stands a small stone structure, now used by a model railroad club, that may have been built by the Winchester & Potomac (opened in 1836, part of the B&O after 1867). On West Boscawen Street, a former Pennsylvania Railroad freight station constructed of brick is now a little theater. Although the tracks of both historic railroads are intact, only the ex-B&O rails are active. [CSX Transportation. Winchester & Western Railroad offices.]

Midwest

Trackside profile of Cincinnati Union Terminal.

Illinois

Illinois's principal city, Chicago, was also the nation's rail capital. More than 20 separate railroads entered the metropolis, and most had their own passenger and freight depots. Today, of the seven principal passenger terminals once standing simultaneously, two remain (though only a half-portion of each). With construction dates ranging from the 1890s to the 1920s, the stations known as Grand Central, 12th Street, La Salle Street, Chicago & North Western, and Wells Street were all razed in the period from the 1950s to the 1980s. Dearborn Station (1885) lost its steep, elaborate roof and the gabled superstructure of its clock tower in a 1922 fire; the train shed was demolished in 1976. (The head house is now an office building.) Union Station has a head house, but its above ground concourse building is gone.

Although mostly still owned by individual freight railroads, Chicago's commuter lines are operated through a preservation-minded agency called Metra. Along three of these lines, a fair number of historic depots remain: the Chicago, Burlington & Quincy (Burlington Northern) to Aurora; the Gulf, Mobile & Ohio (Illinois Central) to Joliet; and the Chicago & North Western running through wealthy North Shore suburbs. At stations where Amtrak stops, noteworthy partnerships for rehabilitation have been forged by the state department of transportation, individual communities, and the railroad.

Early engraving of the Amboy depot with its elaborate chimneys intact.

AMBOY

AMBOY DEPOT
Main and East streets
James Nocquet
1876

The original (c. 1854) headquarters of the Illinois Central's Third Division were separate from the adjacent Amboy station-hotel. When the latter was destroyed by fire in 1875, the IC decided to demolish the headquarters and build a joint building on the site of the burned depot. Spacious and modern, its limestone-trimmed, red brick walls were punctuated by a large number of windows, admitting extensive natural light. A Chicago architect who worked on the IC staff during the 1870s designed the building. Half the first floor was used for crew locker rooms, a conductors' office, battery storage (to power telegraph lines), and baggage. The southeast end comprised passenger services. Accessed by a curved stairway with a walnut handrail, the second floor contained offices of the division civil engineer, superintendent, trainmaster, telegraphers, and payroll and billing clerks, plus a vault for records and money. In 1894, after division headquarters shifted to Freeport, Amboy continued to serve as a crew change point and passenger depot. About 1940, the building was remodeled slightly for conversion to freight and railway express agencies. In the mid-1980s, after IC abandoned the line through Amboy, removed the tracks, and announced impending demolition of the depot, a group of local citizens rescued the building. NR. [Village of Amboy. Museum.]

AURORA

CHICAGO, BURLINGTON & QUINCY ROUNDHOUSE AND MACHINE SHOPS
Broadway and Spring Street
Levi Hull Waterhouse
1856 (full circle completed c. 1866)

Roundhouses (sometimes just segments of a circle) were used historically for maintenance and repair of locomotives and, less often, railroad cars. Built of locally quarried limestone, the Chicago, Burlington & Quincy full roundhouse and adjacent machine shops (where sleeping and dining cars were built) ceased operations in 1974. The city convinced the CB&Q's successor, Burlington Northern, not to demolish the buildings. A joint venture using city, state, federal, and BN funds resulted in the conversion of the machine shops to a commuter rail station, completed in 1988, and augmented by bus, car rental, and taxi facilities. In 1993, after a developer failed to initiate a retail center project for the vacant roundhouse, the city applied for ISTEA funds. If awarded, they would be used for general rehabilitation—to more easily attract an adaptive use. This entire project demonstrates a creative approach to fashioning a modern multimodal facility out of railroad history. NR. [City of Aurora. Transportation center.]

BATAVIA

BATAVIA DEPOT
155 Houston Street
1855

The Batavia depot was originally located on a line from Aurora to Turner's Junction (now West Chicago) that evolved into the Chicago, Burlington & Quincy Railroad. The two-story, board and batten station is Gothic Revival style and not a standard CB&Q design. In 1973, to save it from demolition, 20 Batavia businesspeople jointly purchased the depot. The community raised funds to cover moving costs, and the building was relocated across town. Its new home was a spot owned by the local park district, along Chicago & North Western tracks. Since that time, the rails have been removed, and the right-of-way converted to a bicycle trail. The wing on the depot's north end dates from 1868. NR. [Batavia Park District. Local history museum.]

Batavia depot c.1940s, in its original location.

Chicago Union Station.

December 1924, nearing completion. The templelike concourse (bordering the Chicago River) was razed in 1969 for a highrise office building. Behind it stands the structure that remains today, which contains the station's grand waiting room.

CHICAGO

UNION STATION
225 South Canal Street
Graham, Anderson, Probst and White
1925

Daniel Burnham was scheduled to be the architect for Union Station; but it was not begun until 1913, a year after his death. Completed by his successor firm, the project was a joint venture of the Pennsylvania Railroad, the Chicago, Milwaukee & St. Paul, and the Chicago, Burlington & Quincy. The Chicago & Alton (later Gulf, Mobile & Ohio) was a tenant. The terminal originally consisted of two independent structures. A beautiful concourse (demolished in 1969 for the air rights) was connected to the head house (waiting room and surrounding office building) by a broad, vaulted tunnel under Canal Street. Not surprisingly, the head house exterior —with its Indiana limestone facade and prominent Tuscan columns— bore a strong resemblance to New York City's Pennsylvania Station; the complex was the western terminus of the PRR, principal stockholder in the Chicago Union Station Company.

    Among the station's efficient design features were U-shaped internal driveways that

Early view of the waiting room.

permitted vehicles to unload and turn around without crowding the city streets. Connections to preexisting, narrow gauge railroad tunnels facilitated moving freight to warehouses and stores in the Chicago Loop. The skylit grand waiting room had ornate columns, brass lamps decorated with vines and birds, Henry Hering's sculptural figures, and a color scheme of rose, ivory, and gold. Union Station was a micro-city, filled with stores, restaurants, a nursery, a hospital, and even a basement jail. In the early 1990s, Chicago Union Station Company (now a subsidiary of Amtrak) reversed several decades of grunginess by refurbishing the waiting room, restaurant, and retail facilities for both long-distance passengers and Metra commuters. [Chicago Union Station Company. Train stop and mixed use.]

DECATUR

WABASH DEPOT
780 East Cerro Gordo Street
Theodore C. Link
1901

In 1856, Decatur's first depot was shared by two railroads, the Illinois Central and a predecessor of the Wabash Railway. IC built its own depot in 1900 (razed in 1951). The Wabash moved out of Union Station in 1901 to a new facility just to the east. Designed by Theodore Link, architect of Union Station in St. Louis, the Wabash depot exhibited a classical sense of massing, balance, and details. A breezeway connected the depot to a matching express building. On dedication day inside the terra-cotta-trimmed, yellow brick station, 400 incandescent light bulbs burned to show off the Georgia marble, frescoed walls,

and English-style oak furniture. Outside, a dozen exterior arc lights illuminated a three-story, balconied tower that was the design's focal point (since removed). The public was invited to inspect all of the building, including the second floor, which housed offices of the Wabash's busiest division.

With 3,500 people on the 1927 payroll, this line was once the largest employer in the city. During both World Wars, canteens were operated near or in the depot to feed the troops passing through, who numbered in the hundreds of thousands. The Wabash depot closed in 1971, by then the property of Norfolk & Western. Amtrak's subsequent attempts to revive service failed. The current owner has applied a new roof and is undertaking conversion to an antiques mall. NR. [Privately owned. Vacant.]

DE KALB

DE KALB RAILROAD STATION
200 North 6th Street
Frost and Granger
1891

Noted architects Charles Sumner Frost and Alfred Hoyt Granger were the Chicago & North Western's favorite depot designers from the late 1800s until about 1912. (They were sons-in-law

Wabash depot in Decatur with its three-story tower intact.

DeKalb station, May 1911.

of the railroad's president.) The team worked for several railroads. For example, two major stations in downtown Chicago were from their drawing boards: the La Salle Street Station (used jointly by the New York Central and the Chicago, Rock Island & Pacific) and the C&NW Station. The De Kalb depot was built when the railroad put in a second main line track. It was reconfigured in 1946, at which time the open area between the waiting rooms and the baggage room was enclosed. Passenger service ended in 1971. With a castlelike, octagonal tower facing the tracks, the brick and stone station is now in freight railroad use. [Chicago & North Western Transportation Company. Roadmaster's headquarters.]

DWIGHT

CHICAGO & ALTON STATION
119 West Main Street
Henry Ives Cobb
1892

By the late 1800s, a local sanitarium was drawing patients from all over the country, and Dwight's 1854 depot had become much too small. To design a new structure, the Chicago & Alton hired Henry Ives Cobb, architect of the Chicago Post Office and the University of Chicago's first buildings. Roofed in slate and built of Bedford bluestone, the story-and-a-half depot featured a bold cross gable, accented by fanlights and quatrefoil ornaments. On the inside, beneath the cathedral ceiling, oak was used for both woodwork and furnishings. The roadmaster occupied the second floor. Various alterations have occurred since 1946, including removal of the north-end fireplace and installation of a false ceiling. After passenger service ceased in 1971, the station was used as office and storage space for the Illinois Central Gulf Railroad. In the early Eighties, ICG sold the depot to the village, and the historical society rehabilitated it. The freight station of the same vintage, standing just south of the passenger depot, is now the chamber of commerce. At Lincoln, about 70 miles southwest, stands a larger version of Dwight, built of brick (now a restaurant and Amtrak stop). NR. [Village of Dwight. Train stop and village hall.]

GALENA

GALENA DEPOT
101 Bouthillier Street
1857

A lead-mining center with access to the Mississippi River, Galena was once the premier city of Illinois. General Ulysses S. Grant made two historic departures from this Illinois Central depot—one in 1861 to fight the Civil War and another in 1868 to assume the Presidency. After IC discontinued service a century later (1971), the brick building with arched windows and two Italianate-style cupolas was purchased by a private party, who resold it to the city. The second floor, once the agent's living quarters, houses the chamber of commerce. Downstairs is a visitors center, starting point for a half-mile walking tour of the town, which is filled with more than 60 historic buildings. Original benches grace one of the two former waiting rooms. The old freight section is used by a parcel shipping service. NR District. [Town of Galena. Mixed use.]

GLENCOE

GLENCOE RAILROAD STATION
724 Green Bay Road
Charles Sumner Frost
1891

An 1890 petition by residents of Glencoe pressured the Chicago & North Western for a new depot. As inhabitants of a growing Chicago railroad suburb, they argued that potential home-buyers were "repelled by the unfavorable first impression when they land at the station" including its small waiting room "saturated with dirt and foul odors." The new Glencoe station was one of the early depot designs of Charles Frost. It was executed after his partnership with Henry Ives Cobb had ended, and before his long association with brother-in-law Alfred Granger had begun. The evening of the station's grand opening, a brass band played until midnight, while visitors danced on the waiting room floor. Its walls wainscoted in beaded oak boards, the space was originally heated by stoves. Outside, a gable roof with flared eaves protected the brick

Galena depot c. 1900.

walls, anchored by gently battered, rusticated limestone piers. The cylindrical tower, given a medieval French flavor by its small, second-story windows, housed the ticket office.

In the late 1980s, the station underwent a major rehabilitation funded by Metra Commuter Rail, the village of Glencoe (which leases and operates the depot, and the Glencoe Historical Society. Work included repairing serious water damage that had ruined the original wainscoting, replacing damaged brick and limestone, applying a new cedar shingle roof, and landscaping. [Chicago & North Western Transportation Company. Train stop.]

HINSDALE

HIGHLANDS STATION
County Line Road near Chicago Avenue
c. 1880

The Highlands station was established as a flag stop on the Chicago, Burlington & Quincy in the early 1870s. Reportedly, three families who lived on the east side of Hinsdale requested this service and subsequently built a small, but substantial depot. Rough-faced, square-cut

Highlands station in Hinsdale, 1978.

stone walls were accented by a band of brickwork above the windows, and Eastlake trim filled the jerkinhead gables. The station became a regular stop after 1889. In the early 20th century, when the tracks were raised, the depot received a basement, used for housing a railroad employee. [Burlington Northern Railroad Company. Train stop.]

HOMEWOOD

HOMEWOOD RAILROAD STATION
Ridge Road and Park Avenue
1923

Homewood's earlier station was made of wood and located on the east side of the tracks. In the early 1920s, when the Illinois Central announced plans to demolish it, a local woman made repeated visits to railroad officials in Chicago. She convinced them to donate the depot to the village. The women's club then raised funds to relocate the depot several blocks north, where it became the public library (razed in 1962). The new station was placed on the west side of the tracks, which IC was elevating from downtown Chicago. Designed by the railroad's engineering staff in Mission style, the depot stylistically matched the Ravisloe Country Club located one block west (1916; extant), whose members arrived both by "golfers' specials" and regular commuter trains. Many members built summer homes in the vicinity of the station. The depot's one story was constructed of brick and terra-cotta covered with stucco. The roofline combined a pitched tile roof with lower flat roofs—all with swung gables and parapets—and a narrow bell tower. Today's Metra commuters use a tunnel under the tracks to reach a center platform shelter; the depot itself contains waiting space for long-distance Amtrak passengers. [Illinois Central Railroad. Train stop.]

Joliet Union Station.

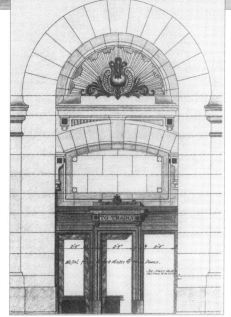

c. 1940.

JOLIET

UNION STATION
50 East Jefferson Street (at Scott Street)
Jarvis Hunt
1912

Prior to construction of Union Station, the four trunk lines that radiated from Joliet had separate passenger stations. The traffic tie-ups on city streets were monumental. In 1906, the city passed an ordinance requiring elevation of the tracks and construction of a union station to serve principally three railroads: Chicago, Rock Island & Pacific; Atchison, Topeka & Santa Fe; and Chicago & Alton (later Gulf, Mobile & Ohio). Trolleys and two interurban lines also stopped at this new location. Architect Jarvis Hunt—nephew of New York architect Richard Morris Hunt and muralist William Hunt—also designed Kansas City Union Station. In Joliet, the depot's relationship to the track intersection resulted in an oblong hexagonal shape, with wings at the extremities. The main Beaux Arts facade, clad in Bedford limestone, faced the center of Joilet. Embarking passengers arrived at the carriage court and entered three arched portals to the ticket lobby. A grand marble

Interior detail, drawn to facilitate restoration work completed in 1991.

stairway led to the hexagonal main waiting room, covered with various marbles, lit by ornate bronze fixtures, and anchored at either end by an interior stone chimney.

Although both commuters and long-distance passengers continued using the station, the years following World War II brought detrimental occurrences, such as installation of a false ceiling that obscured the original 45-foot-high baroque vault, loss of ornate light standards, and eventually, outright vandalism. In the 1980s, the city bought a majority interest in the station and began planning a $6 million restoration and adaptation. The rededication ceremony in 1991 included a banquet for 500 in the old waiting room (with the acoustical tile ceiling removed), which the city hopes will become a restaurant. Amtrak passengers wait on the lower level, while commuters use a glassed-in corridor at track level. Retail businesses are expected to occupy the balance of the station, which also serves the city bus lines. NR. [Jointly owned by Metra Commuter Rail and the city of Joliet. Transportation center and commercial use.]

KENILWORTH

KENILWORTH RAILROAD STATION

Green Bay Road and Kenilworth Avenue
Franklin Burnham (Edbrooke and Burnham)
1891

Kenilworth's commuter station, built by the Chicago & North Western, originally housed both an express service and the post office. The depot was lit by gas and warmed by stoves. Early

newspaper reports described flower boxes around the verandah, geranium and petunia beds, and a fountain entrance that doubled as a horse-watering trough. At first glance, the depot appeared to have the weighty substance of a Richardsonian building—in fact, an illusion, created by a less expensive frame structure enveloped by a stone-arched colonnade. Inside, the men's and ladies' waiting rooms had barrel-vaulted ceilings. A decade later, this depot design was copied in brick and stone by the Chicago, Burlington & Quincy at the Stone Avenue station in La Grange (still in use as a commuter stop). At La Grange, the CB&Q outdid the C&NW by increasing the massive stone arches from two to four. Kenilworth received an

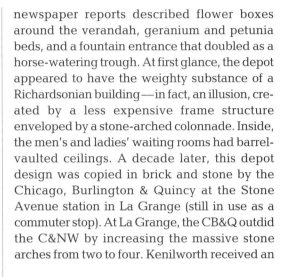

Porch interior after restoration in the 1980s.

Kenilworth station.   1890s.

Lake Forest, one of the largest stations in the Chicago suburbs, c.1900.

extensive restoration in the 1980s, which included re-creating the previously removed agent's bay. [Metra Commuter Rail. Train stop.]

LAKE FOREST

LAKE FOREST RAILROAD STATION
Western Avenue and Deer Path
Frost and Granger
c. 1899

Similar in style to the spacious Tudor Revival residences of many Chicago & North Western passengers, the Lake Forest station was one of the largest in the Chicago suburbs. It was financed by contributions from Lake Forest residents, who included the railroad's president. The architects, Charles Frost and Alfred Granger, both lived in Lake Forest and also designed city hall. Originally surrounded by a park, the depot had a separate ladies' waiting room warmed by a fireplace. The brick inbound depot, with decorative half-timbering in the cross gables, and the outbound station were restored and updated in the 1980s, although the platform canopies were left in their truncated condition. Grant money from the Regional Transportation Authority was supplemented in large part by donations from individuals, businesses, garden clubs, and the Lake Forest Foundation for Historic Preser-vation (which spearheaded the restoration process). To make

the project feasible, the city leased the station from the railroad and assumed responsibility for maintenance and tenant management. Rental income from a bank, barber shop, and tobacconist helps maintain the two buildings. Twenty-one civic groups and 600 volunteers contributed to the project, including the events on Platform Planting Day in 1985, when 130 people from ages eight to eighty installed 10,000 ground cover plants along the station's two 700-foot-long platforms. NR District. [Chicago & North Western Transportation System. Train stop and mixed use.]

LOCKPORT

LOCKPORT RAILROAD STATION
West 13th and Commerce streets
c. 1863

The extant stations at Lockport and Lemont (adjacent stops, eight miles apart) were built of locally quarried dolomite limestone. Positioned along the Chicago & Alton right-of-way, Lockport differed from Lemont by having prominent stone quoins, a larger waiting room, and a freight room. In 1865, President Lincoln's funeral train stopped at this station, which is 100 feet east of what is designated today as the Illinois & Michigan Canal National Heritage Corridor. After suffering from considerable alteration and outright closure, the depot was

A passenger train of the Gulf, Mobile & Ohio (a successor to the Chicago & Alton) at Lockport station.

restored and rededicated in 1989. Windows, wainscoting, and benches re-create the conjectured early appearance of the waiting room and ticket office, an area used today by Metra commuters. The freight section is leased as private office space. [Illinois Central Railroad. Train stop and commercial.]

MATTOON

CLEVELAND, CINCINNATI, CHICAGO & ST. LOUIS STATION
Behind 1632 Broadway
1916

"Big Four" was the nickname of the mouthful Cleveland, Cincinnati, Chicago & St. Louis (eventually part of the New York Central System). Mattoon's economy revolved around the railroad. The city was platted in 1855 at a spot where a predecessor of the east-west Big Four line crossed the north-south Illinois Central. The two railroads shared depot facilities in a hotel, until city council requested that IC help reduce street congestion by depressing its tracks. (The Big Four tracks remained at street level, with the IC trains traveling through an open cut beneath them.) The hotel stop (Essex House) was demolished in 1914. Each line built its own depot, but made sure that bag-

gage and passengers could be easily transferred.

The Big Four station, which had division offices on the second floor, exhibited Beaux Arts classicism in its symmetry and clearly articulated parts. The exterior was sheathed in cement, stone, brick, and terra-cotta. Marquees suspended from chains protected the entranceways. Interior woodwork was oak. After railroad use ended in 1964, the building spent two decades as a warehouse. Development plans, explored since 1983, have not brought an occupant; although a 1993 grant from the state, and availability of special low interest loans, may yet pave the way for private enterprise. The tracks are gone; the 30 acres of rail yard and repair shops are now empty. The Illinois Central station (1916), although partly boarded up, is essentially unaltered and is used by Amtrak. NR. [Privately owned. Vacant—for sale or lease.]

OLMSTED

OLMSTEAD [*SIC*] DEPOT
Front Street and Caledonia Avenue
1872, 1910

Laid out in 1872 by E. B. Olmstead, reportedly the first Presbyterian minister in Southern Illinois, the town of Olmstead lost its *a* in 1940. The station was built by the Cairo & Vincennes Railroad and was later used by the "Big Four" (Cleveland, Cincinnati, Chicago & St. Louis). In 1910, the one-room 1872 depot was moved slightly to the north and incorporated into the southern end of a new station. Important products shipped from Olmsted included chickens, strawberries, mussels (from the Ohio River), and products from the Fullers Earth plant. Principally of board and batten construction with a wood-shingle roof, this combination freight and passenger depot is typical of the simple three-room plan that was a fixture in many American small towns. New York Central (which had absorbed the Big Four) stopped service to Olmsted in 1955, but the tracks remain. In the 1970s, after having used the depot as a storage facility, Edward Lowe (of cat litter fame) donated it to the village. A historical society formed in 1989 expressly to restore the building for use as a local history museum. NR. [Village of Olmsted. Museum.]

ROCK ISLAND

CHICAGO, ROCK ISLAND & PACIFIC STATION
5th Avenue and 31st Street
Frost and Granger
c. 1902

The Chicago, Rock Island & Pacific, whose predecessor (Chicago & Rock Island) arrived in town in 1854, was the first of several railroads to serve the community. By the early 1900s, the CRI&P complex was an important rail center that included a freight depot, laundry building (which also supplied steam to heat the passenger depot), commissary, and a huge roundhouse. Only the passenger depot and a relatively undistinguished baggage and express building remain. Built on a rusticated stone base, the one-story passenger station had decorative brickwork with brackets and dentils, 10 large arched windows, a tile hipped roof, and a 14-foot clock tower (which burned many years ago). In 1952, the CRI&P's 100th anniversary, the railroad decided to "improve" the passenger depot. During this effort, workers converted the middle window on the south side to an entrance, replaced the four grilled ticket booths with one modern desk, put plywood paneling across the wainscoting and the fireplace, removed stained glass from the transoms, and closed off the west vestibule for a restaurant.

The "Rock Island," which never transferred passenger operations to Amtrak, ended service to its namesake city in the late 1970s. The freight railroad which now uses the tracks holds title to the deteriorating depot. In 1993,

the city received phased ISTEA funds to permit stabilization of the exterior, new utilities, and possible re-creation of the tower. Holding an option to purchase, the city expects the depot to become a restaurant. NR. [Iowa Interstate Railroad. Vacant.]

SPRINGFIELD

GREAT WESTERN OF ILLINOIS STATION
1 Copley Plaza
c. late 1850s

Also known as the Lincoln Depot, the station built by the Great Western of Illinois was Abraham Lincoln's departure point for the Presidential Inauguration of 1861. At that time, the depot consisted of a one-story, freight section stretched along the tracks, to which an Italianate, two-story brick addition was soon added. Within a decade, a new combination freight and passenger depot was built a few blocks away; and the Lincoln Depot spent the next century housing a Wabash Railroad freight agency. In the 1960s, the building was being used as a railroad museum, when a serious fire gutted both the one-story former freight section and the head house second floor. A California newspaper publisher acquired the building for a branch office (the one-story section was removed) and re-created the interior space to approximate the Lincoln era. The corporate owners are committed to sharing the depot (one of six Lincoln historic sites in Illinois) with the public. Open to tourists April through August, the depot still sits on an active freight line. [Privately owned. Office and museum.]

UNION STATION
Madison Street between 5th and 6th streets
1898

In 1895, the Chicago & Alton built a new station (greatly altered in 1949, now in use by Amtrak) that was the finest in Springfield. Previously, citizens had boycotted the C&A for its poor facil-

Early postcard view of Springfield Union Station with turreted clock tower (now gone).

ities. The Illinois Central responded competitively by building Union Station, in which it leased space to other railroads, including the Baltimore & Ohio and the Chicago, Peoria & St. Louis. Clad with brick in shades of brown, red, and buff, the limestone-trimmed station had a steep, hipped roof of red-orange tiles. Inside finishes included red oak, Knoxville marble, ceramic mosaics, and bronze. Because of Springfield's status as the state capital and site of the Illinois State Fair, a triumphal arch bearing the inscription Union Station once spanned 5th Street adjacent to the depot. In 1946, IC removed the south porte-cochere and the 90-foot-tall clock tower. Passenger service ended in 1971. The platform area was enclosed in the late Eighties, when a developer spent $4 million converting the station to a retail center. Three years later, Union Station's use changed again, when it became the state historic preservation office. NR [Privately owned. Offices.]

SYCAMORE

SYCAMORE RAILROAD STATION
DeKalb Avenue and Sycamore Street
1880

Built of locally manufactured brick and lit by kerosene, the Sycamore station was the north-

ern terminus of the five-mile-long Sycamore, Cortland & Chicago. Its predecessor was the Sycamore & Cortland built in 1859 to save the town's county seat status—endangered when another railroad chose a route through the area that is now De Kalb. The first depot was wooden. The new one had a two-story main building for passenger services and railroad offices A perpendicular one-story freight wing was built of brick, resting on a limestone-block, raised basement. In the late 1880s, the line was purchased by the Chicago & North Western, which sold the depot 70 years later. Although its red brick is now painted a buff color, and some of the Italianate door and windows openings have been altered, the station's interior retains

Sycamore station with its slate roof and Italianate brackets.

original moldings and wainscoting. Ornamental roof brackets were lost about 1980, when the slate roof was removed; the lightning rods remain. NR. [Privately owned. Warehouse.]

UNION

MARENGO DEPOT
Olson Road, one mile east of Union
1851, 1873

About 1970, the Illinois Railway Museum needed a depot for its four-mile tourist railroad. It did what "real" railroads sometimes did — hauled in a depot from another location. In this case, it was a first generation station from the Chicago & Galena Union (later the Chicago & North Western) located in Marengo, three miles west. Transported in two sections, the depot was reassembled and a new roof applied. The baggage room, added in 1873, was converted to rest rooms with the loading door left intact. In the waiting room, where the museum needed more than one opening for selling tickets, members salvaged a second window from

another station. The depot originally was heated by stoves; plans include rebuilding the two chimneys. Other rail-related buildings at the 56-acre museum site include a signal tower from Spalding and a 1910 rapid transit station from Chicago. The Marengo depot was used as a location for the motion picture *A League of Their Own*. [Illinois Railway Museum. Tourist train stop.]

WILMETTE

WILMETTE RAILROAD STATION
1139 Wilmette Avenue
1873

About 1870, owners of land between Ridge Road and Lake Michigan sought to develop their holdings. In exchange for a share of anticipated real estate profits, the Chicago & North Western began making regular stops at a small wooden depot, constructed by the developers on the west side of the tracks. Within a few years it burned down, and ten subscribers contributed $3,400 to build a new one of fireproof

Wilmette's 1873 station in its first location.

construction in an Italianate style. The brick depot's image was featured regularly in real estate ads, which offered prospective buyers free train tickets to come inspect the building lots. In 20 years, Wilmette's population went from 300 to 3,000. In the 1890s, commuters demanded and got a new station on the east, or inbound side of the tracks (one block north of the old depot), where they could wait in comfort for the morning train. The 1873 depot was relocated to a spot opposite the new station, where it served as a freight house until 1946.

With its platform and canopy removed and arched windows boarded up, it then sat vacant until 1974, when, to prevent demolition, the village obtained it from the railroad. The 55-ton brick structure was transported to property a few blocks away, where its platform and canopy, columns and brackets, were re-created according to 1873 blueprints. About that time, the C&NW built a new commuter station, just north of the 1896 depot, which they then demolished. NR. [Wilmette Historical Society. Restaurant.]

Indiana

More than a dozen major railroad systems passed through Indiana—a state that eastern railroads had to cross as they headed for the hubs of Chicago and St. Louis. A 1989 study conducted by Ball State University revealed that there were approximately 1,500 steam and interurban depots standing in Indiana prior to World War I. Seven decades later, less than 300 remained, including freight depots. (Only 15 of those were functioning in a capacity close to their original use.) Ninety stations were demolished between 1976 and 1986 alone. The downward trend continued, with 19 more gone by 1994. Muncie lost both an 1886 Romanesque Revival union passenger station (razed in 1990 by Conrail) and a 1912 two-story Lake Erie & Western freight depot. The only upward-climbing number has been the percentage of depots converted to other uses—about half of the total that survive.

BEDFORD

SOUTHERN INDIANA RAILWAY DEPOT
Between I and J streets
1899

A Bedford volunteer group called Santa's Helpers keeps busy most days in a former depot, where workers fix up old toys for Christmas giving. Built by the Southern Indiana Railway (later the Chicago, Milwaukee, St. Paul & Pacific), this branch line station was once the furthest point east reached by any of the

western transcontinental railroads. Rock-faced Bedford limestone, in courses of alternating widths, was used for the depot's walls. Typical of many railroad stations, visual interest was concentrated above the eaves—a belcast and tile-covered roof, numerous dormers, and a cross gable with carved stone parapets and finials. After train service ended, the depot was used for many years as a railroad office, until leased in the late 1980s to the elves. It clearly needs maintenance and restoration. A matching stone heating plant once stood just west of the depot. The frame freight station is extant. Two blocks southwest, a 1926 passenger depot of the Chicago, Indianapolis & Louisville (the "Monon Route") is for sale by CSX Transportation. [Soo Line Railroad. Workshop.]

BEVERLY SHORES

SOUTH SHORE LINE STATION
Broadway and U. S. Route 12
Arthur U. Gerber
1929

The heyday of the interurban railroad was from the 1890s to the 1920s. A short-lived, but very prevalent form of light rail, interurbans operated by electricity and traveled on streetcar tracks within the cities they linked. Out in the countryside, they typically ran over private rights-of-way. The "train" (there was no locomotive) consisted of one or two cars; sometimes one car was freight. In town, they almost always loaded passengers from the middle of the street. Protection from the elements was provided by storefront depots or three-sided shelters. Depots similar to those of steam railroads were not altogether uncommon, although they tended to have a single face—oriented toward the street (where the tracks were)—and had less need for an agent's bay window.

Often, interurbans simply shared facilities with conventional railroads. Between towns, they stopped with easy frequency (just about anywhere they were flagged), to deposit mail, milk, packages, and people.

Samuel Insull was a public utilities pioneer and a disciple of Thomas Edison. Despite the massive decline of interurbans that began after World War I, Insull took over and modernized the three major lines out of Chicago. One he reorganized in the 1920s as the Chicago South Shore & South Bend—commonly called the South Shore Line. The Beverly Shores depot was built in conjunction with Insull's decision to upgrade from interurban to heavier standards, similar to those of a steam railroad. The South Shore Line helped promote the Indiana Dunes State Park along Lake Michigan. (That same destination is reached today, along with the Indiana Dunes National Lakeshore, by a modern interurban system—a direct descendant of the South Shore Line.) Built in a Spanish Colonial Revival style, two-thirds of the depot was the ticket agent's residence. The design —similar to several stations built on Insull's Chicago North Shore & Milwaukee and one other on the South Shore (now gone)—was the work of a staff architect. NR. [Northern Indiana Commuter Transportation District. Interurban stop/npa and vacant.]

South Shore Line interurban station at Beverly Shores.

FORT WAYNE

LAKE SHORE & MICHIGAN SOUTHERN DEPOT
Cass Street at Wells Street
1889

Although the main lines of several railroads, such as the Wabash and the New York, Chicago & St. Louis (the "Nickel Plate") served Fort Wayne, the Lake Shore & Michigan Southern entered the city on a branch line (formerly the Fort Wayne & Jackson). Its relatively small, Queen Anne–style station (known locally as the Cass Street Depot) was enhanced by its pleasing location on the banks of St. Mary's River, across from downtown. For part of its career, this was a union station serving railroads that came up from Cincinnati and Louisville. The depot's shingled and wood-paneled exterior walls were topped by a sweeping belcast roof, pierced by rounded corner bays, eyebrow dormers, and two large brick chimneys. Each waiting room had a fireplace. After train service ended about 1940, the depot served first as a warehouse, then as headquarters for a carriage ride business (with horses stabled in the express building), and most recently as a store. A machine shop still

stand just west of the passenger depot (along with evidence of a roundhouse and turntable). Five blocks northeast is the former L&MS brick freight depot and another machine shop. [Privately owned. Commercial.]

PENNSYLVANIA RAILROAD STATION
231 West Baker Street
William Lightfoot Price (Price and McLanahan)
1914

The Pennsylvania Railroad was doing major improvements on its main line to Chicago when the Ft. Wayne station was built (commonly known as Baker Street Station). The preceding depot, division headquarters, and repair shops were two blocks east. (The last parts of that complex were demolished in the late 1970s for a post office.) Because the tracks were being elevated, a pedestrian subway and stairs were built to provide platform access. The architect, William Price, was the brother-in-law of J. J. Turner—first vice-president of a holding company for PRR lines west of Pittsburgh. He designed a series of wonderful stations between the Smoky City and the Windy City, most of which are gone. (Three small combi-

Under construction, the LS&MS station in Fort Wayne.

nation stations by Price still stand in Indiana at Converse, Dunkirk, and Hobart.)

At Baker Street Station, the two-story center block contained a long waiting room with a barrel-vaulted ceiling and wide arched windows. Perpendicular wings had scaled-down second floors that were set back from the main facade and tucked behind three-part lunette windows. The east side contained a restaurant on the first floor with an employee auditorium on the second. The west side housed ticket and baggage services beneath crew locker rooms and the accounting office. Originally built of buff brick trimmed in unglazed terra-cotta, the station got a PRR make-over in 1952. The interior was not disturbed; but on the outside, the railroad replaced the terra-cotta with limestone. To install a conventional hung-gutter system, workers destroyed parapets and balustrades. In 1990, Amtrak rerouted its Pittsburgh to Chicago trains—bypassing Fort Wayne. The city then purchased the building from Conrail in hope of finding a new user. [City of Fort Wayne. Vacant.]

FRENCH LICK

FRENCH LICK DEPOT
State Route 56
John H. Stem
c. 1907

Branch lines of both the Chicago, Indianapolis & Louisville (the "Monon Route") and the Southern Railway used the French Lick depot, which was built primarily for the resort trade. Sidings behind the depot enabled Pullman cars to deliver guests directly to the front door of the massive French Lick Springs Hotel. A New York architect (who may have been related to Allen H. Stem of Reed and Stem) designed the story-and-a-half station with wide arches and leaded glass windows accenting Bedford limestone walls. Porte-cocheres were formed at

Limestone for the French Lick depot was quarried along the Monon line near Bedford.

either end by the extended hipped roof. The vaulted waiting room, surmounted by a clerestory, was rimmed with benches.

The SR tracks are used today by a tourist railroad, operated by the Indiana Railway Museum, which leases a portion of the depot from the resort owner. One block to the north stands the old Monon freight depot (1924), now a maintenance facility for the tourist railroad. [Privately owned. Tourist train stop, museum, and chamber of commerce information center.]

GARY

UNION STATION
Broadway, north of 4th Avenue
1910

By 1906, trunk lines from nine different railroads crossed the planned industrial city of Gary. The chairman of the United States Steel Corporation, E. H. Gary, was involved in decision-making by the railroads about various track alignments (or realignments) and location of new stations. The Lake Shore & Michigan Southern (New York Central System) and the Baltimore & Ohio built Union Station to replace a quick succession of temporary shelters. Wedged between the elevated

Gary Union Station, July 1910.

tracks of both lines, the Beaux Arts–style depot was built of reinforced, cast-in-place concrete, scored to look like stone. A one-story porte-cochere on the west end of the building was capped by a balustrade. Keystones, lozenges, dentils, and garlands were among the many classical details—also made of cast-in-place concrete. Inside, two stories above the main waiting room's marble floor, was a heavily coffered ceiling with a large skylight. Travelers wishing to make connections with the Pennsylvania Railroad could reach the PRR station by taking a streetcar (referred to in a contemporary newspaper as "the Electric Road") down Broadway.

Union Station, suffering both from a fire and the indignity, at one point, of an on-site automobile salvage operation, has stood vacant for many years. A rather ornate express building, connected to the passenger depot by a tunnel, is still standing but empty. The city is negotiating to purchase the property, which it proposes as a mixed use transportation and commercial facility, to include an Amtrak station and a rest stop for the Interstate 90 tollway. [CSX Transportation. Vacant.]

INDIANAPOLIS

UNION STATION
Jackson Place at South Illinois Street
Thomas Rodd
1888

Indianapolis Union Railway, a terminal company co-owned by several railroads, was reportedly the first such "union" venture in the country. In 1853, the company constructed a train barn, encompassing waiting rooms and five tracks. Enlarged in 1866, it was demolished two decades later for the present Union Station. By the 1880s, the Pennsylvania Railroad had gained majority control of the terminal company and thus influenced the selection of Pittsburgh architect Thomas Rodd. His Romanesque Revival design—a head house executed in brick and stone—strongly resembled a cathedral, with twin rose windows and a 200-foot tower. A stylistically unrelated, long-span shed sheltered passengers boarding the trains. Although this union station meant there were fewer tracks through the city, they were still at grade level. Citizens complained about the dangerous interaction among locomotives, vehicles, and pedestrians; but they were essentially ignored until 1899, when a woman drove her buggy into the path of an oncoming train (the crossing guard was on a break). The city enacted a compulsory grade separation ordinance, which was not fully implemented until 1923. Elevating the tracks included a new, two-block-long Bush shed (designed c. 1915 by William Price) above a lower level concourse.

By the 1970s, the station was scarcely used and deteriorating. Only a single ticket window was in operation; and snow was falling not simply on the roof, but through it. The Save Union Station group, which worked to keep people aware of the building's plight, was rewarded by the city's decision to purchase and stabilize the depot. After a decade-long hunt for a developer, Union Station was brought back to life in 1986, when it was rededicated as a festival market-

place and hotel, with train and bus service operating from the south side of the shed. Holiday Inn managed to fit 276 hotel rooms—each different from the other—into the shed's western end. Pullman cars, parked on the tracks, provided additional hotel accommodations. New uses, such as retail shops, a food court, and entertainment facilities, were placed in the more industrial spaces: the loading platform, the baggage area, and the eastern end of the ground-level concourse. The developer endeavored to keep spaces in the head house as similar to tradition as possible, with eateries in previous restaurant locations and offices on the upper floor. Restoration of the head house included massive work inside the barrel-vaulted waiting room, especially on the ornamental and highly varied plaster. The 100-foot-long stained glass skylight, blacked out during World War II, was uncovered. Federal grant money and private funds secured the project, which just made it under the wire before Congress severely altered the rules for rehabilitation tax credits. NR. [City of Indianapolis. Transportation center and mixed use commercial.]

LAFAYETTE

CHICAGO, INDIANAPOLIS & LOUISVILLE STATION
313 North 5th Street
1901

The trains of the Chicago, Indianapolis & Louisville (the "Monon Route") came right down the middle of Lafayette's streets and loaded passengers in a fashion more typical of an interurban line—from a street corner in front of the depot. Built of limestone, the station had neoclassical features such as Ionic pilasters, carved stone, and a flat, balustraded roof. In 1980, after spending two decades adapted to office space, the building was converted to a theater and art gallery. The Monon

Indianapolis Union Station c. 1889.

A train makes its typical street-corner stop at the CI&L station in Lafayette.

freight depot (1878), located at 5th and Salem, is boarded up and neglected. NR District. [Civic Theater of Lafayette. Mixed use.]

CLEVELAND, CINCINNATI, CHICAGO & ST. LOUIS STATION
10 South 2nd Street
1902

Until recently, all three of Lafayette's passenger depots were still standing; the Wabash was razed in 1992. The depot known as the Big Four Station (Cleveland, Cincinnati, Chicago & St. Louis) was also used by the Lake Erie & Western. Both lines were controlled by the New York Central System, and this depot is similar to a Lake Shore & Michigan Southern (NYC System) standard plan. Indiana's one other extant version is at Tipton (LE&W). Complete with the flared, hipped roof and Palladian dormers typical of this design, Lafayette's depot was built on a high limestone base, with maroon brick upper walls and limestone trim.

Because various railroad tracks have historically trisected the city—with one running 14 blocks down the center of 5th Street—the municipality has been involved for decades in a large-scale project to eliminate grade crossings. In 1979, it restored the Big Four depot, including terrazzo flooring, oak trim, and

Early view of the Lafayette CCC&StL depot. The Palladian dormer is typical of this design.

benches. Currently used as headquarters for the track relocation project, the depot will eventually be moved two blocks north to the foot of Main Street. As part of the new Depot Plaza, it will serve as a multimodal center, used by intercity buses and Amtrak (which until recently entrained passengers from mid-street in front of a hotel, as in railroading's early days). [City of Lafayette. Office—future transportation center.]

PRINCETON

EVANSVILLE & TERRE HAUTE STATION
West Broadway at 2nd Street
1875

In 1987, a group of preservationists built a small office for CSX Transportation's signal maintenance crew. It then traded the office for title to the old Evansville & Terre Haute (later Chicago & Eastern Illinois) passenger station, which was scheduled for demolition. The group's ongoing restoration includes removing white paint from the red bricks and re-creating the original wide eaves. The depot's arched door and window openings and round ventilation ports are identical on each set of opposing walls. A companion freight station once stood to the west. Princeton was also served by the Southern Railway (whose predecessor used the E&TH station for a period of time); remnants of its roundhouse and repair shops are extant south of town. The Southern Railway passenger station, which was a few blocks north of the courthouse, is gone. [Princeton Railroad Station, Inc. Vacant—future railroad museum.]

RICHMOND

PITTSBURGH, CINCINNATI, CHICAGO & ST. LOUIS STATION
E Street between 8th and 9th streets
D. H. Burnham and Company
1902

A Second Empire–style train barn preceded this neoclassical station designed by Daniel Burnham's firm. Residents at the time complained that the new one looked like a "store box" and was much smaller than the old depot. Officials explained that interurbans were taking away steam passenger business, and the new waiting room was indeed of sufficient size. Constructed of brick, the depot's

Richmond PCC&StL station, street side.

formal exterior included a terra-cotta frieze and belt course, pedimented gables, and a portico. On the eastern end, a canopy connected the passenger station to a small express building. A division point for the Pittsburgh, Cincinnati, Chicago & St. Louis (later the Pennsylvania Railroad), the depot housed offices on the second floor. The downstairs included a fancy lunch counter and a newsstand (plus in wartime, a U.S.O. facility) that were busy 24 hours a day. An iron, long-span shed (now demolished) covered several stub-end tracks, with through tracks on the outside. In 1988, the nonprofit Urban Enterprise Association purchased the depot from the city (which had rescued it from the railroad). The building has been stabilized, but needs an adaptive use. NR District. [Privately owned. Vacant—for sale.]

ROCKVILLE

ROCKVILLE RAILROAD STATION
U.S. Route 36
c. 1883

Rockville's passenger station was built by the Vandalia Railroad, which became a component of the Pennsylvania system. Its design is very

similar to a PRR standard plan known as "Panhandle System Class C." Because the line ran right down the middle of Virginia Street, residents complained about safety, noise, and air quality. The tracks were realigned; and about three years after the depot was constructed, it was hauled to a new location on the east end of town. Passenger service ended in the late 1930s. In 1972, a nonprofit, tourist promotion group bought the depot, which retains its original Stick Style exterior. Today, tour buses, rather than trains, pick up passengers at the limestone-edged, brick platform. A similar version of this once common depot design stands (in less well-preserved condition) at Frankton. [Parke County, Inc. Office and tourist center.]

SOUTH BEND

UNION STATION
South Street, west of Lafayette Boulevard
Fellheimer and Wagner
1929

Jointly used by the New York Central and the Grand Trunk Western, South Bend Union Station was completed the same year as

South Bend Union Station under construction c.1929.

Central Terminal in Buffalo, N.Y. The NYC hired the same architects, Fellheimer and Wagner, for both projects. A medium-size, brick depot in Art Deco style, South Bend had a curving roofline that foreshadowed the firm's 1933 creation—Cincinnati Union Terminal. Linked to elevated platforms by a wide, underground concourse, the station's waiting room had a 50-foot-high vaulted ceiling, flanked by two-story wings. Trams hauling items from the attached Railway Express Agency building worked their way up four ramped tunnels to the tracks.

Passenger service ended in the early 1970s when Amtrak moved to a boxy new station on the west side of town. A decade later, the South Bend Heritage Foundation lent seed money to an entrepreneur, who rehabilitated the express building for light manufacturing and the passenger depot for offices and a catering service. Two blocks away, at Main and Bronsen streets, stands another former station (ironically sitting adjacent to an old Studebaker factory), built in 1900 by the Terre Haute & Logansport. [Privately owned. Mixed use.]

VEEDERSBURG

TOLEDO, ST. LOUIS & WESTERN STATION
U.S. Route 136
1903

The Toledo, St. Louis & Western station at Veedersburg was built from the same plan as the one at Bluffton, now demolished. The depot was executed in brick to windowsill level with wood above, rather than the more typical all masonry construction of Romanesque Revival. When passenger service ended, the depot was used by railroad maintenance crews. In 1990, after two years spent negotiating the depot's purchase from Norfolk Southern, the current owner began restoring the building for an unspecified use. He removed the dropped ceiling, uncovered the windows, and began researching the depot's multiple color scheme, which he plans to reproduce. The tracks are gone. Also on Route 136 (at Railroad Avenue) is the remaining leg of an L-shaped, board and batten depot, c. 1880, used by the Peoria & Eastern and the Chicago & Eastern Illinois. [Privately owned. Vacant.]

Iowa

By 1900, Iowa had 9,185 miles of track, fourth highest in the nation, but no metropolises. Iowa was heavily traveled because it was part of the land bridge between Chicago and the West. As trains moved through the state, they gathered the products of Iowa's farms —principally livestock and grain. Stock pens and tall, gabled grain elevators were fixtures at nearly every station. Most depots were frame buildings of standard design, although some were replaced by masonry structures as business and population multiplied. Of the numerous trunk lines that webbed Iowa, the Chicago & North Western tended to build the most sophisticated smaller stations—distinguished by structural variations rather than superficial ornamentation. The state's larger stations—for example, the Illinois Central station in Dubuque; the "Rock Island" and Union depots in Des Moines; and Union Station in Cedar Rapids—are all gone.

ATLANTIC

ATLANTIC RAILROAD STATION
Chestnut and 1st streets
1898

Grove City was an established town when the Chicago, Rock Island & Pacific arrived in this area during post–Civil War expansion. After the "Rock Island" chose Atlantic as the site for its station, many Grove City inhabitants pulled up stakes and moved to the newer town. Grove City eventually vanished. Atlantic's first depot (combination freight and passenger) was located a block east of the present structure. When a new one was built, the old wooden one was converted to freight storage and not razed until the 1970s. Atlantic's 1898 passenger depot was constructed of deep orange and buff brick, with marble tile floors and a tile roof. A contemporary newspaper proudly reassured readers that the depot contained no wood, except for the interior trim and wainscoting. It was heated by steam and lit with electricity. As with many depots, the second floor could only be reached via an exterior stairway. Ornamental iron brackets supported the platform canopy that wrapped around the depot and also formed a breezeway (enclosed during the 1960s) to the express building. The cross-gabled second story housed the roadmaster's office. In the early 1990s, a nonprofit organization acquired the depot for an unspecified community use. The building's "island" location, with active tracks and a siding to either side, makes adaptation a challenge. NR. [Atlantic Rock Island Society Enterprise. Vacant.]

BREDA

BREDA RAILROAD STATION
Main Street, east of 1st Street
Frost and Granger
c. 1907

When Breda's 1877 depot was destroyed by fire, it was replaced with Chicago & Northwestern "Combination Depot No. 2." The standard plan was drawn in 1899 by the noted architectural firm Frost and Granger. This once common, but now rare depot is built of wood on a stone foundation. Slate shingles cover the hipped and gabled roof. Despite spending 20 years as a chicken hatchery, the depot retains its c. 1907 floor plan and most materials. In the early 1990s, with financial assistance from the state, a citizens group began restoring the sta-

At the Atlantic station, a variety of horse-drawn vehicles on an unpaved street.

Breda station. Sign on the wall (between the barrel and the man) reads:
BICYCLE RIDING ON THIS PLATFORM STRICTLY PROHIBITED.

tion. Work included rebuilding the wooden gutters and locating original furnishings. Historically, the depot never received electricity or central heating. The unusually meticulous restoration retained this status; the depot uses kerosene lighting and is heated by potbellied stoves (one original to the depot). A National Register nomination is in process. [City of Breda. Visitors center for rail trail.]

CARROLL

CARROLL DEPOT
North West and West 5th streets
Charles Sumner Frost
1896

The Carroll depot and matching American Express building recently escaped becoming a Walmart parking lot, but they are still endangered. The passenger depot was the third in Carroll for the Chicago & North Western (earlier ones had been in the east end of the rail yard). It was one of three that Charles Frost designed in the 1890s for the C&NW's Iowa main line. (Boone and Marshalltown are also

extant.) The floor plan lined up spaces in a straight line: (from east to west) men's waiting room, ticket office, ladies' waiting room, lunchroom, breezeway, and baggage room. Typical of many stations (and sometimes a problem for adaptive use), the rooms each had outside entrances, but no interior passage between them. This arrangement was partly to keep workers from disrupting the decorum of the ladies' area.

Changes over the years to the brick and limestone structure include a kitchen (added in 1906), alterations to the dormers and the corner tower (three small windows and the octagonal roof are gone), and removal of three chimneys and what were probably slate roof shingles. Total demolition is threatened if development pressures continue. The city would like to acquire the depot and the American Express building for a visitors center and the chamber of commerce. Negotiations with the railroad have been difficult, because it insists that the tracks be relocated away from the building, at the city's expense. NR. [Chicago & North Western Transportation Company. Railroad office and storage.]

Illinois Central train No. 105 pulling into the Cherokee station.

CHEROKEE

CHEROKEE RAILROAD STATION
West Maple and South 4th streets
1896

Many of the buildings in the former Illinois Central rail yard at Cherokee are intact, although in poor condition. The approximately 17 remaining structures date to various periods of railroad history through the 1950s, including an enginehouse and machine shop, a turntable, a sand house, and a scale house. By the early 1890s, railroad traffic at this division point was heavy enough to warrant a new passenger station. The old wooden combination station was moved across the tracks and converted to freight-only (extant, but second story removed). IC architects drew plans for an elegant brick passenger station. Its shallow eaves were supported by modillions; a metal cornice was ornamented with an egg-and-dart motif. A companion American Express building (enlarged 1922; extant) was built to the depot's south; a lunch room (1898; razed 1974), was constructed to the north.

In the 1940s, IC made repeated alterations to the passenger depot, including removal of important features that included east side entrance canopies, ornate second-story porches, hipped roof dormers, and leaded glass windows. Because the railroad took pains to match bricks and patch belt courses, these changes are not obvious. In the early Nineties, the city purchased the passenger depot and the express building from the Chicago, Central & Pacific (IC's successor in this territory), and then sold them to a local nonprofit group. Rehabilitation is underway. The tracks are still in use. NR. [Depot Renovation, Inc. Commercial space and future museum.]

COUNCIL BLUFFS

CHICAGO, ROCK ISLAND & PACIFIC STATION
1512 South Main Street
1898

Council Bluffs achieved an important place in railroad history during the 1860s when it became the jumping off point for transcontinental travel to the west. By the 1890s, 15 lines entered the city. By the 1990s, little physical evidence remained of Council Bluff's railroad heritage. The extant Chicago, Rock Island & Pacific station, successor to one that exploded in 1880 (there were two temporary depots), was built with battered brick walls and a tile roof. The station's design balanced a two-story, five-sided tower on the track side with a porte-cochere on the street side. Inside finishes included glazed brick, terrazzo, and oak. In 1954, the "Rock Island" bricked in the breezeway to make more room for freight. Passenger service ended in 1970. Fourteen years later, the local historical society and a group of model railroaders began converting the depot to the Railswest History Center. To make the building suit their needs, they created a passageway between the former men's and ladies' waiting rooms, which originally had only exterior doors. An identical Rock Island depot in Iowa City (NR) has been converted to a law office, retaining original station elements like the ticket window. [City of Council Bluffs. Railroad museum.]

CRESTON

CHICAGO, BURLINGTON & QUINCY STATION
200 West Adams Street
W. T. Krausch
1899

When first built, Creston's Chicago, Burlington & Quincy station was clearly visible from Iowa's prairie. Its imposing two-and-a-half stories were anchored by a stone base. A copper cornice provided a transition between the yellow brick walls and the red tile roof with its six large dormers. By using glass panels (later changed) to roof the steel platform canopy, the CB&Q staff architect avoided darkening the depot's interior. The large general waiting room had a floor of deep red marble, which contrasted with four massive white pillars. Wall treatment combined dark green tile wainscoting with cream-colored, enameled bricks. The ceiling was oak. Besides the men's smoking, ladies' retiring, and lunch rooms, the depot housed numerous railroad offices, including ones for the special agent (who provided security), the timekeeper, the master carpenter, the chief dispatcher, and the superintendent. The Creston yards had a huge stone roundhouse, reportedly the largest in the CB&Q system.

During the 1970s, the city acquired the station for a parking lot. When citizens protested and then voted in favor of a preservation bond issue, the depot was rehabilitated. The main waiting room is intact, functioning now as an informal museum and memorial room. Senior citizens (who are served meals in the old baggage, mail, and express rooms) sometimes congregate on the waiting room's oak benches. The chamber of commerce conducts business through the ticket window. Former division offices on the second floor have become city hall. NR. [City of Creston. Municipal complex.]

A crowd waits under the platform canopy at the Creston CB&Q station.

FORT MADISON

ATCHISON, TOPEKA & SANTA FE STATION
Foot of 9th Street
1910

As tourism blossomed in the late 19th and early 20th centuries, the Atchison, Topeka & Santa Fe heavily advertised its main line heading west through Arizona, New Mexico, and California. Depots such as the one at Fort Madison were built in Spanish Colonial Revival or Mission styles to whet the potential tourist's appetite. Designed by the railroad's chief engineer, the Fort Madison depot (which replaced an 1880s wooden one) was built of brick with a red tile roof. Rounded arches, a square tower, curvilinear dormers, exposed rafters, and an outdoor waiting area enhanced the Southwestern connection. In the mid-1920s, the Railway Express Agency built an adjoining structure of a sympathetic architectural style. Another building was added to the complex in the Thirties when the railroad built a two-story combination freight office/crew-changing-and-sleeping facility. (Its loading dock was destroyed in a 1970s fire.)

In 1968, the city obtained the one-story depot (altered somewhat after a 1945 fire), which it leases to the county historical society.

The interior was damaged in the 1993 Mississippi River flood, when water rose to a level of four feet and soaked the interior for a month. A former Chicago, Burlington & Quincy depot, directly to the northwest, was similarly affected. The city subsequently purchased the CB&Q for an unspecified use. Both the Burlington Northern (CB&Q successor) and AT&SF tracks are still active. Fort Madison was a "Santa Fe" division point; a large enginehouse still stands on the west end of town. NR District. [City of Fort Madison. Museum.]

KEOKUK

UNION DEPOT
200 South Water Street
Burnham and Root
1891

The citizens of Keokuk spent years lobbying for a union station; but not until many small lines consolidated, or were swallowed by larger railroads, was capital available for this undertaking. Officers for the Keokuk Union Depot Company were drawn from several railroads, including the Keokuk & Western (later the Chicago, Burlington & Quincy). For travelers, the depot's opening day meant no more de-

Fort Madison AT&SF station.

Keokuk Union Depot before the tower was damaged by lightning.

crepit train sheds and muddy streets. With the installation of a 200-foot-long macadamized wagon way, a plank sidewalk, and brick platforms, passengers could make a dry-footed approach to the one-story, red brick Victorian station. The exterior was trimmed in stone and terra-cotta; interior finishes included marble, oak, and buff-colored brick. Oak benches in the men's and ladies' waiting rooms were perforated with the words Keokuk Union Depot. Radiators were gilded. The balance of the first floor consisted of a lunch counter, newsstand, ticket office, baggage room, mail room, boiler room, and offices for three express agencies — American, Adams, and U.S. & Pacific. Daniel H. Burnham and John W. Root took no chances on the unreliability of early electricity; they provided for both gas and electric lighting. Just south of the baggage room, an outside stairway led to the tower, which housed rooms for the telegraph operator, station master, and trainmen. The building was capped by a tile roof with copper downspouts, ornaments, and cornices. The corrugated wrought-iron platform canopy was supported by iron columns. A streetcar line and a hack stand completed this late 19th-century transportation center.

In 1939, the central tower with its two clock dormers (which apparently never received clocks) was struck by lightning, then later stripped of its details and chopped down to half-height. The pink marble floors were covered over with terrazzo in a 1949 modernization program that included suspended ceilings and new partitions. Passenger service ended in 1967. About 25 years later, a group of businesspeople acquired the old union depot company and began a partial restoration of the building. At a two-day open house in 1991, a century after the station's first dedication, 3,500 visitors came to inspect and reminisce. [Keokuk Union Depot Company. Special events facility.]

MT. PLEASANT

MT. PLEASANT RAILROAD STATION
418 North Adams Street
1912

For five years, the citizens of Mt. Pleasant squabbled with the Chicago, Burlington & Quincy over the need for a new passenger station. Newspaper editorials referred to the old one as "shameful . . . loafers occupy all the seats, the men's room is seldom fit for men to occupy . . . passengers cannot even secure water to drink . . .the sanitary arrangements are revolting." Lack of space meant that baggage, coffins, and express stood outside in the rain. Citing other towns the "Burlington" had accommodated, Mt. Pleasant finally applied enough pressure to get a new station, one block east of the old one. In a common railroad practice, the blueprints were used simultaneously for a depot at Fairfield (extant), 22 miles west.

Built of pressed brick with limestone trim and a slate roof, Mt. Pleasant had many modern amenities including hot-water heat, electricity, and two "sanitary bubbling" fountains. A general waiting room was augmented by a ladies' retiring room (with rocking chairs) and a men's smoking room. Wainscoting was enameled tile; trim was oak. From the agent's bay window, the operator could see traffic for a mile east and west. Instead of the old system of rods and levers, he activated electrically triggered semaphores. Ample baggage and express areas completed the depot, which was floored in mosaic tile and maple. The preceding Mt. Pleasant depot, purchased by a private party, was hauled away to become a soda pop factory. By 1988, its 76-year-old successor station was suffering from deferred maintenance. The city, Amtrak, and the freight railroad which owns the building cooperated in a repair and beautification project. The endeavor was organized by the depot's devoted caretakers and largely executed by volunteer labor. The railroads jointly provided a new roof and platform. Two other CB&Q depots, moved from Hillsboro and Yarmouth, are installed at the Midwest Old Threshers Museum in Mt. Pleasant. [Burlington Northern Railroad Company. Train stop.]

SHENANDOAH

WABASH DEPOT
North of Ferguson Street in Sportsman's Park
1903

The post–Civil War decades were an era of feverish track laying and vicious competition among railroads. Begun by shrewd and greedy Jay Gould, the Wabash, St. Louis & Pacific Railway (later the Wabash Railroad) needed depots that could be erected cheaply and quickly. The Wabash adopted a one-story, combination freight and passenger station as its standard design. Built of wood, Wabash depots varied principally in applied elements, such as spindled brackets, gable screens, and siding. A cross gable created the agent's bay window, similar to the standard plans of other railroads in Gould's empire (such as the Union Pacific, Missouri Pacific, and Erie). When more square footage was needed, lengthwise extensions could easily be made.

The present Shenandoah depot replaced an earlier standard plan station. Although the Wabash had mostly eliminated gender-segregated waiting rooms by 1900, the arrangement at Shenandoah represented the older concept. Clad in a variety of sidings and shingles, the depot had wide eaves (supported by angle braces) and a Queen Anne–style window (small panes around a large center pane) in each gable peak. By the late 1980s, the depot was derelict, but intact. To beat the wrecking ball, two nonprofit groups rescued the depot from the Iowa Southern Railway and relocated it to a spot where the Wabash right-of-way (now a rail trail) crosses active Burlington Northern tracks. The preservationists later donated the building to the city. About four blocks away, Shenandoah's Chicago, Burlington & Quincy depot (c. 1910) is now a restaurant. NR. [City of Wabash. Visitors center for rail trail.]

Kansas

Kansas railroading was dominated for decades by the Atchison, Topeka & Santa Fe. (Missouri Pacific was runner-up). The Spartan frame depots of earlier years were upgraded as profits rose. The majority were replaced by more attractive standard plans in wood; others, by custom designs in masonry. Typical of most states, a disproportionate number of masonry stations remain standing. This survival rate was lowered by a notorious event that occurred in Herrington in 1988. Under cover of darkness and without a demolition permit, the St. Louis Southwestern Railway (the "Cotton Belt") demolished a former Chicago, Rock Island & Pacific depot and nearby freight house. The community was in the midst of raising funds to rescue the two-story limestone passenger station when the surprise occurred.

ABILENE

UNION PACIFIC DEPOT
Broadway and North 2nd Street
Gilbert Stanley Underwood
1929

In 1867, Union Pacific was the first railroad to reach Abilene. It remained a monopoly until the arrival of the Chicago, Rock Island & Pacific and the Atchison, Topeka & Santa Fe two decades later. UP's first depot was made of wood and stood north of Texas Street. It was replaced in 1880 by a multistory, frame hotel that included a restaurant and depot (razed in 1928). Citizen pressure on UP for a modern station was boosted when the "Santa Fe," with only a branch line into Abilene, constructed new facilities in 1927. For UP's new design, the railroad commissioned Californian Gilbert Stanley Underwood, whose works eventually included at least 20 small to medium-size stations. In a 1930 magazine article, Underwood outlined the concept he used at Abilene. Noting the publicity value of a station at the end of a main street, he emphasized the further advantage created by a naturally divided traffic flow. People regularly had their valises and trunks delivered to the station by

Ornamentation above the entrance to the Abilene UP depot. Dragons flank a cartouche filled with the railroad's shield.

baggage services. Underwood's plan sent automobiles to the east for parking, vehicles carrying baggage or express shipments to the west wing, and pedestrians directly into the tall center section, which contained the general waiting room. The east end contained men's smoking and ladies' retiring rooms. Typical of Spanish Colonial Revival depots, an open-air waiting room was included under the red tile roof. Underwood made extensive use of polychrome terra-cotta (tan highlighted with blue and red) for exterior ornamentation. He also designed the freight depot (extant), just to the west.

In 1985, UP announced that the station was scheduled for destruction, unless removed from the right-of-way. Instead, the city negotiated to lease the building, accept liability, and leave the depot where it belonged. A special advisory committee raised funds to renovate the interior. The building is essentially intact today, despite the loss of original light fixtures, a number of exterior doors, and the ticket office partitions. Abilene has two other extant depots. The AT&SF depot is now in freight railroad use; a relocated CRI&P depot is a museum (both are located off Buckeye Street). NR. [City of Abilene. Civic center.]

BALDWIN CITY

BALDWIN CITY DEPOT
15th and High streets
1907

The ladies' waiting room at Baldwin City had an early air cooling system. Under the floor, copper coils were surrounded with ice, and water was pumped through the tubing. The entire depot was a modern improvement for the community, whose acting mayor lobbied the Atchison, Topeka & Santa Fe to replace an inadequate wooden station. His efforts were rewarded in 1906, when the railroad announced not only plans for a new structure, but also landscaping to beautify the lots east of the depot. Built of limestone-trimmed, buff brick, the station had arched tripartite doors and windows (excluding the freight section). The belcast, hipped roof was originally covered with metal shingles. A carriage entrance led directly to the front-hall ticket window. At some point, possibly when passenger service ended in the 1950s, the men's waiting room was converted to additional freight space and the fireplace removed (the ladies' remained). By the 1960s, freight service too was discontinued. Late in the next decade, the city acquired the building.

It transferred title to the historical society, which pledged to rehabilitate the depot and adapt it to a community center. However, in 1987, an excursion line (which operates over part of the former AT&SF tracks) began using the building. Located next to the ubiquitous midwestern grain elevator, the depot is set up inside as a post–World War II operating station. NR. [Santa Fe Trails Historical Society. Tourist train stop and depot museum.]

CHANUTE

ATCHISON, TOPEKA & SANTA FE DEPOT
111 North Lincoln Avenue
1903, 1917

In Chanute (named for a railroad civil engineer), the Atchison, Topeka & Santa Fe depot not only housed 23 division offices on the second floor, but also had a Harvey House on the north end. The red brick depot, trimmed with cut stone and roofed in slate, was steam-heated and wired for both gas and electric lighting (in case the electricity failed). When the depot proved too small during World War I, the "Santa Fe" nearly doubled its size. At the north end, the enlarged Harvey House contained a bigger kitchen, a dining room, a crescent-shaped, brown marble lunch counter, and an expanded waitress dormitory (upstairs). Silver coffee urns and flatware, finger bowls, and Irish linen were among the amenities that both travelers and townspeople enjoyed. A two-story addition on the south end increased floor space for baggage and Wells Fargo express. The cupola atop the depot was a small storage room. A separate building housed a "Reading Room" (now gone). Reading Rooms combined the functions of a library and social center, which Santa Fe provided for employees in isolated areas. They often included a gymnasium, bowling alley, billiard parlor, auditorium, bunks, and baths.

This trackside view of the Chanute AT&SF depot includes the neighboring Faultless Flour Company.

The depot's booming years had slowed by 1931 when the Harvey House shut down (the Harvey newsstand lasted until the late Fifties). Passenger service ended in 1971. Freight service was moved to a former roundhouse site 12 years later, and the depot closed completely. Purchased by a local businessman to prevent its demolition, the station eventually was acquired by the city. The $2 million dollar renovation, financed completely by private donations (im-pressive in a community with a population of 10,000), included replacing the roof with salvaged tiles of identical manufacture. Formally reopened in 1993, the depot triggered Chanute's downtown revitalization. The Mission-style station that served the Missouri, Kansas & Texas is gone. [City of Chanute. Public library and museum.]

EMPORIA

ATCHISON, TOPEKA & SANTA FE DEPOT
3rd Avenue and Neosho Street
1883, 1926

In 1883, the Atchison, Topeka & Santa Fe replaced a two-story wooden station (at 3rd and Merchant) with a large, Romanesque Revival, limestone building. Four decades later, when this second depot was deemed too small, the railroad enlarged it with Tudor Revival additions that doubled the square footage. Brick wings were built transverse to the original depot. They were linked to each other on the trackside by an arcade, above which peeked the earlier depot wall (amended with its own Tudor dormer). The streetside facade was Romanesque Revival in the middle and Tudor Revival at either end. The expanded depot housed division headquarters, relocated from Topeka, and was augmented by new yard facilities including a 32-engine roundhouse, coal and sand chutes, and sheep feeding barns. A Harvey House restaurant (1880) was located in a separate building. It closed in 1937 and was razed two years later. Amtrak's kiosk now sits on the southwest corner of the Harvey House site.

In 1957, *Santa Fe Magazine* proudly reported the modernization of the Emporia depot. Its "huge, old-fashioned waiting room" was reduced in size to 45 seats. "Outstanding construction features throughout" included suspended ceilings and new movable partitions. Fifty-three windows were bricked up or filled with glass blocks. In 1988, AT&SF moved its division offices to Kansas City and tore down Emporia's concrete platform canopy. Five years later, after trying to sell the depot on the open market, the railroad offered to donate both the

Emporia AT&SF depot

Original Romanesque
Revival structure c.1910

After Tudor Revival
make-over.

depot and land to the city. Citing fiscal problems, the city refused the offer. The building's fate remains uncertain. Emporia also had a fine, c. 1890 masonry depot built by the Missouri, Kansas & Texas, but it was demolished in 1953. [Atchison, Topeka & Santa Fe Railway. Train stop/npa and vacant—for sale.]

LAWRENCE

UNION PACIFIC DEPOT
North 2nd Street (at Maple and Locust streets)
Henry Van Brunt (Van Brunt and Howe)
c. 1889

Lawrence's first Union Pacific depot was a one-story board and batten structure dating from the 1860s. In 1888, after the Union Pacific president visited Lawrence, he commissioned his longtime friend Henry Van Brunt to design new passenger and freight stations. Although Van Brunt and Howe, who originally practiced in Boston, designed a number of stations for UP, most of their business was residential. Their depots tended toward the Richardsonian, but with Queen Anne details of a more domestic nature. Lawrence's passenger station had the flavor of an English country church. Built of Junction City limestone, with red brick and Colorado red stone trim, it had a cross-gabled, hipped roof sheathed in slate. On the west end, supported by cast-iron columns, was a platform canopy (removed after a 1903 flood). Inside, the men's and ladies' waiting rooms were finished in California redwood, with furnishings in light colors. In 1944, the depot was modernized by changing the wooden floors and the brick platform to concrete, moving the ticket office to the west end, combining the waiting

Lawrence UP depot with its flowered walkway and original spire.

rooms, adding an acoustical tile ceiling, and replacing the sliding baggage and express doors with overhead garage versions.

Passenger service ended in 1971. Thirteen years later, after UP discontinued using the building for freight, a local group called the Save the Depot Task Force began a protracted fight to prevent demolition. Its members also successfully resisted UP's insistence that the depot be moved in order to be saved. In 1991, the railroad deeded the depot to the city. Private donations paid for interior stabilization. ISTEA provided funds in 1993 for reconstruction of thetall spire (lopped off in the 1930s) and for completion of the inside. Lawrence's historic Atchison, Topeka & Santa Fe depot (1883) was demolished in the 1950s following a flood and replaced by a modern railroad building. [City of Lawrence. Civic offices and public meeting space.]

LEAVENWORTH

ATCHISON, TOPEKA & SANTA FE DEPOT
781 Shawnee Street
c. 1887

During the 1880s and 1890s, as the major passenger and freight carrier from Kansas to California, the Atchison, Topeka & Santa Fe promoted settlement across the high plains and through the Southwest. In 1887, the company constructed nearly one thousand miles of track in Kansas. The one-and-a-half-story Leavenworth depot, which also served an interurban line, was built in a Romanesque Revival style of rusticated, dark pink sandstone with a slate roof and metal cresting. One of the gable projections that pierced the hipped roof was topped by a tall, corbeled chimney. A circular tower with a conical spire housed the station master's office. About 1944, the AT&SF put an addition on the freight section (south wall). Passenger service ended in the 1930s, and freight in 1982. The tracks are gone. NR. [Privately owned. Restaurant.]

Leavenworth AT&SF depot, 1958.

UNION DEPOT

201 South Main Street
Cobb and Frost
1888

Built on a sloping site, Leavenworth Union Depot had one story facing the street, but two stories on the track side along the Missouri River. Passengers descended iron staircases to reach the covered boarding area. Designed by Chicago architects Henry Ives Cobb and Charles Sumner Frost, the facility was initially planned and promoted by the Union Pacific. The Chicago, Rock Island & Pacific, the Atchison, Topeka & Santa Fe, the Missouri Pacific, and two short lines were members of the building committee. The Romanesque Revival structure was brick with sandstone trim and a red slate roof. The ridge roll and gutters were copper. In 1988, after previously being converted to commercial office space, Union Depot was purchased by the city and made into a community center. The old freight section has meeting rooms and offices; the baggage area is an exercise facility. The men's and ladies' waiting rooms and the ticket office are essentially intact, except for the light fixtures. A gym, racquetball courts, and a swimming pool were installed in a modern addition. NR. [City of Leavenworth. Community center.]

LIBERAL

LIBERAL DEPOT

U.S. Route 83 (Kansas Avenue) and Trail Street
1911

After the Chicago, Rock Island & Pacific arrived in Liberal in 1888, Springfield lost its county seat status to the newly founded railroad community. Liberal's first "Rock Island" depot, a wooden combination hotel and ticket office, burned in 1910. The railroad replaced it with two separate Mission-style structures. Clad in brick and stucco with a red tile roof, the staff-designed depot had a general waiting room, men's smoking room, agent's office, and baggage room on the first floor. Railroad offices were upstairs. To the west was a two-story, T-shaped building that housed the Grier Eating House and the Cimarron Hotel. The first-floor restaurant had a lunch room and dining room that were elaborately hand-decorated by Nelson & Company of Chicago. The second floor of the hotel had 24 guest rooms, furnished with solid mahogany and equipped with private baths. By the late 1930s, both establishments were out of business. The hotel's north wing was removed, probably in the same decade. The Rock Island and successor freight lines used the hotel-eating house and the depot for offices until the mid-1980s. The city is

Cimarron Hotel c. 1914. The Liberal depot is on the far right.

Madison AT&SF depot c. 1908, in its original size and configuration. The freight door is located in an end wall. The loading door that faces the track is marked Wells Fargo & Co. Express.

trying to acquire both buildings—periodically threatened with demolition—for civic use. [Southern Pacific Lines. Vacant.]

MADISON

ATCHISON, TOPEKA & SANTA FE DEPOT
3rd and Boone streets
c. 1879, 1915, 1920

When an Atchison, Topeka & Santa Fe predecessor established a station at Madison, its depot grounds included a privy, stockyard, water tank, wind mill, two tool houses, and a pump house. Madison quickly became a major shipping point for cattle and agricultural goods out of the Flint Hills. The board and batten depot was enlarged twice. In each phase, the wooden pier foundation was extended and the gable walls reattached as new end walls. (The depot's wide eaves are supported by differing bracket styles that testify to the additions.) Originally painted a deep clay red on the outside (later "Santa Fe yellow"), the depot had a simple interior plan. The gabled-dormer bay contained the agent's office, flanked by wait-

ing, baggage, and freight rooms. A Missouri Pacific depot (now gone) stood one block to the east. Passenger service to Madison ended on both railroads in the 1940s. A half-century later, assisted by the state Heritage Trust Fund, Friends of the Depot rehabilitated the AT&SF station, for probable use as a museum and community center. The tracks are gone. NR. [City of Madison. Vacant.]

NEWTON

ATCHISON, TOPEKA & SANTA FE DEPOT
5th and Main streets
1930

Newton's distinction went beyond being a division point for the Atchison, Topeka & Santa Fe. It was also district headquarters for the Fred Harvey Company, which supplied food service for AT&SF trains. At one time in the Newton area, Harvey operated dairy and poultry farms; a creamery; a laundry; and ice, bottling, and produce plants. The depot itself, a triangular-shaped Tudor Revival building, contained a Harvey House restaurant that was a continua-

Street-corner view, Newton AT&SF depot, 1931.

tion of the one that had operated in the predecessor 1899 depot. Newton's Harvey House lasted until 1957, reportedly the longest lived of any in the chain, and then remained open under successive owners until 1980. Designed by the AT&SF engineering staff, the depot's reddish-brown brick walls were accented by stone quoins, window frames, and copings. A slate roof topped the two-story center section. Gothic arches and stepped buttresses formed arcades on both the southeast and northwest facades. Decorative half-timbering — on the trackside exterior and on the restaurant's interior walls — furthered the medieval flavor. Used today by Amtrak, the waiting room and ticket office serve their original purposes. Remaining space was adapted in the early Eighties to commercial usage. NR. [Privately owned. Train stop and offices.]

OSAGE CITY

ATCHISON, TOPEKA & SANTA FE DEPOT
508 Market Street
c. 1912

Osage City's first depot (1869) was enlarged in 1885 to accommodate the coal boom. It was built of wood and located just south of the pre-

sent structure, a Mission-style standard design. The Atchison, Topeka & Santa Fe made frequent use of this pattern throughout Kansas, Oklahoma, and Colorado from about 1910 to 1920. The depot was mostly brick with a rough stucco finish, trimmed in mottled brick, and covered by a red tile roof. Poured concrete "Santa Fe" logos adorned the gable ends of the central projecting pavilions. There were three waiting rooms: general, ladies', and open-air (with built-in concrete settees). Passenger service ended in 1971. In the 1980s, a historical society bought the depot from the railroad. The northeast end contained a badly deteriorated Wells Fargo express office, which the society decided to remove, and a freight section, which it rehabilitated. The tracks are still used by freight and Amtrak trains. NR. [Osage County Historical Society. Museum.]

OTTAWA

ATCHISON, TOPEKA & SANTA FE DEPOT
135 West Tecumseh Street
1889

In the late 1800s, contemporary newspapers stirred up Ottawa's hopes for a grand station by mentioning inclusion of a hotel and Fred

Harvey restaurant, but none materialized. The new two-story depot, built of rough hewn stones, stood alone under its terne metal, hipped roof. At each end, projecting gables were ornamented with low arched recesses and sunburst patterns. The platform canopy was supported by cast-iron posts with decorative corner brackets. In the early 1960s, the Atchison, Topeka & Santa Fe donated the station, little altered through time, to the historical society. Its museum includes period rooms installed in the former second-floor division offices. On the first floor, a model layout reproduces the railroad lines that ran through the county. NR. [Franklin County Historical Society. Museum.]

TOPEKA

UNION PACIFIC DEPOT
Railroad and North Jackson streets
Gilbert Stanley Underwood
1927

With two of three significant passenger depots gone from Topeka (the 1887 Chicago, Rock Island & Pacific and the 1880 Atchison, Topeka & Santa Fe), residents are working hard to ensure the continued life of the surviving Union Pacific depot. UP's first permanent Topeka station was part of an 1872 three-story hotel, just east of Kansas Avenue. In the 1920s, the chamber of commerce spent two years petitioning the railroad for a replacement. It was rewarded with a five-part passenger station of red brick, ornamented in glazed terra-cotta, and roofed in tile. The floor plan included a lofty general waiting room (polychromed in tile and marble), a men's smoking room, and a women's lounge. The far east wing housed a restaurant. Baggage and express were handled from the far west end. A separate freight building (razed in the 1970s) was, like the passenger depot, a Gilbert Stanley Underwood design. His plans called for landscaped parks, reflecting pools, and automobile parking spaces. Opening day was celebrated with a parade (a chronological depiction of "transportation down through the ages") and banquets.

The UP depot was the site of a canteen for World War II troops and of a deluge in 1951, when eight feet of Kansas River water swirled into the waiting room. After passenger service ended in 1971, UP used the depot for freight railroad purposes until 1989. Three years later, vandals set fire to the building. The roof was damaged and the west central portion gutted (principally and ironically the area with the old men's smoking room). A local nonprofit group,

Early view of the Topeka UP depot. Except for awnings above the entranceways, the brick platforms provided no shelter from the elements.

Topeka Railroad Days, decided to expand its mission to include the depot. After obtaining a lease from UP, it was awarded ISTEA funding by the federal government to stabilize the building and begin work on a multipurpose center (most likely including a railroad museum) in the west end. Topeka's small Missouri Pacific station still stands about one block southwest of today's Amtrak station (built by the AT&SF in 1949). At another site in Topeka—Ward-Meade Park—a small AT&SF wooden depot (relocated from Pauline) has been restored and authentically furnished by "Santa Fe" employees and the National Railway Historical Society. An 1885 "Rock Island" freight depot, under consideration for a museum, was heavily damaged by fire and then bulldozed in 1994. NR. [Union Pacific Railroad. Vacant.]

WICHITA

Union Station
701 East Douglas Avenue
Louis Curtiss
1914

Known as the "daylight station" because of its avant-garde window walls, Wichita Union Station was, however, one of the more academic designs of unconventional architect Louis

Curtiss. The station, built primarily to eliminate the deathtrap Douglas Avenue crossing, served four major railroads: the Chicago, Rock Island & Pacific, the Atchison, Topeka & Santa Fe, the St. Louis & San Francisco, and the Kansas City, Mexico & Orient. (Missouri Pacific stayed in its own depot.) Among its amenities were a fruit and candy stand, ladies' retiring room staffed by a mother's helper, and men's smoking room. The Fred Harvey Company operated a newsstand, restaurant, and marble and bronze soda fountain. At the huge opening night banquet, 125 waitresses served 400 chickens, 100 cakes, and bushels of cheese balls. Less than 25 years later, the Harvey dining room was closed; and in 1940, the station's gray Bedford stone exterior was modernized by the removal of much terra-cotta ornamentation. Interior remodeling occurred in the Sixties with installation of a dropped ceiling and metal chairs.

In 1975, the station was acquired by the city, which spent six years and millions of dollars stabilizing the structure and looking for a new user —found when a cable television company purchased the station for its headquarters. Next door is the limestone-trimmed brick "Rock Island" depot (1887; NR), one of Union Station's predecessors, now used as offices. The CRI&P express building is a restaurant. Freight trains still travel the elevated AT&SF tracks. [Privately owned. Corporate headquarters.]

Wichita Union Station with terra-cotta ornamentation intact.

Michigan

In the 19th century, extractive industries like lumber and minerals (particularly iron and copper) brought wealth to Michigan's railroads. They piled some of the profits into huge depots built of stone. These buildings made a good impression on summer vacationers bound for lake resorts. Passenger business was needed more than ever once the natural resources had been depleted. Michigan Central was the most prosperous railroad on the Lower Peninsula—where the most elaborate surviving stations are found.

ALBION

ALBION RAILROAD STATION
300 North Eaton Street
c. 1882

In 1971, Albion's former Michigan Central (New York Central System) station closed, except for a single office used by railroad personnel. Amtrak passengers waited outside. In the mid-1980s, realizing that state funds were available for restoration—but only if the depot were converted to a multimodal facility—a small group of citizens devised a rescue plan. The city would lease the station from Amtrak and then sublet it to the chamber of commerce. The chamber

For valuation purposes, many railroads routinely photographed their depots. Dated in the lower right corner, this picture of the Albion station was taken on April 13, 1920.

would negotiate with Greyhound to help establish a transportation and tourist center. When the owner (Amtrak) approved the concept, an alliance of community and municipal organizations (including the National Trust's Main Street Program in Albion) took charge of the project. Albion College donated architectural and engineering services. Private donations, grants, and in-kind contributions were used for restoration and rehabilitation, including stripping several layers of red paint from the walls (revealing parallel bands of decorative brick) and rebuilding the chimneys. (Replacement of the cast-iron roof cresting was delayed pending acquisition of further funds.) Interior compromises involved lowering the tongue and groove ceilings from 17 to 13 feet and replacing the window sash with insulated replicas. After years as an eyesore, the transformed depot became Albion's symbol of downtown revitalization. [Amtrak. Transportation center and offices.]

ALPENA

ALPENA RAILROAD STATION
10th Street and Fair Avenue
Spier and Rohns
1911

Frederick H. Spier and William C. Rohns of Detroit were German immigrants trained in cathedral design. The firm received many depot commissions from various railroads, including the Michigan Central and the Grand Trunk system. Their railroad stations frequently combined stone and brick with multilevel roofs and rounded-end waiting rooms. When the Detroit & Mackinac Railroad hired Spier and Rohns to design a new depot for Alpena (replacing the old one on Fletcher Street), they incorporated all of these features and capped the entire creation with a dormered, tile roof. A festive banquet accompanied the station's mid-December opening. The depot has been out of service for several decades; its last use was as a warehouse. The tracks, though inactive, remain. In 1994 the building was gutted by fire, making its future uncertain. [Privately owned. Vacant.]

ANN ARBOR

MICHIGAN CENTRAL RAILROAD STATION
401 Depot Street
Frederick H. Spier (Spier and Rohns)
1886

In 1969, a restaurateur, the late Charles Muer (lost at sea in a 1993 accident), purchased Ann Arbor's Michigan Central station. He had difficulty arranging financing for the massive stone Romanesque Revival structure, not only because bankers were unfamiliar with adaptive use, but also because of the deteriorated neighborhood "down by the tracks." In the end, Muer was proven right—within seven years, the restaurant underwent a major expansion (accomplished by taking over the baggage building and enclosing the platform). By then, the station was famous as one of the nation's first large-scale depot-to-restaurant conversions, a success the Muer Corporation repeated at the Pittsburgh & Lake Erie station in Pittsburgh. Amtrak, which for awhile occupied the express building, eventually built a new station just the other side of the Broadway Bridge. When a train pulls in, the passenger cars extend past the restaurant windows. Pleased by the ongoing railroad connection, the diners have established a new tradition. They give the arriving train a round of applause. At another former Ann Arbor station, built c. 1889 by the Toledo, Ann Arbor & North Michigan, the railroad fans are smaller —the depot is now a preschool. NR. [Privately owned. Restaurant.]

Ann Arbor MC station. Romanesque arches, eyebrow dormers, and massive stone walls.

Battle Creek GT depot with its tower domes intact c.1928.

BATTLE CREEK

GRAND TRUNK DEPOT
175 Main Street
Spier and Rohns
1906

At Battle Creek, the new passenger depot of the Grand Trunk (later the Grand Trunk Western) had an inauspicious beginning when the stone masons went on strike for more money. Their work was needed for the first story, clad in rock-faced granite, hauled from New England. The upper story, the curvilinear end and cross gables, and the twin campaniles were brick. Spanish tiles covered both the roof, with its several Hindu-style domes (the two tower domes are no longer extant), and a circular bay. The grand interior included polychrome mosaic floors, white tile walls, vaulted ceilings, half-moon clerestory windows, and multiglobe chandeliers. After passenger service ended in 1971, GTW continued to use the depot as office space for another 17 years. In 1989, a social services agency adapted the station for its headquarters. Although a mezzanine level was added to the waiting room, many features were restored, including stained glass windows (repaired by the original manufacturer), a mural

of the Battle Creek River, and faux marble columns. The large depot dining room is now used for conferences. Both Amtrak and freight trains ply the tracks. [Privately owned. Offices.]

MICHIGAN CENTRAL STATION
55 West Van Buren Street
Rogers and MacFarlane
1888

Ladies who were waiting for Michigan Central (New York Central System) trains at Battle Creek had it easier than the men. They not only had their own waiting room with a fireplace, they also had a retiring room (in the rounded corner projection) and a lavatory, as well. The men's lavatory was located more than 50 feet away from the depot, in the baggage and express building. This new station replaced a less substantial one on North Monroe Street. Battle Creek's promoters gloated that it was 30 feet longer than the depot at Kalamazoo. Their sense of importance was no doubt further heightened by the tall clock tower, massive hipped roof, and porte-cochere supported by a huge arch. Designed by a Detroit architectural firm, the depot was very red and very regional —built of Lake Superior red stone and Detroit red bricks, with an Akron red tile roof. A large

Battle Creek MC station bordering the Battle Creek River.

streetside park (now a parking lot) served as green space for both the depot and the public library. The 1970s and 1980s were troubling decades for the station, with Amtrak moving to a new location and a fire damaging the tower and roof. The tracks were removed as part of a consolidation project, placing all trains passing through downtown Battle Creek on the former Grand Trunk Railway tracks. In 1992, guided by the Secretary of the Interior's Standards for Rehabilitation, businesspeople converted the depot to commercial use. NR. [Privately owned. Restaurant]

BIRMINGHAM

BIRMINGHAM RAILROAD STATION
245 South Eton Street, southeast of
  Maple Road
1931

In the early 1920s, automobile traffic on Woodward Avenue (23 miles long between Detroit and Pontiac) had increased to intolerable levels. The Michigan legislature passed an act to purchase additional right-of-way and widen the avenue. The Grand Trunk Western

voiced opposition, because its tracks ran directly beside the eastern edge of the highway. A little strong-arming (the state had the power to revoke the railroad's charter)—and a large sum of money—motivated the GTW to relocate its tracks one mile to the east. As a consequence, Birmingham received a new station in English Tudor style. Walls were clad in red brick; pseudo-half-timbered gables and dormers were filled with herringbone and basketweave brickwork.; and Vermont slate covered the broad and steeply pitched roof. In 1978, GTW vacated the depot, which became a restaurant. Dining areas include the waiting room with a barrel-vaulted ceiling and the underground, former pedestrian tunnel. NR. [Privately owned. Restaurant.]

CHELSEA

CHELSEA RAILROAD STATION
125 Jackson Street (off Main Street)
Mason and Rice
1880

Chelsea was a 19th-century shipping point for agricultural products, particularly wheat and wool. The town's earliest depots apparently met violent ends; one was destroyed by fire

Chelsea station with roof cresting, finials, and chimneys intact. This valuation photo, taken on August 1, 1919, shows the similarity between Chelsea's wooden depot and the brick one at Albion (*see* page 333).

Boldly accented windows, doors, and transoms distinguish the Columbiaville depot.

and the other by nighttime vandals secretly cabling the depot to a train. Michigan Central's replacement was designed in Stick Style by a prominent Detroit architectural firm. Besides the more usual single agent's bay along the track side, the Chelsea station had bay windows at either end with triple-gable roofs. In the 1980s, a nonprofit group purchased the depot from Conrail. It restored the exterior to the original shades of green, although the station is still missing its roof cresting, finials, and incised chimneys. NR. [Chelsea Depot Association. Chamber of commerce, historical society, and special events facility.]

COLUMBIAVILLE

COLUMBIAVILLE DEPOT
4422 First Street
c. 1893

Although he first came to Columbiaville as a penniless German immigrant, by the 1880s, William Peter had became a millionaire lumber baron. Besides grist, flour, and woolen mills, he built Columbiaville's school, hotel, waterworks, and second depot. Columbiaville's first station was constructed of wood about 1872 by the Detroit & Bay City (later Michigan Central). Peter replaced it with one made of brick from his

own brickyards. The slate-roofed, one-story structure had both Queen Anne and Romanesque elements: round-arched windows and doors, decorative terra-cotta tile insets, leaded and fan-shaped beveled glass. The simply styled interior included men's and ladies' waiting rooms, an agent's office, and a baggage room. Peter donated the depot to the railroad with a deed restriction—no MC passenger trains could go through the station without stopping. Passenger service lasted until 1964. Shared for a time by the public library, the depot is now exclusively a meeting space for the Rotary Club. Although the tracks are gone, shrubs and tall catalpa trees reflect the original landscaping. NR. [Privately owned. Meeting facility.]

DETROIT

MICHIGAN CENTRAL STATION
West Vernor Avenue, southwest of
  Michigan Avenue
Reed and Stem
Warren and Wetmore
1913

Michigan Central's grand station in Detroit was built as part of the Detroit-Windsor tunnel project (Canadian Pacific trains also stopped here). It opened late in December, eight days ahead

New Michigan Central Station,
Detroit, Mich.

Early postcard view of the Detroit MC station.

of schedule, when flames partially destroyed the old depot at 3rd and Jefferson. Located more than two miles from downtown at the portal of the tunnel, the terminal was easily reached by trolley. The site was engineered to avoid the preceding depot's drawback—trains having to back out of the station. Michigan Central was part of the New York Central System; the station's architects were the same firms which collaborated on Grand Central in Manhattan. Passengers crossed the "Depot Esplanade" to the main entrance, which was centered in walls sheathed with granite, blue limestone, light-colored brick, and terra-cotta. The magnificent general waiting room had a 76-foot-high ceiling, massive arches, marble columns, plaster carving, and elaborate light fixtures. It was linked to the skylit concourse by a relatively narrow ticket lobby. In addition, an eastside arcade and a carriage entrance allowed people to reach the ticket office or concourse without passing through the waiting room—an important concept in station design.

Passenger amenities included the usual barber shop, cigar stand, and restaurant. More innovative were the bath and dressing rooms (for out-of-town patrons not wishing to change at a hotel) and the men's reading room, its shelves laden with books and periodicals. A 15-story office building, set back from the street facade, sprouted above the rear portion of the station. A Bush shed covered the tracks, which travelers reached by an underground concourse. Baggage, mail, and express rooms were actually beneath the tracks. Support facilities included a 175-car coach yard, a warming house, a wheel pit, and a two-story building that had quarters for commissary workers, car cleaners, and the Pullman Company.

In the late 1980s, a private developer announced plans to turn the passenger station and office tower (which in its entire history was never fully completed or occupied) into a world trade center. In the meantime, the pipes burst, and Amtrak personnel moved "temporarily" to trailers. The developer's plans, and all the others that have been proposed, fell through. Amtrak is planning a new building elsewhere, while the old endangered station serves no one but vandals and the homeless. NR. [Privately owned. Vacant.]

DURAND

UNION STATION
200 Railroad Street
Spier and Rohns
1903, 1905

Eighteen months after the limestone and brick Durand station opened, the night baggageman discovered a fire in the boiler room. At first contained by the quick-moving fire company, the blaze went out of control after the chief was ordered to cut hoses stretched across the track —a fast passenger train was coming through. All that remained of the depot were the side walls on the northwest end, which were incorporated into the 1905 replacement. The Grand Trunk (later Grand Trunk Western), whose two trunk lines and one branch line crossed at Durand, rebuilt the depot according to the previous specifications, but changed the number and style of dormers and used red clay tile instead of slate for the roof. In the meantime, the Ann Arbor Railroad demolished its nearby depot and moved in with the Grand Trunk .

Durand was an extremely busy junction and division point. As many as 150 passenger and freight trains a day came through (averaging one every 10 minutes). Daily, three thousand passengers changed trains in Durand—a number equivalent to the town's population. By 1974, passenger trains numbered two per day: one Amtrak going east and one going west. That same year, GTW closed the depot. Vandals smashed the windows; rain warped the floors; scavengers stole the marble wainscoting. (The tile roof and all but one dormer had already been lost in a 1965 re-roofing job.) The city acquired the depot in 1979, but vowed to use no tax dollars for repair. Grants and donations supported the clean-up process, which included removing dead pigeons and years of droppings. A restoration worker uncovered decorative stencils and frescoes under layers of paint. After witnessing the 1981 rededication of the waiting room (used by Amtrak), volunteers

restored the dining room to its original size; and local courts began making "depot repair" a frequent community service assignment.

In 1985, a nonprofit group, Durand Union Station, Inc., took over daily and long-term responsibility for the depot. ISTEA funds obtained in the early Nineties were used to make basement repairs, install an elevator, and complete the second floor rehabilitation. Preservation fever is spreading. Five railroad miles southeast, at Gaines, an 1884 dainty, brick depot is being converted to the village's first-ever public library. NR. [City of Durand. Train stop and official state railroad history museum.] *For photo, see page 22.*

FLUSHING

FLUSHING RAILROAD STATION
431 West Main Street
1888

In the 19th century, residents of Flushing campaigned for 24 years to bring the Cincinnati, Saginaw & Mackinaw (later Grand Trunk Western) to their community, which served for a time as the only stop between Saginaw and Durand. The design of the depot included a round-arch pattern, which was repeated in the porte-cochere, the breezeway, and the large agent's bay window, from which decorative half-timbering radiated like a crown. The interior had a large waiting room, divided in the middle by the ticket office, with a fireplace in both the men's and ladies' sections.

In the mid-1960s, the railroad sold the depot. The new owners built a kitchen addition for their depot-turned-restaurant, but were careful to preserve original elements like the ticket office and light fixtures. In 1980, a fire gutted the building. The roof fell in, and the depot remained open to the elements for four years. Successors to the original restaurant owners finally donated the remains to the local historical society, which spent $300,000

After a 1980 fire, early photos like this one were used to guide restoration of the Flushing station.

rebuilding the original floor plan. In 1987, when concerned citizens heard that the 1889 freight house across the tracks was about to be demolished, they relocated it adjacent to the passenger depot for safekeeping. Edmund G. Love immortalized the station in his autobiographical book, *The Situation in Flushing.* [Flushing Historical Society. Museum and cultural center.]

GRAND HAVEN

DETROIT, GRAND HAVEN & MILWAUKEE DEPOT
1 North Harbor Avenue
1870

Located at the mouth of the Grand River, which spills into Lake Michigan, Grand Haven was an important transfer point between train and ferry or flat boat. On a site overlooking the river, the Detroit, Grand Haven, & Milwaukee (later Grand Trunk Western), built a one-story, sand-colored brick depot, circumscribed by a long series of round-arched door and window openings. Passenger service ended in 1955. Twelve years later, the city purchased the

depot from the railroad. For a time, a portion of the building functioned as the United States Coast Guard Museum; it is now leased exclusively to the Tri-Cities Historical Society. The tracks are gone. About four blocks northeast, the Pere Marquette station is vacant and for sale. [City of Grand Haven. Local history museum.]

GRASS LAKE

GRASS LAKE DEPOT
210 East Michigan Avenue
Spier and Rohns
1887, 1992

In the 1890s, author and civil engineer Walter G. Berg described the Michigan Central depot at Grass Lake as "very picturesque and unique," with fieldstone walls of "various shades, with broken faces laid up in rubble-work." By 1980, virtually all that remained were those stone walls—the rest destroyed in a mysterious fire. The former passenger station, used since 1962 by a newspaper publisher, had been poised for conversion to a restaurant. Instead, the condemned shell sat vacant for nine years, always on the brink of demolition, while a community group tried in vain to purchase it. Finally a nonprofit corporation, in part led by the grandson of a turn-of-the-century station agent, succeeded in acquiring both the real estate and grant money for construction.

Three-and-a-half years of volunteer labor resulted in an extraordinary re-creation of the original depot, including woodwork of solid oak. With the original fireplace and mantel back in place (by happenstance, they had been put in storage before the fire), the station was rededicated on September 12, 1992. Although Grass Lake is no longer on its schedule, Amtrak made a special stop that day, just to give the building its deserved railroad imprint. What remains of the lovely depot park—encroached upon over the years by a gas station and convenience store—was landscaped using information gathered from old photographs. The freight house on the track's north side burned in 1974. [Whistlestop Park Association. Community center.] *For photos,* see page 57.

HOWELL

TOLEDO, ANN ARBOR & NORTH MICHIGAN STATION

126 Wetmore Street (at the end of
   Walnut Street)
1886

Howell was already served by the Detroit, Lansing & Northern (later Pere Marquette, then Chesapeake & Ohio) when residents lobbied for a second line, the Toledo, Ann Arbor & North Michigan (later the Ann Arbor Railroad). They thought competition would be good for shipping rates. In fact, rivalry was so fierce that in January 1886, armed workers from the two railroads got in a brawl over access to the spot where their lines would cross. The obligations and hostilities were sorted out in court, and the Howell depot opened that fall. The single-story, brick building—a simple rectangle—was nicely detailed with ornate, curving brackets under the roof overhang; curved cast hoods surmounting the doors and windows; and small oculus windows in the gable ends. The interior

From 1911 to 1924, the Ann Arbor Railroad used gasoline-powered McKeen "motor trains," as seen here at the Howell station.

When this early photo was taken, both of Ironwood's stations were standing: the C&NW depot and (across the tracks) the Wisconsin Central (later Soo Line) depot, which is now gone.

had a ticket office dividing the men's and ladies' waiting rooms and a separate baggage room (partition now gone). Other railroad facilities included an engine house, water tower, coaling station, and stockyard.

"Ann Arbor" passenger service ended in 1950, although the railroad continued freight operations for another two decades. About 1970, a historical society purchased the building, which was restored in part with the assistance of high school students studying curatorial techniques. Freight trains still use the tracks. The 1870s board and batten depot of the Ann Arbor's old rival, the DL&N, stands abandoned about one mile south. NR. [Livingston County Historical Society. Museum.]

IRONWOOD

MILWAUKEE, LAKE SHORE & WESTERN DEPOT
Between Suffolk and Lowell streets
1892

As the iron industry boomed in the late 19th century, railroads pushed into the ore-rich regions of Michigan's Upper Peninsula. Iron-wood was the largest city in the Gogebic Range. The Milwaukee, Lake Shore & Western (soon part of the Chicago & North Western) depot was right in the midst of the activity. In 1892, a new sandstone and red brick station—surmounted by an unusual hipped, cross dormer—replaced Ironwood's frame depot. Its steeply pitched, slate-clad roof continued across a breezeway to the baggage section. On the track side, a 400-foot-long platform extended past the northwest side of the station. Passenger service ended about 1970; freight, in 1981. The city purchased the building, which it leases to the Ironwood Historical Society. Although the C&NW tracks were torn out, the former Soo Line tracks remain, carrying freight and (in the future) tourist trains. (The Soo Line depot, which stood to the north, is long gone.) In celebration of the depot's centennial, the historical society published an extensive book of interviews with people who worked at, lived near, or traveled from the depot. The platform area is paved with new bricks, many engraved with the names of donors who helped fund the depot's restoration. NR. [City of Ironwood. Museum.]

JACKSON

MICHIGAN CENTRAL STATION
Michigan Avenue and Milwaukee Street
1874

The new Michigan Central depot at Jackson did more than accommodate rail passengers. For many Sundays, "union" religious services held at the station brought forth pastors from different churches to preach in the waiting room. Even after increased passenger traffic pushed the worshipers from their interdenominational church, the railroad provided them with meeting space in the car maintenance and repair shop, east of the depot. In 1877, the station experienced a temporary adaptive use. Railroad employees were on strike, and the state militia, which was patrolling the railroad's property, used the depot as its barracks—elegantly trimmed in oak and black walnut. A wood-paneled ticket office, with multiple large windows, projected into the waiting room. The brick, Italianate-style depot, with sections varying from one to two stories, has been refurbished several times—most recently through the combined efforts of civic groups and Amtrak. It still faces Depot Park, spared a parking lot fate when the station agent volunteered his gardening services. [Amtrak. Train stop.]

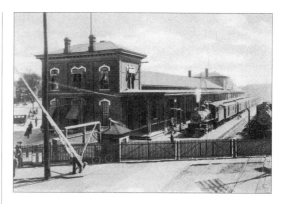

Jackson MC station. The gates stretching across the tracks (relatively unusual for the United States) were most likely installed to control access to the depot.

KALAMAZOO

GRAND RAPIDS & INDIANA STATION
Corner of Pitcher Street and East
    Michigan Avenue
Bush and Patterson
1874

In the railroading boom that followed the Civil War, the Grand Rapids & Indiana (later the Pennsylvania Railroad) was among the new lines entering Kalamazoo. The GR&I was built to satisfy the needs of capitalists to the south, who

Kalamazoo GR&I station c.1895.

wanted to reap profits from virgin white-pine forests to the north. In 1874, an Italianate brick depot was built to replace a wooden one that burned to the ground. It had a deep porch all around and a shallow hipped roof with three chimneys and tiny projecting pediments. Converted to a restaurant about a century later, the building is now closed. [Privately owned. Vacant.]

MICHIGAN CENTRAL STATION
459 North Burdick Street
Cyrus L. W. Eidlitz
1887

The Michigan Central station in Kalamazoo was one of the first modern conversions of a train stop into a multimodal facility. In the early 1970s, preliminary plans were prepared by representatives of Amtrak, several taxi companies, three intercity bus lines, and city, state, and federal governments. The city took title to the depot and surrounding land from Penn Central Corporation. A new bus garage was built on the site of a dilapidated storage building. Restoration work began on the railroad depot, created originally by the same New York architect who designed Chicago's Dearborn Station. (Cyrus Eidlitz was also the first American employer of architect Frederick Spier.) Built of brownstone-trimmed brick, it had a red tile roof with terra-cotta ridge rolls and cresting. The central section incorporated men's and ladies' waiting rooms, a ladies'

toilet room, a ticket office, and a winding staircase to the conductors' room. The benches, wall moldings, and basketweave ceiling were all oak. Outside, long breezeways connected the main depot to two small, detached buildings. One held the men's toilet room, telegraph office, and battery room. The other was for baggage and a second telegraph office. Features like wide sandstone arches, multiple chimneys, ornate gutters, and various types of dormers blended into a hybrid of Queen Anne and Romanesque Revival. NR. [City of Kalamazoo. Transportation center and commercial.]

LAKE ODESSA

LAKE ODESSA DEPOT
Emerson Street near Jordan Lake Avenue
c. 1888

In the mid-1980s, CSX Transportation transferred ownership of the Lake Odessa depot (built by the Detroit, Lansing & Northern) to the local historical society; but the group was required to relocate the building. Moved about three blocks northeast, the small wooden station —with its large, onion-domed turret—would look perfectly at home in Odessa, Russia. Few such fanciful depots exist today; they were the first to be demolished because of their "excessive" architectural details and maintenance

Kalamazoo MC station, track side. The baggage room and telegraph office were in the left dependency; the battery room (to power the telegraph), in the right. As built, the depot received dormers that differed in style and position from this drawing.

Lake Odessa depot on its original site c.1916.

requirements. The roof was originally wood-shingle. The current exterior paint scheme—green Stick Style detailing and white walls—is thought to approximate the original colors. With blueprints in hand, the society has re-created missing elements like the ticket office and roof cresting. Future plans include rebuilding the platform and possibly reinstalling one of the original fireplaces (the other has been destroyed). The group hopes to use this building for its office. Members are considering reconstructing the freight station, which would serve as museum space. Among the famous people who gave speeches at the station were Admiral George Dewey and Theodore Roosevelt. Passenger service ended in 1971. [Lake Odessa Historical Society. Vacant.]

LANSING

GRAND TRUNK DEPOT
1203 South Washington Avenue
Spier and Rohns
1902

Ransom E. Olds was Lansing's pioneer auto maker. In 1904, he announced plans for a new company, Reo Motor Car. He chose a prominent spot for the plant—the south side of the

Grand Trunk (later Grand Trunk Western) tracks, just opposite the recently built passenger depot. The Jacobean Revival station, designed by Spier and Rohns, had an open-air waiting room on the eastern end. Limestone trim contrasted with the redness of brick walls and a tile roof. From the street side, the depot was entered through a 48-foot-high square tower, topped by a battlemented parapet. The original floor plan included a ticket office, men's' smoking and ladies' retiring rooms, and a general waiting room. The latter had an open timbered ceiling, Tiffany enameled brick wainscoting, and mosaic tile floors. In 1942, a freight train loaded with fruit derailed into the station (*see* photo page 41); most of the trackside portion had to be rebuilt. Fruit was on the menu 30 years later when conversion from a depot to a restaurant took place. The tracks are still used by both Amtrak and freight trains. NR. [Grand Trunk Western Railroad. Restaurant.]

UNION DEPOT
637 East Michigan Avenue
Spier and Rohns
1902

Since the 1870s, the Michigan Central and a predecessor of the Pere Marquette had shared a wooden depot on East Michigan Avenue. By the turn of the century, Lansing's economic boom generated the need for a new station. After a spat between the two companies was resolved (MC had adopted plans without consulting PM), construction of the Spier and Rohns design began. Rusticated Bedford limestone was used to windowsill height, as well as for trim of the Tudor-arched doors and windows. The balance of the depot was light brown brick. Chicago-made, Ludowici clay tile covered both the main hipped roof and the conical roofs of two rounded bays. When the depot was converted to a restaurant in 1972, the southern entrance porch was enclosed. The former general waiting room, with its open timber trusswork and boarded ceiling, became the main dining room, supplemented by space in the the old ticket office. (The "ticket window" cashier's office just inside the depot's south door is an imitation.) The kitchen was placed in the baggage and men's smoking rooms. Just above the entrance to the former ladies' waiting room is a railroad clock, inset with marble, believed to be original to the depot. The station's colored glass windowpanes are a modern "antique" application. A small park with benches and ornamental railings once graced the depot's street side. NR. [Privately owned. Restaurant.]

MOUNT CLEMENS

MOUNT CLEMENS RAILROAD STATION
Cass and Grand avenues
1859

Samuel Edison moved his family to Port Huron in 1854. Five years later, his 12-year-old son, Thomas, secured a job on the Port Huron (Fort Gratiot) to Detroit run of the Grand Trunk Railway (later Grand Trunk Western). Thomas Alva Edison was a "train butcher"—a peddler who loaded up with reading material, snacks, and sundries at his base station and sold them from platforms and on board trains. In 1862, at the Mount Clemens station, Edison rescued a three-year-old boy from the path of a runaway box car. In gratitude, the boy's father, who was the Mount Clemens station agent, taught Edison telegraphy, a lucrative communications skill held in great esteem. (Years later, Edison hired his first teacher as a research associate at Menlo Park, N.J.)

Built by the Chicago, Detroit & Canada Grand Trunk Junction Railway, the one-story, Italianate Mount Clemens depot (with a Vermont slate roof) was a standard plan that could be easily lengthened when and where traffic warranted a bigger station. It was almost identical to those built at Fraser, Richmond,

Electric trolley cars and horse-drawn vehicles wait for passengers at Lansing Union Depot.

Mount Clemens, fall 1859. The passenger station is on the right; the freight depot, on the left. Between them is the railroad under construction.

and New Haven (all gone); Smith's Creek (relocated to Greenfield Village in Dearborn); and a number of extant depots in Canada (same design, but stone instead of brick). Mount. Clemens's floor plan (altered over the years) comprised a ticket office flanked by men's and ladies' waiting rooms. Traffic increased dramatically after 1872, when Mount Clemens developed into a popular spa resort, famous for its mineral waters and mud baths.

Passenger service ended in the 1950s. In 1980, the city built a new "maintenance of way" structure for the railroad, and then swapped it for the depot. Local service organizations made contributions such as a coal-burning stove and landscaping. The Michigan Transit Museum (the current tenants) oversaw restoration, which targeted the depot's early 1900s appearance. Work included replication of windows destroyed by the railroad, and rebuilding missing chimneys and the agent's bay. A water tower and separate agent's dwelling once stood adjacent to the depot. NR. [City of Mount Clemens. Museum.]

MUSKEGON

UNION STATION
Western Avenue (at 6th Street)
A. W. Rush
1895

Muskegon's old frame station on 3rd Street was so dilapidated and flimsy, locals called it the "rattle and bang depot." No such disparaging remarks could apply to the substantial masonry building that replaced it. Designed by a Grand Rapids architect (who revised a more elaborate plan by Sidney Osgood), the station's fortress-like appearance derived from its great central tower, with battered walls of reddish brown sandstone and red brick. A corner turret of medieval inspiration bulged from the side of a massive, Romanesque-arched entranceway. The depot's roof was slate. Huge, heavily ornamented fireplaces, bronze and steel grillwork, oak and black ash woodwork, and paneled ceilings filled the interior. All night before the opening, workers transported effects from the old depot to the new one. The next day, trains arrived from both the Chicago & West Michigan (soon to become the Pere Marquette and later the Chesapeake & Ohio) and the Muskegon, Grand Rapids & Indiana (later the Pennsylvania Railroad). William Jennings Bryan arrived a year later to campaign (unsuccessfully) for United States President from the back of a train; Harry Truman had more luck in 1952. Up until 1970, from docks behind the depot, ferry boats carried people and rail cars across Lake Michigan.

In 1977, local officials succeeded in buying the depot and an adjacent express building (now gone), which they sold later to an office furniture concern. The company spent $200,00 on the exterior, but plans for a showroom fell through. A succeeding owner donated the

Solidly impressive, Muskegon Union Station.

depot to the county. In the mid-1990s, the county scheduled an ISTEA-funded project for converting the depot to a convention and visitors bureau, bus stop, and museum. Another extant depot is a block south of Union Station —a small brick structure built by the Toledo, Saginaw & Muskegon (later part of Grand Trunk Western). On the south side of town, GTW's larger, 1930 stone and brick station was demolished in 1965 for a car wash, (now a heliport). NR District. [County of Muskegon. Vacant—future municipal use.]

NILES

NILES DEPOT
598 Dey Street
Spier and Rohns
1892

When the Christmas scene for the 1991 movie *Only the Lonely* was shot, the production designer outlined the Niles Depot in white and colored lights. The community liked the effect so much that it was made an ongoing tradition. Historically, the station was renowned for beautifully sculptured gardens, with NILES spelled out every spring in flowers. Niles was the Michigan Central's last major stop before

Chicago, and officials wanted to impress passengers on their way to the World's Columbian Exposition of 1893. The railroad hired landscape architect John Gipner, who installed a floating garden, trout pond, and gazebo. Greenhouses, established east of the station, provided flowers not only for dining cars, but also for the depot's fine restaurant (part successor to a wooden "eating station"). Train schedules provided enough time for passengers to alight and take a brief stroll through the gardens. Gipner began the practice of passing out flowers or small bouquets to each woman passenger. MC was part of the New York Central System, which tore down the greenhouses in 1935.

The Spier and Rohns design was dominated by a square, pyramid-spired tower nearly 68 feet high. Its five-foot-diameter, three-faced lighted clock was manufactured by the E. Howard Watch & Clock Company of Boston. Massively constructed of Ohio brown sandstone, the station exhibited a full array of Romanesque features including rounded arches and the large, round, general waiting room on the west end. The composition was balanced by a separate baggage and express building on the east end, reached via a covered walkway. The center of the complex housed the dining room and kitchen, with the restau-

Passenger cars with clerestory roofs in front of the Niles depot.

rant manager's apartment above. Oak wainscoting and ceilings, stained glass, brass, and terra-cotta were used throughout the interior. The depot had a large smoking room, but no separate ladies' waiting room. In the late 1980s, the Michigan Department of Transportation and Amtrak undertook a major restoration of the station, which was intact but deteriorating. NR. [Amtrak. Train stop.]

SAGINAW

POTTER STREET STATION
501 Potter Street
Bradford Lee Gilbert
1882

Several railroads once served Saginaw, but only one significant passenger depot remains. Potter Street Station was built by the Flint & Pere Marquette (succeeded by the Pere Marquette and later the Chesapeake & Ohio). The work of a renowned New York architect, the dark red brick depot was trimmed in limestone, terra-cotta, and tile. Two-and-a-half stories tall, the sprawling, grand depot featured square and hexagonal bays, a steeply pitched slate roof, variously styled chimneys and dorm-

ers, and a central, pyramid-roofed tower. Inside, separate oak-trimmed men's and ladies' waiting rooms were gaslit, and transoms were filled with stained glass. Second-floor offices contained fireplaces, sinks, walk-in safes, and brass-ornamented doors. An adjacent powerhouse (extant) had a high hipped roof and a massive, square chimney.

Passenger service ended in 1950. Twenty-six years later, after warding off annihilation (the city considered using a federal block grant for demolition), a nonprofit group acquired the depot from CSX Transportation. The following year, an arsonist set the vacant building ablaze. Preservationists spent several hours persuading fire fighters that there was reason to aggressively battle the flames. By the time the conflagration was extinguished, the roof had collapsed and the second floor was seriously damaged. To fend off the city's bulldozers, the group first secured professional opinions that the building could be salvaged and then obtained a series of restraining orders against demolition. The city and the owners eventually cooperated in obtaining and administering ISTEA funds for repairs. A concept being considered for reuse is a depot museum supported by income-producing rentable space. Listing in the National

Register of Historic Places is pending. One mile east of the passenger depot, a portion of the 1921 brick roundhouse is still standing (used now to repair excursion coaches). Three miles southwest, a small museum has been established in a wooden 1907 Pere Marquette depot, moved from Hemlock in 1983 to prevent its destruction. [Saginaw Depot Preservation Corporation. Vacant.]

ST. JOHNS

ST. JOHNS DEPOT
Railroad Street between Clinton Avenue
    and Spring Street
1920

When a 1920 tornado struck St. Johns, people were apparently not sorry to see the 1857 wooden depot blown apart. They had long complained of its inadequate size. After the twister, the Detroit, Grand Haven & Milwaukee (soon to be Grand Trunk Western) first built a new brick freight house (destroyed about 50 years later). Then the railroad removed the old freight depot and constructed a new passenger station on that site, in effect reversing the previous juxtaposition. The symmetrical passenger depot was made of cut stone and brick with a tile roof. Door and window openings had gently curving stone lintels. The general waiting room had a high ceiling, marble tile floors, and wooden wainscoting. Baggage and express were handled from the far ends of the depot. The station agent took pride in maintaining the grounds, landscaped with trees, shrubs, and flowers. After passenger service ended in 1959, the depot was converted to freight use. In the early Nineties,

the Central Michigan (modern owner of part of GTW) began proceedings to abandon the line. The city expressed an interest in acquiring the depot, but the railroad has, so far, not wanted to sell. A very similar station stands (in neglected condition) at Ionia, 26 railroad miles to the west. [Central Michigan Railroad. Vacant.]

STANDISH

STANDISH RAILROAD STATION
107 North Main Street
1889

Standish was a lumber town. J. D. Standish & Company of Detroit, which owned 17,000 acres of land, platted the village. A sawmill and a wooden depot were among the first buildings established in the early 1870s. About half the Michigan Central trains that passed through Standish were carrying logs; most of the others were carrying laborers going to or from the pineries north of Saginaw Bay. When a new depot was needed, to be placed north of the old one, surrounding farmers contributed their largest field stones. A circular driveway led up to the depot in its parklike setting (now compromised by a gas station). By the 1970s, both passenger and freight service to the depot had ended, although freight trains continued to use the tracks. Abandoned and decaying, the building was saved by being converted to a real estate office. With its broad arches filled by multiple windows, the depot bears a striking resemblance to the fieldstone Michigan Central station at Lawton (also in commercial use), in the southwestern corner of the state. NR. [Privately owned. Commercial.]

Minnesota

In the golden age of railroading, several major railroads were either headquartered in, or passed through, Minnesota. The majority of depots were simple standard plans that allowed the lines to expand rapidly. The wealth generated from logging, mining, farming, and summer resort business made possible the construction of more substantial masonry depots in major cities and county seats.

BEMIDJI

GREAT NORTHERN DEPOT
South end of Minnesota Avenue
1913

Because the area around Bemidji had few navigable streams, rail construction was essential to the region's lumber industry. Great Northern monopolized rail service from 1898 until 1910, when the Soo Line laid tracks into this county seat. Although citizens had long complained about GN's old depot, the arrival of competition was the catalyst for change. The new depot's cruciform plan was executed in reddish-brown brick trimmed in sandstone. Roman-arched windows, transoms with fanlights, and a pedimented gable above the agent's bay gave the one-story, combination freight and passenger depot a neoclassical flavor.

In the early 1990s, Burlington Northern (GN's modern day successor) applied for a demolition permit (which so far has not been issued). As a direct result of the threat to this building, the city formed a preservation commission to make recommendations concerning endangered historic properties. A group of model railroaders have been at work to find an adaptive use for the GN depot, which may eventually be donated to the city—if an organization can be found to take responsibility for liability and insurance. Freight trains still use the tracks. The depot is the mirror image of another station that once stood in Wahpeton, N.D. Bemidji Union Station (1911) is now a restaurant. NR. [Burlington Northern Railroad. Vacant.]

DULUTH

UNION DEPOT
Michigan Street and 5th Avenue West
Peabody, Stearns and Furber
1892

Overlooking Lake Superior, Union Depot replaced an 1870 frame structure on the same site. Built initially for the Northern Pacific and the St. Paul & Duluth railroads, by 1910, the depot accommodated seven different lines. A prominent Boston architectural firm drew the French Norman design (stylistically similar to its work on a large Jersey City, N.J., terminal), executed in brick, brownstone, limestone, and granite. Robert S. Peabody's moniker, "the tower builder," was reinforced at Duluth, where the depot's two robust towers emerged from either side of a triple-arch entry. A cast-iron portico was added in the early 20th century. In 1953, the depot's Pennsylvania green slate roof was replaced with composition shingles. The tall chimneys were severely reduced; roof cresting and weather vanes atop the towers were removed.

In 1967, two years before the last passenger train's departure, a remarkable coalition of civic

Duluth Union Depot and train shed
(removed in 1924) c.1890.

organizations began negotiating for purchase of the depot and adjacent land. A decade later, a new cultural arts complex emerged, partly housed in the former depot and partly in a new addition. A 1945 false ceiling was removed from the 88-foot-high great hall, which now serves both as a lobby between museum areas and as a site for special events. The old immigrants' waiting room, originally connected to a shower room, remains basically as it was, with glazed yellow brick walls and a concrete floor — materials that could be easily hosed down. The Lake Superior Museum of Transportation was installed in a specially designed exhibit space, reminiscent of the long-span train shed removed in 1924. Other organizations which share the former station include a ballet troupe, art institute, concert artists series, symphony orchestra, community theater, children's museum, and historical society. Union Depot's restoration was followed by major revitalization of the immediately surrounding area. NR. [County of St. Louis. Cultural facility.]

HINCKLEY

St. Paul & Duluth Station
Old Highway 61
1894

On September 1, 1894, a forest fire ravaged most of Pine County. Four hundred eighteen people died. Many Hinckley residents were waiting at the St. Paul & Duluth station for a train to carry them to safety. As the area around the depot began burning, they ran a mile out of town — where the train had halted in a clearing — and climbed on board. The engineer reversed his locomotive and backed up five miles to Skunk Lake. The passengers then saved their lives by taking refuge in the water. Back at the depot, the agent stayed posted at his telegraph key until the last possible minute. The final words he tapped out before he died: "I think I stayed too long." He only made it to the doorway. Within two months, the SP&D (later Northern Pacific) station was duplicated, using the original 1871 plans. A two-story main portion and flanking one-story wings housed men's and ladies' waiting rooms, an agent's apartment, a freight section, and a beanery.

About 1970, demolition was avoided when a small group of citizens acquired the depot from Burlington Northern (NP's modern successor). Minnesota Historical Society funds, local contributions, and volunteer labor restored the depot as a 1976 Bicentennial project. BN, whose vice-president was from Hinckley, donated a potbellied stove from another depot, a roll top desk, and telegraph equipment. The second floor is authentically furnished as an 1890s apartment The Great Hinckley Fire destroyed the area's prime economic asset, the forest, which led to the first large-scale reforestation program in Minnesota. The interpretative center now housed in the depot is devoted to the story of the fire and ensuing conservation measures. Hinckley's other station, built for a branch line of the Great Northern, stood about two blocks east; it was razed in the late 1980s. NR. [Hinckley Fire Museum, Inc. Museum.]

LITTLE FALLS

NORTHERN PACIFIC DEPOT
200 1st Street, N.W.
Cass Gilbert
1900

Cass Gilbert was a native of Minnesota. His most famous national commissions include the Woolworth Building in Manhattan and the United States Supreme Court in Washington, D.C. Little Falls's Northern Pacific depot was one of his last designs before moving to New York City. By 1899, Little Falls was a significant lumber processing center. Ten years earlier, NP had shortened the length of its main line by taking a new route along the Mississippi's west bank through Little Falls. The railroad hired Gilbert to design a new station, not to exceed $7,000. He used sandstone, wood, and brick to create a mixture of Shingle and Craftsman Styles. Originally, cedar shingles covered both the steeply pitched roof and the sides of four small dormers. Iron finials bore the NP logo.

Little Falls NP depot as built, with dormers, finials, and cedar-shingle roof.

The exterior color scheme included brown, green, and red paint, and very darkly stained or oiled woodwork. A brick platform surrounded the depot and stretched several hundred feet along the track.

By 1979, passenger service had ended and the depot was being used for freight operations and storage. A fire broke out. With the roof and former ladies' waiting room damaged, Burlington Northern (NP's successor) vacated the building. Following several rounds of demolition deadlines that were extended, the building was acquired by a nonprofit group for eventual community use. The outside has been rehabilitated. Gilbert is known to have designed two other Minnesota depots, Willmar (demolished) and Anoka (radically altered). NR. [Cass Gilbert Depot Society. Vacant.]

MINNEAPOLIS

CHICAGO, MILWAUKEE & ST. PAUL STATION
Washington and 3rd avenues
Charles Sumner Frost
1899

In Minneapolis, behind the decaying grandeur of the Chicago, Milwaukee & St. Paul station, lurks an environmental quagmire: asbestos, lead paint, and petroleum-polluted soil and ground water. But knowing it to be a special historic site that links the Mississippi riverfront to downtown, the city is committed to saving the complex. The head house was designed by Chicago architect Charles Frost in a Renaissance Revival style, almost square in plan, sited on a corner. It replaced a side-loading station that fronted on Washington Avenue. The first story was pink granite, and the upper two floors were orange brick. Terra-cotta wreaths ornamented the bold cornice. On the 3rd Avenue facade, a clock tower rose 140 feet (its elaborate cupola and spire were lost in a 1941 tornado). Inside features included marble

Minneapolis CM&StP station.

1911, with the tower's cupola and spire intact.

The so-called "general" waiting room c. 1905. In reaility, it was filled with huge circular radiators, spittoons, and men (or boys) only.

floors, coffered wooden ceilings, and fireplaces. Abutting the head house was a long-span train shed that protected stub-end tracks. (Trains had to back out of the station and turn on a wye.) A 225-foot-long brick baggage building with a 75-foot-high chimney stood along the north side of the shed. North of the passenger station were separate freight houses: the outbound (demolished) and the inbound (1879; head house portion extant).

Passenger service ended in 1971. The next 20 years were filled with demolition rumors, grandiose plans, and physical disasters that leap-frogged over each other. The saga included a succession of owners, bankrupt developers, a broken partnership, fires, and a bank failure. In 1992, the city finally bought the head house, train shed, one remaining freight house, and 16 acres of land (a tract it had been outbid on years before) from the Resolution Trust Company. Its first task was to

secure the buildings from vagrants. The next steps will be environmental clean-up (which may take decades) and structural stabilization. No decision has been made on adaptive use. Minneapolis had another station designed by Charles Frost—the Great Northern, which was built in 1914 and razed in 1978. NR. [City of Minneapolis. Vacant.]

MINNEHAHA DEPOT
Minnehaha Avenue in Minnehaha Park
1875

In the 1800s, Minnehaha Park and its waterfall were popular tourist attractions, 16 minutes by train from downtown Minneapolis. The Milwaukee & St. Paul (later Chicago, Milwaukee, St. Paul & Pacific) built a diminutive but ornate wooden station to replace an even tinier one from c. 1863. By the turn of the century, there were two small zoos nearby to draw even

Minnehaha depot was built to service a park.

more visitors. One was in a city park and the other was across the street from the depot, in a privately owned attraction called Longfellow Gardens (which included a beer garden along with the animals). In 1964, the railroad donated the depot to the city, which conveyed it to the state historical society. Volunteers from the Minnesota Transportation Museum maintain and staff the building, kept close to its original appearance with a potbellied stove and working telegraph equipment. Freight trains and private rail cars make occasional use of the tracks. NR District. [Minnesota Historical Society. Depot museum.]

RED WING

CHICAGO GREAT WESTERN STATION
West Main and Fulton streets
1906

In 1906, the Chicago Great Western acquired segments of two smaller lines (the Minnesota Central and the Duluth, Red Wing & Southern) and built this two-story brick depot with a tile roof. On either side, the platform canopy extended to a one-story dependency (only the westside baggage building remains). Inside, the general waiting room was supplemented by a smaller ladies' waiting room. Passenger service

ended in 1950; freight, three decades later. Red Wing's residents became somewhat alarmed in 1979, when North Central Food Systems purchased the building for a Hardee's restaurant. Under persuasion from the mayor's office, Hardee's abandoned its usual decorating style and signs to retain the depot flavor. The company even put a railroad museum on the second floor, which originally housed division offices. NR. [Privately owned. Restaurant.]

CHICAGO, MILWAUKEE & ST. PAUL STATION
Levee Street
J. M. Nettenstrom
1905

In the early 1900s, Red Wing's visitors most often arrived by steamboat or train. The Civic League, as part of a general beautification effort, wanted to improve the appearance of the debris-strewn levee along the Mississippi River. The Chicago, Milwaukee & St. Paul agreed to construct a new depot and to contribute money for a park in exchange for trackage rights granted by the city. The old wooden depot was moved to the west side of Broadway and used for freight (since demolished). A member of the railroad staff designed the new passenger station, constructed in two shades of vitrified brick accented with local stone. The roof appears to have been slate. Unlike the more typical platform canopy, the station had a gabled, covered waiting area perpendicular to the depot. Inside the station were oak benches, green walls, and a pale yellow ceiling. The general waiting room had a fireplace surmounted by a large mirror. Although the station had a men's smoking room, apparently there was not a separate ladies' waiting room. Modern amenities included steam heat and both gas and electric lighting.

In 1990, the city purchased the depot from the Soo Line (freight railroad successor to the "Milwaukee Road"), and a local foundation funded the restoration. The original oak wood-

Red Wing CM&StP station c. 1910.

work—long gone—was reproduced using the architect's drawings. Similar wood was used to partition the large general waiting room into two areas—one for Amtrak passengers and one for a conference room. Remaining space is occupied by a private business and the chamber of commerce. NR District. [City of Red Wing. Train stop and mixed use.]

ST. CLOUD

GREAT NORTHERN DEPOT
1715 Breckenridge Avenue
1899

Succeeding two earlier depots (1870s and 1883), the St. Cloud Great Northern depot was situated at a wye between its main line tracks and those of its Osseo branch. An expansive park, filled with trees and delicate flowers, made a sweet approach to the station, heftily built of solid granite blocks. A slate roof capped the depot's simple lines, divided in the center by a cross gable. Angling along the Osseo track was a 240-foot-long covered platform. In 1944, GN modernized the building. Its deep eaves were whacked off and the ceiling lowered in the oak-trimmed interior. In 1971, after Amtrak switched to using St. Cloud's former Northern Pacific station, the GN depot became a freight and yard office. These freight operations (now Burlington Northern) will transfer soon to Minneapolis, thus making the depot's future uncertain. Trains still turn on the wye (particularly necessary since the roundhouse and turntable were destroyed). [Burlington Northern Railroad Company. Freight office.]

St. Cloud Great Northern depot and lunch room, 1907.

NORTHERN PACIFIC DEPOT
555 East St. Germain Street
1909

Graffiti was a problem even in 1909. A contemporary St. Cloud newspaper praised the new Northern Pacific depot for its white enameled brick wainscoting, "which can not be defaced or marked with a pencil." Replacing a dilapidated 1884 building in East St. Cloud, the NP stop was relocated to a more current business and industrial area. The old depot was cut in two and moved 50 yards south to become a freight station (since demolished). A new interlocking tower was built the same year, to prevent collisions where the Great Northern and NP lines crossed.

Built of brown pressed brick, the NP depot had curvilinear gables and false dormers outlined in gray granite. A brick platform surrounded the entire building and stretched almost to the GN crossing. The station was busy enough to warrant three ticket windows opening into the general waiting room. The men's smoking and ladies' waiting rooms were both furnished with comfortable chairs. Red and white terrazzo covered all the floors except the baggage room, where a double thickness of heavy planking could withstand the rolling in and out of trunks and carts. Today Amtrak leases the building, although only two passenger trains a day come through. [Burlington Northern Railroad. Train stop.]

ST. PAUL

UNION DEPOT
4th and Sibley streets
Charles Sumner Frost
1920

In 1879, after 10 years of discussion, the seven railroads that entered St. Paul agreed to form the St. Paul Union Depot Company. By purchasing stock, participating railroads could share in the station's ownership, management, and revenues. Membership remained open to all railroads, current or future. Completed in 1881, the first Union Depot (on Sibley Street south of 3rd) had an elegant head house and a long-span train shed. In 1884, it suffered a fire. Quickly rebuilt, the station burned again in 1913. A new head house was not begun until 1918 because of local problems compounded by the outbreak of World War I. The principal facade of Charles Frost's subdued Beaux Arts design faced 4th Street. A curved driveway

St. Paul Union Depot, 1925.

brought automobiles to the porticoed entrance, which was flanked by two projecting wings. Behind the limestone-clad head house was a vaulted concourse, sheathed in cream-colored brick, which extended south across Kellogg Boulevard. Inside the station, murals, reliefs, and a tile frieze depicted Minnesota's transportation history.

In the 1920s, an average of 20,000 passengers a day used Union Depot; by 1970, the figure was 135. A year later, Amtrak built a new station in the Midway area (accessible to St. Paul and Minneapolis), and Union Depot closed. Ten years of winters and broken pipes caused the decorative plaster ceiling to collapse onto the pink marble floors. A seven-foot tree grew out of debris caught in a skylight. On the lower level, the former immigrants' waiting room was inhabited by the homeless. In 1983, a developer purchased the head house and did substantial rehabilitation, primarily to make space for a number of restaurants. Debt ridden and still not fully occupied, the project is now in the hands of bondholders. Another railroad building in St. Paul, the Great Northern roundhouse on Jackson Street, is being restored by the Minnesota Transportation Museum to shelter and maintain its equipment. NR. [Privately owned. Commercial.]

SLEEPY EYE

SLEEPY EYE RAILROAD STATION
Oak Street Northwest
Frost and Granger
1902

Just east of this Chicago & North Western depot is a granite obelisk—monument to Chief Sleepy Eye for whom the town was named. It was erected the same year as the new depot, which replaced the old one a block east (converted to a freight station). Of the 50 C&NW depots built in Minnesota between 1890 and 1910, 80 percent were wooden and averaged 22 by 77 feet in size. Sleepy Eye's greater dimensions, brick construction, and slate roof indicated the community's position as a railroad center. The ticket office had windows opening into both the ladies' and men's waiting rooms (the western window is now a doorway). Both rooms had splayed, plank ceilings and exposed wooden beams. A baggage room was on the depot's west end; a lunchroom and kitchen, on the east.

After passenger service ended in 1960, the depot was used as a freight agent's office. It closed in 1985, as did the similar depot at New Ulm, 14 miles east (and now essentially aban-

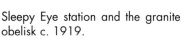
Sleepy Eye station and the granite obelisk c. 1919.

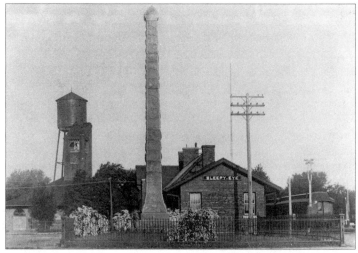

Since the 1920s, the first Duluth & Iron Range train has been on display at the Two Harbors depot.

doned). A group of local residents formed a non-profit corporation, bought the Sleepy Eye depot, and began restoration. Some original items remaining in the depot include the telegrapher's desk, built-in cabinets, a safe, two benches, and baggage carts. NR. [Sleepy Eye Depot Preservation, Inc. Local history museum.]

TWO HARBORS

TWO HARBORS DEPOT
South Avenue off 6th Street
Peter Olson
1907

Transportation of logging supplies, lumber, iron ore, and workers was crucial to Two Harbors's development on the shores of Lake Superior. By the early 1900s, the Duluth & Iron Range Rail Road needed a larger facility for offices and more passenger space. It hired a Duluth architect, whose rectangular, flat-roofed design (in typical division point size and shape) was distinguished by an angular two-story bay, prominent modillioned cornice, and brick belt courses. The names of the railroad and the community were carved into the frieze. The windows were topped by limestone keystones and jack-arch ends. A deep canopy stretched

over the platform. On the first floor, the depot contained baggage rooms, the agent's office, and gender-segregated waiting rooms trimmed in white birch. Upstairs were the division offices. In 1937, following a railroad merger, management activities were transferred to Duluth. Passenger service ended in 1961. The county acquired the red brick building, which housed various cultural and social programs, before usage narrowed down to a history museum and historical society office. Original features include four walk-in vaults and the ticket window. NR. [County of Lake. Tourist train stop, museum, and office.]

WAYZATA

WAYZATA DEPOT
402 East Lake Street
1906

In 1867, when the St. Paul & Pacific (later Great Northern) reached the platted, but sparsely settled village of Wayzata, it laid its tracks along Lake Minnetonka and right down Lake Street. After Wayzata became a popular resort, local officials fined the GN for switching cars and blowing whistles all night, which disturbed hotel guests. In 1893 (according to local lore), hot-tempered James J. Hill, the railroad's president, tore down the depot and moved the stop to a town about a mile east. Wayzata-destined freight and passengers were dropped off at Holdridge for more than a decade, until the embargo was lifted and a replacement Wayzata station was built.

In 1906, Wayzata's new single-story depot projected a slight English Tudor flavor, achieved with stucco and wooden battens. A wood-shingle roof, extending both east and west, created two open-air porches, indicative of the depot's vacation-time lineage. The station's gas lighting was replaced with electricity in 1918. After rail service ended in 1971, the west-end baggage and freight section was converted to office space (at first used by a conservation district and later by the chamber of commerce). The passenger end, domain of the historical society, retains its original contoured oak benches, terrazzo flooring, and white enameled brick wainscoting. In addition to furnishings, the agent's office still has its telegraph and signal equipment. Outside, the platform's brick paving is intact; stucco and woodwork have been finished to early specifications. The one set of remaining rails are still in use. NR. [City of Wayzata. Mixed use.]

WINONA

CHICAGO, MILWAUKEE & ST. PAUL DEPOT
65 East Mark Street
John T. W. Jennings
1888

About 1982, still smarting from the demolition of the Chicago & North Western passenger station two years earlier (the freight station is now a restaurant), Winona community groups began lobbying for maintenance of the Chicago, Milwaukee & St. Paul ("Milwaukee Road") depot. When it first opened nearly a hundred years earlier, the station had a slate roof with jerkinhead gables and flared eaves. The roof was pierced by significant features that are now gone—small Chateauesque dormers and tall corbeled chimneys. Beyond the breezeway, the depot's small annex was topped by a diminutive cupola, which has also been lost. A high peaked gable surmounted the agent's bay. Walls of pressed brick, trimmed extensively with cut stone, enclosed a ticket office, men's and ladies' waiting rooms, and a baggage area. Floors were maple; the ceiling and woodwork were Georgia pine; and the doors were trimmed in bronze. The design was the work of John W. T. Jennings of the railroad staff, who in later years had general practices in Chicago and Madison.

About 1985, the Soo Line acquired the depot from the bankrupt Milwaukee Road. By then, the roof was leaking and the windows were boarded up—a particularly unpleasant situation for Amtrak passengers using the building. The Soo Line soon began major repairs, with the community raising supplemental funds and contributing volunteer labor. The depot's exterior was painted its original color scheme—olive green window frames, dark green doors, and terra-cotta accents. Local gardeners contributed landscaping expertise. Two other late 19th-century Winona railroad buildings remain standing within a few miles of the Milwaukee Road passenger depot—a former C&NW freight house and an enginehouse, built by C&NW predecessor, the Winona & St. Peter (both buildings NR). [Soo Line Railroad. Train stop.]

Missouri

Missouri is home to two railway palaces: St. Louis Union Station, the most expensive rehabilitation of an American historic building at the time it was done, and Kansas City Union Station, the subject of a high stakes law suit and preservation saga. Of the many small depots that once filled the state, more remain from the Missouri Pacific than any of the other major railroads. By contrast, those of the St. Louis & San Francisco (the "Frisco") have mostly been demolished.

BONNE TERRE

BONNE TERRE DEPOT
Oak Street
1909

Bonne Terre's history is imbedded in the St. Joe Lead Mining Company, established in 1864. At first mules and oxen did the ore hauling, augmented by a railroad in 1880. To extend the company's three-foot-gauge line to the Mississippi River, St. Joe chartered a railroad in 1888 called the Mississippi River & Bonne Terre (later Missouri Pacific). The first depot was built 10 years later, north of the present building. When it burned in 1909, mine company carpenters built a larger wooden one, two-and-a-half stories high. A one-story exten-

sion housed freight, express, baggage, and the "colored" waiting room. Both Queen Anne and Stick Style elements were evident in the conical-spired tower, corner posts and braces, and the variety of dormers, wall textures, and colors. The roof was gray slate. Above the first floor waiting rooms and ticket office, the second floor (accessed only by an exterior stairway) housed the railroad and telegraph offices. The depot was once surrounded by a substantial rail yard and used as a shipping point not only for St. Joe's mining operation, but also its freight and cattle company. Regular passenger service was supplemented by frequent excursions arranged for company employees. In 1939, the last passenger train pulled out; freight operations were essentially over by the 1960s. NR. [Privately owned. Inn.]

A Queen Anne tower dominates the Bonne Terre depot.

Boonville MK&T depot c. 1912.

BOONVILLE

MISSOURI, KANSAS & TEXAS DEPOT
320 First Street
c. 1912

Designed by the chief engineer's office of the Missouri, Kansas & Texas (the "Katy"), Boonville was one of four similar Mission-style depots built by the railroad at locations north of the Red River, which included Caddo and Osage, Okla., and Chanute, Kans. Only the smallest, Boonville, remains. One-story with a brick and stucco veneer, the depot replaced an earlier wooden one on the west side of the tracks, which was converted to a freight station (now gone). At both the north and south ends of the depot, extensions of the terra-cotta tile roof formed porticoes—one an outdoor waiting area and the other a baggage platform. The floor plan included general and ladies' waiting rooms, a ticket office, and a baggage room. Converted to storage in the 1960s, the depot has been empty since 1973. When the Missouri River flooded in 1993, the highly successful Katy Trail State Park that goes past the depot suffered $1.5 million damage. The depot's restoration and conversion to trail headquar-

ters were thus delayed. Boonville's other depot, the Missouri Pacific, was demolished in 1987. NR. [State of Missouri. Vacant.]

COLUMBIA

MISSOURI, KANSAS & TEXAS DEPOT
402 East Broadway
1909

When Columbia's new Missouri, Kansas & Texas (the "Katy") depot was built, the old wooden one (1901) was placed alongside it and converted to a freight station (razed in the 1950s). Designed by a railroad employee, the brick station was embellished with terra-cotta egg-and-dart moldings, ball finials, and acanthus leaf tiles. A limestone stringcourse circled the building, with a second one added to the two-story, octagonal tower. The general waiting room was augmented by a ladies' waiting room with a fireplace and a large porch (later enclosed by the railroad). The low-pitched hipped roof was covered in corrugated, red terra-cotta tiles. Passenger service ended in 1958; the railroad sold the building 18 years later. The new owners substantially enlarged the former depot and ornamented the windows with stained glass. The old "Katy" right-of-way has been converted to a nature and fitness trail. NR. [Privately owned. Restaurant.]

WABASH DEPOT
126 North 10th Street
1910

Many of the passengers arriving at the Wabash depot were students or employees of the University of Missouri, some of whose buildings were likewise made of locally quarried rock-faced stone, laid by Scottish immigrants. Red tiles covered the roof. The one-story depot had two entrance porches, but no platform canopy or extended eaves. WABASH was carved in stone on all three sides of the streetside portico; COLUMBIA was carved once on the east side, where four steps led down to the tracks. Parapeted cross gables, at both ends of the main section, gave the building an H-shaped floor plan. The interior, which included both general and ladies' waiting rooms, was finished in mahogany. This building and the preceding station (converted to freight) were acquired in 1977 by the city. After nearly two decades as community meeting space, the older depot is scheduled for demolition (authorities want the land); the newer one serves bus passengers. Freight trains still use the tracks. NR. [City of Columbia. Bus depot.]

HIGGINSVILLE

CHICAGO & ALTON DEPOT
2109 Main Street
1889

Harvey Higgins, who platted the town that took his name, became a director of the Chicago & Alton Railroad. His brick Italianate residence was near the first C&A depot, which burned in 1888. Somewhat oddly, the station was replaced with another wooden one, on a streetscape gradually becoming all brick. The combination freight and passenger station had an agent's office flanked by men's and ladies' waiting rooms. Its three corbeled chimneys were probably vents for coal stoves. Among the goods shipped from Higginsville by rail were wheat, flour, corn, livestock, coal, brick, tile, and shoes. One of the incoming commodities was cheap labor, in the form of children. The youngsters, relocated mostly from eastern cities to the Midwest, were the focus of a charitable undertaking known as "placing out." Higginsville was one of the many stations that received these destitute or orphaned children, who were advertised by aid societies as available for "distribution."

By the 1980s, the C&A depot had not simply been vacant for decades—it was the only one left in the county. A former Higginsville resident purchased the building, which he

Higginsville C&A depot c.1923.

carefully restored both inside and out (with the boost of rehabilitation tax credits) for use as an antiques shop. More recently, the depot was purchased by a local nonprofit group. Green paint, set against off-white siding, highlights the Stick Style details. NR. [Harvey J. Higgins Historical Society. Museum and meeting space.]

JOPLIN

UNION DEPOT

Northeast of Main and First streets,
    behind the post office
Louis Curtiss
1911

Canadian born, Kansas City architect Louis Curtiss was an early proponent of simplicity in design and a straightforward approach to architectural expression. He drew the plans for a number of railroad stations varying in size from the Atchison, Topeka & Santa Fe county seat depot at Snyder, Tex., (c. 1910; extant) to Wichita Union Station (1914; extant). Built on the site of an old mine, Joplin Union Depot (one of his midsize commissions) initially served four major railroads. Missouri, Kansas & Texas sent in the first train on opening day. More than

Louis Curtiss created unique sculptural designs for Joplin Union Depot.

2,000 spectators witnessed the event, followed by a salute of skyrockets and torpedoes — answered by the locomotive's whistle.

The rail yards, roundhouse, passenger and freight stations covered about 30 acres interlaced with seven miles of track. Five acres were set aside for beautification, including a depot park with flower beds and winding walks (now the post office site). A greenhouse on the depot's second floor was used to maintain plants and goldfish over the winter. Built of reinforced concrete, the station was ornamented on the exterior with poured concrete geometric designs; these patterns reoccurred inside on plaster-finished ceilings and walls. The interior color scheme was rose, cream, and green. Floors were terrazzo. In the south wing, the Brown Hotel & News Company operated a dining room and oval-shaped lunch counter.

After closing in 1969, Union Depot fell prey to vandalism and decay. In the mid-1980s, two developers purchased the building from the Joplin Union Depot Company. Their restoration-minded commercial project was only 25 percent complete when it came to an abrupt halt. An ongoing legal battle between the owners and the contractor ensued. Despite having a new roof, the depot is windowless, open to the elements, and obviously endangered. NR. [Privately owned. Vacant.]

KANSAS CITY

UNION STATION

Pershing Road and Main Street
Jarvis Hunt
1914

By the early 1900s, Kansas City had outgrown the Union Avenue Depot (1878). For its new station, the Kansas City Terminal Railway, comprised of 12 equal-owner railroads, selected Jarvis Hunt's Beaux Arts design. (One of the losers in the competition was Daniel H. Burnham.) High ground was selected to avoid

Kansas City Union Station, 1938.

flooding. Facing south, the depot was turned toward a large, two-block plaza—in best City Beautiful tradition. Clad mostly in Bedford limestone with granite trim, the station had a T-shape, the stem of which extended over 16 through tracks. Two levels plus a mezzanine were placed below the grade of Pershing Avenue and four above. On the main level, a grand lobby, 95-feet-high, contained a circular ticket office. The ladies' waiting room was in the east wing, along with a renowned Harvey House restaurant and large lunch room, designed by Mary Colter and then redecorated by her in 1937. Areas for baggage and parcels, and the men's smoking room were in the west wing. The main waiting room and concourse, 352 feet long, was lined with elaborate wooden benches. Interior finishes and features included rosy-brown marble floors and wainscoting, terra-cotta walls, ornate plaster ceilings, electric chandeliers (each weighing 3,000 pounds), giant sconces, and a huge clock. Stairways and elevators in the flanking "midways" led down to track level. Other main-level spaces included a drug store, barber shop, and facilities for immigrants (isolation room, waiting room, and "basket lunch room"). The station also had about 10 stub-end tracks to handle a huge volume of express and mail transfer. Tunnels led to the main Kansas City Post Office across Pershing Road.

Opening day was celebrated by 100,000 people and featured speeches, fireworks, and a 21-gun salute. The station was designed to handle 350 trains per day; the traffic peaked in 1917 at 218. A half-century later, the number was down to about six. For two decades, starting in 1974, Kansas City officials and the real estate developers who had purchased Union Station wrestled over the building's fate. They originally agreed to what seemed like a fair deal—tax abatements on nearby new construction in exchange for rehabilitation of the historic structure. The developers' restoration promise went unfulfilled, and the years went by. Extensive feasibility studies, paid for by the city and by a relentless advocacy group (the Committee for Union Station) considered everything from botanical gardens to a casino. The city had no luck with ballot referendums to raise funds for restoration, partly because there was no clear plan for the station—a building it did not even own. In the meantime, the developers shut off the station's expensive-to-operate heating system. Amtrak personnel and passengers tolerated two years inside a plastic bubble installed in the main hall and then, in 1985, moved to a spot under the Main Street viaduct.

By 1988, the developers had long since failed to meet an already extended deadline for Union Station's restoration. The city filed suit, demanding in excess of $90 million. Although Kansas City was awarded nearly $10 million, collecting the money was unlikely. An out-of-court settlement was reached in January 1994. Twenty acres of land, the station house, and $1.5 million were turned over to a specially formed nonprofit corporation. This group will undertake fund-raising and a development plan that might include returning Amtrak to the station. The principal intended use is "Science City," a project of the Kansas City Museum. NR. [Union Station Assistance Corporation. Vacant.]

KIRKWOOD

MERAMEC HIGHLANDS STATION
1022 Barberry Lane
c. 1895

Meramec Highlands opened in 1895 as a summer resort southwest of St. Louis. It included a hotel (burned in 1926), cottages, a cold sulfur spring bathhouse, and a dance pavilion called Sunset Pagoda. The St. Louis & San Francisco (the "Frisco") station had two-foot thick limestone walls, a porte-cochere, and a steeply pitched roof. The two-story, square tower gave the depot a pagodalike flavor, generated by its

central position, flared eaves, mass, and fenestration. It was topped by a slender pole (later carrying a telegraph cross arm). Inside, both the men's and ladies' waiting rooms had massive, rough-cut stone fireplaces and simply detailed, coved ceilings. Elevated several feet above track level, the depot was fronted on the track side by a stone retaining wall. Originally, the tracks ran through an 1883 tunnel west of the station. After a 1920 train wreck, the tracks were rerouted south to their current location. Train service ended in the early 1930s, and the railroad subsequently leased out the depot as a residence. A serious fire in the 1940s burned through the ceiling of the west waiting room and damaged the roof. Vacant since then, the building received a measure of repairs, after being purchased from the railroad in 1972. [Privately owned. Vacant.]

MISSOURI PACIFIC STATION
Argonne Drive at Kirkwood Road
1893

One of St. Louis County's first planned suburbs, Kirkwood (a former stagecoach stop called Collins Depot) was named for the chief engineer of the Pacific Railroad of Missouri (later Missouri Pacific). The first depot was built in 1853, the same year land sales began.

Meramec Highlands station in Kirkwood c.1900.

Another wooden depot, built 10 years later, was moved slightly to the west when the current station was constructed. A round, tower-like dormer, clad in wooden shingles extended above the agent's bay of the new one-story, stone depot. Decorative metal shingles covered the main roof; its deep flared eaves were sheathed in terne metal. Arriving along a circular driveway, passengers entered the depot through a vestibule. The ticket office was straight ahead, with the men's waiting room to the east, ladies' waiting and baggage rooms to the west.

In 1941, the railroad announced drastic alterations designed to make the depot "conform with contemporary colonial architecture." Plans to remove the Queen Anne tower and to cover the stone walls in asbestos clapboards were scaled down when citizens expressed outrage. Nonetheless, the porte-cochere was widened; two chimneys and the extended east-side canopy were removed. Well maintained today, the depot is leased to Amtrak. NR. [City of Kirkwood. Train stop.]

POPLAR BLUFF

ST. LOUIS–SAN FRANCISCO STATION
303 Moran Street
1928

By the late 1800s, Poplar Bluff had become a major lumbering and wood-products manufacturing area, in particular noted for its stave and barrel plants. A 1927 tornado leveled most of the city's business district, including a large brick depot owned by the St. Louis–San Francisco Railway (the "Frisco"). Its one-story replacement station, built about a half-block north of the old location, was in Spanish Colonial Revival style—chosen to advertise the Frisco's Florida service. Glazed pavers, in shades of brownish red, rose to windowsill height. Bricks were randomly exposed on the

stuccoed walls and two large chimneys to achieve a rusticated effect. On the northern portion, curvilinear gables of the pitched, red tile roof were capped with marble slabs and finials; the freight section roof was flat. On the track side (rails are gone today), copper urn bas-reliefs were placed in niches above some of the windows.

In 1965, the Frisco abandoned this branch line; within five years, the depot was owned by the city, which converted it to a police station. The Moark Regional Railroad Museum leased the building 20 years later. Restoration work in the passenger section included removing the city-installed false walls and ceilings, replicating or reinstalling doors and light fixtures, painting inside and outside with original colors, and making plans to reconstruct the original paddle-type train order board (used to signal locomotive engineers to stop for orders). Poplar Bluff's other depot, built in 1910 by the St. Louis, Iron Mountain & Southern (later the Missouri Pacific), is used today for Union Pacific freight railroad purposes. [City of Poplar Bluff. Railroad museum.]

ST. LOUIS

UNION STATION
Market Street between 18th and 20th streets
Theodore C. Link (Link and Cameron)
1894

St. Louis's first union depot (1875)—a substantial brick and stone, Second Empire design at 12th and Poplar—was declared obsolete in less than 15 years. In 1889, six railroads formed the Terminal Railroad Association of St. Louis (T.R.R.A.), which selected, by competition, the plan of St. Louis architect Theodore C. Link. Born and trained in Europe, Link envisioned a castlelike, medieval gateway to the city named for a French king. Once chosen, Link visited the preceding station daily for six months to better understand passengers' needs. Twenty-two acres of buildings were leveled for the new station, exclusive of main track approaches. Under the site lay the bed of an old mill pond and also the caves and vaults of an old brewery. Complicated foundation work took more than a year. When it opened two years later, Union Station was the largest railway terminal in the world.

The station's principal components were a head house; a concourse (dubbed "the Midway" à la 1893 Chicago World's Columbian Exposition); a train shed (which also sheltered baggage and mail facilities); separate express buildings; and a power plant topped by a switching tower. Rising from the eastern pavilion of the head house, a 230-foot-high, turreted clock tower held the sprinkler system's water tank and also provided fan-driven ventilation for the station. The head house walls were constructed of brick, clad in Indiana limestone on the two principal facades; tan Roman brick and gray brick covered the back. A balconied porte-cochere with bronze and iron electroliers protected the Market Street entrance (removed in 1911 for street widening). Gray Spanish tiles sheathed the roof (replaced in 1955 with red). To the west of the central pavilion was a hotel wing, accommodating both layover passengers and railroad crews. Louis Millet, who worked on the similarly styled interior of the Auditorium Hotel

St. Louis Union Station.

c. 1930. Aloe Plaza, in the foreground, would soon receive a large allegorical fountain designed by Carl Milles. Unveiled in 1940, Meeting of the Waters celebrates the confluence of two great rivers, the Missouri and the Mississippi. It was refurbished in 1985, when Union Station reopened.

The elegant split staircase inside the Market Street entrance. Because of the station's sloping site, Theodore Link devised this connection between the track level (concourse and general waiting room) and the upper level (Grand Hall).

(Adler and Sullivan) in Chicago, was responsible for decorating the head house, including the second-story Grand Hall, filled with gilt, mosaics, marble, scagliola (plaster simulating marble), allegorical stained glass, and many bas-reliefs. Suspended from the 65-foot-high, barrel-vaulted ceiling was a 350-light, two-ton chandelier (sold for scrap during World War II). A huge ladies' waiting room complex to the east was balanced on the west by the men's smoking room and the main and private dining rooms. At track level, one floor below, were general and second-class waiting rooms, the ticket office, barber shop, information bureau, lunch room, and post office. Railroad offices occupied the upper floor on the east side.

The Midway, 606 feet long with a 50-foot clear span, was separated from the tracks by a series of highly ornamental wrought-iron gates. A metal and glass wall, added above the gates in 1924, helped keep out soot and smoke; but the concourse was not heated until 1929. (The wrought-iron fencing was dismantled for a World War II scrap metal drive and replaced by modern doors and windows). Newsstands, locker rooms and a long-lived Fred Harvey restaurant (1896-1970) lined the head house side of the Midway. Civil engineer George H. Pegram designed the station's five-span train shed—606 feet wide, 630 feet long (extended to 810 feet in 1903), and 75 feet high. It covered nearly 10 acres and contained three-and-a-half miles of track. The roof was originally tin-covered wood with a 36-foot-wide skylight. Union Station's more than 30 tracks—increased to 42 in 1929—were all stub-end. Topography dictated a relatively narrow track approach; to enter, trains passed the station and then backed down a wye into the shed. As an indirect (but favorable to passengers) consequence, smoky, cinder-spewing, noisy locomotives remained outside—beyond the roofed-over area.

Union Station's busiest peacetime year was 1920, when an average of 269, mostly long-distance trains arrived or departed every day. In 1971, when Amtrak began operations, the num-ber of passenger trains to St. Louis amounted to six. Compared to some other big cities, St. Louis had little commuter service (and none after the 1960s), which likely accelerated the building's demise as a train stop. Seriously studied ideas for adaptive use began as early as 1945—among them a multimodal center (including airplane landing strips) and an amusement park. In 1974, T.R.R.A. sold the station, which survived a subsequent foreclosure and a change of hands. Amtrak departed to new quarters in 1978. Funded by a federal grant and private investments (rehabilitation tax credits available at the time were critical), a meticulously restored Union Station reopened in 1985. A six-story hotel incorporates several spaces: the old Terminal Hotel, a waiting room and hallway known as the Gothic Corridor, the Harvey Restaurant, and a portion of the shed. The Grand Hall is the lobby. Stores and restaurants fill the rest of the shed and the Midway. Interpretative displays throughout the station depict the building's history. The once-lively surrounding neighborhood, largely demolished during 1950s urban renewal, still awaits resurrection. NHL. NR. [Privately owned. Mixed use.]

SEDALIA

MISSOURI, KANSAS & TEXAS DEPOT
600 East 3rd Street (at Thompson Street)
Bradford Lee Gilbert
1896

Sedalia was served by the Missouri, Kansas & Texas (the "Katy") and the Missouri Pacific, both of which maintained large division operations in the area. For a period of time before its new depot was built, the Katy operated out of a union station (on Main Street—current site of a later MP depot). Bradford Lee Gilbert's design was executed in red brick, with rock-faced limestone up to the first-floor windowsills and bold limestone string courses. Limestone was also used for massive framing of the variously styled windows. The main portion of the

Sedalia Katy depot with tracks still in place.

depot was a two-and-a-half-story, irregularly-shaped half octagon, topped by a slate roof. Spreading southward, the depot telescoped down to sections of decreasingly lower heights. The interior, which the railroad altered significantly in 1943 and 1956, featured a ladies' waiting room (with paneled oak wainscoting and an ornate fireplace), ticket office, large men's waiting room, all-night lunch room (with fireplace and skylight), formal dining room, and baggage room. On the depot's opening day, the dining room menu included boiled lake trout and roast turkey with dressing. Division offices were on the second floors of the north and middle sections. Passenger service ended in 1958, and the depot was used subsequently for railroad offices

and briefly by contractors for the Minuteman Missile system. It currently awaits renewed life, possibly in connection with the Katy Trail State Park (on the old railroad right-of-way), which is expected to run past the building. NR. [State of Missouri. Vacant.]

WARRENSBURG

WARRENSBURG DEPOT
South Holden Street
1890

In 1992, when the Warrensburg depot reopened, Amtrak passengers could get out of the elements for the first time in two decades. The Pacific Railroad of Missouri (a Missouri Pacific predecessor) built Warrensburg's first depot in 1864. It burned 25 years later and was replaced by a Romanesque Revival design executed in locally quarried sandstone. The central, two-story cross gable was flanked by one-story, hipped-roof wings and topped by a wood-shingle roof. The east end had a large, arched window (now a doorway) and two tall chimneys that guarded a gabled dormer (gone). A baggage section and a long covered platform were added later.

Remodeled in 1942 and 1962, the depot closed to passengers about 1970 (a portion con-

A guard flags the crossing at the Warrensburg depot.

tinued in crew use). In 1987, an offshoot of the chamber of commerce formed a nonprofit group, Depot Renovation, Inc. Its goal was to adapt the depot to offices and a meeting space, while restoring a railroad presence. A small waiting room for Amtrak was incorporated into the floor plan. The entire project, which included relaying the brick platform, was accomplished with funds from the community, the state, and Amtrak. Volunteers of all ages and backgrounds contributed labor. A month before the depot was rededicated, Union Pacific (Missouri Pacific's successor) officially donated it to the community. [City of Warrensburg. Train stop and chamber of commerce.]

WEBSTER GROVES

TUXEDO PARK STATION

643 Glen Road (at Tuxedo Boulevard)
c. 1890

Lilburn G. McNair was a grandson of Missouri's first governor. He also was a promoter of both steam and electric railways, a partner in the first St. Louis brokerage firm to have telegraph con-

nections to the New York Stock Exchange, and (with his brother) the largest fruit grower in Missouri. In 1890, he purchased land to build an exclusive commuter suburb that he called Tuxedo Park, modeled no doubt after the like-named community northwest of New York City. McNair provided Missouri Pacific with ground for a railroad station—arrival point for prospective house buyers. Unlike MP's other commuter depots which tended to be frame, the one-story Tuxedo Park station was rough-faced sandstone with raised, red-stained ridges over the mortar joints. An impression of wealth and importance was further exhibited by the deep-set windows, low pyramidal roof, and broad eaves supported by massive wooden brackets. An ornate fireplace dominated the large waiting room. Passenger service ended in the early 1960s. The depot was used for maintaining railroad signal equipment until 1983, when the city took title to prevent its demolition. As yet, no community group has stepped forward to adaptively use the station. Two other depots remain in the municipality: the MP "Webster Groves" stop (now a preschool) and a St. Louis–San Francisco Railway station (now used by Burlington Northern). NR. [City of Webster Groves. Vacant.]

Nebraska

In 1916, Nebraska had some 730 stations (today there are five passenger stops). About 30 depots have been rescued for adaptive use, although not many remain in their original locations. Relatively few Nebraska preservationists have overcome the freight railroads' insistence that the buildings be moved. The state retains only the memory of the station at North Platte (1918), site of a World War II canteen of nationwide renown. Community volunteers provided free food and hospitality to more than six million military personnel during that four-year period. In 1973, citizens were contemplating how the vacant station could be converted to a museum or civic building when Union Pacific suddenly razed the structure. On the vacant land, the railroad dedicated a small park to the canteen's memory—in effect, a depot tombstone.

BEATRICE

CHICAGO, BURLINGTON & QUINCY DEPOT
101 North Second Street
1906

In 1973, by agreeing to install a fence along the tracks, the Gage County Historical Society was able to save Beatrice's former Chicago, Burlington & Quincy depot—in situ—for use as a museum. Burlington Northern (CB&Q's successor) leased the land to the society and donated the depot. Built in the early 20th century of limestone-trimmed Omaha brick, the combination passenger and freight station replaced a wooden structure that was converted to freight-only. The two-story center section of the new depot had a Greek Revival flavor, with pedimented gable ends turned toward both the tracks and the street. A large porte-cochere with keystoned arches and square pilasters was off-limits to horse-drawn cabs; a new rule forced hacks to stand outside the depot grounds. The ladies' waiting room featured rocking chairs instead of benches, which the local newspaper stated would make

long waits "comfortable for the gentler sex." Railroad offices were on the second floor. Covered platforms for passengers and baggage handling connected the main building to its two wings: freight and express to the north and dining room to the south. (The south wing, razed in the 1930s, was reconstructed in 1980.) Beatrice's other two passenger stations, including the Union Pacific depot that stood directly across from the CB&Q, are gone. NR. [Gage County Historical Society. Museum.]

FAIRBURY

CHICAGO, ROCK ISLAND & PACIFIC DEPOT
2nd Street between I and J streets
1914

The week before the Chicago, Rock Island & Pacific depot's grand opening, the local paper announced there would be music, punch, cigars, and dancing, as well as tours given by railroad personnel. When the great day came, the crush of visitors was so overwhelming that many people were unable to get inside. Three

Beatrice CB&Q depot. This 1908 postcard view shows a crowd listening to Republican presidential candidate William H. Taft.

thousand souvenir post cards were distributed. The new depot replaced one built in 1886, two blocks west, that burned in 1911. (A passenger coach served in the interim.) Fairbury was a division point, housing railroad offices on the second floor. A tile roof, with slightly extended eaves supported by Italianate brackets, topped the limestone-trimmed brick walls. Next door, flower-filled Rock Island Park covered two acres. FAIRBURY, NEBRASKA was spelled out in white stones surrounded by lilac bushes.

Once an important stop for the Rock Island "Rocket" trains between Chicago and Denver, the station closed in 1980. The following year, interior artifacts were auctioned off by trustees for the defunct railroad. Local citizens were soon struggling to prevent demolition by the next owners, Mid States Port Authority — recipients of many offers from salvagers who wanted the brick. To raise funds for a liability policy and repairs, the local historical society sold brand new bricks, engraved with the names of donors, which were used for part of a mural wall depicting the Rocket. In 1992, the port authority transferred the deed (via the county) to the society, which then began a volunteer rehabilitation project. Two years later, ISTEA funds enabled the society to begin major work toward opening a museum in the depot. Union Pacific freight trains now use the CRI&P tracks. (The UP passenger depot, a Gilbert Stanley Underwood design, was razed in 1976.) [Jefferson County Historical Society. Vacant.]

GERING

GERING DEPOT
Main and 10th streets
Gilbert Stanley Underwood
1929

In 1928, Union Pacific announced the construction of a western extension to the Gering–Cheyenne Cutoff. Gering was designated a division point, and as such, became eli-

gible for additional station improvements. The old depot, which had been moved early in its history during a dispute over location, was jacked up again and transferred to South Mitchell (a community further west). The new depot, clad in stucco with brick quoins, combined somewhat incongruous elements — a formal, broken-pediment entranceway and a second story of decorative half-timbering. Union Pacific emblems filled both the cartouche above the door and the bull's-eye surmounting the double window. Wall dormers added light and space to the depot's wings.

Passenger train travel through the North Platte River Valley ended in 1971. The city has a long-term lease on the depot, which it has assigned to the Wyobraska Museum of Natural History. Freight trains still use the tracks. Another Nebraska station, the former UP depot at Cozad (now a human resources center), bears a stylistic and proportional resemblance to Gering, although only one story high. The Torrington, Wyo., depot (1926, NR), an Underwood design similar to Gering, is home to the Homestead Museum Foundation. [Union Pacific Railroad. Natural history museum.]

HASTINGS

CHICAGO, BURLINGTON & QUINCY DEPOT
501 West 1st Street
Thomas Rogers Kimball
1902

Hastings was served by several railroads, whose competition may explain the grandiosity of this 18-room Chicago, Burlington & Quincy depot. Its two-story-high main waiting room had eight-foot-high marble wainscoting, a white marble fountain, and ornate gas and electric light fixtures. The east wing held a two-story restaurant. The station was built of light-colored pressed brick on a cut stone foundation and roofed with Spanish tiles. Replacing Hastings's second "Burlington" depot (the first two stations were on Bellevue Avenue), it was designed by Nebraskan Thomas Kimball. His use of Spanish Colonial Revival for Hastings predates by 15 years the extensive post–World War I popularity of this style for depot architecture. The station was remodeled in 1945 and altered again about 1971 for Amtrak. In 1984, Burlington Northern (CB&Q's successor) vacated the depot, which is today in fair condition. NR. [Privately owned. Train stop.]

LINCOLN

CHICAGO, BURLINGTON & QUINCY DEPOT
7th and P streets
1927

The original floor plan for Lincoln's Chicago, Burlington & Quincy depot shows that men's smoking rooms and women's retiring rooms were still being included in station facilities (found here on the south end) as late as the 1920s. Parallel lobbies flanked the main waiting room, noteworthy for its coffered ceiling, marble floor and wainscoting, and terra-cotta walls. The station's exterior was clad in red brick. Engaged limestone columns rose from the second floor to the cornice on the east

facade. Cast-iron canopies suspended from chains sheltered each streetside entrance, while a flat-roofed, freestanding canopy protected passengers on the track side. The previous station on this site was a three-story Victorian Gothic structure of brick and stone.

In the late 1980s, using rehabilitation tax credits, a limited partnership restored and renovated the CB&Q station, including the main waiting room, which is rented for special events. Leased first-floor spaces house an art gallery, the new Amtrak waiting room, and a restaurant (placed in the original dining room location). The upper-floor offices (used by Burlington Northern) have been modernized, while the corridors remain largely as built. [Privately owned. Train stop and mixed use.]

CHICAGO, ROCK ISLAND & PACIFIC DEPOT
1944 O Street
1893

Completed when the Chicago, Rock Island & Pacific first arrived in Lincoln, the red sandstone and brick depot had an open-air platform at one end and a detached baggage room at the other. Its steeply pitched roof was broken by a hipped, cross gable, topped with cresting and finials. Deep eaves swelled into conical-roofed,

Lincoln CRI&P depot, 1920.

rounded bays at either end of the main building. Within the Chateauesque arch of a very large side dormer, the "Rock Island" placed its logo, carved in sandstone. Inside, the centrally located general waiting room was augmented by ladies' waiting and men's smoking rooms.

In the late 1960s, the depot was converted to a bank branch, plus two rental spaces, by adding a harmonious drive-up teller canopy (further remodeled in 1984). The exterior was restored, including removal of paint from the masonry (done by sandblasting when most people were unaware of the damaging effects). Interior partitions now subdivide the once-spacious waiting room, but an abundance of depot furniture and memorabilia—donated by several different railroads—reinforces the ambiance of this early and lasting adaptive use project. NR. [Privately owned. Commercial.]

McCOOK

CHICAGO, BURLINGTON & QUINCY DEPOT
100 North Avenue (Norris and A streets)
1926

McCook's new Chicago, Burlington & Quincy depot opened on an April day in 1926, with evening dancing in the parking lot to a nine-piece railroad orchestra. Fifteen card tables on the second floor were filled with players. Railroad workers were freed of all nonessential tasks to show 3,000 visitors through the depot. One of the marvels on view was in the telegraph office—a new signaling system that "called" the station by using small flashing lights instead of dots and dashes. The rusticated stone and light brown brick station was built just north of its 1882 large, wooden predecessor (immediately demolished); the changed location enabled the railroad to straighten the tracks. West and trackside entrances, sheltered by canopies suspended from chains, led to the double-height waiting room (still used today by

Amtrak) with tall arched windows. The balance of the three-story station was used for baggage and express services, division offices, and crew dormitories. A wide brick platform stretched to the tracks. During World War II, a troop canteen was added to the operations. [Burlington Northern Railroad Company. Train stop and freight railroad facility.]

NORTH PLATTE

HERSHEY UNION PACIFIC STATION
1400 North Poplar Street (Cody Park)
1892

In 1972, a group of retired Union Pacific workers and rail buffs transported the abandoned Hershey station from its original location, 13 miles west of North Platte, to its new home in Cody Park. A UP standard design, the one-story, wooden depot consisted of a single waiting room and a freight section. The agent's office, with its gabled bay window, linked the two areas. Typical of many small-town stations,

UP's combined Cities streamliner No. 103 passing the Hershey depot in its original location. The date is April 30, 1971, the day before Amtrak took over most of the nation's long-distance passenger service.

Hershey had no plumbing; rest rooms were added after the move. These once common stations are now relatively scarce in Nebraska. Few remain on their original sites; and even then, the tracks are gone. The Hershey depot is authentically equipped with a semaphore-type block signal, telephone and telegraph equipment, furniture, and a baggage cart—all donated by UP. In 1992, volunteers enhanced the restoration by applying the original yellow and brown exterior colors, researched through the archives of a local Sherwin-Williams dealer. [City of North Platte. Museum.]

Omaha CB&Q depot.

This 1921 view (taken from the west side of the 10th Street viaduct) shows the station's original appearance.

1930, after remodeling.

OMAHA

CHICAGO, BURLINGTON & QUINCY DEPOT
South 10th Street near Pacific Street
Thomas Rogers Kimball
Graham, Anderson, Probst and White
1898, 1930

In the late 1920s, the Chicago, Burlington & Quincy hired a famous Chicago architectural firm to give a major facelift to its Greek Revival 1898 station—the work of prominent Nebraskan Thomas Kimball. (Kimball was architect-in-chief for Omaha'a Trans-Mississippi and International Exposition, which also opened in 1898.) Graham, Anderson, Probst and White removed the gabled porches and the peristyle (24 of the old columns now form a colonnade near the University of Nebraska football stadium in Lincoln) and ordered new Ionic columns for the center section. Workers extended the building westward to fill the old portico area, while constructing a solid parapet wall around the new flat roof. The "Burlington" station, also used by the Chicago Great Western, sat elevated on a bluff high above the tracks; new ramps and improved stairs breached the previously awkward separation. An overhead walkway (since removed) connected the Burlington station with Union Station on the other side of

Omaha Union Station.

May 1938.

Exit to 10th Street, 1931.

the bluff. Inside, by extracting a circular stairway and raising the ceiling, the architects created a grander scale for the waiting room, while retaining most of the circle and fan motifs of the marble mosaic floor. Fluted moldings, circular gold medallions, and bas-reliefs (containing emblems of four crack Burlington trains) embellished the walls.

Amtrak used this facility for a few years in the early 1970s, before moving to other quarters. Subjected to a number of false starts for adaptive use as a commercial enterprise, the building was empty for decades and suffered water damage and loss of interior fabric. In the mid-1990s, it opened as a farmers and crafts market. Volunteers are attempting restoration. Omaha's first Burlington station also stood on this site—a small Gothic-style building (1870) razed for the current structure. NR. [Privately owned. Vacant—for sale.]

UNION STATION

801 South 10th Street
Gilbert Stanley Underwood
1931

Architect Gilbert Stanley Underwood said of his design for Omaha Union Station, "We have tried to express the distinctive character of the railroad—strength, power, masculinity." Working for the building's owner, Union Pacific, Underwood designed everything from the Art Deco exterior to brass door plates, filing cabinets, and office chairs. UP's passengers—and those of the six other railroads using the station—exited and entered through portals surmounted by sculptures of four railroad workers : a locomotive engineer, a brakeman, a civil engineer, and a mechanic. Glazed, cream-colored terra-cotta sheathed the building's steel frame. Columnettes of faux marble accented the waiting room walls, which were covered in another faux material—Caen Stone. Gold and silver leaf were applied to the sculptured plaster ceiling, from which hung six 13-foot-high chandeliers, sparkling above starburst-patterned terrazzo floors. Within the station's east-end dining room, finishes included simulations of marble, travertine, and patent leather. Wall murals by California artist Joseph W. Keller depicted various stages of transportation history. During World War II, busy Union Station housed a U.S.O. facility.

Two years after Union Station closed in 1971, UP donated the building to the city. In 1975, following the temporary tenancy of a bus company, the Western Heritage Society moved in and soon began an ongoing rejuvenation process. The Redcaps (a museum volunteer group) serve confections from the old soda fountain they restored in the east end of the waiting room. Major renovations scheduled for 1996 include new mechanical systems, as well as new interactive and multimedia exhibits. Two blocks north, a former UP freight house (1890), built of materials salvaged from an 1870 depot, is used as UP's current dispatching center. NR. [City of Omaha. Museum.]

WAHOO

CHICAGO, BURLINGTON & QUINCY DEPOT
431 West 3rd Street
1887

Completed several months before the Chicago, Burlington & Quincy tracks actually reached Wahoo, this wooden depot was typical of many in Nebraska in that the agent's family lived on the second floor. The quarters were spacious for a depot apartment, consisting of a dining room, kitchen, living room, and two bedrooms. In the 1920s, with the installation of water and electricity, a bathroom and pantry were added.

Dripping with icicles, Wahoo CB&Q depot c. 1910. (For exterior view, *see* page 7.)

Flanked by a one-story freight wing, the first floor housed the agent's office and gender-segregated waiting rooms. Among the arriving passengers were children from outlying areas, who routinely took the train to attend high school in Wahoo.

In 1975, the Burlington Northern (CB&Q's successor) donated the depot to the local historical society, but retained the land beneath the building. Nine years later, after BN had abandoned this branch line, the group was able to remove the high chain link fence that the railroad had required as a safety measure. The depot retains its CB&Q paint colors, mineral red with green trim. The brick platform is a reconstruction using old materials. Inside, equipment and furniture, if not original, come from similar stations. The little town of Wahoo had two other depots, Union Pacific and Chicago & North Western (both gone by the 1960s). At Red Cloud stands another two-story wooden CB&Q station (1897). In the 1960s, the Red Cloud depot was relocated 300 feet northwest of its original site, where it became a museum devoted to famous author of regional fiction, Willa Cather. NR. [Saunders County Historical Society. Depot museum.]

North Dakota

Northern Pacific crossed the southern tier of North Dakota; Great Northern went across the northern portion. As the two dominant railroads of the state, they did not directly compete along their main lines (except in Fargo). Where their branch lines fingered through the middle of the state, they tended to build side by side towns, each with a wooden depot. In fact, they overbuilt; most of those towns are gone today with perhaps nothing but a grain elevator and a railroad siding to mark the spot. The state's ever resourceful farmers have taken over many of these depots for storage. One can spot them with some frequency, relocated to the edges of grain fields.

BISMARCK

NORTHERN PACIFIC DEPOT

East Main Avenue between 4th and 5th streets
Reed and Stem
1901

In 1877, one of the larger buildings in Dakota Territory was the Sheridan House, a hotel that also served as a passenger depot. Twenty-three years later, the operators gave up their 99-year lease on the land (owned by Northern Pacific) and physically moved the hotel across the street, to make way for a full-fledged station. Designed by a nationally prominent architectural firm from St. Paul, Northern Pacific's new depot was Mission style. Marble chips were mixed into the station's stuccolike exterior finish; the roof was Ludowici clay tile. A central block contained cherry-trimmed railroad offices and both men's and ladies' waiting rooms. Ladies were made to feel at home with a mosaic tiled floor (covered by a Turkish rug), a massive oak table and sofa, a pier glass, and easy chairs. The east wing contained the main waiting room with walls and floors of terrazzo and gilded radiators. Passengers could drink from the fountain by using a silver mug, suspended from a wall chain. Brass

Bismarck NP depot with original domed towers c.1905.

kick plates on the doors were studded with brass round-headed nails outlining the Monad, which was NP's emblem (a Chinese yin-yang copied from the Korean flag in 1893). Baggage and express were handled from the depot's west end. The depot's wings terminated in square, open-air shelters (enclosed in 1930 and 1955). Twin bell towers were originally domed and crowned by louvered cupolas with belcast roofs. In 1954, the superstructures were replaced by pyramidal hipped roofs, clad in tile, that resembled Tuscan campaniles. At one time post and rail fence surrounded the parklike station grounds. Freestanding Tuscan columns supported the wrought-iron BISMARCK sign and the trackside semaphore.

Amtrak stopped serving Bismarck in 1979. In the early Eighties, private developers bought the station from the Burlington Northern (which still uses the one remaining track). As part of their rehabilitation, the new owners removed layers of paint from the tile walls. They uncovered a band of inlaid mosaic ornamentation and the polychromed Great Monad emblem. The ticket office, now a dining room, retains the wrought-iron window grille and old switching equipment. Another Northern Pacific depot—dating from 1911 and now situated in Bismarck on River Road—was moved 24 miles south from Wilton in 1987. It now serves as a combined riverboat ticket office and restaurant. NR. [Privately owned. Restaurant and offices.]

FARGO

GREAT NORTHERN DEPOT
536 5th Avenue North
Samuel L. Bartlett
1906

The Great Northern assigned Samuel L. Bartlett (apparently a staff member) to design a string of depots across the Dakotas to Glacier Park in Montana. The one-story brick station at

Early view of the Fargo GN depot.

Fargo had a somewhat overpowering four-faced clock tower. According to railroad lore GN president James J. Hill, wanted to outdo the Northern Pacific. Rusticated buff sandstone was used up to the sills of the depot's tall, fan-lit windows. The green tile, hipped roof extended from the east and west ends to form twin open-air pavillions, anchored by hefty square pillars. Passengers waited on a wide brick platform. The American Railway Express Com-pany used a similarly styled building just to the east with a slate roof and green tile trim. In 1993, after several years of vacancy (Amtrak moved to a smaller facility in the late Eighties), the depot was purchased by a private party, who may convert it to a restaurant. Little more than the coffered ceiling remains on the interior. The GN's substantial brick freight station (NR), built in 1902 and enlarged in 1930, stands about three blocks west of the passenger station. NR District. [Privately owned. Vacant.]

NORTHERN PACIFIC STATION
701 Main Street
Cass Gilbert
1898

Fargo was founded by the Northern Pacific in 1871. A year later, the railroad completed the Headquarters Hotel to accommodate both guests and NP employees and also to serve as the depot. Rebuilt after a fire in 1874, the building was destroyed forever by another fire in 1897. The replacement station was designed by nationally known architect Cass Gilbert. Built of brownstone-trimmed, dark brown brick with a red tile roof, the station included a restaurant, a men's waiting room, and an intimately scaled ladies' waiting room with oriel windows and a fireplace. Another fireplace was in the large general waiting room to the east. Baggage was handled from the western, one-story section.

The station ceased operations about 1970. Burlington Northern (NP's successor) donated it to the city for community use. Teenagers treated the depot, converted to a youth center, with less than loving care. A subsequent period of vacancy ended in the late 1970s, when the state and city obtained grant money to remove misguided improvements and restore the building. A local fund drive raised money for landscaping the parking lot (once depot parkland). Workers installed paving bricks (inscribed with donor names) and a fountain. Today, the NP and GN depots, six blocks apart, anchor a historic commercial district, which retains about

half its original buildings. Fargo's third depot within this same area — the 1884 Fargo & Southern (later Chicago, Milwaukee & St. Paul) — was rehabilitated in 1971 after nine years of vacancy — only to catch fire in 1974. It was subsequently demolished. NR. [City of Fargo. Senior center and park district office.]

MANDAN

NORTHERN PACIFIC STATION
401 West Main Street
c. 1930

Mandan's Colonial Revival Northern Pacific passenger station and adjacent, matching cafe replaced their counterparts that burned in 1926. The north and south porticos of the red brick, one-story depot were composed of fluted metal columns and a wooden gallery. The gallery's "union jack" motif was repeated around the fanlit cupola that straddled a gabled, slate roof. Passenger service ended in 1979. Subsequently, the Burlington Northern (NP's successor) leased the depot to the city on the condition that it serve as a Native American

Mandan NP station c. 1948.

arts center. The former waiting room, with its original stone floor, tile wainscoting, and oak woodwork and benches, now serves as the arts association office. The balance of the building is used for other Indian directed operations: a retail store, gallery space, and offices. Out front stands a 1924 equestrian statue of Teddy Roosevelt, who was a frequent visitor to Mandan during his stays in Medora. Although reduced in size, Northern Pacific Park continues to enhance the depot's setting. NP's two-story brick freight house, at the foot of 5th Avenue, N.W., dates from 1911 —built right after completion of the NP's new north-south line. NR District. [Burlington Northern Railroad. Mixed use.]

MINOT

MINNEAPOLIS, ST. PAUL & SAULT STE. MARIE DEPOT

11 North Main Street
William M. Kenyon
1912

The Minneapolis, St. Paul & Sault Ste. Marie (the "Soo Line") used a Minneapolis architect to design its second passenger facility (the first was on the west side of 2nd Street, S.W.). It opened to an all-day-and-evening public reception, accompanied by orchestra music. The story-and-a-half depot was built of patterned brick walls with sandstone trim. MINOT was spelled out in stone blocks on the trackside facade and on the east elevation above the porte-cochere. A pair of shed dormers and a transverse gable pierced the steeply pitched roof, clad in standing-seam copper. The interior spaces—which included a general waiting room with a vaulted ribbed ceiling, a men's smoking room, and a ladies' retiring room—bore finishes of marble, glazed brick, and highly varnished wood. A breezeway on the west side led to the baggage and express annex.

After passenger service ended in 1964, the depot housed offices for Soo Line freight business, Western Union, and the United States Postal Service (which operated out of the main waiting room). Nearly demolished as part of a 1970 proposed urban renewal and street realignment, the depot went through a string of reuses until purchased in 1993 by an American Legion post. (A previous owner did substantial restoration work.) Freight trains use the tracks.

Early streetside view of the Minot Soo Line depot.

The c. 1914 Soo Line freight station still stands about three blocks east. Minot's Great Northern depot (late 1800s) is extant, but drastically altered. NR. [Privately owned. Veterans club and meeting space.]

RUGBY

RUGBY DEPOT
201 West Dewey Street
Samuel L. Bartlett
1907

Railroad stockholders from England gave Rugby its name in 1885. During the early part of the 20th century, the Great Northern billed the town as the gateway to the national parks. Samuel Bartlett designed the one-and-a-half-story passenger depot with Tudoresque gable ends and a transverse gable dormer. A one-story extension housed baggage and express services. Exterior walls clad in brick were accented by limestone that was used for a band running at windowsill level and the gable copings. Interior features included cream-colored tile wainscoting, birch woodwork, and brass electric light fixtures. Water to the fountain was cooled by being run through pipes packed with ice. The depot's grand opening was accompanied by a formal reception and a grand ball. Over the years, special events at the depot included the exhibition of a 55-foot-long whale and a 1939 appearance by the crown prince and princess of Norway. In 1987, the city, the Lions Club, Amtrak, local businesses, and citizens undertook a three-year restoration project. NR. [Burlington Northern Railroad. Passenger train stop and freight crew headquarters.]

WILTON

BISMARCK, WASHBURN & GREAT FALLS DEPOT
1st Street at McLean Avenue
William J. Keith
c. 1900

William D. Washburn was the first president of the Minneapolis, St. Paul & Sault Ste. Marie (the "Soo Line"), a position he resigned following his election to the United States Senate. When his re-election bid for the 1896 seat failed, Washburn toured the Orient for two years. On his return, he bought 115,000 acres of land north of Bismarck. To attract settlers, he built a new railroad—the Bismarck, Washburn & Great Falls. In 1900, the line reached Wilton. East of town, Washburn opened one of the world's largest, underground, lignite coal mines.

Wilton's story-and-a-half wooden depot, designed by a Minneapolis architect, was lengthened by 24 feet in 1907, probably the same year the gable dormer was added. Just above the agent's bay, an unusual square tower, with a vaguely pagodalike character, pierced the roof. The agent's apartment was on the upper floor. The Soo Line (which acquired the BW&GF in 1904) used the depot until 1970. Although demolition was the initial plan, the railroad donated the building to the city in celebration of the United States Bicentennial. Funds were raised from the state's Bicentennial commission and local citizens to relocate the depot in 1976. Placed on city-owned property, several blocks northwest of its old location, the former station was painted the Soo Line scheme of maroon and yellow. It houses a model railroad, a collection of mining tools, and exhibits about the depot. NR. [City of Wilton. Museum.]

Ohio

By the 1870s, all the major eastern trunk lines crisscrossed Ohio, a state that had many rail hubs and led the nation in total number of railroad miles. Cincinnati, for example, long established as a steamboat city, evolved into the north-south gateway for the Great Lakes to New Orleans rail corridor. Over time, in the small-to-medium-size communities, nearly all the first generation depots were replaced by more substantial versions. Two of Ohio's 20th-century metropolises, Cleveland and Cincinnati, produced innovative (but late-in-the-game) designs to the railroad station scene.

ADA

ADA RAILROAD STATION
Central Avenue off Main Street
1887

Since the late 19th century, the wooded area surrounding Ada's depot was known as Railroad Park. Complete with benches, flowers, and a bandstand, it was a pleasant spot from which to watch the flow of main line, Pennsylvania Railroad trains. In 1958, the PRR offered to sell Railroad Park to the village of Ada. The community agreed, but with one condition—the depot had to be part of the deal.

Ada's first station was a depot-hotel. The new one was built in Stick Style, with a slate roof, fancy ridge cresting, corbeled chimneys (venting two fireplaces), stained glass windows, and a gabled platform canopy extending down the tracks. A stone walk led to the preceding depot, which was converted to freight use (and may still be extant, but moved to a different location). Until 1960, a watchman's tower stood elevated on graceful legs beside the Main Street crossing. In 1971, guided by the Hardin County Historical Society, community volunteers began repairing the deteriorating passenger station, which was still partly used by a Penn Central (merged PRR and New York Central) agent. The story-and-a-half building originally housed the telegraph operator in the attic space. Today, that floor is filled with a model railroad layout and memorabilia from Ada's days as a train stop. Amtrak and freight trains continue to roll by. [Community Improvement Corporation. Retail and meeting space.]

BARNESVILLE

BARNESVILLE RAILROAD STATION
300 East Church Street
M. A. Long
1917

During World War I, when Barnesville received a new buff brick (laid in Flemish bond) depot, the old wooden combination station was converted to all freight (c. 1888; razed 1962). The passenger station resembled others on the Baltimore & Ohio line, such as Cambridge and Mt. Vernon (both extant); although not all had Barnesville's curvilinear dormers with spherical finials and leaded glass, quatrefoil windows. The red tile roof contributed further to a Mission flavor. Built as part of a general B&O program to upgrade passenger facilities, the depot was completely devoid of passengers in less than 50 years (1961). In 1983, when CSX Transportation (B&O's modern successor) first petitioned to remove the tracks, Barnesville citizens began pursuing a sales agreement for the depot and associated land. Eight years later, a whirlwind fund-raising campaign by a local development council netted the purchase price of the station, the eight-acre rail yard, and 35 acres of rail bed. A National Trust Preservation Services Fund grant in 1992 helped develop a reuse plan; original drawings, signed by architect M. A. Long, were consulted during the restoration process. The rail yard and depot are used for a museum, community meeting space, special events facility, and farmers market. The track bed has been converted to a recreational trail, flowing through the old stone railroad tunnel that runs beneath Main Street. Adjacent to the depot, volunteers laid 200 feet of track, used to display a wooden, c. 1920 B&O caboose. NR. [Village of Barnesville. Mixed use.]

BUCYRUS

OHIO CENTRAL STATION
700 East Rensselaer Street
c. 1880

Within about five years of its construction, Bucyrus's Ohio Central station came under the ownership of the Toledo & Ohio Central (later New York Central). Just to the north stood Colsan Tower (now gone), where the Pennsylvania Railroad tracks crossed those of the T&OC (no PRR buildings remain in Bucyrus). The T&OC railroad shops in Bucyrus provided many jobs in the community, and the passenger depot provided a proud face for the company. One-and-a-half stories of brick, the depot was anchored on the southeast corner by a two-story stone tower with a conical spire. Cross gables and dormers carried stone coping and finials; the hipped roof bore ridge ornamentation. (The architectural design is strikingly similar to a later building, the Alabama Great

Southern station in Fort Payne, Ala.) An ancillary building to the north (used as a restaurant in the 1920s, now destroyed) was a diminutive version of the depot. Regular passenger service ended about 1930. Between periods of emptiness, the depot was used for storage; today it houses a plumbing business. The interior is surprisingly undisturbed. The fireplace remains; stained glass transoms are stored in the basement, and advertisements and time schedules are still stuck to the walls. The old freight station (substantially altered) stands on the other side of Rensselaer Street. The area was once a hub of railroad activity; another passenger depot, used by the Pennsylvania Railroad, stood about 150 feet southwest of the T&OC passenger depot. It was torn down c. 1930. NR. [Privately owned. Commercial.] *For photo, see page 13.*

CANAL WINCHESTER

CANAL WINCHESTER DEPOT
96 North High Street
1894

The first chapter in Canal Winchester's transportation saga starts in 1828, at the founding of the Ohio & Erie Canal. Situated midway between the state capital and the county seat, the town was later a popular stopover for turnpike travelers. The Columbus & Hocking Valley Railroad (after 1881, the Columbus, Hocking Valley & Toledo) arrived in 1867. Its 1869 wooden station burned down in 1894; within two months, a new one was in operation. Clad in both vertical boards and diagonal, tongue and groove siding, the depot's most outstanding feature was the octagonal waiting room portion. Its cupola had stained glass monitor windows and a finial. The freight section was rectangular. All around the depot, curved Stick Style brackets supported the depot's deep eaves. Inside, wooden benches lined the walls

Canal Winchester depot set amidst the grain elevators and other commercial structures that lined the tracks.

of the waiting room, whose ceiling was tongue and groove, exposed roof decking. The agent's bay originally contained a triangular window, made into a rectangle after the turn of the century.

Passenger service ended in 1949, and the station was closed in the late Seventies. Modernized during a stint as a real estate office and then a craft shop, the depot was empty by the mid-1980s. A local couple donated funds that enabled the historical society to purchase the depot from CSX Transportation. The restoration committee then discovered the structure had dry rot, wood-boring insects, settlement problems, and a leaky roof. As cost estimates rose, five local businesses donated 54 percent of the total restoration expense. The balance came from tickets to scenic railway rides and from individuals, including students at the elementary school and members of a Boy Scout troop. The exterior is painted in historically researched colors—three shades of olive green with red for the window sash. Set into the brick platform is a semaphore signal, believed to be the original. In the former freight section, a model railroad club has a diorama depicting early 1900s Canal Winchester. The future of the adjacent historic grain elevator is uncertain. NR.

[Canal Winchester Area Historical Society. Tourist train stop, community meeting space, and chamber of commerce.]

CINCINNATI

UNION TERMINAL
1301 Western Avenue
Fellheimer and Wagner
1933

Cincinnati was a major north-south rail gateway. By the turn of the 20th century, the city's passenger and freight operations were characterized as a nightmare. Seven railroads used different passenger stations—scattered all over town—and more than 20 freight yards. When spring rains arrived, most of the city's rail facilities flooded. Not until 1927 did the railroads agree to form the Cincinnati Union Terminal Company, composed of the Pennsylvania, the Baltimore & Ohio, the Chesapeake & Ohio, the Louisville & Nashville, the Norfolk & Western, and subsidiaries of the New York Central and the Southern Railway. Besides a passenger terminal, 21 other rail-related buildings were constructed on nearly 300 acres of mostly marshland. Incorporating part of a city park, the location was more than a mile from downtown. Site preparation began in 1929, a few weeks before the stock market crash.

New York architects Alfred Fellheimer and Steward Wagner first developed a conservative concept for the station—their waiting room plan showed long rows of benches and side walls divided by Gothic arches. In 1930,at the behest of the terminal company, Fellheimer and Wagner invited Philadelphia architect, Paul Philippe Cret, to rework the plans, which he made more modern, more exciting, and less expensive. (Cret was also a designer of streamlined trains.) Curves were the order of the day. Entrance was through a monumental concrete and steel, semispherical dome, clad in limestone and marble. Curved, low stepped wings accommodated street vehicles arriving from curving Lincoln Park Drive. A 20-foot-wide, round clock with red neon hands told the time.

Inside the massive rotunda, circular pathways were laid into the terrazzo floor. The information booth and luxurious leather set-

Cincinnati Union Terminal.

Main entrance with cascading fountain and reflecting pool, 1940s. (For trackside view, *see* page 291.)

tees of the concourse were rounded in form and arrangement. Beneath the rotunda's huge dome were ticket offices, shops (including a dress boutique, tailor, and toy store), newspaper stands, restaurants, and a 100-seat newsreel screening room. Natural light from the main facade's windows poured onto the bright yellows, golds, and oranges of the interior paint scheme. Two mosaic murals by German-born Winold Reiss (who was heavily influenced by American Indian art) circled the rotunda. Each

For the north side of the rotunda (above the ticket windows), Winold Reiss created a spectacular mosaic mural depicting the settlement of Cincinnati and its subsequent development. His mural for the south side is a panorama combining elements of United States and transportation history.

was 105 feet long and 25 feet high. One depicted American history; the other, the settlement and development of Cincinnati. Fourteen more mosaics, including a magnificent map, filled the train concourse. Rookwood Pottery tiles decorated the tea room. Chrome, carved linoleum, aluminum, and exotic South Amer-ican woods were among the avant-garde decorative materials. Outside, an innovative scheme of traffic control included underground parking garages and ramps for buses and taxis. The prescient architects even left space for an airplane runway (just beyond the cascading fountain and reflecting pool) and ramps for a proposed rapid transit facility (the line was never built).

Despite the glory of its architecture, Union Terminal, except during World War II, never operated at its full potential. Nationwide passenger service began declining more than a decade before the building opened. The terminal was designed to handle 216 trains a day; when Amtrak moved to another facility in 1972, the indicator board showed only two. The Southern Railway, needing to expand its piggyback freight facility, soon purchased and demolished the train concourse. The Save the Terminal group managed to rescue most of Reiss's concourse mosaics —now installed, ironically, at the Greater Cincinnati International Airport in Kentucky. In 1975, the city bought the remaining head house and leased it for $1 to a developer. His shopping mall, which opened in 1980, soon failed, its demise attributed to the recession, the too far west location, and the decaying neighborhood.

In 1984, a Boston architect, E. Verner Johnson, suggested to the Natural History Museum and the Cincinnati Historical Society that they combine their facilities into a rehabilitated Union Terminal. His concept clicked: the massive basement could handily incorporate two large museums, while upstairs, the rotunda could be restored as a museum unto itself. Voters narrowly passed the bond issue that subsequently provided funds for adaptive use.

The Museum Center at Union Terminal opened in 1990. Within the restored rotunda, the former concourse entrance now leads to an Omnimax domed-screen theater. In 1991, Amtrak returned its Cincinnati operation to Union Terminal. NR. NHL. [City of Cincinnati. Train stop and museums.]

CLEVELAND

CLEVELAND TERMINAL & VALLEY STATION
829 Canal Road
William Stillman Dutton (Dutton and Heide)
1898

The Cleveland Terminal & Valley Railroad was the Cleveland branch of the Baltimore & Ohio. Designed by a local architect, its fortresslike station had a high first story of rock-faced stone, topped by two stories of yellow-orange brick. Both Gothic and Romanesque qualities were displayed in the corner turrets, a corbeled

Cleveland Terminal & Valley station (B&O system) with its mansard roof and tower intact.

cornice, and pointed and round-arched windows. Separate men's and ladies' waiting rooms had mosaic floors and bold paint colors —dark green wainscoting beneath walls of orange-red. An electric elevator rose to the company's general offices, finished in more restful light oak and ecru. Outside, the terrain dropped off sharply on the track side. An unusual elevated shed, incorporated into the railroad trestle, allowed trains to load passengers directly at street level. In the 1930s, after the B&O moved to the new Union Terminal, the old CT&V building became freight offices. Today, despite the absence of its hipped roof and clock tower, the station retains many interior details and fixtures. It is owned by the Sherwin-Williams Company, which is amenable to adaptive use proposals. [Privately owned. Vacant.]

UNION TERMINAL

Public Square

Graham, Anderson, Probst and White

1930

Years of debate and a world war delayed the construction of Cleveland Union Terminal. In 1919, the location of the facility actually had to be put to a public referendum, following a conflict between city planners (who wanted a lakefront station) and the Van Sweringen brothers. The Van Sweringens, owners of the New York, Chicago & St. Louis (the "Nickel Plate"), were building rapid transit lines to their holdings in the suburbs and had already purchased ground for a station in Public Square's southwest quadrant—which became the winning site. The terminal was placed fully underground. Above it, a 52-story office tower (steel clad in limestone) was the tallest building west of New York City. Attached to the tower on the east was Higbee's Department Store; to the west, the 920-room Cleveland Hotel. Altogether, seven buildings stood above the tracks—a total concept for developing air rights over a transportation complex not seen before or since. Except for the

Cleveland Union Terminal, track side in 1953.

post office, all the buildings were accessible from the underground station.

The main entrance to both the terminal and the tower was through a colossal colonnade. Inside, visitors encountered a vaulted, marble-lined hall with seven Jules Guerin murals depicting commerce, industry, transportation, water, fire, air, and earth. Straight ahead were the elevator lobbies for the office tower and the ramps leading down to the "steam" concourse. Paneled in Botticino marble and rimmed by fluted columns, the concourse was lit with chandeliers and an arched, vaulted skylight. (Poking out of the ground south of Prospect Avenue, this clerestory was the only indication of the great railroad facility below.) This level also included two "traction" concourses for rapid transit lines and a 500-seat waiting room. Passageways led to the cab stand, mail, express, and baggage areas. The tracks were one more level below. The principal long-distance trains using the station were those of the New York Central System, the

Nickel Plate, the Erie, and the Baltimore & Ohio. (The Pennsylvania Railroad never used Union Terminal; its lakefront station is now gone.) To fulfill the needs of both travelers and workers in the nearby buildings, the Fred Harvey Company, managed about 175,000 square feet (four acres) of underground stores, restaurants, and service facilities in the terminal.

With a story that mirrors Cincinnati's station, Cleveland Union Terminal was too long in gestation and born too late in railroad history. Dropped immediately into the Depression and then buried by plane and car travel, the station barely had time to hit its stride. By the 1970s, intercity trains were down to one departure and arrival a day; Amtrak moved to a smaller facility on the lakefront. Fluorescent lights and two indoor tennis courts were installed in the steam concourse. In 1977, the Harvey operation shut down. Stalled adaptive use plans and arguments about rebuilding the streets above the station ended when a major local developer announced plans for Tower City Center. Opened in 1990, the hotel-retail-office-transportation complex melds new construction, a rebuilt rapid transit station, and a measure of historic preservation. The most controversial changes were the demolition of the arcade from Public Square to Prospect Avenue, elimination of ramps down to the former station level, and dramatic alterations to the steam concourse (the old skylight was replaced by a barrel-vaulted, glass roof which doubled the vertical space). The English Oak Room restaurant, with its various woods and marbles, was restored as a banquet and meeting space. NR. [Privately owned. Rapid transit stop and mixed use.]

COLUMBUS

TOLEDO & OHIO CENTRAL STATION
379 West Broad Street
Yost and Packard
1895

The remaining depot in Columbus is one of the earliest examples of adaptive use and may also hold the combined record for disasters: two fires (1910 and 1975) and two major floods (1913 and 1959). Built by the Toledo & Ohio Central, the two-story, dark brown brick station was designed by prominent local architects. Its style, described most often as oriental, was more likely rooted in French and Swiss feudal architecture. The most striking feature, a three-and-half-story tower, ornamented with stone quoins and vertical brick openwork, tapered to a compound pagodalike, tile roof. Three see-through clock faces (now gone) kept the pub-

Columbus T&OC station when the tower still bore clock faces.

lic informed of the time. Inside the elegant, barrel-vaulted waiting room was an Italian marble floor, mahogany woodwork, and a cornice decorated with elaborate bas-reliefs.

In 1910, to eliminate a grade crossing, Broad Street was depressed and the tracks elevated to second-floor level. Nearly two decades later, New York Central (successor to T&OC) relocated to Columbus Union Station (an 1897 Daniel Burnham design; razed in 1977). In 1929, a nonprofit service organization, the Volunteers of America, adapted the T&OC depot for its local headquarters. For more than six decades, it has attempted to keep the building in near-original condition. Although the skylight was not replaced after the 1975 fire, the other damaged portions of the waiting room were restored. Fund raising is underway to put clay tiles back on the roof. The building is well used by the community; church services are held there every Sunday. NR. [Privately owned. Offices, community service center, and meeting space.]

DENNISON

PITTSBURGH, CINCINNATI & ST. LOUIS STATION
400 Center Street
1873

For the Pittsburgh, Cincinnati & St. Louis (later the Pennsylvania Railroad), Dennison was a division point about half-way between Pittsburgh and Columbus. Built of rock-faced sandstone and red brick, the depot had among its architectural refinements a corbeled chimney, graceful brackets under the extended eaves, and stained glass windows. Forty acres of rail yards and associated buildings once surrounded the depot. During both World Wars, canteens operated from the station. The first was at the east end (out of a boxcar); the second was in a former restaurant area. Thousands of women volunteers worked round-the-clock to supply free food and smiles to millions of troops passing through. With only five minutes available while the steam trains took on water, canteen workers were often passing items through the coach windows as the train pulled out of the station.

By the 1980s, nothing was left of the station complex but the passenger depot, express building, and sand towers. The roundhouse, machines shops, and water towers were gone. Despite the area's depressed economy, Dennison citizens were determined not to let the last vestige of their railroad and canteen history go. A key source not only of labor, but also inspiration, were students from Buckeye Joint Vocational School. Asked just to repair the roof, they adopted the depot as their annual project for four years. Retired railroad and former canteen workers, as well as local businesses, contributed labor and materials—the equivalent of a half-million-dollar restoration. An addition connects the passenger depot to the express building, used for museum exhibits along with the ladies' waiting and baggage rooms. NR. [Village of Dennison. Tourist train stop, museum, and restaurant.]

FOSTORIA

BALTIMORE & OHIO STATION
500 South Main Street
1907

When the Baltimore & Ohio's replacement passenger station opened in Fostoria, the local paper glowed over the depot's 62 electric lights, "which will respond to the turn of the switch all at once or in groups or singly as the operator may desire." The general waiting room was augmented by a ladies' sitting room and a smoking room for men. Wainscoting was oak; walls and ceiling were painted a soft green. Baggage and express rooms were on the depot's east end. A brick platform extended from Main Street to the separate freight house. In 1992, 50 volunteers completed 1,500 hours of labor refurbishing the depot's interior. Amtrak passengers now wait inside the station, instead of only having access to the platform. Parking facilities and lighting were improved with city funds. A former B&O interlocking tower stands east of the station, where the B&O main line crossed tracks of the New York Central and the Chesapeake & Ohio. Of the many depots that once stood in Fostoria, only the Toledo & Ohio Central (later New York Central) also remains. [CSX Transportation. Train stop.]

GALION

CLEVELAND, CINCINNATI, CHICAGO & ST. LOUIS STATION
127 Washington Street
1900

In 1985, the Cleveland, Cincinnati, Chicago & St. Louis (the "Big Four") station was three days away from demolition when a Galion man stopped by to bid the depot good-by. Its windows were out; the plaster had fallen off; and weeds were in full bloom. Unable to say farewell to his tired old friend, this entrepreneur quickly turned the deathbed visit into a recovery mission — he purchased the station and converted it to commercial use.

Galion was once a Big Four division point. Replacing a smaller wooden structure, the new depot housed offices for civil engineers, the division superintendent, trainmaster, clerks, and stenographers. It was built of both rock-faced and smooth-faced sandstone; the upper story was clad in various styles of wooden siding. The belcast roof had multiple hips, a cross gable, and dormers with Palladian windows. From the depot, workers had a clear view to the rail yard, one mile north. Express shipments were handled from a separate building to the northwest. Galion also had a large Erie Railroad station (razed in the 1980s by Conrail); a limousine service enabled passengers to make connections between the two railroads.

In the 1940s, a freight train demolished the southwest portion of the platform canopy. That same decade, the New York Central (successor to the Big Four) modernized the depot's interior. The original light fixtures and pressed tin sheathing still exist above the dropped ceiling. About 40 freight trains a day cruise past the station on the two remaining tracks. If a proposed Amtrak route from Cleveland to Cincinnati is established, it would come through Galion. The depot's owner has a waiting room in mind. NR. [Privately owned. Restaurant and retail.]

HAMILTON

CINCINNATI, HAMILTON & DAYTON STATION
Henry Street and Martin Luther King, Jr.,
    Boulevard
c. 1860, c. 1888

In the 1860s, tracks of two railroads flanked the Cincinnati, Hamilton & Dayton station. Heading northeast was the CH&D main line from Cincinnati to Toledo; heading west, toward Indianapolis, was the Cincinnati & Indianapolis Junction Railroad. Both lines eventually became part of the Baltimore & Ohio. The one-story section of the present brick building was the original passenger depot. In the late 1880s, the railroad added a two-and-a-half story section with rock-faced stone lintels and dormer windows partitioned by stone mullions (later replaced by double-hung windows). Inside, pressed tin covered the ceilings. The floor plan included a baggage room, restaurant, and ladies' retiring room with fireplace. Between the depot's two sections was a breezeway (now enclosed) for storing baggage carts. The building is currently used for freight railroad purposes. (Inbound and outbound freight depots, two blocks north, were razed.) Amtrak still boards passengers from the platform, but in 1993, vacated its small and vandalized waiting room (just a corner of the original general waiting room). Local citizens would like to see the building at least maintained, if not restored. They are working with city planners to acquire and preserve the station. Hamilton's Pennsylvania Railroad station was demolished in 1991. [CSX Transportation. Train stop/npa and freight railroad facility.]

IRONTON

NORFOLK & WESTERN DEPOT

124 Bobby Bare Boulevard
Edward G. Frye
1907

In the early 20th century, Ironton was in the heart of the Hanging Rock Iron Region, comprising a thousand square miles of Ohio, Kentucky, and West Virginia. Before construction of the Norfolk & Western depot, the ticket office was in the Ironton Hotel. Reflecting the wealth generated by the iron industry, the new depot was a richly embellished neoclassical design. The architect, Virginian Edward G. Frye, designed a number of buildings for the N&W, including the station at Petersburg, Va. (1910; extant but vacant), which is identical to Ironton. Classical elements such as egg-and-

dart molding abounded both on the interior and exterior of the red brick, one-story station. The muntins of the door and window transoms created a "union jack" pattern. The station, which had a freight section in the southeast wing, closed in 1969. N&W donated the depot to the community the following decade. NR. [City of Ironton. Restaurant.]

KENT

ATLANTIC & GREAT WESTERN STATION

152 Franklin Avenue, east of State Route 43
1875

Originally called Franklin Mills, the town of Kent was renamed to honor Marvin Kent, founder of the Atlantic & Great Western (later part of the Erie Railroad). Kent's first depot was a boxcar; the second was a small frame building. When citizens requested a more substantial structure, the railroad's generosity was limited to about 60 percent of the cost—the balance was pledged by the community in a single meeting. Standing above a dam and mill race of the Cuyahoga River (and the parallel Pennsylvania & Ohio Canal), the perfectly symmetrical, red brick depot was built in a

Ironton N&W depot, 1973.

Restored exterior of the Kent A&GW station.

Tuscan Revival style with a slate roof. One-story segments hyphenated the depot's trio of two-story towers. Stone-arched windows on the upper floor were grouped in threes above a platform canopy dripping with pendants. The first floor housed the ticket and telegraph office, men's and ladies' waiting rooms, and baggage and express rooms. Big double doors on the track side led to an elegant restaurant, whose manager lived upstairs. The second floor also provided bunk space and a "Reading Room" for railroad workers (the book collection formed the nucleus of today's Kent Free Library). Just to the south was a wooden freight house (now gone); beyond that were rail yards with shops for building and repairing coaches and freight cars (a few structures remain).

Passenger service ended in 1970. Five years later, the local historical society purchased the boarded up and neglected station. The exterior and upper tower areas were restored, including replicating the woodwork and stripping paint from the brick. The first floor was sympathetically renovated for commercial use. Depots from two other railroads still stand in Kent: the Baltimore & Ohio (separate freight and passenger) and the Wheeling & Lake Erie (combination freight and passenger). NR District. [Kent Historical Society. Restaurant, museum, chamber of commerce, and offices.]

LIMA

PENNSYLVANIA RAILROAD STATION
424 North Central Avenue
c. 1887

Horticulture for the Pennsylvania Railroad station at Lima was supervised by the railroad's head gardener, who worked out of Sewickley, Pa. Driveways to the passenger depot wrapped around circular lawns, filled with immense canna beds. Built of brick, the story-and-a-half depot replaced a long wooden station, just to the east. The platform canopy, pierced by a Victorian Gothic two-story tower, was supported by ornate wooden brackets. The depot's visually stimulating roofline included a corbeled chimney, fancy roof cresting, and highly decorated dormers. Inside, both the ladies' and general waiting rooms had fireplaces; the baggage room was heated by a stove. East of the depot, on the other side of the tracks, a signal tower (c. 1925; extant) was operated by the PRR; the New York, Chicago & St. Louis (the "Nickel Plate") and the Baltimore & Ohio, which crossed here, contributed to expenses.

Lima's PRR freight station was demolished in the late 1980s. The passenger depot, remodeled inside over the years, became vacant after Amtrak's 1991 departure (caused by a rerouting). Three years later, sale to a restoration-minded buyer was underway. South Lima's former Detroit, Toledo & Ironton depot is still standing; the Erie and joint B&O–Nickel Plate depots are gone.[Amtrak. Vacant—sale pending.]

MARION

UNION STATION
West Center Street
1902

Marion Union Station was the joint project of three railroads: the Cleveland, Cincinnati Chicago & St. Louis ("Big Four"—later New York Central), the Hocking Valley (later Chesapeake & Ohio), and the Erie. (The Pennsylvania Railroad maintained a separate station nearby—now demolished.) Expansion was necessary just five years after the new depot was completed, when the railroads doubled the size of the baggage building and constructed a separate express facility. Each leg of the L-shaped depot was parallel to multiple tracks. Grass and flowers lined the streetside approach to the station. Red tiles covered the flaring roof, gabled entrances, polygonal corner pavilion (telegraph office), and bay window.

After passenger service ended in the early 1970s, the depot was boarded up. Over the next 15 years, many of the station's key elements were lost or damaged: brick platforms, protective canopies, marble wainscoting, ornamental plaster, diamond-shaped window panes, and oak benches. In the late Eighties, a nonprofit group formed to purchase the station, which will undergo restoration, including the stained glass skylight over the general waiting room. As part of the museum being planned, the ladies' waiting room will become the President Harding Room, an exhibit about the community's native son. Marion was division headquarters for the Erie, and its shops are still standing to the west. Across the tracks and just northeast of Union Station, Conrail owns and uses a former Erie switching tower. Scheduled to go out of service, that wooden structure may soon be endangered. [Marion Union Station Association. Vacant—future museum.]

OLMSTED FALLS

OLMSTED FALLS RAILROAD STATION
25802 Garfield Avenue
c. 1877

The Lake Shore & Michigan Southern (later New York Central) used a standard design, one-story, board and batten depot for its first-generation stations. One room deep, the long

A man sits beside a hand-operated water pump in this early view of the Olmsted Falls station.

rectangular floor plan typically had men's and ladies' waiting rooms, a ticket office, and a baggage room. Deep eaves supported by large wooden brackets extended from all four sides of the gabled roof. Windows and doors were surrounded by elaborate hood moldings with side brackets characteristic of the Italianate style. At the Olmsted Falls station, large oculus windows pierced both gable ends. The depot was originally located about 1,000 feet to the west, possibly on the opposite side of the tracks. Since 1975, it has been the rented home of the Cuyahoga Valley Model Railroad Club. Other extant examples of this once common design can be found in Ohio, for example at Oberlin (NR), now a preschool, and Oak Harbor, used for storage. [Consolidated Rail Corporation. Meeting space.]

OTTAWA

CINCINNATI, HAMILTON & DAYTON STATION
246 North Taft Street
c. 1890s

An otherwise conventional one-story depot, Ottawa's Chicago, Hamilton & Dayton station (later Baltimore & Ohio) lacked an agent's bay window. Stuck onto the northeast corner, a

three-sided square tower provided a tiny space for the railroad telegrapher, who needed a clear view of the tracks curving north toward Toledo and straight south toward Dayton. Mounted on a pole outside Italianate-style windows was a semaphore, which the operator controlled by levers from inside his office. Originally heated by potbellied stoves, the red brick station had wooden wainscoting with plaster walls above. The waiting room was in the middle, with the baggage and express services in the south end. Findlay, Fort Wayne & Western trains (later part of CH&D) crossed just north of the depot, until the tracks were abandoned in 1918. B&O passenger service ended in the late 1960s. [CSX Transportation. Railroad storage.]

SANDUSKY

LAKE SHORE & MICHIGAN SOUTHERN STATION
North Depot Street (at Carr Street)
Shepley, Rutan, and Coolidge
1892

Sandusky's previous Lake Shore & Michigan Southern station was located farther east on North Depot Street. It became a freight station (now gone) when the new passenger station,

This trackside view of Sandusky shows the triangular gable dormer with Palladian window that was typical of many LS&MS depots.

also used by the Lake Erie & Western, was built. With walls of Amherst buff stone trimmed in blue stone, the depot was designed by a nationally prominent Boston firm. A loggia on the east end connected the passenger facilities to a matching baggage building. Wire snow guards protected waiting passengers from sudden snow slides off the Maine slate roof. Inside, brass combination gas and electric fixtures illuminated the marble water fountains and oak wainscoting. In the west end, the ladies' waiting room was outfitted with cushioned seats, rocking chairs, and rugs, which the local newspaper said "make one loathe to give it up for the noisy, bustling, dirty train." By the 1980s, the depot was a deteriorating eyesore; by the 1990s, vagrants were ripping up the floor boards for firewood. Windows were bricked in to prevent further intrusion. The city, which purchased the station from Amtrak, is seeking a developer to adaptively use the building, with waiting space for travelers as part of the plan. NR. [City of Sandusky. Train stop/npa.]

WAUSEON

LAKE SHORE & MICHIGAN SOUTHERN STATION
Depot Street between Fulton and Brunell streets
1896

Replacing a wooden station, the new rusticated sandstone and brick depot at Wauseon was larger than the typical Lake Shore & Michigan Southern second-generation station. Flanked by small eyebrow dormers, a large gabled dormer pierced the roof—just above the Palladian window arrangement of the agent's bay. The slate roof, with a copper ridge roll, flared into seven-foot-wide eaves supported by large brackets on stone corbels. Inside, the agent's office had ticket windows opening into both the men's and ladies' waiting rooms. The depot was moved 20 feet north early in the 20th century to make way for two more tracks. An additional freight station once stood across the

tracks; a switching tower was to the west. Also used by the Toledo & Indiana interurban line until the 1930s, the depot was out of service by 1960. Acquired by the city for storage a decade later, the former station was put under the stewardship of the Fulton County Historical Society in 1975. Among the station's intact features are the wooden freight platform, Georgia pine interior paneling, and oak woodwork. Wauseon's other two depots, the Wabash and the Detroit, Toledo & Ironton, are gone. Both Amtrak and freight trains use the tracks. NR. [City of Wauseon. History museum.]

YOUNGSTOWN

BALTIMORE & OHIO STATION
530 Mahoning Avenue
1905

In 1905, the Baltimore & Ohio eliminated all its grade crossings through Youngstown. The project included a new station built on a curve overlooking the Mahoning River, with a full view of downtown Youngstown. A substantial, two-and-a-half stories of buff brick with darker sandstone trim and a clay tile roof, the depot featured gabled entry pavilions on both the street and track sides. The tracks were elevated on an embankment; riders alighting from trains saw only the upper story-and-a-half of the station. The double-height waiting room had a ceramic tile floor, decorative pressed metal ceiling, and balconies with wrought-iron railings. Water-powered elevators lifted baggage to the depot's upper (track) level, which also housed railroad offices. Passengers used an underground tunnel to reach the eastbound track.

After B&O service ended in 1971, the depot spent a decade as a freight office, followed by 10 years of vacancy. It was restored through the combined efforts of the city and a commercial tenant, who took advantage of rehabilitation tax credits. When Amtrak rerouted the *Broadway Limited* through Youngstown in the

Youngstown B&O station c. 1915–20.

early 1990s, it placed the ticket office inside the old B&O station. Besides the B&O, Youngstown had three other stations: the New York Central, which is gone; the Erie, in an extant six-story office building plus terminal and the Pennsylvania, whose early station is gone, but whose c. 1950 building still stands. A fourth railroad, the Pittsburgh & Lake Erie, used both the NYC and Erie stations. NR. [City of Youngstown. Train stop and restaurant.]

South Dakota

The vast majority of towns in South Dakota did not merit a masonry depot. As the 20th century advanced and railroad mileage diminished, most frame stations were destroyed, moved, or used for storage. Of the hundreds that existed, perhaps ten remain on their original sites. By contrast, only two or three out of approximately 20 masonry stations have been demolished. South Dakota has no passenger service today.

ABERDEEN

GREAT NORTHERN DEPOT
One Court Street
Samuel L. Bartlett
c. 1906

Facing the county courthouse, Aberdeen's Great Northern depot was designed by Samuel Bartlett with a touch of the medieval English manor. Finely detailed elements included the casementlike windows, modified Tudor arches, decorative half-timbering, and brick quoins on the corners and on door and window surrounds. A long freight section, eventually including two well-matched additions, gave the station an L-shape. Passenger service (which in its final days meant a lone passenger

The Aberdeen GN depot bears a strong resemblance to the C&NW station at Lake Forest, Ill., although the two railroads had no corporate connection.

car attached to a freight train) ended in the 1960s. In 1982, a law firm bought the depot and adapted the building for its use, with the aid of rehabilitation tax credits. The general waiting room, ticket office, and ladies' retiring room spaces are essentially as built. The baggage room (which had a dirt floor) and a fraction of the large freight area have been divided into offices — including the old "warm room" (used to keep in-transit perishables from freezing). Visible on the north side exterior of the brick freight section are ghosts of old advertising paintings. Although the tracks are gone, a portion of the brick platform remains. Three other depots are extant in Aberdeen: Minneapolis & St. Louis (NR), first adapted as a night club, now a supply house; Chicago, Milwaukee & St. Paul Division Headquarters (NR), still in railroad use along with a roundhouse; and Chicago & North Western, rehabilitated for commercial use. NR. [Privately owned. Offices.]

BROOKINGS

BROOKINGS STATION
111 Main Avenue
1905

The former Chicago & North Western building at Brookings is still a station, but the operative word is radio, not railroad. The conversion occurred in 1990, after KJJQ purchased the depot from a freight line that had been using the Brookings station as its headquarters. Attributed to architects Frost and Granger, the very long brick depot originally had a slate roof. Besides the ticket booth and wooden wainscoting, the depot retains original cupboards, office furniture, and a circular radiator. C&NW passenger service ended in the 1960s. [Privately owned. Radio station.]

DEADWOOD

FREEMONT, ELKHORN & MISSOURI VALLEY DEPOT
3 Siever Street
1897

Beginning in the 1870s, the Black Hills around Deadwood were a hotbed of mining activity reached by stagecoach. The goldfields attracted people from all over the world, along with the commercial services needed to support them. Within a decade, two railroads were racing to reach Deadwood: the Fremont, Elkhorn & Missouri Valley (later Chicago & North Western) and the Burlington & Missouri River (later Chicago, Burlington & Quincy). In December 1890, FE&MV won by about a month. A wooden freight depot was completed immediately, but passenger service was ren-

Town of Deadwood c. 1909, viewed from the southwest. FE&MV station (by then the C&NW) is on the right.

dered from a preexisting commercial building. A new passenger station was not dedicated until seven years later, when a story-and-a-half, pressed brick and pink sandstone facility opened. The hipped slate roof, which extended across a breezeway to the baggage building, was bisected by a cross gable with a two-story bay window. The interior had oak wainscoting and white maple flooring. Furniture was shipped in from the east coast. The agent's living quarters were upstairs.

In 1952, after Deadwood's city hall burned, the depot was turned into municipal offices and a fire and police station, complete with barred jail windows. The breezeway was enclosed to garage fire trucks. Forty years later, the city carefully restored the building's original appearance, including a reopened breezeway, new slate roof, and copper downspout system. Originally, the men's and ladies' waiting rooms were completely separated by the ticket office; to visit the opposite sex, one had to first go outside. The restorers created modern, need-driven interior access between the rooms, but deliberately left the openings untrimmed — to avoid muddling the architectural history. Old back-to-back benches from a

depot in Wyoming and antique telegraph equipment are among the items that have been acquired to refurnish the station. Two other noteworthy railroad buildings remain standing in Deadwood. The Chicago, Burlington & Quincy passenger station was razed in the 1950s, but its relocated freight station (c. 1890) has been adapted to a bank. In 1993, ISTEA funds made possible the rehabilitation of a CB&Q enginehouse (built about 1930 with materials salvaged from earlier structures). Plans include restoring its original dimensions and using it for rail trail and transportation purposes. NR District. NHL District. [City of Deadwood. Transit stop, visitors center, museum, and arts council office.]

DE SMET

DE SMET RAILROAD STATION
One block off 1st Street
1906

The setting for six of Laura Ingalls Wilder's autobiographical *Little House* books was De Smet. Wilder made reference to both this station and the preceding one destroyed by fire. Built of wood by the Chicago & North Western, this standard plan, combination freight and passenger station was divided in the center by a gabled-dormer agent's bay. The building had two chimneys; one vented a large potbellied stove. In the 1980s, a private party purchased the depot from the Dakota, Minnesota & Eastern (a short line successor to part of C&NW), whose freight trains still use the tracks. After rehabilitating the structure, the new owners donated it to the community. [City of De Smet. Local history museum.]

HOT SPRINGS

UNION DEPOT
630 North River Avenue
1891

Hot Springs's healing waters and relatively mild climate brought visitors to its numerous mineral baths and hotels. Vacationers and health-seekers came by train, along with workers who fueled the mining, cattle, and quarrying industries. Union Depot made it into Ripley's *Believe It or Not* column as the smallest union station in the world (20 by 50 feet, which is fact large enough to leave room for disbelief). The station serviced both the Chicago, Burlington & Quincy and Chicago & North Western railroads. Built of native Black Hills pink sandstone with a slate roof, the one-story station had a deep, overhanging roof, pierced on the track side by a square, hipped roof tower. A wealthy resident landscaped the station grounds and paid a gardener to keep them maintained. Sleeping cars, parked on a siding, were sometimes used as accommodations, to supplement the 250-room Evans Hotel down the street (1892; now used as senior citizen housing). In 1938, the tracks were permanently washed out in a flood. NR District. [City of Hot Springs. Chamber of commerce office and visitors center.]

MITCHELL

CHICAGO, MILWAUKEE & ST. PAUL DEPOT
210 South Main Street
1909

Mitchell was a division point for the Chicago, Milwaukee & St. Paul (later nicknamed the "Milwaukee Road"). The first depot was built of wood and also housed the fire department. When a brick, neoclassical depot was built, the

Mitchell CM&StP depot. The absence of a platform canopy left passengers and their luggage exposed to the elements.

old one was moved to the east, near the freight house. It was converted to a facility for train dispatchers, conductors, and the roadmaster. Sitting at the lower end of Main Street, the new depot made a memorable impression on visitors to the annual Corn Palace celebration. Although the building was only one story high, its formal, cross-gabled entrance created an unexpected grandness. The keystoned archway was flanked by pilasters and topped by a dentilled pediment. Variations on this configuration were repeated on the trackside facade and in two smaller bays. Oculus windows were centered in the gable ends. The interior included men's and ladies' waiting rooms, baggage and express rooms, a dining room, and lunch counter. After passenger service ended in the 1950s, the depot was used for freight railroad purposes. In the early Eighties, the Milwaukee Road began bankruptcy proceedings. The state took over part of the railroad's holdings (trackage and structures) and sold off the Mitchell depot. The community once had another station (built by the Chicago, St. Paul, Minneapolis & Omaha — a predecessor of the Chicago & North Western) that has been demolished. NR District. [Privately owned. Restaurant.]

REDFIELD

REDFIELD DEPOT
West junction of U.S. routes 281 and 212
1914

Redfield was named for a Chicago & North Western auditor. Replacing an 1891 depot, the station was built in a long, low Prairie Style with tiny eyebrow dormers and classical elements like the cross-gabled, arched entry. On the northeast side, two gargoyles attended the double hung doors, which were protected by a canopy suspended from chains (now gone). The interior had a vaulted, open-beam ceiling, gender-segregated waiting rooms (the ladies were served by a round-the-clock matron), and a dining room. Both Theodore and Franklin

Roosevelt made whistle stop speeches at Redfield. Buffalo Bill and Sitting Bull came through on their way to Washington, D.C. Once a busy division point at the intersection of C&NW's north-south and east-west lines, the station closed in the mid-1960s. It sat vacant and decaying for more than a decade, until purchased by a local feed company, which has since maintained the building. NR. [Privately owned. Commercial.]

SIOUX FALLS

BURLINGTON, CEDAR RAPIDS & NORTHERN DEPOT
210 East 10th Street
c. 1886

Sioux Falls was at one time served by five major railroads. In 1886, Sioux Falls voters passed a bond issue that helped bring one of them, the Burlington, Cedar Rapids & Northern (later the Chicago, Rock Island & Pacific), to their community. Built of rusticated cut stone and wood-shingle siding, the depot's two-story and one-story sections were joined by a covered breezeway, featuring a yawning horseshoe arch to the street. The agent's office and living quarters were on the west side. After passenger service ended in 1950, the "Rock Island" used the depot for storage until 1970. The city bought the land surrounding the station, removed the tracks, and created a park. The building itself was a restaurant for nearly two decades, until purchased by the insurance company housed next door. The depot's future is now uncertain. Another extant Sioux Falls depot, similarly built of local purplish-pink quartzite, is the Illinois Central passenger station (NR), used as private offices. The c. 1910 Great Northern depot now serves the Burlington Northern freight railroad. A 1930 Chicago, Milwaukee St. Paul & Pacific wooden roundhouse, which survived until 1992, burned to the ground when vagrants started a fire to keep warm. NR. [Privately owned. Vacant.]

Sioux Falls BCR&N depot, 1886.

WATERTOWN

MINNEAPOLIS & ST. LOUIS DEPOT
168 North Broadway
1911

Known for most of its history as the Minneapolis & St. Louis (later the Chicago & North Western) depot, this Watertown station was actually cobuilt by the Chicago, Rock Island & Pacific, whose engineering office designed the structure. Built of sandstone-trimmed brick with a simulated slate roof, it replaced an earlier station located one-half block east. Architectural refinements included brick quoins, arched lintels with radiating voussoirs and keystones, stepped gables, and parapeted pavilions. WATERTOWN was carved in stone on three walls.

In the last Dakota land boom, settlers heading for the west side of the Missouri River arrived first at the M&StL depot. Troop trains were common during both World Wars. After passenger service ended in 1960, the depot was used for freight offices and as a crew bunkhouse. In 1985, the county historical society purchased the station from the C&NW. The group restored the building's original floor plan by removing partitions added over the years. The ticket window and much original furniture remains. Railroad workers, invited back to the depot for a chicken dinner, contributed box loads of memorabilia and artifacts. The society added a spiral stair-

A salesperson's sample postcard of the Watertown M&StL depot (labeled as the CRI&P, the railroad that cobuilt the station). Wholesale prices were $1.60 per hundred cards; $15 per thousand.

case inside, to improve traffic flow for classes of school children visiting the station. Outside, a switch locomotive and a Pullman baggage car are displayed on a stub-end track that ties into a freight main line. Watertown was at one time served by several railroads; among them was the Great Northern, whose station was demolished in 1992. NR. [Codington County Historical Society. Railroad museum.]

YANKTON

CHICAGO, MILWAUKEE & ST. PAUL DEPOT
8th and Douglas streets
1905

In the early 20th century, as rail towns sprang up between the James River and the Black Hills, the Chicago, Milwaukee & St. Paul decided to build a new depot at Yankton. The center section of the one-story red brick building housed the waiting room and agent's office under a fairly steep, pitched roof. Shallower hipped roofs covered attached freight rooms to the east and the open-air waiting area, supported by Tuscan columns, to the west. The depot's three chimneys vented heating stoves. After being adapted in the 1970s to law offices, the Prairie Style station was soon acquired by a cable television company. It uses most of the building for its headquarters (the balance is leased), with the old arrival-departure blackboards listing the cable channels. The company president sits in the agent's office, which still has levers to the semaphore pole outside. Freight trains continue to use the single track, running alongside the intact brick platform. Yankton's other depot, the c. 1900 Great Northern, has been relocated to the Dakota Territory Museum. NR. [Privately owned. Commercial.]

Wisconsin

Most of Wisconsin's once prevalent wooden stations are long gone — replaced by masonry depots (a fair number architect-designed) or simply demolished when the towns dried up. A preponderance of the most significant extant depots are the work of Charles Sumner Frost (or his firm), whose father-in-law was Marvin Hughitt, president of the Chicago & North Western. In recent times, the state's successful "rail trail" program has fostered six conversions of railroad depots to trail headquarters: Kendall, Lake Mills, Menomonie, New Glarus, Reedsburg, and Sparta.

ASHLAND

MINNEAPOLIS, ST. PAUL & SAULT STE. MARIE DEPOT
3rd Avenue West (at 4th Street)
1889

In the early 1890s, seven brownstone quarries operated in the Ashland area. Brownstone was an important export, as well as a local building material. The two-story Minneapolis, St. Paul & Sault Ste. Marie (the "Soo Line") depot had massive brownstone walls, randomly laid, with a rusticated finish. Romanesque arches surrounded many of the doors and windows. A large central tower, three stories high, was topped by a pyramidal roof, pierced by louvered dormers. Story-and-a-half pavilions with sloping, cedar-shingle roofs extended from both ends of the hipped-roof main section. Other exterior features included copper roof cresting, a stone chimney, a porte-cochere, and a 400-foot-long covered platform. The passenger section was sandwiched between the express agency on the south end and the northern baggage area. In later years, the Soo Line changed the interior drastically by converting waiting rooms to showers and dormitories. These alterations were reversed in the mid-1980s, when the depot was sensitively converted to a restaurant. Ashland Union Depot (1900; NR), designed by Charles Frost, is now a health club (radically altered). NR. [Privately owned. Restaurant.]

BEAVER DAM

BEAVER DAM DEPOT
127 South Spring Street
Frost and Granger
1901

In 1900, a local newspaper reported — with a sense of outrage — that Beaver Dam's 1882 station was no bigger or better looking than depots built on the Minnesota and Dakota prairies. Beaver Dam passengers waiting for the train were "packed like sardines in a box." The Chicago, Milwaukee & St. Paul responded by having a noted Chicago firm design a new station, which took its architectural cue from a nearby residential neighborhood. Looking like an English cottage, the red brick, story-and-a-half depot was roofed in red tile. Large gable dormers were positioned above tall recessed arches containing double-door entrances. One chimney led to the basement boiler, the other to a brick fireplace in the general waiting room. Men had a separate room for smoking. Easy chairs and settees contributed to the homelike atmosphere. The station closed in the 1940s. Purchased by the city in 1951, it became one of the nation's early examples of adaptive use

when the Dodge County Historical Society leased it for a museum. In 1985, the museum moved next door to a former library building (NR), and the depot was renovated for the chamber of commerce. Despite the suspended ceiling and some changes to freight and baggage doors, the depot retains most of its railroad and architectural features, including the ticket counter, oak doors, pine wainscoting, maple floor, clock, and brick platform. Though unused, the tracks remain. NR. [City of Beaver Dam. Chamber of commerce.]

BRODHEAD

BRODHEAD DEPOT
805 Center Avenue
1881

Edward Brodhead wanted to build a railroad from Wisconsin to the Mississippi River. In the mid-1850s, as chief civil engineer for the Milwaukee & Mississippi (a predecesor of the Chicago, Milwaukee, St. Paul & Pacific), he convinced a half-dozen men to donate both the right-of-way and ground for a depot, located in the sand prairie that would become Brodhead. The first depot, built of wood, was struck by lightning and destroyed by fire. Cream-colored Milwaukee brick was used for the one-story replacement station, designed in an Italianate style with round-arched door and window openings and deep, bracketed eaves. In the gable end of the station's passenger section, a tryptych window surmounted a doorway (later removed) and three full-scale windows; a small rose window highlighted the gable end of the freight section. The floor plan included gender-segregated waiting rooms, separate agent's and telegrapher's offices, and a baggage and cart storage room.

After regular passenger service ended in 1950, the depot continued in freight railroad use. (Travelers could board mixed freight and passenger trains until 1958.) A historical society

Brodhead depot, passenger end. The doorway in this picture was later eliminated, and the second window from the right was relocated to the center.

formed in 1975 and immediately attempted to acquire the depot from the CMStP&P, but the railroad refused to negotiate with a citizens group. In 1980, the city leased the land and purchased the depot for the historical society's use. Freight trains still use the tracks. Extant former depots at Hartland and Boscobel are similar to the design of Brodhead. NR District. [City of Brodhead. Local history museum.]

FOND DU LAC

CHICAGO & NORTH WESTERN DEPOT
182 Forest Avenue (at South Brooke Street)
Charles Sumner Frost
1891, 1916

The previous depot on this site was a train barn built by the Rock River Valley Union Railroad (later Chicago & North Western) in 1851. Made of red brick and locally quarried limestone with a slate roof, the new depot's variations in color and texture were typical of Romanesque Revival buildings. An octagonal tower (with an octagonal spire) formed the agent's bay on the first floor. In 1916, C&NW added 122 feet to the building through extensions to the north and south ends. The rearranged spaces better separated the passenger waiting areas from the railroad's operating departments. The depot

continued to have three waiting rooms — general, men's, and ladies'. The alterations carefully preserved the spirit of Charles Frost's original design. Passenger service lasted until 1971. Today the building lacks interior partitions, which the owner plans to install according to tenant wishes. Fond du Lac's Minneapolis, St. Paul & Sault Ste. Marie depot is without any walls at all — demolished in the 1970s. In nearby North Fond du Lac, where the railroads had their maintenance and repair shops, a number of buildings remain standing. NR. [Privately owned. Vacant — for lease.]

GREEN BAY

CHICAGO & NORTH WESTERN DEPOT
200 Dousman Street
Charles Sumner Frost
1899

In the 1860s, Green Bay's very first Chicago & North Western depot was actually located in Fort Howard (part of Green Bay today); a bridge was built across the Fox River for bringing Green Bay passengers and goods to the depot. In 1898, architect Charles Frost inspected a former freight-yard site, to be used for a new passenger station. Built of brick on a stone base, the depot housed division offices on the second floor. A tall campanile with four clock faces dominated the streetside facade; a long platform canopy extended north and south along the tracks. Enlarged over the years, the depot was also modernized with a big curving ticket counter and linoleum tile floor. Partitions between the ticket office and the men's and ladies' waiting rooms were removed — and then reinstated in 1988 for offices of the Fox River Valley Railroad. Five years later, another freight railroad purchased the depot; but its workers were soon withdrawn. In 1994, the city obtained ISTEA funding for rehabilitation. Plans include a possible commercial venture, with a portion of the building set aside for depot use, should passenger service be reinstated between Milwaukee and Green Bay.

C&NW's 1913 brick roundhouse (originally 40 stalls) and 1940 enginehouse are used today by Wisconsin Central, Ltd., (a late 20th century freight railroad) at North Green Bay. Other significant rail-related buildings in the city include: two Chicago, Milwaukee & St. Paul passenger stations — the Oakland Street Station (vacant) and another occupied by the chamber of commerce; a CM&StP L-shaped service facility (part dating from the 1870s); and the 1898–1910, fully intact Norwood Yard Complex of the Green Bay & Western. [Fox Valley & Western Railroad Corporation. Vacant.]

KENDALL

KENDALLS [*SIC*] DEPOT
North Railroad and White streets
1900

In the 1870s, railroad contractor J. C. Kendall owned a considerable portion of land that was platted as his namesake village. (The community was originally called "Kendalls;" the train stop retained that spelling.) Following a depot fire, the town received a new wooden structure — a large Chicago & North Western standard plan. This version had a separate ladies' waiting room and was embellished by both vertical and horizontal siding, a camel-back hipped roof, and Stick Style details. Two cream-colored brick chimneys rose from the wood-shingle roof. Rail service ended in the 1960s, and the tracks were removed. The following decade, the depot became headquarters for the Elroy-Sparta Bike Trail. Rental bicycles are stored in the former freight section. Installation of period light fixtures and red oak floors was part of the depot's rehabilitation, as well as opening up bricked-in doorways. The wooden ceiling and wainscoting are original. Kendall once had a 14-stall roundhouse; a stone wall marking the turntable site remains. NR. [State of Wisconsin. Rail trail headquarters.]

Green Bay C&NW depot c. 1906. The verticality of the tower balances the horizontality of the long platform canopy.

Madison CM&StP depot with semicircular dormers (now gone).

MADISON

CHICAGO, MILWAUKEE & ST. PAUL DEPOT
640 West Washington Avenue
Frost and Granger
1903

A predecessor of the Chicago, Milwaukee & St. Paul built Madison's first railroad station in 1854. By 1861, the sandstone structure was too small; and the railroad augmented service by using part of the railroad hotel (moved c. 1903; razed in 1967) across the street. The old depot was demolished after Frost and Granger's neoclassical design was built in an adjacent location. Constructed of orange pressed brick above a limestone base, the two-story depot and matching baggage building were joined by a canopied platform. Circular dormers (now gone from both street and track sides) pierced the depot's slate-covered hipped roof. The two-and-a-half-story-high waiting room had a decorative plaster ceiling and fancy rocking chairs. In 1927, the original maple floors of this room and part of the lunchroom were changed to terrazzo. After passenger service ended in 1971, the interior was partitioned into railroad offices. A 1980s adaptive use project, using rehabilitation tax credits, created a restaurant, tailor shop, and commercial office space within the depot. The owners reinstalled a stretch of track, on which a locomotive and four rail cars, rented as retail shops, give the appearance that a train is stopped at the station. Madison had many other rail-related buildings, among them: an additional CM&StP passenger depot (1880s; razed in 1952); three roundhouses (two still standing, but drastically modified); and an extant 1888 Illinois Central freight station (the passenger station was razed in the 1940s). The extant Chicago and North Western depot (NR District) — a c. 1910 Frost and Granger design — has been substantially altered. NR. [Privately owned. Mixed use.]

MAZOMANIE

MAZOMANIE DEPOT
Brodhead Street
1857, 1880

Mazomanie's first depot burned down when only a year old; the fire presumably started in the second-floor kitchen of the eating house. The restaurateurs reopened in the 1857 replacement station built by the Milwaukee & Mississippi (later Chicago, Milwaukee, St. Paul & Pacific). Enlarged in 1880, the wooden depot comprised men's and ladies' waiting rooms, an agent's office, and baggage and express rooms. After passenger service ended in 1960, the depot remained in freight use until 1973. The village purchased the depot 16 years later, with help from the Mazomanie Historical Society. Restoration work included reversing changes made by

Mazomanie depot c. 1920 with its original deep eaves.

the railroad in 1945 (it had shortened the building by 50 feet and chopped six feet off the very deep eaves). Because freight trains still use the tracks, the depot had to be moved about three feet south, to accommodate the width of modern day equipment. Funding sources for the entire project ranged from elementary school children (who delivered a coaster wagon filled with $800 in pennies) to a grant from the federal government. [Village of Mazomanie. Public library and historical society research center.]

MINERAL POINT

MINERAL POINT DEPOT
Commerce Street
1857

In the 1820s, rich deposits of lead just beneath the surface of a Pecatonia Valley hilltop gave Mineral Point its name. (By the 1850s, zinc replaced lead as Mineral Point's chief resource.) Cornish miners — expert stone masons — built cottages of locally quarried buff limestone, the same material used to construct a depot for the Mineral Point Railroad (later Chicago, Milwaukee, St. Paul & Pacific). Two-story walls of large, closely fitted and neatly tooled blocks were pierced by rectangular windows and round-arched doorways. Four chimneys sprouted from the roof. The roundhouse and machine shop (now gone) were also native limestone. Regular passenger service ended in 1950. Today, the right-of-way is a rail trail. The depot remains unused and deteriorating, despite citizens' pressure on the deed holder to sell or restore it. NR District. [Privately owned. Vacant.]

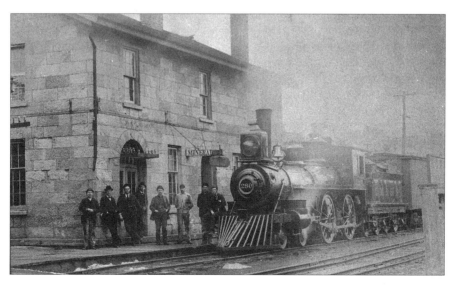

Steam from CM&StP locomotive No. 280 drifts over the Mineral Point depot. This photo was taken c. 1890.

NORTH FREEDOM

ROCK SPRINGS DEPOT

Walnut Street, one-half mile west of the four-
way stop sign in North Freedom
1894

In the early 1960s, the Mid-Continent Railway
Historical Society, which operates a tourist
train, needed an appropriate building for its
ticket office and gift shop. It found one in Rock
Springs — a former Chicago & North Western
station at a stop once known as Ablemans.
Volunteers prepared the donated depot for its
three-mile move by taking off the roof to clear
power lines and by cutting the building into
two sections. When the newly dug foundation
at North Freedom turned out to be five feet too
long, the museum used the opportunity to
enlarge the building in the center. The original
station was similar to those the C&NW built at
Waunakee (1896; extant) and Wonewoc (1888;
razed in 1966), but it predates the C&NW's formal adoption of numbered standard plans.

Clad in both vertical and horizontal
wooden siding, the Rock Springs depot had limited ornamentation, mainly in the form of Stick
Style elements in the agent's bay and end
gables. In 1916, the railroad lengthened the
combination freight and passenger station by 27
feet, and in 1923, replaced the kerosene lamps
with electric lights — an important fire-preven-
tion step. About a half-century later (1970), the
depot suffered a serious fire, just five years after
its relocation to North Freedom. Volunteers did
a second restoration, which was not really complete until the 1980s, when they applied the
C&NW's main line paint scheme — beige with
brown trim. The museum's tourist train runs on
part of a four-and-a-half-mile line (built to serve
iron mines and a quarry) purchased in 1963
from the C&NW. The society displays a large
number of railroad cars in both a 1976 reproduction coach shed and the rail yard. In 1989,
members added a former Minneapolis, St. Paul
& Sault Ste. Marie elevated watchman's tower

to the site. [Mid-Continent Railway Historical
Society. Tourist train stop.]

OCONOMOWOC

OCONOMOWOC DEPOT

115 Collins Street (corner of Summit Avenue
and South Main Street)
Charles Sumner Frost
1896

Albert Earling, future president of the Chicago,
Milwaukee & St. Paul, had a summer home in
the lake area around Oconomowoc. He made
sure that the CM&StP depot was in keeping
with the upper-class resort image that would
impress his friends. Built of split granite boul-
ders trimmed with red sandstone, the new one-
story depot exuded strength and stability; even
the attic windows of the cross gable had split
granite mullions and cut sandstone sills. The
interior layout included ladies' and men's waiting rooms (the latter partitioned for an express
office), an agent's office, and a baggage room.
Upstairs was the agent's living quarters. The
station replaced two successive brick depots.
The first was on the present site; the second
was in another location, deemed too close to
the smelly stock pens.

Passenger service ended in 1972. A freight
agent continued to operate from the nearly
vacant building, while both the city and the
chamber of commerce attempted to acquire it.
In private hands since 1980, the depot has had
intermittent commercial use The gabled platform canopy across the tracks was saved from
destruction by the Ocnomowoc Historical
Society, which leased it from a freight railroad.
A crossing watchman's tower, which originally
stood west of the shelter, was moved one block
east. The group also secured the depot agent's
desk and telegraph equipment by placing
them in a local museum. NR. [Privately owned.
Vacant.]

Postcard view of the Oconomowoc depot shows tile roofing (later changed to flat shingles) and the watchman's tower in its original position.

OSCEOLA

OSCEOLA DEPOT
Depot Street
1916

In 1890, a train wreck destroyed most of Osceola's three-year-old wooden depot; the agent had just left for lunch and avoided the freight car that plowed into his office. The Minneapolis, St. Paul & Sault Ste. Marie (the "Soo Line") boarded up the damaged area and continued operating from one room. Merchants lobbied hard for a masonry depot and were finally rewarded with Standard Plan No.2 — a wire cut, red brick station with a limestone base and white sandstone trim. A pent roof (currently missing) provided shelter from sun and precipitation. The design called for men's and ladies' waiting rooms, an agent's office, a large freight room, and two toilet rooms (the former depot had no plumbing) — all heated by steam. The station was at the base of a limestone bluff overlooking the St. Croix River. At the top, graced by a grove of oak trees, the Soo Line built a park and pavilion. The grove was a popular destination for the families of railroad employees from the Twin Cities, brought by excursion train to the Osceola depot.

After passenger service ended in 1961, a period of varied uses was followed by two decades of vacancy. In 1991, the local historical society began negotiations with Wisconsin Central, Ltd., (which acquired this portion of the Soo Line) to purchase the depot. The society's depot coordinator was anxious that the station be a living depot, not just another restaurant conversion. She contacted the Minnesota Transportation Museum, which — in a new partnership with the historical society — began running excursion trains from Osceola even before the depot sale was concluded. In 1993, the society obtained ISTEA funds to restore the building. Once reopened, plans call for an interpretive center in the baggage area and telegraphers at work in the agent's bay. The group already demon-strates mail pick-ups on-the-fly, in which, as a train pulling an authentic railway post-office car zips past the station, on-board retired postal workers grab a mail sack off the pole. A similar depot is still in railroad use southeast of Osceola at New Richmond. An identical station stood at Elbow Lake, Minn., (razed in the late 1980s). [Osceola Historical Society. Tourist train stop/npa — future depot museum.]

WHITEWATER

WHITEWATER DEPOT
301 West Whitewater Street
John T. W. Jennings
1890

John T. W. Jennings, born and educated in New York City, was an architect for the Chicago, Milwaukee & St. Paul from 1885 until 1893. (Later in his career, he designed nine buildings for the University of Wisconsin.) Other Wisconsin stations credited to Jennings include Monroe and Tomah (both 1888; extant), as well as several built from his standard plans. The Whitewater depot (replacing an 1852 station) was dark red brick with rusticated sandstone forming the base of the walls, the faces of its gabled cross dormer, and various bold trim. A fireplace chimney protruded from the hipped roof, whose deep eaves were supported by curved wooden brackets. Above the trackside double doors were a masonry pair of clasped hands (the meaning is subject to ongoing conjecture). Passenger service ended in 1950. During the depot's subsequent stint as a feed store, the wall between the agent's office and the men's waiting room was removed. In 1973, the city purchased the station (unfortunately sandblasting the walls in the clean-up process) and leased it to the Whitewater Historical Society. In a park adjacent to the depot is a combination decorative fountain and horse watering trough that once stood in front of the wooden freight depot (razed in the 1980s). Freight trains use the tracks. [City of Whitewater. Local history museum.]

WOODRUFF

CHICAGO, MILWAUKEE ST. PAUL & PACIFIC DEPOT
1419 State Route 47 (south of U.S. Route 51)
1930

Seeking to reinforce the Northwoods ambiance so important to tourists, the Chicago, Milwaukee, St. Paul & Pacific built the Woodruff depot in a rustic, picturesque style. Logs for the walls came from trees in the Lac du Flambeau area. At either end of the station, birch letters spelled WOODRUFF against a ragged weathered board. Each board was suspended from a pole cantilevered out from the roof ridge. Inside was a large, open-rafter waiting room with a field-stone fireplace, a men's smoking room, an agent's office, and express and freight rooms. CMStP&P officials arrived for the dedication aboard a special train. A six-course banquet was served in the dining car. About 1959, the railroad sold the depot to an employee who used it for awhile as a summer home. Today the tracks are gone, as is Woodruff's Chicago & North Western depot. [Privately owned. Restaurant.]

Built of logs, the Woodruff CMStP&P depot c.1930s.

Southwest

Atchison, Topeka & Santa Fe station in Santa Fe, N.Mex., c. 1910.

Arizona

Two transcontinental lines crossed Arizona: the Southern Pacific in the southern tier and the Atchison, Topeka & Santa Fe across the north central portion. Still heavily used today for freight operations, these routes are also traveled by Amtrak, which accounts in part for the number of historic stations still functioning. Many were built with a high degree of architectural sophistication, made possible from mining profits. Their styles, Spanish Colonial Revival and Mission, were popular with southwest railroads for tourist appeal and to reinforce corporate identity programs (especially true of the "Santa Fe"). Architects favored these styles because of several features: the arcades that accommodated numerous exterior doorways; the sprawling outline that facilitated a depot's extensive first-floor needs; and the fire-resistant building materials (usually masonry, although some depots were stucco over wood frame). In this warm climate, courtyards and porches made perfect outdoor waiting rooms. Nearly a century later, the size of these buildings (medium to large) facilitates manageable adaptive use costs and flexible floor plans . Unfortunately, a prime example of this station type was lost in 1993, when the Southern Pacific depot at Yuma, which had been an arts center since the mid-1970s, caught fire. (Most of the collection was rescued, but the building had to be demolished.)

AJO

AJO DEPOT
Ajo Plaza, off State Route 85
William M. Kenyon and Maurice F. Maine
1916

One of the oldest, but most isolated copper mining districts in the Southwest, Ajo (originally called Cornelia) was without rail service until 1916. Mule teams were supplanted by iron horses when the Tuscon, Cornelia & Gila Bend built 44 miles of track from Ajo to the Southern Pacific line at Gila Bend. The New

The palm trees were still young when this photo of the Ajo depot was taken c.1921.

Cornelia Copper Company began construction of a company town centered around a plaza — the work of architects William Kenyon and Maurice Maine. The Spanish Colonial Revival depot formed the eastern end of the plaza and connected to the other buildings via a long, tiled arcade. Its single story of stucco-clad, reinforced concrete was highlighted by a domed bell tower. Black and yellow ceramic tiles accented the parapeted loggias on both ends of the depot. The plaza park was filled with benches, palm trees, and a bandstand (extant). In the mid-1980s, the mining and smelting operation was discontinued indefinitely. The Phelps Dodge Corporation, which owns the TC&GB, decided to lease out the depot space, to preserve the structure and generate income. Used briefly by a utility company, the depot now houses a beauty salon, a gourmet coffee shop, and an art gallery. NR. [Privately owned. Commercial.]

CASA GRANDE

CASA GRANDE RAILROAD STATION
Washington and Main streets
1940

In 1937, an oil stove exploded in Casa Grande's 50-year-old depot. As flames raged, the night operator's teen-age son pulled a shipment of dynamite from the freight section, and thus prevented a more widespread conflagration. A boxcar served as the depot until 1940, when the Southern Pacific dedicated a new station. Designed at SP headquarters in San Francisco, the one-story building combined Pueblo form with Navajo-inspired ornamentation. The central and highest section contained the agent's office and waiting and baggage rooms, flanked by a long freight section on the north end and an open-air waiting room on the south. Grooved piers stood beside the passenger entranceways. Bands of diamonds, arrows, and truncated pyramids (painted gold, yellow, and turquoise) decorated the lintels. Interior details

included an arrow pattern, carved into the ticket counter, and a mural of Indian life (subsequently painted over).

In the 1920s, SP built a secondary main line that took long-distance trains through Phoenix and mostly bypassed Casa Grande. After regular passenger service ended in the early 1950s, SP began using the depot for freight offices. Today, the community is concerned about the building's deferred maintenance and possible abandonment; citizens would like to secure a long-term adaptive use. SP maintains that should it offer the station to a civic body, the railroad would require the depot's relocation off-site, which would place it — most undesirably — out of context. [Southern Pacific Lines. Railroad offices.]

CLIFTON

CLIFTON RAILROAD STATION
66 North Coronado Boulevard (U.S. Route 666)
1913

In order to build new freight and passenger depots, the Arizona Copper Company (which owned the Arizona & New Mexico Railway) had to first construct a 10-foot-high slag wall along the east side of the San Francisco River and fill it with earth brought in from the mountains. The buff and reddish-brown brick passenger station was capped with Spanish tiles; wide eaves were supported on gently curving, cantilevered brackets. The second story, of smaller dimensions than the first, was centered so as to form a balustraded roof deck at each end. First-floor spaces included general and ladies' waiting rooms and offices for the station agent, conductors, and Wells Fargo. Division offices were upstairs. In 1921, the A&NM became part of the El Paso & Southwestern (later the Southern Pacific).

The price of copper plunged during the Depression, and in 1932 the mine shut down. To consolidate dwindling business, SP moved the ticket and express offices into the freight building. About six years later, a 1,000-foot-

Clifton station.

c.1940, in restaurant use.

thick body of ore was discovered, and a mammoth mining operation instituted. After seven years of vacancy, in 1939, the passenger station was transformed into the Coronado Inn, complete with two 30-foot neon signs on the verandas, a restaurant on the first floor, and a banquet room on the second. Locals dined, danced, and held community meetings at the popular establishment; travelers sought refreshments there while waiting for the train. In 1967, passenger service ended; the inn operation lasted another 15 years. When a devastating 1983 flood sent the river over its banks, water rose to the eaves of the boarded-up ex-passenger station; the freight depot floated downstream. In 1990, SP donated the depot to the city, which concurrently purchased the underlying land. It now houses the chamber of commerce, a retired persons volunteer program, and an art gallery. A teen center is under consideration for the upper floor. NR. [City of Clifton. Mixed use.]

DOUGLAS

EL PASO & SOUTHWESTERN STATION
14th Street (at H Avenue)
1913

The Phelps Dodge Corporation named the town of Douglas (established in 1900) for a metallurgist and mining engineer, whose advice brought the company good copper yields in the

Motor No. 1 making a stop at the depot c. 1920. The A&NM used this rail bus for hauling passengers and small parcels on days when it chose not to expend fuel and labor on a steam train.

Arizona Territory. The year before Douglas was founded, to avoid paying the high rates charged by the monopolizing Southern Pacific, Phelps Dodge purchased the newly formed Arizona & Southeastern Railroad. The line's name was soon changed to the El Paso & Southwestern. Douglas's first permanent depot was on the current site of the Railroad Y.M.C.A. (1905, 1918; NR), designed by noted St. Louis architect Theodore C. Link. (That depot was moved four blocks north in 1904 and then razed nine years later.) In 1913, the EP&SW built an expensive new depot, paid for entirely in cash from mining profits. To make a "national statement," the railroad deliberately selected the Beaux Arts style, rather than a regional Mission or Spanish Colonial Revival. This choice was reportedly influenced by Dr. Douglas's daughter-in-law, who was also instrumental in bringing a California landscape architect to develop the depot's three-acre grounds. He spent six months working on Douglas and on the similarly styled depot in Tucson (NR; now a restaurant).

The walls of the two-story brick depot were clad in brick and terra-cotta; the roof was clay tile and terne metal. Two-story-high Tuscan columns created recessed entrances on both the track and street sides of the station. Each end of the depot was flanked by a large, square porch. Inside the station, a second-floor circular gallery provided an exceptional view of the stained glass rotunda. French doors opened onto exterior balconies. The depot served a variety of passengers including mine workers, copper company executives and their families, and troops who stopped at the World War II canteen. Passenger service ended in the 1960s, and the building went into a leaky, deteriorating decline. In the 1980s, the city bought the depot from Southern Pacific (the "monopolizers" had gotten hold of the line in 1924). Largely with funds seized from drug traffickers, the building was gradually restored — including the stained glass (stored away for years) and the ornate outdoor water fountains. It reopened in 1993. NR. [City of Douglas. Police station and public meeting space.]

FLAGSTAFF

FLAGSTAFF RAILROAD STATION
1 East Santa Fe Avenue
1926

In 1882, Flagstaff's first depot consisted of two box cars, soon replaced by a frame building that burned within a few years. Its 1889 successor (extant, but endangered), built of local sandstone by the Atlantic & Pacific, became the freight station in 1926. That year, the Atchison, Topeka & Santa Fe established a new passenger depot one block west, on the opposite side of the tracks. Designed by a member of the AT&SF engineering department, the Tudor Revival depot had tricolored walls of dark red, bright red, and orange bricks. The roof covering was slate (unfortunately removed in 1989). Twin cross-gables were filled with decorative half-timbering (using redwood planks and stucco) and had diamond-paned windows on the second floor. Other period revival elements included jerkinhead gables and tall corbeled chimneys.

Flagstaff station, September 1955.

The asymmetrical building housed a baggage and express area in the east end, with a women's suite (including a large octagonal bay and fireplace) on the west end. The general waiting room and agent's office were in the center section. Early fluorescent fixtures and recessed wall sconces with shell-shaped reflectors (all extant) illuminated the interior. Outdoor protection for passengers was provided by a flat-roofed, brick porch, rather than either deep eaves or a freestanding canopy. The platform was vitrified brick laid in a herringbone pattern. In the early 1990s, the city purchased the station from the AT&SF. Restoration plans include replication of the interior fir doors. Amtrak's waiting room will be transposed to the baggage area. [City of Flagstaff. Train stop and visitors center.]

GRAND CANYON

GRAND CANYON RAILROAD STATION
South Rim, Grand Canyon National Park
Francis Wilson
1910

In order to attract more passengers to the South Rim of the Grand Canyon in the early 1900s, the Atchison, Topeka & Santa Fe developed a luxurious hotel called El Tovar (1905; extant). Passengers originally debarked at a board and batten depot located on the wye (that building was moved to the site of the present station in 1905). The "Santa Fe" soon hired Santa Barbara architect, Francis Wilson (responsible for the home of Santa Fe's president), to design a replacement station. His plans specified log

Grand Canyon station.

In this early view, letters within the front gable show the original spelling, Grand Cañon.

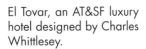

El Tovar, an AT&SF luxury hotel designed by Charles Whittlesey.

construction using Ponderosa pine from local sources. The upper story was finished in wooden shingles stained dark brown. Beneath the tiny shuttered attic windows, tall copper letters spelled out Grand Cañon (changed to Grand Canyon shortly after the depot opened). The agent's living quarters were on the second floor. Downstairs, the chandeliers in the waiting room and the dark stained, log-slab wainscoting echoed elements of El Tovar. Much of the depot's interior hardware bore the stylized letters GC (a fair amount has been stolen).

Regular passenger service ended in 1968, and the Santa Fe vacated the building a year later. After a series of legal proceedings, the National Park Service acquired the property in 1982. The depot, located about 160 yards from the canyon's rim, served consecutively as a construction office, an interpretative center, and a concession stand for hiking equipment. In 1989, Grand Canyon Railway purchased the 64-mile line and restored steam passenger operations from Williams to the South Rim. Its trains stop at Grand Canyon Station, which the Park Service (with an office upstairs) substantially restored, including the wood-shingle roof. The first floor houses the railroad's waiting and baggage rooms. Because the depot's original benches were removed to an outdoor porch at El Tovar, the Park Service has made replicas. NR. [National Park Service. Train stop and park office.]

KINGMAN

KINGMAN RAILROAD STATION
4th and Andy Devine streets
1907

Kingman was named for a civil engineer and surveyor on the Atlantic & Pacific (a predecessor of the Atchison, Topeka & Santa Fe). After the railroad reached Kingman in 1883, the town quickly became a major shipping and trading center for silver, gold, and cattle. The first depot was a boxcar; the next, a two-story wooden building. Trains still made meal stops along this section of the "Santa Fe," which was a slower stretch, not double tracked until the 1920s. Passengers hurried into an "eating house" on the north side of the track to catch a meal before the train pulled out. In 1901, Santa Fe built a new Fred Harvey restaurant. Five years later, fire destroyed the wooden station house, replaced within a year by today's Mission-style depot.

Parapets hid the flat roof of the long, narrow building. Its one-story, reinforced concrete walls were covered with pebble-dash stucco; a raised Santa Fe herald was applied to each curvilinear gable. The floor plan included men's and ladies' waiting rooms, divided by the agent's office. Baggage and freight rooms accounted for half the total square footage. A large, diamond-shaped pane was centered in each exterior door transom and upper window sash. With minor alterations and its original brick platforms intact, the station remains in use by Amtrak as well as the railroad that built it. The Fred Harvey restaurant, closed in 1938, was demolished following World War II. At Seligman, the next division point east of Kingman, a somewhat opposite situation exists; the depot is long gone, but the vacant Harvey House hotel (last used for freight railroad purposes) remains standing. [Atchison, Topeka & Santa Fe Railway Company. Train stop and freight offices.]

PHOENIX

UNION STATION
401 West Harrison Street
William H. Mohr
1923

By 1915, Phoenix had outgrown its two, territorial-era passenger depots: Arizona Eastern (later Southern Pacific) and Atchison, Topeka & Santa Fe. Both were located near 1st and

Phoenix Union Station c. 1924.

Jackson streets. In 1920, after the Arizona Corporation Commission formally ordered the railroads to decide on new sites and types of buildings, the railroads agreed on a union station concept. They chose architect W. H. Mohr (noted for the 1916 AT&SF station in San Bernardino, Calif.), whose plan was published in the local paper even before the location (covering more than a city block) was announced. A continuous series of arches surrounded most of the building and united a central two-story section with single-story wings. Phoenix's warm climate was reflected in the seating capacity of the depot's two waiting rooms. The interior one (with a two-story-high coffered ceiling) had benches for 36 people; the open-air waiting room in the east wing held 48 seats. (This wing —site of a World War II canteen—is now enclosed for garages.) The long west wing housed baggage and express services. Landscaping appropriate to a semitropical climate surrounded the steel and reinforced concrete depot, which was clad in stucco and roofed with Spanish tiles. Among the notable interior features were red tile floors and terra-cotta-clad pilasters with composite order capitals.

Opening day festivities included the arrival of civic groups on elaborately decorated trains, band music, and a congratulatory telegram from President Calvin Coolidge. Another celebration was held in 1926, when the Southern Pacific completed a new main line that passed through Phoenix (previously served by spur lines only). That day, the Queen of Transportation (and her 14 princesses) presided over an 850-voice chorus supported by a band of 300. Today, Amtrak uses the waiting room and ticket office of the depot, while the balance of the building is occupied by its owner and restorer, Sprint Corporation. [Privately owned. Train stop and offices.]

PRESCOTT

PRESCOTT DEPOT
Sheldon Street at Cortez Street
1907

About a quarter-century after trains first arrived in Prescott, the Santa Fe, Prescott & Phoenix (later Atchison, Topeka & Santa Fe) constructed a new depot of reinforced concrete clad in punctuated stucco. The two-story,

Mission-style station exhibited graceful simplicity in its smooth columns, arcades topped with iron railings, and curvilinear gables. The first floor plan consisted of men's and ladies' waiting rooms (each with a fireplace), a ticket office, and a newsstand. The baggage and express building was reached via a breezeway. Passenger service ended in 1962, although the line carried freight for another two decades. Subsequently, numerous attempts at adaptive use failed, principally because of difficulties with land ownership and access. In the late 1980s, a developer solved these problems and —using Secretary of the Interior's Standards— carefully restored the building. Work included reviving the original paint scheme: cream-colored exterior walls, red-orange pillars and window jams, and orange window sash. The worn, red pantile roof was removed and reapplied, supplemented by replacement tiles from the original manufacturer. Although two new but compatible buildings to the north and east filled quickly with retail tenants, finding occupants for the historic depot was a slow process; by the early 1990s, a restaurant and a florist shop were in place. The tracks are gone. NR. [Privately owned. Commercial.]

WICKENBURG

WICKENBURG DEPOT
216 North Frontier Street
c. 1895

Rail passenger service to Wickenburg ended in 1962. Two decades later, the Atchison, Topeka & Santa Fe set a demolition date for the Wickenburg depot—right after the 4th of July. Local citizens favored a different Independence Day treat. To convince the railroad to donate the depot to the town, they obtained a $5 million liability policy, holding AT&SF harmless in the event of any accident or derailment. The community then raised substantial restoration funds, used initially to lift the depot off its rot-

ting railroad-tie foundation and build new concrete footings.

Built in the late 1800s, this standard plan station, clad in vertical and horizontal siding on the passenger end, is simple board and batten construction on the freight end. Asbestos shingles, in a diamond pattern, cover the roof. Inside, the walls and 12-foot-high ceiling of the passenger room and agent's office are sheathed in wood. When the depot was converted to chamber of commerce offices, the loading doors on the freight end were shoved back into pockets. A new door and window were inserted to provide light and access to the room. The original doors can still be rolled shut for security purposes (or to create a screen for showing slides). Worker manuals, paperwork, flags, and freight scales remain—left behind by the railroad. Painted red for many years, the depot is now its original exterior colors of cream and chocolate brown. [Town of Wickenburg. Offices and information center.]

WILLCOX

WILLCOX DEPOT
125 South Railroad Avenue
c. 1880

Willcox was a major shipping and receiving point for mining and ranching industries and for the army. Sheathed in six-inch-wide redwood shiplap (made possible by railroad shipments from California), the depot today is a rare, first-generation, on-site survivor along this Southern Pacific route. Built on a massive redwood foundation, the two-story center section housed the waiting room and agent's office on the first floor, with living quarters upstairs. A large, one-story freight and baggage section extended to the south. In 1914, an addition on the northwest end provided more waiting room and office space. Subdued exterior ornamentation came from Stick Style details and from brackets supporting the wide eaves. Since

1985, the city has been trying to acquire the station, possibly for a railroad museum. SP has expressed a willingness to sell the deteriorating building. But the city would also have to pay the cost of moving the depot off the right-of-way—a relocation that would compromise the massive redwood foundation and the building's historical context. Amtrak and freight trains still use the tracks. [Southern Pacific Lines. Storage.]

WILLIAMS

FRAY MARCOS HOTEL AND DEPOT
Grand Canyon Boulevard
Francis Wilson
1908

Williams, named for a local trapper and hunter, is 40 miles from the Grand Canyon. Although the Atchison, Topeka & Santa Fe main line passed through town, 19th-century sightseers had to take a stagecoach to reach the canyon's south rim. In 1901, the "Santa Fe" bought and lengthened a bankrupt ore-hauling line, thus making the Grand Canyon accessible by rail. Six years later, Francis Wilson (who would subsequently design the Grand Canyon station)

drew up plans for the Williams depot. It was combined with a Harvey House restaurant and hotel called Fray Marcos, named for the priest who accompanied the 1540 Coronado expedition. Italian Renaissance in style, the complex was built of reinforced concrete—including the floors, interior walls, and ceiling. A one-story depot was located on the east end, connected by a breezeway to the two-story Harvey House.

In 1958, the cutoff from Williams Junction to Crookton was completed, which eliminated the main line past Williams (the main line tracks became a branch line to Prescott and Phoenix). By the time the station closed in the 1960s, the depot's colonnaded entry was still standing; but the balconies on the hotel were gone, and the balustraded parapets on both buildings had been infilled. Roof leaks in subsequent years destroyed the plumbing and electrical systems. In 1989, a newly formed Grand Canyon Railway resurrected steam operations on the defunct line. A year later, it partially restored the Williams complex, which now houses a waiting room, crew change rooms, and ticket and train dispatch offices. The railroad is considering reestablishing a restaurant in the old Harvey dining room (now a museum), putting a museum in the lobby and north wing, and converting the upstairs guest

Fray Marcos Hotel in Williams. AT&SF hotels frequently included an Indian Room, filled with native handicrafts.

Panoramic view of the Winslow station with La Posada in the center and the AT&SF depot on the right (in front of the smokestack).

rooms to GCR offices. On the south side of the tracks stands the possible predecessor of the current station—a brick freight depot that may have originally served passengers. [Grand Canyon Railway. Train stop and museum.]

WINSLOW

WINSLOW STATION AND LA POSADA HOTEL
East 2nd Street
Mary E. J. Colter
1930

The famous symbiotic relationship between the Atchison, Topeka & Santa Fe Railway and the Fred Harvey Company increased passenger traffic and promoted the Southwest as a tourist destination. Hotels were placed at "hub" cities from which tourists, who usually arrived by train, were taken on day trips in "Harveycars" (touring buses) to various sites. From Winslow, one could visit places like the Painted Desert and the Hopi Villages. Just before the 1929 stock market crash, construction began on a new combination Harvey House hotel (the old one became a dormitory for Harvey Girls) and railroad station. The project was undertaken by Harvey's chief resident architect and decorator, Mary Colter. On each of her projects,

Colter invented an elaborate history that guided her design. Using the instincts of a stage-set designer, she created La Posada ("resting place") to look as though the 150-year-old ranch of a wealthy Spanish don had been converted to a hotel—with furnishings and grounds intact.

Colter imagined that materials and labor would have been locally obtained and that across generations, the building expanded. To give furniture and finishes a timeless and unique appearance, she combined valuable antiques with hand-hewn items made in an on-site workshop. Colorful designs, hand painted onto plaster panels, and wrought ironwork appeared throughout the building. In the dining room, the ceiling was finished with exposed log beams covered by branches to simulate indigenous adobe construction. The Harvey newsstand and lunchroom were brightly decorated with Spanish tiles. Colter selected the fabrics and Navajo rugs that decorated each of the more than 70 guest rooms and suites.

Covering 11 acres, the complex was landscaped with orchards and shade trees—a paradise in the desert—and a sunken garden with petrified wood fountains. Colter's penchant for creating ambiance by faking decay was manifest in a stone "ruin," apparently representing an actual early Mormon settlement. It was incorporated into the adobe, stone, and weathered board fencing that surrounded the property. A colonnaded walkway linked the E-shaped hotel to the depot, roofed in red tile. Both were built of reinforced concrete clad in pale pink, punctuated stucco. The depot's floor plan included a general waiting room; men's smoking and ladies' retiring rooms; and ticketing, baggage, and express areas.

La Posada flourished despite the Depression; but within 25 years, the Santa Fe's dwindling ridership forced the 1959 closing of La Posada. The furnishings were auctioned off and Mary Colter's interiors either mutilated or condemned to life behind dropped ceilings and wallboard. The Santa Fe converted the hotel to division point offices, which it remained until the railroad departed the building in the early 1990s. The depot (open only at train arrival times) continues to be used by Amtrak. A special emergency arrangement between the city and AT&SF allows community volunteers access to the grounds to maintain the landscaping. In 1994, the city applied for ISTEA funds. If obtained, the money would go toward acquisition and restoration of La Posada for a combination of uses, including municipal offices and a railroad museum. NR District. [Atchison, Topeka & Santa Fe Railway Company. Train stop and vacant hotel.]

New Mexico

Fred Harvey facilities were common in the early days of New Mexico railroading. They were built not only for passengers, but also to serve railroad workers in isolated locations. The fancier Harvey Houses associated with later tourism were mostly second generation buildings—often the work of Mary E. J. Colter. One of the most famous and splendid, the Alvarado, stood in Albuquerque. The hotel was demolished in 1970; the remaining truncated portions of the depot burned in 1993. Colter lived just long enough to see her American Indian–inspired masterpiece hotel in Gallup—El Navajo—torn down in the late Fifties for a parking lot. The extant depot portion is currently undergoing rehabilitation for a transportation and cultural facility. A survey undertaken by the state has located approximately 100 depots left standing in New Mexico. A small number are still on original sites; few of those retain tracks.

CHAMA

CHAMA DEPOT
Just east of State Route 17 (Terrace Avenue)
1899

The Rocky Mountain region was once laced by an extensive network of three-foot-gauge railroads that supported the area's mining camps. After the silver market dwindled and trucking superseded rail transport, most of the system was dismantled. One portion that remains—a 64-mile section of the former Denver & Rio Grande Western—is owned by the two states it meanders through, Colorado and New Mexico. Now called the Cumbres & Toltec Scenic Railroad, it runs on coal-fired steam power and is operated by a private concessionaire. At the headquarters town of Chama, many early trackside structures not only remain, but also function

Chama depot, October 1973.

as built: a 1924 coaling tower; portions of the 1899 combination roundhouse, boiler house, and machine shop; oil and sand houses; a c. 1897 double-spout water tank; an 1880s log bunk house; stockyards (1888, enlarged 1915); and a combination freight and passenger station. The one-story wooden depot (replacement for a two-story one that burned) once included

living quarters for the agent. In the 1970s, to better accommodate passengers, the scenic railway placed rest rooms in the baggage area and removed part of the freight platform. NR. [Cumbres & Toltec Scenic Railroad. Tourist train stop and railroad operating offices.]

CLOVIS

CLOVIS DEPOT
South end of Main Street, one block south of U.S. Route 60
Myron H. Church
1908

Partially opened for service in 1907, the Belen Cutoff enabled the Atchison, Topeka & Santa Fe system to avoid the mountain passes at Raton and Glorieta. Approximately one dozen virtu-

Clovis depot.

Styled to match the depot, the outdoor snack bar (on the far right) served coffee and sandwiches.

Gran Quivira, September 1951. Display windows, left and right of the hotel entrance, promoted New Mexico products.

ally identical masonry depots were built along the Cutoff. They differed principally in size. Conceived by a Chicago architect, the design was grounded in the typical floor plan of a one-story AT&SF depot: a single waiting room, the agent's office, and a freight room. The Cutoff stations, however, each had second stories, to provide living quarters for the agents' families. Rounded archways, low overhanging roofs, and buttressed walls gave the depots a Mission flavor. The Clovis station was built of stuccoed reinforced concrete with a red tile roof. It had an open-air waiting area on the east end (enclosed at some point for a "colored" waiting room and later used as office space). A separate express building, made of brick, was demolished in the 1970s; but a Harvey House hotel, Gran Quivira, still stands, as well as a c. World War I general office building, still used by the railroad. AT&SF would like to donate the depot and Harvey House to the city, but so far the community has not taken the offer. [Atchison, Topeka & Santa Fe Railway Company. Vacant.]

COLUMBUS

COLUMBUS DEPOT
Intersection of state routes 11 and 9
1909

The Columbus depot was a stop on the El Paso & Southwestern (later Southern Pacific), a line owned by the Phelps Dodge Corporation principally for hauling copper ore to its smelters in El Paso, Tex. A temporary depot was used for six years until the existing, two-story standard plan was built. In 1916, Mexican revolutionary Pancho Villa attacked both the village and the Camp Furlong military outpost north of the railroad tracks, an incident in which 18 people died. The depot took a number of hits—a bullet stopped the clock at 4:20 a.m. Because no one was on duty at the station, army personnel had to break down the door to use the telegraph. In World War II, 40 trains a day stopped

at the depot to take on coal and water. By 1961, train service had ended; four years later the tracks were gone. The village acquired the depot and surrounding structures and sold what was readily movable (for example, worker homes, pump houses, and the water tank). In 1975, the village donated the depot to a community group, which had formed expressly to save the station. Southern Pacific contributed the land. A brick and stucco "section" house (used for bunking railroad workers) still stands east of the depot. [Columbus Historical Society. Local history museum.]

LAS CRUCES

LAS CRUCES DEPOT
Las Cruces Avenue and Mesilla Street
c. 1910

Made of wood, the first Atchison, Topeka & Santa Fe depot in Las Cruces was moved to Anthony, Tex., in 1910 (depot no longer extant). The new one, brick covered in pebble-dash stucco, was a standard design that presented a more substantial appearance, appropriate for a county seat. The terra-cotta-clad roof extended into deep eaves, broken on the track side by the agent's bay with its round-arched window. Stepped and sloped parapets (some with the AT&SF herald worked into the coping) and wrought ironwork contributed to a Spanish Colonial Revival flavor. In 1961, using concrete block, the railroad lengthened the freight section, but attempted to match the surface finish to the earlier portion. After passenger service ended, freight use continued until the 1980s. Scheduled for demolition, the depot was saved the following decade, when city council members (at the behest of preservation-minded community groups) acquired both the depot and the land beneath it. Although a new use for the entire building has not been determined, the city anticipates restoring the

AT&SF combination passenger and freight depot at Las Cruces.

agent's area to operational appearance. Freight trains still use the tracks. NR District. [City of Las Cruces. Vacant.]

LAS VEGAS

LAS VEGAS DEPOT
Railroad and Lincoln avenues
1898

Las Vegas was a major shipping point for livestock and wool from New Mexico and parts of Texas. The Atchison, Topeka & Santa Fe chose Las Vegas as a division point and put up the usual complement of service and maintenance buildings. In the late 1800s, erection of a new passenger station, designed by a member of the railroad staff, was accompanied by construction of the Castañeda, a trackside Fred Harvey hotel. Located across a park north of the depot, the Castañeda was from the drawing board of California architect Frederic Louis Roehrig. Both buildings were relatively simple in massing with an overlay of Mission elements. Named after a soldier in Coronado's army, the Castañeda was built of brick over a wooden frame. Its U-shaped design combined a series of round-arched arcades along the wings

and courtyard with a baroque central tower and wooden balconies. The Castañeda was the site of an annual event, reoccurring until 1948 —Teddy Roosevelt's Rough Riders (later "and Cowboys") Reunion. At the first gathering in 1899, the whole town turned out to meet Governor (of New York) Roosevelt's train.

The story-and-a-half brick depot (later stuccoed) had the same tin tile roofing material and curvilinear parapets as the hotel, but its hipped dormers (now gone), pent-roof platform canopy, and fanlight windows made a statement more East Coast than Spanish Colonial. By 1911, much of the traffic that had passed through Las Vegas was diverted to the Belen Cutoff. Although AT&SF built a new 34-stall roundhouse south of the passenger depot in 1917 (extant), Las Vegas was already in economic decline. The railroad moved its shops to Albuquerque after World War II; the Castañeda closed in 1948. Nearly demolished in the 1960s, the hotel is now in private hands, partly used for a pool hall, tavern, and apartments. South of the depot stands the former Gross, Kelly and Company warehouse (now adapted to office use), which exemplifies the structures built by the wholesale and shipping firms whose development followed the railroads. Amtrak trains stop twice a day at the passenger depot, which

Las Vegas depot.

Trackside view with the hotel in the background.

Hotel Castañeda c. 1905.

is being considered for conversion to a multi-modal center. [Depot, owned by Atchison, Topeka & Santa Fe Railway Company. Train stop.] [Hotel, privately owned. Mixed used.]

MAGDALENA

MAGDALENA DEPOT
108 Main Street
1915

Magdalena's first depot was an 1885 standard design that stood somewhat west of the current station. (The old depot has been relocated and is now a residence on Chestnut Street.) The new and bigger wooden station was also based on a stock plan, but built with an extended freight room to store bales of wool (which were frequently stacked on the loading dock, as well). Near the depot were both livestock pens and wholesale establishments to handle supplies for ranchers and miners. Specifications for the depot called for shiplap siding painted standard yellow, tin roof shingles, and the typical Atchison, Topeka & Santa Fe gabled agent's bay.

In the mid-1970s, the branch line to Magdalena was abandoned and the tracks removed. The village soon adapted the building to serve as both municipal offices and the public library—without covering over the wooden wainscoting of the waiting room, the rough unpainted lumber of the freight room, or the iron bars of the ticket window. Some original oak furniture, the loading platform, and even the outdoor privy remain. NR. [Village of Magdalena. Municipal use.]

PORTALES

PORTALES DEPOT
North of West Commercial Street and North
 Avenue A
1913

About 1900, the Atchison, Topeka & Santa Fe gained control of the Pecos Valley & Northeastern Railway, which it absorbed completely in 1912. The "Santa Fe" remodeled some of the existing depots it acquired into Mission style— the style also used for the brand new AT&SF depots on the line. At Portales, Santa Fe totally replaced the old 1901 board and batten depot with a building of stucco-clad brick walls topped by a red tile roof. The railroad's herald, a cross within a circle, was worked into the peaks of the gable ends. Shallow relief decorations, in the form of inverted crosses, surrounded the windows and freight doors. Unlike most of the other depots on the Pecos Valley branch, Portales did not have a breezeway. Inside was a large freight room, an agent's office, and a small waiting room. AT&SF vacated the building in

the 1980s when it consolidated freight operations. Although the depot is intact, its future is uncertain. [Atchison, Topeka & Santa Fe Railway Company. Vacant.]

RATON

ATCHISON, TOPEKA & SANTA FE STATION
1st Street and Cook Avenue
1904

Located precisely at the south end of the Raton Pass (NHL), Raton owes its existence to the railroad. As an Atchison, Topeka & Santa Fe division point, Raton had major locomotive servicing facilities, a two-story board and batten depot, a separate freight house, and a Fred Harvey restaurant (necessary for feeding railroad workers in this isolated area). By 1900, as many as 60 trains a day came into the busy rail yard. AT&SF constructed a new stucco-over-brick, Mission-style depot, probably designed by Charles Whittlesey, architect for El Tovar hotel at the Grand Canyon. The geometrically varied building included a square tower, curvilinear parapets, a hexagonal room, and a semi-hexagonal arcade. Distinctive red-tile-covered spires (removed in the 1920s) poked above the tower and the south end polygon.

Early view of the Raton AT&SF station with its spires intact.

Today most railroad structures are gone from Raton, except for the 14-room, multilevel depot; an adjacent, similarly styled Wells Fargo express building (1910); and the Reading Room —a former recreational facility (vacant, northwest of the depot). Amtrak passengers use the unrestored waiting room on the north end of the building. [Atchison, Topeka & Santa Fe Railway Company. Train stop and freight railroad offices.]

SANTA FE

ATCHISON, TOPEKA & SANTA FE STATION
500 Guadalupe Street
c. 1909

The Atchison, Topeka & Santa Fe main line never made it to Santa Fe. Besides certain economic and political considerations, the route from Raton to Santa Fe was deemed too mountainous for efficient trunk line construction and operation. The town thus lost the position of dominance it once held on the old Santa Fe Trail, despite the spur line completed from Lamy to Santa Fe in 1880. The first depot, a rectangular wooden structure, was replaced as part of the AT&SF general upgrading of facilities in New Mexico. Built about 200 yards northwest of the old station, the second one repeated the railroad's frequently used Mission style with light-colored stuccoed walls, arched openings, and a tile roof. The ticket office and a lobby separated the men's and ladies' waiting rooms. A baggage and express wing to the north balanced an open-air waiting room on the south. Facing the tracks were two broad archways divided by a parapeted cross gable. AT&SF remodeled the first depot into a freight station (razed in the 1970s).

In 1926, buses replaced conventional passenger service between Lamy and Santa Fe. Yet, one could still ride a "mixed train" (combining both freight and passenger cars) or, in later years, get a seat in the freight train caboose. Today this former AT&SF branch is owned (outside the rail yard only) by the Santa Fe Southern, a short freight line that also pulls tourist trains on round trips to Lamy. Directly southeast of the AT&SF station stands another depot (now a restaurant), known commonly as the Denver & Rio Grande station, although it was originally a union depot built by the Santa Fe Central. To the west is the Gross, Kelly and Company warehouse (now retail stores) designed by the renowned architectural firm of Rapp and Rapp. AT&SF has vacated the rail yard, which is expected to undergo redevelopment either by the city or by its private owner (a real estate company spun off from the railroad). [Privately owned. Tourist train stop and freight offices.]

···TRACK ELEVATION···

This plan for the AT&SF station at Santa Fe was drawn by the department of the chief engineer in 1908. (For photo, *see* page 413.)

TUCUMCARI

TUCUMCARI DEPOT
North 2nd Street and East Railroad Avenue
1926

In 1902, a third transcontinental route from Chicago to Los Angeles was formed when the El Paso & Southwestern (later Southern Pacific) and the Chicago, Rock Island & Pacific connected at Santa Rosa, N.Mex. In 1907, the junction was shifted 70 miles northeast to Tucumcari. Wood was used for Tucumcari's first depot and separate restaurant building, which were outgrown in less than two decades. The replacement depot was apparently built and owned by the "Rock Island," although it contained furniture belonging to joint occupant, the Southern Pacific. A medium-size, single-story building, it was constructed of stuccoed brick (the base of exposed brick may have been added later). Both the cross gables and end gables had curvilinear parapets in a Spanish Colonial Revival style; the roof was red tile. A bench-lined breezeway linked the waiting room and ticket office to the express and mail section.

The Van Noy Interstate Company operated a round-the-clock restaurant concession at Tucumcari called the Interstate. Located in the depot's west end, it had both a lunch counter and a formal dining room with linen and silver service. Waitresses were housed in a dormitory across the rail yard. Tucumcari was a crew change point for railroad workers, who frequented the Interstate along with the passengers. Typical of many depot restaurants, the dining room was the nicest social spot in town, and the only one large enough to accommodate banquets and large meetings. During each World War, a free canteen for service personnel operated from the Tucumcari stop. The whole community frequently turned out to greet the troop trains. Passenger service ended in 1968. The depot evolved into a yard office for the Southern Pacific's freight operation; its interior spaces have been subdivided over the years. The machine shops, roundhouse, and other steam servicing facilities are gone. [Southern Pacific Lines. Railroad offices and storage.]

Oklahoma

All preserved depots in Oklahoma are by necessity adaptive uses — the state has no regular passenger service. These former stations represent various eras in Oklahoma's history, from depots constructed during the Territorial era (statehood occurred in 1907) to those constructed during 20th-century days of booming oil production. The tracks in Oklahoma are still active with freight trains; and statewide enthusiasm for railroad history has produced a number of significant restoration projects.

BRISTOW

BRISTOW DEPOT
Between 6th and 7th streets, east of Main Street
1923

In the early 1980s, Burlington Northern planned to demolish the Bristow depot (built by the St. Louis–San Francisco). The city filed suit to prevent the destruction. A group of citizens, mostly members of the Bristow Historical Society, persuaded BN to transfer the depot's ownership to the city, with a lease on the land. The railroad's unyielding condition was that the society erect a permanent structure separating the depot from the tracks. Eighteen hundred people bought bricks, individually engraved, used to build a six-foot-high wall between the trains' path and the station house and to pave the platform. Construction of a streetside entrance canopy (also required by BN) and general rehabilitation were funded by $750,000 in private contributions. The tile-roofed depot was the second for Bristow. (The first one, built of wood in territorial days, was demolished for the present structure.) Behind its red brick walls were "white" and "colored" waiting rooms, a ticket office, and a freight and baggage room. Passenger service ended in 1967. [City of Bristow. Local history museum and chamber of commerce.]

CHICKASHA

CHICAGO, ROCK ISLAND & PACIFIC DEPOT
East end of Chickasha Avenue
c. 1910

In 1986, the Chickasha chapter of the Antique Automobile Club of America purchased the empty and deteriorating Chicago, Rock Island & Pacific depot. Although 35 feet had been lopped off the north end for a highway overpass and the marble stripped from the elaborate lavatories, the depot was worth saving. Chickasha's first "Rock Island" depot was a box car; the second, a depot-hotel. Designed on a cruciform plan, the present building was built with a three-and-a-half-story-high center section flanked by two-story wings. Monumental arches, surrounded by terra-cotta ornamentation, dominated both the street and trackside elevations. Textured brick rose to windowsill level, surmounted by walls of stucco mixed with crushed quartz aggregate. Spanish tiles covered the roof.

In 1993, the auto club was awarded ISTEA funds, which will be used for restoration and for adaptation to a transportation museum. South of the depot, the famous Geronimo Hotel (a J. J. Grier inn and meal stop) was razed in 1937, but a separate express building still stands. A few blocks northwest, the Atchison, Topeka & Santa Fe depot is now a newspaper office. Chickasha was once served by four major railroads. NR. [Chickasha Antique Automobile Club, Inc. Vacant—future transportation museum.]

Chickasha CRI&P depot (right), Geronimo Hotel (center), and rail yard (left).

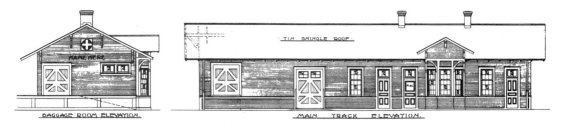

AT&SF standard plan, Frame Depot No. 4 for Branch Lines, dated 1910, was used for the Davis depot.

DAVIS

DAVIS DEPOT
1st Street and State Route 7
1911

The Davis depot is a typical—and once very common—standard plan of the Atchison, Topeka & Santa Fe, most easily recognized by the gabled, hexagonal agent's bay. A one-story, combination freight and passenger station, it replaced a boxcar depot. Clad in narrow, horizontal wooden siding, the building exhibits elements of Colonial Revival styling in the six-over-six window panes, pedimented lintels, and hooded gable. In the station's active era, an interior ticket window opened into the "white" waiting room; the agent sold tickets to "colored" passengers through an outside window. The depot had no plumbing.

After passenger service ended, the AT&SF used the station for freight purposes for about 20 years. In the early 1980s, the city gained title to the building and leased the land from the railroad. The north end (waiting rooms and agent's office) now serves as a museum. The south end (former freight section) is a youth center. Interior features remain intact, including the railroad's telegraph and telephone equipment. Atop the roof, shingled in a diamond pattern, is the one remaining chimney of the two that vented the depot's coal stoves. Extant depots at Pauls Valley (undergoing restoration) and Lindsay (chamber of commerce and teen center) are AT&SF standard designs, very similar to Davis. [City of Davis. Museum and youth center.]

ENID

ATCHISON TOPEKA & SANTA FE DEPOT
North Washington Street
1927

Depots remain standing from two of the three railroads that served Enid (the 1907 St. Louis & San Francisco station was demolished in the

Streetside postcard view of the Enid AT&SF depot.

1960s). The Atchison, Topeka & Santa Fe depot replaced a c. 1904 station. Tudor Revival style, in red brick with a red tile roof, the new station had "white" and "colored" waiting rooms on the east end. After passenger service ended in 1955, the depot was used first as a freight office and then by an auto parts company. In the early Nineties, in preparation for a restaurant that never materialized, a private owner removed the suspended ceiling and repaired the depot's doors and windows. The city obtained ISTEA funds in 1993 to purchase the passenger station, which will become part of a transportation theme area. Plans include using the depot for a restaurant and as a ticket sales office for the privately owned, nonprofit Railroad Museum of Oklahoma (already housed in the AT&SF freight station across the street). The city's proposal includes buying equipment for a new scenic railroad through Oklahoma, with Enid as one of the stops. [Privately owned—sale pending to city of Enid. Vacant.]

CHICAGO, ROCK ISLAND & PACIFIC DEPOT
Owen K. Garriott Boulevard between Grand and 2nd streets
1928

By 1889, the Chicago, Rock Island & Pacific had built across the Cherokee Outlet from Kansas to Old Oklahoma. Enid was opened to settlement via a land run in 1893. But because of a rumored land grabbing scheme, the United States secretary of the interior moved the chosen townsite three miles south, which left the already established railroad station well outside the planned community. A feud (including the sabotage of railroad bridges) developed between the "Rock Island" and the town; only an act of Congress brought resolution. South Enid won the dispute, and the railroad relocated the station stop. The current building, third on the site, is a one-story structure with stuccoed walls above a brick base, curvilinear parapets, quatrefoil windows, and a clay tile

roof. A breezeway connected the separate baggage building to the passenger station, which had racially segregated waiting rooms, ladies' retiring and men's smoking rooms, and a newsstand.

Passenger service ended about 1968. During the 1970s and 1980s, the Enid chapter of the National Railway Historical Society worked to restore the building, which it had an option to buy. But the Rock Island went bankrupt and the depot was sold to a private party. The new owner chose not to undertake asbestos removal; the station is now empty and deteriorating. NR. [Privately owned. Vacant.]

GUTHRIE

ATCHISON, TOPEKA & SANTA FE DEPOT
Between Oklahoma Avenue and Harrison Street
1902

Guthrie was the territorial capital and the first state capital of Oklahoma. Thousands of homesteaders, participating in the open land run of 1889, arrived by train at Guthrie's first Atchison, Topeka & Santa Fe depot—which later washed away in a flood. Built directly across the tracks on higher ground, the brick replacement station—essentially a long, one-story depot with a two-story cross gable near the center—housed "colored" and "white" waiting rooms, baggage and express rooms, and a Harvey House restaurant. It opened as a union depot, for a period of time serving five railroads besides the "Santa Fe."

After 1979, when Amtrak discontinued passenger service, the depot was used for AT&SF freight offices. The county historical society (which acquired the building in the Eighties and eventually the land beneath it, as well) received ISTEA funds in 1993. The group used an early photograph to guide the exterior restoration. Adaptive use plans include a restaurant and a vaudeville-type theater.

Freight trains still ply the AT&SF tracks. Guthrie's Chicago, Rock Island & Pacific depot, at one time converted to a feed store, is now vacant as well as trackless. NR District. [Logan County Historical Society. Vacant—rehabilitation in progress.]

HUGO

ST. LOUIS & SAN FRANCISCO DEPOT
North B and West Jackson streets
Charles Roquette
1914

Hugo was platted at the junction of two railroads: the St. Louis & San Francisco and the Arkansas & Choctaw. In 1902, SL&SF purchased A&C. Hugo became a division point (and the county seat), complete with a roundhouse. Hugo's second consecutive depot, a c. 1911 wooden station with a handsome clock tower, burned in 1913. The "Frisco's" staff architect specified fireproof materials for the next one: steel, red brick, concrete, terra-cotta, and tile. The large depot had facilities for express and baggage, a Harvey House restaurant, a newsstand, a ticket office, and racially segregated waiting rooms. Upstairs were railroad offices, dormitories for Harvey Girls and trainmen, and a large public meeting space.

Passenger service ended in 1960. After Frisco sold the station, it was used as a salvage yard and a wood chip factory. In the 1970s, county residents formed a historical society to save the depot (purchased from a private party). The group restored and reopened the restaurant, which serves breakfast and lunch under the old name, Harvey House (the original closed during the Depression). The horseshoe-shaped counter was reconstructed, based on a six-foot-long surviving portion. The balance of the depot is a local history museum. A new freight line bought the abandoned right-of-way, on which both freight and tourist trains now run. NR. [Choctaw County Historical Society. Tourist train stop and mixed use.]

OKLAHOMA CITY

UNION STATION
300 Southwest 7th Street
1931

In the 1920s, Oklahoma City voters passed a public improvement bond issue. Part of the funds were used to purchase a new railroad right-of-way, thus removing the tracks of the Chicago, Rock Island & Pacific and the St.

Opening day at Oklahoma City Union Station, July 15, 1931.

Louis–San Francisco from the center of town. The "Rock Island" and the "Frisco" moved into a new two-story station. Designed with a Mission-style outline, the depot was veneered in quarry-faced limestone, rather than the more usual stucco. Spanish Colonial Revival features included an arcade with keystoned arches, curvilinear gable dormers, a tile roof, and a bell tower with a hemispherical dome. Chandeliers hung from the vaulted ceilings of two large waiting rooms ("white" and "colored") that were trimmed in solid walnut and birch and floored in terrazzo. The walls combined stucco, marble, and brick. A Frisco employee designed and oversaw construction of a rock garden in a court leading to the baggage wing. It contained 100 different kinds of rock from all over the world, a goldfish pond, and 50 varieties of plants.

Following the end of passenger service in 1967, the station was used for railroad offices and express handling until 1973. A private party restored the building, but a bank foreclosure brought another round of vacancy. In 1989, the local transit authority purchased Union Station. Fortunately, the previous owner had managed to install an island of offices within the depot that did not adversely affect the architecture. The transit authority is developing plans for a multimodal facility including buses and light rail. Oklahoma City's other large extant depot (built one year later than Union Station) is the Art Deco–style Atchison, Topeka & Santa Fe—now vacant and under consideration for ISTEA funding. NR. [Central Oklahoma Transpor-tation and Parking Authority. Offices.]

SHAWNEE

ATCHISON, TOPEKA & SANTA FE DEPOT
614 East Main Street
1904

With stone walls two feet thick, a crenellated tower, stepped gables, and a curving colonnade, Shawnee's Atchison, Topeka & Santa Fe depot could be mistaken for the corner of a medieval castle. The tower—source of much speculation as to its origin and purpose—appears from the blueprints to have been used for ventilation. Round niches at the top, initially meant for clock faces, were filled with "Santa Fe" heralds instead. Located on a branch line (right-of-way problems derailed plans for a trunk line), the depot was roofed in red tile and surrounded by brick paving. Inside, the floor was braced with railroad ties and surfaced with a mixture of cement and cinders. As passenger traffic dwindled, interior spaces were reassigned. The high-ceilinged ladies' waiting room, which once had a curved window seat, became the freight office;

Early view of the Shawnee AT&SF depot with its miniturreted tower

the baggage room became the warehouse. Subsequent changes occurred when segregation laws required a "colored" waiting room.

After passenger service ended in the 1960s, AT&SF continued to use the depot for freight purposes. Within 15 years, the city bought the station, which it leased to the Historical Society of Pottawatomie County. Freight trains still use the tracks. Near them is buried "Santa Fe Bo," an independent dog and frequent train traveler, who always started and ended his trips from the Shawnee depot. The roundhouse (south of the North Canadian River) burned in 1957; fire destroyed the freight house, north of the passenger depot, in 1971. Shawnee's Missouri, Kansas & Texas and Chicago, Rock Island & Pacific stations are long gone. NR. [City of Shawnee. Museum.]

STILLWATER

STILLWATER DEPOT
400 East 9th Street
1900, 1915

In the late 1800s, Stillwater was an energetic young town, home to the Agricultural and Mechanical College, but 20 miles from the nearest railroad access. The territorial legislature's intent to relocate the school was averted when locals convinced the Atchison, Topeka & Santa Fe to service their community. The first combination freight and passenger depot, built of wood in 1900, was remodeled 15 years later when a large brick addition occurred. Roofed in thick wooden shingles (stained green), the new section had the "Santa Fe" logo worked into masonry above the end gables and the agent's bay.

After spending the 1980s as a restaurant, the depot was auctioned off to a group of local businesspeople determined to save it, despite having no specific plans for its use. The former station is now owned by a national organization of current and former college band members. Many original features remain: "white" and "colored" ticket windows with TICKETS carved into the wood trim, leaded glass windowpanes, and pull chain toilets. An open-air waiting area, glassed in by the restaurant, retains its old masonry benches. A similar depot in Cushing is still standing, but vacant. NR. [Privately owned. Organizational headquarters.]

TULSA

UNION DEPOT
1st Street and Cincinnati Avenue
1931

Crowd estimators counted 60,000 visitors at the elaborate grand opening of Tulsa Union Depot. An all-day radio broadcast accompanied the festivities, including a parade, banquet, and dancing. Tulsa was previously served by separate stations: Missouri-Kansas-Texas, Atchison, Topeka & Santa Fe, and St. Louis–San Francisco (the "Frisco"). Union Station's construction was part of a massive project to elevate the streets above the railroad tracks. The Frisco's chief architect designed the depot with neoclassical massing, an arcaded portico, and octagonal towers—all overlaid with Art Deco motifs. Reinforced concrete walls were faced with variegated Bedford limestone. Elaborate marquees shielded racially segregated entrances. Inside, high-ceilinged waiting rooms at viaduct level incorporated clerestory windows, marble and travertine walls, and floors of marble inlaid with terrazzo. Vermilion neon letters spelled out the words of directional signs encased in statuary bronze frames. The depot's lower level accommodated baggage handling, dog kennels, a mail room, and the station master's office. A mezzanine provided facilities for redcaps and train porters.

In 1967, Union Depot closed. For 15 years, the elements, pigeons, scavengers, and vagrants ruined the interior. The chandeliers were stolen, and the only marble left intact consisted of pieces too high for jackhammering thieves to reach. Real estate developers pur-

Tulsa Union Depot.

Streetside entrance c.1950s.

1931 view with boarding platforms visible beneath the viaduct.

chased the depot from the Tulsa Urban Renewal Authority. The new owners overcame the city's master plan—demolition for a parking lot—by adapting the structure for office space. Although an additional floor was inserted into the former main waiting room, the company repainted the interior in the original color scheme. In 1983, the project received an award from the National Coalition of Art Deco Societies. The construction company for the renovation was the same firm that built the building. [Privately owned. Commercial offices.]

WAURIKA

WAURIKA DEPOT
Railroad and Meridian streets
1912

The first train stopped at Waurika in 1902, the same year the town was established. The Chicago, Rock Island & Pacific built a new division point station a decade later, set directly over the 98th Meridian (the old boundary between Oklahoma and Indian Territories). After passenger service ended in the 1950s, the railroad continued to operate a radio communications system at the depot, until the facility closed in 1980. Aided by a donation from a former train conductor, the city acquired the red brick depot in 1984. Three years later, the Depot Restoration Committee formed, with a mission to raise funds and find a use for the boarded-up station. Today the large general waiting room, with its marble floor and high ceiling (given added light through arched upper windows) is a special events facility. The former baggage and freight areas are the reading rooms of the public library; the small "colored" waiting room is used for the librarian's office. [City of Waurika. Library and community meeting space.]

WAYNOKA

WAYNOKA DEPOT AND HARVEY HOUSE
Waynoka and Cleveland streets
1910

In the late 1800s, the Atchison, Topeka & Santa Fe established a shipping station and section house in Waynoka. The area remained relatively quiet until "Santa Fe" made it a division point in 1907. The railroad constructed a roundhouse and repair shops, a depot, and (at nearby Broadway Crossing) a Reading Room—a 100-bed employee dormitory, including a library, tennis court, and gymnasium. The Fred Harvey organization built a restaurant at the same time, and soon railroad workers and waitresses swelled the earlier cowboy and farmer population. Both the depot and restaurant were essentially Spanish Colonial Revival, featuring horseshoe-arched arcades and gables with curvilinear parapets; but the red brick walls and Queen Anne windows with leaded glass deviated from a more usual interpretation of the style. Roofed in red clay tile (slate on the Harvey House), the depot had an open-air waiting room on the north end and segregated waiting rooms in the central block.

In 1929, Transcontinental Air Transport (TAT) began the first through service between New York and Los Angeles. A fly-by-day, train-by-night jaunt, it combined travel on the Pennsylvania Railroad, AT&SF, and Ford Trimotor planes. One leg was the flight from Columbus, Ohio, to the Waynoka airstrip. Buses (called "aerocars") brought passengers to the Harvey House for culinary refueling before boarding a Santa Fe train to Clovis, N.Mex. Amelia Earhart, an officer in the company along with Charles Lindbergh, was aboard the first westbound trip. For the 16 months that TAT lasted, Waynoka—population 2,300—was small but famous.

The restaurant closed in 1937. After the original Reading Room was demolished, that facility was installed in the Harvey House, which later housed AT&SF offices, as well. In 1986, the depot became the museum of the Waynoka Historical Society. ISTEA funds were approved in 1994 to remove tan paint from the exterior walls and restore both buildings. The following year, the historical society raised in excess of the 20 percent matching funds required of the recipient. AT&SF then donated the land, the depot, and the Harvey House to the city, which in turn conveyed the entire package to the historical society. The depot's south end retains its floor scales and loading dock. The roundhouse, which was one-half mile north of Broadway Crossing, is gone. Freight trains still use the tracks. NR. [Waynoka Historical Society. Museum in depot: future museum and restaurant in Harvey House.]

1950s view of the Reading Room (formerly a Harvey House) at Waynoka. The depot is on the far left.

Texas

Before World War II, perhaps 800 stations existed in Texas. The survey director at the state historic preservation office estimates that 50 years later, 100 remained on their original sites. Beginning in the 1980s, interest in depot preservation rose markedly. Some stations, like one in the community of West, which had been moved out of town years ago to become an antiques shop, were actually hauled back to the tracks and restored.

AMARILLO

ATCHISON, TOPEKA & SANTA FE STATION
Southeast 4th Avenue and Grant Street
1910

In the late 1800s, the Atchison, Topeka & Santa Fe expanded into Texas through acquisition of preexisting railroad charters. One of these evolved into a line known as the Panhandle & Santa Fe Railway, a subsidiary of AT&SF. Its stuccoed, Spanish Colonial Revival depot, designed by an unidentified AT&SF staff member, included waiting rooms segregated by both race and gender and a Harvey House restaurant that operated lunch and dining rooms. The second floor housed railroad offices and the Harvey Girls dormitory, separated by the upper portion of the waiting rooms. A park surrounded the station. South of the passenger depot were a freight station and an express building (both extant). Numerous alterations and additions occurred over the years, as the needs of the Harvey House and the railroad shifted.

After passenger service ended in 1971, the depot went through a period of freight use and then vacancy. In the early 1980s, a private party purchased the building and converted it to a restaurant and small shops, which closed less than a decade later and have not reopened. West of the depot, AT&SF steam

Early view of the Amarillo AT&SF station. When sunshine heated the wide brick platforms, the depot's archways provided shade.

Brownsville SP station, 1929.

locomotive No. 5000 (a piece of historic equipment listed in the National Register) is still on display. Dubbed "Madam Queen" after a character on the *Amos 'n Andy* radio show, it was built in 1930 specifically to expedite fast freight trains over the Belen Cutoff. Amarillo had two other stations—the Chicago, Rock Island & Pacific (gone) and the Fort Worth & Denver (altered beyond recognition). Freight trains still ply the AT&SF tracks. NR. [Privately owned. Vacant—for sale.]

BROWNSVILLE

SOUTHERN PACIFIC STATION
641 East Madison Street
Leonard B. McCoy
1929

Missouri Pacific was already established in Brownsville, when Southern Pacific began extending into the Rio Grande Valley. An SP staff member designed a one-story, Spanish Colonial Revival depot with copious cast-stone ornamentation and ironwork. Clad in light-colored stucco and roofed in red clay tiles, the depot originally had open-air waiting areas on the northeastern and southeastern ends and a 400-foot-long platform canopy. Interior finishes included tile floors and wainscoting, stenciled

beams, and decorative tile around the "colored" and "white" water fountains. In 1952, the depot was leased to the Gulf Pacific Cotton Agency for offices. Upon the agency's departure, vagrants took over. The city bought the depot in the early 1980s and turned over operation to the Historic Brownsville Museum Association. The similar, but less elaborate, SP station at McAllen, is now a law office. At one point, Brownsville had two Missouri Pacific depots; both are gone. NR. [City of Brownsville. Local history museum.]

BROWNWOOD

BROWNWOOD DEPOT
Washington Avenue and Adams Street
1909

The Gulf, Colorado & Santa Fe (later Atchison, Topeka & Santa Fe) arrived in Brownwood in 1885. The first depot—located directly opposite the present station—burned in 1892. A wooden replacement station arrived in sections, loaded onto 10 flat cars from Paris, Tex. When the "Santa Fe" built a new masonry depot less than 20 years later, the old station (now gone) was relocated two blocks east. In 1911, the Fred Harvey system constructed a stuccoed brick restaurant and hotel east of the passenger depot, connected by a tile-roofed loggia. The coffee shop and dining room were augmented by a tea room with Prairie Style stenciling and English oak woodwork. Guest rooms were upstairs. The passenger depot, its facades pierced by tall, Romanesque arches, had a "white" waiting room on the east end and a two-story, skylit tower for the agent and telegrapher in the center. The west end housed the baggage room, express agency, and "colored" waiting room. East of the building was a fenced garden with flowers, shrubs, and trees. Walkways and street paving were brick. The restaurant closed following World War II. When passenger service ended in 1968, the depot was used as a freight agency for six years and then —after a period of boarded-up vacancy— as a restaurant and night club. A nonprofit group purchased the station in the early Nineties. It is seeking funds to restore the building for civic, cultural, and restaurant use. NR. [Brownwood Civic Improvement Foundation. Vacant.]

COUPLAND

COUPLAND DEPOT
Hoxie Street
c. 1885

Coupland's very small Missouri, Kansas & Texas depot is in its fourth location. The initial site was Boggy Creek, two miles north of what became Coupland. Within a few years, the board and batten, combination freight and passenger station was moved to a spot just east of Coupland (where county road number 1466 crosses the tracks). After train service ended about 1952, a farmer bought the building and moved it to his property, where it served first as a tenant house and later as a hay barn. In 1975, the Coupland Community Club decided that restoring the depot would make a good Bicentennial project. It found a spot to place the building (a few blocks west of the old east-of-Coupland location) and took the depot for its

third ride. The roof was decayed, the walls rotted, and the windows gone. Thoroughly restored, the building contains some of its original furnishings, including the stove, safe, telephone, telegraph key, timetables, and typewriter. [Coupland Community Club. Depot museum.]

DALLAS

UNION STATION
400 South Houston Street
Jarvis Hunt
1916

Prior to the construction of Union Station, Dallas was served by nine railroads operating from five depots. Stock in the Union Terminal Company, formed in 1912, was equally apportioned among eight of those railroads (the ninth became a tenant). Jarvis Hunt of Chicago (architect for Kansas City Union Station) designed a Beaux Arts building, sited to overlook Ferris Plaza—both its style and setting responsive to the nationwide "City Beautiful" movement. Before construction began, eight acres were cleared of a flour mill, grain elevator, and several warehouses. The nearness of Trinity River precluded construction of a passenger tunnel; instead a "midway" was built over the tracks connecting the second floor waiting room with the platforms. (In 1947, after construction of the river levee, this arrangement was replaced by a tunnel under the tracks.)

Above the depot's granite base rose a stark white facade of enameled, combed brick and terra-cotta. Six huge columns soared to an ornamental balustrade at the roof line. The lower level housed ticket and baggage handling facilities. The middle level included a grand general waiting room, men's smoking room, several smaller waiting rooms, elegant dining facilities, and an information kiosk made of brick and cast iron with a marble

Architect's rendering of Denison Union Depot.

counter. Union Terminal Company occupied the third floor. From 1947 to 1950, a Fort Worth architect supervised major station renovations, which drastically altered the use of interior spaces. In 1972, the city purchased the terminal and leased much of the depot to commercial ventures. Of the initial train facilities, only the westernmost butterfly shed and two tracks remain. The original waiting room is essentially intact and used by Amtrak. NR. [City of Dallas. Train stop and commercial.]

DENISON

UNION DEPOT
100 block of West Main Street
Henry T. Phelps
1911

About 1870, officials of the Missouri, Kansas & Texas (the "Katy") wanted to place a new town near the proposed Red River crossing. When the town of Sherman refused to provide the necessary financial inducements, the railroad and a local investor teamed up to purchase land further north. They laid out the town of Denison, named for the Katy's vice-president, just before the first train came through. The first two depots were wooden and stood north of today's location. To house its division headquarters, MK&T needed a bigger station. Conceived to accommodate multiple railroads, this new station was also used by the St. Louis & San Francisco (two other railroads decided not to join in). San Antonio architect Henry T. Phelps designed a Beaux Arts brick building with red granite and terra-cotta trim. Mirror-image Roman arches dominated both the east and west facades of the three-story center section. Two-story, symmetrical wings repeated the arch motif and the bold entablature of the main building. The station's daylight-filled central waiting room was circled by an interior balcony. A "colored" waiting room, a restaurant, and an express agency were among the depot's other facilities.

After passenger service ended in the mid-1960s, the Katy continued to use the station for offices. Purchased by a developer in the Eighties, the depot now houses two restaurants, a railroad museum, radio and television stations, shops, and offices. Numerous commercial and institutional buildings from the 1800s and early 1900s remain in the immediate area. NR District. [Privately owned. Mixed use.]

EL PASO

UNION STATION
Coldwell and San Francisco streets
D. H. Burnham and Company
1906

Both the Santa Fe and Chihuahua cattle trails passed through El Paso, located on the Mexican border. By the 1880s, the community was a thriving rail center. Passenger travel had an international flavor; the El Paso Union

El Paso Union Station with its original spire (removed in 1941 and reconstructed in the 1980s).

Passenger Depot Company was formed in 1903 not only by six United States railroads, but also the National Railways of Mexico. Travelers who were between connections at the new Union Station spent time in a lofty central waiting room, 45 feet high, with massive square columns and clerestory windows. Doors on the west wall opened into a Harvey House restaurant. At the second floor level, a gallery with a simple balustrade gave access to railroad offices. The station was designed by a nationally prominent Chicago architectural firm. Its neoclassical exterior was remodeled in 1941, when the railroad applied a Spanish Colonial Revival make-over. The spire was removed from the six-story campanile, the depot's red brick walls were painted white, and the roof was surfaced in clay tiles.

In the 1970s, Southern Pacific nearly sold the building to speculators interested in demolition. The city took action and in the Eighties used a federal grant to restore the station's pre-1941 appearance. Today, the local transit authority occupies the office space and Amtrak uses the waiting room. Three other depot structures remain in El Paso: a former Texas & Pacific combination freight and passenger station; a former SP freight depot; and a c. 1930 Atchison, Topeka & Santa Fe freight depot (still in railroad use). NR. [City of El Paso. Train stop, offices, and special events facility.]

FORT WORTH

TEXAS & PACIFIC STATION
West Lancaster Avenue and Main Street
Herman C. Koeppe (Wyatt Cephas Hedrick)
1931

The Texas & Pacific terminal complex was built as part of a major grade separation project. The centerpiece was a 13-story passenger station and office building, replacement for a red brick, Romanesque Revival structure (rebuilt after a 1904 fire; demolished in the 1930s). The chief designer was Herman Koeppe, who was employed by a prominent Fort Worth architect. Additional structures included an adjoining express and commissary building; an eight-story inbound freight warehouse and sales building; and an outbound freight house (demolished in the 1980s for redevelopment that never occurred). The combination station and office building was clad in polished granite, Bedford limestone, and rough-textured

Main waiting room at Fort Worth T&P station. (For exterior view, *see* page 43.)

brick. Art Deco geometric and plant motifs decorated both the terminal and its huge companion, the T&P Warehouse (extant.) The skyscraper's ground floor contained a large central waiting room plus smaller segregated waiting rooms, the stationmaster's office, a restaurant, and an elevator bank. Spectacular decorative elements included gold leaf and enamel on cast-plaster ceilings, ornate chandeliers, white marble floors, and reddish brown marble wainscoting. Mezzanine and second-floor levels housed railroad offices. A two-story concourse stretched across the track side of the station.

In 1967, the station shut down, and nonrailroad tenants began moving out. About a dozen years later, a developer rehabilitated the office space for commercial use. Subsequently the intact Art Deco waiting room was readied for Amtrak, scheduled to transfer its service from

Forth Worth's Union Depot in the late 1990s. ISTEA funds will facilitate the addition of other modes of transportation. Retail shops are planned for the first floor. NR. [Privately owned. Commercial use and future multimodal facility.]

UNION DEPOT

1501 Jones Street
1900, 1938

About five blocks northeast of the T&P station, stands Fort Worth Union Depot (also known as the Santa Fe Depot). Built by the Fort Worth Union Passenger Station Company, it served more than a half-dozen railroads over its lifetime, including, most recently, Amtrak. Its striking two-tone appearance was achieved by intricate masonry work. Courses of limestone were inserted between rows of red brick on the first floor as well as between voussoirs of the round and flat-arched window openings. A diaper-patterned, horizontal band girdled the station between the first and second floors. Limestone was also used for quoins and window trim. A low-pitched, hipped roof covered in tile was tucked behind parapeted gables. In the main waiting room, two stories high, handpainted window glass (later removed to a museum) depicted the evolution of regional transportation.

Fort Worth Union Depot with features now gone: the iron eagles (perched on balls above the gables) and the streetside portico.

During a major exterior and interior remodeling in 1938, the streetside portico was taken off and replaced by a marquee. At the same time a two-story Atchison, Topeka & Santa Fe freight depot (still standing) was built just north of the passenger station. Constructed of reinforced concrete and polychrome brick, its floor plan included a cold storage room for perishables, a Fred Harvey supply room, and offices for the freight agent, division superintendent, and special agent. By the 1990s, the passenger station's last tenant, Amtrak, had made plans to move from Union Depot to Fort Worth's former Texas & Pacific station—thus leaving the Santa Fe building with an uncertain future. In 1993, it was listed as one of the 10 most endangered structures in Texas. The depot is owned by a development company that was spun off from AT&SF. NR. [Privately owned. Train stop—soon to be vacated.]

GAINESVILLE

GULF, COLORADO & SANTA FE STATION

California Street, one block east of Lindsay Street

1902

The first depot of the Gulf, Colorado & Santa Fe (Texas subsidiary of the Atchison, Topeka & Santa Fe) was a small wooden structure. In 1901, the chief engineer's office drew plans for a replacement station of reddish orange brick with curvilinear gables, rock-faced stone trim, and a Ludowici clay tile roof. A depot park bor-

Gainesville GC&SF station.

The second story was once used as dormitory and apartment space.

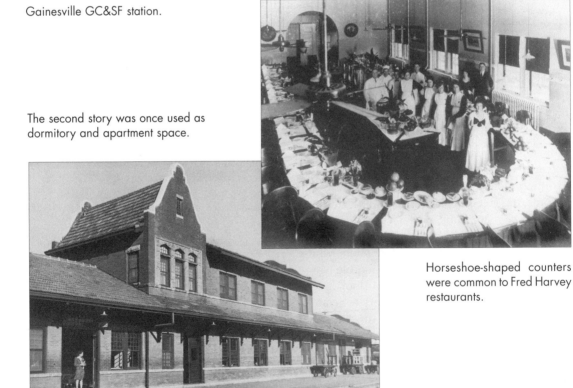

Horseshoe-shaped counters were common to Fred Harvey restaurants.

dered the west side. Gainesville processed massive livestock and cotton shipments; freight was handled from a separate facility (now gone) about a quarter-mile north. The passenger depot had racially segregated waiting rooms, a baggage area, and a Fred Harvey restaurant. A refrigerator room kept food cool with a 700-pound block of ice. The center portion of the depot had a second story, with dormitory rooms for the Harvey waitresses and an apartment for the manager. The restaurant closed in 1931. During World War II, Gainesville saw unprecedented passenger traffic, after an infantry training facility was built at Camp Howze. By 1971, only two passenger trains a day came through; by 1979, none. Two years later, the city acquired the depot from the railroad. Despite a feasibility study and grant applications, no new use has been found. Gainesville's other passenger station, the Missouri-Kansas-Texas, is gone. NR. [City of Gainesville. Vacant.]

GALVESTON

UNION DEPOT
25th Street and The Strand
Robert McKee (1931 addition)
1913, 1931

Galveston used makeshift stations between the town's first railroad activity in the early 1860s and construction of the first union station in 1874 near 23rd Street and Avenue A. Subsequent undertakings occurred in the vicinity of 25th Street and The Strand, where the Union Passenger Depot Company built a four-story red brick station (now gone) as the first in a series of evolving plans. The depot that stands today is the combination of an eight-story structure from 1913 and a later 11-story tower and north wing. The El Paso architect who designed the 1931 addition extended cream-colored terra-cotta tiles across both portions to create a unified appearance. The main floor included segre-

gated ticket windows and waiting rooms and a Harvey House restaurant. Grass and oleander trees were planted in an area that adjoined the platforms and the baggage and express buildings. Upper floors housed corporate offices of the Gulf, Colorado & Santa Fe (Atchison, Topeka & Santa Fe system).

In the mid-1960s, AT&SF transferred its administrative operations to other cities and shortly thereafter, passenger service ended. The building was vacant and in danger of demolition, when a local philanthropical foundation acquired it, restored it, and transferred ownership to an affiliated nonprofit group. The first floor is a large railroad museum; the waiting room is home to 36 life-size statues known as the "Ghosts of Travelers Past." (*See* photo, page 50.) On a multiacre tract behind the station, the museum exhibits antique rail cars and locomotives. A Houston to Galveston tourist train stops at the station several times a week. Offices for nonprofit and government agencies occupy the depot's upper floors. [Shearn Moody Plaza, Inc. Tourist train stop, museum, and offices.]

HOUSTON

UNION STATION
501 Crawford Street
Warren and Wetmore
1911, 1912

In 1905, four railroads united to form the Houston Belt & Terminal Railway Company. It handled "switching" between 16 railroads that moved within the city limits. (Switching consists of moving cars from one track to another, or to different positions on the same track—essentially the make-up and break-up of trains.) A union passenger station and multiple union freight terminals were planned. HB&T purchased an 18-acre site for this enterprise; blocks of single family residences and a synagogue were cleared for the new construction. One of the new freight depots was three blocks long.

New York City's Warren and Wetmore were hired to design the passenger building. The initial structure was three stories high—the first two clad in white terra-cotta, the third in brick. Almost immediately, more office space was needed. Two stories were added, and the hipped roof replaced with a flat one. The first train arrived in 1910 before the depot's completion. At the dedication the following year, an orchestra played for 10,000 celebrants. The depot was decked out in flowers; Harvey House waitresses wore their usual black dresses and heavily starched aprons. The building cost $540,000 ($45,000 went for three kinds of marble used in the waiting rooms and restaurant).

In the 1960s, the station was remodeled. The ceiling height of the barrel-vaulted waiting room was reduced from 45 feet to 10, and the grand space partitioned into offices. The restaurant was converted to a waiting room. The following decade, Amtrak consolidated its two Houston operations and began using only the small Washington Avenue Southern Pacific depot (1959 dull substitute for a 1930s Art Deco delight). Since then, none of the rumored plans for Union Station's adaptive use have materialized. Among notable visitors to the station over the years were the Duke and Duchess of Windsor, President and Mrs. Franklin Roosevelt, and an elephant who got loose from a circus train (the pachyderm crashed through the wrought-iron platform gate and watched the passengers scatter). NR. [Houston Belt & Terminal Railway Company. Railroad offices.]

LUBBOCK

Fort Worth & Denver South Plains Station
19th Street and Avenue G
Wyatt Cephas Hedrick
1929

The Fort Worth & Denver South Plains (the "Denver Road")—a subsidiary of the Chicago, Burlington & Quincy—was a latecomer to rail-

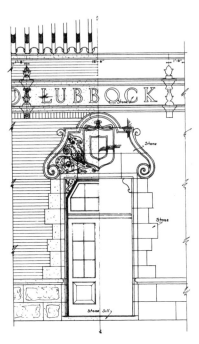

Detail of center doorway at the Lubbock FW&DSP station.

roading. Chartered in 1926, the 204-mile system of branch lines stretched southwest through the South Plains region, with Lubbock at the end of the line. Depot construction did not begin until after the tracks were laid, so that materials could be shipped in over the Denver rails, rather than by truck or another railroad. Fort Worth architect Wyatt Hedrick designed all the Denver stations. They were built on the "unit system"—specialized crews moved in assembly line fashion from one depot to the next, similar to the construction of tract houses. Hedrick was responsible for the Spanish Renaissance Revival buildings at Texas Technological College in Lubbock. He used the same style for the asymmetrical Lubbock depot, which featured a low-pitched roof covered in red clay barrel tiles, carved stonework, and decorative window grilles. The combination freight and passenger station included baggage and express rooms, a ticket office, and racially segregated waiting rooms.

After the railroad abandoned the depot in 1953, it was used as a warehouse and then as a salvage yard. In the mid-1970s, a private party converted the limestone and light tan brick station to a restaurant. Although interior plaster was removed to expose the masonry walls (a typical 1970s idea of instant antiquity), woodwork was repaired and refinished, and a new kitchen wing was designed to lend visual continuity to the whole. The tracks are gone. Lubbock's 1911 Atchison, Topeka & Santa Fe depot—a Louis Curtiss design very similar to the extant Snyder station—burned in 1953. NR. [Privately owned. Restaurant.]

MARSHALL

TEXAS & PACIFIC STATION
North end of Washington Avenue
1912

The Texas & Pacific station and rail yards in Marshall once comprised 57 buildings, where 3,000 people worked. The city was platted with the depot at one end of Washington Avenue and the courthouse at the other. Built in Mission style, the two-story, red brick passenger station was square and symmetrical, unlike the more typical rectangular, asymmetrical depots of southwestern designs. Both the passenger depot and express building sat in the middle of a wye. During the early 1900s, before T&P had dining cars, trains made 45-minute buffet meal stops at Marshall. On their way west by train, settlers—300 to 400 at a time—crossed the tracks to the elegant 1896 Ginocchio Hotel (NR), where they dined on trestle tables set up in the lobbies and ballroom.

In the mid-1970s, Union Pacific, which by then owned the passenger depot, abandoned the building. UP subsequently demolished the express building and the c. 1900 repair shops (the 1871 shops had been destroyed by fire in 1971). Amtrak continued to stop, but passengers

had no access to the station's interior. Citizen concern for the structure reached a critical point in 1988, when UP applied for a demolition permit; the city's preservation committee fortunately voted for a delay. Two years later, after solving safety and liability issues (the depot is surrounded by three active tracks), a nonprofit group called Marshall Depot, Inc., secured a lease from the railroad. The group stabilized the building, and plans are under consideration for a multimodal center and museum. UP has requested permission to demolish the one remaining water tower, north of the depot. NR District. [Union Pacific Railroad. Train stop/npa.]

NACOGDOCHES

HOUSTON, EAST & WEST TEXAS STATION
State Route 21
1910

One of Texas's oldest settlements, Nacogdoches was named after a Caddo Indian tribe. The community was already thriving when the first railroad arrived in 1883—the Houston, East & West Texas (later Southern Pacific).

Nacogdoches passenger station, built by the HE&WT. Successor railroad, SP, was already using the depot for freight purposes when this 1974 photo was taken.

Tracks run on two sides of this one-story former passenger depot, which has a multihipped roof covered in tile. Flaring eaves form deep platform canopies. Capped by a tent roof with a finial, the polygonal agent's bay and dormer still provide a view up and down the line. Most other buildings in the railroad complex—a freight depot, express office, and coaling station—are gone. A grocery warehouse, has been converted to a restaurant. Passenger service ended in the mid-1950s. An identical brick depot at Orange suffered a fire and is on Texas's list of most endangered buildings. NR. [Southern Pacific Lines. Freight railroad office.]

PARIS

UNION STATION
1100 West Kaufman Street
1910

Because Paris was a junction point on a major passenger route (Dallas to St. Louis), Union Station was relatively large for the size of the community. The passenger depot was owned by the Paris & Great Northern (subsidiary of St. Louis & San Francisco); the rail yard was mostly owned by the Gulf, Colorado & Santa Fe (subsidiary of Atchison, Topeka & Santa Fe). Passengers typically remained on the train, while locomotives of the "Frisco" and the "Santa Fe" were exchanged. Each line supplied personnel for the depot on an alternating five-year basis. (Texas Midland also used Union Station at one time.) The present structure is the second depot on the site. Built of red brick with joints thinly "buttered," the story-and-a-half depot had marble lintels and a prominent center tower (totally ornamental and without access). The clay tile roof was pierced by several hipped dormers, which went into unused attic space. Only the biggest dormer over the agent's bay served a functional purpose, lighting what was probably the conduc-

tors' room. Marble wainscoting embellished parts of the interior, which included (from north to south) a "white" waiting room, ticket office, "colored" waiting room, baggage-cart breezeway, and express annex. The Fred Harvey newsstand appears to have been a kit installation, bearing decorative details such as trefoils, totally unlike the style of the depot.

By 1960, passenger service on both the Santa Fe and Frisco had ended. About a quarter-century later, a newly formed freight railroad acquired the building, which was not needed for its operations. The railroad stabilized the empty structure and relocated its tracks to create space for automobile parking, in the hope of attracting an adaptive use. Paris also has a former Texas & Pacific depot, which was struck by a tornado in the 1950s; the remaining half was reconfigured into a smaller combination freight and passenger station. [Kiamichi Railroad Company. Vacant—for sale or lease.]

QUANAH

QUANAH, ACME & PACIFIC STATION
Mercer Street
C. H. Page and Brothers
1909

Quanah Parker, son of a Comanche chief and a white mother, was an investor in the Quanah, Acme & Pacific Railway (later controlled by the St. Louis–San Francisco). Austin architects designed the QA&P station in a Spanish Colonial Revival style. The two-story building, with stuccoed frame walls and a Ludowici red tile roof, was constructed on a cruciform plan. Square towers, three stories high, connected the intersecting wings. A racially segregated waiting room in the rotunda contained a winding staircase to the upper floor. The 20-room building included the railroad's general headquarters. Electricity for lighting the depot was generated at the roundhouse.

Passenger service ended in the 1960s. Late in the following decade, vandals and scavengers began desecrating the leaking, abandoned station. The county historical society, having just restored an 1894 jail immediately west of the depot, convinced the railroad to donate the station. Both buildings now house local history collections, including a room devoted to the QA&P. In the Nineties, the society acquired an express building, northeast of the passenger station, plus land for a depot park. Although the QA&P rails are gone, freight trains still use nearby Burlington Northern tracks, formerly Fort Worth & Denver City. The FW&DC depot, within sight of the QA&P, was demolished overnight by BN in the late 1980s. Quanah is also home to two relocated depots (now restaurants) from Medicine Mound and Chillicothe. NR. [Hardeman County Historical Society. Museum.]

SAN ANGELO

KANSAS CITY, MEXICO & ORIENT STATION
700 South Chadbourne Street
1909

In 1888, the Gulf, Colorado & Santa Fe was the first railroad into San Angelo. A second line was promoted by mining and railroad entrepreneur Arthur Stilwell, whose Kansas City, Mexico & Orient Railway started laying track just after the turn of the century. At San Angelo, the KCM&O built depots and repair shops. The red brick passenger station, two stories high with a belcast, hipped roof, housed waiting rooms segregated by race and gender, a baggage room, a ticket office, a dispatcher's room (in a trackside square tower), and division offices. By the 1930s, Atchison, Topeka & Santa Fe owned both GC&SF and KCM&O. In 1947,

San Angelo KCM&O station in March 1985.

The well-restored passenger depot bears the emblem of successor railroad AT&SF.

At the companion freight station, a two-story, freight agent's office is attached to a long wooden freight room and loading dock. This once relatively common plan was also used for combination stations, in which case the ticket office and passenger waiting room were in the two-story portion.

it consolidated operations into the KCM&O complex (and demolished the GC&SF buildings). Passenger service ended in the 1950s; freight, in the early Eighties.

Later that decade, after confronting the railroad's demolition plans, the city convinced AT&SF to donate the two remaining structures. Historic Orient–Santa Fe Depot, Inc., helped the city obtain a grant to repair the passenger station roof, which was resurfaced with the original tiles and matching replacement pieces. Volunteers contributed more than 6,000 hours of labor to restore the depot's exterior. Across the street, the freight station was converted to a senior citizens center. Aided by 1994 ISTEA funds, the city plans to use the passenger depot as offices for its municipal transit company and for a railroad museum. The platform canopy is intact, and freight trains still use the tracks. NR District. [City of San Angelo. Mixed use.]

SAN ANTONIO

INTERNATIONAL & GREAT NORTHERN STATION
West Commerce and Medina streets
Harvey L. Page
c. 1908

The cornerstone for the new International & Great Northern (later Missouri Pacific) station was laid at a ceremony in the fall of 1907. Railroad and city officials then adjourned to the architect's home for breakfast, where he described his plans for the building. The outline of the depot was that of a Greek Cross, defined by a central dome from which four barrel vaults radiated. At each corner was a three-story campanile; curvilinear parapets swept from one to the other. In its active years, the depot was advertised as the "Gateway to Mexico," because the luxurious *Texas Eagle*

San Antonio I&GN station.

Above the entrance, a stained glass, rose window incorporates the railroad's emblem.

Copper-topped dome with eight-foot-high Indian statue.

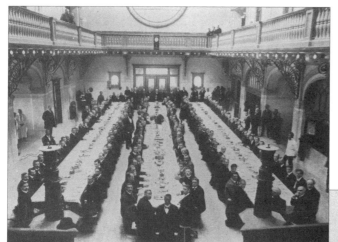

San Antonio GH&SA station (SP system).

Opening day, February 1, 1903. The San Antonio Business Men's [*sic*] Club held a banquet at the depot.

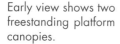

Early view shows two freestanding platform canopies.

stopped at San Antonio before completing the journey from St. Louis to Laredo.

After the station closed in 1970, it was subjected to 15 years of failed development plans and massive scavenging. Fortunately, the City Employees Federal Credit Union purchased the depot in 1985. It added a wing to the core of the building, which was put back to near original condition. Among the changes were a tile floor (instead of terrazzo) and a wooden (rather than iron) railing for the gallery and the grand stairway. Artisans relied on old photographs and the few remaining colored shards to re-create a stained glass window landscape, depicting a pair of Indians in the foreground with a Spanish mission in the distance. Other restoration included replacing copper sheathing that had been stripped from the dome's roof and reproducing the multiglobe lamps that stood on the rotunda floor. Missing from atop the dome was an eight-foot statue of an Indian shooting an arrow toward Fort Sam Houston. Stolen during the station's years of abandonment, it was surreptitiously returned, apparently by the thieves. NR. [Privately owned. Financial institution.]

GALVESTON, HARRISBURG & SAN ANTONIO STATION
1174 East Commerce Street
Daniel J. Patterson
1903

In 1877, the Galveston, Harrisburg & San Antonio (part of Southern Pacific) was the first railroad built into the city. Its depot at Austin and 10th streets was replaced by the current building, described at the dedication luncheon as being of Spanish Renaissance style. The stuccoed walls were washed in a light ochre with arches trimmed in red brick, and a red tile roof. Baroque sculpture embellished the second-story windows of two substantial, square towers. Art glass ornamented large round windows at opposite ends of the main hall (one window has been replaced with a stucco panel). The north window depicted a magnificent sunset, with the targeted opening date, 1902, in Roman letters beneath the words SUNSET ROUTE. (Opening day was delayed nearly a year, because construction materials were late in arriving.) The south window contained the Texas lone star seal. Other features were a vaulted and coffered ceiling—painted in light yellow, cream, and gold; a skylight; and ornate plasterwork. A balcony opened onto second-floor offices, which were reached by a grand stairway. The platform—long enough to handle 16-car trains—was sheltered by a wood-framed roof with iron columns and delicate bracketing. To the south, a baggage and mail facility linked the passenger depot to the express building. Designed by an SP architect, the station was altered many times over the years. It was restored in the 1980s to its c. 1940 configuration and serves as an Amtrak stop. San Antonio's third major depot, the 1917

Missouri, Kansas & Texas Station, was demolished in 1968 for a parking lot. NR. [VIA Metropolitan Transit. Train stop.]

TEAGUE

TEAGUE RAILROAD STATION
208 South 3rd Avenue
1907

About 1905, an official of the new Trinity & Brazos Valley Railway (later the Burlington–Rock Island) selected the village of Brewer for a division point. Rechristened Teague to honor a family name of the same official, the community received a two-story depot of buff brick trimmed with red brick, a red tile roof, and a modest campanile. Reportedly the first non-wood structure in town, the depot was designed in Renaissance Revival style. Inside was an octagonal rotunda (the main ticketing area) and three waiting rooms designated Ladies, Gents, and Colored. The depot also held a baggage room, restaurant, and railroad offices. Train watching was such a popular pastime in Teague (and everywhere else) that a crowd of 100 gawkers at arrival time was not unusual.

Teague station, July 1965.

In April 1917 (the month the United States entered World War I), GC&SF employees purchased a huge American flag, which they hoisted over the station at Temple.

Passenger service ended in the mid-1960s. Later, the Burlington Northern (the freight railroad currently using the tracks) donated the depot to the city. The building reopened as a museum with its globe chandeliers and much of the furniture intact, although the outside archways had been enclosed and a partition added to the portico's north end. The T&BV roundhouse still stands just south of the depot. An adjacent log house is a recent transplant. NR. [City of Teague. Railroad and local history museum.]

TEMPLE

Gulf, Colorado & Santa Fe Station
315 West Avenue B
1910

Temple was named for the chief engineer of the Gulf, Colorado & Santa Fe (Texas subsidiary of Atchison, Topeka & Santa Fe). The present station replaced a two-story wooden structure, companion to a large Harvey House hotel, also made of wood. Nearby, a 275-acre

Harvey-owned farm supplied dairy products, hogs, and chickens to the company's Texas operations. Although plans for an even bigger, masonry Harvey House were drawn in the early 1900s, only the two-story brick and stucco depot was built. (The wood-sided Harvey House closed in 1933 and was subsequently destroyed.) A trackside loggia protected waiting passengers from the sun. Brickwork versions of the railroad's herald—a cross within a circle—were liberally applied to the exterior walls. The installation of two "depot parks" reflected the railroad's landscaping policy—a garden for the station grounds at every county seat or other prominent locale. The first-floor layout included (from west to east) a baggage room, a ticket office, "white" and "colored" waiting rooms, and a telegraph office. The dispatcher's office was upstairs.

The Temple yard included a full complement of railroad and service buildings and a separate freight depot. Only a brick warehouse (southwest of the passenger depot) remains. AT&SF vacated the depot in the early 1990s; Amtrak passengers continue to use the waiting room. The city would like to acquire the station,

Early view of B-RI station at Waxahachie.

possibly to make the empty portions a museum. Temple has two other former stations: a wooden 1907 GC&SF depot (relocated from Moody in 1973 to serve as a museum) and a 1912 Missouri, Kansas & Texas depot on its original site (donated in 1993 to the Railroad and Pioneer Museum by the Union Pacific). [Atchison, Topeka & Santa Fe Railway Company. Train stop.]

WAXAHACHIE

TRINITY & BRAZOS VALLEY STATION
Between College and Rogers streets
c. 1907

The Burlington–Rock Island (successor to the Trinity & Brazos Valley) was so named because of its joint ownership by the Chicago, Burlington & Quincy and the Chicago, Rock Island & Pacific. In the early 1960s, the railroad leased its former passenger depot at Waxahachie to a manufacturing concern for office space. The one-story yellow brick building, with bold, red brick accents, is roofed in red tile. On the track side is a three-story, octagonal tower—originally a combination agent's bay and telegrapher's office. With its crenellated parapet, the tower appears to have migrated from a castle wall. A very similar depot was built 31 railroad miles south at Corsicana (extant, in railroad use). To the east of Waxahachie's passenger depot is a wooden freight station. A simple Missouri, Kansas & Texas depot stands across the parking lot. The town's charming Houston & Texas Central (later Southern Pacific) depot is gone. NR District. [Burlington Northern Railroad Company. Manufacturing office.]

West

At the Union Pacific station in Salt Lake City, Utah, the gift shop sold newspapers, cigars, pennants, souvenir dishes, and Navajo blankets. The table in the foreground bears an artistically arranged pile of fruit.

Alaska

The Alaska Railroad was operated by the United States government until 1985, when the state took over. The tracks go from Seward to Fairbanks, and passengers can board most anywhere by flagging the train. The railroad's 1942 headquarters and depot building in Anchorage continues to serve passengers; its upstairs was converted to commercial office space after the administration moved to a new structure in the early 1990s.

SEWARD

SEWARD DEPOT
501 Railway Avenue
1917

By the 1910s, private enterprise had clearly tried and failed to provide a rail link between Alaska's resource-rich interior and the year-round port at Seward. Congress authorized a commission that would build a railroad through the Alaska Territory and connect two existing short lines, which the commission took over. Seward was the initial headquarters for the Alaska Engineering Commission, responsible for the design of its Arts-and-Crafts–style depot, completed two years after railroad construction began. Covered in eight-inch-wide

Seward depot, 1936.

clapboards, the station was roofed in wooden shingles. A 12-foot overhang at the south end created an outdoor waiting area. The interior layout included a waiting room (finished with beaded board wainscoting), ticket office, trainmen's hall, and a large baggage and freight area. In 1923, President and Mrs. Warren Harding visited Seward and before their departure, spent a half-hour mingling with the large crowd at the depot. They gave everybody with a camera the chance to snap a picture. The Hardings then proceeded to Nenana, where the President drove in the golden spike, marking completion of the Alaska Railroad. Only eight stations were initially built along this 460-mile-long railroad; three survive. The one at Nenana (NR), was a twin to the Seward depot. Constructed in 1922, Nenana was enlarged in 1937, when a second story was added for the agent's living quarters.

In 1928, new dock and rail facilities were completed at the foot of Fifth Avenue, and the Seward depot was moved from its original location on Adams Street to this new site. After a 1964 earthquake forced rebuilding of Alaska's infrastructure, a new train stop was established several blocks away. The 1917 railroad station became a passenger depot for the Alaska Marine Highway (a system of state-operated ferry routes). The structure appears essentially as built, except for changes to the original freight opening and the roofing material. NR. [City of Seward. Ferry depot.]

Skagway depot. The WP&Y office building is on the left.

SKAGWAY

SKAGWAY DEPOT
Broadway and 2nd Avenue
1898

The distance from the steamship dock at Skagway to Whitehorse in the Yukon Territory was only 110 railroad miles, but construction was very difficult. The climatic conditions varied from sub-zero temperatures and deep snow in winter to flooding and mud slides in summer. Civil engineers were challenged by the terrain: chasms to span, mountains to tunnel, and steep grades to climb. Labor and materials had to be brought in by sea. Once the route opened, thousands of prospectors rode the narrow gauge rails into gold country. They departed from the two-and-a-half-story Skagway depot, which was clad in horizontal tongue-and-groove siding. When the building first opened it contained a ticket office, waiting room, and baggage room on the first floor with offices above. Within 10 years, it was enlarged and connected to the adjacent general office building. About 1970, the White Pass & Yukon Route vacated its historic depot for a new building next door. (WP&Y discontinued freight service in 1982, but operates as a tourist railroad in the summer months.) The National Park Service acquired the old depot and office, which

it made into headquarters for the Klondike Gold Rush National Historical Park. Both structures wear early color schemes: dark red body with yellow trim for the depot; yellow body with dark green trim for the office. NR District. NHL District. [United States Department of the Interior. Visitors center.]

WASILLA

WASILLA DEPOT
Parks Highway and Knik Road
1917

The area around Wasilla had both mineral resources and arable land. The Alaska Engineering Commission established a townsite at the intersection of the Alaska Railroad and the wagon road from Knik to the Willow Creek gold mines. The single-story, wooden depot included living quarters for the agent's family. Originally bearing a cupola, it was designed in Bungalow style, with ribbons of windows letting in light. Today, the Lions Club subleases the depot from the city, whose officials rent it from the railroad. Restored during the 1976 Bicentennial, Wasilla is one of three historic stations left along the line. Access to the depot's interior can be arranged through the Lions Club. NR. [Alaska Railroad. Train stop/npa and meeting space.]

California

Despite being the freeway capital of the world, California has begun devoting attention to rail. Through a program administered by the state department of transportation, grant money is available for multimodal installations, including the station buildings themselves —both new and old. The historic ones are frequently Spanish Colonial Revival or Mission styles, popular with the railroads because they conveyed the image of "exotic California" to new arrivals. A fair number of mid-size communities retain two or more depots. Typically, at least one of them is a restaurant.

ALTURAS

ALTURAS DEPOT
3rd and East streets
1908

The three-foot-gauge Nevada-California-Oregon Railway went from Reno, Nev., into the remote northeastern corner of California. Alturas was briefly its northern terminus, and the depot was built just after the line's completion. Made of locally quarried stone, the story-and-a-half, Queen Anne station—with belcast roof, jerkinhead gables, fancy cresting, patterned shingles, and single eyebrow dormer— would have looked at home in New England. Both the end gables and the trackside cross gable had small round windows (two later replaced by rectangular versions). The station's original location was 12th and Oak streets, which was near the company's yards northwest of town, but inconvenient for the public. In 1915, the building was dismantled—with each stone numbered—and reconstructed eight blocks closer to downtown. In 1917, after selling off the southern portion of its line to Western Pacific, N-C-O relocated its headquarters from Reno to Alturas. The railroad built a Mission-style general office building (NR), which still stands at 619 North Main Street and is owned by the Elks Club. After passenger service ended in 1938, Southern Pacific (which bought N-C-O in the Twenties) used the depot for crew housing. A local club

Alturas depot c.1910–12 on its original site at 12th and Oak streets.

Early view of the AT&SF complex at Barstow. The hotel and restaurant are in the two-story section; the depot is on the left.

acquired it in 1962 for its meeting space. The group also rents out the depot for wedding ceremonies and community gatherings. Freight trains still use the tracks, changed in 1928 to standard gauge. NR. [Alturas Garden Club. Clubhouse and special events facility.]

BARSTOW

ATCHISON, TOPEKA & SANTA FE COMPLEX
685 North First Street
Francis W. Wilson
1911

Fire and natural disasters have plagued Barstow's Atchison, Topeka & Santa Fe facilities since 1887, when the first Harvey House burned to the ground. By 1909, two more had followed suit. The "Santa Fe" then launched a major upgrading program that included new passenger facilities, a power house, roundhouse, and oil and water stations. To protect its investment and prevent recurring floods, the railroad rechanneled the Mojave River. In 1910, the depot-hotel complex known as Casa del Desierto (House of the Desert) began its phoenixlike rise from the ashes with a new Harvey House of brick and reinforced concrete, designed by Santa Barbara architect Francis

W. Wilson. Blending Spanish and Moroccan elements, he produced a trio of structures connected by arcaded pergolas and spacious verandas. On the east end was the hotel and restaurant, distinguished by its meals and service—and famous for its ice cream. Made in the hotel's own plant, the frozen delicacy was not only peddled to train passengers on the platform, but also supplied to dining cars and other Harvey Houses in the region. The one-story, centrally located passenger depot contained men's and ladies' waiting rooms and baggage and express facilities. Both World Wars brought heavy traffic to the station. In 1943, the original dining room veranda was partly enclosed for throngs of armed forces. At the same time, the Harvey system's first-ever, self-service cafeteria provided round-the-clock food for AT&SF employees.

In 1962, the western portion of the complex—a three-level combination trainmen's dormitory and recreation hall—was demolished. Several of the pergolas and the courtyard were destroyed as well. About eight years later, all restaurant and hotel operations ceased. The upper floor of the Casa del Desierto was closed off; Santa Fe's construction offices took over the space below. A small building at the southwest end of the lawn—headquarters for the Santa Fe "bull" (special detective)—was razed in 1976. In the late Eighties, AT&SF made plans to demolish the hotel. It was rescued by the city's purchase of the land and the railroad's agreement to donate all remaining historic buildings. Restoration was well underway when an earthquake struck in June 1992. Four of the hotel's towers were damaged and much face brick loosened. A federally approved seismic retrofit was deemed necessary. Altogether, the Harvey House project was set back about three years. The depot remains in use, primarily as an intercity bus agency, although Amtrak passengers have access to the waiting room. Plans for the Harvey House include a restaurant, offices, and retail space. NR. [City of Barstow. Transportation center and future commercial facility.]

BERKELEY

SOUTHERN PACIFIC STATION
3rd Street near University Avenue
1913

Southern Pacific's Berkeley station replaced a wooden structure located at 3rd and Delaware streets. Designed in Mission style by an unidentified staff architect, the stucco-on-wood-frame building was originally landscaped with palms and aloes. An arcade formed a lengthy open-air waiting area. When Amtrak began operations in 1971, the company chose Oakland rather than Berkeley for its East Bay passenger station. Five years later, the SP station reopened as a Chinese restaurant. The owners enclosed the arcade with glass. They added interior paneling and light fixtures salvaged from the Alaska Commercial Building in San Francisco (1908; razed in 1975). The restaurant contains a photo exhibit on the contributions of Chinese immigrants to early California history, especially to the railroads. Berkeley's Atchison, Topeka & Santa Fe station (1904), located 12 blocks east on University Avenue, was designed in Mission

Pretending to "row" a baggage wagon, the University of California crew at the Berkeley SP station, 1949.

style, but with somewhat more unusual Moorish detailing. Also a restaurant, it has been substantially altered. [Privately owned. Restaurant.]

BURLINGAME

SOUTHERN PACIFIC STATION
Burlingame Avenue and California Drive
J. B. Mathisen and George H. Howard, Jr.
1894

In the early 1890s, members of the just opened Burlingame Country Club were not satisfied with the small depot-shelter at Oak Grove. They appealed to the Southern Pacific to build a new station. Persuasion was not difficult; some of the club members were officials of the railroad. The agreement stated that the club would be responsible for the station design and any costs over those of an "ordinary depot." Two local families donated the land. Two club members—architects Mathisen and Howard—volunteered their services. Their design was likely inspired by fellow member A. Page Brown, who had drawn national attention to the Mission style by his work at the World's

Early view of the Burlingame SP station, before the arcade was extended.

Columbian Exposition in Chicago. Burlingame is one of the first times this style was used for a railroad station. Balloon frame walls were clad in diagonal redwood siding, then covered with galvanized chicken wire and textured stucco to simulate adobe. Handmade roof tiles were salvaged materials from two authentic, but decaying missions. The depot's southeast end held the agent's living quarters. The baggage area, at the opposite end, received an additional arcaded platform in 1909. To reach the station, which stood in the midst of an open field, carriages and early automobiles traveled what is now Burlingame Avenue, bordered with eucalyptus and cypress trees. In 1983, local citizens formed the Save Our Station organization to rescue the deteriorating depot, by then a stop on the CalTrain commuter line. Private contributions and government funds were used for restoration. Burlingame is among several other splendid (and each different) small depots found on the former SP line between San Francisco and San Jose. NR. [State of California. Train stop and chamber of commerce.]

CALISTOGA

SOUTHERN PACIFIC DEPOT
1458 Lincoln Avenue and Fairway
1868

Calistoga was the northern terminus of the Napa Valley Railroad (eventually Southern Pacific). Three principal buildings stood by the

Special excursion train stopping at the Calistoga depot, June 1947.

railroad tracks: the depot, a distillery, and a winery. Besides exporting agricultural products, Calistoga imported tourists, who took advantage of the skating rink, race track, and mud and sulfur baths, all of which were attractions promoted by a local real estate developer and officer of the railroad. The story-and-a-half depot was clad in shiplap siding. The interior consisted of a waiting room, agent's office, and freight area. A produce shed and platform were located south of the main building. Regular passenger service ended in 1929, although excursion trains and freight service continued for several decades. In the mid-1970s, a private party purchased the depot from the Southern Pacific and rehabilitated it to house a restaurant, shops, and chamber of commerce. Antique rail cars on a short stretch of go-nowhere track contain additional retail space. The parking lot was once a livestock pen; a turntable and enginehouse stood nearby. NR. [Privately owned. Commercial.]

CARLSBAD

CARLSBAD DEPOT
Carlsbad Village Drive west of State Street
1887

Carlsbad was originally called Frazier's Station, named for a sea captain who settled in the area. Frazier decided the well water on his property had curative powers over his chronic rheumatism. He offered his water to railroad passengers traveling between Los Angeles and San Diego from a water barrel near the depot, over which was posted the sign, Alight, Drink, and Be Happy. One happy person was a German-born midwesterner, who settled in the area and bought Frazier's land. After having the mineral water chemically analyzed, he determined that it matched the product of Well No. 9 at a famous spa in Karlsbad, Bohemia. An eight-page, nationally circulated brochure produced an influx of tourists. Frazier's Station got a new

name, a new depot, and a new hotel. For a period of time (1907–24), the Atchison, Topeka & Santa Fe called the station stop "Carl" to avoid confusion with Carlsbad, N.Mex. The wooden, combination freight and passenger depot, with its flared roof, Stick Style ornamentation, and fancy roof cresting was similar to a number of other AT&SF stations all built in 1887, including Encinitas (extant, but relocated), Escondido (extant), and San Marcos (razed in 1953). After "Santa Fe" vacated the Carlsbad depot in 1960, the building served as the chamber of commerce for a number of years. Restored in the late 1980s by the city, the station now sports authentic AT&SF colors of mustard with dark green trim. Passenger and freight trains use the tracks. NR. [City of Carlsbad. Convention and visitors center.]

CLAREMONT

ATCHISON, TOPEKA & SANTA FE STATION
1st Street between Yale and Harvard avenues
1927

Claremont's first Atchison, Topeka & Santa Fe station (1887) was a fairly substantial wooden structure just west of the current depot. Pomona College was established the same year. By the 1920s, because more colleges had been built and the citrus industry was booming, AT&SF was motivated to update facilities. Its staff architect (presumably William H. Mohr) produced a basic Spanish Colonial Revival design—with the usual stucco walls and red tile roof—made outstanding by elaborate surface details cast in concrete. The two-story, balconied center section contained the waiting room. Passengers entered through double doors that had the "Santa Fe" herald worked into the panels. Windows were protected by skillfully turned wooden bars. The one-story west wing was an open-air waiting room, entered through Moorish arches. The east wing held the ticket office and baggage and freight rooms.

Claremont AT&SF station when its brick platform was intact. The railroad's herald, a cross within a circle, is part of the door design.

In the late 1960s, AT&SF closed the building and removed the herringbone-pattern brick platform. Vandals set to work spray painting the exterior and setting a fire in the baggage room. In 1989, after two private developers failed to carry out plans for the depot, the city purchased it. Restored with funds from the state department of transportation, the station was rededicated in 1992 as a stop on the Metrolink commuter line. The stencils on the beamed ceiling were repainted; and from the few remaining tiles in the waiting room, a local ceramic artist was able to make duplicates. A restaurant for the west end is in the planning stages. Claremont's 1917 Pacific Electric (later Southern Pacific) station was demolished in 1968. NR. [City of Claremont. Train stop and future restaurant.]

GLENDALE

SOUTHERN PACIFIC STATION
400 West Cerritos Avenue (at Railroad Street)
MacDonald and Couchot
1924

In the 1880s, when Southern Pacific needed land for a station, a local man donated a piece of his huge ranch, reportedly on the condition that he could flag down any train for his friends returning to Los Angeles. The first depot was wooden, and the stop was called Tropico (the towns of Tropico and Glendale consolidated in 1918). In the 1920s, SP built a new depot in order to expand operations at this strategic location. Important trains that had heretofore merely passed through Glendale now made it a scheduled stop, thus eliminating the need for suburbanites to use the downtown Los Angeles station. Celebrities were often photographed boarding trains at Glendale, a convenient station for travel to Burbank and Hollywood. The San Francisco partnership of Kenneth MacDonald, Jr., (architect) and Maurice Couchot (structural engineer) gave the Spanish Colonial Revival depot elaborate baroque entrances, massive carved doors studded with hammered brass nails, and extensive ironwork. Walls were reinforced concrete, plastered inside to look like old adobe. At the south end, an open-air waiting room (enclosed later for a lunch room) received a lattice-work covering of redwood girders and cedar logs. Open space

Baroque trackside entrance to the Glendale station, October 1994.

and eucalyptus trees surrounded the building. The depot was modified and expanded in the Forties and Fifties.

When Amtrak took over passenger service from SP in 1971, the station had fallen on dreary times. Between train arrivals, the Amtrak agent began to spruce up the depot. With help from volunteers over the next 15 years, he put the ticket office back in its original position, repaired cracked plaster, painted, landscaped, and even found appropriate light fixtures and furniture salvaged from other stations. To his delight, in 1989, the city purchased the depot from SP. As a transportation hub, it now serves Amtrak long-distance trains, Metrolink commuter trains, and two bus lines. The city plans additional uses for the station, such as a possible restaurant for the baggage and freight area. The Glendale station has been used as a location in numerous motion pictures, in particular the 1944 version of *Double Indemnity*. [City of Glendale. Transportation center.]

GOLETA

GOLETA DEPOT
300 North Los Carneros Road
1901

About 1900, the railroad track through the Goleta Valley was shifted north. A new station

site was needed, and the Kellogg family— owners of a walnut packing house, creamery, and agricultural land—donated the ground. Southern Pacific put up Standard Plan No. 22, a 3,000-square-foot wooden building that housed a waiting room, agent's office, and baggage and freight rooms. SP built dozens of these depots, but few remain. The agent's bay contained a special window, likely used for handing out train orders to engineers and conductors. A two-bedroom upstairs apartment provided living quarters for the agent's family. The depot's redwood siding was painted "SP colonial yellow;" trim was brown and the window sash white. Redwood gutters accented the cedar-shingle roof, pierced by brick chimneys (destroyed, possibly in a 1925 earthquake). Famous "name trains" rushed passed the depot, which was serviced only by slower-moving "locals."

Passenger service ended in the 1960s; freight, a decade later. A clause in the deed stated that if the railroad agency ever closed, the land reverted to the Kelloggs. An eight-year legal battle ensued between the family and SP, during which time the boarded-up depot was heavily vandalized. Interior redwood paneling was ripped from the walls and set afire to keep the resident vagrants warm. In 1981, with legal issues concerning the land still unresolved, the community was informed that the only option for saving the building was to

Goleta depot c. 1955 on its in-service site, west of Kellogg Avenue, south of the tracks.

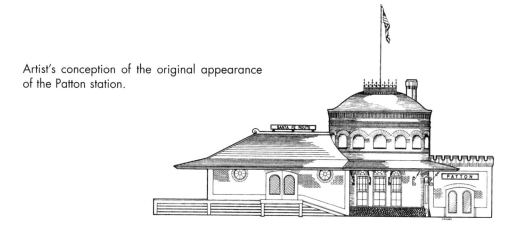

Artist's conception of the original appearance of the Patton station.

move it. Sawed in half and hauled three miles to a park, the station was restored largely with private donations of money, materials, and skilled labor — boosted by government and foundation grants. Appropriate railroad artifacts and memorabilia, including signal equipment and the original GOLETA signs, made their way home again. Three hundred feet of standard gauge track were installed to provide a measure of context. [Institute for American Research. Railroad museum.]

HIGHLAND

PATTON STATION
Highland Avenue and Victoria Street
Benjamin Franklin Levet
1898

The Patton stop was originally known as Asylum. A state mental hospital stood nearby, its buildings begun in 1890, but mostly destroyed in a 1933 earthquake and later demolished. The name of the station was changed to Patton, honoring the hospital commissioner, when a brick combination freight and passenger depot replaced the previous wooden one. The design is credited to Benjamin Levet, the Atchison, Topeka & Santa Fe civil engineer responsible for the extraordi-

nary La Grande Station (an 1893 predecessor of Los Angeles Union Passenger Terminal), of which Patton was an odd, diminutive version. Patton also resembled the asylum buildings, all set in an isolated rural setting. In 1938 the station operations shut down; the tracks were totally removed by 1980. The breezeway was enclosed years ago and the depot's bricks were coated with green paint, which has since been removed, unfortunately by sandblasting. Today's tenants, owners of a farmers market and gift shop, found the blueprints inside the depot, which show that the floor plan of the core building is essentially intact. [Privately owned. Commercial.]

KELSO

KELSO DEPOT
Kelbaker Road
c. 1924

Located in the heart of the East Mojave Desert, the Kelso depot was rescued in 1992 when the federal government purchased it. For the preceding seven years, the Kelso Depot Fund (based in Barstow) provided the support that kept bulldozers and vandals at bay. In the days of steam locomotives, trains stopped at Kelso to take on water from its deep wells. A roundhouse serviced the helper engines that pushed trains up the steep grade to Cima. The commodious Spanish Colonial Revival depot was primarily a trainmen's hotel—providing meals and accommodations for Union Pacific crews—and secondarily a freight and passenger station. Its large basement rooms were available to the community for square dances and church services. At various times the space even held a school and a courtroom. The lush grounds, irrigated to produce grass and trees, for years provided a major flyway stop for birds from Mexico. Currently, the Bureau of Land Management is stabilizing the depot, which will become a visitors center and museum. The tracks remain active. A stylistically similar depot stands at Caliente, Nev. [United States Department of the Interior. Vacant.]

KENWOOD

KENWOOD DEPOT
314 Warm Springs Road
c. 1888

Originally called South Los Guilicos, the depot at Kenwood was constructed of locally quarried,

pink and gray basalt—the same stone shipped to San Francisco for paving. Richardsonian Romanesque elements appeared in the rounded arches of the door and window openings, the rounded agent's bay, and an eyebrow dormer above the porte-cochere. A stone chimney vented the brick waiting room fireplace. The depot was built to accommodate trains on both the east and west sides, but tracks to the west side never materialized.

In 1936, Kenwood's Grange Hall was destroyed by flames. Four years later, at the behest of a women's club, the Kenwood Improvement Club used the $1,000 fire insurance payment to buy Kenwood's abandoned railroad depot from the Southern Pacific (controller of Northwestern Pacific) and make repairs. At some point, a kitchen and rest rooms were added to the west side of the building (through two of the arched doorways) and the baggage room partition was repositioned. During World War II, the depot was put in service as a first aid station, complete with cots and medical supplies, in case an air raid occurred. Today a successor to the Improvement Club runs the depot. Funds for maintenance come from dues, fund-raisers, and rental fees. The tracks have been gone since 1941. A wooden

Kenwood depot c.1910s. The bit of roof visible on the far right belonged to a store (now gone) owned by the station agent.

Los Angeles Union Passenger Terminal.

Alameda Street entrance, 1944

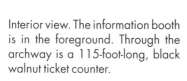

Interior view. The information booth is in the foreground. Through the archway is a 115-foot-long, black walnut ticket counter.

freight depot exists across the road to the north, opposite the site where a water tank stood. Kenwood's passenger depot bears a stylistic resemblance to the one at San Carlos. [Kenwood Community Club. Special events facility.]

LOS ANGELES UNION PASSENGER TERMINAL

800 Alameda Street
1939

Construction of a union station for Los Angeles was decades in the planning—delayed repeatedly by conflicts over its location, real estate costs, and unfulfilled plans for a network of ele-

vated tracks. After scorning the results of a voter referendum, the railroads appealed the mandates of various regulatory bodies until finally forced—by a United States Supreme Court decision—to comply with the site first selected, adjacent to the city's original Spanish Plaza. Construction and operating costs were shared (unevenly) by the Southern Pacific; the Atchison, Topeka & Santa Fe; and the Union Pacific. A committee of architects from the three railroads (with John and Donald Parkinson of Los Angeles as consultants) came up with a design that both expressed the city's Spanish heritage in its overall style and conveyed modernity through its layout and Art Deco details.

Travelers not arriving by the two streetcar lines found plenty of parking spaces for their automobiles, either in a parking lot out front or the underground garage. They entered the station, made of steel clad in reinforced concrete, through a 50-foot-high arch, inset with colored mosaic tiles, ornamental concrete, and patterned glass. An information booth was centered in the huge foyer, in turn flanked by the ticket concourse and an open-air arcade. Straight ahead, the waiting room featured carved wood and leather settees, mosaics, travertine, and marble. Acoustical tiles, on the upper walls and within the ceiling coffers, alleviated a chronic problem of cavernous rooms— the echo that made hearing train announcements difficult. Tall windows and 10-foot-diameter chandeliers provided illumination. On the north and south walls were bronze-framed doors, leading to landscaped patios (many original plantings exist today). Fred Harvey facilities included a restaurant, cocktail lounge, luncheonette, soda fountain, news and cigar stand, barber and retail shops—all decorated by the renowned Mary Colter. A utility annex, which contained a baggage room, the arrival and departure lobby, and Railway Express, stretched across the track side of the terminal. Another important part of the station complex was the giant United States Post Office Terminal (extant across Macy Street). A pedestrian tunnel took passengers under the tracks and then up ramps to the train platforms. Three days of celebration surrounded the station's opening. *Romance of the Rails*, a show portraying California's transportation history, played in a specially erected amphitheater along the tracks. Floats and 10 brass bands were part of a parade attended by a half-million people.

The depot's initial heyday was short-lived. After World War II, Los Angeles began expanding its airport operations. Union Station was especially hard hit by diminishing long-distance rail travel, because the terminal had no commuter trains to swell its activity level. Although train service was never discontinued, in the 1960s, the restaurant and other passen-

ger amenities shut down. Then in 1990, voters approved funding for a comprehensive commuter rail system to serve Southern California. Union Station—already experiencing an increase in the number of Amtrak arrivals—became a hub for Metrolink trains and a stop on both the new Red Line subway and a modern trolley system. The current owner, Catellus Development Corporation (a spin-off from AT&SF), plans to develop parts of the 75-acre site. The interior of the station retains its original features. NR. [Privately owned. Transportation center.]

MENLO PARK

MENLO PARK DEPOT
1100 Merrill Street
1867

As early as 1863, the Menlo Park Villa Association was advertising 800 acres of lots for sale, in tracts of not less than five acres. The trip from San Francisco—which was three hours by carriage—would be only 80 minutes by rail, once the line was built. Numerous wealthy families (like the Leland Stanfords) began moving into the area. In 1867, the San Francisco & San Jose (soon acquired by Southern Pacific) completed a small wooden depot, 22 by 41 feet, which housed the agent's office and gender-segregated waiting rooms. The town's first telephone exchange was installed at the depot in 1884. Sheathed in horizontal redwood siding, the simple cottagelike station received Stick Style and Shingle Style embellishments toward the end of the 19th century. Enlargements over the years included an open-air waiting shed (later partly enclosed), added to the north end to accommodate World War I troops from nearby Camp Fremont. After 1960, the chamber of commerce occupied the building, while commuter trains continued to stop outside. The California Department of Transportation purchased the station from SP in 1987. Rehabilitation included applying the depot's 1917 paint scheme—yellow, amber, brown, and white; but the public expressed displeasure at the results, and the colors were covered over. A c. 1917 baggage and express building (now home to a model railroad club) has been relocated north of its original position to allow more commuter parking spaces. NR. [State of California. Train stop and chamber of commerce.]

OAKLAND

SOUTHERN PACIFIC 16TH STREET STATION
16th and Wood streets
Jarvis Hunt
1912

After the 1906 San Francisco Earthquake, the Southern Pacific undertook a massive program of improvements (including changing SP's suburban lines from steam to electric). At the preceding 16th Street Station (an 1870s two-story wooden structure), main line trains often caused delays for commuters when they blocked the path of local trains. SP solved this problem by elevating the suburban tracks from 11th to 28th Streets (about a half-mile to either side of the station). Two days after the new station opened,

the chamber of commerce staged a 500-vehicle automobile parade through downtown, followed by a Saturday evening reception at the depot. Designed by a noted Chicago architect, the building was Beaux Arts style, a clear departure from SP's more usual regionalism.

Cladding at the base of the exterior walls was a polished, silvery-gray granite; upper walls were specially cast, granite-patterned brick and terra-cotta. Red mission tiles covered the roof behind a classical parapet. Suspended from chains, a huge metal marquee protected the main entrance. Finishes for the three-story-high waiting room included California marble and polychromed molded plaster. The room was illuminated by high arched windows and by fishscale-patterned electrified globes, hung from rosettes in a coffered ceiling. Large color photographs of California scenes (Mount Shasta and Lake Tahoe) were added to the the north and south walls in 1929, to accompany an ornate clock and a large SP herald. The west side of the room opened onto the main line platforms; stairs and elevators rose to meet the elevated tracks for suburban trains. After local service ended in 1941, the upper level platforms were closed and the trestles dismantled.

Although very deteriorated from years of deferred maintenance, the station continued to

Oakland SP station, Wood Street side. The loop track was used for electric trains to uptown Oakland. On the other side of the building were grade-level, main line tracks for steam trains and elevated tracks for electric suburban trains.

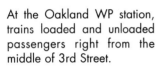

At the Oakland WP station, trains loaded and unloaded passengers right from the middle of 3rd Street.

serve SP long-distance trains (Amtrak after 1971), until the Loma Prieta Earthquake shook the building in 1989. Closed since then and not weather tight, the station suffers ongoing water damage to its numerous original features. In the early Nineties, the city applied for ISTEA funds to study reuse of the building. Because a new freeway alignment—a result of the earthquake collapse of Interstate 880—will give better automobile access to the station, SP is now considering development of its 20-acre site. In 1994, Amtrak relocated from its temporary shelter to a new multimodal facility next to Jack London Square (a move that was planned prior to the earthquake). The tracks at the SP station are scheduled to be eliminated; and the 16th Street interlocking tower, just north of the station, will go out of service. Four SP shop buildings are in the path of the new freeway, three will be moved to a railroad museum in Rio Vista Junction. [Southern Pacific Lines. Vacant.]

WESTERN PACIFIC STATION

3rd and Washington streets
William H. Mohr
1910

Western Pacific was the third transcontinental connection for Oakland; its depot was completed ten months after the last spike was driven. A huge triumphal arch across the tracks,

just east of the station, was part of the enthusiastic celebration on opening day. WP had successfully broken Southern Pacific's more than 40-year monopoly of the waterfront, and city officials (who regained control of valuable development along the shore line) were grateful. Designed by William H. Mohr (presumably a WP staff architect), the tall one-story depot formed an E shape—a center pavilion flanked by somewhat lower, stepped-back inner and outer wings. The waiting room had a high, coffered ceiling and glazed tile wainscoting. According to a 1909 floor plan, an express room in the west wing and a baggage room in the east wing had no interior connections to the waiting room; access was from the front arcade. WP trains came right down the middle of 3rd Street, and passengers boarded in trolley car fashion—from the street. Tickets were purchased through the ornately grilled windows of a polygonal, outside ticket booth (similar to that of a movie theater).

When Oakland's 159th Division returned from World War I, the soldiers were greeted at the Western Pacific station by a large crowd, including actress Mary Pickford in a colonel's uniform. In 1949, WP inaugurated its *California Zephyr*, a luxurious, glass-domed train, with schedules designed to take advantage of the scenery. After the last *Zephyr* run in 1970, the station was sold to a private party. When the owners applied for a demolition permit four years later, the city planning director delayed the issuance—the first such action under a new landmarks preservation ordinance. Commercial tenants since then have ranged from offices to a disco. In 1991, the depot was made available to a nonprofit group, which is considering a mixture of uses, including office, retail, and performing arts facility. NR. [Privately owned. Vacant.]

PALO ALTO

UNIVERSITY AVENUE STATION
95 University Avenue
1941

Palo Alto's fourth successive depot was built in conjunction with a grade separation project (a highway underpass beneath the tracks). The one-story, reinforced concrete building, clad in stucco, was pure Streamline Moderne. The style was a variation on Art Deco, inspired both by new streamlined locomotives and by optimistic visions set forth in science fiction. Southern Pacific's designer (presumably chief architect J. H. Christie) used these concepts, not only in the depot's composition and massing, but also in the curved corners and horizontal striping that expressed speed and power. Other Moderne elements included porthole windows, glass blocks, and hexagonal light fixtures of frosted glass and silver-toned metal. Above the ticket counter was a large John A. MacQuarrie mural; its central theme was Leland Stanford's dream of a university, interwoven with transportation and historical elements. Only one major change to the depot occurred over the years. A colored ceiling border of superimposed chevrons outlines the long-gone lunch counter that operated from the northeast corner of the waiting room. In 1982, the local transit district built a bus transfer island between the depot and the Hostess House (NR), a 1918 structure relocated from nearby Camp Fremont after World War I. Workers also landscaped the site and repaired the depot, which serves both commuters and Stanford University students. [Stanford University. Train stop.]

PERRIS

PERRIS DEPOT
State Route 74 and D Street
Benjamin Franklin Levet
1892

In 1885, a subsidiary of the Atchison, Topeka & Santa Fe ran into a dispute with land owners near its temporary boxcar station at Pinacate.

Opening day festivities at the Perris depot, 1892.

The railroad decided to move its stop about a mile north, to a site local developers named in honor of the Santa Fe's vice-president and chief civil engineer Frederick Perris. But the young town soon lost its main line status, when a new through line bypassed the station. The citizenry, nonetheless, lobbied for a replacement to the wooden warehouse then serving as a depot (extant today, but relocated). The new station was designed by Perris's son-in-law and financed by a local businessman, who traded it to the railroad in exchange for property along Main Street. A one-story brick building, it had a high cross-gabled center section, with long wings running parallel to the tracks. A false observation tower surmounted the trackside semicircular bay. Queen Anne–style small panes of colored glass adorned the upper window sash. Travelers came and went through round brick archways that rested on short Romanesque columns, while seasonal farm products (including Perris's famous potatoes) were loaded from the raised freight platform. Passenger service (a single coach attached to a freight train) ended on this branch line in the early 1950s. In 1971, AT&SF donated the station to an outdoor railroad museum located nearby. The depot houses displays belonging to yet another group, the Perris Valley Historical and Museum Association. An occasional freight or tourist train uses the track. NR. [Orange Empire Railway Museum, Inc. Local history museum.]

RIVERSIDE

ATCHISON, TOPEKA & SANTA FE STATION
Santa Fe Avenue between University Avenue and 7th Street
1927

In the 1920s, the Atchison, Topeka & Santa Fe decided to replace the 1886 wooden depot that stood alongside the canal in Riverside. The new depot's exterior image was essentially Pueblo, a southwestern style resembling Indian dwellings of New Mexico and Arizona. Inside, the look was more typical of the day—Spanish Colonial Revival. Suspended from the waiting room's wood-beamed ceiling were ornate wrought-iron chandeliers. The floor was red brick. In 1927, the city, AT&SF, and Union Pacific agreed to establish a park between Riverside's two depots, on the former homesite of the community's founder. The park served as an outdoor waiting area for both stations, which were further interconnected by vine-covered pergolas made of reinforced concrete to simulate what would normally be logs. Passenger service ended in 1968. After many years of vacancy, the depot is undergoing plans for conversion to commercial use. Both AT&SF and UP trains travel the tracks. [Privately owned. Vacant.]

SAN PEDRO, LOS ANGELES & SALT LAKE STATION
3751 Vine Street
1904

The San Pedro, Los Angeles & Salt Lake (later Union Pacific) followed the old Mormon Trail connecting Los Angeles to Salt Lake City. Built the same year the first train arrived, the Riverside depot was somewhat similar to other Mission-style stations along the line. Two stories high, with the obligatory stuccoed walls and red tile roof, the depot included four towers and a five-room agent's apartment with fireplaces and Oregon pine paneling. A large open-air waiting room on the north end was enclosed in 1943.

Passenger service ended in 1971. Three years later, UP vacated the depot. (It eventually abandoned the trackage as well; UP trains now go past Riverside's Atchison, Topeka & Santa Fe depot.) A serious fire broke out in 1982, followed by rebuilding and a proposed commercial adaptive use (unful-

Riverside SPLA&SL station c. 1930, then owned by the successor railroad, UP.

filled when the owner went bankrupt). The depot is now part of a 270-acre site — the Riverside Marketplace redevelopment project —that includes the former AT&SF station and several historic buildings related to citrus packing. The local redevelopment agency is negotiating to purchase the UP Depot. [Privately owned. Vacant.]

SACRAMENTO

SOUTHERN PACIFIC STATION
401 I Street
Bliss and Faville
1926

In 1863, the Central Pacific (predecessor to Southern Pacific) broke ground at Sacramento for its history-making transcontinental line. Vast rail yards were filled with every kind of building and equipment necessary for the fabrication of locomotives and rolling stock. Today the buildings are empty and the site has been declared a 244-acre toxic wasteland. The SP passenger station is trapped within the clean-up and redevelopment plans. Designed by a San Francisco architectural firm, whose partners met while working for McKim, Mead, and White in New York, the Renaissance Revival building succeeded at least two earlier SP stations. Its three-story-high, structural steel framework was faced with Italian sienna-colored brick, trimmed with

In this c. 1940s view of the Sacramento SP station, a photographer had his lights and camera set for a shot of the waiting room east wall. His subject was the mural by John A. MacQuarrie, which depicts Sacramento's pivotal role in railroad history.

terra-cotta. The waiting room had a 60-foot-high domed ceiling, marble floors, and Philippine mahogany woodwork. Sunlight streamed through 35-foot-high windows filled with leaded, amber-colored glass. On the east wall, a mural by San Francisco artist John A. MacQuarrie depicted the 1863 groundbreaking ceremony of the Central Pacific. The north wing contained a restaurant, reportedly modeled after the Palace Hotel cafe in San Francisco. Train dispatchers and general division offices were on the upper floors.

Ten long-distance and corridor trains (plus Amtrak buses) stop here per day. In the early 1990s, the state spent several thousand dollars reversing years of deferred maintenance to the building. Nonetheless, SP, with city officials' apparent support, plans to relocate the train tracks to an undeveloped area and build a new depot at that location (for SP's tenant, Amtrak). The old station, minus its train tracks, would be adapted to a nonrailroad use as part of a very long-range, toxic clean-up and commercial investment project. Opponents of this plan believe the railroad station—symbol of the industry that made Sacramento—is best preserved by maintaining its original function. The large Railway Express Agency building next to the depot is part of this conflict; a section of it has already been demolished for a new city-owned federal courthouse. Sacramento's other extant depot, built by the Western Pacific in 1909, is attributed to noted architect Willis Polk, who was the west coast liaison for Daniel Burnham. Now a restaurant, between J and K Streets, it remains adjacent to active tracks. NR. [Southern Pacific Lines. Train stop.]

SAN BERNARDINO

ATCHISON, TOPEKA & SANTA FE STATION
1170 West 3rd Street
William H. Mohr
1918

San Bernardino's first depot was a boxcar. It was replaced about 1887 by a large, two-and-a-half-story frame station that also housed division headquarters and an eating house. In 1916, a spectacular blaze destroyed this building, as well as other railroad property. Heat melted the huge iron doors of the depot's supposedly fireproof vault, and 30 years of records for the Atchison, Topeka & Santa Fe (Los Angeles Division) were destroyed. Two years later, a new reinforced concrete station was completed just west of the old depot. At the throttle of the first train was the same AT&SF engineer who had opened the preceding station, three decades earlier. Trains of the Los Angeles & Salt Lake (Union Pacific system) also used the new facility.

San Bernardino AT&SF station under construction, 1918.

The Mission-style building, designed by a company architect, had four domed towers anchoring the center portion. A 330-foot-long trackside arcade extended past the station's two-story, asymmetrical wings. Pale green trim and a red tile roof made a crisp statement against white stuccoed walls. Inside, extensive tiling in shades of brown, gray, and green were used in the wainscoting of three waiting rooms (general, ladies', and men's smoking), above quarry tile floors. Harvey House dining and lunch rooms were on the depot's east end (with living quarters above). This area was enlarged in 1921. Baggage and express were handled from the west end, with division headquarters on the second floor and the tower floor. The superintendent's suite had space for nearly 40 desks. The station's modern amenities included a tube system, by which telegrams could be distributed among the many offices (without need of a messenger boy) and a state-of-the-art telephone system for dispatching trains.

In the early 1990s, ownership of the depot was transferred to the local transportation authority. Eventually the San Bernardino Economic Development Agency will become a joint owner and begin the process of finding an adaptive use. Amtrak continues to occupy the waiting room. (Metrolink passengers wait on platforms, newly installed in the parking lot.) Across the tracks, the many remaining AT&SF buildings (locomotive shops, roundhouse, power plant, and administration building) are scheduled for demolition. [San Bernardino Association of Governments. Train stop and mostly vacant.]

SAN CARLOS

SAN CARLOS DEPOT
559 El Camino Real
1888

In the 1880s, the San Carlos Land Company promoted its new townsite by advertising its

The restored track side of the San Carlos depot, May 1987.

handy commuter access via the Southern Pacific. The company erected a depot as the first permanent building. Its Richardsonian Romanesque style bore noteworthy resemblance to the buildings under construction at Stanford University. (Speculation exists that Charles Coolidge of Boston, architect for the school, also designed the station.) At various times, the one-story depot also served as the community's first church, library, and post office. Its separate passenger and baggage buildings were joined by a covered breezeway. Both were built of large sandstone blocks from a quarry south of San Jose. The hipped, slate roof had sawn redwood ridge cresting and sheet metal finials. A round, trackside tower housed the ticket office on the first floor; the agent-operator slept in a tiny bedroom just above. Ladies did their waiting in a polygonal bay at the northwest end of the depot.

Exterior changes first occurred following the 1906 earthquake, with enclosure of the entrance porch. A few decades later, the streetside porte-cochere was removed. After railroad usage ceased in 1967, the depot served various commercial purposes, during which time most interior elements were removed, such as the ticket counter and light fixtures (the general waiting room fireplace remains). The state of California undertook an extensive restoration of the exterior (including paint colors) in the mid-1980s and rehabilitated the interior as a restaurant and a waiting space for commuters. Just a few years later, the stone chimneys were damaged by an earthquake. They were rebuilt using sandstone blocks salvaged from buildings at Stanford University. NR. [State of California. Train stop and restaurant.]

SAN DIEGO

ATCHISON, TOPEKA & SANTA FE DEPOT
Kettner Boulevard and Broadway
Bakewell and Brown
1915

San Diego's Atchison, Topeka & Santa Fe passenger station was built large enough to handle crowds coming to the Panama-California Exposition held in Balboa Park. The first train ticket was issued by the "Santa Fe" clerk who,

San Diego AT&SF depot in the 1940s, before demolition of the forecourt.

nearly 30 years earlier, performed the same act at the High Victorian style station next door. When the old depot was razed (the day after the new one opened), a crowd of 2,000 watched two Santa Fe locomotives, cabled to the tower, begin the demolition. The new building was also referred to as Union Depot, because San Diego & Arizona trains (later San Diego & Arizona Eastern) used it from 1916 until 1951.

Designed by noted San Francisco architects John R. Bakewell and Arthur Brown, Jr., in Mission style, the San Diego depot was constructed of steel, brick, and concrete, clad in stucco and roofed with red tile. A trolley loop swung past the Broadway side of the station. Most people entered through the large, handsome forecourt. Its gable-roofed arcades and open-air waiting area led to the depot's monumental single archway, flanked by twin, colorfully tiled Moorish towers. (The entire forecourt was demolished in 1954 for an automobile parking lot.) Centered on the south wall was a huge bifacial clock (visible outside and inside), replaced in 1949 by a Santa Fe medallion. The interior floor plan included a vestibule with marble-capped, Mexican onyx wainscoting; a general waiting room with a long series of rounded arches, a redwood ceiling, bronze chandeliers, back-to-back oak benches, and oak and polychrome tile wainscoting; men's smoking and ladies' waiting rooms; and a Fred Harvey restaurant (closed in the 1930s).

By the mid-1960s, passenger service was down to six trains a day. Proposing to build a huge apartment and office complex on the site, AT&SF sought a demolition permit. The railroad sold the depot's numerous interior clocks; a huge 1910 oil painting of the Grand Canyon went to a Denver restaurant. City council and the public resisted demolition; and in 1982, the railroad announced it would instead refurbish the depot and develop the adjoining 15 acres. Today the station's multimodal service incorporates Amtrak trains and Mexicoach Bus

San Jose SP depot, soon after opening in 1935.

Lines with the San Diego Trolley (light rail vehicles that began operating in 1981, mostly on the old San Diego & Arizona Eastern right-of-way). The office and research library of a local railroad museum are housed in the original ticket office and part of the former baggage and express building, connected to the depot's north end by a 650-foot-long trackside arcade. In 1990, the depot's ownership was transferred to Catellus Development Corporation, title holder to AT&SF real estate no longer used by the freight railroad. NR. [Privately owned. Multimodal facility.]

SAN JOSE

SOUTHERN PACIFIC DEPOT
65 Cahill Street
1935

San Jose's new Southern Pacific station was part of a grade separation and track realignment project that had been under consideration for 30 years. The objective was to get rail traffic off 4th Street. The project included replacing the 1872 Market Street Depot that stood about a mile northeast of the present building. An SP architect (probably J. H. Christie) produced a design that combined Italian Renaissance Revival massing with elements of Streamline Moderne. The exterior walls of structural steel were clad in tapestry brick of varied colors; the roof tiles were multihued terra-cotta. Three tall, rounded arches filled the three-story center section, which was flanked by two-story, symmetrical wings. On the street side, passengers entered beneath a cantilevered steel and concrete marquee.

Caen Stone, applied to the waiting room walls, surmounted the marble wainscoting. A floral pattern was stenciled onto the beams of the coffered ceiling. Within an arch at the north end of the room, a mural by noted San Francisco artist John A. MacQuarrie depicted the colonization of the Santa Clara Valley entwined with a view of modern San Jose. Ornamental plaster grilles flanked both the mural and a Moderne clock located on the south wall. The marble ticket counter included rippled glass, maple ticket files, and lights supported on tubular brass arches. Today, these features are essentially intact, as are the umbrella platform canopies outside. The station site is enhanced by the existence of utilitarian structures of the sort that rarely survive: a water tank, a board and batten switchman's shack, and a car cleaners' shack. In 1994, the state rehabilitated the station, which serves both long-distance and commuter trains. Eventually, a modern trolley service will also stop at the depot. About a block to the west stands a former Western Pacific depot, moved and enlarged in 1922. NR. [State of California. Train stop.]

SAN JUAN CAPISTRANO

SAN JUAN CAPISTRANO DEPOT
26701 Verdugo Street
1894

Within a block of the famous Mission San Juan Capistrano, the Atchison, Topeka & Santa Fe built a depot imitative of the decaying ecclesiastical structures. The design is attributed to the railroad's civil engineer Benjamin Levet. It was preceded by a wooden station, possibly in a different location. In the mid-1970s, the one-story-depot with a two-story bell tower became a restaurant. The seating and service areas were expanded by glassing in the station's arcade and by placing a series of old railroad cars beside the depot. The complex was linked together by a 10-foot-wide enclosed platform that extended beyond the old freight depot, now the restaurant's bar. Authentic features that were retained include wooden loading doors, a brick fireplace in the waiting room, and interior walls made of stone rubble from one of the mission's churches. Red roof tiles, originally plucked from the mission, were returned to their rightful owner, and replacement tiles were installed on the depot. The exterior walls suffered a different fate. Lime-plaster stucco, peeling from the depot's bricks, was removed by sandblasting. (The historically correct and less harmful process would have been restuccoing.)

In 1988, the city acquired the property. Two years later, it leased the depot to a new restaurant company, which undertook a seismic retrofit, asbestos removal, and overall rehabilitation. The lease requires the restaurant to keep the building unlocked during hours of train service and make restrooms accessible to Amtrak passengers. Amtrak is expected to open a ticket office in two of the antique box cars. Freight and Metrolink commuter trains also use the tracks. NR District. [City of San Juan Capistrano. Train stop and restaurant.]

SANTA CLARA

SANTA CLARA DEPOT
Railroad Avenue and Benton Street
1863, c. 1877

Both the local farming industry and Santa Clara College existed before the arrival of the San Francisco & San Jose (later Southern Pacific). The school invested financially in the line and also influenced the specific location of the depot. The initial structure was a 24-by-50-foot rectangle—one of the largest of the line's

A fenced garden faced the San Juan Capistrano depot in 1894.

Santa Clara depot c. 1912.

standard plans—sheathed in redwood board and batten siding. Windows and doors had slightly pedimented casings. About 1877, this passenger depot was moved across the tracks (probably for safety and convenience because the town lay on the west side of the rails) and tacked onto a freight shed. An agent's bay was added and the freight section lengthened. More than a century later, the state took over the line's commuter trains (now called CalTrain) and subsequently bought the depot. The South Bay Historical Railroad Society became tenants in the freight and baggage end. It traded painting and fix-up jobs for five years of free rent. The state obtained grant money for major work like a new roof. Santa Clara is reportedly the oldest continuously operating depot in California. NR. [State of California. Train stop and railroad museum.]

SANTA ROSA

NORTHWESTERN PACIFIC DEPOT
4th and Wilson streets
1904

In 1993, the city of Santa Rosa acquired the former Northwestern Pacific depot (Southern Pacific system), which had been built by a predecessor, the California Northwestern. The municipality's first step was to shovel out ankle deep piles of pigeon droppings and dead birds.

The next step was to apply for ISTEA funds. The money will be used to upgrade the mechanical systems and perform a seismic retrofit. In 1903, a wooden depot on the same site was destroyed by fire. Its story-and-a-half successor was the work of Northern Italian immigrants. These masons used the same locally quarried, basalt stone for the c. 1915 express building across the street, two nearby hotels, and the depot in Kenwood (all extant). After passenger service ended in the 1950s, the railroad remodeled the interior of the depot for administrative and engineering offices, which occupied the building until the early Eighties. Boarded up since then, it awaits new life, possibly as a combination multimodal and interpretative center. The original depot park, long maintained by the city, continues to separate the depot from the street. Southeast of the NWP station stands the former Petaluma & Santa Rosa interurban depot, extensively remodeled during a 1978 restaurant conversion. NR District. [City of Santa Rosa. Vacant.]

SONOMA

SONOMA DEPOT
270 1st Street West
1880, 1977

The Sonoma Valley Railroad (eventually Southern Pacific) was a narrow gauge line, three feet wide. After the San Francisco & North Pacific took over, it converted the line to standard gauge (in 1890) and moved the wooden depot from its Spain Street location. The railroad added a freight room and an attic apartment for the agent. After passenger service ended in the 1950s, the railroad used the depot for storage. Purchased by the city in 1975, it was placed in the National Register of Historic Places the same year. The following January, when refurbishing was nearly complete (a Bicentennial project), the station was gutted by a 4 a.m. fire, most likely arson. The city committed the fire insurance payout to a proposed rebuilding project—provided the community could raise matching funds in three months. A combination of county money and individual contributions met the goal. Then a severe windstorm blew down the depot's shell. Salvaging the pieces and armed with measured drawings (made by an architect in the early 1970s), the community went forward with rebuilding. The reconstructed waiting room and ticket office house a research library. Museum exhibits fill the freight end. The railroad right-of-way is now a bike trail, but a stretch of track (with three pieces of rolling stock) remains adjacent to the depot. Despite the 1976 destruction by fire and wind, the depot was never removed from the National Register. NR. [City of Sonoma. Local history and railroad museum.]

STOCKTON

ATCHISON, TOPEKA & SANTA FE STATION
735 South San Joaquin Street (at Taylor Street)
1900

In the late 1800s, Stockton was the northern terminus of the San Francisco & San Joaquin Valley Railroad, part of the Atchison, Topeka & Santa Fe system. Staff engineers designed the depot in a Mission style similar to the much larger station in Fresno (1899, NR). Entering through the streetside porte-cochere, passengers walked into a vestibule—the first floor of a three-story, square tower. Straight ahead was the ticket counter. To the left and right were the ladies' and men's waiting rooms, each with a fireplace and a window into the agent's office. The floor plan included baggage and express rooms and a large outdoor waiting room (enclosed in 1961) with back-to-back benches and a Fred Harvey newsstand. An arcade along the track side provided additional shelter. Red tiles capped the two-story station as well as the four rectangular pillars that punctuated the arcade. Original elevations show that a matching structure, described as a "tavern," was planned for the west side of the depot, but never built. About a mile northeast of the AT&SF station (in use today by Amtrak), two other depots remain, although neither is in good condition—Western Pacific and Southern Pacific. [Atchison, Topeka & Santa Fe Railway Company. Train stop.]

WILLITS

WILLITS DEPOT
East Commercial Street
Dan DeShiell
1916

The original depot at Willits was a fairly substantial frame building with a two-story bay window. In the early 1900s, Mendocino County residents felt this structure was too ordinary to impress the tourists who came to see the area's redwood trees. Officials of the Northwestern Pacific (originally a subsidiary of both Southern Pacific and Atchison, Topeka & Santa Fe) agreed. For three years, local lumber companies set aside specially selected, clear-grain redwood to use for the new station. The story-and-a-half depot was completed in 1915 and opened for business the following year. Designed by a local architect-builder in Arts and Crafts style, it was all-redwood construction. The gabled roof had deep overhangs, which on the track side formed a waiting porch, supported by eight squared, redwood columns. Carved trim ran the length of the roof, just under the eaves. A wide shed dormer let light into the attic space. Separate men's and ladies' waiting rooms were a significant improvement over the preceding single arrangement. A Willits newspaper reported that women and children had preferred waiting outside, even in bad weather, to being with "rough men."

The depot is still used today by the same lines or their successors. One, the California Western, continues to operate both passenger trains and its famous "Skunk" rail-motor cars on the serpentine, 40-mile Redwood Route from Fort Bragg to Willits. Two ancillary structures, both redwood, stand next to the depot: to the west, a former restaurant (neither of the original lines had dining cars) and to the east, a building possibly used for baggage. The building directly across the tracks belonged to the old Northwestern Redwood Lumber Company, whose owners were also directors of the railroad. The NWP enginehouse is gone. [Southern Pacific Lines. Train stop.]

Colorado

In Colorado, one solution to negotiating the mountainous terrain was development of narrow gauge railroads. The rails were closer together than the 4 foot, 8-1/2 inch standard gauge, and the trains they carried were similarly scaled down. Because curves could be sharper and tunnels smaller, railroad construction costs were substantially reduced. Many of the extant depots in the state shared not only in the story of these narrow gauge lines, which enabled mine towns to boom, but also in the saga of Colorado's more monumental battle—the physical struggle and corporate competition to reach beyond the Rocky Mountains.

ANTONITO

DENVER & RIO GRANDE DEPOT
U.S. Route 285
1880

As the Denver & Rio Grande built west toward Durango, work trains laden with ties and rails rode past the newly built Antonito depot. A two-story structure of lava rock quarried in Trinidad, Colo., it had a half-octagon waiting room on the north end and a baggage room on the south end (added in 1917). Decorative wooden brackets supported the roof's extended eaves. Other rail-related buildings included a wooden freight depot, stockyards, an ice house, enginehouse, water tank, coal dock, and section and bunkhouses. By 1951, all regular passenger service on the Denver & Rio Grande Western (a merger of the D&RG and the Rio Grande Western) had ended. The passenger depot then spent many years in freight service. For at least 20 of the most recent years, the community has approached the railroad (most

Antonito D&RG depot in 1885. The fourth adult from the right is the agent.

recently the Southern Pacific) about obtaining the station for a museum, but without success. [Southern Pacific Lines. Storage facility.]

COLORADO SPRINGS

ATCHISON, TOPEKA & SANTA FE STATION
555 East Pikes Peak Avenue
c. 1918

The Atchison, Topeka & Santa Fe station in Colorado Springs was preceded by an 1889 union depot made of stone. The present two-story brick building, in Jacobean Revival style, also served the Colorado & Southern. Passenger service ended in 1971, and the abandoned station soon suffered from vandalism and the ravages of two fires. During the late 1970s, a developer rehabilitated the depot, including the Harvey House dining room, for restaurant and office space. The project went to foreclosure. The current owner leased the Harvey House space to a church, for which the high arched ceiling and multicolored skylights made an appropriate setting. A large outdoor waiting area on the north end (now glassed in) and the balance of the square footage (with an inserted second floor) became offices. To the south, the separate freight house is vacant. New office

Colorado Springs AT&SF station c. 1920s.

Midland Terminal depot at Cripple Creek in 1949, shortly after abandonment. In the foreground is the road bed where the rails have just been removed.

buildings stand in the former track area. Colorado Springs's other depot, built in 1887, was used by the Denver & Rio Grande (also the Chicago, Rock Island & Pacific, and the Colorado Springs & Cripple Creek District Railway). Enlarged and converted to a restaurant and retail complex in the early 1970s, it still stands on Sierra Madre Street along active freight tracks. [Privately owned. Church and commercial.]

CRIPPLE CREEK

MIDLAND TERMINAL DEPOT
5th Street and Bennett Avenue
1894

In 1896, two disastrous fires, a few days apart, destroyed nearly every building in the gold mining town of Cripple Creek. The lone (but scorched) survivor was a railroad station, built of brick and reddish-brown sandstone by the Midland Terminal Railroad. Three stories high, it was set against a hillside. The lower level, with rugged, round-arched doorways, was possibly used for storing freight. (The separate freight station, located to the north, is now gone.) The middle story, at track level, contained both men's and ladies' waiting rooms. A cantilevered oak stairway led to the upper floor —originally offices, but later converted to an apartment for the agent. A two-story, round tower faced the tracks, balanced on the west facade by a three-story square pavilion.

The standard gauge MTRR ceased operations in 1949. A few years later, two local investors (who coincidentally were founders of the American Ballet Company) bought the depot and established a nonprofit organization to oversee its future. The museum that opened in 1953 houses artifacts from Teller County and the Cripple Creek Mining District. Stations for several railroads once served Cripple Creek, but the Midland Terminal depot is the only one extant and on its original site. A wooden station next door—departure point for the Cripple Creek Narrow Gauge Railroad tourist line—has been relocated twice, first from Anaconda to Bull Hill and more recently, to Cripple Creek. [Cripple Creek District Museum. Local history museum.]

DENVER

MOFFAT STATION
15th and Bassett streets
Edwin Moorman
c. 1905

David Moffat, originally from New York State, was very important to Denver's development. He started the first bank and the first electric company. He was also a director of the Denver

The Welcome Arch (now gone) made an elegant entrance to Denver Union Station. The arch had been erected in 1906, in front of the 1894 central portion of the depot. It remained standing after the new central portion was completed in 1915, but was junked by the city in 1931.

& Rio Grande (later Denver & Rio Grande Western)—a line that shared in the ownership of the city's Union Station. But Moffat was also building his own railroad, the Denver, Northwestern & Pacific, begun in 1903. The occupants of Union Station (with Edward Harriman as the ringleader) denied access to Moffat's line, and he was forced to build his own small terminal several blocks to the west. Designed by a Denver architect, the square, one-story depot was constructed of red brick trimmed boldly in terra-cotta, with unusual banded globes above the parapet. Its three neoclassical facades were virtually identical. A freight warehouse and loading dock extended from the rear. By the 1940s, long after Moffat's death, his line became part of D&RGW; and train service was switched from Moffat's namesake depot to Union Station—the very building from which his trains had been banned. Used for awhile as railroad offices, Moffat Station has been essentially vacant for decades. In 1995, arson destroyed the entire freight extension and seriously damaged the front portion of the building. Coincidentally, an automobile viaduct, which obscured the station, had recently been removed. [Privately owned. Vacant.]

UNION STATION
17th and Wynkoop streets
1881, 1915

By the 1870s, there were at least four railroad stations in Denver. To transfer from one line to another, passengers and freight had to move along dusty and muddy roadways. Union Station brought them under one roof, owned by a terminal company in which Union Pacific held the majority interest. Within a decade virtually every railroad (except David Moffat's line) availed themselves of the facility. Outside the door, a web of tracks, stretching nearly to the Platte River, accommodated both narrow gauge (primarily mountain-bound) and standard gauge trains. The initial Union Station was two-and-a-half stories of rough-hewn, pinkish-gray lava stone, trimmed with pink sandstone and topped by a Victorian Gothic clock tower. Plans called for finishing the various gaslit railroad offices with black and French walnut. Two wings added in 1892 brought the station's length to 880 feet. Two years later, a fire destroyed the center portion housing passenger services. This section was rebuilt in nonharmonizing red sandstone, with a tower 40 feet taller than the one before. In 1914, the old terminal company was disbanded and reorganized by a new group of six railroads (equal owners) that demolished the 1894 center section and built the Beaux Arts version standing today. Made of Colorado granite on a steel frame, it is flanked by the original 1881 wings (1892 additions are gone).

The station has since received numerous expansions and alterations. The most recent occurred in the 1990s. Installation of a new high-speed bus lane required changes to the 1916 pedestrian tunnel and to the platform canopies. At the same time, lean-tos were removed that had obstructed the building's facade. Amtrak continues to use the station's three-story waiting room (minus its ornate chandeliers and bench-back candelabras) and a newly renovated wing, but much of the building is vacant. For years, city planners tried (fortunately with no success) to get Amtrak relocated to the outskirts of town. The tides appear to have turned—the city is now studying Union Station as a potential multimodal center. With a new baseball stadium just two blocks away (on part of the old Union Pacific yard) and the historic Oxford Hotel revived, Union Station's neighborhood is back to life. NR. [Denver Union Terminal Corporation. Train stop and offices.]

DURANGO

DURANGO DEPOT
South end of Main Avenue
1881

The Silverton Branch of the Denver & Rio Grande was once part of an extensive network of three-foot-gauge railroads built to service the region's silver mines (hauling both workers and ore). In the mid-20th century, the system (some of which had been converted to standard gauge) began unraveling, until only two sections remained. Both are now tourist lines: the Cumbres & Toltec (owned by Colorado and New Mexico) and the privately owned portion called Durango & Silverton, which operates coal-fired steam trains (freight as well) through Colorado's San Juan Mountains. The Durango depot is essentially a long one-story building, broken in the center by a two-story cross gable. The upper portion was occupied at one time by the Rio Grande Southern. Covered in clapboards, the station has simple pedimented window frames. The windows originally extended nearly to the floor, but most were shortened during the 1930s. The interior has been reconfigured for offices, rest rooms, and a gift shop. The current single waiting room was once

Durango depot. This early view shows the first-floor windows when they extended nearly to the floor and the breezeway, which is now enclosed for the D&S gift shop.

divided into separate spaces for men and women. NR District. [Durango & Silverton Narrow Gauge Railroad. Tourist train stop and railroad headquarters.]

GLENWOOD SPRINGS

DENVER & RIO GRANDE STATION

7th Street between Cooper and Blake avenues
c. 1905

The first Denver & Rio Grande passenger depot (1886) at Glenwood Springs was originally a construction office for the railroad. After about 20 years, D&RG built a new depot five blocks to the east on land donated by the city. The local newspaper concurred that its community was too important a place for "the rickety old affair which has been called a depot." The second one's material and style were similar to the Hot Springs Lodge (extant, directly across the Colorado River)—both made of Frying Pan River red sandstone. Because the depot and tracks were set against the Colorado River bank, the streetside entrance was on a level

above the waiting rooms. A jerkinhead cross gable formed the center portion of the building, flanked by medieval brick towers with flared, pyramidal roofs. Passengers descended an interior brass-railed stairway to wait for their trains on long oak benches, which remain in place today. In 1990, Amtrak (the depot's tenant) preserved the original roofing material by removing and relaying all the reddish-brown tiles. A Colorado Midland depot once stood two blocks to the west. [Southern Pacific Lines. Train stop.]

GRAND JUNCTION

DENVER & RIO GRANDE STATION

Pitkin Avenue and First Street
Henry J. Schlacks
1906

Grand Junction's first depot, a log structure, was replaced in 1884 with a Queen Anne–style wooden station. In less than two decades, the Denver & Rio Grande built a larger, buff brick building, just to the south that was used by the

Street side of the Glenwood Springs D&RG station. The entrance led to the upper floor.

Grand Junction D&RG station, 1910.

Colorado Midland and two smaller lines, as well. Designed by a Chicago architect in a French Renaissance style, the station's exterior was finely ornamented with terra-cotta foliated designs and floral patterns. The agent's office was in a one-story square pavilion projecting from the station's track side. A glass-roofed canopy, suspended from chains, partially sheltered the brick platform. Inside, the principal space was a large, oval-shaped waiting room with a fireplace. The ladies' retiring and men's smoking rooms formed the streetside corners of the station. From the vestibule, an ornate, oak stairway (since removed) led to mezzanine offices. Sometime in the 1920s, the railroad installed a true second floor, in the process removing the stained glass of the arched waiting room windows and covering over the ceiling's ornate plasterwork.

In 1992, citing a leaking roof in the depot, Amtrak moved into a commercial building next door. Southern Pacific (which bought D&RGW) sold the building two years later to the son of Amtrak's current landlord. Through a combination of funds from the National Trust for Historic Preservation, the Colorado Historical Society, and ISTEA, the owner was able to put on a new red tile roof (with materials obtained from the original manufacturer) and commission a feasibility study. Volunteers helped with preliminary interior work. The plans for the depot involve restoring the waiting room and mezzanine (for conversion into a restaurant and a railroad museum), but apparently do not include space for Amtrak. A diaper service occupies the one-story baggage and express wing. NR. [Privately owned. Train stop/npa and commercial.]

GREELEY

Union Pacific Station
7th Avenue between 8th and 10th streets
Gilbert Stanley Underwood
1930

In 1991, Amtrak reinstated its *Pioneer* route from Seattle to Chicago. Closed since passenger service was discontinued in 1983, Greeley's former Union Pacific station had a grand rededication ceremony to celebrate its return to operations. Trains first arrived in Greeley in 1869, via the Denver Pacific, a UP predecessor. The first three successive depots included a boxcar, a hotel, and a frame or log depot. The present station (also used by the Colorado & Southern) replaced a stone one just to the south built in 1883. Designed in Collegiate Gothic style by a nationally prominent architect, the one-story brick depot had four pedimented entrances surrounded by terra-cotta blocks. Each round arch above the doors was filled with an oculus, inset with a UP shield. A low platform of brick pavers surrounded the building. A separate brick freight depot was built across the tracks. Inside the passenger depot, motifs of folk-Germanic influence (foxes, birds, stars, and quatrefoils) were stenciled onto window and door surrounds, the ticket counter area, oak benches, and the exposed kingpost truss system. Today, except for a few changes to interior partitions and removal of baggage and express room doors, the depot is essentially intact. NR. [City of Greeley. Transportation center.]

LEADVILLE

UNION PACIFIC STATION
7th and Hazel streets
1893

In the mining town of Leadville, there were once three stations serving passengers. The Colorado Midland burned in 1936; the Denver & Rio Grande was demolished in the 1960s. The remaining depot (built by a Colorado railroad controlled by the Union Pacific) saw its last passenger train in 1937, after which it was used solely as a freight station. In 1988, a tourist railroad purchased all that remained of the line,

a 14-mile stretch from Leadville to Climax. To regain access to the granite-trimmed, red brick depot (which it bought from the city), the railroad laid approximately 300 yards of missing track. Restoration of the depot (guided by the original blueprints) included the wood-shingle roof, window sash, moldings, and Texas pine wainscoting. The project was honored by two statewide merit awards. The railroad also owns an active roundhouse (a half-mile north on Sawmill Road), built in 1883. Converted to three standard gauge stalls in 1940, it originally had six places for narrow gauge locomotives. NR District. [Leadville, Colorado & Southern Railroad. Tourist train stop.]

LOVELAND

COLORADO & SOUTHERN STATION
Railroad Avenue between 4th and 5th avenues
Charles B. Martin
1902

Loveland's first station consisted of tents for the agent and the section gang. A small red brick depot was built in 1878 by the Colorado Central, a predecessor of the Colorado & Southern.

Stanley Steamers wait for passengers at the Loveland C&S station.

Described as a shack, the building's freight section was so overcrowded that livestock were often placed in the waiting room. A contemporary newspaper said passengers had to open the door timidly—for fear of letting out a flock of sheep or a small herd of cattle. C&S built a new depot across the tracks. Bricks from the old station were used to pave the platform. Designed in a Romanesque Revival style by a railroad staff member, the buff brick depot consisted of freight and passenger sections joined by a breezeway. The depot's architectural features included broad arches for both exterior and interior openings, Ionic columns and pilasters, leaded glass transoms, eyebrow dormers, and built-in mahogany furniture. Separate waiting rooms for men and women opened, via a small arcade, directly onto the train platform. When the depot was converted to a restaurant in 1981, a patio room was added to the west side of the building. In 1993, the building became a retail store. NR. [Privately owned. Commercial.]

MONTROSE

MONTROSE DEPOT

Main Street and North Rio Grande Avenue
1912

The Denver & Rio Grande arrived at Montrose in the 1880s. Soon the pioneer settlement developed into an important supply and outfitting point for the numerous mining camps in the San Juan Mountains. In 1912, a new depot was built just south of the preceding wooden station, which was converted to handle freight only. Of stuccoed frame construction, the Mission-style passenger station had similar street and trackside facades—arched arcades broken by stepped parapets. Curvilinear wall dormers pierced the eaves of the main roof. In a park just south of the depot, D&RG planted a dozen shade trees. For the station's opening night banquet, a local church prepared food for at least 350 people. Passenger service ended about 40 years later. Since the mid-1970s, the depot has been home to the Montrose Historical Society, which leases it from the city. The building also served as a bus depot until the late Eighties. Except for a second floor inserted into the once high-ceilinged ticket area (flanked by lower height men's and ladies' waiting rooms), the depot maintains a good level of integrity, including original freight room scales, ticket office cupboards, toilet room fixtures, and yellow-green stained glass. The society was able to locate matching clay tiles to repair the roof. Freight trains occasionally use the tracks. NR. [City of Montrose. Local history museum.]

PUEBLO

UNION DEPOT

Victoria and B streets
Sprague and Newell
1890

In 1887, the Pueblo Union Depot & Railroad Company was formed by five railroads. David Moffat (Denver & Rio Grande) was president. Directors included representatives of the Chicago, Rock Island & Pacific, the Atchison, Topeka & Santa Fe, the Missouri Pacific, and a predecessor of the Colorado & Southern. Thus all Pueblo passenger service was soon brought under one roof. Designed by a Chicago architectural firm, the Romanesque Revival structure was massive, comprising Manitou red sandstone, a heavy slate roof, and a 150-foot-high clock tower. From the street side, passengers entered through a double door in the base of the tower. The first floor included waiting rooms, baggage services, a large restaurant (employing over 30 waitresses), and a bakery. Among the decorative elements were mosaic tile floors, wooden wainscoting, stained glass windows, allegorical bas reliefs, and half-ton wrought-iron chandeliers. Railroad offices occupied the second floor, topped by two attic stories of hotel rooms (later offices and dormitories).

The station was subjected to a number of floods over the years. The most devastating occurred in 1921, when several feet of water trapped trains in the yards and penetrated the building. Four years later, the station received repairs and major alterations. The immigrants' waiting room was converted to a baggage area, an addition for mail was built to the east, men's and ladies' waiting rooms were combined into one, and the slate roofing was removed. The most dramatic change was to the structurally damaged clock tower, which had to be lowered by 30 feet—necessitating removal of the west face of the Seth Thomas clock. (The north face was damaged in the 1950s by a gunshot.) Passenger service ended in 1971. The depot remained in railroad use until sold to a private party, who subsequently lost the building in the recession of the 1980s. The next entrepreneurs were more successful, giving the station new life as a retail, dining, special events, and apartment complex. Freight trains still use the tracks. NR. [Privately owned. Mixed use.]

SILVERTON

SILVERTON DEPOT
10th Street
1882

Located 45 railroad miles from Durango, Silverton was the northern terminus of a Denver & Rio Grande branch (later Denver & Rio Grande Western). In the 1950s, the railroad sought to abandon the line; but the Interstate Commerce Commission refused permission, because tourist ridership was on the upswing. To discourage railroad business, the D&RGW first converted the Silverton depot to a trucking facility. The next step was demolition plans, but the railroad was persuaded to donate the building to the San Juan Historical Society. In 1975, the group was using the depot to store museum artifacts when someone dynamited the freight end. (The perpetrator was never found.) Partly by using materials salvaged from the explosion, the society rebuilt the damaged area. The group also reroofed the depot with wooden shingles and painted it the "Rio Grande" color scheme of yellowish-tan and brown. The depot's simple exterior has vertical boards to windowsill level,

A multifaced clock tower peeks over the roof at Pueblo Union Depot.

D&S coal-fired steam engine No. 473 pulling into Silverton, 1983.

clapboards above, pedimented door and window openings, and heavy brackets supporting the deep roof overhangs. About half the windowpanes are still old wavy glass. A circular window adorns the gable end of the waiting room, which contains benches and a stove (probably brought from other depots in the Rio Grande system), and the original two ticket windows. During the 1970s and 1980s, the depot was leased to a publishing house. The journey back to railroad use began when the Durango & Silverton (the tourist operation that bought the branch line) subleased space for a ticket office. The railroad eventually purchased the entire building. The attic space has been remodeled for crew sleeping quarters. NR District. NHL District. [Durango & Silverton Narrow Gauge Railroad. Tourist train stop.]

TELLURIDE

TELLURIDE DEPOT
4 West San Juan Avenue
1891

Telluride was named for tellurium, the semimetallic matrix containing silver and gold, found on mountainsides above the San Miguel River. Before the arrival of the three-foot-gauge Rio Grande Southern, Telluride's "freight line" consisted of ox-drawn wagons pulled across Horsefly Mesa to Montrose. Less than a half-century later, the transportation system had regressed to another sort of "animal." Starting in the 1930s, the financially strapped railroad tried an alternative to steam trains—gasoline-powered "galloping geese." A goose was the front half of a Buick or Pierce-Arrow (or a bus) married to a freight car. The whole contraption rode on the rails. The line was fully abandoned in 1952; and the combination freight and passenger depot, which had been lengthened and remodeled over time, sat essentially vacant for 40 years. When the current owner took title in 1991, the foundation and flooring were gone. He had the building jacked up and temporarily moved 40 yards away. After workers built a full basement, they set the depot back down in its original location. The wooden station is now outfitted in a wood-shingle roof and one of the early RGS color schemes—maroon and yellow with brown trim. With its large Queen Anne dormer and brick chimneys intact, the depot opened for adaptive use 100 years after the first train came to town. The tracks are gone. [Privately owned. Restaurant and microbrewery.]

Hawaii

Railroads in Hawaii were built primarily for the sugar industry. Most of the major plantations had private railways, which they used for transporting workers to the fields and sugar cane to the factories. Common carriers then took the bagged sugar (in later years, bulk) to the docks for shipment to California refineries. They also hauled canned pineapples and passengers. The few depots that remain have all been converted to other uses (like the one at Paia on Maui—now a surfboard shop), because the state has no regular train service.

HONOLULU

OAHU RAILWAY & LAND COMPANY DEPOT
333 North King Street
Guy Rothwell
1927

Started in 1889, the Oahu Railway and Land Company opened up the areas of western and northern Oahu for cultivating sugar. Besides hauling freight, the railroad provided plantation workers with easy access to Honolulu. In the 1920s, the OR&L built a new Mission-style station of stuccoed concrete to replace an earlier frame depot. Designed by a Honolulu architect and engineer, the two-story, L-shaped depot was surrounded by a first floor arcade and capped by a tile roof. A four-sided clock tower with a wrought-iron balcony and a crenellated battlement dominated the station's north facade. After OR&L abandoned the depot in the 1940s, it served as a bus station until being rehabilitated in 1976 for offices. Although the interior has been modified, original tile work remains visible in some areas. NR. [State of Hawaii. Offices.]

OR&L depot in Honolulu, 1946.

Idaho

Most of the main line stations in Idaho started out as crude structures, thrown up as railroads hurried to reach the west coast. These were typically replaced by more substantial buildings after the turn of the 20th century. By contrast, branch line depots—found in more remote farming and mining towns—were built under less pressure. Standard plan, combination freight and passenger stations of sufficient size and sturdiness, they lasted until train service came to an end. Some stations in Idaho were nothing more than milk sheds, where cans were stored until a local passenger train came by to collect them.

BLACKFOOT

BLACKFOOT DEPOT
130 Northwest Main Street
1913

When the Oregon Short Line (Union Pacific system) needed a better depot at Blackfoot, the railroad first relocated the 1895 wooden station and converted it to strictly freight use (that structure is now gone). The new station, with brick structural walls, was faced with pink and gray stone quarried from nearby Rexburg. The roof was probably wood shingle. In relief lettering, artisans carved BLACKFOOT into the agent's bay and O.S.L.R.R. above the streetside entrance. The floor plan included an express office, baggage room, men's smoking room, general waiting room, newsstand, and ticket office. After passenger service ended in 1971, UP used the depot for freight railroad business. Sixteen years later, the city acquired the station, which now houses Idaho's World Potato Exposition. Freight trains still use the tracks. NR. [City of Blackfoot. Museum.]

BOISE

BOISE RAILROAD STATION
2603 Eastover Terrace (south end of Capitol Boulevard)
Carrère and Hastings, Shreve, Lamb and Blake
1925

In the early 1880s, the Union Pacific main line (built by a subsidiary, the Oregon Short Line) bypassed Boise by 12 miles, when the community failed to post the required bond. The future state capital got only a stub-end branch line and a wooden depot, located a short distance from the present station. The next depot was a stone structure at 10th and Front streets (which stood until 1948). In 1925, after decades of disputes and fund raising, Boise residents were rewarded with through service and a new station of impressive style and proportion. A showpiece at the end of a grand boulevard, the depot combined Boise sandstone, white stucco, and orange roof tiles into a multilevel Spanish Colonial Revival design, the work of a New York City architectural firm. With its exposed trusswork, tall windows, back-to-back pewlike benches, and rows of chandeliers, the two-story-high waiting room exuded a distinctly ecclesiastical quality. On a hillside below the depot, the railroad planted trees and flower gardens.

Boise station.

A crowd welcomes the first main line train, April 25, 1925. The tower did not yet have clocks.

The waiting room, 1974.

In 1969, UP converted the one-story baggage wing to offices; two years later, its last passenger train pulled out of the station. (Amtrak reinstated service in 1977.) The Morrison Knudsen Corporation purchased the depot in 1990. The company's meticulous restoration included stripping, cleaning, and reinstalling roof tiles; reconstructing the copper downspout system; and repairing the campanile's chimes (installed in 1927 to honor UP's Edward H. Harriman). To give the public a spot for viewing the Treasure Valley, MK added an elevator and stairway inside the nearly 100-foot-tall tower, previously inaccessible to visitors. Forty-five thousand paving bricks were pulled up, cleaned, and reinstalled. Corner guards of cast iron were forged to re-create those missing from the baggage room doors. MK used locally quarried sandstone to create a new entrance for Amtrak passengers. High on the walls of the original waiting room (used now for functions held by charitable and nonprofit organizations), painters restored the trim colors of blue, vermilion, and yellow. The Barkalow Brothers newsstand, concealed since 1962, was uncovered and found surprisingly intact. NR. [Privately owned. Train stop, special events facility, and corporate offices.]

The curves of this decorative fountain contrast with the angular patterns in the tile floor and dado.

Early view of the Nampa depot with its red tile roof (now gone) and full complement of ornate finials.

NAMPA

NAMPA DEPOT

12th Avenue South and Front Street
1903

By 1900, the volume of Oregon Short Line (Union Pacific system) business at Nampa had rendered the old wooden depot outmoded. A staff architect designed a new brick and sandstone building of moderate size with an imposing French Renaissance entrance and a red tile roof. In 1925, after an even bigger depot was built directly across the tracks (a Gilbert Stanley Underwood design razed in 1987), the old station was converted to railroad offices. The county historical society acquired the one-story depot in 1973 and removed the numerous partitions that the railroad had added. Guided by an old photograph, the group reconstructed the agent's office and ticket window. The ladies' waiting room had retained its fireplace, accented by a large onyx disc above the mantel. Union Pacific still owns the land beneath the depot. Amtrak passengers wait under a small shelter across the tracks, just west of the 1925 depot site. NR. [Canyon County Historical Society. Train stop/npa and museum.]

NEW MEADOWS

NEW MEADOWS DEPOT

U.S. Route 95
H. W. Bond
1911

New Meadows was the northern terminus of the Pacific & Idaho Northern (Union Pacific system), a line important for shipping cattle, sheep, farm products, and timber. The red brick depot, which had a one-story freight office on the west end and the railroad's headquarters on the second floor, was designed by an architect from Weiser. He also drew plans for a nearby mansion, home to the railroad president. (Located northeast of the depot on Route 95, the house is now a hotel, with red bricks painted yellow.) Rail service ended in 1979. The head of a nearby logging concern purchased the station grounds and, rather than see the expected demolition go forward, donated the depot to the local historical society. A small public library is housed in the former ladies' waiting room, although much of the building is unused. As determined by a feasibility study undertaken in 1993, substantial rehabilitation would be necessary to realize the facility's full potential. The track is gone. NR. [Adams County Historical Society. Library and partly vacant.]

Pocatello depot on
November 27, 1923.

Street side.

Track side with platform
canopy (now gone).

POCATELLO

POCATELLO DEPOT
300 South Harrison Street
Carrère and Hastings
1915

Pocatello was an important stop on the Union
Pacific main line. Although the first depot was
a boxcar, the second one was a substantial and
handsome wooden station (1886), demolished
after the present depot was built. Designed by
the predecessor of the firm that would work on
Boise's station nearly a decade later, it was clad
in gray stone on the first floor with red brick
above. The station housed offices for UP's
Montana and Idaho divisions. Renaissance
Revival in style, the three-story center section
contained a large waiting room with a balcony
at the second-floor level, ticket office, stationmaster's room, newsstand, and barber shop. A
two-story east wing had baggage and express

facilities, a mail clerk's office, and a waiting
room for "emigrants." Dining facilities were in
the two-story west wing. A platform canopy
(since demolished) that extended from the
north side of the building was an unusual feature for Idaho, where stations tended to be built
without exterior shelter. Although passenger
service was initially discontinued in 1971,
Amtrak began serving Pocatello six years later.
Passengers do their waiting on the original oak
benches. [Union Pacific Railroad. Train stop
and freight railroad offices.]

SANDPOINT

NORTHERN PACIFIC DEPOT
Railroad Avenue (east end of Cedar Street
    Bridge)
1916

Northern Pacific was the principal developer of
the town of Sandpoint, located on Lake Pend

Oreille, a place where sand was collected for use on the entire system. (Locomotive engineers use sand to keep wheels from slipping on a steep grade or to help get a heavy train moving from a standstill.) The story-and-a-half brick depot, possibly the third on the site, exhibits a Tudor flavor in its cross gable dormers and the moderately pointed arches of door, window, and porte-cochere openings. A crenellated agent's bay protrudes from the depot's track side. Amtrak passengers use the original waiting room, which has white tile with black mortar wainscoting and slate floors. An old cart and scale remain in the baggage room. NR. [Burlington Northern Railroad Company. Train stop and freight railroad agency.]

SHOSHONE

SHOSHONE RAILROAD STATION
304 North Rail Street
Gilbert Stanley Underwood
1929

The Shoshone station was at a junction of the Union Pacific main line and a branch that went north into mining country. (In the 1930s, UP developed this silver mining area into the Sun Valley resort.) A new passenger station replaced a wooden one that was moved east about three blocks to be used for freight only

(razed in the 1970s). The east half was the baggage and express wing, equipped with wide double doors of rustic design. The passenger end had a baroque pedimented doorway with urn finials and a terra-cotta UP shield. Exterior finishes for the walls were stucco, brick, and decorative half-timbering; the roof was tile. In 1977, Amtrak reinstated passenger service that had been discontinued for seven years. Today, travelers wait in a small shelter near the historic station. Should UP vacate the depot, the city would be interested in acquiring it for a museum. NR District. [Union Pacific Railroad. Train stop/npa and equipment storage.]

WALLACE

NORTHERN PACIFIC STATION
6th and Pine streets
c. 1901

Wallace's Northern Pacific station was built from stock plan No. 281-1. With its round tower capped by a conical spire, the design resembled the corner of a French chateau. The walls comprised a cut stone base, brick first floor, and pseudo-half-timbered second story. The steeply pitched hipped roof was wood shingle. Burlington Northern (NP's successor) vacated the station in 1980. Within a few years, the depot faced what seemed like certain

Architect's rendering of the Shoshone station, track side.

Wallace NP station in its original location, 1952.

destruction, dictated by its location in the path of a highway realignment. To the rescue came an Idaho silver baron, who formed the Northern Pacific Depot Foundation expressly to raise funds and look for an alternative solution. In 1986, the state department of transportation relocated the depot from the north bank of the Coeur d'Alene River's south fork to a plot immediately across the river. The department sponsored the depot's restoration, completed according to the Secretary of the Interior's Standards for Rehabilitation, and donated it to the city. It now houses a museum that focuses on the area's railroad history, which was critical to the development of the lead and silver mining industry. NR. [City of Wallace. Museum.]

Montana

Montana's extant depots reflect the state's economic heritage: precious metal mining, farming and livestock production, lumber extraction, and tourism—all expanded and made more lucrative by the arrival of five major railroads. Today in several of the larger communities that were served by more than one line, more than one depot remains—saved by adaptation to nonrailroad uses. A fair number of small wooden depots are still standing in rural locations—ghostly guideposts along trackless right-of-ways.

ANACONDA

MONTANA UNION RAILROAD DEPOT
Front and Main streets
1890

The Butte, Anaconda & Pacific Railway was built by copper king Marcus Daly, who felt he was being gouged by the Montana Union Railroad (formed through a pact between Union Pacific and Northern Pacific). BA&P first took away MU's business and then moved into its depot, a brick and rusticated stone structure

with a hipped roof and polygonal agent's bay. BA&P's own station on Commercial Street was converted to freight use only and subsequently razed in the late 1930s. Passenger service ended in the mid-Fifties, and the station was converted to a retail lumber outlet the following decade.

The BA&P rail yard retains an extraordinary number of intact facilities, including a locomotive repair and machine shop; a building housing both the blacksmith and boiler shops; a warehouse; houses for sand, oil, and hoses; a paint shop; shops for carpenters, plumbers, and electricians; and a wrecking crane house. An 1893 roundhouse (enlarged in 1907) and original turntable are in use by the Rarus Railway, a successor to part of the old BA&P. Rarus also occupies the 1897 BA&P general office building at 300 West Commercial Street. NR District. [Privately owned. Commercial.]

BILLINGS

NORTHERN PACIFIC DEPOT
Montana Avenue between North 23rd and
   24th streets
1909

In 1882, Billings was named for the president of the Northern Pacific, the railroad that created the town. Passenger trains stopped at the 1883 Headquarters Hotel, which served as a depot and eating house. (Hotels proliferated in Billings. The historic district surrounding the present depot still contains about eight of them.) By the early 20th century, Billings was a rail hub, with the lines of four railroads extending in 10 different directions. NP built a new passenger complex, consisting of a one-story depot flanked by a baggage building to the east and a beanery to the west. The sandstone-trimmed, buff brick buildings were designed by the office of NP's chief civil engineer. Georgian Revival elements included a pedi-

Billings NP depot, 1970.

mented portico and Palladian windows. Chicago, Burlington & Quincy trains also stopped at this location, which was sometimes known as Union Station.

The buildings have been vacant since Amtrak discontinued service in 1979. ISTEA funding, obtained by the city and the Billings Preservation Society in the early Nineties, will be used to stabilize the structures through asbestos removal and a new roof, once a property management agreement is worked out with the current owner. An additional grant is being sought to fully restore the smallest building, the beanery, to attract a tenant and also give the community a sense of the potential for the entire site. A portion of the 1992 movie *Far and Away* was shot in the depot. Freight trains still use the tracks. NR District. [Burlington Northern Railroad Company. Vacant.]

BUTTE

CHICAGO, MILWAUKEE & ST. PAUL STATION
1001 South Montana Street
1917

The silver and copper mining industries attracted several railroads to Butte. The last of the transcontinentals to arrive on the scene (in 1908) was the Chicago, Milwaukee & St. Paul. John D. Ryan—besides sitting on the board of the "Milwaukee Road"—was president of both the Anaconda Copper Company (which owned the Butte, Anaconda & Pacific Railway) and the Montana Power Company. At first, the Milwaukee Road shared the BA&P depot, but technology changed its needs. By the mid-1910s, CM&StP had followed the lead of the 26-mile-long BA&P and electrified this part of its line. (The vastly longer Milwaukee Road electrification extended from Harlowton, Mont., to Avery, Idaho.) Compared to steam, electrification was an easier operation, especially under severe winter conditions. Furthermore, in any weather, it required fewer locomotives to pull heavy loads

Architect's rendering of the Butte CM&StP station.

uphill. For passengers, electrification meant less smoke and cinders.

The Milwaukee Road's new red-tile-roofed passenger station was touted as being the cleanest in the Northwest. The two-story central portion of the building was clad in pressed St. Louis brick on a structural steel frame. The main entrance was through the base of a five-story-high square tower. At the top, a four-sided Seth Thomas clock kept time. Beneath the dials, which were each more than six feet wide, Milwaukee Road emblems were worked in white letters against a red and yellow background. Waiting rooms and a restaurant were on the first floor; railroad offices, upstairs. Interior finishes included marble floors and oak and burlap paneled walls.

To the west, a one-story wing held baggage, express, and mail rooms, plus a clubroom and general quarters for employees. Umbrella sheds, about 500 feet long, protected a portion of the red brick platforms that reached more than 700 feet down the six tracks, which are now gone. This union depot was eventually shared with the BA&P, whose c. 1895 depot (in use today as a warehouse on Utah Street) had become too small. After passenger service ended in the 1950s, the Milwaukee Road depot was converted from a railroad station to a television station. NR District. NHL District. [Privately owned. Television studio and offices.]

NORTHERN PACIFIC STATION
800 East Front Street
Reed and Stem
1906

Besides Grand Central Terminal in New York City, Reed and Stem worked on more than 100 railroad stations. Their design for Butte's Northern Pacific station (also used by the Union Pacific) was relatively simple. The two-story, limestone-trimmed, red brick building contained waiting rooms, men's smoking and ladies' retiring rooms, and ticket and administration offices. A mezzanine circled the upper portion of the general lobby. Down below, the NP herald was laid into the tile floor. Baggage was handled from a building to the west; meals were served from a building to the east. Six square brick pillars supported the platform canopy.

Amtrak stopped serving Butte in 1979, and the depot was boarded up. The following decade, after a hail storm damaged the station's green tile roof (probably not original), water penetrated the station. A private party purchased the depot in the early Nineties. Preservation work and a reuse plan are under consideration. The NP freight depot still stands on South Arizona Street, two blocks north of another former passenger station, the Great Northern (now in manufacturing use). NR District. NHL District. [Privately owned.

Commercial uses in ancillary buildings; main building vacant.]

DILLON

DILLON DEPOT
South Montana Street
1909

Dillon was named for the president of the Union Pacific, parent company of the Oregon Short Line. In 1907, Dillon's mayor complained to the OSL about the inadequacy and location of its depot. The railroad subsequently undertook major improvements, including rearranging rails and switches for a new brick passenger station on the town side of the tracks. Built in the Arts and Crafts style, the story-and-a-half depot was given a gently sloped, hipped roof with wide eaves. A large cross gable with multipaned windows and numerous hipped dormers (the latter removed during a 1970s reroofing) created a chaletlike appearance. Inside were two waiting rooms (general and women's), a ticket office, and a baggage room. After passenger service ended in 1971, UP used the depot for freight railroad purposes. In the late Eighties, the railroad donated the building (but not the land it sits on) to the county. The Beaverhead County Museum Association is in charge of operations. NR. [County of Beaverhead. Museum and visitors center.]

GREAT FALLS

CHICAGO, MILWAUKEE & ST. PAUL DEPOT
River Drive North
1915

When the latecomer Chicago, Milwaukee & St. Paul (in the 1920s, nicknamed the "Milwaukee Road") arrived in Great Falls, it was time for one-upsmanship in depot construction. The Great Northern had been in town since the 1880s. Its most recent station (1910) sat adjacent to a large park. The CM&StP chose a site on the opposite side of the park, within view of the GN clock tower. (The Civic Center, built in the 1930s, now blocks the sight lines.) The disproportionately high tower of the Milwaukee Road station was not only visible from great distances across the city, it also bore large, mosaic tile heralds on all four sides. Inside the station, sheet metal ducts, concealed in the ceiling beams of the general waiting room, provided ventilation by circulating air up through this same tower. The depot was designed by an unidentified member of the railroad's bridges and buildings department. A contemporary newspaper noted that the depot was pleasantly distant from the switch yards and other "noiseome [sic] and smoky things" typically associated with rail operations.

In the early 1970s, after 15 years of vacancy, the station was converted to a restau-

Dillon depot when still in service.

rant and shops. Unfortunately, decorative wall plaster and tile wainscoting were stripped to expose the brick walls. The retail venture failed, and a new owner plans to use the building for offices. Great Falls's Great Northern depot (NR District) was remodeled into headquarters for the local gas company which retained the polygonal clock tower, yet installed incompatible doors and windows, and tore out the faded, but intact interior. The GN freight depot (1913) and the express and commissary building (1917) are extant, but endangered. NR. [Privately owned. Vacant.]

HARLOWTON

HARLOWTON DEPOT
U.S. Route 12, just south of Harlowton
1908

As the Chicago, Milwaukee & St. Paul pushed west, it utilized at least a dozen different standardized depot plans. Harlowton's "Standard Class A Passenger Station" was a design for larger towns. (Other extant examples, in their original locations, are at Alberton and Deer Lodge.) Clad in beveled lap siding on the upper portion of the walls, the depot had vertical boards below, which were covered with fiberboard in the 1970s. The roof overhang was supported by chamfered knee braces, with ends sawn in an ogee pattern. Geometrically scored paving bricks (now gone) formed the platform. The roof was wood shingle; exterior paint colors were orange and maroon. The original floor plan, enlarged and modified over the years, consisted of a waiting room, ticket office, beanery, and baggage and express areas. The 1907 wooden freight house was demolished in 1994, but other buildings remain in the yard, including the c. 1910 yardmaster's office and the c. 1915 steam room (where, for example, dining car garbage cans were cleaned).

Harlowton's place in railroad history was reinforced in 1916, when the CM&StP electrified the line from Harlowton to Avery, Idaho, for extra power over the Rocky Mountains. At the time, this was the longest stretch of electrified line in the nation; Thomas Edison described it as an "unmatched technical marvel." Trains stopped at Harlowton to exchange motive power; the roundhouse with attached machine shop (extant) serviced both steam (later diesel) and electric locomotives. Passenger service ended in the early 1960s. After freight service ceased about 1979, the tracks were removed. In 1994, the city began restoring the depot. Part of the planned adaptive use includes a diorama and model railroad depicting the Harlowton Yard. NR District. [City of Harlowton. Vacant— future museum.]

LIVINGSTON

LIVINGSTON DEPOT
200 West Park Street
Reed and Stem
1902

Once known as the "Gateway to Yellowstone," Livingston was both a Northern Pacific division point and the junction for a branch line south to the national park. The very first depot, built of wood, burned. The next one, a substantial two-and-a-half-story brick building, stood across the tracks from the present depot's location. A nationally prominent midwestern firm, Reed and Stem, designed the third station to impress tourists. A curving colonnade joined the three buildings that formed the station complex. Clad in red brick with terra-cotta and buff brick trim, the Italian Renaissance Revival–style structures sported NP's Great Monad emblem as a design motif throughout the composition.

In 1979, after Amtrak rerouted passenger service, the Burlington Northern freight railroad (successor to NP) used parts of the deteriorating building for offices. Simultaneously, it began closing down its maintenance shops—a loss of 1,000 jobs in a community of 7,000 people. Despite economic woes, the city accepted

The curving colonnade at the Livingston depot.

BN's donation of the passenger station as the only way to prevent demolition of this handsome and visible element of the area's railroad heritage. The Livingston Depot Foundation formed to take over both fund raising and complete management of the complex. The project required nearly $1 million worth of work, including seismic reinforcement. Restoration involved removing most of NP's 1947 alterations—like the false second floor inserted into the high-ceilinged waiting room—and reworking plaster, marble, and mosaic tile. The two-story main building was converted to a museum focusing on western history. The old beanery on the east side has been revived as a

restaurant; the baggage building on the west houses the chamber of commerce and a rental hall. Freight trains still use the tracks. NR District. [City of Livingston. Mixed use.]

MISSOULA

CHICAGO, MILWAUKEE & ST. PAUL STATION
South Higgins Avenue
J. A. Lindstrand
1910

Missoula's Chicago, Milwaukee & St. Paul station was completed just after the railroad finished laying track across Montana. It was designed by a member of the CM&StP bridges and buildings department. Pedestrians and vehicular traffic approached the buff brick depot from a gradually descending road, across a small creek lined with deciduous trees. Capped by a Spanish tile roof, the depot was essentially two stories (with a one-story baggage and express building), made vastly more imposing by two square towers—one three stories and one five stories high. Converted to a restaurant and shops about 1980, the station saw its second adaptive use in the early Nineties as home to the Boone and Crockett Club, a century-old, hunter-conservationist

Missoula CM&StP station when still in service. The right-of-way (now a rail trail) paralleled the Clark Fork River. The one-story building accommodated baggage and express.

group founded by Theodore Roosevelt. The right-of-way is now a riverfront trail. At the opposite end of Higgins Avenue, freight trains still go by Missoula's Northern Pacific station (NR), used today for a restaurant and offices. NR. [Privately owned. Organizational headquarters.]

WEST GLACIER

BELTON STATION
U.S. Route 2, Glacier National Park
1935

The Great Northern stop at West Glacier was originally called Belton. Two boxcars (one for the agent to live in) constituted the 1892–93 station, located on a curve east of the present depot. Railroad magnate James J. Hill and his son Louis decided to build tourist accommodations at Belton to promote the "American Alps." In 1910, on the boxcar site, the railroad constructed a simple, standard design depot. Passengers walked under a grape arbor to reach the Belton Chalet (a cluster of four buildings now in the National Register). In 1935, GN moved the old depot about 100 yards to the west to become the baggage and express section of a new passenger station. Rough-hewn siding, which extended over the entire building, and exposed purlins under the deep eaves

reinforced the intended rustic appearance. The center portion, formed by a jerkinhead cross gable, adjoined a large open-air waiting area on the west.

In 1991, the Burlington Northern (successor to GN) donated the building to the Glacier Natural History Association, which removed inappropriate 1950s partitions. The waiting room (available to Amtrak passengers in the summer when traffic is the heaviest) is the association's retail book outlet. The ticket office, containing original furniture, and the baggage room provide office and warehouse space. NR. [Glacier Natural History Association. Train stop and organizational headquarters.]

WEST YELLOWSTONE

WEST YELLOWSTONE DEPOT
Yellowstone Avenue between Dunraven and
    Canyon streets
c. 1909

Union Pacific began through service to Yellowstone National Park in 1908. Fourteen years later, the existing concrete passenger depot, clad in lava rock excavated from the railroad right-of-way, was joined to the west by two compatible structures—a baggage building and a large dining lodge. Trains

Early view of the west entrance to Glacier National Park. On the far left is the 1910 Belton depot, which in 1935 was moved about 100 yards to the west (beyond the right edge of this photo) and integrated into the new station.

West Yellowstone depot in 1928.

UP locomotive No. 529 pulling a passenger train into the station.

A rusticated, one-story dining lodge of oversized proportions.

arrived in the morning for breakfast and departed in the evening after supper. The dining lodge and a 1927 dormitory were designed by noted architect Gilbert Stanley Underwood. The original floor plan of the depot (architect unknown) included offices for both the station agent and Pullman representative. Wings that angled out from the depot's main section contained waiting and dressing rooms for men and women—each with a large fireplace.

Passenger service, which had never operated in the winter because of snow drifts, ended completely in 1959. Two years later, the town accepted the railroad's donation of the station buildings, including a large water tank now used by the municipality. In 1972, the depot reopened as the Museum of the Yellowstone. The baggage building was converted to the town office, police station, and jail. The dining lodge, rehabilitated through volunteer labor, came back to life in the 1980s as a multipurpose facility that houses the public library, a museum

for the Federation of Fly Fishers, an art gallery, and a special events facility (where high school graduation exercises are held). The lodge's largest space, the Mammoth Room, has a 45-foot-high ceiling and a walk-in fireplace. Trackless since 1981, the roadbed now serves as an unofficial recreational trail. NR District. [Town of West Yellowstone. Mixed use.]

WHITEFISH

WHITEFISH DEPOT
North Central Avenue
Thomas McMahon
1927

The Great Northern arrived at the southern end of Whitefish Lake about 1904. Its first station combined freight and passenger services with a lunch room. In 1927, GN built a new combination division office and passenger depot of substantial size, designed in a style referred to at the time as "Alpine." The plans were drawn by Thomas McMahon (apparently a GN staff member). The depot's timber walls were sheathed in wooden siding on the lower level, with decorative half-timbering from the second story into the gambrel eaves. Cedar shingles covered the roof, pierced by massive dormers (both peaked and gambrel) and multi-windowed shed dormers.

In the late 1980s, Burlington Northern (successor to GN) decided to acquire a prefabricated structure and vacate the deteriorating 60-year-old building. The local historical society came up with a wise alternative that the railroad accepted in 1990. BN transferred the depot's title to the preservation group and also donated the money it had allotted for a new building. The historical society used those funds to renovate the upper story-and-a-half of the old depot and then leased that space back to BN. The first floor, with some of its original partitions rearranged, is shared by Amtrak and the depot's nonprofit rescuers. [Stumptown Historical Society. Train stop, freight railroad offices, and museum.]

Nevada

Railroads in sparsely populated Nevada were tied to the boom and bust of precious metal mining. Of the perhaps two dozen railroad structures that remain, less than a handful belong to the fabled Virginia & Truckee (NHL). A short line started in 1869, V&T suffered a blow in 1991, when its Carson City shops were demolished, despite years of local preservation efforts.

CALIENTE

CALIENTE DEPOT
100 Depot Avenue
Parkinson and Parkinson
1923

Caliente was a busy railroad center—a division point for servicing Union Pacific steam equipment, as well as a terminal for "helpers" (extra locomotives that assisted trains up the nearby steep grades). A frame structure with a stucco veneer and a red tile roof, the depot-hotel was designed in Mission style by noted Los Angeles architects John and Donald Parkinson. The preceding building was destroyed by fire. The new one included two restaurants—an elegant dining room (now Amtrak's waiting room), and a more casual beanery. Caliente's hotel served both railroad crews on layover and travelers. By the 1940s, diesel locomotives were rendering steam engines obsolete. Diesels did not need water, coal, or frequent servicing as steam locomotives did, and could be run in multiples—typically eliminating the need for helper engines and extra crews. In 1948, UP transferred its division facilities to Las Vegas. In time, the Caliente roundhouse, water tank, and Reading Room (a combination clubhouse and dormitory) were destroyed.

About 1970, in lieu of demolition, UP rented the depot to the city (eventually transferring title) and agreed to a long-term lease on

Caliente depot when it still contained hospitality facilities: two restaurants and a hotel.

the land. Taking care to retain interior features, the city installed its own offices in the depot. Remaining first-floor space is used today by several entities, among them the public library, chamber of commerce, and a county arts organization. Enough funds for restoration are an ongoing concern, but various sources (including ISTEA) continue to support improvements. A small community college is planned for the second floor. NR. [City of Caliente. Train stop and mixed use.]

CARSON CITY

WABUSKA DEPOT
South Carson Street (U.S. Route 395) at
    Fairview Drive
1906

In 1900, Southern Pacific purchased a narrow gauge line (the Carson & Colorado) running through Wabuska. Six years later, because of a copper mining boom, the 1881 C&C depot was inadequate for increasing traffic. Railroad carpenters constructed a new wooden, combination freight and passenger station, which remained active until 1979. In the early Eighties, SP donated the building to the Nevada State Railroad Museum, which moved it to Carson City. Oriented to the north as it

was in Wabuska, the depot is adjacent to one mile of track used for tourist rides. Tickets are sold from the agent's office. Painted SP yellow with brown trim and capped by a wood-shingle roof, the depot wears a replica of its original sign, stating elevation above sea level and mileages to the original termini in California— Keeler and San Francisco. Still on its original 1872 location in the center of town, Carson City's Virginia & Truckee passenger depot (and after 1896, general headquarters) has undergone fairly radical alterations since entering private hands in 1952. NR. [Nevada State Railroad Museum. Tourist train stop.]

Wasbuska depot in its original location.

ELY

EAST ELY DEPOT
1100 Avenue A (at 11th Street East)
1907

The Nevada Northern was a short line railroad, carrying copper from mines west of Ely to a smelter in nearby McGill, and then on to Southern Pacific connections at Cobre. Passenger service provided transport for mine workers, school children, and people on the first leg of wider travel. The railroad's headquarters were in East Ely, in a station that was rusticated stone on the first floor, with stucco cladding above. Curvilinear gables dominated both the street and track sides of the building. Embedded into the wall, seven circles, each bearing one stone letter, spelled out the station name. The first floor housed the agent's office, men's and ladies' waiting areas, and a baggage and express room. Railroad offices were upstairs.

Passenger service ended in 1941. Seventeen years later, the Kennecott Copper Company acquired the assets of the railroad, which continued to haul freight until 1983. The copper company then donated the entire complex—45 acres of land, more than 30 buildings, rolling stock, track, and the railroad's voluminous records—to the White Pine Historical Railroad Foundation. The foundation subsequently turned over ownership of the passenger depot, nearby wooden freight house, and NN papers to the state. Virtually every item of the passenger station remains intact, from oak desks and filing cabinets to black ceramic telephones. Ely is home to two other historic NN depots, both built in 1907. One is the relocated Cherry Creek depot, hauled 50 miles in 1990 to the White Pine County Museum. The other is the still on-site Ely depot, located one railroad mile southwest of the *East* Ely Depot. Now called Old Requa Depot, it was converted to a senior center in the late 1970s. NR. [State of Nevada. Tourist train stop and depot museum.]

GOLD HILL

GOLD HILL DEPOT
Main Street
1872

The Virginia & Truckee made money by hauling two commodities: precious metal ore from the famous Comstock mines and timber from Carson City (first sent down flumes from Lake Tahoe). The Gold Hill depot was built to accommodate a curve in the track; one long side of the depot was straight and the other rounded. A wood-shingle roof stretched across the large board and batten freight end, as well as the smaller passenger section (clad in horizontal siding). After a mining depression occurred in the early 1900s, V&T began an intermittent decline. The Gold Hill depot was closed from 1916 until 1921 and finally abandoned in the late Thirties. In 1946, V&T conveyed the depot to the county. The building continued to deteriorate until a preliminary restoration was begun in 1974 by the Carson City Railroad Association. Further restored in the early 1990s, the depot is now a stop on a tourist railroad operating from Virginia City to Gold Hill (expected to reach Carson City by 1996). The Comstock Historic Restoration Foundation used an 1890 photograph for its work on the interior, which includes resurrection of a complete set of telegraph equipment. At the next stop north, Virginia City, a small V&T passenger depot (c. 1869) and a freight depot (1877) are both in private hands; the main Virginia City terminus was demolished for firewood after World War II. NR District. NHL District. [County of Storey. Tourist train stop and museum.]

RENO

NEVADA-CALIFORNIA-OREGON DEPOT
325 East 4th Street
Frederick J. DeLongchamps
1910

The years from 1906 to 1912 were moderately prosperous for the 238-mile-long, narrow gauge line known as the Nevada-California-Oregon. By 1917, red ink forced the railroad, whose southern terminus and headquarters were in Reno—to sell off part of its holdings to Western Pacific. (The balance of the line was absorbed by Southern Pacific in 1928.) Included was a two-and-a-half story, brick depot, built just seven years earlier, which had replaced a smaller brick station about two blocks southwest. (The very first N-C-O depot —wooden, damaged by fire, and relocated— is reportedly extant as a warehouse on North Park Street.) The new depot's designer was Frederick DeLongchamps, one of Nevada's best-known architects, whose career included numerous government and university buildings. At the N-C-O depot, he made bold use of concrete for quoins, keystones, sills, and curvilinear gables. Red tiles covered the shallow hipped roof, pierced by broad, shed dormers and supported at the eaves by large

Reno N-C-O depot, 1910.

double brackets. First-floor door and window openings were Roman arches filled with fanlights.

After train service ended in 1937, WP used the depot for offices. In private hands since the Fifties (for many years home to a liquor distributor), the building is now empty. Just to the east stands the N-C-O enginehouse and machine shop (1889, NR), used today as a warehouse. At Lakeview, Ore., the northern terminus of the N-C-O is also extant (1912, NR). Another DeLongchamps design, it bears a strong resemblance to the Reno depot. NR. [Privately owned. Vacant.]

SOUTHERN PACIFIC STATION
135 East Commercial Row
1926

Southern Pacific built its fourth consecutive Reno station (the first was 1868) in a stucco-clad, nearly symmetrical design. It also served the Virginia & Truckee, whose trains pulled up on the south side. Five tall, rounded arches formed door and window openings—repeated in mirror image on both sides of the building. On the SP (north) side, a deep marquee suspended by chains provided limited shelter for waiting passengers. Red tiles covered the roof of the station's center section, which had Palladian windows within its gable ends. To each side were stepped-down wings. Large, torch-like sconces provided the only exterior illumination. Inside lighting was provided by chandeliers suspended from a high, coffered ceiling. Floor and wall materials included terrazzo, marble, and an application of Caen Stone. Seating was on back-to-back wooden benches, still used today by Amtrak passengers. An unsympathetic, cinder block addition on the western end of the building served for a time as a casino, but is now vacant. Across Lake Street and to the east, the express building (most recently a restaurant) is also empty;

Reno SP station.

A baggage porter pulls a heavy-laden wagon past locomotive No. 295 in this c. 1935 photo.

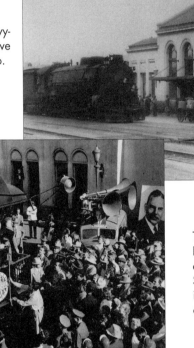

The year is 1948. Making a whistle stop at Reno, Governor Earl Warren of California campaigns for vice president of the United States. Posted next to the sound truck is the image of Republican presidential candidate Thomas E. Dewey.

but the freight depot has been converted to retail shops. [Southern Pacific Lines. Train stop.]

RHYOLITE

RHYOLITE DEPOT
Golden Street, four miles west of Beatty on U.S. Route 374
1908

Rhyolite is a ghost town near Death Valley National Park. Founded in 1905 as the center of the Bullfrog Mining District, within two years, Rhyolite had a population estimated between 10,000 and 15,000. Then the stock market panic of 1907 began pushing the mines toward bankruptcy from over-speculation. Only 700 people remained in Rhyolite in 1910; by 1920 desertion was essentially complete. Other than stone foundations and brick fronts, few structures survive today. One is a house almost entirely built of beer bottles; another is a picturesque railroad station. The Mission-style, masonry depot, constructed by the Las Vegas & Tonopah Railway, had men's and ladies' waiting rooms, a baggage room, and agent's living quarters (above the ticket office). The station went out of service in 1918. Revived twice—as a saloon and then as a casino—the trackless depot stands mostly unused and deteriorating, its interior stripped. Owned by a gold mining company, the depot is surrounded by a chain link fence to prevent further vandalism. (Many of the structures in Rhyolite have been dis-

Rhyolite depot, 1930s.

mantled for salvage or hauled away in entirety.) The owners are considering stabilizing the building and making it available to a nonprofit group for an interpretative center. | Moviemakers occasionally use the depot as a location; one example is the 1988 film *Cherry 2000* (with a Saloon sign slapped on the front). [Privately owned. Vacant.]

Oregon

Until 1883, when Oregon's first transcontinental rail link-up occurred, isolation was the chief deterrent to the state's growth. Attracted by subsidy land programs, settlers— mostly from other states—came by train. The depots that welcomed them were predominantly built of wood, provided by the state's own dense forests.

BAKER CITY

SUMPTER VALLEY STATION
Broadway Avenue
1903

The Sumpter Valley narrow gauge railroad, owned by stockholders in a number of lumber companies, was at first used solely for hauling logs from the Blue Mountains. Passenger service was added in 1896, which eventually necessitated construction of a one-story, wooden freight and passenger station at Baker City. This service ended in 1937; the tracks were torn out about 15 years later. Union Pacific, whose standard gauge tracks paralleled Sumpter Valley's through Baker City, had its own depot (1911), which it demolished in 1961. UP's communications office moved into a trailer. Three decades later, an unusual tale of modern day depot recycling unfolded. The city obtained 1993 ISTEA funds to purchase the old Sumpter Valley station (not used as a depot in more than 40 years). Plans are to relocate the building from the west to the east side of the tracks (and rotate it 180 degrees), to the spot where Amtrak's plastic shelter sits. Amtrak and UP will both move into the depot. A third tenant will likely be Sumpter Valley Railroad Restoration (business office only)—a tourist line that operates in the valley of the Blue Mountains on part of the old SV right-of-way. [Privately owned—sale pending to city of Baker City. Vacant—future train stop and railroad offices.]

BEND

BEND DEPOT
Kearney and Division streets
1912

Because of the area's isolation and the difficult terrain presented by the Deschutes River Canyon, no tracks reached Bend until the second decade of the 20th century. Construction of the Oregton Trunk Railway was marked by the violent competition (and eventual compromise)

Bend depot.

The express building that dates from c. 1924 had not yet been built when this photo was taken. Its forthcoming site is adjacent to the depot, about where the automobiles are parked.

of the Union Pacific and the Great Northern, both of which wanted a route into the area's lucrative Ponderosa pine forests. GN tycoon James J. Hill (then 73) drove in the golden spike at Bend's 1911 ceremony, marking the railroad's arrival. Both the Bend depot and its twin at Redmond (1912; extant) were scheduled to be made of wood, but the OTR agreed to masonry if locals would provide the material. "Tuff" is a light pink or charcoal gray stone composed of compacted volcanic ash—two-thirds the weight of sandstone, easy to work, and available from local quarries. Built of the pink version (environmental effects have darkened it), the Bend depot was a one-story Arts and Crafts structure with a hipped roof and a porte-cochere. Transoms and upper window sash were multiple small panes (as many as 20). Stone carvings included the 1911 cornerstone and the word BEND above the telegrapher's bay window. Men and ladies waited in separate rooms. A baggage room was on the north end, and a large freight house (razed in 1986) stood across the tracks. About 1924, an American Railway Express Company building, clad in vertical siding and stucco, was built 80 feet south of the passenger station.

In the early 1990s, both the Bend and Redmond depots became candidates for relo-

James J. Hill driving the golden spike, 1911.

Eugene OE station c. 1914.

cation. The state department of transportation intends to put a highway through the Bend site and move the depot's owner, Burlington Northern, to a new building. Sixteen miles north, the Redmond depot (also BN property) is simply surplus. The nearby city of Prineville, which operates a municipally owned, 18-mile-long freight line (a private excursion train also runs on the rails) obtained ISTEA and state funds to move the two depots and the express building to the Prineville area—an endeavor planned for 1997. The structures will be restored and recycled into museums and train stops, anchoring both ends of the City of Prineville Railway. [Burlington Northern Railroad Company—pending transfer to city of Prineville. Future freight railroad headquarters, tourist train stop, and museum.]

EUGENE

OREGON ELECTRIC STATION
5th Avenue and Willamette Street
Doyle, Patterson, and Beach
1914

The Oregon Electric Railway, an interurban line, grew from the battle between two steam railroad magnates, James J. Hill (Great Northern) and Edward H. Harriman (Southern Pacific). GN's extension into the Willamette Valley, via the Oregon Electric, cracked SP's mo-

nopoly of the region. Built two years after OE arrived in Eugene, the red brick station was designed by a noted Portland firm in Georgian Revival style. North and south facades of the central block each had three tall, arched entranceways, sheltered on the street side by a copper-clad, iron marquee. Attached to the high-ceilinged waiting room were lower, symmetrical wings housing baggage, ticketing, and express areas. Decorative elements included brick wainscoting, oak paneling, fluted pilasters, and terrazzo floors.

After passenger service ended in 1933, the depot was used first for office and storage space and later as a museum. In the late 1970s, during a restaurant conversion, architects consulted the original blueprints to reconstruct the wooden balustrade that was missing from the roof and to take out the false ceiling that had been installed in the waiting room. Many coats of paint were removed from the brick exterior (unfortunately by sandblasting). NR. [Privately owned. Restaurant.]

SOUTHERN PACIFIC STATION
4th Avenue and Willamette Street
1908

One block north of the Oregon Electric station stands a former Southern Pacific station, the third on the site. A one-story building, made of brick laid in Flemish bond, the depot was probably a standard plan. The SP design staff used simple Richardsonian elements. A belcast hipped roof extended into a seven-foot-wide overhang, pierced on the track side by a squat, rounded agent's tower. Diamond-shaped panes of colored glass accented the tower windows and the streetside dormers. Massive tongue and groove, cross-braced doors led into the furnace and baggage rooms. Extensive landscaping (a rose garden and a rookery with ferns, palms, and flowers) elicited approval from a contemporary newspaper, which declared the park a definite improvement over the previous barns, cigar signs, garbage and manure piles. Today the lawn is a parking lot; but the depot itself is little changed, except for a suspended ceiling. Amtrak passengers wait in the original waiting room. Other former railroad buildings at the site include an express office to the east, a bunkhouse (moved from its previous location at the west end of the depot grounds), and a freight house. [Privately owned. Train stop.]

HOOD RIVER

OREGON-WASHINGTON RAILROAD & NAVIGATION COMPANY STATION
110 Railroad Avenue (1st and Cascade streets)
1911

The Oregon-Washington Railroad & Navigation Company station (Union Pacific system)

replaced an 1882, two-story frame structure on the same site. Built in the Arts and Crafts style, the new story-and-a-half depot was stucco over pressed brick, with a red metal-shingle roof. Its gable ends and dormers were filled with decorative half-timbering. The interior had a general waiting room, a men's smoking room, and a ladies' retiring room with Mission-style rocking chairs and large leather couches. A baggage and express room on the depot's west end survived the 1918 impact of a runaway locomotive.

In 1968, UP purchased Mount Hood Railroad, a feeder line built in 1906 by the Oregon Lumber Company. UP consolidated operations into the O-WR&N depot and, in 1971, razed the MH station. The following decade, UP sold the MH line to local entrepreneurs, who operate both a freight and summer tourist train operation. Their interior restoration of the old O-WR&N depot, using the original blueprints, included exposing the 16-foot-high vaulted ceiling, taking vinyl off the pink marble baseboards, and repainting in original colors—dark green for the lower walls and pastels for the upper walls and ceiling. Exact copies of the station's benches were made based on a surviving model. Custom light fixtures duplicated the conjectured styles of the originals. In the late 1980s, Amtrak stopped using a plastic shelter that had served passengers since 1977 and moved back into the depot. At Pendleton, 135 railroad miles to the east,

A water tank stood adjacent to the Hood River O-WR&N station.

stands a 1910 O-WR&N depot (now a museum, NR District) that is similar to Hood River. NR. [Mount Hood Railroad Company. Amtrak and tourist train stop, freight railroad offices, and special events facility.]

PORTLAND

UNION STATION

Foot of Northwest 6th Avenue
Van Brunt and Howe
1896

In the 1880s, railroad magnate Henry Villard made plans for a union station designed by McKim, Mead, and White. Workers got no farther than the foundation (the site was where the main post office is today) when Villard fell into financial trouble. He later regained part interest in the Northwest Pacific Terminal Company, whose owners (Northern Pacific, Union Pacific, and Southern Pacific) decided on a different location, previously intended for a freight depot. To promote the economic development of Portland by contributing a large portion of the Union Station site and rail yard, Captain John Couch donated his 15-foot-deep lake (part of his 1845 claim). The equivalent of 22 city blocks, it was subsequently filled with gravel, sand, and ship's ballast. An architectural firm with offices in Boston and Kansas City (and a favorite of UP) designed the red brick station combining Queen Anne and Romanesque elements. The 150-foot-high clock tower received a four-sided Seth Thomas clock. (A century later, station personnel still hand-crank its 900-pound weights back into position every week.) Among the station's amenities were a separate waiting room for "emigrants," a men's smoking room, a huge, curved newsstand, and dining facilities. Monetary constraints caused the terminal company to forego a steel and wood, long-span train shed. (Platform canopies were added later.) By 1922, every passenger railroad serving Portland (except the Oregon Electric) used Union Station.

Portland Union Station c. 1920s.

Between 1927 and 1930, the station's interior received a major remodeling, an early work of noted Portland designer, Pietro Belluschi. He opened up the main waiting hall by eliminating its cast-iron columns and the mezzanine level. Italian marble was applied to the walls and floors, and travertine arches were added to the reconfigured baggage area. Dormers permitted more natural light to reach the second- and third-floor offices. During World War II, the Terminal Company provided special waiting space for mothers with children under age two. Called "the baby lounge," it was staffed by volunteers from the American Association of University Women. In 1987, the Portland Development Commission purchased Union Station and 31 acres of former rail yard. PDC's depot rehabilitation included restoring the painted flower patterns of the waiting room's coffered ceiling, reopening the pre-1925 phone booths, and repairing the red metal tile roof. Immense, blue and gold neon GO BY TRAIN and UNION STATION signs (installed in 1948) still light up the tower. The waiting room is

Prairie City depot. Curtains are visible in the windows of the agent's second-floor apartment.

used by Amtrak, with the balance of space leased to about 40 restaurant, retail, and office tenants. Union Station's interlocking tower, built of brick in 1914, continues to function from its location about 700 feet southeast of the depot. NR. [City of Portland. Train stop and commercial.]

PRAIRIE CITY

PRAIRIE CITY DEPOT
Main and Bridge streets
1910

Prairie City was the western terminus of the three-foot-gauge Sumpter Valley Railway. Clad in shiplap siding and diagonally laid tongue and groove boards, the station was originally surrounded by a small lumber mill, stock pens, and warehouses (this area is a park today). A jerkinhead cross gable reached from the agent's office up to his second-floor apartment. Wooden shingles covered the roof; on the wraparound platform canopies, they formed decorative patterns. The ground floor had one room each for passengers, freight, and combined baggage and express, but no plumbing.

Regular passenger train service ended in the 1930s. For the next decade, people bought tickets and rode in the freight train caboose. The depot was used for a while as a group foster home and then sat vacant and vandalized for many years. In the 1970s, city and county officials were considering demolition, when a

citizens group formed to raise funds and coordinate restoration (some of it volunteer). The city, which has a long term lease on the depot, moved a local history museum into the building in 1984. The tracks are gone. NR. [County of Grant. Museum.]

SALEM

SOUTHERN PACIFIC STATION
500 13th Street, S.E. (at Oak Street)
1918

Salem's first depot was built in 1871, about 100 feet from the present structure. It burned in 1885. The replacement station (c. 1889 Queen Anne style) was due for an upgrade when it too caught fire. For the third go-round, Southern Pacific built a station clad in buff brick with a tall, single-story center section and two lower wings. Ionic columns framed the recessed, round-arched windows of the street facade. Shelter on the track side was provided by a marquee suspended from chains. An unburned portion of the old station was moved around to the north end of the new passenger station and incorporated into a c. 1920s express building (now boarded up and in need of rescue). In the early Nineties, the city obtained ISTEA funds to buy the depot from Southern Pacific and expand it into a multimodal facility. The waiting room (with a lowered ceiling) is currently used by Amtrak. [Southern Pacific Lines — sale pending to Salem Area Transit District. Train stop.]

Utah

Although four major railroads traversed Utah, only two went through areas of significant population—the Union Pacific and the Denver & Rio Grande. Most of the depots left standing are masonry descendants of the original wooden depots; and most of them are along UP tracks—often still bearing freight and passenger traffic.

BRIGHAM CITY

OREGON SHORT LINE STATION
800 West and Forest streets
1907

After years of citizens' complaints, the Oregon Short Line (Union Pacific system) agreed to replace Brigham City's c. 1891 wooden depot (successor to an even earlier station). The railroad moved the old one across Forest Street, to the east side of the tracks, and converted it to a freight warehouse (razed in 1969). Clad in rock-faced concrete block, the new county seat passenger depot was designed in Arts and Crafts style. Its belcast, multihipped, wood-shingle roof was pierced by numerous dormers that repeated the outline of the main roof. A cross gable created a polygonal agent's bay on the track side and an arched entrance on the street side. The high-ceilinged interior included men's and ladies waiting rooms, and baggage and express facilities.

Today, although Amtrak trains use the tracks, they no longer stop at Brigham City. In the early 1990s, Union Pacific (whose workers occupied the depot) made plans for a new structure. UP donated the old depot to the Golden Spike Association, which annually reenacts the 1869 transcontinental railroad ceremony at Promontory Summit (31 miles west). The group is steadily at work returning the building to its original appearance. NR. [Golden Spike Association. Depot museum.]

Brigham City OSL station c. 1907.

CEDAR CITY

CEDAR CITY DEPOT
North Main Street, north of State Route 56
1923

Although the railroad arrived in Iron County in 1905, the closest rail service to Cedar City remained 33 wagon miles northwest at Lund. Fifteen years later, Union Pacific announced plans for a spur line to accommodate the many tourists drawn to the scenic beauty of southern Utah. Bedecked with stars and stripes, the first train to Cedar City discharged President and Mrs. Warren G. Harding, who proceeded by automobile to Zion National Park. The passenger depot, which officially opened a few months later, was a one-story, stone and brick building, with rounded arches outlining the passenger and baggage entrances and the windows of the agent's bay. Transoms and upper window sash were filled with small panes of glass. UP engaged directly in the tourist business by operating hotels and bus tours to the canyons. Sightseers boarded motor coaches from an L-shaped shelter (1929) attached to the depot's south end. By the 1940s, Cedar City passenger service had already diminished; and most of the time, residents had to take a UP-operated bus to catch the train at Lund.

Used for two of today's ubiquitous commercial enterprises—a pizza parlor and a service station-minimarket (at the bus end)—the depot nonetheless retains its benches and architectural features. The freight station and most of the "balloon track" (an arc used to swing trains around and head them the other way) are gone. NR. [Privately owned. Commercial.]

LOGAN

LOGAN DEPOT
600 West Center Street
1895

Approached from the street side, Logan's former Union Pacific depot looks like an English cottage, except for the double baggage doors at either end. Constructed by the Oregon Short Line, the story-and-a-half building of gray-white, rock-faced sandstone has window surrounds and quoins of pressed red brick. On the street side, the projecting bay, with four high, square windows, is topped by a very broad gable clad in pseudo-half-timbering. On the west side, the wood-shingle hipped roof extends over the platform and then north and south down the tracks. The interior includes the former men's and ladies' waiting rooms, ticket office, and agent's upstairs apartment (originally offices).

Upon vacating the depot in 1986, UP first offered it to the city; but officials claimed they

Touring cars at the Cedar City depot, 1926.

Early streetside view of the Logan depot.

had no funds for restoration or maintenance. In 1993, the railroad donated the building to a group formed especially for its preservation. The tracks are still active. UP maintains a freight office in one room, which it retained the right to use in perpetuity. The preservation group is raising funds to restore the balance of the building for a restaurant and a museum devoted to local history, especially transportation. It plans to furnish the apartment with artifacts supplied by descendants of the depot agent and to paint the exterior trim in the original colors of crimson and gold. If the group's application for ISTEA funding is successful, a proposed extension of the Logan River recreational trail would pass by the depot. [Logan Depot Foundation. Freight office and future mixed use.]

MORGAN

MORGAN DEPOT
98 North Commercial Street
1926

The Morgan depot is a small and simple version of a distinctive Union Pacific style that varied by size, number of stories, and level of sophistication. A design built in masonry (in this case, stuccoed walls inlaid with herringbone-pattern red brick), the archetypal features

were flush eaves (no cornice or roof overhang), gabled bays on both the street and track sides, raised basement, tile roof, and UP polychrome shields. Constructed the same year the line was double-tracked, the Morgan depot succeeded a wooden station that was converted exclusively to freight use and still stands about one block to the northwest. After closing the three-room depot in 1982, UP donated it to the city. The municipality in turn leased the building to the county economic development office; but that organization dissolved in the mid-1990s, thus leaving the depot's future uncertain. The ticket booth, wavy glass window panes, oak benches, flooring, and woodwork are intact. Each day, two dozen freight trains go by the station. [City of Morgan. Vacant.]

OGDEN

UNION DEPOT
Wall Avenue and 25th Street
Parkinson and Parkinson
1924

In 1869, the golden spike ceremony at Promontory Summit signified the linkage of eastern and western railroads—the birth of transcontinental train travel. Passengers could now cross the country by rail, although not

Twin streetside entrances at Ogden Union Depot include fine masonry details and wrought-iron light fixtures.

without changing trains at three places: Chicago, Omaha, and Promontory. The third transfer point soon shifted to Ogden, whose first depot was a one-story, board and batten structure erected by the Union Pacific and painted bright red. In 1889, the Ogden Union Railway & Depot Company (owned by UP and Southern Pacific) dedicated a new, multi-dormered depot with a clock tower, designed by Van Brunt and Howe. It was destroyed by fire 34 years later; the present building is built on the old one's foundation. For the replacement, a Los Angeles architectural firm used pink and buff brick to look like Cordova tile. Two arched entrance porches were ornamented with bright blue mosaic tile and heavy wrought-iron chandeliers. The main structure was Italian Renaissance Revival style. Mail and trainmen's buildings were less ornate.

In the early 1970s, UP and SP were contemplating demolishing or selling Union Depot (which had also been served by the Denver & Rio Grande Western). But a stipulation in the original deed dictated that the land be used for rail passenger service in perpetuity; otherwise it reverted to Brigham Young's descendants. After six years of negotiations, the railroads donated the three buildings to the city with a

50-year lease on the underlying land. Renovation was carried out by a nonprofit corporation with federal, state, local, and private funds. The two-story-high grand waiting room, with open truss ceiling, was restored and adapted for civic and theatrical uses. Other spaces were provided for Amtrak, two museums, freight railroad offices, an art gallery, and convention and meeting rooms. Added later were two more museums, a restaurant (in the original dining room space), a model railroad store, an office for the arts council, and an information center operated by the United States Forest Service. NR. [City of Ogden. Train stop and mixed use.]

PARK CITY

ECHO & PARK CITY STATION
Heber Avenue and Main Street
1886

Union Pacific's engineering office in Omaha, Neb., designed a wooden Queen Anne–style depot for the affiliated Echo & Park City Railroad, a three-foot-gauge line in silver mining country. The floor plan included a single waiting room and an agent's office of equal size, baggage and express rooms, and a large freight section. The agent's apartment on the second floor included a substantial balcony, from which presidential candidate William Jennings Bryan reportedly spoke to a crowd of 3,000 in 1897. (Some descriptions have him standing on a ladder.) Upper window sash were bordered with small panes of colored glass.

The depot had been vacant for about a decade when much of the southern portion was destroyed by a 1985 fire. A subsequent rebuilding for a restaurant did not accurately reproduce the exterior. This situation was corrected by new owners in 1993, who replaced the original baggage room doors and reconstructed the

Several well-dressed people have come onto the balcony to pose for this photo of the Park City E&PC station.

front porch. The tracks are gone, as is the Denver & Rio Grande depot, which stood about a block northwest of the E&PC (UP) station. [Privately owned. Restaurant.]

SALT LAKE CITY

DENVER & RIO GRANDE STATION
3rd South and Rio Grande Street
Henry S. Schlacks
1910

The center portion of Salt Lake City's Denver & Rio Grande station (built also to serve the Western Pacific) housed a splendid waiting room, 58 feet high. The east and west walls were each filled by three immense arched windows. Light poured through green opalescent glass onto a color scheme of brownish-red and gray walls with a dark brown ceiling. The ticket office, newsstand, and telegraph and telephone offices were centered in the room. Wings housed men's smoking and ladies' retiring rooms, and baggage, express, and parcel rooms. Railroad offices were upstairs. For exterior surfaces, Chicago architect Henry Schlacks used white marble, terra-cotta, red brick, and red roof tiles.

In 1977, the Utah State Historical Society was in need of a new home. Rather than

Salt Lake City D&RG station. Most of the conveyances are horse-drawn in this early street-side view.

Salt Lake City UP station, 1924. A large UP shield has been erected above the cornice.

undertaking or leasing new construction, the state government acquired the vacant and run-down "Rio Grande" station. Workers chemically cleaned the exterior, performed a seismic retrofit, and retained as many original exterior and interior features as possible, including the bathroom sinks. The waiting room now houses the state historical society museum. A restaurant is in the north wing, site of the station's old tea and dining rooms. Besides housing the society's office, meeting, and library space, the depot still has its railroad connection; in the mid-1980s, Amtrak established a waiting room in the former baggage wing. NR. [State of Utah. Train stop and mixed use.]

UNION PACIFIC STATION
South Temple at 400 West
Daniel J. Patterson
1909

Original plans for the Union Pacific station were published as early as 1903 in a Salt Lake City newspaper. The architect of this French Renaissance Revival design was a *Southern Pacific* staff member (at the time, Edward Harriman controlled both SP and UP). Built of reinforced concrete, clad in cut gray sandstone and brick, the station included many decorative elements such as twin streetside towers, carved stone gargoyles, fancy metal cresting on a black-slate mansard roof, and circular dormers. The most impressive interior space was an ornate, skylit waiting room with a vaulted ceiling. Above each of the five trackside entrances, San Francisco artist Harry Hopps installed a stained-glass window depicting a western or transportation-related theme. For the north and south walls, fellow San Franciscan John A. MacQuarrie painted two murals: *This is the Place*, commemorating Brigham Young's arrival in Salt Lake City and *Driving of the Golden Spike*, honoring completion of the first transcontinental railroad. Express facililties were in the basement; railroad offices, on the second floor.

After moving into a building north of the depot in 1988, UP donated its Salt Lake City station to the state. The railroad stipulated that the structure be used for some arts-related project. Since that time, the Utah Arts Council has used the cosmetically well-preserved, former station as office space and storage for its permanent collection. The council is investigating the possibility of converting the building to a unique art-science discovery center. NR. [State of Utah. Offices and fine arts storage.]

Washington

In 1883, completion of the first northern route, transcontinental railroad—the Northern Pacific—ushered in a flood of settlers to Washington Territory. A decade later, the Great Northern arrived, determined to crack the NP monopoly. The rivalry and intermingling of these two railroads (influenced by the Union Pacific and the Chicago, Milwaukee & St. Paul) affected the location and style of stations, as well as the layout of communities they served.

BELLINGHAM

GREAT NORTHERN STATION

Foot of D Street
F. Stanley Piper
1927

In the 1890s, the Fairhaven & Southern (Great Northern system) went right across the tidal flats of Bellingham Bay. A trestle held both the tracks and the depot. In 1902, GN abandoned the trestle, filled the land, and relocated the tracks. GN's new brick depot with a wood-shingle roof burned in 1924. (Its companion freight station, built of wood in 1905, still stands.) Designed by a local architect, the next passenger station had one-story brick walls, a Spanish tile roof, and sophisticated decorative elements. The streetside entrance to the waiting room was recessed behind an arcade of three semicircular arches, faced in glazed terracotta. Ornamentation consisted of Corinthian capitals and raised tendrils. Inside the waiting room, the tendril motif was repeated on the tall curved opening of the ticket cage. Wrought-iron circular chandeliers were suspended from a high, beamed ceiling. A geometric Indian motif, used frequently by Great Northern, was painted along the lower edges of four wooden, boxed girders. Brass strips formed a diagonal pattern in the terrazzo floor, laid in two shades of gray.

The depot's wings housed the agent's office, baggage and express services, and a ladies' retiring room. Outside the agent's bay, a long freestanding platform canopy was pierced by a semaphore mast (both canopy and signal are now gone). Amtrak, which suspended service to this station in the early 1980s, is scheduled to return to Bellingham in the Nineties, but probably will stop in another part of the city. Besides GN, Bellingham had two other major steam railroads—the Northern Pacific and the Chicago, Milwaukee & St. Paul. (A former Pacific Northwest Traction Company station is now a bus depot.) [Burlington Northern Railroad Company. Freight railroad offices.]

Bellingham GN station, streetside entrance.

CENTRALIA

UNION DEPOT

Railroad Avenue between Pine
   and Magnolia streets
1912

In 1912, Centralia's new depot opened with a kind of intermodal christening — bottles of champagne dropped onto the roof from an airplane. The Spanish tiles sustained minor damage. Transcontinental and regional rail lines radiated from Centralia, nicknamed "Hub City." Northern Pacific's first two stations, both wooden, were built in 1880 and 1905. The third successive station was a union depot, shared by the Great Northern and the Oregon-Washington Railroad & Navigation Company, among others. Passengers walked across herringbone-patterned bricks to reach the depot, built of brick above a Tenino sandstone base. The depot's central portion, which housed waiting, ticketing, and baggage facilities, was surmounted by a large cross gable with half-round attic windows. Additional light was admitted through gabled dormers, which were removed at some time before 1925. Breezeways led to the depot's north and south wings. Interior features included terrazzo floors, enameled white tile wainscoting, oak benches, and a massive, ornate wooden stairway.

In 1993, the state negotiated transfer of the depot's ownership from Burlington Northern (GN's successor) to the city. ISTEA funds were used to begin restoration, including removal of the dropped ceiling. In addition to continued operation as an Amtrak stop, the facility will become a transfer point for the city's bus network. If BN vacates its space (now used by maintenance crews), the city expects to add commercial uses to the depot. NR. [City of Centralia. Transportation center.]

CHEHALIS

CHEHALIS DEPOT

599 Northwest Front Way
1912

The twin cities of Centralia and Chehalis were four railroad miles apart on the busy corridor between Portland and Seattle. Both Great Northern and Union Pacific rented space in the Chehalis depot, built by Northern Pacific. It was smaller than the one in Centralia; and its cross gable and parapeted end gables were curvilinear rather than peaked. Brick walls were sheltered by a slate roof.

Lacking any railroad use today, Chehalis's preservation story, as a case study, contrasts with that of Centralia. In the early 1970s,

In this early view of the Chehalis depot, hotel-owned conveyances wait to pick up incoming guests.

Burlington Northern (a 1970 merger of several railroads) decided to raze the Chehalis depot. Thinking that a new home for the Lewis County Historical Museum was more desirable than a parking lot, determined citizens enlisted support ranging from county commissioners to United States senators. It took two rounds of negotiations (BN reneged on its first promise not to seek demolition), a fence agreement, and a museum-only use restriction to produce a lease between the county and the railroad. Rehabilitation funds came principally from the United States Department of Commerce and private donations. Among the railroad artifacts on view today are the depot's freight scale and an 1873 telegrapher's key (first used at a station three miles away). Both freight and passenger trains still ply the tracks. NR. [Burlington Northern Railroad Company. Museum.]

DAYTON

OREGON RAILWAY & NAVIGATION COMPANY STATION

222 East Commercial Street
1881

The town of Dayton did not grow in the expected direction—the population expanded to the east instead of the west. In 1889, the Oregon Railway & Navigation Company (later Union Pacific), decided to relocate its tracks. The railroad moved the depot directly across the 40-foot-wide Touchet River, apparently by placing it on roller logs, pulled by a horse and winch.

In 1971, UP closed the depot and stripped it of all wiring, plumbing, and fixtures in preparation for demolition. Dayton Historical Depot Society convinced the railroad to give it both the building and land. Federal, state, and private funds were used for restoring the graceful Stick Style depot. Work began with the foundation (deteriorating because of an underground spring), followed by replacement of the

cedar-shingle roof with like materials. Volunteers rebuilt the second-floor balcony that wraps around three sides of the depot, and the ground-floor boardwalk. Paint donated by Union Pacific returned the depot to its original colors—mustard body with two shades of brown trim. Exterior doors were reproduced, using the one remaining example as a guide. The society refinished the original oak benches and decorated the station agent's upstairs apartment in 1880s style. Available for private and civic functions, the depot's museum exhibits railroad memorabilia and local items (in particular, century-old furniture manufactured in the area) and photographs of Columbia County. Dayton's other depot—Northern Pacific—has been relocated from its site northeast of the OR&N station and altered beyond recognition. NR. [Dayton Historical Depot Society. Museum.] *For photo, see* page xiv.

ELLENSBURG

NORTHERN PACIFIC STATION

606 West 3rd Avenue
Reed and Stem
1910

By the early 1900s, Ellensburg was the center of a prosperous agricultural region and home of a state-chartered college. The frame, two-story Northern Pacific depot (1886) was perceived as a civic embarrassment. It was relocated along the tracks to the southeast, where it stands today in industrial use. Renowned Minnesota-based architects, Reed and Stem, designed the new depot as a smaller version of the one at Yakima (c. 1910, NR). Spanish Colonial Revival style, with a large curvilinear cross gable, the depot had a two-story center section and one-story wings. The walls were reddish brown brick, and the roof was likely clay tile. Interior finishes included terrazzo floors and enameled white tile wainscoting. The waiting rooms and lunch room had beamed ceilings. Division

Ellensburg NP station. This early view shows the open south end (now enclosed), roof cresting (now gone), and full complement of chimneys.

headquarters were on the second floor. Nearby were a water tower, stock pens, and a round-house (the latter destroyed by fire in the 1950s). In 1934, the railroad remodeled the depot by enclosing an open area on the south and reducing the size of the central waiting room, probably for additional office and freight space. The changes were made almost invisible by carefully matched materials.

After the Burlington Northern (NP's successor) abandoned the depot in the 1980s, it was converted to a restaurant and winery with the ticket window retained for serving food. The building's use has since changed to offices. Freight trains occasionally ply the tracks. Ellensburg's Chicago, Milwaukee & St. Paul depot (1907) was demolished about 1963. NR. [Privately owned. Commercial.]

ISSAQUAH

ISSAQUAH DEPOT
Rainier Avenue North
1889

The arrival of the Seattle, Lake Shore & Eastern Railway (soon Northern Pacific) turned Issaquah into a coal and logging boomtown. The combination freight and passenger station (the stop was first known as Gilman) had separate men's and ladies' waiting rooms, made smaller within a decade to provide living quarters for the agent.

The exterior was sheathed in shiplap and tongue and groove siding; wood shingles covered both the main roof and the cross gable.

Regularly scheduled passenger service ended in the 1920s, and the railroad abandoned the building in 1962. A private party gutted the interior, changed the windows, and covered the exterior in modern siding for use as a warehouse. More than two decades later, the city purchased the deteriorating depot and leased it to the Issaquah Historical Society. Its meticulous, ongoing restoration includes removing the dropped ceiling, reconstructing the ticket booth, reinstalling partitions, and replicating missing millwork. All work has been based on early photographs, blueprints, and existing material fragments. Over the years, the railroad repeatedly filled the soft ground and raised the tracks. Because the historical society wanted to re-create the original height relationship of depot to track level, the group jacked up the building and built a new platform to meet it. Remnants of paint were analyzed to reproduce the original exterior colors—a bright violet-red body, green trim, and white window sash. NR. [City of Issaquah. Vacant—future museum and special events facility.]

SEATTLE

KING STREET STATION
303 South Jackson Street
Reed and Stem
1906

Seattle's first depots were rickety buildings located on the waterfront. In the 1890s, the city had two major railroads, Northern Pacific and Great Northern. Their competitive presidents dragged city council into a decade of arguments over which location and what level of architectural sophistication a joint station should have. The case was settled when GN's James J. Hill acquired control of NP in 1901. He built a depot where he had planned—on the south side of Jackson Street; a mile-long

The elegant interior of Seattle King Street Station in 1907.

tunnel carried the tracks under the business district to reach the waterfront. Despite his selection of Charles A. Reed and Allen H. Stem (later of Grand Central Terminal fame) as the architects, Hill opposed the idea of spending money for a "fancy depot." King Street Station was three stories high on the track side (two on Jackson Street); carriages and hacks could deliver passengers directly to the lower train level. Its outstanding feature was an exceedingly high clock tower (used for storing records), derived from a campanile in Venice's Piazza de San Marco. Constructed of granite and red brick with terra-cotta and cast-stone

ornamentation, the depot's so-called plainness was relative to 1906 standards for ornateness.

In the 1960s, the two railroads utilized tax incentives available for modernization of stations. GN replaced the platforms and umbrella sheds. NP made interior changes, including lowering the waiting room ceiling, trading chandeliers for fluorescent lighting, and covering (or possibly replacing) the marble with plastic laminate. (In the lobby at the base of the tower, evidence exists of the marble wainscoting, mosaic banding, and plaster walls.) The second and third floors, modified several times, were used as freight railroad offices into the late 1980s. Amtrak occupies the first floor. In 1994, the city began studying the feasibility of a multimodal facility for King Street Station. NR. [Burlington Northern Railroad Company. Train Stop.]

UNION STATION
South Jackson Street and 4th Avenue South
Daniel J. Patterson
1911

The Oregon-Washington Railroad & Navigation Company (Union Pacific system) was a latecomer to Seattle. The depot it built on reclaimed tidal flats became known as Union Station because it was shared by the Chicago, Milwaukee & St. Paul. Designed in Beaux Arts style by the same architect who worked on Salt Lake

Seattle Union Station (with Oregon-Washington sign on its pedimented facade). The clock tower of neighboring King Street Station is in the background.

City's Union Pacific station, the depot was constructed of reinforced concrete clad in dark red brick with a tile roof. Pale stonework and terra-cotta provided contrast. Three-story-high office wings flanked an even taller center section. The ceiling of the barrel-vaulted grand waiting room was formed by six arched ribs that intersected two longitudinal beams. Tiny, naked light bulbs outlined this configuration — its center filled with colored glass skylights. Furnishings consisted of back-to-back oak benches, foot-high brass spittoons, and potted palm trees. Rimming the waiting room were a men's smoking room, barber shop, ladies' waiting and retiring rooms, a news and parcels room, ticketing and baggage facilities, and an immigrants' waiting room. A concourse at the back of the building led via stairways to the track level. Passengers were sheltered under umbrella platform canopies.

Union Station's busiest year was 1945, with the return of World War II troops from the Pacific arena. "Milwaukee Road" passenger service ended in 1961; Union Pacific, a decade later. During the Seventies, successive plans for government offices and a multimodal facility died. UP was set to restore the building as commercial office space, but subsequently decided to divest itself of nonrailroad real estate. The building remains unused, except for the first floor (leased to a caterer). NR. [Union Pacific Railroad. Mostly vacant — for sale.]

SNOQUALMIE

SNOQUALMIE DEPOT
109 King Street
1890

In 1889, a year before Washington gained statehood, the Seattle, Lake Shore & Eastern (later Northern Pacific) opened a new line into Snoqualmie Valley. Huge stands of cedar and fir trees now had a way to reach the marketplace, and people could travel to Seattle in a few hours. Construction through the rugged Cascade Mountains lay ahead of the railroad. To convince investors that it was solvent, the SLS&E decided to build an impressive station. The construction contract specified that the Snoqualmie depot be completed in 90 days. Although the railroad never made it further east, the station handled countless tourists arriving for a visit to Snoqualmie Falls.

After regular passenger service ended in the 1920s, the depot handled only freight. A half-century later, a local railroad historical association acquired the depot and about six miles of track. Using federal and county grant money, the group restored the wooden, story-and-a-half depot, which had been seriously altered over the years. Work included reconstructing the octagonal agent's bay and tower, removing the dropped ceiling, and reestablishing the original floor plan. Within the curved

Early view of the combination passenger and freight station at Snoqualmie.

West elevation (Pacific Avenue side) of Tacoma Union Station c. 1912.

east side of the depot, the museum bookstore now occupies the former men's waiting room. The freight room houses the museum's interpretative exhibit and rest rooms, and tickets for tourist trains are sold from the ticket office. Interior walls on the passenger end are clear, tongue and groove fir, installed diagonally. Most of the depot's original architectural features — such as eyebrow and gable dormers, decorative barge boards, fish scale shingles, and stained glass windows — have been preserved or restored. The fancy ridge cresting is next on the list. NR. [Puget Sound Railway Historical Association. Tourist train stop and museum.]

TACOMA

UNION STATION
Pacific Avenue and 19th Street
Reed and Stem
1911

On a spring day in 1911, the governor of Washington and the president of Northern Pacific joined a crowd of 25,000 to celebrate the opening of Tacoma's Union Station (used also by Great Northern and Union Pacific). Designed by nationally prominent architects, the depot glowed with a 90-foot-high, copper-sheathed dome that rested on four barrel vaults, intersecting at right angles. A large car-

touche was applied to each intersection. Masonry work included dark red brick walls (laid in Flemish bond with black mortar) and limestone (used for the cornice and the monumental arches of the street and trackside facades). The depot was built against an embankment; only two stories of the three-story office wings were visible from Pacific Avenue. Inside the rotunda, floors were mosaic tile and terrazzo; walls were Italian marble, up to balcony height. Spaces surrounding the general waiting room included a restaurant, baggage room, men's waiting room, and ladies' suite. Atop the ticket windows was a marble-faced clock made by Joseph Mayer and Brothers of Seattle. Flights of marble stairs led down to a skylit and windowed concourse stretching over the canopied tracks.

Burlington Northern (the last railroad owner) and Amtrak both vacated Union Station in the early 1980s. The city put a construction fence around the station, located in a blighted area. Within 18 months, a "Save Our Station" group grew to 1,500 members, many of them senior citizens whose memories would not let Union Station die. Numerous proposals arose and faded away, until the deteriorated, scavenger-stripped building was acquired by the city in 1987. To the north, Tacoma constructed a new courthouse, connected at track level to the former station, which also houses courtrooms (in the old restaurant and ladies' waiting room area) and other court-related facilities. The three-story-high rotunda is available for special events, and a cafe operates from the old concourse level. The area around Union Station continues to bounce back, with a new museum being built to the south and historic warehouses across the street undergoing adaptive use for college classrooms. NR. [City of Tacoma. Mixed use.]

TENINO

NORTHERN PACIFIC STATION
399 West Park Street
Luther Twichel
1914

In 1914, Northern Pacific rerouted its Tenino to Tacoma main line. Tenino's wooden, combination freight and passenger depot was relocated and put into temporary service at the junction of the original main line (demoted to branch line status) and the new one. NP commissioned a Tacoma architect to design a more substantial depot. His plan specified native sandstone (blocks and veneer), one of the community's most significant resources. Masons achieved a striped effect by alternating courses of rock-faced and smooth stone, as well as varying the height of the layers. Cedar shingles covered the gabled hip roof, which flared slightly into a

deep overhang. The depot's two sandstone chimneys were crowned with decorative caps. Most doors and windows, including the large wooden freight doors, had rounded transoms.

After passenger service ended in the 1950s and freight the following decade, Burlington Northern (NP's successor) intended to demolish the depot. In 1975, citizens raised funds to move the one-story building to a site just east of the first station's location, adjacent to the pre-1914 main line. The South Thurston Historical Society operates a local history museum in the depot. A telegraph key inside the agent's bay and the original semaphore signal on the outside help retain the railroad flavor. In the 1990s, BN began procedures to abandon the right-of-way (which will eventually become a recreational trail), and the depot lost all but a short stretch of its adopted tracks. NR. [City of Tenino. Museum.]

TOPPENISH

TOPPENISH DEPOT
Asotin Avenue
1911

Toppenish's first station was a combination depot and post office. The second one, across the tracks and northwest of today's station, was wooden and deemed too small. Its replacement

Tenino NP station. The white numbers and letters indicate that the railroad used this photo to appraise the various elements of its property. Today such valuation records can be a rich source of information on depots.

This early view of the Toppenish depot shows the now-missing dormers that will be re-created.

was a story-and-half brick structure with a tile roof and brick platform. It had open-air shelters at either end and a curvilinear cross gable. The floor plan included a waiting room with a terrazzo floor and oak trim, an agent's office, and express and baggage areas.

After passenger service ended in 1985, the depot was boarded shut. In 1992, the Yakima Valley Rail and Steam Museum worked with the city to obtain ISTEA funding for both acquisition and restoration of the depot and a park to the east. The station will be painted in original Northern Pacific colors. Funds will also be used to reconstruct the depot's small gable dormers with lunette windows. Other extant buildings are the freight depot (recently converted by the museum to an enginehouse) and the section foreman's residence. Freight trains still use the tracks. [City of Toppenish. Railroad museum.]

WALLA WALLA

NORTHERN PACIFIC STATION
416 North 2nd Avenue
1914

By the 1870s, Walla Walla had become a major trading center for the prosperous wheat belt of southeastern Washington and northeastern Oregon. The combination of a pioneer steam railway and river barges made possible the shipment of wheat to ocean ports. Within two decades, Walla Walla was connected to two transcontinental main lines: the Union Pacific (via the Oregon-Washington Railroad & Navigation Company) and the Northern Pacific (via the original Washington & Columbia River line). In 1914, NP announced improvements for its Walla Walla facilities, including a new passenger station to replace the wooden one at East Main and Palouse streets. Designed by the home office in St. Paul, Minn., the brick depot had a story-and-a-half central block, flanked by one-story wings, and a freight annex extending from the north end. A separate freight depot (now gone) stood across the tracks and to the east. On the track side, a three-story-high square tower lit by 17 double hung windows dominated the composition. (The tower's first floor now has doors instead of windows.) Interior spaces included a separate ladies' waiting room (south wing), a baggage room, and an express storeroom.

In the 1980s, after several years of abandonment, the depot was converted to a retail and restaurant complex. A one-story addition off the south end reflects the roof pitch and form of the north annex. Completed according to the Secretary of the Interior's Standards for Rehabilitation, the project qualified for tax credits. Among the features retained were wooden benches, porcelain fixtures (moved to new rest rooms), maple and tile floors, tongue and groove wooden ceilings, and the exposed brick walls of the two freight rooms. A parking lot covers the old right-of-way. The O-WR&N depot (1907) is gone. NR. [Privately owned. Commercial.]

Wyoming

Following an eight-year absence, Amtrak returned to Wyoming in 1991. A year later, preservationists joined with city and state officials to launch Tracks Across America, a program to promote and preserve history along the 400-mile-long transcontinental route — ranging from the trails of pioneer migration to industrialized modes of transportation. Roundhouses, depots, sheep warehouses, and coal mining facilities are among the structures still standing that commemorate the state's railroad heritage. This kind of project encourages retention of the everyday buildings so casually and commonly demolished — the links to understanding the way people lived.

CHEYENNE

UNION PACIFIC STATION
15th Street and Capitol Avenue
Van Brunt and Howe
1887

In 1885, the *Cheyenne Daily Sun* editorialized on the need for a new Union Pacific depot. Apparently passengers avoided the existing wooden one as if it were a "cowshed." Work on a new depot began the following year. A time capsule placed inside the 2,500-pound cornerstone included a book of poems entitled *Black Mammy*. Van Brunt and Howe (who relocated from Boston to Kansas City, Mo., in 1886) formulated a Richardsonian Romanesque design, extending over more than a city block. Red and gray sandstone, quarried at Fort Collins, Colo., covered the two-and-a-half-story iron and wooden frame. A miniturreted clock tower more than 120 feet high, emerged from the slate-covered roof. Red oak was used extensively on the interior, including the ladies' waiting room, which the *Sun* described as having an "old-fashioned fireplace. . . making the spacious

Cheyenne UP station, 1908. The exposed platform of this substantial depot provided a wide area for baggage carts and passenger circulation, but no shelter from the elements.

Evanston depot, street side in 1908.

and elegant room appear cheerful and home-like." Waiting rooms for "gents" and "emigrants" (who ate at a separate lunch counter) were said to be equally well appointed. The second floor of the east wing housed division offices. On the north and east ends stood a park (replaced in 1940 by a bus depot) with flowers, trees, and a water fountain that accommodated both horses and dogs. In 1922, a story-and-a-half "eating house" of matching sandstone was added to the depot's east end (converted in 1948 to an office and meeting facility known as Hicks Hall). Seven years later, the interior received an Art Deco updating. Other alterations included elimination of the carriage passageway that extended through the building and the addition of a concourse.

After passenger service ended in 1971, UP partitioned the depot for offices. When the railroad vacated the building in 1990, citizens formed the Wyoming Transportation Museum Corporation, expressly to save the depot. With UP's pledge to transfer the station to a city-county entity, the group has obtained state grant money and raised matching funds toward rehabilitation. The objective is to create a facility exploring the impact of railroading and other forms of transportation on the history of the West. Southwest across the tracks, seven stalls remain of an 1890 roundhouse, about one-sixth its orig-

inal size (now used for storing UP's collection of historic, functioning locomotives, but not open to the public). NR. [Wyoming Transportation Museum Joint Powers Board. Vacant—future museum.]

EVANSTON

EVANSTON DEPOT
10 10th Street
1900

In 1868, the first train arrived in Evanston, which soon became a division point along the Union Pacific main line. Evanston today is a county seat of about 12,000 people in a still isolated area. Every year, with admirable dedication, community members hold the "Renewal Ball." Proceeds go to restoring Depot Square, a three-block area that comprises commercial buildings from 1880 to 1930. Evanton's UP depot is a highly ornamented structure, compared to the relatively plain buildings nearby. One story high, the depot has a double-level hipped roof (lower on the baggage and express end) that extends into deep eaves, supported by substantial wooden brackets. A medieval-looking cross gable forms the streetside entrance. Its stepped parapet surmounts a round-arched entrance, flanked by twin turrets. A freight depot once stood about 500 yards to the east.

In 1983, Amtrak discontinued service through Evanston. Two years later, UP donated the depot to the city. Restoration took nearly four years, while a public-private partnership continuously worked at fund raising. A retired architect donated his services, and using the original blueprints, oversaw such projects as rebuilding the missing fireplace and installing new tongue and groove floors. The depot originally had separate waiting rooms for men and women, which are now available for community and private functions. In 1991, when Amtrak revived the *Pioneer* route through Wyoming, it leased the depot's former baggage-express area (complete with original scales) as its new Evanston waiting room. NR District. [City of Evanston. Train stop and special events facility.]

RAWLINS

RAWLINS DEPOT
North Front and 4th streets
1901

Rawlins was founded as a Union Pacific division point in 1868. The livestock industry benefited from the railroad's presence as did the developing mineral industry. Rawlins Metallic Paint Company produced "Rawlins red" (a color used extensively by UP) from locally mined, red hematite ore. By the turn of the 20th century, the town's 1868 depot had been outgrown. A granite-trimmed, rock-faced brick station was constructed north of the tracks, just south of the downtown area. Its architectural features combined Prairie Style and more traditional elements, such as Gothic-arched windows in the pagodalike tower. Interior trim and wainscoting were oak. Within a dozen years, the railroad built an eating house of matching

materials to the east. (Parts of the restaurant structure were rebuilt after a 1920s fire.) In the early 1940s, UP made changes to the depot's floor plan, such as combining the gender-segregated waiting rooms into one. The railroad enclosed the breezeway to the eating house and converted it to offices and locker rooms.

In 1994, UP donated the depot to the city. A state community block grant was used to temporarily repair the asbestos roof, until money becomes available for a historically accurate, black slate replacement. ISTEA funds, matched by the city, provided an environmental study and architect's rendering. Amtrak passengers now wait in an adjacent shelter. Once rehabilitation is completed (partly with volunteer labor), the city hopes to provide space for a waiting room, the chamber of commerce, the downtown development authority, and a museum. NR. [City of Rawlins. Train stop/npa and vacant.]

RIVERTON

RIVERTON DEPOT
1st and Main streets
1907

A half-century after the Union Pacific had pushed through southern Wyoming, the central part of the state was still without rails and without white settlement. In 1906, the federal government opened up about 100,000 acres of land, awarded to homesteaders by lottery and claimed by squatters rights. At a bend in the Big Wind River, government surveyors staked out a townsite, cut diagonally by a railroad right-of-way. Settlers camped out across the river. On the designated August morning, en masse, they rushed into town to stake their claims. About two weeks later, the Chicago & North Western laid down tracks. In the first railroad shipment was lumber for a depot, erected by railroad crews once they completed the line to Lander. The one-story station was clad in drop siding and housed (from north to south) an express agency, storage room, men's waiting room, ticket office, women's waiting room, and agent's living quarters.

In the early 1970s, the C&NW abandoned the line and demolished the big railroad bridge south of Riverton (tracks remained until the early Nineties). The railroad sold the depot and land to a private party, who promised the railroad he would raze the building. He later offered it to a citizens group—provided the members would move it off-site. Determined to keep the depot and its brick platform where they belonged, the group secured grant money, private donations, and an interest-free loan—and bought the property. Restoration, using almost all volunteer labor, began in 1976. A fire damaged the south-end living quarters, which were then remodeled rather than restored. The group had difficulty keeping up its financial obligations; in 1993, a local man—equally committed to preservation—purchased the depot. NR. [Privately owned. Chamber of commerce and restaurant.]

ROCK SPRINGS

ROCK SPRINGS DEPOT
501 South Main Street
1900

Located on the main line of the Union Pacific, Rock Springs supplied the railroad with large quantities of high quality bituminous coal. The present brick depot was built during an era of a general upgrading by the railroad. Reportedly, UP president Edward H. Harriman visited the town and insisted not only on a new station, but also on the addition of two small parks to either side. Carloads of topsoil were hauled in and seeded, converting the arid land to lawn. UP made the old 1868 depot into a freight house (replaced in 1910 by a brick version that is still standing). Designed by the UP's engineering office in Omaha, Neb., the new passenger station had a cut stone base, brick walls, and a slate roof. The street side was entered through an enclosed vestibule with brick pilasters and an ornamented pediment. On the track side, above the agent's bay, a

Rock Springs depot in 1906, six years after construction. The adjacent Depot Park contains a curled hose and one small tree.

Palladian window filled the single large dormer. Interior spaces included express and baggage rooms, a men's waiting room, a central "boarding lobby," and a women's waiting room with a polygonal alcove. UP altered the interior in 1922 and 1941, probably to accommodate more crew facilities. In the early Nineties, UP donated the depot to the city, which now leases it to Amtrak. (Passenger service was reinstated in 1991.) The eastern wall of the station suffers from two large cracks, caused by past underground coal mining. The city has applied to the Abandoned Mine Lands Fund for money to make repairs. NR District. [City of Rock Springs. Train stop.]

SHERIDAN

SHERIDAN DEPOT
Broadway between 4th and 5th streets
1912

In 1911, officials of the Chicago, Burlington & Quincy arrived in five private rail cars to view the railroad's facilities at Sheridan. They went directly to the roundhouse, walked through the rail yards, and then inspected the two-story wooden depot. Built c. 1892, it stood opposite the Sheridan Inn (1893, NR). An announcement immediately followed the visit: a new station would be built. The old depot was relocated about a half-block north, where it was connected to other buildings for use as a yard office and freight warehouse (extant). The move was accomplished by placing the depot on skids and pulling it with a switch engine, traveling along track laid specifically for the event. The replacement passenger station was dark red brick with a block-and-a-half-long brick platform. Its large single waiting room had white tile wainscoting, a high, beamed ceiling, and big globe lights. Marble stairs led to railroad division offices on the second floor. Express shipments were handled from the depot's south end. Opening day was celebrated with speeches, tours of the building, and a public dance.

After passenger service ended in 1969, the depot went through alternating periods of use and vacancy. In the early 1990s, a local entrepreneur purchased it from the railroad. He adapted the first floor to a restaurant and placed retail shops upstairs. Freight trains still use the tracks. A similarly styled CB&Q depot stands at Casper, remodeled in the Nineties for freight railroad use. [Privately owned. Commercial.]

Epilogue:
Permanent Derailment

Demolition of Union Station, in Portland, Maine, August 31, 1961. A wrecking ball has just hit the 138-foot-high, Chateauesque clock tower.

Some demolitions hit harder than others. For decades after the destruction, people remember the pain as if it were yesterday. Whether the depot was a simple, frame way station or a granite terminal of cathedralesque grandeur, mourners never pass the desecrated site without thinking of the long-gone station—the soul and vitality of an old friend, extinguished by a seemingly incurable illness. Perhaps today, people speculate, one could marshal support and find a countermeasure before that fatal swing of the wrecking ball. But in the Fifties, Sixties and Seventies, there was little sympathy for railroad stations.

For many Americans in those years—particularly families with generations of workers on the railroad payroll—the loss of a depot turned them squarely toward reality. The hole left in the streetscape confirmed that America's once dominant transportation industry had been, at best, sidelined and, at worst, totally excluded from the game. The startling emptiness expanded in communities with more than one station, when in the space of a few years, all the depots were gone. With them went more than roofs and walls. People were deprived of a tangible connection to both their personal memories and, on a grander scale, to over 100 years of American history. In most places, little evidence remains of the monumental impact railroads had on our development—from westward expansion to the outcome of wars, from technological, architectural, and engineering innovations to the growth of nationwide commerce. Some communities have at least drawn inspiration from the rubble of a smashed depot. They began preservation organizations like Greater Portland (Maine) Landmarks, whose founding was a direct response to the 1961 demolition of that city's Union Station.

This chapter is a photo tribute to a dozen lost depots—a tiny sampling of the thousands obliterated in the second half of the 20th century. Yet it commemorates every station that felt the rumble of a train. Each one represented an intersecting point in what was once a nation of railroads. Today we inhabit the Automobile Age, and the pressure to replace historic structures with highway ramps, parking lots, and shopping centers continues unabated. May the memories found on these pages strengthen our resolve to seek out vigorous, creative solutions for adapting the past to the present.

PORTLAND, MAINE

UNION STATION

location: Near St. John Street and Park Avenue

architects: Bradlee, Winslow, and Wetherill

original railroads: Boston & Maine, Maine Central, Portland & Ogdensburg (later part of MC), and Portland & Rochester (later part of B&M)

built: 1888

lost: Razed in 1961

on site today: Shopping center

Portland Union Station.

A gabled train shed stretched the full width of the granite head house.

The waiting room with its ornate, polygonal ticket booth.

GRAND TRUNK STATION

location: India Street, near Fore Street

architects: Spier and Rohns

original railroad: Grand Trunk

built: 1903

lost: Razed in 1966

on site today: Water treatment plant and parking lot

Early view of Portland Grand Trunk station (the tower was removed in 1948). On the interior, its main waiting room included a vaulted ceiling, marble walls, gold and rose panels, and a mosaic tile floor.

SALEM, MASSACHUSETTS

EASTERN RAILROAD STATION

location: Washington and Norman streets (Ripley Plaza)

architect: Gridley Bryant

original railroad: Eastern Railroad (later Boston & Maine)

built: 1847; rear portion rebuilt after 1885 fire

lost: Razed in 1954

on site today: Vehicular intersection

A locomotive steams out of the Eastern Railroad station, right into the streets of Salem. As built, the station had a wing that jutted into Washington Street on the left and a gable-roof train shed on the right; both were gone by the time this turn-of-the-century photo was taken.

CUMBERLAND, MARYLAND

QUEEN CITY RAILROAD STATION AND HOTEL

location: Harrison Street at the CSX railroad tracks, just north of I-68

architect: Attributed to Thomas N. Heskett

original railroad: Baltimore & Ohio

built: 1872

lost: Razed in 1972

on site today: Post office and Amtrak prefabricated station

The platforms and canopies had not yet been built in this early view of the Queen City Station and Hotel in Cumberland. The interior of the red brick, Italianate building included a 400-seat dining room that converted to a ballroom.

PHILADELPHIA, PENNSYLVANIA

BALTIMORE & OHIO STATION

location: Southwest corner, 24th and Chestnut streets

architect: Frank Furness

original railroad: Baltimore & Ohio

built: 1888

lost: The station was in private hands when damaged by a fire in the early Sixties.
Razed in 1963

on site today:
High-rise apartment building

B&O station in Philadelphia.

The track-level main waiting room combined the industrial flavor of riveted steel with the ornateness of Victorian ironwork.

The main entrance was through a porte-cochere on the south side of Chestnut Street. Inside were the comforts of a large 19th-century railroad station: rocking chairs and massive fireplaces.

ATLANTA, GEORGIA

TERMINAL STATION

location: Spring and Mitchell streets

architect: P. Thornton Marye

original railroads: Southern; Atlanta & West Point; Central of Georgia; Atlanta, Birmingham & Atlantic; and later Seaboard Air Line (relocated from Atlanta Union Station)

built: 1905

lost: Razed in 1972

on site today: Richard B. Russell federal office building, adjacent to Norfolk Southern corporate headquarters and rail yard

Atlanta Terminal Station with its long-span train shed (far left, replaced by butterfly sheds in 1925). After a c. 1940 lightning strike, the baroque superstructures of the two tallest towers were removed.

BIRMINGHAM, ALABAMA

TERMINAL STATION

location: 26th Street at 5th Avenue

architect: P. Thornton Marye

original railroads: Birmingham Terminal Company, composed of five tenants owning equal amounts of stock: Southern; Alabama Great Southern; Central of Georgia; St. Louis & San Francisco; and Illinois Central

built: 1909

lost: Razed in 1969–70

on site today: Vacant land

At Terminal Station in Birmingham, 5th Avenue passed under the building. This majestic and intricately detailed station remained intact on the interior and exterior until its demolition. New construction planned for the 11-acre site has never materialized.

CHICAGO, ILLINOIS

GRAND CENTRAL STATION

location: Wells and Harrison streets

architect: Solon Spencer Beman

original railroads: Built by a subsidiary of the Wisconsin Central, but used principally by the Baltimore & Ohio (the eventual owner). The station also served Chicago Great Western and Pere Marquette trains.

built: 1890

lost: Razed in 1970

on site today: Vacant land

Chicago Grand Central Station.

1927 photo. From a brownstone base, the station's brown brick tower rose to a height of 247 feet. Its bell was inscribed with the words I RING FOR ALL.

In this early interior view, men waited on oak and cane benches and tall rocking chairs. The elegant room included columns with foliated capitals, two-story windows (ornamented in the arches with stained glass), red and white marble floors, and pale pink and gray marble walls.

MILWAUKEE, WISCONSIN

CHICAGO & NORTH WESTERN STATION

location: Wisconsin Avenue at the lakefront

architect: Charles Sumner Frost

original railroad: Chicago & North Western

built: 1889

lost: Razed in 1968 (for expressway ramp that was never built)

on site today: Remained vacant land until early 1990s, when it became part of the new O'Donnell Park.

Situated at the end of Milwaukee's main street, the C&NW station bordered on Lake Michigan. The depot's clock tower was surmounted by a 30-foot-high iron spire and a weather vane.

UNION STATION (ALSO KNOWN AS EVERETT STREET STATION)

location: Everett Street between 3rd and 4th streets

architect: Edward Townsend Mix

original railroads: Chicago, Milwaukee & St. Paul and Wisconsin Central (later Soo Line)

built: 1886

lost: Already slated for demolition when gutted by fire in 1965

on site today: Office building

Union Station, Milwaukee, on November 14, 1935. Its gabled train shed, 600 feet long by 100 feet wide, covered five tracks.

ALBUQUERQUE, NEW MEXICO

ALVARADO HOTEL AND DEPOT COMPLEX

location: First Street at Gold Avenue, S.W.

architect: Charles F. Whittlesey

original railroad: Atchison, Topeka & Santa Fe

built: 1902

lost: The hotel closed and was demolished in 1970. The depot was destroyed by fire in 1993 (Amtrak train still stops).

on site today: Gravel parking lot

Alvarado Hotel and Depot in Santa Fe, c. 1908. On the left, the AT&SF depot with its original tower (altered in 1912 following a fire and then again in 1944). The hotel is on the right.

SAN FRANCISCO, CALIFORNIA

SOUTHERN PACIFIC STATION

SP station in San Francisco.

location: 3rd and Townsend streets

architect: Architectural Bureau of the Southern Pacific Company

original railroad: Southern Pacific

built: 1915

lost: Main part (waiting room) was razed in 1975; remaining offices, in 1976–77 (for a freeway ramp that never materialized in this location). A new station (used by Caltrans) was built nearby in 1975 at 4th & Townsend streets, former location of storage tracks for the historic station

on site today: Storage lot for recreational vehicles

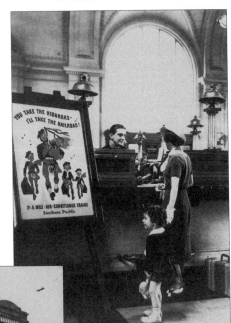

Exterior c. 1918. Today a wonderful collection of restored depots lines the tracks between San Jose, Ca., and San Francisco; but the most substantial station, this Mission-style anchor, is gone.

Interior, 1938. This SP publicity photo includes an advertising poster that proclaims YOU TAKE THE HIGHROAD—I'LL TAKE THE RAILROAD! 2 CENTS A MILE AIR-CONDITIONED TRAINS.

Further Reading

Alexander, Edwin P. *Down at the Depot: American Railroad Stations from 1831 to 1920*. New York: Bramhall House, 1970.

_____. *On the Main Line: The Pennsylvania Railroad in the 19th Century*. New York: Bramhall House, 1971.

Anderson Notter Finegold, Inc. *Recycling Historic Railroad Stations: A Citizen's Manual*. Washington, D.C.: U.S. Department of Transportation, 1978.

Bach, Ira J., and Susan Wolfson. *A Guide to Chicago's Railroad Stations: Present and Past*. Athens, Ohio: Ohio University Press, 1986.

Bailey, Shirley R., and Jim Parkhurst, comps. *Early South Jersey Railroad Stations*, Millville, N.J.: South Jersey Publishing Co., 1981.

Beauregard, Mark W. *Railroad Stations of New England Today*. Vol. 1, *The Boston & Maine R.R*. Flanders, N.J.: Railroad Avenue Enterprises, 1979.

Berg, Walter E. *Buildings and Structures of American Railroads*. New York: John Wiley & Sons, 1893.

Bernhart, Benjamin L. *The Outer Station, Reading, Pennsylvania*. Reading, Pa.: Benjamin L. Bernhart, 1991.

Blardone, Charles, ed. *The Chestnut Hill and Fort Washington Branches*. Philadelphia: Philadelphia Chapter, Pennsylvania Railroad Technical & Historical Society, 1982.

Boothroyd, Stephen, and Peter Barney. *Railroads in Early Postcards*. Vol. 2, *Northern New England*. Vestal, N.Y.: The Vestal Press, 1992.

Bradley, Bill. *The Last of the Great Stations: 50 Years of the Los Angeles Union Passenger Terminal*. Glendale, Calif.: Interurban Press, 1992.

Brooker, Kathleen Ann. "Railroad Depots in New Mexico: Southwestern Styles and the Masonry Tradition." Master's thesis, University of New Mexico, 1981.

Bryant, Keith L., Jr. "Cathedrals, Castles, and Roman Baths: Railway Station Architecture in the Urban South." *Journal of Urban History* 2, no. 2 (February 1976): 195–230.

_____. "Railway Stations of Texas: A Disappearing Architectural Heritage." *Southwestern Historical Quarterly* 79 (April 1976): 417–440.

_____. "Urban Railroad Architecture in the Pacific Northwest." *Journal of the West* 17 (October 1978): 12–20.

Bye, Ranulph. *The Vanishing Depot*. Wynnewood, Pa.: Livingston Publishing, 1973. Reprint. Souderton, Pa.: Indian Valley Printing, 1994.

Cavalier, Julian. *Classic American Railroad Stations*. San Diego, Calif.: A. S. Barnes, 1980.

Cavalier, Julian. *North American Railroad Stations*. Cranbury, N.J.: A. S. Barnes, 1979.

Cincinnati Chamber of Commerce. *The Cincinnati Union Terminal Pictorial History*. Cincinnati: Cincinnati Chamber of Commerce, 1933. Reprint. Cincinnati: The Cincinnati Historical Society, 1987.

City of Phoenix Planning Dept. and Don W. Ryden Architects. *The Union Station: Phoenix' Portal to the Nation*. Phoenix, Ariz.: The City of Phoenix Historic Preservation Commission, 1990.

Condit, Carl W. *The Port of New York*. 2 vols. Chicago: The University of Chicago Press, 1980–81.

_____. *The Railroad and the City: A Technological and Urbanistic History of Cincinnati*. Columbus, Ohio: Ohio State University Press, 1977.

_____. "The Steel Frame: Skyscrapers and Railroad Terminals." In *American Building: Materials and Techniques from the First Colonial Settlements to the Present*. Chicago: The University of Chicago Press, 1968.

Culp, Edwin D. *Stations West: The Story of the Oregon Railways*. Caldwell, Idaho: The Caxton Printers, 1972.

Diehl, Lorraine B. *The Late, Great Pennsylvania Station*. New York: American Heritage Press, 1985. Reprint. Lexington, Mass.: The Stephen Greene Press, 1987.

Dixon, Thomas W., Jr. *Chesapeake & Ohio Standard Structures*. Clifton Forge, Va.: The C&O Historical Society, 1991.

Douglas, George H. *All Aboard! The Railroad in American Life*. New York: Paragon House, 1992.

_____. *Rail City: Chicago USA*. San Diego, Calif.: Howell-North Books, 1981.

Droege, John A. *Passenger Terminals and Trains*. New York: McGraw-Hill, 1916. Reprint. Milwaukee, Wis.: Kalmbach Publishing, 1969.

Drury, George, comp. *Guide to Tourist Railroads and Railroad Museums*. Waukesha, Wis.: Kalmbach Publishing, 1995.

_____, comp. *The Historical Guide to North American Railroads*. Waukesha, Wis.: Kalmbach Publishing, 1985.

Edmonson, Harold A., ed. *Railroad Station Planbook*. Milwaukee, Wis.: Kalmbach Publishing, 1977.

Finnegan, Thomas. *Saving Union Station, Albany, New York*. Albany, N.Y.: Washington Park Press, 1988.

Forest, Kenton, and Charles Albi. *Denver's Railroads: The Story of Union Station and the Railroads of Denver*. 2d ed. Golden, Colo.: Colorado Railroad Museum, 1986.

Gilbert, John F., comp. and ed. *Crossties to the Depot*. Vol. 1. *Virginia Railroad Stations*. Raleigh, N.C.: Crossties Press, 1982.

Grabowski, John H., and Walter C. Leedy, Jr. *The Terminal Tower, Tower City Center: A Historical Perspective*. Cleveland: Western Reserve Historical Society, 1990.

Grant, H. Roger. *Kansas Depots*. Topeka: Kansas State Historical Society, 1990.

_____. *Living in the Depot: The Two-Story Railroad Station*. Iowa City, Iowa: University of Iowa Press, 1993.

Grant, H. Roger, and Charles W. Bohi. *The Country Railroad Station in America*. Sioux Falls, S.D.: The Center for Western Studies, 1988.

Grant, H. Roger, Don L. Hofsommer, and Osmund Overby. *St. Louis Union Station: A Place for People, A Place for Trains*. St. Louis, Mo.: The St. Louis Mercantile Library, 1994.

Grattan, Virginia L. *Mary Colter: Builder Upon the Red Earth*. Flagstaff, Ariz.: Northland Press, 1980.

Grow, Lawrence. *On the 8:02: An Informal History of Commuting by Rail in America*. New York: Mayflower Books, 1979.

_____. *Waiting for the 5:05: Terminal, Station, and Depot in America*. New York: Universe Books, 1977

Gustafson, Lee, and Phil Serpico. *Coast Lines Depots: Los Angles Division*. Palmdale, Calif.: Omni Publications, 1992.

[Hankey, John, and Ruth Falkenberg]. *Railroad Depot Acquisition and Development*. Information Series No. 44. Washington, D.C.: National Trust for Historic Preservation, 1989.

Harwood, Herbert H. "Philadelphia's Victorian Suburban Stations." *The Railway History Monograph* 4, no. 3 (July 1975): 1–48.

Hayman, John C. *Rails Along the Chesapeake: A History of Railroading on the Delmarva Peninsula, 1827-1978.* N.p.: 1979.

Highsmith, Carol M., and James L. Holton. *Reading Terminal and Market: Philadelphia's Historic Gateway and Grand Convention Center.* Washington, D.C.: Chelsea Publishing, 1994.

Highsmith, Carol M., and Ted Landphair. *Union Station: A Decorative History of Washington's Grand Terminal.* Washington, D.C.: Chelsea Publishing, 1988.

Hines, Thomas S. *Burnham of Chicago: Architect and Planner.* New York: Oxford University Press, 1974. Reprint. Chicago: The University of Chicago Press, 1979.

Kovl, David R. *Michigan Rail Preservation.* 3 vols. Orion, Mich.: David R. Kovl, 1990–94.

Lewis, Edward A. *New England Country Depots.* Arcade, N.Y.: The Baggage Car, 1973.

——————. *Reading's Victorian Stations.* Strasburg, Pa.: The Baggage Car, 1976.

Lord, Robert F. *Downeast Depots: Maine Railroad Stations in the Steam Era.* Collinsville, Conn.: Robert F. Lord, 1986.

Macdonald, Fiona. *A 19th Century Railway Station.* New York: Peter Bedrick Books, 1990.

Meeks, Carroll L.V. *The Railroad Station: An Architectural History.* New Haven, Conn.: Yale University Press, 1956.

Middleton, William D. *Grand Central: The World's Greatest Railway Terminal.* San Marino, Calif.: Golden West Books, 1977.

Nathan, Adele Gutman. *Famous Railroad Stations of the World.* New York: Random House, 1953.

Newell, Dianne. *The Failure to Preserve the Queen City Hotel, Cumberland, Maryland.* Washington, D.C.: The Preservation Press, 1975.

Palmer, Richard, and Harvey Roehl. *Railroads in Early Postcards.* Vol. 1, *Upstate New York.* Vestal, N.Y.: The Vestal Press, 1990.

Parker, Edward C., *Next Stop: St. Louis Union Station.* St. Louis, Mo.: The Patrice Press, 1989.

Parker, Francis H. *Indiana Railroad Depots: A Threatened Heritage.* Muncie, Ind.: Ball State University, 1989.

Passenger Terminals and Stations Designed by Kenneth M. Murchison. New York: Kenneth M. Murchison, 1921.

Pollard, Bill. "Railroad Eating Houses Along the Rock Island." *Rock Island Technical Society 1991 Digest* 11: 66–101.

Pounds, Robert E. *Santa Fe Depots: The Western Lines.* Dallas: Kachina Press, 1984.

Price, James N. *The Railroad Stations of San Diego County: Then and Now.* San Diego: Price & Sieber, 1988.

Reisdorff, James J., and Michael M. Bartels. *Railroad Stations in Nebraska: An Era of Use and Reuse.* David City, Neb.: South Platte Press, 1987.

Reusing Railroad Stations. 2 vols. New York: Educational Facilities Laboratories, 1974–75.

Richards, Jeffrey, and John M. Mackenzie. *The Railway Station: A Social History.* New York: Oxford University Press, 1986.

St. Louis Union Station: A Monograph by the Architect and Officers of the Terminal Railroad Association of St. Louis. St. Louis, Mo.: National Chemigraph Co., 1885. Reprint. St. Louis, Mo.: St. Louis Station Partners, 1985.

Sandy, Wilda, and Larry K. Hancks. *Stalking Louis Curtiss.* Kansas City, Mo.: Ward Parkway Press, 1991.

Schivelbusch, Wolfgang. *Geschichte der Eisenbahnreise.* Munich: Carl Hanser Verlag, 1977. English trans. *The Railway Journey: Trains and Travel in the 19th Century.* New York: Urizen Books, 1977. Reprint. Berkeley, Calif.: The University of California Press, 1986.

Scull, Theodore W. *Hoboken's Lackawanna Terminal.* New York: Quadrant Press, 1987.

Sherman, Joe. *A Thousand Voices: The Story of Nashville's Union Station.* Nashville, Tenn.: Rutledge Hill Press, 1987.

Stanford, Linda Oliphant. "Railway Designs by Fellheimer and Wagner, New York to Cincinnati." *Queen City Heritage* (Cincinnati Historical Society) 43, no. 3 (Fall 1985): 2–24.

Steam Passenger Service Directory. Richmond, Vt.: Great Eastern Publishing, 1995.

Stilgoe, John R., *Metropolitan Corridor: Railroads and the American Scene.* New Haven, Conn.: Yale University Press, 1983.

Taber, Thomas T. *The Delaware, Lackawanna & Western: The Road of Anthracite in the Nineteenth Century.* Muncy, Pa.: Thomas T. Taber III, 1977.

Taber, Thomas T., and Thomas T. Taber III. *The Delaware, Lackawanna & Western: The Road of Anthracite in the Twentieth Century.* 2 vols. Muncy, Pa.: Thomas T. Taber III, 1979–81.

Thayer, Preston. "The Railroad Designs of Frank Furness: Architecture and Corporate Imagery in the Late Nineteenth Century." Ph.D. diss., University of Pennsylvania, 1993.

Thomas, George E., Jeffrey A. Cohen, and Michael J. Lewis. *Frank Furness: The Complete Works.* New York: Princeton Architectural Press, 1991.

Thomas, Larry, ed. "St. Louis Union Station Centennial." *TRRA Historical & Technical Society Newsletter* 7, no. 3-4 (March 1994).

Underkofler, Allen P., ed. *The Philadelphia Improvements.* Parts I and II. Langhorne and Bryn Mawr, Pa.: Philadelphia Chapter, Pennsylvania Railroad Technical & Historical Society, 1979–80.

Van Metre, T. W. *Trains, Tracks and Travel.* New York: Simons-Boardman Publishing, 1926.

Van Trump, James D. *Station Square: A Golden Age Revived.* Pittsburgh: Pittsburgh History & Landmarks Foundation, 1978.

Wakefield, Manville B. *To the Mountains by Rail.* 3d ed. Fleischmanns, N.Y.: Purple Mountain Press, 1989.

Ward, Ralph. *Southern Railway Depots.* 2 vols. Asheboro, N.C.: Ralph Ward, 1991–94.

Wayman, Norbury. *St. Louis Union Station and Its Railroads.* St. Louis, Mo.: The Evelyn E. Newman Group, 1987.

Ziel, Ron, and Richard Wettereau. *Victorian Railroad Stations of Long Island.* Bridgehampton, N.Y.: Sunrise Special, Ltd., 1988.

Information Sources

The following organizations and agencies can supply information on subjects covered in *Great American Railroad Stations*. Additional sources of advice include state historic preservation offices, local historical societies, state transportation departments, and historical and technical societies for various railroads.

Atchison, Topeka & Santa Fe Archives
Center for Historical Research
Kansas State Historical Society
6425 S.W. 6th Avenue
Topeka, KS 66615

Hays T. Watkins Research Library
B&O Railroad Museum
901 W. Pratt Street
Baltimore, MD 21223

California State Railroad Museum
111 I Street
Sacramento, CA 95814

Colorado Railroad Museum
P.O. Box 10
Golden, CO 80402

Intermodal Surface Transportation Efficiency Act (ISTEA)
CAMPAIGN FOR NEW TRANSPORTATION PRIORITIES
National Association of Railroad Passengers
Suite 308
900 2nd St., N.E.
Washington, DC 20036

SURFACE TRANSPORTATION POLICY PROJECT
Suite 300
1400 16th Street, N.W.
Washington, DC 20036

Interstate Commerce Commission Valuation Records
Civil Reference Branch
National Archives and Records Administration
Washington, DC 20408

National Railway Historical Society
P.O. Box 58153
Philadelphia, PA 19102

National Trust for Historic Preservation

HEADQUARTERS
1785 Massachusetts Ave., N.W.
Washington, DC 20036

DEPOT PRESERVATION PROGRAM
Mountains/Plains Regional Office
Suite 1100
910 16th Street
Denver, CO 80202

LIBRARY
Architecture Building
University of Maryland
College Park, MD 20742

Nevada State Railroad Museum
Capitol Complex
Carson City, NV 89710

Railroad Museum of Pennsylvania
P.O. Box 125
Strasburg, PA 17579

Railroad Station Historical Society
430 Ivy Lane
Crete, NE 68333

Rails-to Trails-Conservancy
Suite 300
1400 16th Street, N.W.
Washington, DC 20036

Railway & Locomotive Historical Society
P.O. Box 215
East Irvine, CA 92650

Steamtown National Historic Site
150 S. Washington Avenue
Scranton, PA 18503

Union Pacific Historical Museum
1416 Dodge Street
Omaha, NE 68179

Walker Transportation Collection
Beverly Historical Society and Museum
117 Cabot Street
Beverly, MA 01915

Photographic Sources

Abbreviations refer to the following collections:
AAR—Association of American Railroads
B&O RM—The Hays T. Watkins Research Library, B&O Railroad Museum
CSRM—California State Railroad Museum
HABS—Historic American Buildings Survey, National Park Service
HAER—Historic American Engineering Record
HHH—Herbert H. Harwood
KSHS—Kansas State Historical Society
LC—Library of Congress
NRHS—National Railway Historical Society
SI—Smithsonian Institution
SYR—Special Collections, Syracuse University Library

100 YEARS OF GLORY
x SI, no. 2395. **xiv** Dayton Historical Depot Society. **2** Hagley Museum and Library. **3** AAR. **4** top, Hagley Museum and Library; bottom, Stoughton (Mass.) Historical Society Archives. **5** upper and lower, J. E. Bailey, photo, SYR. **7** top, Saunders County Historical Society; bottom, Donald Weiser Collection. **8** John D. Burger photo, Jay Williams Collection. **9** Photograph Archives, Utah State Historical Society. **10** KSHS. **11** top, South Dakota State Historical Society; bottom, C&O Railway Historical Society Collection. **13** top, William A. Steele; bottom, Courtesy of Photographic Archives, University of Kentucky Libraries, Louis Edward Nollau photo. **14** left, Hyman Myers, AIA; right, Frank Weer Collection. **16** LC. **17** Robert M. Vogel Collection. **18** B&O RM. **19** top, LC; bottom, Courtesy, Georgia Dept. of Archives and History. **20** HHH photo. **21** William B. Barry photo, SYR. **22** Durand Union Station, Inc. **23** Union Pacific Museum Collection. **24** Minnesota Historical Society. **25** The Peale Museum, Baltimore City Life Museums. **26** top, Jack E. Boucher photo, HABS; bottom, Ward Kimball photo. **27** left, author's collection; right, Frank Weer Collection. **28** Courtesy, Georgia Dept. of Archives and History. **29** SI. **30** top and bottom, Frank Weer Collection. **32** H. B. Harmer photo, Frank Weer Collection. **33** Joe Horton Studio Historic Collection. **34** Courtesy Boston Public Library, Print Dept. **35** LC. **36** Railroad Museum of Pennsylvania. **37** author's collection. **38** SI, no. 58676. **39** Joe Horton Studio Historic Collection. **40** J. E. Bailey photo. **41** top, Donald Weiser Collection; bottom, Leavenworth Photographics. **42** LC.

BEYOND THE GREAT DEPRESSION
43 left, Donald M. Cohen photo; right, W. D. Smith Commercial Photography. **44** Lower Merion Historical Society Collection. **45** top and bottom, KSHS. **46** top and bottom, from the McKim, Mead, and White Collection, Division of Drawings and Archives, Avery Architectural and Fine Arts Library, Columbia University in the City of New York. **47** left, from the McKim, Mead, and White

Collection, Division of Drawings and Archives, Avery Architectural and Fine Arts Library, Columbia University in the City of New York; right, Norman McGrath, Photographer.

SAVE THE DEPOT!
49 Drawing by Draper Hill. **50** Jim Cruz photo. **51** John Kuehl photo. **53** top, Steve Rosenthal Architectural Photography; bottom, Security Pacific Collection/Los Angeles Public Library. **55** top, AAR; bottom, Kalmbach Publishing Company. **56** Richard C. Allen. **57** both, Whistlestop Park Association. **59** Hagley Museum and Library. **61** LC. **62** Chestnut Hill Historical Society. **63** Lower Merion Historical Society Collection. **64** SYR.

NEW ENGLAND
67 Millis Historical Commission. **68** Leroy F. Roberts Connecticut Railroads Collection, Historical Manuscripts & Archives Dept., University of Connecticut Library. **69** top, The Connecticut Historical Society, Hartford; bottom, Charles B. Gunn photo, The Connecticut Historical Society, Hartford. **70** Leroy F. Roberts Connecticut Railroads Collection, Historical Manuscripts & Archives Dept., University of Connecticut Library. **71** Boston Public Library. **72** Merwinsville Hotel Restoration, Inc. **73** Peter H. Flynn. **74** Andrew C. Koval Collection. **75** Charles B. Gunn photo, The Connecticut Historical Society, Hartford. **76** Robert F. Lord Collection. **77** Robert F. Lord Collection. **78** Robert F. Lord Collection. **79** Robert F. Lord Collection. **80** Robert F. Lord Collection. **81** Both, Robert F. Lord Collection. **82** Robert F. Lord Collection. **84** Belmont Historical Society. **85** The Bostonian Society/Old State House. **86** Howard D. Goodwin Collection. **87** Chatham Railroad Museum. **88** William Bullard photo, Dennis Le Beau Collection. **89** Boston Athenaeum. **90** *Buildings and Structures of American Railroads,* by Walter G. Berg, 1893. **91** left, LC; right, Donald S. Robinson photo, Walker Transportation Collection, Beverly (Mass.) Historical Society. **92** Millis Historical Commission. **94** Cervin Robinson photo, HABS. **95** Earle G. Boyd photo, HHH Collection. **96** Swampscott Historical Commission, Stuart P. Ellis photo. **97** Courtesy of the Society for the Preservation of New England Antiquities. **98** top, Wayland Historical Society; bottom, Worcester Historical Museum. **100** Courtesy of the Society for the Preservation of New England Antiquities. **101** author's collection. **102** Walker Transportation Collection, Beverly (Mass.) Historical Society. **103** Walker Transportation Collection, Beverly (Mass.) Historical Society. **104** Walker Transportation Collection, Beverly (Mass.) Historical Society. **105** Roberta Niesz. **106** top, Collection of Boston & Maine Railroad Historical Society; bottom, Walker Transportation Collection, Beverly (Mass.) Historical Society. **107** Walker Transportation Collection, Beverly (Mass.)

Historical Society. **108** Walker Transportation Collection, Beverly (Mass.) Historical Society. **109** top, Howard D. Goodwin Collection; bottom, NRHS Library, Philadelphia. **110** Pettaquamscutt Historical Society. **111** Howard D. Goodwin Collection. **112** Courtesy of the Rhode Island Historical Society. **113** NRHS Library, Philadelphia. **114** Images from the Past, Bennington, Vt. **115** Photograph by Dana D. Goodwin, Collection of Boston & Maine Railroad Historical Society. **116** Courtesy Vermont Historical Society. **117** Jack Armstrong photo, HHH Collection. **119** Courtesy Vermont Historical Society. **120** top, Claire Johnson; bottom, photograph by Dana D. Goodwin, Collection of Boston & Maine Railroad Historical Society. **121** Shelburne Museum, Shelburne, Vt. **122** Windsor Station Restaurant.

MID-ATLANTIC
123 Western Maryland Railway Historical Society. **124** Caley Historical Postcard Collection. **125** Delaware State Archives. **126** Caley Historical Postcard Collection. **127** Frank Weer Collection. **128** Hagley Museum and Library. **130** top, Graham, Anderson, Probst & White, successor to D. H. Burnham & Company; bottom, LC. **132** top, HHH Collection; bottom, B&O RM. **133** top, SI, photo no. 54317; bottom, B&O RM. **134** Steve Rosenthal Architectural Photography. **135** anonymous. **137** Western Maryland Railway Historical Society. **138** Ellicott City B&O Railroad Station Museum. **139** William P. Price. **140** HHH photo. **141** Brother Andrew C. Fowler, HHH Collection. **142** William Edmund Barrett, HAER. **143** Ken Payson and Jonathan Fine drawing, HAER. **145** top, New Jersey Transit; bottom, William B. Barry photo, SYR. **146** Edward H. Weber photo. **147** *Buildings and Structures of American Railroads,* by Walter G. Berg, 1893. **148** left, Watson B. Bunnell photo, SYR; right, William B. Barry photo, SYR. **150** Courtesy, Liberty State Park. **151** top, Targa Investments, Inc.; bottom, New Jersey Transit. **153** Watson B. Bunnell photo, SYR. **154** William B. Barry photo, SYR. **155** both, Steve Rosenthal Architectural Photography. **156** SYR. **157** top, SI; bottom, Edward T. Weber photo. **158** New Jersey Transit. **159** SI. **160** Hagley Museum & Library. **161** SI. **162** Edward T. Weber photo. **163** Timothy C. Truscott Collection. **164** John T. Goodnough. **165** Edward H. Weber photo. **167** Buffalo and Erie County Historical Society. **168** top, Fort Edward Chamber of Commerce; bottom, CSRM. **170** top, Greensburgh Historical Society; bottom, Messick, Cohen, Waite Architects. **172** NRHS, Central New York Chapter. **173** top, SI; bottom, The Middletown Historical Society and the Wallkill Precinct. **174** HHH Collection. **175** HHH photo. **176** WPA-FWP no. 35, Municipal Archives, Dept. of Records and Information Services, City of New York. **178** both, D&H Collection, New York State Library. **179** SI. **180** NRHS, Rochester Chapter. **181** J. Heatley photo, Society for the Preservation of Long Island Antiquities. **182** top, Timothy C. Truscott Collection; bottom, Ron Ziel Collection. **184** SYR. **185** top, Frey Collection, Oneida County Historical Society; bottom, HHH photo. **186** HHH photo. **188** left, Edward H. Weber photo; right, Frank Weer Collection.

189 author photo. **190** J. E. Green photo, Courtesy Delaware County (Pa.) Historical Society. **192** Western Maryland Railway Historical Society. **193** Edward H. Weber photo. **194** Edward H. Weber photo. **195** R. A. Newbegin photo, HHH Collection. **196** top, Lebanon County Historical Society; bottom; Frank Weer Collection. **198** Frank Weer Collection. **199** left, Robert Skaler Collection; right, Lower Merion Historical Society Collection. **201** both, Frank Weer Collection. **202** Graham, Anderson, Probst & White. **203** top, Graham, Anderson, Probst & White, from the D. Garth Wise Collection; bottom, Hagley Museum and Library. **204** Frank Weer Collection. **205** both, Pittsburgh History & Landmarks Foundation. **206** both, Pittsburgh History & Landmarks Foundation. **207** Frank Weer Collection. **208** N. Dale Wakefield, Sr., Collection, Courtesy Friends of the East Broad Top. **209** top, CSRM; bottom, Watson B. Bunnell photo, SYR. **210** Ken Murry photo. **211** top, SI; bottom, Edward H. Weber photo. **212** Frank Weer Collection. **213** top, Frank Weer Collection; bottom, Hagley Museum and Library. **214** HHH photo. **215** C&O Historical Society Collection. **216** West Virginia Division of Culture and History. **217** both, Hays T. Watkins Research Library, B&O RM. **218** C&O Historical Society Collection. **219** top, Jeffrey R. Hollis; bottom, Hays T. Watkins Research Library, B&O RM Railroad Museum. **221** C&O Historical Society Collection.

SOUTH
223 C&O Railway photo, C&O Historical Society Collection. **225** both, Courtesy, Historic Chattahoochee Commission. **226** H. E. Monroe Collection. **227** Eric Overbey Collection, University of South Alabama Archives. **228** HAER. **229** David Harris photo. **230** CSRM. **232** John P. Vander Maas Collection, University of Iowa. **233** John P. Vander Maas Collection, University of Iowa. **234** top, Clifton E. Hull; bottom, Quapaw Quarter Association. **236** Bruce Lyndon Cunningham, Artist. **237** Arkansas Historic Preservation Program. **239** Florida State Archives. **241** Historical Museum of Southern Florida. **242** top, John Parks Drawing, HABS; bottom, Florida State Archives. **243** top, L&N Collection, University of Louisville Archives; bottom, Florida State Archives. **244** both, Jack E. Boucher photo, HABS. **247** Frank Weer Collection. **248** top, Frank E. Ardrey photo, HHH Collection; bottom, Middle Georgia Archives. **250** top, drawn by Roland David Schaaf, HAER; bottom, drawn by John Gregory Albers, HAER. **252** C&O Historical Society Collection. **253** L&N Collection, University of Louisville Archives. **254** *Buildings and Structures of American Railroads,* by Walter G. Berg, 1893. **255** L&N Collection, University of Louisville Archives. **256** C&O Historical Society Collection. **258** A. E. Brown photo, Louis A. Saillard Collection. **259** top, C. W. Whitbeck photo, Louis A. Saillard Collection; bottom, Watson Memorial Library, Northwestern State University of Louisiana. **261** Mary Eleanor Kerr Wyatt. **262** Courtesy Mississippi Department of Archives and History. **263** Frank A. Brooks, Jr. **264** top, Collection of Thomas H. and Joan W. Gandy; bottom, Vicksburg Foundation for Historic Preservation. **267** Greensboro Historical Museum.

268 North Carolina Division of Archives and History, Marchant photo. 269 North Carolina Division of Archives and History. 270 North Carolina Division of Archives and History. 271 both, Historic Salisbury Foundation. 274 South Caroliniana Library. 275 Ann M. Stringer, artist. 276 LC. 277 Tennessee Overhill Heritage Association. 278 William T. Turner Collection. 279 James E. Thompson photo. 280 left, William T. Turner Collection; right, Joe Horton Studio Historic Collection. 281 Courtesy of Photographic Archives, University of Kentucky Libraries, Louis Edward Nollau photo. 283 C&O Historical Society Collection. 284 Virginia State Library and Archives. 285 Norfolk & Western Ry. Photograph Collection, Virginia Polytech Institute and State University Libraries. 286 The Library of Virginia. 287 The Library of Virginia. 288 Historic Staunton Foundaion. 289 H. Reid, C&O Historical Society Collection. 290 Edward H. Weber photo.

MIDWEST

291 The Cincinnati Historical Society. 292 Charles H. Stats Collection. 293 Batavia Depot Museum. 294 left, David R. Phillips, Chicago Architectural Photographing Co.; right, Graham, Anderson, Probst & White, successor to D. H. Burnham & Company. 295 Andrew C. Koval Collection. 296 George Krambles Collection. 297 Illinois Historic Preservation Agency, Galena State Historic Sites. 298 Edward H. Weber photo. 299 top, NRHS Library, Philadelphia; bottom, A. M. Kinney Associates. 300 left, Chicago and North Western Historical Society; right, A. M. Kinney Associates. 301 LC. 302 Roberta Niesz Collection. 304 top, Lincoln Library; bottom, A.W. Johnson photo, George Krambles Collection. 305 Wilmette Historical Museum. 307 Indiana Dunes National Lakeshore. 308 Walter Sassmanshausen Collection. 309 LC. 310 Calumet Regional Archives, Indiana University Northwest. 311 HABS. 312 both, Tippecanoe County Historical Association. 313 Curt Teich Postcard Archives/Lake County (Ill.) Museum. 314 Courtesy of the Northern Indiana Historical Society. 316 Roberta Niesz Collection. 317 Roberta Niesz Collection. 318 Roberta Niesz Collection. 319 Roberta Niesz Collection. 320 Roberta Niesz Collection. 321 Keokuk Junction Railway. 323 Martha Hagendorn-Krass photo, KSHS. 325 Charles Sesher Collection. 326 left, KSHS; right, R. Scott Thomas Collection. 327 both, KSHS. 328 KSHS. 329 KSHS. 330 KSHS. 331 KSHS. 332 KSHS. 333 Allen County (Ohio) Historical Society. 334 Bentley Historical Library, University of Michigan. 335 Willard Library. 336 top, Willard Library; bottom, Allen County (Ohio) Historical Society. 337 Columbiaville Historical Society. 338 Courtesy, State Archives of Michigan. 340 Flushing Area Historical Society. 341 Bentley Historical Library, University of Michigan. 342 Courtesy, Michigan State Archives. 343 top, Jackson District Library; bottom, Kalamazoo Public Library. 344 *Buildings and Structures of American Railroads*, by Walter G. Berg, 1893. 345 CSRM. 346 Lansing Public Library. 347 Michigan Transit Museum. 348 Muskegon County Museum. 349 Courtesy, Michigan State Archives. 352 Northeast Minnesota Historical Center, Duluth, Minn.

353 Morrison County Historical Society. 354 left, Photo: Hibbard, Minnesota Historical Society; right, Minneapolis Historical Society. 355 Milwaukee Road Collection, Milwaukee Public Library. 356 top, Minnesota Historical Society; bottom, Photo: Hill, Great Northern Railway Collection, Minnesota Historical Society. 357 Photo: C.P. Gibson, Minnesota Historical Society. 358 Minnesota Historical Society. 359 Lake County Historical Society. 361 State Historical Society of Missouri, Columbia (artist unknown). 362 Wayne Lammers Collection, Boonville, Mo. 363 Henry J. Higgins Historical Society. 364 Hal Sandy photo. 365 Phelps D. Murdock, Jr., James A. Schaid, AIA, and Missouri Valley Collection, KCMO Public Library. 366 Missouri Historical Society, St. Louis. 368 left, Missouri Historical Society, St. Louis; right, St. Louis Public Library. 370 top, Katy Trail Sedalia, Inc.; bottom, State Historical Society of Missouri, Columbia. 372 Gage County Historical Society. 374 Nebraska State Historical Society. 375 Francis Gschwind. 376 both, Western Heritage Museum. 377 both, Bostwick-Frohardt Collection, owned by KMTV and on permanent loan to Western Heritage Museum, Omaha, Neb. 378 Saunders County Historical Society. 379 Photo by Frank B. Fiske, State Historical Society of North Dakota. 380 State Historical Society of North Dakota. 381 Photo by Leo LaLonde, State Historical Society of North Dakota. 382 State Historical Society of North Dakota. 386 R. Kile Codner photo, Donald Weiser Collection. 387 both, The Cincinnati Historical Society. 388 Cleveland Public Library Photograph Collection. 389 Robert Runyan photo, HHH Collection. 390 Allen County (Ohio) Historical Society. 393 Edward H. Weber photo. 394 Mosser's Studio, Kent, Ohio. 395 Allen County (Ohio) Historical Society. 396 Allen County (Ohio) Historical Society. 398 B&O RM. 399 Chester A. Groseclose, Jr., Collection. 400 J. E. Stimson photo, Wyoming State Museum. 401 South Dakota State Historical Society. 403 top, Siouxland Heritage Museums; bottom, Codington County Historical Society. 406 The Brodhead Historical Society. 407 The State Historical Society of Wisconsin neg. no. WHi (X3) 38533. 408 Milwaukee Road Collection, Milwaukee Public Library. 409 top, The State Historical Society of Wisconsin, neg. no. (G5) 1360; bottom, Mineral Point Historical Society. 411 CSRM. 412 Roberta Niesz Collection.

SOUTHWEST

413 Photo by Jesse L. Nusbaum, Courtesy Museum of New Mexico, neg. no. 66658. 414 Phelps Dodge Corporation. 416 left, Risdon Collection, Arizona Historical Society/Tuscon; right, Magma Copper Co. 417 KSHS. 418 top, National Park Service; bottom, Courtesy Special Collections, University of Arizona Library. 420 Research Div., Arizona Dept. of Library, Archives and Public Records, Phoenix. 422 Courtesy Special Collections, University of Arizona Library. 423 Courtesy Special Collections, University of Arizona Library. 425 top, Vernon J. Glover photo, Courtesy Museum of New Mexico, neg. no. 56681; bottom, both, KSHS. 427 Rio Grande Historical Collections, New Mexico State

University Library. **428** both, Courtesy Museum of New Mexico; top, neg. no. 35877; bottom neg. no. 14705. **429** Raton Museum. **430** AT&SF Railway. **432** Western History Collections, University of Oklahoma Library. **433** top, KSHS; bottom, Frank W. Campbell Collection, Railroad Museum of Oklahoma. **435** photo by Waterhouse, Archives & Manuscripts Division, Oklahoma Historical Society, no. 19270.32. **436** Western History Collections, University of Oklahoma Library. **438** both, Tulsa Historical Society. **440** KSHS. **441** DeGolyer Library, Southern Methodist University, Dallas, Ag 94.956, H. D. Conner photo. **443** C. J. McManus Collection. **444** City of El Paso, Office of Historic Preservation. **445** top, Donald M. Cohen photo; bottom, W. D. Smith Commercial Photography. **446** left, KSHS; right, Cooke County Heritage Society. **448** The Depot Restaurant and Bar. **449** Charles Conniff photo, HHH Collection. **451** both, Don Abbe photo, Texas Historical Commission. **452** left, Courtesy of San Antonio Conservation Society; right, Joseph K. Brown photo, Courtesy of San Antonio Conservation Society. **453** both, Courtesy of San Antonio Conservation Society. **454** DeGolyer Library, Southern Methodist University. **455** KSHS. **456** Ellis County Museum.

WEST
457 Photograph Archives, Utah State Historical Society. **458** Anchorage Museum of History & Art. **459** Yukon Archives, H. C. Barley Collection, Vol II. **460** Courtesy, Modoc County Museum. **461** CSRM. **462** Henry E. Bender Collection. **463** top, CSRM; bottom, Marilyn McCoul, Calistoga Depot. **465** top, Claremont Heritage Council; bottom, Herb Holman photo, California Dept. of Transportation. **466** Southern Pacific Lines. **467** Lee Gustafson/Phil Serpico Collection. **468** Sonoma County Historical Society. **469** left, California State Library, Arnold Hylen photo; right, CSRM. **471** Vernon J. Sappers Collection. **472** CSRM. **473** Stan Kistler Collection. **475** top, Union Pacific Museum Collection; bottom, California State Library. **476** William B. Garner. **477** California State Library. **478** CSRM, Frank E. Meitz photo. **479** Southern Pacific Lines. **480** California State Library, C. B. Waite photo. **481** South Bay Historical Railroad Society. **484** top, Courtesy, Colorado Historical Society, F11,483; bottom, Local History Collection, Pikes Peak Library District. **485** Courtesy, Colorado Historical Society, Mattes Collection, F36,950. **486** The Denver Public Library, Western History Department. **487** La Plata County Historical Society. **488** Courtesy, Colorado Historical Society, F24.652. **489** Courtesy, Colorado Historical Society, F35,030. **490** From the Collection of the Loveland Museum/Gallery. **492** Courtesy, Colorado Historical Society, F4821. **493** Dell A. McCoy photograph, San Juan County Historical Society. **494** CSRM, Paul Darrell Collection. **496** top, Idaho State Historical Society, no. 3000; bottom, both, Duane Garrett photo, HABS. **497** Idaho State Historical Society, no. 60-159.4.

498 both, Union Pacific Museum Collection; left image no. 500598; right image no. 500598A. **499** Union Pacific Museum Collection, image no. 72-14. **500** James M. Frederikson photo. **501** Elmer Treloar photo, HHH Collection. **502** Milwaukee Road Collection, Milwaukee Public Library. **503** Union Pacific Museum Collection. **505** top, Livingston Depot Foundation; bottom, Milwaukee Road Collection, Milwaukee Public Library. **506** Haynes Foundation Collection, Montana Historical Society, Helena, Mont. **507** Haynes Foundation Collection, Montana Historical Society, Helena, Mont. **509** top, Union Pacific Museum Collection; bottom, Nevada Historical Society. **511** Nevada Historical Society. **512** left, AAR; right, Special Collections, University of Nevada–Reno Library. **513** Nevada Historical Society. **514** both, Deschutes County Historical Society. **515** Courtesy of Lane County Historical Museum. **516** Oregon Historical Society, ORHi —80980. **517** Oregon Historical Society, ORHi— 17468. **518** Oregon Historical Society, ORHi—17656. **519** Utah State University Special Collections, C-1245. **520** Photograph Archives, Utah State Historical Society. **521** Photograph Archives, Utah State Historical Society. **522** Union Pacific Museum Collection. **523** both, Photograph Archives, Utah State Historical Society. **524** Photograph Archives, Utah State Historical Society. **525** Image no. 5061, J. W. Sandison Collection, Whatcom Museum of History and Art, Bellingham, Wash. **526** Courtesy Lewis County Historical Commission, Chehalis, Wash. **528** Kittitas County Historical Society, photo by Pautzke. **529** top, Special Collections, University of Washington Libraries, photo by Lee, neg. no. 20053; bottom, Pemco Webster & Stevens Collection, Museum of History & Industry. **530** Special Collections, University of Washington Libraries, photo by LaRoche, neg. no. 138. **531** James M. Frederickson. **532** Warren W. Wing Collection. **533** Eric G. Nelson Collection. **534** J. E. Stimson photo, Wyoming State Museum. **535** J. E. Stimson photo, Wyoming State Museum. **537** J. E. Stimson photo, Wyoming State Museum.

EPILOGUE
539 Don Johnson Photography. **541** left, Maine Historical Society; top and bottom, Maine Historic Preservation Commission. **542** top, Peabody Essex Museum; bottom, B&O RM. **543** top, Cervin Robinson, HABS; middle, B&O RM; bottom, Courtesy Georgia Department of Archives and History. **544** top, Joe Horton Studio Historic Collection; bottom left, from E. S. Hand, *Grand Central Passenger Station at Chicago*, Courtesy The Art Institute of Chicago; bottom right, B&O RM. **545** top, C&NW Historic Photo Collection, Milwaukee Public Library; bottom, Milwaukee Road Collection, Milwaukee Public Library. **546** top, The Albuquerque Museum, photo by William Henry Jackson, Denver Public Library Collection; bottom left, Tom Gray Collection; bottom right, Denver Public Library, Western History Dept.

Index

THE OPTIMUM SAILBOAT

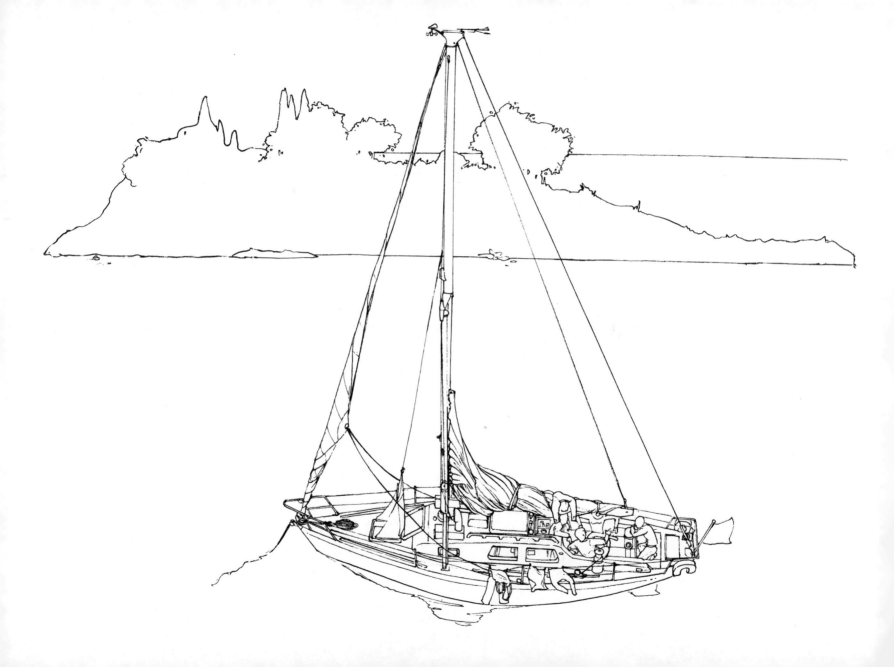